Hong Kong Cinema

HONG KONG CINEMA

The Extra Dimensions

Stephen Teo

 Publishing

First published in 1997 by the
British Film Institute
21 Stephen Street, London W1P 2LN

The British Film Institute exists to promote appreciation, enjoyment, protection
and development of moving image culture in and throughout the whole of the
United Kingdom. Its activities include the National Film and Television Archive;
the National Film Theatre; the Museum of the Moving Image; the London Film
Festival; the production and distribution of film and video; funding and support for
regional activities; Library and Information Services; Stills, Posters and Designs;
Research; Publishing and Education; and the monthly *Sight and Sound* magazine.

British Library Cataloguing-in-Publication Data
A catalogue record for this book is available from the British Library

ISBN 0–85170–496–4
     0–85170–514–6 paperback

Cover designed by Andrew Sutterby

COVER STILLS: **Front** – (top) Pak Suet-sin and Yam Kim-fai in a typical pose from one
of their many Cantonese opera films (courtesy of the author), (bottom left) Bruce
Lee in *Game of Death*, 1978 (Courtesy of Media Asia Group. Copyright Star TV.),
(bottom right) *The Wicked City*, 1992 (Film Workshop/Golden Princess); **Back** –
Chicken and Duck Talk, 1988 (Hui's Films Prod. Co.).

Typeset by Fakenham Photosetting Ltd, Fakenham, Norfolk

Printed in Great Britain by St Edmundsbury Press, Bury St Edmunds, Suffolk

Contents

Foreword

One can draw considerable satisfaction from the achievements of Hong Kong cinema over the past year or so. Inroads have been made into the American market on account of the Jackie Chan and Michelle Yeoh phenomena; Wong Kar-wai pictures have gained a substantial art-house following; John Woo, Ringo Lam and Tsui Hark have joined the ranks of Hollywood action directors. However, within the domestic market, the Hong Kong film industry is in crisis and has been for the last four years. Its market share has shrunk by as much as 40% and box-office earnings have dropped. Ironically, as Hong Kong cinema has become better known internationally, its predominance in the domestic market has increasingly been eroded by Hollywood. For the first time in 20 or even 30 years, Hollywood movies have gained a secure foothold in the Hong Kong market. In 1993, the year when the crisis can be said to have begun, *Jurassic Park* became the highest-grossing film of all time at the Hong Kong box office.

The Hong Kong film industry advanced towards the nineties in a spirit of optimism. Some 66 million tickets were sold in 1988 (although this figure dropped to 44.8 million in 1989). In the late eighties, Hong Kong cinema's first new wave began to mature after a period of consolidation. At the same time a younger, second wave of filmmakers (Clara Law, Stanley Kwan, Wong Kar-wai) courted international recognition. In this period, the industry underwent certain structural changes, notably as a result of the introduction of a classification system in the wake of a new censorship bill. (The relaxation of censorship norms coincided with a more liberal attitude towards sexual matters in the wider society, as was exemplified by the legislative council's decriminalisation of homosexuality in 1990.) Liberal censorship laws gave rise to a new genre of soft-core entertainment known as 'Category Three' movies (restricted to adults).

As the nineties progressed, however, the picture began to change: the boom in property prices spelt the end of the big cinema halls; the exhibition sector began to streamline its operations by demolishing old-fashioned cinemas seating over a thousand people and replacing them with multiplexes boasting state-of-the-art technology in sound, projection and seating. This programme of replacement was the most fundamental structural change to occur in the film industry, but while it brought Hong Kong cinemas in line with international practices and standards, it has had the consequence of contracting the market. The number of cinemas increased but admissions went steadily down. This can be attributed to the fact that theatre owners have routinely increased admission prices. At the same time, the costs of producing a movie have rocketed to new heights in the face of stars' demands for high salaries (big names are often paid about US$1 million per movie).

It is easy to blame the crisis on macroeconomic structural changes in the market (in fact, due to the crisis, the market responded in 1997 with some remedial measures such as reducing ticket prices from HK$50 to HK$30 on Tuesdays). Arguably, though, this is to ignore the problem of the poor quality of productions: the relatively unregulated state of the industry has always tended to lead to over-production in a search for quick profits and short-term gains. There is always the problem of 'audience fatigue' and the fact that Hong Kong's changing demographics mean that a new breed of teenagers are now propping up the film industry. That the crisis has continued over the last four years indicates that there are no easy solutions. The Hong Kong film industry is caught in a potentially deadly cycle: the market has been shrinking at the same time as costs (ticket prices, production budgets, star salaries) have spiralled inexorably upwards – partly in response to the diminished audience's demands for 'added value'. Over the last four years, added value has not been found in Hong Kong cinema and audiences have turned instead to Hollywood blockbusters for satisfaction.

Efforts have been made to ameliorate this situation. In 1996 the industry began to shift its emphasis away from A-List big budgeters by concentrating on low-budget, quickly-made, independent-based productions starring unknowns and cashing in on the teenage market. UFO pictures such as Peter Chan's comedies (*He's a Woman, She's a Man* and its sequel, plus the Maggie Cheung-Leon Lai romancer, *Comrades, Almost a Love Story*) led a minor recovery which was capitalised upon by the P.U. production company with its B-movie thrillers (*The Third Full Moon, The Day That Doesn't Exist*). Then there were the 'triad kid' movies inspired by comics (*Young and Dangerous* and its sequels) as well as numerous imitations (*Once Upon a Time in Triad Society,* and its sequel); even the Wong Kar-wai art films (*Chungking Express, Fallen Angels*) have done modestly well at the local box office. However, the crisis seems to have become ingrained as a kind of philosophical coming-to-terms with the handover and, perhaps, with the realisation that Hong Kong cinema will never be the same again as it faces integration with China. All eyes are now turned to the Mainland Chinese market, hoping that it will offer the Hong Kong film industry a way out of its malaise. Though the Chinese film market has itself shrunk considerably, it remains formidable: the figure of 5 billion tickets sold annually is being brandished about. More players are entering the Chinese market as the country reforms its distribution structures, breaking a state monopoly over foreign movie imports (the country's major studios are now awarded permits to distribute overseas films).

In the nineties, Hong Kong filmmakers jumped on the bandwagon of co-productions with China. Industry insiders see China evolving as the most important market for Hong Kong movies, eventually eclipsing traditional markets such as Taiwan and Southeast Asia. While a number of Hong Kong filmmakers have gone into China to make their own films, a few have poured money into films made by established Chinese directors of the calibre of Chen Kaige (*Farewell My Concubine*), Zhang Yimou (*Raise the Red Lantern*) and Huang Jianxin (*Back to Back, Face to Face*). The bulk of co-productions are run-of-the-mill escapist entertainments (with an accent on violence) which rarely encounter censorship problems. But China has blown more hot than cold with regard to censorship and the issue of 'independent filmmaking.' China has, in fact, cut down on the number of co-productions with Hong Kong in the past two years, though for reasons which are not entirely clear. Restrictions are imposed on filming and on distribution rights; in some cases, Hong Kong filmmakers are unable to get their negatives out of China for cutting and post-production. Last year, the number of co-productions dropped to about ten from forty to fifty in previous years. Bureaucracy and censorship loom as the greatest obstacles to greater co-operation and may yet prove to be the bamboo pole that breaks the back of the Hong Kong film industry after the handover. So far, Chinese filmmakers have been in the firing line in terms of the censorship debate: in 1994, the Chinese authorities issued an official blacklist of 'independent' directors including Tian Zhuangzhuang, the acclaimed director of *The Blue Kite*, and Zhang Yuan. Their films are officially banned and any showings at international film festivals arouse the ire of the Chinese authorities, often leading to punitive action (such as banning directors from attending festivals and withdrawing films).

Hong Kong filmmakers clearly have something to worry about if China's current tendency to censor films and her intransigent attitudes remain unaltered after the handover. Blacklisting directors and banning movies spell the death of creativity for filmmakers who continue working in the system. For those Hong Kong directors who have worked in China, an overriding desire to see China take its rightful place in the community of civilised nations is tempered by scepticism about the future of their home city as it returns to the embrace of the Motherland. The events of recent years have not inspired optimism and may serve to discourage film investment in China. Certainly, not all Hong Kong filmmakers have been seduced by the rush for co-productions with the Mainland and not all filmmakers are convinced that China offers them a lifeline. Even those filmmakers who see China as the Hong Kong film industry's 'saviour' acknowledge that there are numerous difficulties to overcome, arguing that restrictions have to be lifted and censorship relaxed before any breakthroughs can be achieved. On the other hand, the Hong Kong film industry has struggled against the odds in the past to become the world's third largest film industry. No one would be foolish enough to dismiss it as a spent force. The post-handover film industry of Hong Kong could take off yet again and conjure up another miracle in the face of great adversity.

This book offers a history of Hong Kong cinema in the post-war period. It is an extraordinary history of survival and success against the odds, a history which is inseparably bound up with Hong Kong's economic miracle. It is a book which I had long wanted to write, having ruminated long and hard on the subject during my work as English editor with the Hong Kong International Film Festival – specifically with the editing of its annual retrospective catalogues. The catalogues offer the only systematic studies of Hong Kong cinema anywhere. They have gone some way to redressing the critical neglect of Hong Kong cinema, but there is still much ground to cover, not least because of the lack of archival resources. Until only recently, there have been no concerted efforts to conserve Hong Kong's cinematic past. A film archive has now been established in the territory but it remains to be seen whether the work of conserving, restoring, duplicating and subtitling classic works of Hong Kong cinema can take off in any substantial way. In the meantime, a large tract of Hong Kong's cinematic history, particularly the films of the 30s, remains *terra incognita*.

In writing this book, I set out to strike a balance between information and analysis: I have tried to inform the reader for whom Hong Kong cinema is relatively unfamiliar and then to usher him or her into the realm of the films themselves. Wherever possible, analysis is undertaken according to the tenets of auteurism: the theory that a film is made by an author, essentially the director. At the same time, the book offers a contemporary portrait of the territory's cinema, taking into account its historical and aesthetic background, and illustrating it with empirical observations of motifs found in the works of certain filmmakers who may not necessarily have a coherent enough body of work to be labelled auteurs. It also looks at Hong Kong cinema's link to the history and tradition of Chinese cinema as it existed in Shanghai during the golden age of the 30s, thus demonstrating the distinguished tradition from which it came. With the handover on 1 July 1997, Hong Kong cinema comes full circle. If it integrates successfully into the Chinese film industry, it will have the chance to give back as much as it has taken from the tradition of Chinese cinema.

In venturing upon auteurist analysis, I am mindful of the frequently stated comment by some formalist critics that Hong Kong cinema 'lacks a theory' and that true formalist-auteurist analysis is impossible so long as Hong Kong cinema is seen as inferior and negligible. (I am equally aware that there are theoreticians who believe that the only way an 'inferior' Hong Kong cinema can really be studied is through formalist criticism.) The lack of work in the field means that the task for critics is a complex one: it may involve working out a formula which combines aesthetics and theory to fit the circumstances of development that marked Hong Kong cinema, it may require an analysis of the continuity of themes in the work of a certain director or variations in the many genres of Hong Kong cinema, as well as their evolution into mixed genres, it may mean clarifying the political and social contexts under which films were made. It may even mean imposing a Western theoretical grid on the structures of Hong Kong cinema.

The lack of a proper critical and historical perspective on Hong Kong cinema is a liability which I hope to correct in the following chapters. But it will need more than just one book to solve the problem. The historical gap is still too wide. The lack of subtitled prints of old classics and the commonly held belief that old Hong Kong cinema is of dubious aesthetic quality has meant that only modern contemporary works have had exposure. The conflict between style and content has arisen partly because of this gap and it may have inadvertently perpetrated the fallacy that Hong Kong movies are unabashedly 'modern' or 'post-modern'. For a time, such a fallacy kindled the notion that Hong Kong movies were startlingly terse, anti-intellectual, non-historical, non-political and without discourse of whatever shade. They could only be appreciated for their surface gloss, their play on generic formulas. Thus, style came to submerge content.

Today, the growing popularity of Hong Kong movies has spawned another myth based on the universal principle. Having earned greater recognition, Hong Kong movies are no longer alien; their film language is now easily understood. Western audiences have acculturated themselves to the exotic quality of Hong Kong movies; the Hong Kong cinema is now as universal as Chinese food. When critics address themselves to such gener-alisations, they are essentially referring to the best crop of works produced by the film industry. Quality is underwritten in the works of directors who may be considered auteurs. My contention is that the nature of this quality is still largely misunderstood. And as Hong Kong cinema returns to the fold of Chinese cinema, the nature of Hong Kong cinema itself may change. My book hopefully prepares the reader for such a contingency.

In closing, I would like to thank my fellow critics, Paul Fonoroff, Law Kar, and Li Cheuk-to, for rendering assistance in the formulation and writing of this book. I am grateful to the Hong Kong Urban Council, the Hong Kong International Film Festival and the Hong Kong Film Archive for ultimately making this book possible. I also want to express my appreciation to Mika Siltalla, Paul Willemen, and Ling Mei Lim-Petcher for making constructive editorial suggestions. Finally, I am indebted to my wife, Bea Fung, for her invaluable assistance and support during the writing of this book.

Part One

Northerners and Southerners

Chapter One

Early Hong Kong Cinema: The Shanghai Hangover

THE BEGINNING

The development of cinema in Hong Kong cannot be dissociated from the development of cinema in the Chinese Mainland. Hong Kong was one of the birthplaces of Chinese cinema.[1] It produced in 1909 the earliest two-reeler comedies: *Right a Wrong with Earthenware Dish/ Wa Pen Shen Yuan* and *Stealing the Roasted Duck/ Tou Shao Ya*, both adapted from the repertoire of Chinese operas. The director was a Chinese theatre actor-director and amateur film enthusiast named Liang Shaobo, but his producer was an American national, one Benjamin Brodsky, who had established the Asia Film Company in Shanghai.[2] Brodsky had his eyes on the Mainland Chinese market when he started making his films in Hong Kong, thus setting in motion the first linkages between Hong Kong and Shanghai, two cities developing nascent film industries.

In 1913, Li Minwei, a theatre director, made *Zhuangzi Tests His Wife/ Zhuangzi Shi Qi*, an adaptation of a Cantonese opera (Li himself had to play the part of the wife because of a taboo against women appearing in the theatre). Li had founded a dramatic troupe, the Ching Ping Ngok, with Liang Shaobo. Together with Liang Shaobo, his brother Li Beihai and cousin Li Haishan, Li established the Minxin Company (or the China Sun Motion Picture Company) in Hong Kong in 1923, thus initiating the rudiments of a film industry in the territory. However, in 1924, the Minxin Company had re-located to Guangzhou after its application to rent land to build a studio was rejected by the Hong Kong government. They produced a feature film, *Lipstick/ Yanzhi*, which was released in Hong Kong's New World Theatre in 1925. That year, a general strike was called in Hong Kong and Guangzhou. The company was greatly affected by the strike (all film activity including the production and exhibition of films came to a stop) and Minxin once again re-located in 1926, this time to Shanghai. The company was incorporated into the Lianhua Film Company (known in English as United Photoplay Services) in 1930.

Li Minwei was an avid documentarist and photographer. He is better known today for his archival footage of Dr Sun Yat-sen, the founder of the Nationalist Party (the Kuomintang, henceforth abbreviated as KMT) and leader of the Chinese Revolution of 1911 which toppled the Qing Dynasty and put China in the direction of its republican destiny. In the 1920s, Sun was still leading the revolution: his mission was to unify the country under the principle of *tianxia weigong*, translated by KMT party stalwarts as 'the goal of great commonwealth'. Li Minwei followed Dr Sun as he went about achieving this goal and, between 1926–8, photographed the statesman in his last efforts to consolidate the revolution through the 'Northern Expedition' – an attempt to rid northern China of its warlords and unify the country under KMT rule. However, Sun died and it was left to his successor, Chiang Kai-shek, to lead the Northern Expedition.

Li Minwei's documentary footage of Dr Sun Yat-sen, Chiang Kai-shek and other KMT leaders has survived as the standard photographic records of the historic personalities of early republican China. This footage may be seen in *A Page of History/Xunye Qianqiu*, an edited version of the original material shot by Li and passed down to his descendants. Li's backing for Sun's republican philosophy and political aims is the first instance in Chinese film history of a film-maker using the new medium of film to propagate a political cause. It was Li who raised the slogan 'Save the Nation Through Cinema!'. As a producer, Li also supervised the production of fictional feature films, significant precursors of the film industry that would develop: his 1927 version of *Romance of the West Chamber/Xi Xiang Ji* (known in export versions as *Way Down West*), was an outstanding example of a fantasy martial arts genre movie in the silent era. Made in Shanghai, it foreshadows the films of King Hu and Tsui Hark, showing that the early Shanghai cinema is the legitimate precursor of the modern Hong Kong film industry.

When the Minxin company became a part of the Lianhua company in 1930, Li personally supervised the production of the company's initial projects: *Spring Dream in the Old Capital/Gudu Chunmeng* (1930), *Wild Grass/Yecao Xianhua* (1930) and *Love and Duty/Lian'ai yu Yiwu* (1931). These silent classics shared the common theme of love in a feudal setting and all three featured Ruan Lingyu (dubbed China's Garbo) in the best parts of her career.[3] The trilogy secured Lianhua's reputation as the most prestigious and important studio in Shanghai.

The force behind Lianhua was Luo Mingyou, a Hong Kong-born, Peking-educated theatre manager turned producer. He established the North China Film Company in 1927 and controlled the distribution circuit and theatre business in five northern provinces. Luo had brought together investors from Peking, Shanghai and Hong Kong to start the Lianhua company. Luo and Li merged their companies with a third company, the Da Zhonghua Bai He Film Company, and took in another partner, the printing magnate Huang Yicuo.[4] The head office was initially in Hong Kong and the company's largest investor was reported to be the local tycoon Sir Robert Ho Tung, who was named the managing director. The head office was re-located to Shanghai in 1931. By then, it was clear that China's biggest metropolis was proving to be a greater magnet for film talent than Hong Kong. However, the company maintained a branch studio

4

in the colony even as Shanghai became the Mecca of Chinese film-making, initiating the golden age of Chinese cinema in the 30s, with Lianhua playing a major role.

The golden age lasted several years, coming to a premature close when China became embroiled in war from 1937 onwards: first in the anti-Japanese war, then, after the defeat of Japan, in the civil war between the Nationalists and Communists which lasted until 1944. During the war period, Chinese film production continued in various cities, not least in Shanghai itself. After the fall of Shanghai on 13 August 1937, the Japanese occupied all sections of the city except the foreign concessions which were seized only in December 1941 after Japan's declaration of war on the Western powers. With the first stage of Japanese occupation in 1937, many of Shanghai's film talents dispersed to Hong Kong and other Chinese cities, but some remained behind in what became known as the 'Orphan Island': the foreign concessions still free of Japanese control. There, Shanghai's filmmakers continued their activities as before but with the Japanese keeping a watchful eye on them.

With the city's total capitulation in 1941, what remained of Chinese film-making in Shanghai came under Japanese control. The Japanese had built their own film-making facilities in Manchuria and Peking and soon took over production facilities in Shanghai as well. In 1942, they set up a coalition of all film companies under a 'United China' rubric that later came to be known as 'Huaying', the abbreviated form of the Chinese name for the United China Motion Picture Company Limited (or Zhonghua Dianying Lianhe Gufen Youxian Gongsi). Chinese historians and critics under the communist regime have long considered Huaying a 'sham' Chinese company and looked with disfavour on all those who worked for it. The Shanghai film industry under the Japanese has remained a historical 'black hole', the issue being sensitised by post-war political recriminations against those film-makers who had stayed behind to work in Huaying and who were consequently regarded as collaborators or traitors. Further light can only be shed on this period by research undertaken under more favourable political conditions.[5]

As China dug in to fight a war with Japan, film-makers on the Mainland were forced to make films on the move – in Wuhan, Chongqing, Hong Kong. A new genre appeared in Chinese cinema: the 'national defence' movie. These were patriotic war films that recreated images of the Japanese overrunning Chinese villages, committing atrocities, and the heroic resistance of the Chinese against the foreign invaders. National defence movies were made not least in Hong Kong where many film-makers from Shanghai had fled after the Japanese occupied the Chinese sections of the city in 1937.

The history of Hong Kong cinema in the pre-Pacific war period is at best a sketchy one because of the almost total lack of extant films. From the sources available, we know that a quite advanced film industry had developed in the colony by the early 30s as the territory recovered from the crippling effects of the general strike which began in June 1925 and lasted until October 1926 (the film industry took until 1929 to resume normal production of films). Among the leading production companies were the Hong Kong branch of the Lianhua studio, managed by Li Beihai, which employed directors Liang Shaobo and the Chinese American Kwan Man-ching, who had returned to Hong Kong and China armed with experience in Hollywood. Kwan was also one of the supervisors of the 'Overseas Lianhua' branch based in America where, in 1933, he and a fellow Chinese American Chiu Shu-sun (also known under his Americanised name of 'Joseph Sunn') founded the Grandview (Daguan) Company. It was Grandview which produced, in America, one of the earliest Cantonese talking pictures, *The Singing Lovers/ Gelü Qingchao* in 1934 (the first Cantonese talkie was *White Gold Dragon/ Baijin Long*, produced in 1933 in Shanghai by the Tianyi Company). The next year, Grandview was established in Hong Kong where it became one of the best-resourced studios in the territory, joining the ranks of the major film companies Universal, Nanyue and Tianyi, all established in Hong Kong a year earlier.

Tianyi was perhaps the best known of Grandview's competitors. Originally based in Shanghai, the studio had made its name through its prolific production of escapist martial arts fantasies popular throughout China. However, such films were considered morally decadent in conservative circles (they were certainly not all that well regarded by leftist progressives either) and the government moved to ban them. In 1933, Tianyi had a great success with *White Gold Dragon*, the first Cantonese talking picture ever made, which was so successful in the Cantonese-speaking regions of southern China that studio boss Shao Zuiweng thought it opportune to move his studio away from Shanghai and closer to the Cantonese world where he could continue to produce his 'morally decadent' pictures in Cantonese to meet the growing demand. He moved to Hong Kong. It not only saved the studio's fortunes but pointed the way for the territory to become a viable centre of movie production. At the same time, it ushered in the era of sound movies. Tianyi, and companies such as the China Sound and Silent Film Production Company (founded by the tireless Li Beihai), led the way in the production of local sound movies which first appeared in Hong Kong in 1933.[6]

The use of Cantonese was to spark a contentious debate among nationalists and aroused the opposition of Mandarin-language purists. In 1936, the KMT government in Nanjing passed an edict banning Cantonese movies. This was appealed against by Cantonese film-makers in Hong Kong and Guangzhou.[7] Due to the outbreak of war with Japan in 1937, the government, with more pressing matters on its hands, conveniently closed its eyes to the edict. Cantonese movie producers in Guangzhou, the ones most affected by the edict (Guangzhou had developed into a major centre of Cantonese movie production in the mid-30s) simply moved down to the British-controlled colony, and Hong Kong emerged as the base for Cantonese movies with a sizeable overseas market in Southeast Asia and America. In this way, Hong Kong's film industry counted on the use of Cantonese dialect as a selling point. In 1935–7, it is estimated that a total

6

of 157 Cantonese films were produced in the territory. Before 1935, an average of only four Cantonese films had been produced per year since the arrival of sound.[8]

Of the production companies making Cantonese movies in Hong Kong, Grandview occupied the largest studio space and employed some of the most prestigious film-makers, including its founders Chiu Shu-sun and Kwan Man-ching, both directors in their own right. They established reputations as major directors of Cantonese films and exerted an impact on future Cantonese film-makers such as Lee Sun-fung, Ng Cho-fan, Ng Wui and Lee Tit, who were all given their first big breaks as fledgeling talents by Grandview. However, practically none of the early films produced by the company has survived, including the award-winning 'national defence movie' *Lifeline/ Shengming Xian* (1935), directed by Kwan Man-ching. Chiu, who supervised all of Grandview's productions, himself directed the well-regarded national defence movies *Hand-to-Hand Combat/ Rou Bo* and *48 Hours/ Sishiba Xiaoshi* in 1937, the year when full-scale war broke out between China and Japan.

The anti-Japanese war stimulated Hong Kong's film industry as film-makers rushed to put out national defence movies. As the mainstream film industries in China fell under the control of the Japanese, Hong Kong was the only place where patriotic national defence movies could be made freely (even though the Japanese exerted pressure on the British authorities to ban or censor them). Historians have usually pointed to the outbreak of war on the Mainland as a turning point in Hong Kong's film history. It led to the growth of the local film industry as Hong Kong absorbed migrants fleeing Shanghai. In fact, the migration flow had started earlier, and the historical intercourse between Hong Kong and Shanghai went much deeper than is suggested by the consequence of migration due to the cataclysm of war (although political uncertainties caused by the incursions of the Japanese army into China from 1931 onwards would have played their part).

The re-location of the Tianyi studio in 1933–4, triggered by domestic political factors (the threat of a ban on the martial arts fantasies and tales of superstition that were the staple products of the studio), was an event of perhaps greater significance than the migration of directors during wartime Shanghai. Tianyi's move to Hong Kong would see the Shaw Brothers (including Runde, Runme and Run Run) expanding and establishing an empire in Southeast Asia which they oversaw from their headquarters in Hong Kong. The original Tianyi Company evolved into several companies, each more famous than its predecessor. In 1936, a fire destroyed the Tianyi studio and out of its ashes grew the Nanyang Company, managed by Runde Shaw (Shao Cunren) who was recalled from Singapore by elder brother Shao Zuiweng. Runde later re-organised his company into Shaw and Sons. In 1956, Run Run Shaw (Shao Yifu) established the Shaw Brothers studio, the most famous of the various film-making enterprises of the Shaw Brothers.

Thus, Tianyi's move to Hong Kong (as well as the cross-Pacific move of the Grandview Company) was a prescient one, signalling Hong Kong's vast potential as a production and distribution base from which a company like Tianyi (and its subsequent clones) could export their Shanghai-produced Mandarin films and Hong Kong-produced Cantonese films to Southeast Asia and other key markets with large Chinese communities. Directly or indirectly, the Shaws brought along other members of the Shanghai film-making fraternity. The Nanyue Company was founded by Zhu Qingxian, a pioneer of sound recording in the Shanghai film industry who had invented his own recording apparatus for talking pictures. Directors and scriptwriters who had associated with the Tianyi Company in Shanghai also made the move to Hong Kong. They included Su Yi (who ran the Universal Company), Tang Xiaodan, Wen Yimin and Hou Yao. These film-makers were well entrenched in Hong Kong by 1937 when members of the 'progressive' movement in Shanghai cinema started pouring into Hong Kong to continue their struggle: the burning issue of the day being the anti-Japanese war and the need to propagate the war effort of the Chinese people.

THE IMPERATIVES OF WAR

When the Japanese army overwhelmed Shanghai in 1937, Hong Kong was virtually used as a rearguard station for Shanghai-based film-makers until it too came under the yoke of the Japanese in December 1941. Probably the most prominent director to make the southward migration was Cai Chusheng, a Cantonese born in Shanghai. The latter became the first Chinese film-maker ever to win a prize in an international film festival, in Moscow in 1935, for his *Song of the Fishermen/Yuguang Qu*. One of Cai's briefs as an émigré director of the patriotic left was to make anti-Japanese propaganda films from Hong Kong. He complied with films such as *March of the Partisans/Youji Jinxing Qu* (1938; Cai wrote the script, his Shanghai colleague Situ Huimin directed), and *Orphan Island Paradise* aka *Devils' Paradise/Gudao Tiantang* (1939).

March of the Partisans was banned by the Hong Kong government because of its anti-Japanese propaganda (under colonial policy, the British sought to be neutral in the Sino-Japanese conflict) but the ban was lifted in 1941. The film is set in a Chinese village overrun by Japanese soldiers. A young man, Wang Zhiqiang (played by Cantonese actor Lee Ching) is injured while trying to organise the men into a resistance group. After his recovery, he joins the guerrillas in the mountains while his girlfriend is captured by the Japanese. The last shot sees the hero reunited with his girlfriend who is mortally wounded during a guerrilla attack on the Japanese base.

As part of the propaganda, the film portrayed 'good' Japanese characters: soldiers who question their involvement in the China war, and turn against their fellow soldiers as the guerrillas attack. The production of this film represented a significant occasion for Hong Kong's screen professionals (much of the cast included Cantonese-speaking actors then making their first impressions on the screen) to work with their Mandarin-speaking cousins from the more sophisticated Shanghai film industry.

8

Although the standard line in cinema history books published in China states that Hong Kong cinema only produced 'national defence movies' as a result of the infusion of Shanghai émigrés such as Cai Chusheng, Tang Xiaodan, Su Yi, Situ Huimin and others, the fact was that many local Hong Kong film-makers were just as keen as their émigré colleagues to contribute their talents to making anti-Japanese war propaganda films, as is borne out by the Grandview productions directed by Chiu Shu-sun and Kwan Man-ching. Chiu's *48 Hours* was heralded in *The Grandview Film News* (the company newsletter), as a 'spectacular national defence epic' in which major stars worked without pay and box-office receipts would be contributed to meet defence needs in the front lines. A film made along similar principles was *At This Crucial Juncture/ Zuihou Guantou* (1937), a voluntary effort by the territory's major stars and directors to raise funds for the Hong Kong Film Industry Aid Relief Association (founded by film celebrities after the Marco Polo Bridge Incident, which sparked off the anti-Japanese war on the Mainland). None of these 'national defence' films by Hong Kong's own film personalities has survived. Critical writings have thus tended to focus on those, including *March of the Partisans*, *Orphan Island Paradise* and *Ten Thousand Li Ahead*, which were made by prominent Shanghai expatriates.

Orphan Island Paradise, directed by Cai Chusheng, is set in Shanghai during the Orphan Island period. The film centres around a group of young patriots who operate as an assassination squad targeting Chinese traitors and collaborators. In an otherwise tedious propaganda exercise noteworthy only as one of the first Mandarin films ever made in the territory, there is one exuberant sequence in which Cai showed a flash of genius: assassins, dressed in tuxedos and wearing eye-masks, gate-crash a New Year's Eve party and proceed to gun down their victims identified by their devil-horn caps; the sounds of pistols are disguised by popping balloons and drum rolls while the party is in full swing.

Hong Kong cinema suffered a kind of inferiority complex particularly when its film-makers were forced to compare themselves with their Shanghai counterparts. Quality and artistry were aligned with the notion of spreading social consciousness or propaganda messages. This was undoubtedly a legacy of the left-wing tradition of Shanghai film-making. However, there were many Cantonese artists who campaigned for higher quality films in the 30s as the feeling spread that Hong Kong cinema was fast sinking into mediocrity as production output increased. Consequently, the 'clean-up cinema movement' gained popular support. Film scholars generally point to three 'clean-up' movements in Hong Kong cinema: the first in 1935, instigated by a group known as the Overseas Chinese Education Association; the second in 1938, initiated by major film personalities (producers and distributors) concerned with the edict to ban Cantonese movies; and the third occurring in 1949, instigated by film-makers who sought to improve the quality of Cantonese movies.

The 'national defence films' of Cai Chusheng and other Shanghai directors were indicative of the principles that precipitated the second clean-up movement in 1938. They were rousing and patriotic. They possessed a national outlook with messages to unite and defy the enemy. The common feature of all the 'clean-up movements' was the factor of outside influences. Hong Kong's film-makers were motivated by events that occurred, and decisions made, outside the territory. The anti-Japanese war in China brought Shanghai's major film-makers to the territory and the interaction between them and Hong Kong film-makers set the pattern of development of the latter's film industry. War resuscitated patriotic and nationalistic feelings among Hong Kong's film-makers and sowed the seeds for the theme of nationalism that would feature in later Hong Kong movies.

However, even with the flow of talent from Shanghai to Hong Kong in 1937, the territory did not entirely overcome its reputation as a regional industry, secondary to Shanghai (one, moreover, which produced dialect films). The central government's edict to ban Cantonese dialect films did not help the industry's morale either. Most of the film-makers in this first migration were veterans of the left cinema movement in Shanghai, inspired by writers (such as Xia Yan) who belonged to the Communist Party. In Hong Kong, they were concerned above all else with China's plight in the war. For this reason perhaps, the Shanghai film-makers harboured a certain patronising, even contemptuous, view of Hong Kong.

Cai's *Ten Thousand Li Ahead/Qiancheng Wanli* (1941) is representative of this trend. Its characters are Mainlanders living in exile in Hong Kong, experiencing hardships and oppression typical of a crass capitalist society. Hong Kong residents are shown as fun-loving, materialistic and indifferent to the calamity engulfing China. At the film's conclusion, the Mainlanders turn their backs on Hong Kong as if to say 'good riddance' and march back to China to help the war effort. Cai himself marched north when Hong Kong fell to the Japanese in 1941. He returned briefly to Hong Kong after the war (to participate in yet another 'clean-up movement' of Hong Kong cinema) but left soon after to become the communist regime's top administrator in film affairs.

With the fall of Hong Kong in December 1941, the territory's film-making community quickly dispersed, some joining fellow artists in the interior of the Chinese Mainland, others forced to make a living performing live in variety troupes. Before and after the fall of Hong Kong, the Japanese tried but failed to gather together Hong Kong's film artists in another clone of the 'Huaying' conglomerate in Shanghai. Throughout the period of the Japanese occupation which lasted three years and eight months, Hong Kong's film-making community stopped making films altogether. The only film made in Hong Kong during the war was *The Attack on Hong Kong/Xianggang Gonglüe Zhan* (1942) aka *The Day of England's Collapse/Yingguo Bengkui zhi Ri*, a Japanese propaganda film that featured one local star, the fledgeling actress Tsi Lo-lin, who was flown to Japan to shoot her scenes. The actress later asserted that she was coerced into making the film. The resistance of Hong Kong's film community to make a single film for the occupiers proved so successful that there was no repeat of what happened in Shanghai after the war. There, those film-makers who remained behind and continued to make films under the Japanese occupation faced accusations of collaboration with the enemy. In contrast, there was no recrimination, fear and reprisal in Hong Kong. This paved the way for a rapid recovery of the Hong Kong film industry, which once more benefited from a second wave of migration of those Shanghai film artists who were tainted by suspicion of collaboration with the enemy and threats of retribution.

The immediate post-war years were marked by a sense of uncertainty. The peace was short-lived and China was torn apart once again by civil war. This produced a further third wave of migration of the Shanghai film community into Hong Kong, including leftists fleeing the 'white terror' of the KMT government and politically unaligned artists who just wanted to flee a city wracked with financial and political instability. This migration wave undoubtedly contributed to the development of a fully-fledged Mandarin cinema in Hong Kong, quite separate from the Cantonese cinema for which the territory was known. Despite the distinctive qualities of each of these cinemas, the industry largely operated on the basis of vertical integration, with film studios or production companies controlling distribution and owning theatres outright. As Cantonese production soared, major Mandarin studios operated their own Cantonese production units. Many stars and directors worked in both Mandarin and Cantonese cinemas. In the final analysis, Hong Kong was still a regional centre for Cantonese movie production. With the migration of Shanghai film talent between 1946 to 1950, Hong Kong would transform into the regional centre for the production of Mandarin movies as well, effectively replacing Shanghai as the Hollywood of the East.

THE RISE OF HONG KONG'S MANDARIN CINEMA

Hong Kong's film industry as we know it today came into its own only in the 50s as it recovered from the war. The civil war of 1946–9 brought about a further migratory wave of Chinese film-makers from Shanghai to Hong Kong. This time, the talents who migrated were broader and included producers, stars and directors. Two key figures, the producers Li Zuyong and Zhang Shankun, although they had aimed to establish themselves in Shanghai when the civil war had ended, were instrumental in creating a veritable Hollywood in Hong Kong in the immediate post-war years. They established the Yonghua studio in 1947. Zhang Shankun eventually fell out with Li and threw his weight behind a rival studio, Changcheng (or Great Wall), established in 1949. Other Mainland entrepreneurs (theatre magnate Jiang Boying among them) had come to Hong Kong in 1946 harbouring the same ideas as Li Zuyong and Zhang Shankun. They formed a company named Da Zhonghua (or Great China) which started promisingly but folded after making just over 40 films in little more than two years. The majority were Mandarin movies directed by and starring ex-Shanghai luminaries such as Zhu Shilin, Yue Feng, Wang Yin, Butterfly Wu, Zhou Xuan, Yuan Meiyun (all of whom had worked in Shanghai during the 'Orphan Island' days and through the Pacific War). One of the best, a land-

11

mark of Mandarin film production and representative of the company's commitment to grand production values and glamorous casting in the early post-war period, was He Feiguang's *Madame X/Mou Furen* (1947). The film is notable today for showcasing the talents of its neglected director, He Feiguang, who had worked in Chongqing during the war, making the remarkable 'national defence' film *Protect My Country/Bao Jiaxiang* (1939).

Madam X starred Butterfly Wu, a former superstar of the Shanghai cinema. She plays the eponymous madame, in her own words 'a third-rate Peking Opera actress' who had climbed the social ladder by marrying a warlord. Her old flame from ten years ago, a counterfeiter masquerading as a rich overseas Chinese businessman (Wang Hao), turns up and blackmails her. The production values reflected the sophisticated tastes of its Mandarin-speaking artists who obviously were keen to make an impression on their audiences in order to facilitate the quick recovery of the film industry. The studio's commitment to grand design and excellent performances was borne out in the films Zhu Shilin directed for them. *Where is My Darling?/Yuren Hechud* (1948) has elaborate sets, including a rich mansion and a haunted building. The plot centres on the budding romance between a rich man's son and the chauffeur's daughter. Aware of his social status, the chauffeur tries to stop the affair, but the daughter masquerades as a high-class lady to go on a date with the young man who then insists on escorting her home. Not willing to divulge her real identity, she walks into a large house where a night watchman attempts to rape her. There follows an exciting 'haunted house' sequence in which she frenziedly tries to escape from her assailant, being chased through deserted halls and corridors. Zhu's masterly style is evident in his direction of the excellent ensemble cast of veteran character actors, all members of the Shanghai exodus who became a familiar repertory group by way of Zhu's Hong Kong films. The social interplay between the servants evokes Renoir's comedies. The class theme is prominent, with the line 'We are all equal' becoming a leitmotif. Zhu directed four films for Da Zhonghua: *Two Persons Unsympathetic to Each Other/Tongbing Bu Xianglian* (1946), *You're Smart in One Way, I in Another/Ge You Qianqiu, A Dream of Spring/Chun zhi Meng* (both 1947) and *Where is My Darling?*, all of them focusing on women who are made to suffer because of their gender and status.

Da Zhonghua's films typified the development of the immediate postwar Mandarin cinema in Hong Kong, their production values demonstrating that they addressed the Mainland market. Essentially, the Da Zhonghua productions were Shanghai movies made in Hong Kong. While they were shot in Hong Kong, the films' characters and settings were usually specified as Shanghai, avoiding any reference to Hong Kong. On the other hand, the fact that Da Zhonghua was based in the territory reflected the uncertain conditions then prevailing in the Mainland's film capital as a result of the civil war. The founders of Da Zhonghua were business people who were hedging their bets, putting their money in Hong Kong and waiting for conditions to stabilise in China before moving back.

Like his entrepreneurial contemporaries, Li Zuyong had an inkling that the cinematic ground of Chinese cinema would shift away from China, but perhaps even he could not have foreseen that Hong Kong would become the centre of Chinese film production for the next two decades. Li's plan in starting Yonghua Studio betrayed the same rear-guard mentality displayed by Da Zhonghua's founders: he also used Hong Kong as a base whence to address China as the main market, intending to return to Shanghai when peace resumed, supposedly under a nationalist government. Li encouraged talent from Shanghai to join his studio, including left-wing film-makers, many of whom were later deported by a jittery Hong Kong government for instigating a crippling strike in the studio in 1952.[9]

Li's first two films, typical of the producer's ambitious approach, were epics on a grand scale: *Soul of China/Guo Hun* and *Sorrows of the Forbidden City/Qinggong Mishi*, both released in 1948. They dealt with historical subjects, contained themes of national salvation and were made on huge budgets. *Soul of China* depicts the fall of the Song Dynasty as the Mongols began to engulf China and focuses on the Song loyalist Wen Tianxiang's futile attempts to save the dynasty. His patriotism is portrayed in terms of a morbid preoccupation with suffering and he dies a martyr after rejecting all overtures by the Mongols to win him over to their side.

Sorrows of the Forbidden City is a more assured work with a tight script by Yao Ke and efficiently directed by Shanghai veteran Zhu Shilin. The film concentrates on the last decade of the 19th century in which the reformist Manchu Emperor Guangxu was out-manoeuvred by the Empress Dowager Cixi. The emperor's attempt at a palace coup in 1898 failed, resulting in his virtual imprisonment within the Forbidden City by the Empress Dowager, who assumed full power. Both films were released at the height of the civil war between the Communists and the Nationalists, and the theme of salvation and history could not hide a bias towards right-wing conservatism. Wen Tianxiang's steadfast loyalty to the Song Dynasty in *Soul of China* conjured up a political parallel with the Communist–Nationalist stand-off in the civil war. As the film portrayed it, the choice was clear: loyalty to the old regime, and martyrdom rather than capitulation.

Although *Soul of China* and *Sorrows of the Forbidden City* were released in the Mainland (the latter film was heavily criticised in the prelude to the Cultural Revolution), subsequent films produced by Li's Yonghua Studio were banned, which proved to be a crippling blow for Yonghua. Financial problems in addition to a workers' strike forced Li Zuyong to seek financial help in Singapore and Taiwan. The company was restructured, as was its approach to distribution. Now that China had become a closed market, Hong Kong cinema began to cultivate what would become its 'traditional' markets in Southeast Asia (primarily Malaysia and Singapore), Taiwan and other overseas Chinese communities in the West.

With Yonghua's failure to establish itself as the premier studio in Hong Kong, the early 50s saw the dispersal of Shanghai talent into several smaller companies, some of which were managed as film-making co-operatives. The film community in this period was roughly divided between 'left' and 'right' tendencies. Political sensitivities were exacerbated by the

Communist Party's victory in the civil war and the self-exile of the nationalist government in Taiwan. Both the Communists and the Nationalists vied for influence over film-makers in Hong Kong and got their funding agencies to support film companies in the territory. When Yonghua went into financial crisis in 1955, Li Zuyong turned to the Nationalists to bail him out. Left-wing studios such as Fenghuang grew out of a Chinese-initiated co-operative film-making movement known as the Southern China Film Culture Movement which was active between 1949–52. American funding sources also got into the act: the Asia Film Company was established with American money from an agency known as the 'Free Asia Association'.[10]

THE LEFT CINEMA TRADITION

In the turbulent years following the Second World War (1946–9), the civil war took a spiritual toll on the Shanghai film-makers who had come to Hong Kong. For many, it was like a hangover after a night of bad dreams. Others felt despair and homesickness. Those who had worked for the Japanese-controlled United China Motion Picture Company during the 'Orphan Island' period would have felt a sense of reprieve at having left Shanghai.

After the war, a few had been publicly branded as traitors or collaborators in a blacklist issued by the authorities in 1946. Shunned by colleagues in the industry, film-makers who were affected, whether or not their names appeared in the blacklist, found it expedient to leave, prompted by fears of persecution. Others simply felt no compulsion to stay because of the instability of the times and went into voluntary exile in Hong Kong. By 1949, these film-makers were facing the new decade with the realisation that exile was permanent, which showed in their films. Veteran directors from that period, such as Zhu Shilin, Bu Wancang, Ma-Xu Weibang, Yue Feng, Li Pingqian, Gu Eryi, Wang Yin, Tu Guangqi, never quite surmounted the traumatic separation from their native Shanghai. That sense of separation stemmed from the geographic, linguistic and cultural differences between Shanghai and Hong Kong. But the Shanghai directors who took over the Mandarin film industry in Hong Kong in the 50s did not apparently feel any need to address these differences. They took their Mainland experience and aesthetics for granted. To them, Hong Kong was, at least in aesthetic terms, a carbon copy of Shanghai.

However, the Cantonese and Mandarin cinemas remained parallel film cultures. Hong Kong was the natural home of the Cantonese cinema after the war. After all, its residents were native Cantonese. Even among those who were not, the Cantonese dialect was the *lingua franca* in the territory and had the effect of assimilating all non-Cantonese Chinese families. In the 30s, with the arrival of sound cinema, Hong Kong became the centre for Cantonese film production. By the 50s, the wave of migratory film talent from Shanghai and the newcomers' relative indifference to the Cantonese language and cinema had profoundly modified the Hong Kong cinema's Cantonese identity. The Hong Kong depicted by the Mandarin directors was an abstract, cardboard city, using Hong Kong locations

14

dressed up as the streets and quarters of Shanghai or other northern cities. Characters behaved like typical Shanghai residents, their dialogue laced with Shanghai-isms. The styles, themes and content of Hong Kong's Mandarin films evoked the classics of Shanghai cinema of the 30s.

One director who did acknowledge Hong Kong's existence in its own right was Zhu Shilin, although even he could not completely wipe out traces of the Shanghai tradition in his work. Zhu came to Hong Kong in 1946 but not until the 50s did he produce works set in Hong Kong tackling the problems of daily living in his adopted city. In his first years in Hong Kong, Zhu worked for Da Zhonghua (Great China), a company which was, as its name implied, basically eyeing the Mainland market – and so were rival companies such as Yonghua and Great Wall. The films they produced catered to a China-wide audience. In 1948, Zhu directed *Sorrows of the Forbidden City/Qinggong Mishi* for Yonghua. Like his colleague Bu Wancang's *Soul of China/Guohun*, released the same year, Zhu's film was an allegorical work that addressed modern China's dilemma in the civil war. The political situation in the Mainland was to exert an impact, directly or allegorically, on the work of other Shanghai film-makers. While *Soul of China* and *Sorrows of the Forbidden City* could be construed as being critical of the Communists by arguing for a vague nationalism to inspire all Chinese patriots, other directors took a more partisan approach.

Many of the left film-makers who made the southward migration remained committed to propaganda briefs. The precedent had been set in 1937 during the period of all-out Japanese aggression in China by the first migratory wave of 'progressive' film talent from Shanghai to Hong Kong. The priority then was for the Left to instil patriotic anti-Japanese sentiments to rally all Chinese behind the war effort. In late 1948, a wave of left-wing film-makers arrived in the territory to continue the battle for hearts and minds, since conditions in Shanghai were not conducive to their propaganda designed to win over the middle class and intellectuals to a new United Front against imperialism and feudalism. This wave included Cai Chusheng, Ouyang Yuqian, Shi Dongshan, Wang Weiyi, Wu Zuguang, Cheng Bugao and Gu Eryi.

Ouyang Yuqian's *Wild Fire and Spring Wind/Yehuo Chunfeng* (1948), was produced by one of the more strident left-wing outfits, a small company called Da Guangming (Grand Motion Picture Company). The story is set in Hangzhou during the Sino-Japanese war and deals with the back-stage drama of an old teacher infatuated with the beautiful lead actress of a theatrical troupe. It is reminiscent of Sternberg's *The Blue Angel*, but links that film's theme of moral decay to a quest for national salvation: the narrative charts the slow degeneracy of the central character (played by actor-director Gu Eryi) who descends to the worst kind of moral degradation by engaging in espionage activities to aid the enemy. Gu's performance is the best thing in the film, but director Ouyang's *mise en scène* and his focus on characterisation are equally impressive, giving some substance to the melodrama.

Ouyang was not so lucky with his next film, *The Way of Love/Lian'ai zhi*

Dao (1949), produced by another small left-wing company, Nanqun. It is an austere, stagy romance set against the turbulent background of China's recent history: from the Northern Expedition of 1927 to the Second World War. The film's characters are lower middle-class intellectuals, targets of the United Front propaganda strategy; and is typical of the 'petit-bourgeois' romances made by leftist directors who tried to make a point about class distinctions and political loyalty. Zhu Shilin's *Where Is My Darling?/Yuren Hechu*, made for Da Zhonghua in 1947, addresses much the same theme but in the form of a comedy. The classic of this type of romance advocating class struggle is *Spring River Flows East/Yijiang Chunshui Xiang Dong Liu*, made in 1946 in Shanghai, co-directed by Cai Chusheng and Zheng Junli.

The majority of the 1948 left-wing migrants returned to China after the establishment of the People's Republic, some voluntarily, others were deported by the Hong Kong government after the 1952 strike at Yonghua. One or two stayed behind, but the left-wing cause in Hong Kong in the 50s continued to advance under the helmsmanship of directors such as Li Pingqian and Zhu Shilin. Ironically, both were considered politically incorrect pariahs by the Left in Shanghai because of their status as 'Orphan Island' film-makers. Nevertheless, these two Shanghai veterans worked for left-wing studios in the territory, such as Great Wall, Longma and Fenghuang.

Founded in 1949, the force behind Great Wall was Zhang Shankun, a producer of 'Orphan Island' repute not known for leftist views. In fact, he had felt compelled to leave Shanghai because of accusations of collaboration with the Japanese. During the war, Zhang had produced the infamous *Eternal Fame/Wanshi Liufang* in 1942 for 'Huaying' in Shanghai. The episodic film told of Imperial Commissioner Lin Zexu who disrupted the opium trade in Guangzhou and provoked the Opium War with Britain. Among the many directors recruited to direct episodes were Zhang himself, Zhu Shilin, Bu Wancang and Ma-Xu Weibang. His contacts both in Shanghai and Hong Kong were impeccable and despite a reputation for political ambivalence, he devoted his time and talent to a company which aligned itself with the Left, and mobilised Shanghai talent to join the company although Zhang held no official position in it. In the beginning, the company saw itself as a nationalist studio, producing works in the mould of the left-wing traditions of 30s Shanghai.

Although Great Wall gradually acquired a more ideological label and became the leading studio of the left in Hong Kong during the 50s (Zhang left the studio after it was restructured in 1950), many of its artists were not seen in an ideological, austere mould. A star like Bai Guang, a sultry songstress employed by Great Wall under the aegis of Zhang Shankun, was hardly of the austere school. The films of director Li Pingqian, who worked throughout his career for Great Wall, were generally light and frivolous even when they professed to deal with momentous themes such as China's political destiny, as exemplified by *A Strange Woman/Yidai Yaoji* (1949), starring Bai Guang. Its plot was derived from *Tosca*. Bai's character is known as

Xiao Xiangshui (or Little Perfume) who gives herself to a brutal warlord (played by Yan Jun) in order to save the life of her lover, a revolutionary. Any mention of a revolutionary cause in the period would refer to that of the anti-Qing bourgeois revolution of 1911 and the efforts by the Nationalist Party to consolidate its rule over the whole country in 1927 through the Northern Expedition. Setting the story in the pre-1949 era made the point that revolution was a bipartisan cause. The film lovingly creates the mood and decadent atmosphere of Peking under the rule of rapacious warlords. The memorable performances of Bai Guang and Yan Jun (enjoyable as the warlord) give the film a feeling of high camp.

Li Pingqian (who also went by the handle of Jack Li) made thrillers, melodramas, opera films and comedies. In comedy, Li is remembered for satires tinged with rebuke against capitalist excess, such as *The Awful Truth/Shuohuang Shijie* (1950), a screwball farce set in Shanghai during the inflationary last days of the KMT regime, and *Tales of the City/Duhui Jiaoxiang Qu* (1954), about an unemployed young man who wins the lottery and is fawned upon by friends and foes alike. Of these farces, *The Awful Truth* is a genuinely zany satire brilliantly scripted by Tao Qin, who became one of the best Mandarin directors in the 50s and 60s. It bristles with an irrepressible pace and energy, mercilessly lampooning the corruption and materialism of a collapsing regime. Its portrait of money-crazy speculators and con-men who cajole, trick and cheat each other has definite contemporary resonances. As Hong Kong experiences integration with China in 1997, the events of the late 40s depicted in *The Awful Truth* parallel that of China in the 90s: inflation, speculation, decadence and corruption marking an economy beset by unbridled growth exacerbated by government inefficiency and political uncertainty.

The Awful Truth is one of Li's made-in-Hong Kong masterpieces carrying unmistakable Shanghai brushstrokes. Another is *Laugh, Clown, Laugh/Xiao Xiao Xiao* (1960), a tragi-comedy set in Tianjin during the anti-Japanese war which tells the story of an accountant who loses his job but hides the truth from his family, pretending to go to work every day. Together with another out-of-work colleague, he performs *xiangsheng* on stage (a Chinese form of a stand-up comic act relying on Mandarin patter). His wife and daughter's dismayed humiliation when they discover the truth underlines the traditional low status accorded to stage performers. The film features a superb central performance from Bao Fang as the accountant. Despite his problems, the character remains optimistic and forward-looking. As in *A Strange Woman*, where Bai Guang gave her own renditions of scenes from Peking opera, the *xiangsheng* sequences demonstrate Li's affinity with the northern Chinese performing traditions. Being northerners – from the perspective of the southern Cantonese residents of Hong Kong – the Shanghai directors felt closer to traditions which they considered to be representative of Mandarin-speaking culture.

The left in Hong Kong, of which Li Pingqian and Zhu Shilin were perhaps the best representatives, branched out into various 50s genres. Directors such as Yuan Yang'an, Cheng Bugao, Tao Qin, Gu Eryi and Yue

Feng ensured quality and style. They were employed by Great Wall, where Yuan Yang'an was also the general manager. Gu Eryi, one of the founders of the Da Guangming company which produced *Wild Fire and Spring Wind*, made *The Victims/Xiehai Chou* (1951) for Great Wall, a *noir*ish melodrama employing Shanghai stars Li Lihua, Tao Jin and Han Fei to good effect in a story set in Macao. The film features song segments (aka *chaqu*) in both Cantonese and Mandarin. Scenarist Tao Qin made his debut as a director at Great Wall with *Father Marries Again/Yijia Chun* (1952), showing how a typical middle-class Mandarin-speaking family adjusts to life in their adopted city. It tells of a widower, an architect, who decides to re-marry but meets with opposition from his sister and two daughters. Both films used characters and places that reflected proximity to Hong Kong.

Zhu Shilin, who worked mostly for Longma and Fenghuang, both companies which he had founded, tackled issues of more relevance to Hong Kong in films such as *Spoiling the Wedding Day/Wu Jiaqi* (1951) and *Festival Moon/Zhongqiu Yue* (1953) while also coming up with an excellent genre piece in *Flower Girl/Hua Guniang* (1951), faithfully based on Guy de Maupassant's short story, *Boule de Suif.* Zhu transposes it to the Sino-Japanese war on the Mainland: a group of bourgeois evacuees flees the Japanese and finds itself sharing a bus with a prostitute or 'flower girl' (played by Li Lihua). They are stopped by Japanese troops whose commander orders the prostitute to spend a night with him. When she refuses, he holds up the group, and it is up to her to get her fellow passengers out of their predicament by acquiescing to the order.

Like Li Pingqian, throughout his Hong Kong career Zhu tended to alternate between 'entertainments' and films with a more didactic intent. His mature work came in the 50s, when he was well established in Hong Kong cinema following critical acclaim for the Yonghua super-production *Sorrows of the Forbidden City* (1948), a breakthrough in his career. Nevertheless, Zhu's work remained rooted in the classicism of Shanghai's golden age. This influence can also be understood in the light of ideological principles guiding the production companies (Longma, Great Wall and Fenghuang) for whom Zhu worked in Hong Kong – left companies working with credit from the Bank of China, one of the Peking government's official agencies operating legally in the territory. The link to the Mainland was therefore more than superficial. With this background, the aesthetic link to Shanghai was conspicuous, particularly for the films that could be described as left-wing social classics.

In films such as *Spoiling the Wedding Day/Wu Jiaqi* (1951, co-directed with Bai Chen), *Mr Chen vs Mr Chen/Yiban zhi Ge* (1952), *Festival Moon/Zhongqiu Yue* (1953), *House-Removal Greetings/Qiaoqian zhi Xi* (1954), *Between Fire and Water/Shuihuo zhi Jian* (1955), Zhu evokes the community spirit inherent in the social realist tradition of Shanghai as defined by *Crossroads/Shizi Jietou* (1937), *Street Angel/Malu Tianshi* (1937) and *Crows and Sparrow/Wuya yu Maque* (1949). With both eyes focused on social issues troubling Hong Kong in the 50s, it is remarkable that Zhu never lost sight of the need to put humour into his films. The number one problem plaguing the community was the housing problem. To this, Zhu added the themes of identity and class-consciousness, conditions exacerbated by the lowly status of refugee existence. Zhu's characters are exiles in Hong Kong struggling to belong to a community in transition. His masterpiece, *Festival Moon*, is about precisely such an exile (played by the comedian Han Fei, another Chinese exile) and his attempt to maintain a dignified existence in the face of society's humiliations.

Zhu is remembered today as a socially conscious but conservative and classical director of Mandarin pictures, a view reinforced by his three last works, *The Eternal Love/Tongming Yuanyang* (1960), *Thunderstorm/Lei Yu* (1961) and *Garden of Repose/Guyuan Chunmeng* (1964). All three were adaptations from theatrical or literary sources. All have deep tragic elements. *The Eternal Love*, the best of the three, tells the story of a young man who gains merit as a scholar but fails to live up to his potential because of rigid social conventions and taboos. The end comes when he discovers that his mother, supposedly a widow, had not been as chaste as had been made out. Unknown to the son, she had secretly kept a lover by her side all these years, a man whom the son knew as his 'uncle' but who was, in fact, his father. Fearing scandal, the son makes all the wrong decisions, leading to a tragedy of Jacobean dimensions underwritten by the film's formalism which suggests the rigid structures of a tradition bearing down on its characters. His last film, *Garden of Repose/Guyuan Chunmeng* (1964), was an adaptation of a Ba Jin novel about decadent and decaying families in wartime China. Ever the consummate artist, Zhu turned Ba Jin's customary anti-feudalism and family-centred concerns into an intricately designed melodrama, shot in wonderful Eastmancolour. The vivid colour and art direction in the classic style of 'studio realism' are the film's most striking features. A wintry scene is an occasion to design a remarkably open interior set, displaying a snowfall in the background through open windows. The characters are indifferent to the weather: indeed, the view of falling snowflakes and the positioning of the characters inside the house are designed to convey nothing more than the characters' feeling of numbness and emotionally frigid state of mind.

Garden of Repose also works well as a melodrama, but it sinks under its own weight of ideological didacticism. Its characters suffer and behave with the typical forbearance of symbolic good and bad figures who represent life's cruel forces and its beacons of hope. The only difference here is that the characters seem less optimistic. The work is characteristic of that aspect of Zhu's classicism which is essentially metaphoric and symbolic, detaching itself from the realism of the social contexts. Little wonder that the film was attacked by Hong Kong's left-wing press. In China itself, the director's *Sorrows of the Forbidden City* was later seized upon by Mao-inspired leftists who launched an avalanche of criticism against the film as a prelude to the Cultural Revolution. No doubt, Zhu's status as an 'Orphan Island' film-maker, and one, moreover, who worked in the notorious Huaying, did not help his defence.

Li Pingqian too made his share of such classically symbolic melodramas:

Marriage Affair/Men, released in 1951, and *Forever Waiting/Wangfu Shanxia*, released in 1957. Both films followed the correct ideological line in deprecating the feudal family, while propounding a feminist ideology: the central characters of both films are women who are given a raw deal by men.

Li and Zhu could be seen as the finest exponents of classical didacticism. But this was, in fact, a common trait in the melodrama genre at the time, both in the Cantonese and the Mandarin cinemas, to some extent regardless of left or right ideologies. The inclination to preach or to arrive at a social-conscience message was a temptation too few film-makers resisted. Hong Kong was not the affluent society in the 50s and 60s that it would become in the 70s and 80s. China was politically unstable. The country preyed on the minds of Hong Kong's people, many of whom were refugees who had fled the Mainland, but who felt a patriotic attachment to it nevertheless. Hong Kong cinema tended to reflect the conscience of Chinese society at this time. The left-wing studios were the quickest to take up this particular banner, but they were also mindful of the principle of entertaining the masses even while making politically required (and correct) message films.

They usually worked in the classical areas of Mandarin-speaking culture, particularly the costumed genres (historical epics, opera films, martial arts swordfighting films), but also contemporary melodramas, thrillers and comedies. Films with contemporary settings were inspired by the left-wing tradition of Shanghai cinema *circa* the 30s: classics such as Wu Yonggang's *The Goddess/Shen Nü* (1934), Sun Yu's *The Big Road/Da Lu* (1934), and Shen Xiling's *Crossroads/Shizi Jietou* (1937). These works impressed Chinese audiences with their social introspection and social criticism, qualities which became recognised as hallmarks of the left's film tradition equating political consciousness with cinematic classicism. Shanghai veterans who were already working in the 30s, such as Li Pingqian and Zhu Shilin, continued this tradition in Hong Kong, as did more consciously political directors such as Cai Chusheng, Ouyang Yuqian and others from the 1948 migration wave who chose not to stay in Hong Kong. While Li and Zhu came across as the more stalwart directors of Hong Kong's left-wing studios, others, such as Cheng Bugao and Yue Feng, were skilled craftsmen whose early work evoked a leftist conscience but who gradually turned to more routine genre films. They are remembered for their realist classics of the 30s: Cheng for *Spring Silkworms/Chun Can* (1933) and Yue for *Angry Tide of China's Seas/Zhongguo Hai de Nu Chao* (1933).

Yue Feng evolved from realism (albeit of the studio variety) in his early years in Shanghai to a more conscious use of style and design in his Hong Kong films for the left-wing Great Wall studio as well as distinctly non-political studios such as MP and GI and Shaw Brothers. Yue, along with directors like Tao Qin, Yi Wen and others of the studio era of the 50s, is one of the most under-rated Hong Kong film-makers. He was no visionary, but he was an unassuming, meticulous director who adopted a wholly sympathetic attitude to his characters, particularly women. It was no accident that Yue worked with some of Hong Kong's most memorable female stars: Li Lihua, Bai Guang, Lin Dai and Zhou Xuan. In Hong Kong in 1947, his first films were stolid melodramas: *Three Women/San Nüxing* (1947), *An Unfaithful Woman/Dangfu Xin* (1949), *The Flower Street/Hua Jie* (1950), and *Modern Red Chamber Dream/Xin Honglou Meng* (1952), all of which centred around women characters and espoused a strong feminist theme.

Three Women, produced by the Da Zhonghua company, stars Li Lihua in one of her first films in the territory following a wartime career as a teenage star in 'Orphan Island' Shanghai and the film industry under Huaying. It was Yue Feng, a fellow Orphan Islander and ex-Huaying employee, who had introduced a 16-year-old Li Lihua to cinema audiences by directing her first film, *Three Smiles/San Xiao* (1940). Her performance as an independent career woman who brings up the daughter of a prostitute in *Three Women* was one of the most direct feminist statements in Hong Kong cinema at the time. But the film is stilted and heavy-handed, its theme redolent of left-wing Shanghai cinema, ironically made more precious by a melodramatic style.

Yue's women are typically portrayed by Li Lihua and Lin Dai, his two favourite actresses who were both adept at exuding strength of character underneath a veneer of feminine charm. They embark on a quest for social understanding and, above all, equal relationships with men. The feminist theme lies at the heart of Yue's films, from the early Great Wall message 'melodramas' such as *An Unfaithful Woman* and *Modern Red Chamber Dream* to later, glossy Shaw Brothers films such as *Madam White Snake/Baishe Zhuan* (1962), *Lady General Hua Mulan/Hua Mulan* (1964), *The Last Woman of Shang/Da Ji* (1964) and *The Lotus Lamp/Baolian Deng* (1965). The style and pacing of the films, particularly in his later work for the Shaw Brothers, show a meticulous craftsman at work. The films he made for Great Wall show a director of mellow, classical tastes who was willing to go along with political circumstances and conform to the ideological line of the studio. In this respect, *Modern Red Chamber Dream* is a fitting example of how a classical director could function within the limits of Marxist ideology. It is a modern-dress adaptation of the classic novel *Dream of the Red Chamber*. Its main plot – the arrival of Lin Daiyu (played by Li Lihua) to the Jia mansion which is presided over by a kindly but traditionalist grandmother, and Daiyu's romance with Jia Baoyu (played by Yan Jun) – is turned into an ideological tract on feudalism and class struggle. The modernisation of the classic endows the Jia family with a capitalist feature: the patriarch is a financial speculator ever mindful of what political events will do to the stock market. The ending has the Jia family abandoning their household – and Lin Daiyu – as the nationalist regime collapses; the servants and Daiyu gather on the porch to watch the rising of a new sun as the soundtrack brims over with the sound of soldiers marching past. The setting is Shanghai, although the film looks and feels like it could have been set in Hong Kong, no doubt to prick the conscience of Hong Kong audiences. However, like most of the films coming out of the left-wing studios, the attack on capitalism was mitigated by the traditional emphasis on high feudalism as the left's most conspicuous *bête noire*. Capitalism and feudalism were portrayed as a way of life that grew out of their mutual embrace: *Modern Red Chamber Dream* was an example of how the left-wing studios encoded such an equation into their brand of ideological aesthetics.

However, the ideological underpinning did not detract from the director's more positive sympathies for the characters of Lin Daiyu and her rival in love, Xue Baochai (played by Ouyang Shafei). In them, both the director and his stars expressed their leanings toward classicism. The ideological straitjacket imposed on the production was clearly an obstacle which hindered the exercise of a modern interpretation of a classic, but Yue showed that he could adapt his own idealism, and his bias for female protagonists, to the requirements of the studio. Yue's adapatability survived his switchover to a non-ideological studio such as Shaw Brothers, for whom he made two splendid melodramas: *Street Boys/Jie Tong* (1960) and *The Deformed/Jiren Yanfu* (1960). In these two films, Yue proved his worth as a director with a social conscience even while being employed by a studio well known for its superficial gloss and espousal of the good life.

A film such as *Modern Red Chamber Dream* illustrates an anomaly in early 50s Hong Kong cinema that was an outcome of the exodus of Shanghai talent. The anomaly involved a large degree of expediency in the adjustments of careers and political outlooks. As a result of their southward migration, many stars and directors not normally considered radical first worked for studios that were politically to the left: in this category were stars such as Li Lihua, Yan Jun, Zhou Xuan, Bai Guang, and directors such as Yue Feng, Bu Wancang and Tao Qin. These artists became well established in the Hong Kong film industry and many later migrated to Taiwan. They were undeniably idealistic in their younger days. At times, their work conveyed a certain sentiment for regional folk culture or espoused a broader patriotism – especially in movies about the anti-Japanese war and other allegorical works dealing with the civil war that called for the audience to take sides. Yue's *The Flower Street* is representative of that genre of patriotic-nationalist works.

The Flower Street stars Zhou Xuan as the daughter of a stage performer, Xiao Hu (played by Yan Jun), who goes missing at the start of the anti-Japanese war. The story begins during the Northern Expedition in 1927 (the campaign by Chiang Kai-shek to rid northern China of its warlords and to unify the country under the nationalist government), when Daping (Zhou Xuan) is born. Her name means 'great peace' and signifies the hope that the end of the warlords will usher in an era of peace for China. But the country enters into a period of more turbulence when war with Japan ensues. In Xiao Hu's absence, Daping and her mother are forced into a life as itinerant performers. Then, one day, Xiao Hu turns up as nonchalantly as he had disappeared and resumes his career as a performer, but he falls foul of his own nationalistic pride when he is forced to sing pro-Japanese propaganda songs. Xiao Hu subverts the lyrics and comes up with a patriotic rendition condemning the Japanese invasion. He is beaten up but survives. The film ends on an upbeat note as war ends and the family is reunited amidst invocations for lasting peace in the country.

In common with films such as Li Pingqian's *A Strange Woman* (1949) and *Laugh, Clown, Laugh* (1960), Zhu Shilin's *Flower Girl* (1951), Tu Guangqi's *Little Phoenix/Xiao Fengxian* (1953), Li Hanxiang's *Red Bloom in the Snow* (1956), and Yue's own *Golden Lotus/Jin Lianhua* (1957), *The Flower Street* is notable for its evocation of cultural life in the early republican era. *Golden Lotus*, made for the MP and GI studio, is much superior to *The Flower Street*, which it resembles. Lin Dai gives a wonderful performance in it as a songstress – the role which Zhou Xuan played in the earlier film but without Lin's stylised mimetic expressiveness in showing all the human senses and emotions. All of these films advocate a nationalism that is a mixture of a newly-found patriotism and a resurgence of Chinese folk culture, here equated with northern forms, styles and dialect. The culture is presented against the background of war when it is perceived to be threatened by Japanese propaganda, lending urgency to its task of instilling morale and pride in the people.

Such a tendency among Chinese directors in Hong Kong and Taiwan may be termed 'cultural nationalism' – a term which stands as the opposite of 'cultural imperialism'.[11] The Shanghai émigrés were particularly prone to such cultural nationalism because of the perception among overseas Chinese audiences that Mandarin-speaking artists personified the most representative and highest form of Chinese culture. Certainly directors such as Li Pingqian, Zhu Shilin and Yue Feng exploited this perception to show their talents by creating period atmosphere and portrayals of northern culture, the staple forms being Peking opera, as well as various other theatrical and street performing styles.

Cultural nationalism is one part of the legacy the Shanghai film-makers bequeathed to Hong Kong cinema. It defers to the purist side of Chinese culture. But as interpreted by Hong Kong cinema, cultural nationalism catered to only one side of the Chinese psyche. The other side hankered for modernisation and the good life, Hollywood-style. Even in their heyday in the 30s, the Shanghai directors were just as prone to delve into Western (meaning Hollywood) styles in efforts to 'modernise' Chinese cinema.[12] Hong Kong cinema naturally benefited from the expertise and sophistication of the Shanghai film-makers in integrating Chinese tradition with the urge for modernisation: cultural nationalism on the one hand and, on the other, a kind of aestheticised materialism. The two-faced nature of Chinese film-making became much more marked in Hong Kong and it may be argued that as the Shanghai émigrés settled down to life in the territory, they became adept in juggling these two aspects of cinema which gradually grew to complement each other.

THE RIGHT'S RESPONSE

The left-wing studios may have believed themselves to be in the frontline in presenting tradition as positive nationalism and modernisation as the great urge of all Chinese. But in truth, the environment in Hong Kong was more pluralistic and the left had to contend, and compete, with other independent studios and companies to the right of the political spectrum. The

Shanghai film-makers who migrated to the colony reflected the left–right divide that prevailed in the Mainland and, as the left-wing studios began to make films along ideological lines, they came up against more consciously right-wing companies purveying anti-communist ideology. Such companies were the right's equivalent of the left-wing studios, operating under the sponsorships of the Nationalists now based in Taiwan, and even American agencies. A representative case was the Asia Film Company, established in 1953 with American funding.[13]

The films of the Asia Company reinterpreted left-wing dramas, themes and preoccupations from a right-wing perspective. Hence, a film like *Half Way Down/ Ban Xialiu Shehui* (1955, directed by Tu Guangqi) was the right's response to a film like Zheng Junli's classic Shanghai tenement drama *Crows and Sparrows/Wuya yu Maque* (1949). Tenement films, long the province of the left, made use of slum settings and dealt with communities trying to survive in dire economic circumstances. Usually they ended in an affirmation of unity and purpose: to survive and carry on the struggle. That structure is adopted by the makers of *Half Way Down* which similarly revolves around a slum community, but its characters are intellectuals and former middle-class, 'smart' people now living as refugees in Hong Kong's Tiu Keng Leng (Rennie's Mill) resettlement centre, reserved by the government for Chinese soldiers and low-ranking officials of the Nationalist government. The characters are imbued with the spirit of exile – like the professor who carries a pouch of Chinese earth wherever he goes. Such behaviour accords with the standard slogan of the Nationalists, 'recover the Mainland', which underpins the propaganda message of the film.

In other Asia-produced films such as Tang Huang's comedy of manners *Life With Grandma/ Man Ting Fang* (1955) and Bu Wancang's Chekovian tragedy *The Long Lane/ Chang Xiang* (1956), feudal attitudes are once again attacked. The former is about a grandmother who interferes in the lives of her grandchildren; the latter deals with a family shattered by a tragic secret: many years ago, the mother had abandoned her baby daughter in order to adopt someone else's son. *The Long Lane* is set in Peking and once again successfully evokes the mood and atmosphere of a northern culture. *Life With Grandma* is set in Hong Kong and its characters are northerners who had come to Hong Kong to escape life under the Communists. They are shown growing used to life in the territory and, indeed, becoming more Westernised. However, the film had to contain a character who is an obsequious traditionalist: a grandmother (played by Wang Lai) whose role in life is to remind her grandchildren of the need to observe tradition and cultural propriety. She is accordingly nicknamed 'The antique' by her grandchildren.

Perhaps the right's foremost cultural-nationalist was Ma-Xu Weibang. In 1949, he worked for the Great Wall company which, when overseen by Zhang Shankun, was not the classical left studio it later became. At Great Wall, Ma-Xu directed *A Maid's Bitter Story/ Qionglou Hen* aka *The Haunted House* (1949), his first film upon settling in the territory. *A Maid's Bitter Story* was his Hong Kong masterpiece, made with one of the biggest budgets ever given a production at that time (nearly bankrupting Great Wall since it was a box-office disaster). *A Maid's Bitter Story* offers indisputable proof that Ma-Xu had obsessions instead of themes.

Born in 1905, Ma-Xu started his career in Shanghai in the 20s, eventually rising to fame with the horror classic, *Song at Midnight/Yeban Gesheng* (1937). In 1941, he made a sequel, *Song at Midnight, Part II/Yeban Gesheng Xuji*. Both films are masterworks in which Ma-Xu grandly displays his singular obsession: the face and its disfigurement. The hero (based on the *Phantom of the Opera*), is an actor-revolutionary, named Song Danping, who commits himself to fight feudalism, autocracy and warlordism. Song's face is disfigured in an act of jealousy by a warlord, Song's rival for the love of a landlord's daughter. His subsequent predicament as a lovelorn 'phantom' living in a dilapidated theatre is an indictment against the corruption and oppressiveness of pre-war Chinese society. *Song at Midnight* was a hit with Chinese audiences as particularly patriotic young students identified with a hero both physically and spiritually deformed by the age he lived in.

Ma-Xu (his double-barrelled surname being the result of his acceptance of his wife's family as his progenital family; his own surname was Xu) was to return again and again to his obsession with physical deformity in Shanghai-produced films such as *The Leper Girl/Mafeng Nü* (1939), the two-part *Qiu Haitang* (1943), and Hong Kong-produced titles such as *A Maid's Bitter Story* (1949) and *The Python and the Beauty/Dumang Qingyuan* (1957). Disfigured faces, animal symbolism, unfulfilled and unconsummated love, all such motifs amounted to a cry in the dark, a hope for redemption and better days as well as a lament for China. Ma-Xu's characters were victims of history, of great political events such as war and revolution, but he used tragedy only when the world around him was descending into chaos. His view of China's fate was essentially pessimistic, understandably so in the light of contemporary events.

The face and its disfigurement, physical wholeness deformed by spiritual infirmity, madness and role-playing, are all motifs developed to the hilt in *A Maid's Bitter Story*. Stylistic traits from *Song at Midnight* are here too: melodramatic songs communicating one's innermost thoughts, Gothic chiaroscuro and art direction utilising a Chinese sensibility as in the exquisite set of a Chinese mansion with waxing-moon motifs (in this respect, the film's alternative title *The Haunted House* is perhaps more evocative). Ma-Xu's first Hong Kong production was enough to qualify him as a major talent, but he was not always given the chance to develop in his own way or to work consistently in the horror genre. He had an erratic career, slotting tame melodramas (with often overt anti-communist messages, such as 1955's *New Song of the Fishermen/Xin Yuguang Qu*) in between penny-dreadful horror films. He was more in control on *Booze, Boobs and Bucks/Jiuse Caiqi* (1957), starring Grace Chang, a screwball musical comedy. He ended up making Amoy-dialect opera films and died in a car accident in 1961.

Ma-Xu's best work bears the unmistakable stamp of his personality, even though some scenes did not work due to the technician's carelessness or lack of skill. His obsessions dominated his films. His characters were extensions of his own personality. Obsessive and preoccupied with personal pain, they stalked empty chambers and hallways, consumed with revolutionary zeal to rescue China, but personal tragedies always got in the way. Ma-Xu was a visionary with a highly refined sense for expressionist imagery, able to find a visual style to match the intensity of his personal obsessions.

A Maid's Bitter Story provides a key towards a better understanding of how Hong Kong exploited Shanghai talent and how far such exploitation tied in with the creation of Hollywood-style studios and the contradictory need of some individual talents to go beyond the house-styles of those studios. Ma-Xu eventually had to relent, perhaps realising that the special characteristics of Hong Kong were at last beginning to make themselves felt in Hong Kong's cinema, characteristics that could be defined roughly by the title of his own *Booze, Boobs and Bucks*. By the mid-50s, the evidence suggests that Hong Kong's Mandarin cinema was beginning to overcome its Shanghai hangover, as Hong Kong's settings and, more importantly, lifestyle began to be integrated into the territory's film. The left-wing tradition became less prominent in the second half of the 50s as the Hong Kong film industry moved towards accommodating market conditions rather than ideological and patriotic imperatives. The left-wing studios had to face up to a right-wing backlash, formally instituted with the establishment of the KMT-affiliated Hong Kong and Kowloon Cinema and Theatrical Free Enterprise General Association which advocated the boycott of left-wing films in the crucial Taiwan market. Economic pressure was put on the left studios to secure market niches other than the China market which began to shrink away. This meant competition with studios of the apolitical right as represented by Shaw Brothers and MP and GI, studios which were soon to monopolise market positions in Taiwan and Southeast Asia. The Hong Kong film industry was moving in the direction of a more conventional and refined glamour industry, producing works that would not risk political censorship in their new markets. In time, the left followed suit.

Mandarin film-makers in the early 50s displayed a political ambivalence which the left exploited as cultural nationalism by bringing into play nostalgia and homesickness for the Mainland. The Shanghai film-makers shared a general feeling of goodwill towards their country of birth and if a film expounded on a nationalist theme from a left perspective, none felt compelled to object strongly. Thus, there was no feeling of irony when those stars and directors initially associated with the left later switched to the right as their careers became more established. The most enigmatic figure from this period was producer Zhang Shankun, a man who personified both the business and artistic sides of Chinese cinema during his days in Shanghai and his 'exile' in Hong Kong. Zhang was not a showman in the mould of a Li Zuyong or Run Run Shaw, but a smart operator who knew enough about cinema as art for an aesthetic sensibility to permeate his productions. He was credited with the direction of films which he produced, a classic example being *What Price Beauty?/ Xiao Bai Cai* (1954), starring Li Lihua, and co-directed by Yi Wen.[14] The film shows the maturing of the

Shanghai style in Hong Kong, not as a successful hybrid but as a pure trans-plant. More importantly, it tells a story with no ideological blinkers despite the fact that it is a story that easily lends itself to different ideological interpretations (indeed, film-makers in the Mainland have made their own version of the story). The setting is the late Qing period when social eti-quette and sexual mores were still untainted by the influence of modern thought. Xiao Bai Cai (Li Lihua) is the beautiful wife of a tofu hawker. She and a doctor named Yang Naiwu, are wrongly accused of murdering her husband. Both are innocent of the crime and of conducting an illicit love affair, although the doctor is attracted to the woman. The real culprit is the local magistrate's son who desires Xiao Bai Cai and, when spurned, con-spired to take his revenge on her. During their ordeal in court, the two innocent defendants fall in love. They are acquitted; Xiao Bai Cai earns a further pardon from the Dowager Empress which effectively clears her of all social stigma. But instead of doing the expected thing by marrying the doctor, she enters a nunnery. The production is infused with the kind of sedate stylisation associated with the masters. The acting and the black and white photography complement the staid *mise en scène*: the feeling is one of invocation, sadness and a sense of reverence for the old. The style is half of the message; the other half may be glimpsed in the performances of Li Lihua and Huang He as the wrongly-accused couple: both render per-formances of quiet passion and genuine pain when they are tortured to extract confessions. In the end, as the truth comes out and they are acquit-ted, their pain lingers because society dictates that one's loyalty be paid to the past (to a dead husband) and to the community to keep it free from scandal. Hence, Xiao Bai Cai goes to the nunnery and Yang Naiwu is left alone to grow old.

It is possible to see how the theme of exile, pain and a reverence for the past could have been more relevant to the right-wing than an ideological battle with the left over issues such as anti-feudalism and nationalism. Zhang Shankun was the right man to show political and ideological ambivalence. In Shanghai during the war, he kept the film industry alive by means of back-room manoeuvres and machinations with the Japanese (and was subsequently accused of collaborating with them). In his Hong Kong career, he went against the grain to produce works powered by emotion and a moral sense of right and wrong based largely on conservative values. In Hong Kong he associated with left-wing film-makers but later dissociat-ed himself from the left to become his own producer and director. He knew his audience and entertained them with movies which were, as far as he could control, ideologically ambivalent but emotionally true.

NOTES
[1] The earliest film activity ever recorded in the territory took place in 1898 when a team of cameramen-representatives from the Edison Company came to Hong Kong on their trip around the world to present Edison's Vitascope exhibitions. The Edison team took cinematic records of Hong Kong Government House, the Hong Kong Regiment, the Sikh Artillery and miscellaneous street scenes. A selection of

these Edison shorts were presented at the 12th (1988) and the 19th (1995) Hong Kong International Film Festivals.

[2] Jay Leyda's *Dianying, Electric Shadows: An Account of Films and the Film Audience in China* (Cambridge, Mass.: MIT Press, 1972) is still the only book in English which offers a relatively detailed account of the early history of Chinese cinema. See also I. C. Jarvie's *Window on Hong Kong: A Sociological Study of the Hong Kong Film Industry and Its Audience* (Hong Kong: Hong Kong University Press, 1977) which offers a good account of pre-war Hong Kong cinema. In Chinese, the two standard histories are Cheng Jihua's *Zhongguo Dianying Fazhan Shi/ History of the Development of Chinese Cinema* (2 vols, Peking, 1963) and Du Yunzhi's *Zhongguo Dianying Shi/ History of Chinese Cinema* (2 vols, Taipei, 1972).

[3] All three films were long considered lost but a print of *Love and Duty* was recently discovered in the Chinese Consulate in Uruguay and brought 'home' to the Taipei Film Archive where it was restored. The film was shown at the 1996 Hong Kong International Film Festival and revealed to be a masterpiece of silent Chinese cinema.

[4] The full name of the company was the Lianhua Production and Printing Company.

[5] For a rare account in English of this period of Chinese cinema history, see Poshek Fu's essay 'The Struggle to Entertain: The Political Ambivalence of the Shanghai Film Industry under Japanese Occupation 1941–45', HKIFF catalogue, Urban Council, 1994.

[6] Hong Kong's first all-sound movie was *A Fool's Marriage/ Shazai Dongfang*, produced in 1933 by the China Sound and Silent Motion Picture Production Company established by Li Beihai, who also directed the film. Earlier that year, Li had also produced and directed *Conscience/ Liangxin*, a part-sound movie.

[7] See the bi-monthly Chinese-language film magazine *Art Land/ Yilin*, nos 1 and 3, 1937, for articles debating the official banning of Cantonese and defending the use of the dialect. *Art Land* was first published in February 1937.

[8] See Yu Mo-wan's *Eighty Years of Hong Kong Cinema/ Xianggang Dianying Bashi Nian*, in Chinese, published by the Hong Kong Regional Council, 1994.

[9] For an account of Li Zuyong and the Yonghua Studio, see Law Kar's essay 'The Shadow of Tradition and the Left-Wing Struggle', HKIFF catalogue, Urban Council, 1990.

[10] Law Kar, op cit.

[11] The apogee of cultural nationalist films is Hou Xiaoxian's recent release *The Puppetmaster/ Ximeng Rensheng* where the accent is on regional folk culture and its propagation against a background of Japanese colonialism. In Hou's case, the political-patriotic sentiment is largely absent perhaps because of Taiwan's ambiguous status with respect to China.

[12] In this regard, Frank Borzage's influence on Chinese *wenyi* melodramas deserves closer study.

[13] That same year also saw the establishment of the Hong Kong and Kowloon Cinema and Theatrical Enterprise Free General Association (Gang Jiu Yingju Ziyou Hui), a federated union of KMT-affiliated right-wing groups within the film industry. The association is presently headed by actress Tong Yuejuan, widow of producer Zhang Shankun (the late actors Wang Yuanlong and Wang Hao were ex-presidents of the association).

[14] Although Zhang's creative input could not be underestimated, critics and scholars have tended to credit the achievements of *What Price Beauty?* to Yi Wen.

Chapter Two

Shanghai Redone: Les Sing-Song Girls in Hong Kong

While the sense of exile continued to exert itself as nostalgia for the motherland, keenly felt in films with historical subjects set in ancient dynastic eras or the early republican era (1911–27), Hong Kong's Mandarin cinema began to evolve a unique, fabricated style that was partly Shanghai, partly Hong Kong, reaching its apex in the late 50s and early 60s. Its most representative form was the musical which evolved from the phenomenon of the famed sing-song girls, a feature of Shanghai life ever since its development as a treaty port from the middle of the 19th century. Mandarin cinema took this particular Shanghai tradition of sing-song girls to heart and, in the great majority of its productions, regardless of genres, featured a tune or two.

Writer Eileen Chang, ex-Shanghai resident and one of the most evocative writers on her native city, explained the term sing-song girl in her annotations to the late Qing dynasty novel *Haishang Hua Liezhuan* (a title which may be translated as 'Shanghai Blossoms' or, more literally, 'Ocean Blossoms'),[1] set in the brothels of old Shanghai and detailing the lives of high-class prostitutes and their clients. The novel, written by Han Ziyun, used dialogue in the *wu* dialect (the basis of Shanghainese) in which *xiansheng*, Mandarin for a scholar or gentleman, refers to a high-class prostitute adept at singing opera and popular tunes and at narrating stories or poetry from the classics while attending to the men with wine or tea. In Shanghainese, *xiansheng* is pronounced 'xi-shang' which was corrupted (or misunderstood) by European revellers partaking of Shanghai's night-life as 'sing-song'. This term then entered the lexicon of popular culture and became understood in the West as a unique institution of the greatest Chinese treaty port. It was perhaps the one enduring, human feature of Shanghai's epithet as a 'wicked city'.

The character of the sing-song girl encapsulates the materialist and cultural-nationalist tendencies of the Chinese. In cinema, the sing-song girl is both performer and entertainer, a tamer and more cultured version of a street whore. Throughout the past forty years of its post-war development, Hong Kong cinema featured variations of the sing-song girl. One of the best reminders of the Shanghai antecedence of Hong Kong's Mandarin cinema was Zhou Xuan, who personified the type. In her, audiences saw a bitter-sweet personality who could only have been created by the Shanghai film industry. The exploitative side of that industry tried to integrate aspects of the personal lives of the stars into their films. Ruan Lingyu, the silent actress known as the Chinese Garbo was the archetype of the tragic stars: her real life was just as flawed as her various screen lives. She was devastated by malicious gossip about her personal life and committed suicide because of it. Zhou's life was equally marked by tragedy: she had a history of mental depression brought on by a broken marriage and subsequent affairs with men who turned out to be rogues and cheats. She spent her last years in a mental hospital in the Mainland where she died in 1957, aged thirty-nine.

Zhou gained immortality in the 1937 classic *Street Angel/ Malu Tianshi* where she sang the song 'Four Seasons' and the ballad of the 'Tianya Songstress' (meaning 'the Songstress of the World', an epithet usually applied to Zhou Xuan herself). Her Hong Kong films, such as *An All-Consuming Love/ Chang Xiangsi* (1947) directed by He Zhaozhang, *Song of a Songstress/ Genü zhi Ge* (1948) and *Orioles Banished from the Flowers/ Huawai Liuying* (1948), both directed by Fang Peilin, and *Waste Not Our Youth/ Mofu Qingchun* (1948) directed by playwright Wu Zuguang, were thrifty melodramas set in Shanghai or some unspecified locality in the Mainland. Although none of these pictures was particularly distinguished, all capitalised on the singing voice of Zhou who was dubbed *Jin Sangzi*, 'the Golden Throat'.

Zhou's musical films were actually melodramas and comedies with *chaqu*, that is to say, inserted musical numbers of the star-singer plying her trade. *Chaqu* sequences came complete with subtitles of the song's lyrics appearing line by line as the song was sung, very much like modern-day karaoke laser discs. The intention was to encourage viewers to sing along with the stars. *An All-Consuming Love* featured Zhou as a housewife whose husband is called away to war. The husband's best friend is requested to look after Zhou and, inevitably, affection grows between them. The *chaqu* episodes were successfully integrated into the melodrama, with Zhou playing a character whose singing voice sees her through bad times during the war (she becomes a nightclub singer). *Chaqu* sequences tended to have a life of their own. The most appealing aspect of *Orioles Banished from the Flowers*, a static comedy about heterosexual jealousy, was precisely the *chaqu* segments which continue to inspire nostalgia for Zhou Xuan. The same was true of *Waste Not Our Youth*, a ghost-comedy adapted from Pu Songling's *Liaozhai Zhiyi* (*Strange Tales from a Chinese Studio*), in which Zhou portrayed a country lass who falls in love with a boy from a rich family. The two lovers are separated due to family objections and she later appears as a ghost to guide him back to her. *Song of a Songstress* is probably the most interesting of Zhou's films released in the period of 1947–8 because of its semi-biographical premise. She portrays Zhu Lan, a nightclub singer whose affections for a painter are complicated by the advances of a rich, obnoxious playboy. The plot progresses from light-heartedness to soap-operatic tragedy as the playboy is revealed to be the son of the man who had killed Zhu's mother during an attempted rape when she was working for him as a maid. Zhu was brought up by foster parents who kept the mother's death a secret (Zhou herself had an unhappy childhood among foster parents).

As one of the first singing stars in Chinese cinema, Zhou Xuan's popularity influenced the vogue for singing stars and Mandarin songs. She was a rather poor actress but a singer of golden-throat distinction. Today, her songs have outlasted the sad and tragic dimensions of her personal life and acting career. From the modest *chaqu* episodes of her films sprang a tradition of Mandarin-pop as well as the development of the full-fledged musical genre, which in Chinese is known as *gechang pian*: a genre that is differentiated from *chaqu* or *xiqu* (which refers to the opera film, not to a modern musical). Hong Kong's Mandarin cinema of the 50s was particularly blessed with a string of female singing stars who sang and composed in the style of Zhou Xuan, appending their own signatures, of course. These included Bai Guang, Zhou Manhua, Zhong Qing, Lin Cui and the best of them all, Ge Lan, also known as Grace Chang. To a greater degree than Zhou Xuan, these stars possessed sex appeal and were also far more convincing actresses as tragediennes or comediennes.

Bai Guang began her singing and acting career in Shanghai in 1942. She came to Hong Kong after the war and earned her stardom in a series of *femme fatale* roles. In Yue Feng's *film noir*-cum-karaoke musical (*chaqu*) *Blood-Stained Begonia/Xieran Haitang Hong* (1949), Bai struts her sexy stuff (and voice) as a *femme fatale* whose deviousness ruins her husband. The Begonia is the sobriquet adopted by Bai Guang's husband (played by Yan Jun) for his secret life as a cat-burglar. He leaves as his calling card after each burglary, a red begonia flower. The Begonia has a self-pitying streak; he resorts to crime only because he is driven to it by his flamboyant wife who is as improvident with men as she is with money. The Begonia is framed by his wife and her lover for a theft he did not commit. He escapes the trap, confronts his unfaithful wife and her lover, killing him before surrendering to the police. The next scene is a standard sing-along with Bai Guang: a montage of flower-symbolism and mock-melancholia which seems to suggest that the Begonia is greatly missed. The Begonia eventually escapes from prison to kill his wife when she threatens to take their daughter away from her respectable adoptive family. *Blood-Stained Begonia* is a *film noir* with good moments, all having to do with the Bai Guang character. In her other Yue Feng film that same year, *An Unfaithful Woman/Dangfu Xin*, Bai played a prostitute wrongly accused of murder. The presiding judge (Yan Jun again) turns out to be the man she had loved as a servant girl: he is the son of the landlord who had employed her. The plot was adapted from Tolstoy's *Resurrection*.

In *Song on a Rainy Night/Yuye Gesheng* (1950), directed by Li Ying, Bai starred as a newly arrived migrant in the territory who becomes the most sought after escort girl-cum-cabaret singer. In a scene at the beginning, she trips on the stairs while going up to an apartment, a rather too obvious moment of significance to telegraph her misbegotten life-to-come as a woman who cannot resist the materialistic life. By the end of the film, she is a cripple shunned by her former benefactors and patrons. *Song on a*

Rainy Night had a leftist agenda: the sing-song girl gets her social come-uppance and reforms. Ever since the golden age of Shanghai cinema, the character has fascinated left-wing film-makers who saw in the sing-song girl contradicting qualities of beauty and depravity which to them illustrated what was wrong with Chinese society. Moreover, the sing-song girl exuded sex-appeal, an attribute which both left-wing and right-wing film-makers exploited.

Bai Guang is counted among a group of beautiful Chinese stars of the 50s and 60s that included Li Lihua, Li Mei, Zhang Zhongwen and Lily Ho. They were styled 'sour' beauties with sex appeal in contrast to the 'sweet' stars, of which Zhou Xuan was one. The singing stars of the 50s were all prone to sweetness, but Bai Guang was one of the first to stand out as a kind of terrible beauty, the epithet she earned in 1949 after the Chinese title of the Li Pingqian film she starred in, *Yidai Yaoji*, which may be translated as 'the bewitching beauty of all ages' (the English title is less bewitching: *A Strange Woman*). Interestingly, both the sweet and the sour beauties of Hong Kong in the 50s proved to be more appealing than many of the male leading stars. One of the characteristics of Mandarin cinema in this period, which remained valid until the late 60s, was the supposedly romantic but effete leading man, so pathetically weak and ineffectively romantic as to be a wimp of all ages.

Zhou Manhua was the leading lady of *Long Live the Bride/Xinniang Wansui* (1952). She had a career in Shanghai as a singing star modelled on Zhou Xuan; both stars worked for the same production company from 1939 to 1941 during the 'Orphan Island' period. Zhou Manhua moved to Hong Kong in 1950 where *Long Live the Bride* was her first film, playing a woman who stands up for her right to choose her own husband, defying her father who wants her to marry a rich man's son. A comedy examining social mores and the issue of the modern woman, *Long Live the Bride* is an early example of a Mandarin musical in the *chaqu* style, showing that the influence of Zhou Xuan was hard to shake off, although the film did also try to incorporate American dance forms (the jitterbug) and big band music (Glenn Miller) then in fashion. In fact, American influence was to become pervasive in the genre.

Li Lihua, a radiant 'sour' beauty who got her start in 'Orphan Island' Shanghai in 1940 and who would outshine her rivals by the end of the 50s, gave one of her most memorable performances as the prostitute Xiao Fengxian (Little Phoenix) in *The Little Phoenix/Xiao Fengxian* (1953), directed by Tu Guangqi. The story is based on the real-life romance between Xiao Fengxian and the famed revolutionary general Cai Songbo (played by Li's husband, Yan Jun). The plot centres on Cai and Xiao Fengxian's conspiracy to undermine the rule of Yuan Shikai, first president of the Chinese Republic (founded 1911) who sought to proclaim himself emperor. Li's Xiao Fengxian is a classic sing-song girl: well-versed in poetry, an able performer of opera skits, and so beautiful that generals and states-men vie to risk their reputations and careers over her.

Li Lihua and Ge Lan were the co-stars of *Red Bloom in the Snow/Xue*

Lihong (1956). Li plays Xue Lihong, an opera actress and folk-songstress who keeps company with other itinerant players in a small northern town; among them is strongman Jin Hu (Luo Wei), her former lover. Now unhappily married to another man, she contrives to seduce Jin Hu and prevent his affections for Hehua (Ge Lan) from turning into real love. The film captures well the mood of northern street culture in the China of the 1930s, with good ensemble acting from a supporting cast of Mandarin actors of northern Chinese origin, including the young King Hu. It marked the debut of director Li Hanxiang, who went on to specialise in films of northern Chinese settings and subjects.

Red Bloom in the Snow is a melodrama with its few musical sequences integrated into the narrative as skits performed by its characters. Thus Ge Lan performs a folk version of northern 'rap', keeping time and rhythm by beating a drum, one more proof of the versatility which would help her become a star; Li Lihua performs a watered-down sketch of a classic *huadan* role in Peking opera. In that sense, the thin line dividing the musical from other genres (usually melodrama) continued to grow thinner. However, *Red Bloom in the Snow* was still not a true musical even though the plot was reminiscent of *Cavalliera Rusticana*. The setting, characters and story-telling mode were suitably *verismo*, but not quite appropriate for the leap into fantasy required by the Hollywood musicals that Hong Kong cinema was trying to emulate.

Up to this point in the mid-50s, the Mandarin musical of the standard karaoke variety was already crooning its way out of fashion. The vintage stars such as Zhou Xuan, Bai Guang and Zhou Manhua were going through – or had already experienced – turning points in their careers (as a result of illness, Zhou Xuan's career was practically over by then). Gradually, modern dance sequences were integrated into the stories and more spicy popular songs soon become the order of the day. This called for a setting, and a city, which audiences could recognise as modern and in keeping with the times. Hong Kong fitted the bill. By the mid-50s, the words Hong Kong actually appeared in the dialogue and was referred to by characters as a real city rather than a vague urban locality standing in for Shanghai.

In *Songs of the Peach Blossom River/Taohua Jiang* (1956), co-directed by Wang Tianlin and the producer Zhang Shankun, a standard city boy-meets-country girl plot confers a new status on Hong Kong, the adopted city of most, if not all, of the cast and crew. Hong Kong comes into its own as a place of both the mind and the heart. The man, Li Ming (Luo Wei), comes from Hong Kong and is in the countryside to study and collect folk songs. He meets a spritely lass, Jin Lirong (Zhong Qing), otherwise known as the Wild Cat and who is the best local singer. In this country spot, folk songs and music are a mark of pride and honour, and a man can get his girl by knowing how to sing. Hong Kong is referred to as a kind of wonder city where new gadgets like records and phonographs brighten up the lives of the residents. Music and Hong Kong, the city, are thus important and integral motifs in the film. For perhaps the first time, there was actually an attempt to break the mould of the karaoke-episode musical even though the format was still preserved. The characters now sang to each other instead of the usual solo episodes punctuating the picture. Now, music and songs sprang forth naturally as a function of both scene and plot. Zhong Qing became a star with the film. Her rise to stardom was preceded a few years by that of Ge Lan, her classmate from acting-school who grew up in Shanghai and came to Hong Kong as a teenager in 1949 (they were both talent-spotted by director Bu Wancang, who trained and gave them their debuts in his film, *Seven Sisters/ Qi Zimei*, 1953).

The writing was on the wall: the musical genre was about to change from the *chaqu* format to the *gechang* format, and nothing signified the change better than the rise of Ge Lan to musical stardom. By the time *Mambo Girl/ Manbo Nülang* was released in 1957, the Mandarin musical was in full swing as signified by the film's opening sequence of a robustly choreographed mambo dance. The close-up of Ge Lan's legs, one foot in front of the other in dance notation, and the crane back revealing the whole ensemble in a joyful rendition of tribal dance, signals the maturity of the musical in Hong Kong cinema. *Mambo Girl* moves from one musical set-piece to another and wastes no time in getting on with the melodramatic plot. By the third musical number, Ge Lan, the happy Mambo Girl, has learned that she was abandoned at an orphanage by a fallen woman and that her unique dancing and musical talents are the result of a 'wild' pedigree. Ge Lan is excellent, both as a dramatic actress and a musical star. She shifts from joyous Mambo Girl to crestfallen orphan searching for mother (whom she finds working as a toilet lady in a nightclub) without missing a beat. The film is masterfully directed by Yi Wen. In Ge Lan, Hong Kong cinema found its most representative musical star-cum-actress and with *Mambo Girl*, Hong Kong cinema produced its first musical masterpiece.

Nearly as good as *Mambo Girl* is Wang Tianlin's *The Wild Wild Rose/ Ye Meigui zhi Lian* (1960), a transposition of Bizet's *Carmen* to the nightclub milieu of Hong Kong. Ge Lan is the Carmen character, a mankiller with a soft heart named Miss Deng. She takes pity on a sacked colleague in the nightclub band she sings with and sells her services to a client to obtain money to pay for her friend's wife's medical treatment. In the next breath, she seduces a young piano player (Zhang Yang, the wimpiest of all romantic leading men) and causes his downfall from innocent, virginal babe to a crazed and jealous wreck. Ge Lan's rendition of the Habanera (translated into Chinese with modifications, but with the cries of 'L'amour, L'amour' intact) is a high point, but for this critic at least, the 'Jajambo' number is more like the real Ge Lan: funky, animalistic, with an element of camp but still stylish and graceful.

The Mandarin musical as it existed in the late 50s was a very eclectic genre. Even though it developed into a major genre by Hong Kong cinema standards, one cannot escape the feeling that it remained a pale shadow of Western musicals. Western influences, particularly from Hollywood, were pervasive. Add Western opera, jazz, rock and roll and all other strands of popular music as it developed from the 60s onwards, and you have a strange but beguiling mixture. In addition, there was a whiff of cultural stolidness to the Mandarin musical which could bewilder audiences, particularly foreigners unused to the fact that the Chinese artists were trying their darndest to be as Western as possible. Hong Kong cinema was relying on its Shanghai artists to generate a unique type of entertainment utilising Western motifs and fashions (in the Hong Kong style) while mobilising traditional Shanghainese sing-song entertainment.

The Mandarin musical suffered from being too eclectic, but it could not be faulted for its effort at drawing on as many sources as possible in its attempts to entertain the masses. While it developed, the Mandarin musical relied on its female performers to sing the ballads, a tradition it never really abandoned even when it was incorporating Western influences. This practice resulted in a lack of convincing male musical stars. The nearest the Mandarin musical ever got to one was Peter Chen Hou, who was called upon to put on dancing shoes and sing at the same time. He worked hard in both departments but the results were, at best, average.

A Shanghainese who came to Hong Kong in 1950, Chen became known for his light performances in memorable Mandarin comedies produced by the MP and GI studio. His roles in Yue Feng's *The Battle of Love/Qingchang Ru Zhanchang* (1957), Tao Qin's *Beware of Pickpockets/Tifang Xiaoshou* (1958) and Yi Wen's *The Loving Couple/Xinxin Xiangyin* (1960) typecast him as a romantic leading man in light comedies (his leading ladies were Lin Dai, Lin Cui and Ge Lan, respectively). These comedies were close cousins to musicals and Chen appeared to be a natural for that genre too. He was at the right place at the right time, appearing in a spate of musicals when the genre was being refurbished as glossy, modern entertainment. He was in *Mambo Girl* playing Ge Lan's male admirer and dancing student. Thereafter, he was seen in Eastmancolour as the romantic foil to Li Mei and Zhang Zhongwen, playing two rival sisters in *Calendar Girl/Longxiang Fengwu* (1959), the first musical in colour, directed by Tao Qin with stylistic panache and an eye to the colour scheme. Chen's character functions as the inconspicuous leading man, someone whom the female leads could fall back on like a useful tool around the house. All he needed to do was to be nice and provide occasional comic relief. He was also needed as the male partner in dance scenes but the effect it generally had was to put the women in greater relief. In *Hong Kong Nocturne/Xiangjiang Huayue Ye* (1967), directed by Inoue Umetsugu, a Japanese director employed by Shaw Brothers, Chen had a rather more substantial role as the husband of Zheng Peipei, one of the three female leads (the other two were Lily Ho and Qin Ping). *Hong Kong Nocturne* shows how much the genre missed out in not being able to nurture suitable male partners for the sweet and the sour musical beauties of Hong Kong cinema. The story centres on three sisters who go their separate career paths after quitting their father's magic act. All three meet the men of their dreams but only one – the Zheng Peipei character – actually gets to marry her man. However, in the course of the narrative, Zheng's husband dies in a plane crash. The theme of the story is the happenstance of ideal men and how they must act as the moral nerve centres of women's lives. Consequently, their existence as moral-conscience figures is emphasised rather than their physical presence. Such a philosophical-moral theme is quite unprecedented in the musical genre.

The Mandarin musical failed to secure male stars as a viable alternative to its female stars. Few leading men ever carried a musical picture. The image of weak and effeminate romantic leading men became the norm, much in contrast to the women. *Hong Kong Nocturne* was one of the last of the Mandarin musicals before it turned to martial arts swordfighting and kung fu pictures. The heroic archetype was changing and sometimes, even within a single movie, one could see the opposition of the weak romantic hero against the emerging macho hero. A representative film was Tao Qin's *My Dreamboat/Chuan* (1967), a musical-melodrama based on a novel by the popular Taiwanese writer Qiong Yao. The story deals with mismatched love among young couples. Tang Kexin (Lily Ho) is betrothed to soft-spoken Du Jiawen (Yang Fan) but she falls in love with Jiyuan (Jin Han), a gruffly outdoors type. This precipitates a tragedy as Jiawen marries the virtuous Xiangyi (Jing Li) and, accordingly, sinks into depravity as he gambles away his father's fortune. The film ends with the tragic deaths of Jiawen, his wife and his father, but leaves a hopeful note as Kexin and Jiyuan adopts Jiawen's daughter for their own. Director Tao Qin, a professional, glossy artist, expertly bisects the story into two moods: the first half is a high-spirited, tuneful youth movie featuring musical setpieces centred around a Christmas party and a hunting frolic in the mountains; the second half is an appropriately high-strung melodrama that ends in tragedy. The setting is Taiwan: the characters are typical *waishengren* – non-Taiwanese Mandarin-speaking Mainlanders who have settled in the island following the communist victory. The protagonists, in keeping with Qiong Yao's style, become psychological wrecks as the arrow of love finds the wrong targets. That this first generation of Mainlanders in Taiwan finds little fulfilment in their private lives symbolises the difficulty of adapting to life in another land (the symbol of the boat indicates destiny as well as the pain of exile). However, it is the opposition of the male heroic stereotypes in the film that poses the most interesting problem. The sexy Lily Ho chooses the strong outdoors man. Her former lover, the weak romantic hero, understandably falls into depression and marries the wrong woman. The strong macho hero wins out but tragedy results.

My Dreamboat was the swansong of the romantic melodrama as well as the musical (in its composite form). The star, Lily Ho, was the object of desire for the two heroic types presented in the film. Interestingly, she would feature in another major film that dealt with the changing male heroic image, Zhang Che's *The Singing Thief/Dadao Gewang* (1969). Zhang Che, the director of such martial arts classics as *The One Armed Swordsman/Dubi Dao* (1967) and *The Golden Swallow/Jin Yanzi* (1968) did *The Singing Thief* as a combo kung fu-musical almost as if to disprove the musical's exposure of man's effeminate nature. In his martial arts movies, Zhang Che seemed to be exorcising the soft male image of bookish gentility and effeteness. In *The Singing Thief* he was apparently completing the exorcism by tackling a musical where the hero is adept in martial arts and also idolised by women.

Employing Taiwanese singer Lin Chong to fill in the lead role, Zhang came up with a curious hero, at least in terms of his sexual image. Pan (Lin Chong) is the reformed ex-cat burglar now employed as a solo singer in a nightclub; he is falsely suspected of a series of robberies where a red carnation, his usual signature, is left at the scene of the crime. With the relentless cop 'Bulldog' Pao on his trail, he seeks the help of Guoji (Luo Lie), a pal from the old days, to catch the real culprit. Help also comes from an unexpected quarter: the beautiful Darling Fang (Lily Ho), a rich playgirl who is mesmerised by Pan. She keeps film clips of Pan's performances which she projects onto a screen in front of her bed, an example of karaoke madness before its time. The height of karaoke ecstasy is reached when she makes love to Pan in the bed as the film is running. But Pan's sexuality may be as artificial as the celluloid gracing his lovemaking with Darling. The scene is a little lacking in feeling. One can feel more sexual heat in Pan's first meeting with Guoji, characterised by looks, glances and knowing smiles (all motifs which predominate in scenes between male heroes throughout Zhang's oeuvre). The revelation that Guoji is the traitor results in a duel scene (set inside a film studio) that lacks any of the ramifications of male bonding or concealed gay love found in Zhang's espousal of the code of *yi*.[2] Hence, this is a film which is only partly successful in creating a male image that is macho but sensitive, a kind of idealised hero whose sexuality is tempered by an underlying old-world sensitivity. Kinky sophistication and gay undercurrents (as strong as they are in a Zhang Che martial arts movie) underline the film's sexual perspective. The male image was however not really redeemed by Zhang Che's stress on man's martial prowess; in effect, the image developed was that of the romantic hero, the last vestige of the Shanghai tradition concomitant with sing-song girls and rooted in the traditional performing arts, particularly opera and the *wenyi* melodramas.[3] So ingrained was the weak scholarly image of the male hero that by the late 60s, audiences were more than happy to see Chinese screen counterparts of Western action heroes such as John Wayne, Clint Eastwood, Charles Bronson, Alain Delon and Sean Connery – all of whom were hugely popular in Hong Kong. Before the male image was rescued by the martial arts genre, it suffered more pummelling in pictures such as *Sun, Moon and Star/Xingxing, Yueliang, Taiyang* (1961), *Love Without End/Bu Liao Qing* (1961), *The Blue and the Black/Lan yu Hei* (1964) and *Till the End of Time/Heri Jun Zailai* (1966). These films were all soapy melodramas which featured karaoke musical segments in the true, time-honoured tradition of a song in every film. The Mandarin musical had come to the end of a cycle by reverting back to the hyphenated combinations. The musical in its integrative form where music, songs, characters and plots were inter-related to each other, survived only for a short period in the late 50s. The 60s saw glossiness come in, as exemplified in *Hong Kong Nocturne*. But that picture also confirmed that the made-in-Hong Kong musical could not transcend the emphasis on plot when it should have been on songs and music. The tunes were not catchy enough, the music was mediocre.

37

Was this an epitaph for the Mandarin musical? The answer to such a question would have to be set against the decline of the musical in Hollywood itself and what has developed in Hong Kong cinema since then. Mandarin pop evolved into Cantonese pop. MTV came into its own and developed technically and aesthetically within a niche of electronic gadgetry which rendered the old-style film musical obsolete. The musical tradition lives on in MTV and karaoke. In Hong Kong cinema, there are extensive uses of both styles in films of practically all genres. The musical genre itself was revived briefly in the 80s in Tsui Hark's *Shanghai Blues/Shanghai zhi Ye* (1984) and *Peking Opera Blues/Dao Ma Dan* (1986). They are modern examples of the hyphenated musicals of old: combos of comedy, adventure, the woman's film, plus the extra bonus of MTV giving an already eclectic genre a postmodern tinge. The titles of Tsui's films, putting the spotlight on Shanghai and Peking opera as they do, are apposite. They indicate that Hong Kong cinema is a stylistic hangover of old cinematic and theatrical traditions. In cinematic terms, Shanghai had left its indelible mark, and no movie brat of modern Hong Kong cinema, as Tsui Hark is, could ever hope to rub it out. Anita Mui is the contemporary reincarnation of the classic sing-song girl (she is also the modern version of a sour beauty). Her performance as Fleur, the Cantonese variant of a sing-song girl, in Stanley Kwan's *Rouge/Yanzhi Kou* (1989) is right out of the Shanghai brothels as depicted in the novel *Shanghai Blossoms*. Fleur embodies all the traits of the memorable sing-song girl: talent, beauty (with a subliminal touch of the seductive vamp), and a taste for tragedy. More glamorously, in Tony Au's *Au Revoir, Mon Amour/Heri Jun Zai Lai* (1991) set in Shanghai in 1941 on the eve of the Japanese takeover of the city, Mui plays 'Mui Yee', a high-class *chanteuse* if not exactly a classic sing-song girl who acts as a neutral bridge between her nationalist lover (played by Tony Leung Ka-fai) and a Japanese agent who loves her. Mui's version of a Shanghainese sing-song girl once again fulfils the role that has been attributed to such characters by Hong Kong film-makers. Mui Yee is no standard bearer of nationalism; rather, she is a medium, a character who does not appear to harbour any political affiliations, thus able to make nationalism all the more accessible by wrapping it in abstract or cultural terms. *Au Revoir, Mon Amour* is a stunning showcase for Anita Mui who soothes the senses with her crooning, lit with loving care by four of Hong Kong's best directors of photography. The film and Mui's performance contrive to be an *hommage* to Shanghai by exploiting all the generic signs and conventions of 'Shanghai' films: the night life in the foreign concessions; the brutal underworld; a standing Japanese army confronting young patriots eager for battle; and above all, a sing-song girl. Mui's interpretation of the character shows how far and how complete Hong Kong had absorbed Shanghai.

NOTES
[1] See 'The Complete Collection of Zhang Ailing', vol. 10, entitled *Haishang Hua Kai* (Hong Kong: Crown Publishing, 1992) [in Chinese].

[2] Cf. the chapter on John Woo.

[3] Wenyi is an abbreviation of *wenxue* (literature) and *yishu* (art), both considered soft or weak occupations for men but which nevertheless have a hallowed tradition in China.

Chapter Three

The Early Cantonese Cinema

THE OPERA CONNECTION

As the Shanghainese film-makers consolidated their positions in the Hong Kong film industry, the division of the industry into two different streams became more pronounced. The Mandarin language pictures produced by the Shanghainese film-makers competed directly with Cantonese dialect pictures produced by a parallel film industry from the early pre-war period right up to the 70s.[1]

The first Cantonese dialect film was an opera film, *White Gold Dragon/ Baijin Long* (1933), starring Sit Kok-sin, a famous Cantonese opera star of the period. *White Gold Dragon* broke all box-office records in Hong Kong and Guangzhou, the two major Cantonese speaking cities, and set off the production of a wave of opera films which reached a peak in 1939. Film historian Yu Mo-wan has estimated that a quarter of the output in the 30s were opera films.[2] Chinese opera and cinema had been closely linked from the outset. The first Chinese film made by Chinese artists was in Peking in 1905 when Peking opera actor Tan Xinpei put three scenes from the opera *Dingjun Mountain/Dingjun Shan* on film. In Hong Kong too, the earliest films were comic farces adapted from Chinese opera. In both the silent and sound periods, Chinese cinema utilised opera's appeal in order to attract greater crowds, producing a genre of opera films that capitalised on the love of traditional *xiqu*. In the 50s, as Cantonese cinema boomed in the atmosphere of post-war recovery, the opera film became so popular that it could be seen as an emblem of the times. Audiences wallowed in the traditional stylisation of the opera film, singing along with the stars as the lyrics appeared in subtitles on the screen! The opera film was distinguished by remarkably intuitive acting and frankly acknowledged theatricality. The genre is best remembered for its stars, and none typified the opera film more than the divas Yam Kim-fai and Pak Suet-sin, who forged a screen partnership in more than fifty films from 1951 to 1967.

Yam was typecast as male scholars, roles which had been her specialty in the opera theatre where she had begun performing at the age of fourteen. Opera actors were trained in performing particular character-types and often specialised in one role or type throughout their careers; so convincing was Yam as a male impersonator that she was forever stereotyped as male scholars or *sheng*. Her scholars were romantic foils to Pak's demure, sometimes flirtatious, *dan* characters (*dan* being the category of female

40

roles which could be impersonated by male actors). Yam and Pak delighted audiences with their acting and singing styles (actors developed singing styles by means of various vocal pitches, and acting styles through specialised gestures, movements and facial expressions).

Both of the stars appeared separately in opera films and other genres as well, and chalked up credits in literally hundreds of films. The astonishing quantity says something about the production-by-numbers process of the Cantonese film industry. Opera stars were routinely employed by film producers to double up as movie stars in non-opera films. Their popularity threatened to swamp legitimate screen actors, thus giving rise to the famous 'ling-xing conflict' – 'ling' being the name applied to opera actors while 'xing' meant movie stars or the legitimate dramatic actors of the screen. The conflict led to a crisis in Cantonese cinema; the question of which set of aesthetics (drama or opera) should prevail was never satisfactorily resolved. The crisis provoked legitimate screen actors to hone their own skills since they were the ones accusing opera film producers and actors of lowering standards. So prevalent was the sense of mediocrity that legitimate screen actors and directors felt as if Cantonese cinema was dominated by amateurs.

The prolific output of Cantonese opera films, combined with their theatricality and lack of technical finesse, have made it difficult for critics to assess the films. But they have attracted a cult following among devoted fans and critics who accept Cantonese opera on its own terms and who feel that, in some cases, it has fused well with the film medium. One of the most popular cult items, constantly revived on early morning television is *The Purple Hairpin/Zichai Ji* (1959), starring Yam-Pak (the abbreviated form of Yam Kim-fai and Pak Suet-sin), directed by Lee Tit, with a libretto by Tong Dik-sang, considered the finest librettist in the business. In the best opera films, the theatricality of the form provides a quiet, mellow backdrop to the plot, the lyrics and the performances conveying a subtle but heady flavour which to connoisseurs is rather like tasting a wine of ancient vintage.

Based on the legend of a Tang dynasty courtesan Huo Xiaoyu, made into an opera by the famous Ming dynasty librettist Tang Xianzu, the plot tells of the romance between Huo (played by Pak Suet-sin) and the scholar Li Yi (played by Yam Kim-fai). They first meet and fall in love when Li Yi happens to pick up a purple hairpin belonging to Huo. However, Li is betrothed without his consent to a magistrate's daughter. The lovers are separated due to the machinations of the magistrate, but the intervention of a man in a yellow robe allows them a brief reunion before Li Yi is held incommunicado once again.

The Purple Hairpin works out as a happy combination of the talents of director Lee, librettist Tong and performers Yam-Pak. Tong Dik-sang's Cantonese libretto is a literary masterpiece in itself, but with Lee's *mise en scène* and the matchless performances of Yam-Pak, the film becomes an outstanding example of the genre. In the Yam-Pak combination, Yam exerted the greater appeal, bordering on camp worship, to opera cultists. Director Lee said of Yam Kim-fai, who died in 1989: 'She was one of a kind. People still adore her, even now. She wasn't really pretty in real life but always appeared very handsome when she played men. She had a quality that was rare, even among male actors – she knew how to play men who were consumed by love. Her voice wasn't that outstanding technically but her singing was always pleasing to the ear. Ordinary women in the audience took her as their prince.'[3] The Yam-Pak partnership reached its peak in 1959, the year of *The Purple Hairpin* and three other now-classic Yam-Pak films: *Tragedy of the Emperor's Daughter/Dinü Hua* directed by Tso Kei (remade by John Woo in 1967 as *Princess Cheung Ping*, starring Yam-Pak protégées Loong Kim-sang and Mui Suet-si), *Butterfly and Red Pear/Dieying Hongli Ji*, directed by Lee Tit, and *The Fairy of Ninth Heaven/Jiu Tian Nü*, directed by Mok Hong-si. Their last film together was *Tragedy of the Poet King/Li Houzhu* (1968), directed by Lee Sun-fung, after which they both retired from the theatre and the screen.

Yam was paired with other opera greats in her career: notably with Fong Yim-fen in *The Tragic Story of Leong San-pak and Chuk Ying-toi/Liang Zhu Henshi* (1958) and *Snow Storm in June/Liu Yue Xue* (1959), both directed by Lee Tit. Yam again played scholar-lovers to Fong's demure maidens. But Fong cast the greater shadow in these two films – in fact, Yam's roles were essentially supporting parts. In *The Tragic Story of Leong San-pak and Chuk Ying-toi* Fong did her own impersonation of a male scholar. The story is the famous one of a female scholar, Chuk Ying-toi (played by Fong) who disguises herself as a male in order to obtain an education in the most prestigious university. There she falls in love with a fellow student, Leong San-pak (played by Yam). Finally, in order to put things right, Chuk reveals that 'he' is really a girl. But their affair falls foul of family opposition; they commit suicide and are transformed into a pair of butterflies.

Cantonese cinema employed a pantheon of opera stars: fans today recall with fondness retired actresses such as Yu Lai-chen, Lo Yim-hing, and two others who went by the marvellous stage names (after an opera style or character) of Fung-wong Noey (The Phoenix Lady) and Hung-sin Noey (The Red Thread Lady); actors Mak Bing-wing, Lo Kim-long and Lam Ka-sing, who often played martial or scholarly roles; or memorable character actors Boon-yat On, Liang Tsi-pak, Leong Sing-po, Lee Hoi-chuen (the father of Bruce Lee) who specialised in playing generals, magistrates and fools. Their versatility was wide-ranging for they were often called upon to fill character roles in all the genres of Cantonese cinema. Most of them built careers as legitimate screen actors while developing parallel careers on the opera stage. Ma Si-tsang was one of the opera greats who became well known for his non-opera screen roles: primarily as the warm-hearted father in Ch'un Kim's *Parents' Hearts/Fumu Xin* (1955), and as the jealous husband in Lee Sun-Fung's *Broken Spring Dreams/Chuncan Mengduan* (1955), a Cantonese version of *Anna Karenina* set in Macao and Hong Kong. His wife, Hung-sin Noey, was an equally famous opera actress who is remembered for her many 50s melodramas. Although immensely popular in the 50s and 60s, the opera film virtually disappeared from Hong Kong cinema in the 70s, although occasionally, one or two films are produced, such as John Woo's 1976 version of *Dinü Hua, Princess Cheung Ping*, and Chor Yuen's *The Legend of Lee Heung-kwan/ Li Xiangjun* released in 1989. Cantonese opera has gone home to the stage. One reason for the disappearance of the opera film was Hong Kong's newly found affluence in the 70s and 80s: the emerging middle class could now afford tickets for the theatre whereas in the 50s audiences found it cheaper to see their favourite opera stars on the screen. A new generation of film audiences was changing tastes and trends: in the 70s, martial arts kung fu films dominated the screen.

CANTONESE REALISM

The 'legitimate', non-opera, 50s Cantonese cinema fought a battle on two fronts: the invasion of opera actors and the competition posed by Mandarin cinema. The post-war Mandarin cinema in Hong Kong started off on a grand scale, as evidenced in Li Zuyong's two aforementioned epics. These and other big budget productions such as Ma-Xu Weibang's *A Maid's Bitter Story* encouraged the perception that it was the Mandarin cinema which produced the legitimate 'A' features in the Hong Kong film industry. In contrast, Cantonese cinema was home-grown poverty-row product. But if Cantonese cinema was materially poor, it made up for this with richness of spirit. Talent was not lacking; indeed it faced up to the challenge of invigorating the Cantonese film industry, an objective which had always been the goal of Shanghai-based Cantonese film-makers such as Cai Chusheng when he came to Hong Kong in 1937 and in 1948, as it was also that of overseas Cantonese veterans Kwan Man-ching and Chiu Shu-sun (both residents of the United States and both founders of the Grandview Company, one of the most important pre-war production companies), who resumed directing careers in Hong Kong to hasten the post-war recovery of the industry.

By 1950, the rush to produce Cantonese pictures had snowballed into a production boom as the recovery stimulated both Mandarin and Cantonese cinemas. But even in its heyday, the Mandarin cinema could not equal its Cantonese counterpart in terms of output. In fact, the 50s were something of a renaissance era for Cantonese cinema, with an average annual production of over 150 films (some unconfirmed sources double the figure). Production peaked in the years 1960–3 but fell dramatically by the end of the 60s.[4] These figures suggest that Cantonese cinema was a popular medium of mass entertainment, but quality could not possibly keep up with quantity.

The earliest Cantonese movie to receive serious praise was probably Wang Weiyi's *Tears of the Pearl River/ Zhujiang Lei* (1950), heavily influenced by the left-wing tradition of Shanghai film-making. The producer was none other than Cai Chusheng, a veteran of that tradition who had returned to work in Hong Kong as the Chinese left's roving director-ambassador. This time, Cai's task was to liaise with other 'progressive' and 'new democratic' artists in Hong Kong and to launch yet another 'clean-up cinema' campaign. He succeeded in starting a film movement under the aegis of a

43

production company, the Southern Film Company (or Nanguo). This 'clean-up' campaign, like the earlier one, sought to uplift the professional and moral standards of Cantonese cinema. His *Tears of the Pearl River* for Nanguo set the trend.[5]

The film convincingly depicts the lives of uneducated peasants in a Guangdong village. The peasants are first seen celebrating victory over Japan in the Second World War, but it soon becomes clear that they are being oppressed by the village bigwig, a rapacious landlord (played by Cheung Ying) who bribes his way into earning a commission to eradicate 'bandits' in the mountains. The main protagonist is the peasant nicknamed 'Big Bull' (played by Lee Ching) who is forced to run away from the village, leaving his wife to cope alone with the landlord. Big Bull escapes to the city where he is tricked into the army. His wife comes to the city to search for him and is, in turn, tricked into becoming a prostitute.

This type of communist propaganda plot soon became standard fare on the Mainland. However, the splendid acting by a cast of professional Cantonese screen actors and the production values, high for the time, were impressive. The film's penultimate shot (Cheung Ying's landlord lying bruised on the ground while the shadows of his oppressed peasants fall on him as they walk past) is just one of the film's striking visual scenes. Although mostly praised because of its adherence to Shanghai-style quality film-making closely associated with the left, *Tears of the Pearl River* should be appreciated as one of the most successful examples of the way regional traits and characteristics can be used to force a Cantonese film idiom.

The next Nanguo production, *Tragedy in Canton/Yangcheng Henshi* (1951), was cinematically less successful but ideologically more radical than *Tears of the Pearl River*. Set in Guangzhou in the period from the anti-Japanese war to the civil war, the film dealt with a father and son conflict that reflected the state of a Mainland engulfed in civil strife ending with the defeat of the old-order patriarchy. The film was overseen by Cai Chusheng, who returned to the Mainland before production was finished. Director Lo Dun and scenarist Kuk Lau completed Cai's radical vision. Both Lo Dun and Kuk Lau had worked together in another highly regarded Cantonese film a few years earlier, *Everlasting Regret/Ci Hen Mianmian Wu Jue Qi* (1948), produced independently. A third partner was actor Cheung Ying, who produced *Everlasting Regret* and was cast as the revolutionary son in *Tragedy in Canton*. Like all the so-called 'progressive films', praise for *Everlasting Regret* and *Tragedy in Canton* came mainly from the left and centred on the movie's 'realist' depictions of social oppression, corruption, feudalism and suffering. Mainland writers Mao Dun and Ke Ling were both struck by the 'uncompromising sobriety' of *Everlasting Regret*.

The left-wing films of the Nanguo Company in the euphoric early years after the establishment of the People's Republic instigated a style of political soap opera in Cantonese cinema stressing social caricature and allegorical references to the civil war. A representative example was *An Illusion of Paradise/Tiantang Chunmeng* (1951), directed by a co-operative of

Cantonese artists, which seems on the surface to tackle the traditional bug-bear of leftist politics, the feudal family. However, the film draws an analogy between the family it depicts and a KMT which is corrupt to the core. The story is set during the last days of Chiang Kai-shek's government. One of Chiang's cronies (played by Ng Cho-fan) goes to Hong Kong to plan an escape route, bringing his whole family with him, including a wife, two mistresses and a spendthrift son. The plot deals with the manoeuvrings of the family members and the patriarch's deceitful handling of funds obtained from a rich relative. He is in turn cheated of the funds by another crony of the Generalissimo.

These left-wing films fostered an impression that the Cantonese cinema was at last overcoming its mediocrity. However, the debate over dialect films had not ceased in the early 50s and there remained a general feeling that Cantonese cinema was inferior to Mandarin cinema. The left-wing as represented by the outsider Cai Chusheng (but also by such key figures within the Hong Kong Cantonese film industry as Ng Cho-fan, Cheung Ying, Lo Dun, Ng Wui, Lee Sun-fung, Lee Tit and Chun Kim) took the initiative to shatter that public perception by producing Cantonese films that were equal in quality to Mandarin films. In turn, they created another myth: that left-wing Cantonese films represented quality and lofty content.

This was, of course, not true since the post-war recovery of the film industry was largely funded and overseen by organisations and personalities who were, if not apolitical, far from sympathetic to the communist cause. The Cantonese cinema possessed studios such as Grandview which were dedicated to entertainment even though they remained prone to didacticism, warning against superstitious or feudal thinking. Grandview's *Ghost Woman of the Old Mansion/ Guyuan Yaoji*, released in 1949, was a perfect example. A ghost story clearly inspired by classic Hollywood horror films, *Ghost Woman* was indicative of the quality strand of Cantonese film-making which all Cantonese film artists aspired to regardless of political affiliation. Production values were high and the film cried out for comparisons with Ma-Xu Weibang's classy Mandarin horror thriller *A Maid's Bitter Story/ Qionglou Hen*, released the same year, which reportedly almost bankrupted its studio (Great Wall) because of its high costs and subsequent box-office failure.

Fortunately, the leftist line in Cantonese film-making was not a hard ideological one. While they were not neutral, many of its actors and directors could hardly be considered true communist believers. Their cinema was oriented more towards social themes and issues, veering away from ideology while remaining tainted by a didactic intent, which meant that the attempt to relate to common people usually came across as genuine and sincere. Outstanding examples were *Kaleidoscope/ Renhai Wanhua Tong* (1950), a multi-episode film ranging from contemporary morality tales to historical pieces. It was produced by the South China Film Industry Workers Union and involved the talents of all the major directors and stars of the Cantonese cinema at the time. *The Kid/ Xilu Xiang* (1950) was directed by Fung Fung and featured child star Bruce Lee in his first major role. Both films, though didactic in intent, were genuinely unpretentious though ambitious entertainments that depended on hard-hitting caricatures and depictions of social problems to 'educate' the public.

By 1952, the Cantonese cinema was operating with renewed confidence via the establishment of the Union Film Enterprises Ltd (or Chung-luen), the production collective of the South China Film Industry Workers Union which had earlier produced *Kaleidoscope*. In line with its aim to improve quality, Chung-luen was founded partly as a house union of legitimate film workers reacting against the influx of opera actors into the film industry to make opera films, leading to the 'ling-xing' conflict. In a speech, actor Ng Cho-fan, on the 'xing' side and one of the founders of Chung-luen, later explained the conflict in these terms:

> As producers regarded the opera as the only legitimate form of drama, opera films soon dominated the market. This situation was not without opposition. Many socially-conscious film-makers felt that the cinema should entertain as well as educate audiences to be ethical, to serve the community, to be patriotic and to take pride in their cultural heritage. This was also Chung-luen's stand.[6]

The sense of crisis fostered by the 'ling-xing' conflict also coincided with the third 'clean-up' campaign initiated in 1949 by Cai Chusheng and other leftist film-makers under the banner of the Southern China Film Culture Movement, of which many of Chung-luen's founders were members.

Chung-luen's first production was an adaptation of novelist Ba Jin's attack on feudalism, *Family/Jia* (1953), directed by Ng Wui. Its second production was Ch'un Kim's *The Guiding Light/Kuhai Mingdeng* (1953), a deft melodrama with yet more 'educational' properties, as the advertising hype put it. More enduring examples of Chung-luen's style and content were films such as *In the Face of Demolition/Weilou Chuniao* (1953), directed by Lee Tit, and *Parent's Hearts/Fumu Xin* (1955), directed by Ch'un Kim. The plot of *In the Face of Demolition* centres on a teacher, Mr Lo (played by Cheung Ying), who moves into a ramshackle communal apartment. The co-tenants include a dancehall girl, a down-at-heels Taipan, a taxi driver, their assorted families and other low-life characters. Through Mr Lo's relationships with these characters – first, as a fellow tenant, then as a rent-collector – we see the dynamics of an insecure community desperately trying to unite and surmount their difficulties. The line 'one for all, all for one' is uttered more than once in the movie. Life in the apartment is obviously a metaphor for life in Hong Kong, then in the middle of a housing crisis caused mainly by the influx of refugees from the Mainland. Director Lee Tit handled the drama with an eye to mundane detail, drawing convincing performances from his ensemble cast. The themes of unity and sacrifice return obsessively in left-wing realist cinema. Lee Tit, however, put the emphasis on personal redemption in an almost existentialist manner, way-laying the standard invocation of personal sacrifice for the collective good. The focus is on Mr Lo's personal dilemma as he turns from initial acceptance by the community to alienation from it. This personal dilemma becomes almost a theme in itself, forming the crux of the film's thematic structure.

Similar dilemmas of redemption and ethical responsibility were explored in Ch'un Kim's *Parents' Hearts*, a family melodrama which centres on a father and his relationship with his two sons.[7] The film presents a moving portrait of life in Hong Kong in the 50s through the struggles of a working-class father to raise his sons. Conflict with the eldest son ensues and the film turns into a heartfelt critique of traditional father and son relationships. *Parents' Hearts* is a profound work which confirms Ch'un's reputation as perhaps the major directorial talent working in Cantonese cinema at the time. Chung-luen was clearly an outfit which could provide the environment for the sort of serious film-making found in Ch'un's work. The company gathered the cream of Cantonese talent, including Ch'un himself, Lee Sun-fung and Lee Tit; actors Ng Cho-fan, Cheung Ying, Cheung Wood-yau, Pak Yin, Hung-sin Noey and Zi Luo-lien. However, these talented film-makers dispersed after only three years, although the company continued to make films until 1964. Ch'un went on to set up several production companies, such as Kwong Ngai, founded in 1955, for which he made some of his most important films, including *Moon Under the Palm Grove/ Yelin Ye* (1959), a melodrama set in Malaysia and Singapore, and *Intimate Partners/ Nanxiong Nandi* (1960), a prototype for Cantonese buddy-buddy movies. Under the banner of other companies which he had a hand in founding, Ch'un made *A Mother's Tears/ Cimu Lei* (1953), a classic melodrama which is interesting for its restrictive sets and use of flashbacks, and one of his best works, *Neighbours All/ Jiajia Huhu* (1954), a family picture revolving around conflicts between a wife and her mother-in-law. Ch'un turned to Mandarin pictures in 1965, directing for Shaw Brothers in the last five years of his career. In the mid to late 60s, Cantonese cinema declined and Ch'un's career reflected this – just as it had reflected its rise. As outputs for a major studio, Ch'un's films were impersonal, glossy exercises that betrayed a sense of professional burn-out. Ch'un committed suicide in 1969.

By 1972, Cantonese production was virtually at a stand-still. Although Ch'un's career symbolised the peaks and troughs of Cantonese movies, it really represented only one aspect of that cinema. His melodramas dealing with the family marked the beginnings of a realist school even though he gave in to more conventional forms of romantic melodramas in the end. The realist strain of Cantonese cinema continued indomitably, often with modifications – or concessions – to the demands of other genres. In tackling a genre such as the family melodrama, directors often had an opportunity to deploy neo-realist effects while simultaneously indulging the sentimentality of the genre.

As its name implies, the family melodrama is a genre of films set in domestic households centring on the family as a social unit, either revolving around father and son relationships, such as Ng Wui's *Father and Son/ Fu yu Zi* (1954), or variations of that relationship – with mothers and other family members, such as Chor Yuen's *Parents' Love/ Kelian Tianxia Fumu Xin* (1960). Matters of family ethics, marital fidelity, relationship between husband and wife, loyalty and jealousy of siblings and relatives, fil-

47

ial obligations of sons and children, respect for elders, these are the central concerns. Some of the finest Cantonese examples of the genre in the 50s are Lee Sun-fung's films. The feudal morality of a traditional family is dealt with in his *Spring/Chun* (1953); heterosexual conflicts and the traditional roles of the man and woman in forming the family are the themes of *A Flower Reborn/Zaisheng Hua* (1953), *Cold Nights/Han Ye* (1955), *Lone Swan/Duanhong Lingyan Ji*, and *Broken Spring Dreams/Chuncan Mangduan* (1955); the extended family and its internal contradictions are satirised in *A Man of Prosperity/Fada zhi Ren* (1956); a father and son relationship forms the crux of *The Orphan/Renhai Guhong* (1960), one of Bruce Lee's early films made in Hong Kong as a teenage actor. Like Ch'un Kim, Lee's main strength lay in bringing out social themes in films which would otherwise fall squarely within a generic formula. He tried his hand at all the customary Cantonese film genres, including the melodrama, the family film, the ghost film and the martial arts swordplay film.

Humanity/Rendao (1955), is remarkable for presenting a portrait of Chinese peasantry with antinomian values: the idea that human faith rules over all moral-secular constraints. It is a tale of a young farmer from Shanxi province (despite its northern Chinese setting, the film is spoken in Cantonese) who leaves his family and wife to go to Peking for his university education. In the capital, he falls for another woman whose rich father, a rice merchant, hoards rice in anticipation of higher prices as northern China undergoes a drought. He marries into this rich family, forsaking his own family in Shanxi and practically leaving them to die of hunger. The farmer then develops a bad conscience, but not too late for him to reject his rich wife in Peking and return home to his village in time to save his starving wife. Throughout we see the farmer's crisis of conscience which is contrasted with the unshaken faith of his father, mother and wife in Shanxi. They remain convinced that he will return and be their salvation. A remake of an earlier Shanghai film made in 1932, Lee's work contains a fascinating sub-layer of ritualistic ceremony and symbolism in which we sense the burden of tradition weighing down the protagonists. Certain scenes are invested with such clarity of action that we cannot miss their significance: when the whole family gathers around a table on which the father breaks open a pot containing his life savings with which he will send his son to university; or the funeral of the father who dies of hunger; the son taking off his Western suit and putting on his Chinese peasant gown. As played by Ng Cho-fan, the son's moral ambiguity and the restoration of his conscience symbolise the struggle of all sons as they strive to be educated and modern while attempting to withstand the weight of tradition. Ng Cho-fan's performance accentuates the 'weakness' in the son's character.

Such weakness of character, symbolising the burden of tradition, is a recurrent motif in Ng's performances in other Lee Sun-fung films, such as *Cold Nights*, a fine adaptation of another Ba Jin novel. Ng plays a tubercular intellectual, a typically weak husband with a domineering mother, whose wife is a modern-minded Nora straight from Ibsen's *A Doll's House.*

She leaves the husband; he dies and, by his graveside, she is reconciled with the mother-in-law. It is an ending in which the force of tradition comes off stronger than ever because the protagonist, a woman who is identified with modernity, cannot be seen to win. Even in the absence of the husband/son, the family must carry on. In *The Orphan*, ethical responsibility is seen as a natural consequence of family building. Ng Cho-fan is the headmaster of a reform school for boys. A teenage pickpocket (played by Bruce Lee, who gives a wonderfully mannered performance) is entrusted to his care. A father and son relationship develops. The older man's belief that human nature is essentially good and that it is the depth of parental responsibility towards children which determine the character of the next generation, is the movie's ethical anchor. As a film about juvenile delinquency, it not surprisingly locates a possible solution to the problem in the family and focuses on the moral strength of patriarchy.

That the realist tradition in Cantonese cinema ultimately homed in on the family seemed entirely appropriate. In a traditionalist Chinese society, the constancy of the family provides each individual with a sense of social well-being as well as with his or her moral codes. Any individual who operates outside the family risks being condemned to social limbo. The genre of family pictures was whittled down to the nucleus of the family, and a subgenre of father and son films developed, exemplified by Ch'un Kim's *Parents' Hearts* and, in the 80s, by Allen Fong's *Father and Son*. Social responsibility was clearly put in the hands of the father whose duty was to groom his eldest son into inheriting his mantle. The son's filial duty was all important: a rejection of the father was tantamount to biting the hand that feeds. This theme is still current, even in the face of pervasive modernisation and Westernisation.

As Hong Kong cinema developed into two parallel industries making either Mandarin or Cantonese pictures, each industry seemed to acquire a distinct personality. Mandarin cinema embraced the capitalist system and its lifestyles. It looked more sophisticated than its Cantonese counterparts, with more luxurious sets and more glamorous stars, revelling in fantasy, myths, historical legends and musicals. Cantonese cinema tended towards social issues, attacking the feudal system, commenting on patriarchal values and reaffirming the family. By focusing on pressing social problems, it evolved a realist tradition. However, the different 'personalities' of the two cinemas were not exclusive, as can be seen in the social-realist films of Mandarin director Zhu Shilin and, later, in the fantasy-thrillers of Cantonese cinema. But in the 50s, the division reflected the political realities of the day. As local Cantonese film-makers in this period felt compelled to highlight social issues in Hong Kong while holding patriotic sentiments about the motherland, they tended to fall into the leftist camp. Mandarin directors were more sharply divided along partisan lines into supporters of either the Communist Party or the KMT. Both camps, however, professed patriotism and love for the motherland.

The Hong Kong cinema was also large enough to accommodate 'neutral' studios which produced both Mandarin and Cantonese pictures, and films which blurred the ideological divide. The most interesting of the 'neutral' studios was probably Grandview, largely dedicated to Cantonese features but occasionally coming out with prestigious Mandarin ones. Run by the forward-looking veteran Chiu Shu-sun and members of his family, Grandview's products in the 50s were designed to prove to the world that Cantonese cinema was as good as its Mandarin counterpart, particularly when judged in the technical department. Grandview was the company that made the first Cantonese colour movie, *Madame Butterfly/Hudie Furen* (1948), the first Mandarin colour movie, *Heavenly Souls/Caifeng Zhan Youlong* (1949), the first 3-D movie, *A Woman's Revenge/Yunü Qingchou* (1953) and the first CinemaScope movie, *New Yu Tangchun/Xin Yu Tangchun* (1954). The 3-D and CinemaScope movies were directed by Chiu Shu-sun himself, perhaps betraying the fact that Chiu was an American citizen who made it his lifetime mission to bring Hong Kong cinema into the frontlines of cinematic development. Such, ultimately, was also the mission of all those directors who migrated to Hong Kong in the various periods of the development of the film industry.

The Hong Kong film industry undoubtedly benefited from the presence of the northerners, regardless of their political persuasions, who were now honorary, if not native, Hong Kongers. Hong Kong absorbed the talents of the Shanghai film industry so completely that works produced in Hong Kong gained a distinct identity. The territory itself was to exert its own reality over the Shanghai migrants. This reality was its capitalist lifestyle overseen by a British colonial government and the underlying ideological precepts based on such a lifestyle. Ultimately, this meant the prevalence of the right-wing political line, a fact signified by the rise of two major studios which dominated the film industry in the late 50s: Shaw Brothers, under the leadership of Run Run Shaw; and the MP and GI (Motion Picture and General Investment, or Dianmao) under the leadership of Singapore-based Malaysian tycoon, Loke Wan-tho. However, left-leaning studios continued to co-exist with their right-oriented counterparts, and to persist with their political line, although this was muted by their adherence to the issue-oriented realist tradition characterised by a non-ideological tendency. As for Cantonese cinema, it developed in no less unique a fashion: it was virtually the only Chinese dialect-speaking cinema successfully to carve out substantial markets in the region and to earn recognition for its brand of aesthetics based on dialect, home-grown issues, and an orientation towards realism. Later, it tried to emulate Mandarin cinema by turning to fantasy, romance and escapism, but it did not succeed in outgrowing its conservative image. It could not compete with Mandarin cinema which dominated the mainstream industry. As a result, Cantonese cinema experienced a brief decline in the early 70s.

CANTONESE FOLLIES

In the 80s, Hong Kong cinema became the domain of modern special effects, fast-paced action and sex, attributes which Hong Kong critics call *chauk-tou* (or *xuetou* in pinyin, which could roughly be defined as gimmickry, trickery, or the urge to amuse and play to the gallery). This is not to say that *cheuk-tou* was entirely missing in the Cantonese cinema of the 50s and 60s: in the opera film, for example, it was there in Lung To's early 60s films with the use of optical special effects, split-screen, matte painting techniques and hand-drawn animated effects. With such techniques, primitive by 90s standards, the opera film moved into the realm of the martial arts genre, sharing the common features of period settings and some element of fantasy.

The martial arts film was a separate genre, but in the 60s, under the influence of opera, it was very theatrical in its action choreography. In fight scenes, actors moved operatically, that is to say, mimetically, as if they were going through prescribed motions. Apart from the stylised choreography of action scenes, the Cantonese cinema's martial arts genre was otherwise much more influenced by the literary tradition of long, serialised novels. Special effects were invariably incorporated into the fabric of the genre to make it resemble legends, fantasies and fairytales. Examples were Ling Wan's *Burning of the Red Lotus Monastery/Huoshao Honglian Si* (1963) and *Buddha's Palm/Rulai Shanzhang* (1964). These films featured heroes skilled in swordfighting and the art of emitting deadly rays from their palms; they populated a mythical land of demons, magicians and evil followers of profane cults or dynastic families. The heroes existed to put order into chaos and to set things right. Adapted from long novels, martial arts films were usually released in two parts, with the first part concluding in a cliffhanger followed by an off-screen narrator's voice asking rhetorical questions, pondering over the fates of the characters, and finally reminding audiences that Part Two was to be released soon and not to miss it. The serial tradition of the martial arts genre was also evident in a long series featuring the comparatively more mundane adventures of the Cantonese kung fu legend, Wong Fei-hung, portrayed by Kwan Tak-hing, who has made the role his lifelong career. Wong Fei-hung is known to 90s audiences as the hero of Tsui Hark's *Once Upon a Time in China* series. But throughout the 50s and 60s, he was a household name, the benevolent hero of nearly 80 films. The series began in 1949, with Wu Pang's *The True Story of Wong Fei-hung/Huang Feihong Zhuan.* Kwan Tak-hing's Wong was a martial artist *par excellence:* someone who fought in the true Shaolin tradition – not for the sake of fighting but to help the weak and to uphold a righteous cause. Wong moulded kung fu into a hybrid of Confucianist values, nationalist feeling and defensive martial arts. He was also a medical practitioner who knew the value of life. Like the swordplay fantasy films, the Wong Fei-hung series typified the operatic tradition of martial arts choreography which required actors to mime the gestures of combat. Kwan Tak-hing was himself a highly trained kung fu martial artist, as were his fellow actors, primarily Tso Tat-wah (as Wong Fei-hung's number one disciple) and Shek Kin (as the master's perennial opponent). These actors established the kung fu tradition which required actors skilled in martial arts to physically perform their arts on screen. Their actions always stemmed from their patriotism and the heroes were the very embodiments of virtue. Wong Fei-hung is the prototype of the heroes created by Bruce Lee in the 70s.

51

Because of the emphasis on actual physical skills, the Cantonese kung fu films were not as conscious of *cheuk-tou*. In certain films, *cheuk-tou* took the form of light comic interludes, particularly in the interplay between two of Wong's disciples: a buck-tooth stutterer and a fat butcher. The comedy genre is perhaps the one genre where *cheuk-tou*, in the form of slapstick, would find a natural home. This is the case with the comedies produced in the 80s by the company known as Cinema City founded by comedians Karl Maka, Dean Shek and Raymond Wong. Cinema City's comedies came up with a genuinely liberal *cheuk-tou* formula mixing slapstick, special effects, action stunts and sex in films such as *Chasing Girls/ Zhui Nüzai* (1981) and *Aces Go Places/ Zhui Jia Paidang* (1982). In the 50s, comedy had to rely on much less. The budgetry and technical limitations of Cantonese cinema meant that slapstick was not even a predominant style in the early 50s comedies. Actors usually tried their best to give a semblance of slapstick through the playing of pranks and practical jokes, but the accent was on character and dialogue.

The 50s comedies were not free of realist influence. By adopting a didactic, moralising tone, comedies with contemporary settings echoed the social-realist melodramas. However, they transcended them by satirising behaviour and sexual mores. An exemplary series of comedies made in 1950 featured as its lead character a business broker named Lai (played by Cheung Ying) and satirised the greed and lasciviousness of the emerging middle class, capturing the social scene as accurately as any social-realist melodrama. Broker Lai was typical of a breed of Hong Kong businessmen who started out as small-time brokers making deals and earning commissions. Often, these deals turned bad or were revealed as outright confidence tricks. The first film in the trilogy, *Broker Lai and the Smart Fei-tin Nam/ Jingji La yu Feitian Nan* (1950), directed by Mok Hong-si, has Lai entangled in a web of deals brokered by his wife, his mistress and his rival, Fei-tin Nam (played by Yee Chau-shui, one of Cantonese cinema's most memorable character-comedians).

The characterisations of the selfish and uncouth businessmen and women in the Broker Lai series were perhaps the earliest manifestations of the 'little-men' characters who would turn up in later Cantonese comedies such as Ch'un Kim's *Intimate Partners/ Naniong Nandi* (1960), Michael Hui's films of the 70s and the comedies of Karl Maka and Dean Shek in the 80s. All these characters were determined to elevate their social status by hook or by crook. They presented shrewdness and greed as virtues in a society oriented towards profit, and took a very pragmatic view of money and sex. In *Broker Lai and the Smart Fei-tin Nam*, Lai is married but thinks nothing of carrying on an affair with a socialite for the sake of business; his wife, meanwhile, conducts an affair with Fei-tin Nam, Lai's rival. Petty disputes and face-saving measures were also typical of the little-men skin-flint personae. In *The Misarranged Love Trap/ Baicuo Mihun Zhen* (1950), Broker Lai and his wife are caught in a game of one-upmanship as Mainland relatives on both sides of the family come to stay in their Hong Kong apartment. The relatives provoke a series of absurd disputes and contests as husband and wife bicker over who should stay in their house.

The satirical vein of Cantonese comedies against greed and hypocrisy continued with films such as Ng Wui's *Money/Qian* (1959), which centres on a bag of stolen money passing through the hands of several characters; and Tso Kei's *The Chair/Jinshan Dashao* (1959), about the frantic search for valuables hidden in a chair (based on a Russian story which was also the basis of Mel Brooks's *The Twelve Chairs*). It was seen in grand fashion in *The Grand Party/Haomen Yeyan* (1959), collectively directed, written and acted by members of the left-leaning South China Film Industry Workers Union, including directors Lee Sun-fung, Lee Tit and Ng Wui; and actors Ng Cho-fan, Cheung Ying, Pak Yin and Lee Ching. Eager to show off a valuable diamond ring, a wealthy couple invites relatives and friends to a grand party. So as not to appear too po-faced, the husband comes up with the pre-text of honouring his father's scholastic beard. However, the father lives in a squatter hut, ignored by his rich children. He is too skinny to be pre-sentable, so his family contrives to fatten him up and resorts to all sorts of methods to make him look prosperous.

Social satires provided one strand of Cantonese comedies; another con-sisted of situational and physical farces which made household names of a group of Cantonese character actors and comedians, among them Yee Chau-shui, Sun-Ma Si-tsang (also called Sun Ma-tsai), Tang Kei-chen, Sai-gua Pao, Leong Sing-po (also famous as a Cantonese opera actor), Tam Lan-hing and Ko-lou Chuen. Most of these comedians deployed physical features to comic effect: Leung Sing-po and Tam Lan-hing were fat; Tang Kei-chen was thin; Ko-lou Chuen was tall and deep-voiced; Yee Chau-shui's gaunt face had a hooked nose; Sai-gua Pao had buck teeth and spoke with a stutter (he also provided comic relief in the Wong Fei-hung films). But they were genuinely talented and versatile actors who were also called upon to perform dramatic roles in other genres. They created comic characters who made otherwise slipshod films memorable. An example is Yee Chau-shui's restaurant waiter Chow Sun-yuk in *A Comet of Laughter Lands on Earth/Xiaoxing Jiang Diqiu* (1952). Chow Sun-yuk is a pun on a Cantonese expression which literally means 'whole body shaking'; Chow had a phobia for music which made him shake and shiver uncontrollably. The obese comedians Leung Sing-po and Tam Lang-hing were paired in Tso Kei's sur-realistic *The Romance of Jade Hall/Xuan Gong Yanshi* (1957), set in a mythical snow kingdom ruled by a Snow Queen, with characters singing a medley of melodies, Cantonese opera style; Leung and Tam were a class act, per-forming sight gags and a humorous operatic duet. Sun-Ma Si-tsang and Tang Kei-chen were the classic Two Fools in a series of slapstick comedies. The titles said it all: *Two Fools in Hell/Liang Sha You Diyu, Two Fools in Paradise/Liang Sha You Tiantang* (both 1958). Sun-Ma, who is also a re-spected Cantonese opera performer, was the fool-incarnate of a cartoon character, Mr Wong, made popular in Shanghai in the 30s. The film was *Mr Wong's Adventures with the Unruly Girl/Wang Xiangsheng Qi Zheng Yanzhi Ma* (1959).

Non-comedians also tried their hands at comedy. Perhaps one of the most influential Cantonese comedies is *Intimate Partners* (1960), starring dramatic actors Tse Yin, Wu Fung and Nam Hung, directed by Ch'un Kim. Tse and Wu play a couple of buddies down on their luck. Tse is on the point of suicide when he meets Wu, an old friend whom he tries to rob. They team up and start to re-organise their lives by becoming brokers, counting on Wu's simple philosophy: 'If there is hope, there is a way; if there is a way, there is hope'. They climb the ladder of success; meet an orphan girl (played by Nam Hung) and both fall in love with her. The two male leads gave good comic performances but it was their buddy-buddy characterisations which have lasted. They created the *pak-dong* prototypes (*pak-dong* being the Cantonese expression for buddies, or partners) which provided Michael Hui with the basis of his partnership with his brother Samuel Hui in his 70s comedy films. In the 80s, the comedy-adventure series which took off from *Aces Go Places/Zui Jia Paidang* (1982), also evoked the *pak-dong* spirit.

Of equal importance was the aura of fledgeling materialism which Ch'un depicted with his typically tender sensibility. Here Ch'un took a leaf from Mok Hong-si's Broker Lai films by putting his characters against a background of unpitying materialism – their mean-spirited 'little-men' mentality contributing as much to their downfall as it also stimulated them into facing the future with renewed confidence. These little men were skin-flints, miserly, exploitative, shrewd, calculating: qualities which could be turned into virtues if they were vices, and to vices if they were virtues, depending on the environment and their stations. Ch'un had a propensity to portray hard times, and his vision of 'little men' was fundamentally humanistic.

The Hui Brothers (primarily Michael and Samuel; third brother Ricky was sidelined in the early films) developed the 'mean little-men' aspect of the *pak-dong* spirit with greater satirical resonance in the 70s. By then, Hong Kong had become even more materialistic; the little men of the 60s might have become the middle class of the 70s, but their ranks continued to swell due to the influx of refugees from the Mainland, and times became meaner as people scrambled to make a living. The buddies played by Tse Yin and Wu Fung were a more sedate version than that provided by the Hui Brothers (Michael, in particular, was adept at portraying incorrigible niggardliness), but their *pak-dong* spirit stemmed from the same circumstances of economic survival.

As society became more business-minded and *laissez-faire* in the 60s, Cantonese cinema took to making 'black comedies', developing mixed genres, a practice which has survived into the 90s. One of the most interesting films of the 60s was *Humanity/Ren* (1960), directed by Lau Fong, who masterfully balanced comedy, drama and thriller elements in a weird but workable pastiche, never far away from self-parody. The film's title (not to be confused with Lee Sun-fung's 1955 film *Humanity/Ren Dao*) refers to the office-staff of a trading company, from the lowliest positions to the topmost executives. A tone of eccentricity is struck from the outset. The company is hiring women as secretaries and each candidate is submitted to stringent tests: the interviewer suddenly whistles into the girls' ears or goes berserk around the office breaking things, just to test the girls' reactions under stress. If they remain calm and reserved, they are hired. The girls who make it are assigned to deliver parcels to addresses around the city. A dramatic segment involves the husband of one of the newly-hired secretaries who sells his daughter to feed his addiction to drugs. Another sub-plot concerns the office janitor who poses as the head of a department in order to impress his son, a returned graduate who is under the impression that his father is an executive. The film ends as a farcical thriller: the company director is revealed to be a drug trafficker who has hired the girls to become unwitting couriers. When the girls and an honest executive (Ng Cho-fan) discover the truth, they are kidnapped and kept under cover as the villain schemes to get rid of them. The drug problem, family ethics, the rise of a white-collar business class, the preoccupation with status and face are themes tackled in one fell swoop. As a pastiche, a genre not attempted before in Hong Kong, *Humanity* is a precursor of trends which developed more fully in the 80s and 90s.

The series of thriller-parodies which director Chor Yuen came up with in the 60s were more in keeping with modern norms. *The Black Rose/Hei Meigui* (1965) inspired the 90s postmodern films with its evocation of 'antique' Cantonese cinema. This was the film to which the 1992 release *92 Legendary La Rose Noire* referred. *The Black Rose* has its antecedents in comic books and, not surprisingly, lends itself well to parody. The Black Rose is a cat burglar. Actually there are two of them: a pair of orphan sisters who grew up in a circus and whose parents committed suicide after being exploited by corrupt managers. The elder sister, Chan Mei-yu (played by Nam Hung), has vowed that the poor would never be oppressed by the rich. With her younger sister, Mei-lai, they put on black tights and balaclavas to become modern Robin Hoods, robbing the rich to help the poor, leaving a black rose as their calling card after each robbery. The concept of two related criminals acting as one was a wonderful idea with great potential for visual thrills. Chor Yuen rose to the occasion. The opening scene is a marvellous set-piece in the mansion where the Chan sisters live. Mei-yu, a wealthy socialite wooed by sugar daddies when she is not a cat burglar, gives a fancy-dress party to entertain her rich friends. She appears as the Black Rose, immediately arousing fear and excitement among the party-goers. The police storm in and surround her. Calmly, she takes off her mask to reveal her identity and everyone is relieved to know that it is a practical joke. As the atmosphere relaxes, there is a blackout. The Black Rose strikes again and a precious jewel is stolen. A private detective, Cheung Man-fu (played by Tse Yin), employed by an insurance company, is assigned to investigate. Cheung and the police devise a plan to catch the Black Rose in the act of stealing a jade piece owned by one of Miss Chan's sugar daddies. But, once again, the Black Rose outwits her foes with another marvellous show of theatricality involving bandaged faces à la *The Invisible Man* and a blundering cop. However, soon Cheung suspects that Miss Chan is the Black Rose and, predictably, they become allies, with a hint that they might become lovers as well. By joining forces with the Black Rose, a folk heroine,

Cheung becomes as idealised a character as his ex-opponent. *The Black Rose* is the kind of cult film that stimulates caricaturists and parodists. The sequel a year later, *The Spy With My Face/ Hei Meigui yu Hei Meigui*, went further into the realm of pulp-fiction with James Bond-like sets and situations accentuating the element of parody, especially since the sets were Cantonese counterfeits. The director Chor Yuen showed himself to be a director who was conscious of cinema as an elastic form by injecting new styles into old genres.

TOWARDS GENERATIONAL CHANGE

The prolific Chor Yuen straddled generations at crucial points in the development of the post-war Cantonese cinema: when it reached the height of its popularity in the early 60s and when it declined in the late 60s. Chor bridged the 50s and 60s as a second-generation film-maker who inherited the mantle of first-generation Cantonese directors such as Ch'un Kim, Lee Sun-fung, Ng Wui and others. The son of actor Cheung Wood-yau, Chor (his real name was Cheung Bo-kin) entered the industry in 1956 as a writer and assistant director and was associated with Ch'un Kim, for whom he scripted *Autumn Comes to the Purple Rose Garden/ Ziwei Yuan de Qiu Tian* (1958), a melodrama which harked back to the *wenyi* tradition (a romantic style of melodrama). Chor made his directing debut in 1958. One of his first films was a social-realist melodrama, *Parents' Love/Kelian Tianxa Fumu Xin* (1960), which recalled Ch'un Kim's *Parents' Hearts* (1955) in its central theme of a father trying to raise his family in hard times. In the early phase of his career, Chor specialised in *wenyi* melodramas such as *Eternal Regret/Niehai Yihen* (1962), *Remorse/Yuanlai Wo Fu Qing* (1965) and *Winter Love/Dong Lian* (1968), featuring archetypal *wenyi* roles for actresses Pak Yin, Ka Ling and Josephine Siao playing women with some secret to hide in their relationships with men. These films displayed Chor Yuen's capacity for stylisation: the decor and acting were manifestly theatrical, subjected to the director's design (*Winter Love* is exceptional in this regard). Always keen to experiment, Chor was typical of young film-makers everywhere who bridged generations: schooled in the old formulas, he was eager to make his mark with new styles. *The Black Rose* was typical of Chor's penchant for experimentation, as were other parodies such as *The One Million Dollar Inheritance/ Yichan Yibai Wan* (1966) and *I Love Violet/ Wo Ai Zi Luolan* (1966), a remarkable pastiche of comedy, *wenyi* melodrama and psychological thriller.

The most significant of Chor's new style films was *The Joys and Sorrows of Youth/ Lengnuan Qingchun* (1969), as astonishing youth movie about the lives of university students, rich and poor, in late 60s Hong Kong. Each character conforms to a 'type' whose transgressions fit their stations. There is the spoilt rich student, Tommy Hu, a spendthrift and a show-off (he is driven to campus in his father's Rolls-Royce) who causes his father's bankruptcy in the end; Tommy's sexy girlfriend Angel (played by Tina Ti) who becomes a prostitute; and Angel's mother, an ex-whore who jumps down from a building upon discovering her daughter plying her own trade.

There is the poor student Hoi-kit (played by Tsang Kong) who must smuggle dope to earn his keep. His roommate, the upright Siu-fan (Chu Kong) feels betrayed when he learns the truth about Hoi-kit's activities. There is the ruthless King (Fung Tsui-fan) who forces David (Ch'un Pui) to rape Tommy Hu's sister. The women include the virtuous sister of the villainous David (played by Nam Hong) who spends most of her time in church and whose last scene in the movie is to pray for a miracle to save Hoi-kit's life. Wounded in a knife fight, Hoi-kit is taken to the chapel to wait for the ambulance – he dies at the point of Nam Hong's supplication. The movie successfully integrates the familiar youth-movie motifs from knife fights to chicken runs passed down from Nicholas Ray's *Rebel Without a Cause*. Chor Yuen's experimental techniques were illustrated, first, by his own Lubitsch-like appearance in a prologue to explain his characters and setting, and through a radical montage technique punctuating crucial moments in the narrative.[8] The radical style and subject matter complemented the times. The film was released two years after the 1967 riots inspired by the Cultural Revolution, an event which deeply marked Hong Kong youth. The film was also one of the last-ditch efforts to save Cantonese cinema from its sure decline in the late 60s. *The Joys and Sorrows of Youth* was produced independently by Chor and the young actors of his cast who were beginning their careers. The company they formed was named 'New Films' which symbolised their awareness that Cantonese cinema was fast becoming outmoded, unable to compete with its sophisticated Mandarin counterpart.

Unable to stave off the decline of Cantonese cinema, Chor turned to directing Mandarin films in the 70s. For Shaw Brothers, Chor turned his hand to martial arts and opera films. They were interesting choices. As a Cantonese director, Chor had focused on genres with contemporary settings, particularly the melodrama. For his Mandarin films, the director decided that he would be best served by genres with period settings. The martial arts films were an action genre which did not intimidate Chor; in fact, he was to develop a 'new wave' style for martial arts films, as witnessed in *Confessions of a Chinese Courtesan/Ai Nu* (1972) and *The Magic Blade/ Tianya Mingyue Dao* (1976). Audiences were treated to new elements: a vengeful lesbian heroine in the former film, and brilliant swordfighting choreography combined with a lyrical, dreamlike mood in the latter. To press home his versatility, Chor also made an opera film, *Farewell to a Warrior/Zhu Men Yuan* (1974), sung in the Chaozhou dialect. Fittingly, Chor was called upon to direct *The House of 72 Tenants/Qishi'er Jia Fangke* (1973), the film which revived the Cantonese dialect cinema in the early 70s. This film, and Michael Hui's which appeared in the mid-70s, paved the way for the eventual assimilation of Cantonese in Hong Kong cinema as a younger generation of film-makers emerged in the 80s.

Chor Yuen is the one director who best typifies the mock-modern aura of 60s Cantonese cinema in films such as *Winter Love* and *The Black Rose*. The mock-modernism, indeed the counterfeit Western decor and romantic styles of Chor's works are the ultimate form of modernisation which characterised the turning point when Hong Kong was on the road to capitalist modernisation. Chor formed the link between the old generation of Cantonese directors and the new generation who would make their mark from the mid-70s onwards, from Michael Hui to the new wave directors of the 80s. Today, Chor is a veteran director who has increasingly turned to acting in the films of his younger colleagues. His recent directorial output has been marked by a return to his favourite genre, the melodrama, and the traditional opera film. In melodrama, Chor inherited a tradition developed by a master, Ch'un Kim. Like Ch'un's, whom he understudied as an assistant director, Chor's best melodramas are stylish, thematically emphatic works conveying the intelligence and personality of an *auteur*, demonstrating that the Cantonese cinema's melodrama genre mobilised the finest talents, such as Ch'un Kim, Lee Sun-fung and Chor Yuen, who developed a fine tradition of dramatic romances about star-crossed lovers (the *wenyi* tradition) and family-centred melodramas which examined father and son relationships. As one of Cantonese cinema's brightest young talents, Chor continued the classical tradition but promoted a new aesthetic. Other directors from his generation followed the same artistic path, notably Lung Kong, an actor who joined the industry in the late 50s and turned director in 1966 with *The Broadcast Prince/Boyin zhi Wang*. Lung became known for his tendency to deal with pertinent social themes. One of his best films was *The Story of a Discharged Prisoner/Yingxiong Bense* (1967) which told the story of an ex-convict, Lee Cheuk-hung (played by Tse Yin) who tries to rehabilitate himself in society but is harassed by a police inspector (played by Lung) and a one-eyed crime boss (Shek Kin), both of whom attempt to enlist Lee into their ranks as an informer and as a safe-breaker respectively.

The Story of a Discharged Prisoner was re-worked by John Woo nearly twenty years later as *A Better Tomorrow/Yingxiong Bense* (1986) where the lead character becomes a misunderstood hero ostracised by society. Lung's directorial career focused on films which tackled acute social problems such as prostitution, juvenile delinquency and the malaise of drugs and disease. Lung briefly rejuvenated the Cantonese industry with entertaining genre films such as melodramas, thrillers and comedies which also had something to say about social problems. Like his contemporary Chor Yuen, Lung produced a youth movie as a prefatory work signalling the revival of Cantonese cinema: *Teddy Girls/Feinü Zhengzhuan* was released in the same year as Chor's *The Joys and Sorrows of Youth*. Josephine Siao plays Josephine Tsui, a rebellious girl who prefers a reform school after a fight with boys in a discotheque rather than the guardianship of her mother and her shady lover (played by Lung Kong himself). *Teddy Girls* is one of Hong Kong cinema's most inspired studies of 'Ah Fei' (the Cantonese term for wayward youths). Despite the didactic note which permeates the narrative (as represented in the character of the rector of the reform school, played by Tsang Kong), the main strength of *Teddy Girls* lies in its characterisations, particularly of the lead protagonist. Josephine is a visceral character who retains redeeming features even as she resorts to violence. She acts out of a strong belief of personal justice, defending herself from male arrogance, whether perceived or felt. In the end, she escapes to seek revenge on Lung Kong whom she blames for her mother's suicide. Right from the start, the audience is made to sympathise with Josephine. Actress Josephine Siao embodies the character with strong physical traits (best seen in the outstanding opening scene in the disco) and she gives a most impressive performance without ever going over the top. *Teddy Girls* remains one of Lung Kong's best films, not only because of its ardent sense of social commitment, but because of the director's skilful deployment of melodramatic elements with a genuine flair for stylisation, giving it a timeless beat even as it dances to the specific time-rhythm of the late 60s.

Films such as *The Joys and Sorrows of Youth* and *Teddy Girls* as well as a whole new line of Cantonese youth films that critic Law Wai-ming has labelled 'A-Go-Go' films, featuring such teenage icons as Chan Po-chu and Josephine Siao, typified the generational change that was to overcome the film industry in Hong Kong. When seen in the Cantonese cinema, the 60s certainly was a decade of mixed emotions, filled with social problems underpinned by the drugs culture, fears sparked by the 1967 riots (with its links to the leftist fanaticism of the Cultural Revolution running rampant on the Mainland) and heady optimism inspired by Western rock music and the rise of the hippy movement. The Cantonese cinema certainly tried its best to adapt to the changes but ultimately could not compete with the financial might and star-allure of the Mandarin studios nor with the equally powerful threat represented by television. Towards the mid-60s, the market for Mandarin movies had been revitalised with the emergence of a non-traditional source of Mandarin movies: Taiwan. The intense competition between Hong Kong and Taiwan for the Mandarin market in Southeast Asia effectively wiped out whatever gains Cantonese cinema might have made with its successful teenage movies or fantasy-martial arts movies which predated the rise of the genre in Mandarin cinema by a few years. However, the death-knell for the Cantonese cinema was truly sounded with the debut of local television production and programming in 1967. Towards the end of the decade, local television programmes in the Cantonese language effectively became the most popular entertainment medium for Cantonese-speaking audiences, co-opting the new Cantonese film stars of the 60s along with the veteran performers of earlier decades.

Cantonese cinema experienced its decline as Hong Kong modernised. As it turned out, the decline was brief, lasting for all of the two years between 1971–2 until the fall of 1973 when the Cantonese dialect was heard again in cinema screens in Chor Yuen's *The House of 72 Tenants/Qishier Jia Fangke*. The following year, the comedies of Michael Hui proved that the revival of Cantonese was not short-lived. When the new wave emerged, Cantonese was practically the only language heard in Hong Kong movies, a situation that remains true today.

As the generation of veterans from Shanghai retired or died, a younger generation of film-makers began to take over. This new generation grew up with both feet firmly planted in Hong Kong, and a new cinematic identity based on Cantonese dialect grew with them. Contemporary Hong Kong cinema is a hybrid, a child of the two major streams, the Mandarin and Cantonese cinemas of the 50s, as well as Western influences. But as a source of warm childhood memories, Cantonese cinema did exert a lasting impact on the minds of the generation that took over the reins of the film industry in the 80s.

NOTES

[1] Mandarin and Cantonese cinemas were the two most important streams. A third cinema, which may be classified under 'Other Dialect' is beyond the scope of this book; examples of the dialect-films in this category are Amoy and Chaozhou films.

[2] Yo Mo-wan, 'The Development of Hong Kong's Opera Film', HKIFF catalogue, *Cantonese Opera Film Retrospective*, 1987 [in Chinese]. Yu states that 378 films were produced in the 30s, of which 91 were opera films.

[3] Interview with Lee Tit, HKIFF catalogue, *Cantonese Opera Film Retrospective*, 1987.

[4] Statistics gleaned from filmographies of Mandarin and Cantonese cinemas published in HKIFF catalogues, 1986, 1987, 1989.

[5] See Lin Nien-tung's article 'Some Trends in the Development of Post-War Hong Kong Cinema', HKIFF catalogue, *Hong Kong Cinema Survey 1946–68*, 1979.

[6] Speech given during a 1956 UN cultural meeting held in Hong Kong. See also Yu Mo-wan's article, 'A Study of Zhonglian Film Company', HKIFF catalogue, *Cantonese Cinema Retrospective (1960–69)*, 1982.

[7] See Chapter 4 for a full discussion of the father and son cycle of family melodramas in Cantonese cinema.

[8] The use of a radical montage technique as a precursor of new-wave cinema also marked the Taiwanese cinema in the late 60s. Bai Jingrui's *Home at Taipei/Jia Zai Taibei*, released the same year as Chor's *Joys and Sorrows of Youth* (1969), is a similarly pivotal work. In many respects, it is an even more stylistically radical film than Chor's work in its use of multi-character episodic narrative, split-screen, tilted angles, jump cutting, etc.

Chapter Four

Father and Son

Like a long forgotten diary written during one's childhood that is discarded as one grows up and then re-discovered later in adulthood, the cycle of films in Cantonese cinema dealing with relationships between father and son instantly evokes powerful memories. The titles *Father and Son/Fu yu Zi* (1954), *Parents Hearts/Fumu Xin* (1955), and again *Father and Son/Fuzi Qing* (1981), are simple, straightforward, and in the original Chinese, softly sentimental (the 1981 film for example translates as 'Love Between Father and Son'). The emotions they stir up are far deeper, more complex and ambivalent.

The father and son relationship when portrayed in cinema immediately strikes chords in the audience. No extraordinary references to literature, drama or cinema are necessary when a viewer can feel at one with the protagonist on the screen. One is struck by how close the issues and emotions are to real life even when toned down or portrayed in the abstract. The relationship is invariably one of conflict, with the father seeking to extend the past into the present, and the son straining to break away. In the process, both are engulfed in phobia and obsession, each recriminating against the other.

The father and son cycle links contemporary Hong Kong cinema with the old Cantonese cinema. Surely it is no flight of fancy to view the new generation of directors as the son and the old Cantonese cinema as the father. One of the directors of the Hong Kong new wave, Allen Fong, evoked this analogy in his first feature, *Father and Son/Fuzi Qing*, released in 1981. The analogy is implicit in the historical development of Hong Kong cinema itself, but Fong may have been the first director in the new wave to make it explicit. *Father and Son/Fuzi Qing* shows that the new wave is rooted in the past: continuity is maintained by recalling the conventions and themes of the family melodrama which enjoyed wide currency in the 50s and 60s but which became moribund in the 70s and 80s.

There are more than incidental similarities between Fong's film and the 1954 Cantonese picture entitled *Father and Son/Fu yu Zi* directed by veteran Cantonese actor-director, Ng Wui. While the two films are quite different in style, there is an uncanny link between them. In returning to the well-worn conventions of the family melodrama and attempting to work within its bounds, Fong acknowledges a debt to the previous generation. But while

Father and Son/Fuzi Qing is bound by the conventions of an old genre, it also attempts to stand outside that genre, codifying within it a message that the new generation has 'made it' and that it will achieve something new.

In both economic and social terms, the survival of the new generation in Hong Kong was ensured by the efforts of the responsible elders in preserving the family unit at all cost. Throughout the 50s and 60s, Hong Kong worked its way to the economic success of the 70s. In those decades, life was hard and families barely subsisted. Many were refugees who had escaped Mainland communism to forge a new life in the colony. Survival meant not merely escaping from poverty, but, more importantly, doing so with the sacred institution of the family intact. Sacrifice, humiliation and punishment were foregone conclusions in the battle to preserve the family. The central figure in this drama was usually the father. Nothing was too much or too little for the father to suffer.

Women who go to see the father and son films may be forgiven for concluding that the films contain more than a hint of misogyny. The description of women in these films conforms to a traditional outlook: women serve and bolster the patriarchal system. The mother is often crucial to the integrity of the family. Although she and other female members of the family appear peripheral and dispensable, they actually incarnate, positively or in an inverted manner, the values the family is supposed to represent; women play a crucial role, and yet, they appear subservient and secondary in many of the narratives. This seeming paradox in the genre actually formed the basis of a critique of social conventions.

There is also a cycle of films involving father and daughter, or mother and daughter, which may best be understood as inverted relationships: they are surrogate forms of the central father and son relationship. In order to uphold the family name and honour, the daughter takes up the role of the son, behaving in the fashion characteristic of the 'Hua Mulan syndrome'. Hua Mulan was the eldest daughter in a military family without male offspring. The legend has her preserving family honour by distinguishing herself on the battlefield against the Mongols, dressed as a man.[1]

Fong's film strives for a critique of the family, specifically a critique of the old father and son subgenre within the family melodrama with its emphasis on the social fact that eldest sons in Chinese families are the most privileged members. Yet, it also seeks to maintain a link with the past: to realise the precept contained in the Chinese proverb *chengxian qihou* (to evoke the past so as to inherit its legacy). To gauge how successfully Fong has achieved the critique as well as the attempt to forge a thematic continuity with old genres, it may be helpful to examine the notion of a 'thematic continuity' in terms of the relation between Fong's *Father and Son/Fuzi Qing* and the Cantonese classics, Ng Wui's *Father and Son/Fu yu Zi* (1954) and Ch'un Kim's *Parents' Hearts/Fumu Xin* (1955).

First, a critique of a genre such as the Cantonese family melodrama would involve an explanation of social norms in Chinese society as portrayed by the film-makers. Second, the meanings embedded within the films themselves should be critically analysed for the ways in which the generic conventions inflect the inscription of these social norms. It then becomes possible to work out a dialectical relationship between generic and social conventions. It is in the father and son subgenre of the family melodrama that the dialectic between genre and society is most pointed and carries the most didactic weight. In Cantonese cinema, the family melodrama's inherent pedagogic value directly informs its aesthetic qualities because of its apparent commitment to the integrity of the family as an institution.

The family nexus and the father and son theme are not unique to the melodrama. Indeed, one can work out a whole category of kung fu martial arts films which deal with fathers and sons, and its closest approximation of such relationships, the master and disciple relationship. The kung fu genre contains its own narrative conventions which put the traditional father and son relationship on a different level from that of the contemporary melodrama. Lau Kar-leong's *Executioners From Shaolin/Hong Xiguan* (1977) and a more recent film such as *New Legend of Shaolin/Hong Xiguan* (1993), co-directed by Wong Jing and Yuen Kwai, both contain a father and son relationship featuring the Shaolin hero Hong Xiguan and his son Wending. The premise of these two films is a tale of revenge drawing on the conventions of the fantasy genre rather than directly seeking to engage with contemporary social patterns. Male relationships in kung fu movies do activate themes such as male bonding and homoeroticism, to name but two,[2] which inflect the text's functioning at various levels. However, in kung fu movies where fathers and sons are prominent, such as those featuring the young Wong Fei-hung and his father Wong Kei-ying in Yuen Woo-ping's *Drunken Master/Zui Quan* (1978) and *Iron Monkey/Shaonian Huang Feihung zhi Tie Houzi* (1993), the central father and son relationship is tangential to the action. The kung fu genre in Hong Kong cinema remains committed to choreographic form and style even though it has the potential to explore the ethical tenets of family relationships or the nature of heroism *vis-à-vis* the security of the family, as in the idea of collective action versus individual heroism, for example.

In contrast, the melodrama offers us the possibility of a theory based on linkage. The theory is that genre and society are linked in a continuity of form and substance based on social reality. Fong's *Father and Son* serves as the best example of a recent work in Hong Kong cinema which can provoke critical thinking about Hong Kong cinema and its reflective relationship to society. The father and son theme runs through a series of films, from the old to the new, implying a progression of living history. Films produced in the 50s were used as points of reference. Allen Fong's *Father and Son/Fuzi Qing* starts where Ng Wui's *Father and Son/Fu yu Zi* leaves off. The substance of the theme remains the same although the characters have changed. In his critique of the old generic conventions and, by implication, of the older social conventions, Fong introduces explicitly autobiographic elements and provides greater interplay between the son and other family members, giving more attention to the sister. Through her Fong points out that the patriarchal ideology underpins some of the Chinese family's ills – although it has played a role in the economic growth of Hong Kong and thus in the family's relative prosperity.

A fundamental aspect of the patriarchal ideology is the father's authority together with an emphasis on the first male child of the family at the expense of the other children. This fundamental truth is underlined in a dialogue at the beginning of *Father and Son/Fuzi Qing*. The father has died and Ka-hing, the eldest son, has returned from America for the funeral. His sister, Ka-hei, meets him at the airport and they take a taxi home:

> *Ka-hei*:   He loved you most of all.
> *Ka-hing*:   He loved all of us.
> *Ka-hei*:   Yes, of the love he gave you, what was left over he gave to us.

In spite of this bitterly angry statement, the film is mainly a tale of how the father goes about his life-long obsession of securing the education of his eldest son. The father's efforts create a sense of guilt in the son who dreams of becoming an actor and a film-maker. The father's plans are nearly thwarted by the son's youthful intransigence as well as by his own low economic status due to inadequate educational qualifications: his lack of English prevents him from earning a promotion. But it is finally the father's own obstinacy which proves to be the key factor in breaking down the son's resistance to his authority; this, and the unstated demand that the daughter, Ka-hei, sacrifice her own ambitions for higher education. She does so ostensibly because she has studied enough to work as a nurse to support the family, but in reality her wages make it possible for the father to send Ka-hing to America. Another daughter is married off to a factory manager as part of the plan to secure more funds for Ka-hing's education. The women in the family are no more than sacrificial lambs at the altar of the patriarchy.

Although their perspective is secondary, the presence of the women is, nevertheless, important. Ka-hei's remark about the 'left-over' love which the father bestows on the rest of the family is strong enough for us to cast a critical look at the ideology of the patriarchy and of paternalism. Fong shows that materialistic progress in the ordinary Chinese family has not lessened the conservative, even reactionary, nature of patriarchy's role in preserving the family. Part of this materialistic progress was achieved by putting the women to work, thereby perpetuating the power of patriarchy, handing authority from father to son.

In Fong's film, the father achieves his ends by manipulating his son's as well as anyone else's feelings of guilt. As Ka-hing grows older, his rebelliousness is submerged by the feeling that he should not be unworthy of the sacrifices and humiliations suffered by his father. Ka-hing's love for the movies is at first only an escape from a humdrum childhood characterised by total obedience to an autocratic father as well as meaningless rote-learning in school, but it later crystallises into a real chance of employment as a film-maker. His father's opposition to his chosen *métier* is a foregone conclusion. Ka-hing's experiences with his father would surely have jolted the memories of many people in the audience who themselves are embroiled in real-life soap operas involving fathers and sons. It certainly jolted mine, bringing to the surface a childhood experience of my father's opposition to my love for the movies, the sense of guilt that overcame me when I was caught playing hooky in order to see a movie. Expecting punishment, I was surprised when none was given. This was one of the first examples of 'uncharacteristic' behaviour I could remember from my father, but it was an even more formidable form of punishment for all that as I was later told that he had wept. The sense of guilt that engulfed me was like the heavens caving in on me.

The father in Fong's film exploited the sentiment of guilt more than he evoked love. This seems to me a very characteristic form of behaviour among Chinese fathers. They are brusque and taciturn and never show emotion except when angry. They may be sentimental at times, but only for reasons of self-interest and self-preservation. A son's feelings towards his father can only be based on guilt, not affection. Filial love as seen by the father means discipline, punishment and rote-learning. It means deference to the father because 'father knows best'. In Fong's film, the son eventually accepts this maxim. The paradox in all father and son relationships and their history of conflict is lodged in this final acceptance of the father by the son. It is as much a part of the convention in the genre of the family melodrama as the principle in other genres that heroes never die. Because of the classic simplicity of the generational clash between father and son, it is easy to read into it the symbolism of a clash between tradition and modernity.

In the narrative of *Father and Son/Fuzi Qing*, the son's progress is cut off at the point when the father dies after suffering a stroke on receiving the happy news of his son's graduation from an American university. The film is structured on the flashback of the son as he arrives back in Hong Kong for his father's funeral; it ends at the airport with the son taking off in a plane, his future secured by a place at an American university. Presumably, the son's growth is ensured with the education he will receive in a liberal, progressive Western country. But the paradox of the father and son conflict means that the son's liberation through education is a result of the father's dictate that the son go overseas to study. To put it simply, tradition dictates that things should change and become modern. But imagine the trauma which arises from this fundamental contradiction: when the son returns as a 'modern man', he soon discovers that tradition expects yet more deference, yet more compliance. The contradiction will become more vicious as the son begins to question this process. As the son becomes more critical, tradition becomes more repressive.

Fong and other directors in Hong Kong's new wave have extensively explored the patriarchal tradition and its related motifs, such as national-ism and identity, the search for which was indicated by the rise of the new wave itself. Because of Hong Kong's own awkward position in history, this search for identity naturally became a central motif in the work of its most sensitive directors. It meant that the Hong Kong cinema had evolved from linkage and continuity to maturity and independence. In expressing their own identity, the new wave directors had to tackle the history of Hong Kong, or the lack of it. Tradition and culture provided the link with China and its history, and were thus absorbed as indispensable motifs. But Hong Kong was also ruled as a British colonial entrepôt, and administered by professional civil servants appointed by the British Crown. As a society, it had evolved a role for itself as a medium for cross-cultural exchange between East and West. And as it developed into a sophisticated economy, an understanding grew of Hong Kong as a unique place with a culture all its own. Tradition, or the link with China, was dissolved as Hong Kong gradually exerted its own identity. Yet no matter how hard it tried, Hong Kong could not escape the clutches of China. Between 1982 and 1984, the period of intense negotiations between Britain and China concerning the fate of Hong Kong after 1997, the territory had to endure the squint-eyed gaze of the Chinese fatherland. Implied in the father's squint-eyed gaze was all that Chinese tradition and custom demanded: consensus, deference, discipline and obedience. Hong Kong faced the realisation that it would eventually have to cope with the patriarchal tradition of China and forgo the liberalism it had inherited from its Western rulers.

There has always been some acceptance among Hong Kong inhabitants of China as a source of cultural tradition and romantic myths. It is at the level of East–West adaptation and political ideology that differences exist in each other's perception of Chinese culture. But tradition itself seemed inviolate; the structures of patriarchy remained intact in the transition from China to Hong Kong, and in the passing of the old to the new, even though Hong Kong, as the son to China's father, has largely gone its own way. Thus we may look at the 'link' between Fong's *Father and Son/Fuzi Qing* and Ng Wui's *Father and Son/Fu yu Zi* and Ch'un Kim's *Parents' Hearts/Fumu Xin* to confirm that patriarchy has not changed its spots. The films by Ng and Ch'un are significant works in their own right although they become more complex and richer when compared with Fong's reinterpretation of the father and son motif. Fong's film also shows that despite materialistic progress in the post-war years, tradition is still the lodestar guiding Hong Kong to its destiny. No one can argue with conviction that Fong is a radical film-maker in his methods; yet he is unique among the new wave directors for going his own non-commercial way. He is also singular in his understanding of how tradition links the intangible past with the present. The past appears intangible because succeeding generations in Hong Kong rely too much on the new, on the sense of contemporaneity and modernity.

The same may be said of Ng Wui and Ch'un Kim. Although it is true that Ng Wui, on the evidence of his film, was not as technically proficient as either his contemporary Ch'un Kim or the new-generation director Allen Fong, he was just as preoccupied with the realism which animates both Ch'un and Fong's films. Ng was one of those directors trapped within the poverty-row system which marked Cantonese film-making in the 50s but who nevertheless sought to endow their work with social relevance. It is pertinent to remind readers once again that Ng's contribution to

Cantonese cinema is not founded on any great claims of auteurism or craftsmanship. If we must compare Fong's *Father and Son/Fuzi Qing* with Ng's *Father and Son/Fu yu Zi* in terms of technique and style, there would be no doubt that many would find Fong's film superior. Ng's technique, like those of most directors in the Cantonese cinema of the period, tended to falter. However, because Fong made an explicit reference to Ng Wui's film and to the conventions of the family melodrama, his point of view was really limited to that set of thematic continuities which Ng had codified in his own film.

Ng Wui started as an actor in 1940 with the Grandview (Daguan) Company and directed his first film the following year. He began his career in a company that was known for its pictures that reflected the turbulence of the times and the need to instil patriotic and other social-conscience messages. Ng's best work was done in the 50s, a period of post-war recovery that saw many people embedded in poverty trying to rebuild their lives. The family was the basic source of Ng's characters. The film that best reflected Ng's preoccupation with the family is *The Prodigal Son/Baijia Zai* (1951), a superb, funny satire of the traditional father and son relationship based on the biblical parable. Cheung Ying plays a spoiled layabout son who squanders away the money remitted by his working migrant father in America. He separates from his wife (Pak Yin), a virtuous woman who can no longer put up with the taunts and bullying of her mother-in-law (Wong Man-lei) and the infidelities of her husband. The father (Lo Dun) returns home without the anticipated fortune of a man who has gone to the 'Gold Mountain' and gradually discovers that his son is a 'bai-kar-tsai' (one who will cause ruin to the whole family). The father starts a laundry and hires Cheung's separated wife as a worker. Impressed by her hard work and honesty, he learns the truth about the reasons for the separation. After being disowned by his father, the son redeems himself by going back to the family fold and working in the family business without being asked. Though spoiled by a soundtrack composed of a classical hodgepodge by Western romantic composers, this last sequence works entirely without dialogue so as to underline the motif of personal redemption, thus making it less didactic up to a point. However, in its depiction of the father and son relationship, it is automatically assumed that the father holds the moral high ground and the son is a transgressor of the family ethical system (that is, to work hard and be frugal, be a good husband, a filial son, etc.). Thus, *The Prodigal Son* conforms to the didactic tradition in films of the period, but this no doubt reflected the strength of the family system in Chinese society.

The Prodigal Son was only one of numerous films in the Cantonese cinema which dealt with the family system in the immediate post-Chinese civil war years, the most noteworthy of which included Fung Fung's *The Kid/Xilu Xiang* (1950) and Ch'un Kim's *The Guiding Light/Kuhai Mingdeng* (1953). These films looked at the family from different angles, mostly anchored in the potential collapse of the family system due to societal factors or harsh economic conditions. In both films, Bruce Lee was featured as an orphan searching for father figures and a stable home. In fact, *The Kid* was Lee's first starring role as a child star.

Ng Wui was certainly not averse to attacking the family system, as he did in his next film *Family/Jia* (1953), adapted from the famous novel by Ba Jin about the conflict between feudal and progressive values (or, seen in another way, about the lasting legacy of feudalism). As interpreted by Ng Wui, Ba Jin's novel contained more ideological arguments concerning the decline and death of feudalism than the end of the family system *per se*. *Family* was the first production of the Chung-luen Company which was set up to elevate the quality of Cantonese cinema by injecting social conscience and high production values. The film belonged to the left-wing tradition but it was less radical in its attack on the family than a film like *Tragedy in Canton/Yangchen Henshi* (1951), directed by actor Lo Dun (the father in *The Prodigal Son*). Set in Guangzhou during the anti-Japanese war right through to the civil war, *Tragedy* deals with a father and son conflict (the father is a warlord, the son a revolutionary).

Somewhat daringly for a Cantonese production of the period, the film dispenses with allegory and clearly grounds the conflict in a political context. However, the film's radical centre lies not so much in its avowed leftist tendencies as in its depiction of the total collapse of the father and son relationship. The father puts the son in jail, and, in the final climax, pulls out a gun to shoot at him. Unlike most family melodramas, the film offers no chance of a reconciliation. The father is an all-out villain, possessing not a trace of moral fibre (he also rapes his adopted daughter). Significantly, *The Prodigal Son* and Ng's subsequent *Father and Son/Fu yu Zi* (1954) were grounded in milder economic arguments that reflected the daily concerns of families in the modern environment of Hong Kong. Both films were about the survival of families, one line of the thematic continuity that carried through to the new wave cinema – and indeed to the ubiquitous postmodern comedies of the 90s featuring Stephen Chiau in the role of the son to Ng Mang-tat's father figure. In contrast, *Tragedy in Canton*, which ups the ante in both ideological and melodramatic stakes being a production of a company (Nam Kwok) set up by left-wing artists, is today largely a curiosity in Cantonese film history, at least when seen by contemporary film-makers.

Father and Son/Fu yu Zi stars Cheung Wood-yau as a widower who has to raise a young son on a meagre income. Like the father in Fong's film, he is blocked from promotion because of a lack of educational qualifications and influential contacts (the person who is promoted over him is a classmate of the boss's son). The film dwells on the father's unceasing efforts to put his son in a prestigious school. In the process, he meets up with the forces of snobbery – the emerging middle class – in the urban landscape of 50s Hong Kong. The film ends with the father coming to terms with his own status and allowing his son to go to a less prestigious, more community-oriented school. Allen Fong has enlarged upon the plot of Ng's film. The most important advance in Fong's *Father and Son/Fuzi Qing* is the inclusion of a strong female character within the family household: the sister Ka-hei, who acts as the conscience of the family. In Ng's *Father and Son/Fu yu Zi*, the father and son relationship virtually dominates the whole film; and the feeling it generates is consequently more desperate. But even in Ng's film, a conscience figure is never far away, and as in Fong's film, that figure is a woman. Also, as in Fong's film, she opens up a possible critique of the intensity of the father and son relationship if not of the patriarchal system itself.

This conscience figure is the sister of the father: the boy's aunt. She provides a focus of sanity and reason in the ridiculously unbalanced father–son relationship, with the father overwhelming the son. She is a self-sufficient figure who attempts to moderate the father's excesses. On another level, she personifies the paradox in the system. While acting as a conscience, she is the measure of moral justification for the father and son relationship. In her character lies the substance of the conservative tradition in the Chinese family system. As the father grooms the son for manhood, it is the woman who must offer support as the tacit member in a patriarchal conspiracy. Naturally, as times change, this character type is most prone to become outdated because the role of women has undergone tremendous change: she can no longer be represented as simply a bystander. By the 80s, the passive woman already signifies the moribund conventions in the family melodrama as a genre. In his *Father and Son/Fuzi Qing*, Allen Fong engages with a version of 'the passive woman', but his creation, the sister Ka-hei, is a much more bitter manifestation. This link with the past offers a historical perspective on how things have (or haven't) changed.

Fong is really paying a price for looking back into the past: the price of *chengxian qihou* (to evoke the past so as to inherit its legacy). This is also the price of thematic continuity, the nature of the exercise requiring that one gives way to generic forms and conventions. Fong is not the only director caught in the impasse of a suspension of time in the present (represented by the father's death at the start of the film where the only future is that of a funeral) for a look into the past. Such temporal tensions and generic conventions also mark the work of even younger directors such as Stanley Kwan (in *Rouge/Yanzhi Kou* and *Actress/Ruan Lingyu*) and Wong Kar-wai (in *Days of Being Wild/A Fei Zhengzhuan*, where time is actually an integrated motif). In the pursuit of thematic continuity, film-makers either fall prey to or transcend the forms and conventions of genre. One method in which they transcend moribund conventions is to respect the integrity of present time by changing old conventions and adding new things. A work which looks back to the past gains more value if it is seen as relevant to the present, if old conventions are adjusted to the needs of a contemporary audience.

One cannot deny that Ng Wui's *Father and Son/Fu yu Zi* was relevant to its times – the 50s. Its virtue lies in its contemporaneity with the generic themes of the period which draw upon Hong Kong's poverty and economic backwardness. This is a common feature of most Cantonese films belonging to genres closely corresponding to the society of their time: the melodrama, the thriller, even the musical. It is important to realise that the desire for social relevance was a paramount aspiration among Cantonese film-makers of that period, much more so than compliance with the dictates of an entertainment-oriented industry.

Ch'un Kim's *Parents Hearts/Fumu Xin*, released in 1955, is even more resolute in its feeling of contemporaneity and is arguably the best of the father and son films. Again, the central relationship is that of a father, a Cantonese opera actor laid off by his company and who becomes a street performer with his eldest son, a student who earns a scholarship to go and study in Macao. Ch'un Kim builds up this relationship on a more equal footing to reflect the eldest son's more advanced age. Unlike the sons in Fong's and Ng's films, Ch'un's is more independent, more capable of making his own decisions. He puts off higher education so that he can work to support the family rather than defer to the father's wish that he continue his education despite the lack of money. This leads to a psychological war with the father and the fact that the son is absent from the screen most of the time makes the psychological clash even more formidable. The father, played affectingly by Cantonese opera star Ma Si-tsang, is warm-hearted to a fault and never overbearing. Ma's performance is a convincing portrayal of paternal heroism, but he is not without his weak side. This point is put across once again by introducing a female character who acts as a counterpoint to the father: the mother, played by Wong Man-lei, an actress often typecast in matronly roles, who gives an acidic portrayal of the character. Mother appears to resent the relationship between father and son. Practical and tough-minded, she even shocks her eldest son into acting like a stranger to her. We know soon enough that her unusual behaviour is brought about by a terminal illness. Like Ka-hei in Fong's film, the mother's presence, and paradoxically her absence when she dies two-thirds into the film, makes her the conscience of the family. Her tough-mindedness is offset by the warm-heartedness of the father, whose paternalism then appears more of a social duty reluctantly assumed. The father and son relationship is soft-centred and aligned to other psychological factors in a wider family relationship. The father is weak, the mother is strong, the son is wilful but basically filial.

Ch'un Kim delineates not one but two father and son relationships in *Parents' Hearts/Fumu Xin*. After the eldest son's departure to Macao, the film shifts into a second father and son relationship as the focus falls on the youngest son, played by child star Yuen Siu-fai (the son in Ng Wui's *Father and Son/Fu yu Zi*). Ch'un contrasts these two relationships, one a 'failed' relationship, the other an 'ideal' one. The father teaches his youngest son all sorts of acting tricks and begins to mould the boy in his own image. But in the Chinese tradition, it is still the eldest son who must carry the burden of filial duty, although this does not mean that the youngest son is let off the hook: he is expected eventually to step into the shoes of the eldest son. It is a dilemma that proves too much for the young boy. He shows talent for performing on stage but is bound too tightly by the desire to maintain a harmonious relationship with his father, and burdened by having to make

70

up for the brother who has broken father's heart. When the boy is given the chance to perform on stage, he fails and becomes a laughing stock. The presence of his father off-stage and the burden of having to live up to an ideal relationship prove too much to bear.

Ch'un adopts a sympathetic tone to the younger son's dilemma which reveals the true message of the film: the family unit is never ideal and relationships remain superficial if they are not formed on the basis of understanding and trust. Ch'un implies that Chinese tradition itself militates against such ideal relationships. The weight of this message is carried by the characterisations, most importantly by the interplay between characters and gains veracity through the successful handling of *mise en scène*, underlining the perception of a sense of contemporaneity. If any film can, this one transcends the generic elements of the family melodrama.

Parents' Hearts/Fumu Xin can be distinguished from Fong's *Father and Son/Fuzi Qing* by its respect for temporal integrity and its hard-nosed approach to the father and son relationship. While Ch'un does not lack sentiment, he draws out the unwritten tension between his characters, allowing us to differentiate what is sensitive from what is sentimental. Perhaps it is a pity that Allen Fong did not take *Parents' Hearts* as his model as Ch'un Kim was obviously a more sophisticated director than Ng Wui. His talent was more symptomatic of the times as *Parents' Hearts* proves. The film's importance now lies in its provision, rather than mere reflection, of a template for the pattern of thematic continuities in the family melodrama.[3]

The articulation of thematic continuity is necessitated by changes and variations in the genre through the passage of time. A film such as Lee Sun-fung's *The Orphan/Renhai Guhong* shows how the dynamics of the father and son relationship change along with the times. The father (played by Ng Cho-fan) is a widower who lost his son in the chaos of the Second World War. As if to compensate for the loss of his family, he becomes the headmaster of a reform school for young offenders and orphans, firmly believing that the older generation has a moral duty to rear and teach the young. In themselves, young delinquents have no guilt: their delinquent behaviour represents the failure of their elders. While Ng Wui's *Father and Son* and Ch'un Kim's *Parents' Hearts* depict the father's economic burden in bringing up his children, *The Orphan* depicts a moral burden as well as the malaise of juvenile delinquency in Hong Kong as it developed into an industrial society. Released in 1960, *The Orphan* closes one era and looks forward to a new one. It is today mostly remembered as the film in which Bruce Lee (as the teenage delinquent who turns out to be the headmaster's long lost son) gave his most memorable performance in Hong Kong before he left for America. However, the movie marvellously evokes a time when social conscience was a cinematic composite of realism and melodrama, while the film's heart is firmly located in its portrayal of the father and son relationship and the survival of the family unit.

The father and son genre continues to resonate in the Hong Kong

71

cinema of the present, as in Lawrence Ah Mon's *Gangs/ Tong Dang* (1988), Lau Chen-wei's *Love and the City* (1994) and Ah Mon's *One and a Half/ Gen Wo Zou Yi Hui* (1995). The first two films are examples of how Hong Kong's melodramas mesh together distinct strands from different genres (such as the gangster film). The development of genres in the 90s has also given rise to warmed up versions of old father and son films, as in the postmodernist comedies featuring Stephen Chiau and his older sidekick Ng Mang-tat.

The contradictions inherent in the father and son relationship are such that both protagonists seek to embrace but succeed only in further alienating each other. Behind every father and son film lies the truth that the ending is never perfect. Another generational conflict looms, as sons are bound to grow up to become fathers. The cycle will go on *ad infinitum.*

NOTES

[1] Film versions have been made of Hua Mulan, dubbed the 'lady general', both by the Shanghai and Hong Kong cinemas.

[2] This is particularly so in Lau's *Executioners From Shaolin.* See Chapter 7 for a fuller discussion of this film and the homoerotic theme in the films directed by Lau and other key masters of the genre.

[3] It has taken more than thirty years for the father and son film to reach its (pro-visional) apex in Chinese cinema, and it happened not in Hong Kong but in Taiwan, with Edward Yang's *A Brighter Summer Day/ Guling Jie Shaonian Sharen Shijian* (1991).

Chapter Five

The Romantic and the Cynical Mandarins

THE STUDIO MOGULS AND THEIR SCREEN ALTER EGOS
Two remarkable men dominated the Hong Kong film industry in the latter half of the 50s. They were the respective commanders of, on the one hand, MP and GI, and Shaw Brothers on the other, two rival studios which played decisive roles in forging the Hong Kong film industry into a cohesive force while at the same time competing fiercely for markets in Hong Kong, Taiwan and Southeast Asia. The boss of MP and GI was Dato Loke Wan-tho (the title of Dato is one conferred by Malaysian royalty for services rendered to the community) a rare species among ethnic Chinese Malaysian business magnates. He was a dandified Cambridge-educated scholar and aesthete who also possessed good business acumen. The boss of Shaw Brothers was (later Sir) Run Run Shaw, a shrewd promoter and Cecil B. DeMille-type showman who was no less an aesthete and a true connoisseur of film. He once went out of his way to arrange a private showing on a steenbeck of Pasolini's *Salo*, which was banned in the territory. Shaw often boasted that he saw more films in a day than critics saw in a week.

Loke Wan-tho headed the Singapore-based Cathay Organisation which bought into the financially troubled Yonghua studio in Hong Kong in 1955. Cathay revamped Yonghua and set up its own company in 1956 calling it Motion Picture and General Investment (MP and GI), the legal name of the studio.[1]

Run Run Shaw was the youngest of the Shaw Brothers who went south from Shanghai to Hong Kong and Southeast Asia to build up a film-producing and distributing empire. The eldest brother, Shao Zuiweng, had established a branch of their Shanghai studio, Tianyi, in Hong Kong in the 30s. This studio was managed by second brother Runde (or Shao Cunren) and was later re-named Nanyang, becoming Shaw and Sons in 1950. Run Run (Shao Yifu) was in Singapore with his brother Runme (Shao Renmei), acquiring property to turn into theatres and overseeing distribution. In 1957, he returned to Hong Kong to start a new company, Shaw Brothers. It is this latter company which came to be regarded as the one and only company which the Shaw Brothers established. In fact, each of the Shaw brothers evolved and set up separate companies within the Shaw empire.

Loke's and Shaw's studios were representative of the momentum in Hong Kong towards greater industrialisation and manufacturing in the late 50s. Investments from overseas Chinese communities and businessmen stimulated the territory's economy into becoming a source of supply for manufactured goods, including movies. Hong Kong-made films catered to all overseas Chinese communities in Southeast Asia, especially Singapore and Malaysia (a region familiar to both Loke Wan-tho and Run Run Shaw), Taiwan and Hong Kong. The demand was for Mandarin films, which stimulated the overseas Chinese's sense of kinship and nostalgia for Chinese culture by utilising stories from Chinese legend, myth and history. At the same time, contemporary feel-good films encouraged audiences to have a positive attitude towards the modern world and enabled them to partake, in their imagination at least, of prosperous lifestyles beyond their dreams. The period 1956 to 1964, when MP and GI was restructured and officially re-named Cathay following the death of Loke Wan-tho in a plane crash, was a time of stability and the heyday of Mandarin cinema enabling the two major studios to consolidate their economic power and market positions, becoming virtually synonymous with Mandarin cinema.

The two studios developed production methods as effective as Hollywood's, invoking fantasies of modernity and glamour. The sophistication of Mandarin cinema during this period was due to excellent technical standards and the professionalism of Shanghai film-makers who had migrated to Hong Kong after the war. They were now employed on a contract basis by either of the two studios, after early periods at smaller companies now sidelined by the two 'majors'. Directors such as Bu Wancang, Tao Qin, Yi Wen, Tang Huang, Wang Tianlin, Yue Feng, Yan Jun and Li Hanxiang[2] were in large measure responsible for the glossy look and polished styles which became associated in the public mind with films produced by the two majors.

The studio system put into operation by Shaw Brothers, MP and GI, and their amalgamation of Shanghai and Hollywood styles was perhaps best represented by their musicals and comedies. MP and GI classic musicals such as Yi Wen's *Mambo Girl/Manbo Nüang* (1957) and Wang Tianlin's *Wild, Wild Rose/Ye Meigui* (1960) were the top of the line, but films such as *Our Sister Hedy/Si Qianjin* (1957, directed by Tao Qin), *Air Hostess/Kongzhong Xiaojie* (1959, directed by Yi Wen), *Cinderella and Her Little Angels/Yunchang Yanhou* (1959, directed by Tang Huang) and *Sister Long Legs/Changtui Jiejie* (1960, directed by Tang Huang), were bright and sprightly efforts influenced by, and in some cases were re-workings of, many a Shanghai and Hollywood comedy or musical. Although MP and GI produced outstanding films in other genres, they are now remembered mostly for their musicals starring Ge Lan and comedies featuring a host of beauties from Lin Cui and Ye Feng to Lin Dai.

Shaw Brothers enticed a number of its rival studio's stars and directors to join them in the common task of making optimism and fantasy part of everybody's lives. Ex-MP and GI director Tao Qin and stars Peter Chen Hou and Lin Dai made one of the best, *The Love Parade/Hua Tuan Jin Cu*

(1963). Peter Chen Hou starred in a series of contemporary comedy-musicals for Shaw, usually directed by Tao Qin. But the studio is perhaps best remembered for tearful romantic melodramas and historical epics rather than for cheery musicals and comedies. Chen Hou himself was required to make the transition from light leading man to romantic tragedian in one of Shaw's best-known melodramas, *Till the End of Time/ Heri Jun Zailai* (1966), directed by Ch'un Kim. Shaw made the genre a specialty because of its previous success with Tao Qin's *Love Without End/ Bu Liao Qing* (1961), starring Lin Dai, one of the studio's greatest assets as a tragic star. She committed suicide in 1964, aged thirty.

Romantic melodramas in Hong Kong cinema of the 50s and 60s tended to be heavy, cheerless love stories. In *Love Without End*, Lin Dai, although also an adept comedienne, was in perfect form as the foremost tragedienne of the early 60s. She played Li Qingqing, a nightclub songstress who falls in love with wimpish Guan Shan portraying a businessman whose business is saved from bankruptcy because Qingqing procured a loan for him by becoming a gangster's moll. Director Tao Qin may be compared to Otto Preminger for his careful Scope compositions and unassuming directorial style. His command of actors was superb, enabling both Lin Dai and Guan Shan to give possibly their best performances ever, hitting just the right notes of tragedy and romantic love. In the film, Qingqing dies from leukaemia just when love means never having to be separated from your man. After singing the unforgettable melody of the title (in Chinese, it means 'The Love I Cannot Forget'), she leaves him in order to die alone. *Love Without End* is sentimental kitsch but played with conviction.

Tao's next epic romance-tragedy, *The Blue and the Black/ Lan yu Hei* (1964), also starred Lin Dai and Guan Shan. It was set in Tianjin against the background of the anti-Japanese war. Lin plays Tang Qi, an orphan living with her aunt's snobbish family, the Gaos. Her love affair with Zhang Xingya (Guan Shan), distant cousin and fellow orphan adopted by another foster family, meets with opposition from both families. Tang Qi leaves the Gao family to work as a nurse; she is raped by a lascivious doctor and becomes a nightclub singer while her lover Xingya, unable to make up his mind whether to elope with Tang Qi, enlists in the army to fight the Japanese. Guan Shan gave yet another classic 'romantic wimp' perform-ance – a man so indecisive and given to weeping that the characterisation verged on caricature. Yet such weak romantic heroes were the norm at the time, being regarded as virtuous characters. Lin Dai's presence as the strong, self-sacrificing woman, and Guan Shan's tearful hero make *The Blue and the Black* an irresistible melodrama, enhanced by Tao Qin's expert direction and widescreen *mise en scène*.

Ch'un Kim, who directed *Till the End of Time*, was a specialist in these melodramas called *wenyi pian*.[3] Although *Till the End of Time* was a remake of a 1954 Cantonese melodrama, *Love in Penang/ Bin Cheng Yan*, Ch'un's source of inspiration was closer to something like Jean Negulesco's *Humoresque* (1947, produced by Warner Brothers whom the Shaws clearly were emulating) with Joan Crawford as a married woman in love with John

Garfield's concert violinist. The film plays like a variation of the *Humoresque* theme, with its lovers similarly star-crossed. The woman is a singer (Jenny Hu) and the man a songwriter (Peter Chen Hou) from a rich family whose father opposes the union. They marry, he is disowned by his father, and as a result of straining to make ends meet by writing songs twenty-four hours a day, he goes blind. The woman goes back to the nightclub, is discovered and becomes a big movie star. Meanwhile, the man broods, thinking himself a failure both as husband and artist, and he leaves his wife.

Hong Kong cinema in the 50 and 60s, both in its Mandarin and Cantonese streams, was characterised by romantic leading men of a specific type and behaviour. The Chinese romantic hero possessed charm, sensitivity and culture, but he was also effete, bookish and ineffectual. Shaw's *Love Without End, The Blue and the Black* and *Till the End of Time* illustrate this wimpish aspect of the male romantic actor. Peter Chen Hou and Guan Shan were only two in a long line of leading men of the period who exuded sorrow, pain and weakness as the necessary ingredients of romanticism. In Cantonese cinema, Ng Cho-fan exemplified this romantic type. In Mandarin cinema, MP and GI had a near-monopoly of actors playing the weak romantic hero, such as Zhang Yang, Zhao Lei (who later worked for Shaw) and Lei Zhen who all vied to be the dullest and weakest of the lot. Zhang was the star of *Sun, Moon and Star/Xingxing, Yueliang, Taiyang* (1961), directed by Yi Wen, which set the trend for romantic epics such as Shaw's *The Blue and the Black*. Zhao Lei appeared in many period films, memorably in Wang Tianlin's superb version of *The Story of Three Loves/Tixiao Yinyuan* (1964) from the Zhang Henshui novel. Lei Zhen was featured in many comedies and melodramas. Thin and thoughtful, he was, in the eyes of many women, an ideal romantic type. That such a type dominated cinema screens in the region for well over a decade may be attributed to various factors: the flowering of a romantic age following a period of war and national disaster; the appeal of the type to the intellectual aesthete in Loke Wan-tho who was himself the very picture of a scholarly and dandified gentleman (or a *shaoye*) well liked by the actors he had under contract. Run Run Shaw also cultivated the image of a cultured Chinese *shaoye*, but he was competing with Loke, and whatever Loke utilised in his pictures, Shaw was determined to match. Hence, Shaw Brothers had their own romantic leading men: Guan Shan, Qiao Zhuang, Paul Zhang Chong and Chen Hou when he was not working in comedies. In the early 50s, before the dominance of the two major studios, there were actors like Wang Hao, Huang He, Luo Wei or Yan Jun who best represented the type; on the left-wing side, there were actors such as Fu Qi, Gao Yuan and Bao Fang.

The tradition of the effete romantic hero had been established in literature and theatre. Character roles in Chinese opera and the traditional theatre were divided into *wen* (meaning civil) and *wu* (meaning martial). On the *wen* side was the *shusheng* (or scholar), a role with a performing tradition which passed into cinema through the opera film and other period films. The *shusheng* was also found in literature and one can go back as far as the days of Confucius to establish the lineage. The predominance of the *shusheng* type of protagonist led to variations of the weak, tubercular heroes created by writers such as Ba Jin and Cao Yu, who used their characters to symbolise China's subjugated and weak condition which prevailed for about a hundred years from the Opium Wars to 1949.

The weak hero, physically and spiritually emaciated, gave rise to another interesting variation: the Ah Q character created by Lu Xun in his short story *The True Story of Ah Q/A Q Zhengzhuan*, published in 1921. The story triggered the so-called 'Ah Q syndrome', a condition peculiar to Chinese manhood characterised by weakness and defeatism – a condition so deeply ingrained that defeat is even viewed as a form of victory. Ah Q was a caricature of a Chinese loser, a fool who aspired to be smart and strong but forever remained a fool because society looked down on his aspirations. The character could not make up his mind whether to pass from the realm of *wen* (civil) characteristics into those of *wu* (martial) and was caught somewhere in the middle. Actor Guan Shan achieved prominence by portraying Ah Q in Yuan Yang'an's *The Story of Ah Q/A Q Zhengzhuan* (1958; Guan won the acting prize in the Locarno Film Festival that year). He typified the weak romantic man thereafter in films such as *Love Without End* and *The Blue and the Black*, playing up-market versions of Ah Q.

The classical *shusheng*-type prevailed in films with period settings, either historical epics recounting tales of weak emperors and their strong-minded concubines, or love stories set in ancient dynasties with a touch of myth and legend, usually adapted from opera. Such genres were staples of the two studios but Shaw had an edge over its rival because it had the best directors for these films. Yue Feng's *Madam White Snake/Bai She Zhuan* (1962), *Lady General Hua Mulan/Hua Mulan* (1964) and *The Lotus Lamp/Baolian Deng* (1965) were examples of Shaw's taste for classicism: the stories were all popular myths and legends, also adapted for opera, and all featured romances between effete scholar types and ladies of distinction.

True to opera convention, such roles could also be portrayed by women. In Yue's films, actresses Ling Bo (in *Lady General Hua Mulan*) and Zheng Peipei (in *The Lotus Lamp*) were employed in *fanchuan* roles: that is, roles requiring the actor to play the opposite sex – in this case, women playing male *shusheng* types. Ling Bo became known for her *shusheng* roles, first winning praise for her performance as the lovelorn scholar Liang Shanbo in Li Hanxiang's *The Love Eterne/Liang Shanbo yu Zhu Yingtai* (1963). Liang falls in love with fellow scholar Zhu Yingtai, a woman who puts on male attire in order to get an education so that she can sit for the imperial examinations, a practice reserved only for males. Yingtai reveals her true identity and Shanbo swears to marry her, but the marriage is made impossible by the opposition of Yingtai's father who has arranged for her to marry someone else. The lovers commit suicide and are transformed into a pair of butterflies. A folktale which has been adapted into numerous opera versions, Li turned *The Love Eterne* into a form of Chinese operetta known as *huangmei diao*.

The Love Eterne was Shaw's biggest money-spinner of the time and still holds the record as the studio's most constantly revived film. It started the fashion for *huangmei diao* films, most of which starred Ling Bo and consolidated Li Hanxiang's status as Shaw's foremost director of historical costume films, being assigned to the big-budgeted items: *The Kingdom and the Beauty/Jiangshan Meiren* (1959), *Yang Kwei Fei/Yang Guifei* (1963), *Empress Wu Tse-tien/Wu Zetian* (1963), *Beyond the Great Wall/Wang Zhaojun* (1964), *The Empress Dowager/Qingguo Qingcheng* (1975) and *The Last Tempest/Yingtai Qixie* (1976). Shaw Brothers thrived on the period film that had *chaqu* episodes sung in the *huangmei diao* mode and it prompted rival Cathay to jump on the bandwagon: they hired actor-director Yan Jun to make their own version of the Liang Shanbo and Zhu Yingtai legend starring Yan Jun's wife, Li Lihua, and You Min.

Li Hanxiang was not the only prominent director of period films at Shaw Brothers. Yan Jun's *The Grand Substitution/Wangu Liufang* (1965) and Gao Li's *Inside the Forbidden City/Song Gong Mishi* (1965) were splendid examples of the genre and both put Shaw's repertory of veteran character actors to good use. The genre emphasised the classical division between *wen* and *wu* and finely balanced both types, often favouring female actors to impart both characteristics. The biggest star in this period, actress Ling Bo, even became famous for her impersonations of male scholars and warriors. Li's historical films focused on strong female protagonists. Li Lihua played concubines of emperors who rose to become virtual rulers of the empire in *Yang Kwei Fei* and *Empress Wu Tse-tien*. Lin Dai played benevolent concubines of weak emperors in *The Kingdom and the Beauty* and *Beyond the Great Wall*. Her characters were prone to sacrifice their lives for the sake of the empire.

The men in Li's films were of the fragile *shusheng* type, which also applied to emperors and other ineffective or indecisive protagonists. Li usually employed Zhao Lei to play such roles, and so perfectly did Zhao endow his dyspeptic scholars and emperors with the required weaknesses that one could well conclude that the actor was Li's alter ego. Before he became a director, Li had dabbled rather unsuccessfully in acting. His northern Chinese background (Li was born in Liaoning Province in 1926) and years spent in Beijing studying at the city's Art Academy would have stood him in good stead to play roles such as those acted by Zhao Lei. Instead, it gave him a good grounding to direct these roles: he excelled at sketches and drawings which he made to bring out the right characterisations. As a director, Li Hanxiang was quite the opposite of a weak-kneed *shusheng*. He was ambitious and developed a grand vision of cinema commensurate with his direction of epics and romantic melodramas.

After his time in Beijing, Li went to Hong Kong in 1948 and found jobs in the film industry, initially as a bit-player. His career progressed faster behind the camera: he worked variously as art director, set designer, scenarist and assistant director until he got his big break on a Yonghua production, *Golden Phoenix/Jin Feng* (1955), which was nominally directed by Yan Jun, the star of the movie, but was actually directed by Li, who also wrote the screenplay.[4] A pastoral romance that doubled as a mood piece with added musical numbers (*chaqu* episodes), *Golden Phoenix* was distinguished by the memorable performances of its female lead, Lin Dai, and a strong supporting cast including King Hu as a stammering scald-head. Good location work (exterior scenes shot in Hong Kong's New Territories), superb art direction (recreating northern Chinese small-town markets and mansions in the early republican era) and editing, made it a superior production from a studio facing its demise and determined to go out with a bang. Li gradually settled into the director's chair with *Red Bloom in the Snow/Xueli Hong* (1956), a melodrama about sizzling passion in a northern Chinese town in the 30s, made for an independent company. Li's depiction of the itinerant life of travelling players conferred a strong northern Chinese atmosphere to the movie, repeating his successful integration of mood, characterisations and set designs. He had an excellent cast, all from northern Chinese backgrounds, including his favourite actress Li Lihua who would appear in several more of his pictures. Li signed on with the Shaws almost immediately after making *Red Bloom in the Snow* and blossomed into a front-rank director of Mandarin features, adept at both melodramas and costume pictures. *The Kingdom and the Beauty* (1959) was his breakthrough work, combining epic and romantic themes, tackling both drama and history and incorporating folk elements of northern Chinese performing styles. Stylistically, Li's period films were gracefully executed: his fondness for camera movement effected through tracks and cranes and his elaborate *mise en scène* combined to give an impression of Li as an almost Mizoguchian stylist. But Li was also an eclectic, even mercurial, artist and his style changed over time. In two contemporary melodramas, *Rear Entrance/Hou Men* (1960) and *The Coin/Yimao Qian* (1964), Li absorbed the conventions of Chinese melodrama as seen, for example, in the films of Zhu Shilin, while the influence of Douglas Sirk may also be discerned. *Rear Entrance* employed two ex-Shanghai stars, Wang Yin and Hu Die (aka Butterfly Wu), as a childless middle-aged couple whose adoption of a girl is jeopardised when her natural mother turns up to reclaim her. However, the melodrama is ploddingly didactic; and his heavy-handed approach also marks *The Coin*, a film about a young doctor's guardian who obstructs their marriage. Again, heavy moralising permeates the film.

   The tendency to rate Li's historical epics higher than his melodramas is justified by the splendid *Empress Wu Tse Tien/Wu Zetian* (1963), a superior example of the *gongwei* (or palace chamber) drama, a subgenre of the historical epic. *Gongwei* epics deal with political intrigues at the highest echelons of the imperial court: empresses and eunuchs intriguing to usurp the powers of rightful claimants or vying to exercise power behind the throne. The title role is played by Li Lihua with feminist panache, portraying the first *de facto* empress in China's history as a ruthless ruler who could still be magnanimous and was ever ready to strike a blow for feminist principles. *Empress Wu Tse Tien* was to be Li's swansong for Shaw Brothers in the first phase of his directing career from 1956 to 1963. He left Shaws in 1963 and embarked on the most ambitious phase of his career in

Taiwan where he set up his own production company called Guolian (the Grand Motion Picture Company). Li's ambition was grand indeed: he wanted his own studio as well as to direct pictures of a grand design that would be commercial, artistic and remembered for all time. He also dreamt of turning Guolian into the centre of Mandarin film production in the region, which made him instrumental in revitalising the Taiwanese film industry, laying the groundwork for the emigration of Mandarin-speaking film talent from Hong Kong to Taiwan.

The year 1964 was a watershed for the Mandarin cinema in Hong Kong. Li, the Shaw Brothers' brightest talent, was now in Taiwan running his own studio while Taiwan was speeding up its own production of Mandarin-language films. In June of 1964, Loke Wan-tho was killed in a plane crash in Taiwan. Loke's passing was a blow to MP and GI: it came at a time when the Shaws' studio was gaining ascendancy in the war for markets. MP and GI did not recover from the shock of Loke's death. Many of its stars felt that it was the passing of an era: with Loke gone, there was no one around with Loke's aesthetic tastes to motivate them. MP and GI even lost its name; it was re-named Cathay (after its parent organisation in Singapore) and carried on with business as usual. Although it continued to produce films until 1970, the magic was lost.

The restructuring of MP and GI into Cathay, the establishment of Guolian and the entry of Taiwan into the Mandarin film market encouraged greater plurality in the regional film scene in the second half of the 60s. While it was probably in its most advantageous position during this time, the Shaw Brothers studio also lost some of its best talent. Li Hanxiang was the first to go; then Raymond Chow, the production chief, left in 1970 and bought the facilities of Cathay, reconstituting them under the banner of his own company, Golden Harvest, changing the traditional studio-based type of production to one of independent production companies and signalling the beginning of the end for the big-time studios, although Shaw's would continue to produce films until 1985 (the studio is now used primarily to make television serials). Golden Harvest adapted itself to an independent production system where stars and directors could agree to mutually profitable deals with the studio and call the shots. Bruce Lee, for example, worked for Golden Harvest and not Shaw Brothers; Michael Hui and Jacky Chan followed suit. Raymond Chow has since put the name of Golden Harvest on international marquees, branching out as the producer of Hollywood blockbusters such as *The Cannonball Run* (1981), *Teenage Mutant Ninja Turtles* (1990) and their respective sequels.

Loke Wan-tho's death also presaged the death of the effete romantic hero. Genres such as historical epics and romantic melodramas went out of fashion by the late 60s. By 1966, Hong Kong's Mandarin cinema was mining gold with other genres – primarily the action genre of swordfighting films which emphasised a more realistic kind of violence and required a new breed of hero. Historical epics and melodramas featuring romantic protagonists would henceforth become the domain of the Taiwanese film industry.

The films which Li Hanxiang made for his own Guolian studio testified to his own romanticism: Li's move to Taiwan signified Hong Kong cinema's move away from the romantic tendency. It would be fair to say that Li had a good run in his Guolian days although he ultimately went bankrupt (after which he hung on as an independent film-maker for a couple of years before he returned to the Shaw Brothers fold in 1972). He got to direct a number of films and produced several more, giving new directors their first big break. Song Cunshou's *The Dawn/Poxiao Shifen* (1967) and Li's own *The Winter/Dong Nuan* (1967) are two works bearing the Guolian emblem which regularly appear in most Hong Kong critics' Ten Best lists of Chinese movies.

Li is justly proud of *The Winter*, proclaiming it a movie that a studio such as Shaw Brothers could never have produced. It is a socially conscious look at life in a working-class slum in Taipei, centering on Wu, an inarticulate but sensitive hawker (played by Tian Ye) and his love for the woman next door, Ah Jin (Gui Yalei). The scenes which see their relationship develop from unspoken yearnings to deep love are handled with impressive spontaneity. Although often praised for its 'realism', *The Winter* is a melodrama in the *wenyi* formula which it invoked by putting at its centre a romance between ill-matched lovers struggling to find happiness. Li is, of course, no stranger to *wenyi*, but unlike his previous works in the genre which are weighed down by dogmatic Confucian ethics, *The Winter* contains an assured sense of realism which Li had shown only once before – in his first film, *Red Bloom in the Snow*. *The Winter* can also be seen as the precursor of works in the realist mould which would be developed by Taiwan's new wave directors such as Hou Xiaoxian.

Like many would-be moguls, Li over-reached himself. His folly at Guolian was the two-part historical epic *The Beauty of Beauties/Xi Shi* (1965), an impressive production that was thrown off-balance by undue emphasis on production values and design.[5] Its huge costs were not recovered by a modest box-office success in the domestic Taiwan market and it failed in Hong Kong as well as in the important Southeast Asian market. Li soon fell foul of creditors and saw his dream-studio placed in receivership. He was on the verge of personal bankruptcy when three director colleagues (King Hu, Li Xing and Bai Jingrui) offered to help revive his credit by proposing to make an anthology film called *The Four Moods/Xi Nu Ai Le* (1970), with Li contributing a forty-minute episode entitled *Happiness/Xi*. It was to be Li's last film in the romantic mode showing only vestiges of the innocence Li had possessed as an artist. His episode dealt with a kind-hearted ghost who befriends a poor fisherman. The ghost is condemned to haunt the area where the fisherman works until he is reincarnated by 'redeeming' his spirit with another person's. He waits by the fisherman's hut for 'opportunities' to present themselves. Two women come along planning to commit suicide, but the ghost's kind-heartedness prevents him from taking advantage of human frailty. He is finally rewarded and makes his way to Heaven. *Happiness* was a throwback to good will, hope and optimism, but as a short episode in a portmanteau film, it represented the beginning of a new career style for Li. From then on, Li would compose his movies as short, self-contained episodes, a series of which (sometimes three, sometimes four) would make up a feature. In effect, Li churned out short stories; writing his own scripts and sometimes acting in and designing his own films as well.

Li's directing career seemed to be back on track with his return to Shaw Brothers, but his style and preoccupations had in fact changed almost completely. Throughout the 70s, Li made a long series of films about prostitutes, whoremongers, rip-off artists and all manner of shady characters cheating and hustling their way through life. These films made as episodic vignettes bore titles such as *Legends of Cheating, Cheating Panorama, Tales of Larceny, Cheat to Cheat,* and so forth. Perhaps chastened by his experience as a failed mogul and then having to work for a genuine one, Li developed into a Hong Kong cinema hack, honing a sharp sense of cynicism and using that as the basis for his aesthetics in the 70s. It was as if Li was acknowledging his own failure as an artist as well as attesting to the 70s as a decade of greed and big spending. When it became an established cinematic style, Li's cynical aesthetics influenced other directors in the Shaw Brothers stable, notably Cheng Gang and Zhang Zengze, who switched from directing martial arts movies to films about sex and gambling; Lui Kei, originally employed as an actor in Shaws' Cantonese branch, became a director of softcore sex comedies in the 70s, as did He Fan, who was, like Lui an ex-actor turned director.

Apart from episodic narratives, Li's cinematic style of the 70s is characterised by an inordinate and irreverent use of the zoom lens and wide-angle lens. In Li's hands, the zoom was a heady sort of instrument, while the wide angle tended to be a fisheye which could cover every aspect of Li's designs but which was an ugly, distorting lens, made even more so by the CinemaScope aspect ratio which was the standardised format at the time. The zoom and the fisheye illustrated the creative style of the hack phase of Li's career, although there were exceptions such as *The Warlord/Da Junfa* (1972), *The Empress Dowager* (1975) and *The Last Tempest* (1976). The last two were *gongwei* films which Li had made consistently throughout his career and was perhaps his most favoured genre.

Li developed a series of historical diptychs, including *The Beauty of Beauties/Xi Shi* (1965/66), made in Taiwan for his own Guolian studio and released in two parts; *The Empress Dowager/Qingguo Qingcheng* (1975) and *The Last Tempest/Yingtai Qixie* (1976) for Shaw Brothers; *Burning of the Imperial Palace/Huoshao Yuanming Yuan* (1983) and *Reign Behind the Curtain/Chuilian Tingzheng* (1983), co-productions with China shot in Beijing's Forbidden City and which were made for his own independent company after his departure from Shaws in 1982. These latter films, beginning with *The Empress Dowager,* all dealt with the life of the last Dowager Empress of the Qing Dynasty, Ci Xi, the real wielder of power in the Qing court, who stymied reforms. These epics were the last works to show Li in his element: an eye for historical detail; an obsession with *objets d'art* (often genuine ones taken from Li's own collection); a feeling for the restrictiveness of court life which concubines and empresses strive to transcend, often falling into sexual transgressions in the process; a facility at portraying the ruthless politics and petty jealousies of eunuchs, usurping empresses and ineffective emperors. Even though Western readers may recognise these elements from Bernardo Bertolucci's *The Last Emperor* (1987), it was really Li who made these elements staple components of the genre. Li in fact made his own version of the life of Emperor Puyi, entitled *The Last Emperor/ Huo Long* released in 1986.

On closer analysis, Li's dramatic sense tended to be uneven. A preoccupation with artifacts in his historical epics resulted in sets which bear an unfortunate resemblance to museum chambers. The cluttered sets did not blend with Li's dramatic treatment or his unfortunate handling of the widescreen: on this score, any comparisons of Li and Bertolucci would be invidious. Li could have done with the services of a Vittorio Storaro. Through his attention to detail, Li undoubtedly transmitted a cinematic sense. Occasionally, the acting of his principals proved his skills as a dramatist. As a result, his historical epics often contain isolated scenes of outstanding drama in between variable sections of postcard views. Like an apostate monk in a Shaolin monastery, Li could still reveal a formidable talent while at the same time cynically foregoing his convictions as an artist. Such cynicism was the hallmark of his non-epic films such as *The Warlord* and *Sinful Confessions*. There was a vulgarity in their style and subject matter, but Li's energy, exuberance and craftsmanship still shone through. Whatever one may think about Li's 'cynical' films, they show him to be in tune with the boom-and-bust spirit of the 70s. In the period of the full flowering of Li's aesthetics of the cynical (between 1972 to 1982), he depicted Hong Kong as one of the most wicked cities in the world, exuding the atmosphere of *fenghua xueyue* (literally, 'Wind, Flowers, Snow and Moon' which denotes opulent decadence and bohemian charm). His characters were effete but no longer romantic. *Fenghua xueyue* was abbreviated into *fengyue*[6] and came to denote a new generic mixture of soft-core pornography and light farce, a field which Li made his own in the 70s.

As a northerner, Li possessed a northerner's fascination with the exotic *jiangnan* (the south) reflected in the *fengyue* movies where Hong Kong is presented as an endless source of pleasure and material wealth. Although the settings of Li's *fengyue* films alternated between contemporary and period eras, the origin of these films goes back to Li's career in the 60s, to the *huangmei* opera film *The Love Eterne/ Liang Shanbo yu Zhu Yingtai* (1963), the historical epic *The Kingdom and the Beauty/ Jiangshan Meiren* (1963) and the period ghost story *The Enchanting Shadow/ Qiannü Youhun* (1960). These films formed a generic bridge to Li's later *fengyue* films and were the first steps in his engagement with the erotic, addressing sexual desire and hinting at promiscuity, homosexuality and necrophilia. All had women as central characters.

The women of Li's *fengyue* films exploited their sexuality and functioned as sexual objects of male desires. The titles of the *fengyue* films are self-explanatory: *Illicit Desire, That's Adultery, Facets of Love, The Happiest Moment,*

Crazy Sex, Love Swindlers and *Moods of Love*. The worst of the *fengyue* films assume that sex is vulgar, a form of human behaviour in the same register as spitting and farting. Although his *fengyue* films took into account amorality, fetishism and other forms of perversions, Li's pulp sensibility was too far advanced to make anything of them. Instead, he created a morally corrupt world far removed from the realist-romanticism of *The Winter*. Thus Li's aesthetics of the cynical paints a Hong Kong drowning in crass commercialism and vulgarity – a society of philistines. With few exceptions, notably films by Ann Hui, Tony Au and Stanley Kwan, Hong Kong cinema never fully recovered its romantic spirit.

NOTES

[1] People who find it a mouthful prefer to call it Cathay, but the two companies are quite distinct.

[2] He did not come from Shanghai but can be regarded as belonging to that tradition.

[3] *Wenyi* is an amalgam of the Chinese words for literature (*wenxue*) and art (*yishu*).

[4] As claimed by Li himself in his enjoyable two-volume memoirs written in Chinese, *Sanshi Nian Xishuo Congtou* (Hong Kong: Tiandi Publishers, 1987). [The title may be translated as *Recollections of Thirty Years*.]

[5] There are a great many parallels between Li's career and that of Francis Ford Coppola, including the Zoetrope-like enterprise of Guolian and his coming to grief through, oddly perhaps, a failure of nerve in the realm of aesthetics. For his wonderfully stylish cinematic experiment *One From the Heart*, Coppola couldn't quite bring himself to reduce the storyline to a bare minimum and the film fell between two stools, as did Li's grand stylistic experiment.

[6] The *fengyue* strain actually stems from Chinese literature's classic novels such as *The Golden Lotus/Jin Pingmei*, dealing with sexual escapades which Li adapted into a *fengyue* movie in 1974.

PART TWO
Martial Artists

Chapter Six

The Dao of King Hu

The images of a King Hu film are now so familiar to most people as to be emblematic of Hong Kong martial arts movies in general. Leaping swordsmen and knight-ladies, whirling, somersaulting and free-falling in mid-air as they cross swords and exchange punches, radiate an exhilarating sensation of pure movement and scarcely give the eyes time to rest before beginning another dizzying sequence of action and reaction.

King Hu's films first graced the screens of Western art cinemas in the mid-70s. For a time, Hu was the only director from Hong Kong to be taken seriously by Western critics. He remains, to a large extent, the only director from the generation before the new wave whom the West knows something about. His international renown has superseded the reputations of most of his contemporaries including Li Hanxiang, Zhang Che, Zhang Zengze, Cheng Gang, Ch'un Kim, Chor Yuen, not to mention older veterans such as Tao Qin, Bu Wancang or Yue Feng, who all deserve to be better known. This is not to deny Hu's talent, but rather to point out the discrepancies that still exist in achieving a comprehensive understanding of Hong Kong cinema, particularly the period of the 50s and 60s when Hu was developing his career in Hong Kong's Mandarin cinema.

Hu obviously did not spring out of a vacuum but his unique images and breathless pace seem to indicate that he had. He committed himself to a particular genre – the martial arts swordfighting movie (*wuxia pian*) and was instrumental in transforming that genre from a half-moribund state to a vibrant, exciting and exotic action picture format. The momentum of creativity he sustained from 1965 to 1980, with at least seven features and an episode in an anthology film, resulted in an outstanding body of work that transcended the norms of the *wuxia pian*. His career declined together with the martial arts genre itself as it evolved into new hybrid forms.

He is a stylist, more concerned with the plasticity of images than with ideas. In both the realms of images and ideas, however, Hu is now perceived as a director who has fallen victim to a generation gap. He cannot easily identify with the new-generation film-makers in Taiwan, such as Hou Hsiao-hsien and Edward Yang, who have purposefully dealt with the modern realities of Taiwanese society. In Hong Kong, Hu's indomitable *sang froid* expressed in his ability to execute images of mounting complexity is admired, but even here, he has been surpassed by a new generation of directors such as Tsui Hark and Ching Siu-tung, both of whom have created, as in *Swordsman/ Xiao'ao Jianghu* (1990), images even more protean and quick-footed than Hu's. The fact that Hu has stuck to period subjects almost always set in the Ming dynasty indicates that he is a director who relies on the conventions of genre and myth. His affinity with ancient history is a sign of his alienation from the present, a condition exacerbated by exile from his northern Chinese roots. Hu was born in Beijing in 1931 and came to Hong Kong in 1949. Like other northern Chinese directors who put down roots in Hong Kong, Hu's status in the Mandarin cinema was founded on his northern cultural background. As mentioned before, the work of these northerners capitalised on the use of Beijing-accented Mandarin and allusions to the performing tradition of Beijing opera and other styles from northern China, such as the *bangzi qiang* (clapper opera) and the *huangmei diao* (melodious tunes sung in recitative mode). Their stories were usually taken from historical sources or legends and mounted as elaborate costume dramas, or from more contemporary northern Chinese settings in the late Qing or early republican era (1911–27, after which China came under the military dictatorship of Chiang Kai-shek). Cut off from his roots, Hu could only return to them in cinematic milieux corresponding closely to the northern Chinese landscape. While in exile, Hu shot his films which needed classic northern Chinese settings in South Korea and in the mountain regions of Taiwan. It was not until *The Painted Skin/ Hua Pi zhi Yinyang Fawang* (completed in 1992 but still unreleased in Hong Kong at the time of writing) that Hu at last returned to film in his beloved Beijing. Consequently, Hu's explorations of the past are also a form of coming to terms with his exile in Hong Kong and Taiwan. His baroque and always colourful treatment of themes of transcendentalism, materialistic struggle and spiritual existence is a manifestation of his experience of exile. The theme of exile itself is made into an abstraction, never directly addressed as a motivating force but discerned only in the motif of the Dao, the urge to clock up more mileage in the Way, the Path, the Road. The only tangible evidence of this abstraction lies in the images themselves. These, Hu deploys with deftness and confidence, using a masterful command of technique to express the abstraction of movement attaching to the exilic experience.

Audiences will also be familiar with the dictum of the martial arts genre most often invoked in a King Hu work: if the Dao (good) stands one feet tall, Mo (evil) stands ten feet taller. Hu uses the cliché of a Manichaean struggle between good and evil that has the effect of continually reinforcing one's familiarity with the genre. Such familiarity is important because Hu is the most musical of martial arts directors. He composes his work like a symphonic piece where the recapitulation of a theme is imperative to its enjoyment. If the listener remembers the theme, his enjoyment of the piece is all the more enhanced. This explains why movement is so incessant in a King Hu film. All the running, the jumping about, the leapfrogging, the aviating, are but variations of the Manichaean theme: it is the closing in and catching up of the distance between the Dao and the Mo (good and evil) so that combat may take place and the Mo annihilated. The dictum also implies that Mo/Evil must never be underestimated and that the Dao/Good must never be complacent. The Dao also means the Way or the Path, the road travelled in doing right, suggesting a moral dimension to his tales. In his essay 'The Path of the Traveller',[1] critic Sek Kei suggested that the movement in Hu's films, impelled both by cinematic technique and the action of his characters, is a continuous attempt to transcend nature:

> It does not necessarily lead anywhere. The content of his films is a stepping stone towards the generation of movement, it does not constitute the theme. Hu does indeed touch on themes of nationalism, history, knight-errantry, Confucianism, the supernatural, Zen, even the world of spirits, but these are not themes the director really wants to explore. They are the pretext for achieving a free and unfettered state.

Sek Kei is skeptical about claims for Hu as an auteur if such claims are based on the thematic content of the director's works. In another essay about Hu,[2] British critic Tony Rayns examined four of the director's best films in terms of their plot, syntax, action and imagery. Except for the section on plot, which points out that Hu's films are not given to conventional plotting and that 'his approach to questions of dramatic construction owes nothing to the genre's usual stark functionalism', the other sections do not even hint at content or themes, which is perhaps indicative of the Western admiration for the director. The essay indicates that Hu's films are admired for their use of non-linear and non-conventional plot, syntax, action and imagery. Rayns also states that the 'extraordinary consistency' of Hu's work makes it a cinch for auteurist analysis. Hu's work has indeed remained consistent, but his critical stock fell in the 80s, a period he spent largely in Taiwan, completing only two features and an episode in an anthology film. In the 90s, he has so far completed one more feature. His career appears to have lost its way amid new trends and developments in the Hong Kong, China and Taiwan cinemas.

In Hu's most typical films, the inn is a recurrent setting signifying transience, with tableaux and design flexible enough to provide a stage for life-and-death struggles and thus to compel movement and action which, because of the very restrictedness of the spaces, become even more emphatic. It is significant that the inn is not seen as a microcosm, but as a stage for sheer movement, a kind of mythical environment where the rules of gravity and the natural world are suspended in favour of a protean mobility. Hu's consciousness of space is, however, a liberating experience as his camera tries to transcend the limitations of the set.

The Fate of Lee Khan/Yingchun Ge zhi Fengbo (1973) represents Hu's highest achievement in liberating movements within the confines of an inn. A mobile camera pans and tracks a remarkable company of waitresses, who are actually skilled martial artists, as they frolic in the Yingchun Inn awaiting the arrival of the Mongol prince Lee Khan. Whether they are warding off the advances of a lascivious customer or stealing a pearl from the headgear of an unsuspecting guest, or stopping bandits from robbing customers in the inn and making a dash for the door by gracefully leaping from table to table, the waitresses are like dazzling, fast-moving pieces on a checker board. Set in the last days of the Mongol Yuan Dynasty when Chinese patriots were trying to reassert Han Chinese power and to establish the Ming Dynasty, the film revolves around the visit of the Mongol Prince Lee Khan to the Yingchun Inn and the attempts by the patriots to retrieve a vital map in his possession.

Anger/Nu, the episode in the anthology film *The Four Moods/Xi Nu Ai Le* (1970), is also exemplary in its use of the inn-space. Lasting only forty minutes, *Anger* is the film in Hu's oeuvre most clearly indebted to Beijing opera. Inspired by a classic Beijing opera, *The Midnight Confrontation/Sancha Kou*, the whole film is staged to evoke theatre by means of its confined settings and a soundtrack punctuated with a characteristic *bangzi* (wooden clapper) beat. The plot's exposition is virtually dependent on a continuous sequence of action, acrobatic stunt work and precise, choreographic movement. In common with his other inn films, *Anger* is about a group of patriots fighting for a cause and trying to rescue a captured comrade. The inn in *Anger* is a 'black inn', a base for criminal activities managed by a husband and wife team. They take in, as guests for a night, four guards from the Ministry of Punishment who are escorting a prisoner named Jiao Zan, an upright official. Later, a lone stranger, Ren Tanghui, appears to rescue the prisoner. The innkeeper and his wife form an alliance with the guards to do away with both Ren Tanghui and Jiao Zan, and to share in the rewards, a bag of silver kept by Ren plus reward-money from the guards' patron who wants Jiao dead. At the sleeping hour, the husband and wife carry out their plan to kill Ren Tanghui, but their attempts are foiled by Ren who proves to be a superior tactician and swordsman. A cat-and-mouse situation develops as the innkeepers, the guards, Ren Tanghui and Jiao Zan attack and evade each other, with opposing sides muddled and at cross purposes. When Ren and Jiao recognise each other, they seize the offensive and gradually subdue the guards. As dawn breaks, the innkeeper receives reinforcement from members of his gang; they are, however, defeated by Jiao Zan. The innkeeper is killed accidentally by his wife.

The innkeeper's wife is the most memorable figure in the film even though she is on the wrong side of the law. She resembles a type of female warrior heroine often featured in Hu's pictures. Her attractiveness as a character lies in the fact that she reflects a grey side in the moral division of Dao and Mo. In King Hu's films, this sort of Manichaeism is supra-normal: only super-heroes and super-villains seem to fit into the realm of Dao and Mo. Shades of grey also infuse Hu's characters in *The Fate of Lee Khan* (the small band of patriotic women who are also pickpockets and thieves) and the character of Fan Dapei (played by Yue Hua) in his first martial arts film, *Come Drink With Me/Da Zui Xia* (1965).

90

Fan Dapei's sobriquet, 'The Drunken Knight' (which is the literal meaning of the Chinese title *Da Zui Xia*) confers on him an amoral dimension. He is, nevertheless, a hero and a superior swordsman on the side of the Dao. His antithesis is the evil monk Liao Kong, who returns from travelling in the *jianghu* (mythical rivers and lakes, a term to denote the criminal underworld) to face off the hero in a last-ditch fight. *Come Drink With Me* is a transitional film in which Hu was feeling his way towards a more distinctive personal style in the martial arts genre. In the 60s, the genre was considerably influenced by imported Japanese martial arts films which became popular for their accent on realistic violence and the elaborate swordfighting choreography. A hint of Japanese influence in *Come Drink With Me* is quite apparent, but Hu consciously works against it by stressing a unique style of action choreography based on Beijing opera. The picture is an assured work. Its mood is mythic and romantic, reflected in the nicknames of its characters: Golden Swallow, Drunken Knight, Jade-Faced Tiger. Golden Swallow (played by dancer-actress Zheng Peipei) undertakes a mission to rescue her brother, an official in the Magistracy who has been kidnapped by a gang of outlaws led by Jade-Faced Tiger. At the inn where she first appears, Golden Swallow tackles an advance group sent by Jade-Faced Tiger to intercept her. She is helped by Drunken Knight, Fan Dapei. They join forces to defeat Jade-Faced Tiger and the monk Liao Kong, who has been called in as the only man able to deal with Drunken Knight. The mood and characters recall Nicholas Ray's *Johnny Guitar* (1954), where the baroque touches perfectly mirror the mythic world of lonely gunfighters, boss-ladies, outlaws and lynch-mob posses in the Western genre. In *Come Drink With Me*, similar touches draw out the world of deadly knight-ladies, evil monks draped in saffron robes and scraggy heroes with mystical prowess in the martial arts. Like *Johnny Guitar*, the film shifts settings from the inn's interior to a waterfall hideout. Both films create a colourful mythic environment allowing the dream-like nature of cinema to emerge. In *Come Drink With Me*, movement and action are mapped out in a precise manner which can only be called stylised, but which had no direct parallels with Hollywood or the Japanese samurai epics which influenced it.

In Hu's next film, *Dragon Inn*, patriots set out to rescue the family of another upright official condemned to prison by the Dongchang (a repressive organisation of the Ming Dynasty, variously translated into English as East Wing, East Agency, Securitate or Gestapo). The patriots, including a nimble knight-lady (played by Shangguan Lingfeng), holed up inside an inn, keep the Dongchang at bay. The head of the Dongchang, the eunuch Cao Shaoqin (played by Bai Ying), comes to the scene to deal personally with the patriots. This was Hu's first film made in Taiwan and his first real success. It achieved great impact in Southeast Asia and Hong Kong and created in its wake a new trend in the martial arts genre, rather like Bruce Lee's films had done in the early 70s. Hu's style was imitated and swordfighting knight-ladies and all-powerful eunuchs became stereotypes in the genre.

Hu's influence on the martial arts genre can also be seen in the later films of Tsui Hark and Ching Siu-tung. In fact, he employed the talents of latter-day luminaries in the martial arts genre such as Sammo Hung and Yuan Biao, either as martial arts instructors/directors or as stuntmen and actors. Even director Ann Hui has worked as Hu's assistant. The one film bridging the evolution of martial arts styles from Hu's generation to the new generation is *The Valiant Ones/Zhonglie Tu* (1975). A slim plot about the efforts of patriots to stop the pillage of China's southern coastal regions by Japanese pirates provides an excuse for the exercise of action styles never before seen in the genre. The film is almost neatly divided into two discernible action styles: one composed of Hu's Beijing opera-derived choreography and directed by Hu's usual martial arts choreographer, Han Yingjie; the other consisting of sharp-edged fluctuations of movement and action as demonstrated in the climactic end-scene where Hakatatsu, the Japanese pirate (played by Sammo Hung) meets his match in the taciturn Chinese master-of-all-martial-arts, Wu Jiyuan (Bai Ying). This incredible scene points to later developments in the Tsui Hark-Ching Siu-tung mould best seen in *Swordsman* and the 1992 sequel *Swordsman II/Xiao'ao Jianghu zhi Dongfang Bu Bai*. It is also characteristic of many action scenes choreographed by Sammo Hung in his own martial arts pictures. Of all King Hu's films, *The Valiant Ones* is the only one which is somewhat adrift from Hu's preoccupations with the nature of existence. Movement seems to be employed for its own sake, for the sheer enjoyment of it. *The Valiant Ones* is the closest thing to a *divertissement* that Hu ever achieved. Once again, the abstraction of movement is in prominent relief, but it mirrors a blurred vision, a journey to nowhere, as if an itinerant fatalist had embarked on a long, winding journey in search of a free and unfettered country. At every stage in the journey, the traveller traverses 'well-worn paths marked by outstanding changes and constant development', writes Sek Kei. 'In this unceasing journey, it is possible that the traveller may have threaded through wrong paths, or that he may have been going around in circles, making no real progress. It is also possible that he will never find his destination. In the very notion of movement lies the real meaning of fatalism.'[3]

Hu's Buddhism is an explicit cultural element which allows Chinese culture to exist on a less nationalistic and more metaphysical plane, in so far as Buddhism is an integral part of Chinese culture. However, in order to understand Hu's Buddhist motifs in their proper perspective, one must consider what lies behind the urge for his characters to move and act the way they do. As if to emphasise the spiritual side of life, Hu delights in a supernatural universe haunted by ghost-spirits and a mystical force capable of giving human beings inhuman strengths and abilities. In *A Touch of Zen/Xia Nü* (1971), the monk Hui Yuan (played by Roy Chiao) is shown to possess extraordinary powers which he, however, uses discreetly. He glides down to the realm of mortals from high up in the mountains, the sun behind him, his feet barely touching rocks, leaves and blades of grass. His powers stem from the sun and from the whole of nature around him. In

Raining in the Mountain/Kong Shan Ling Yu (1979), the female retainers of the Master Wu Wai levitate across stony cliffs and rocky crags, sharing the same energy which empowers Hui Yuan.

A Touch of Zen was adapted from a story in the famous anthology of ghost stories and weird tales, *Liaozhai Zhiyi* (translated into English by Herbert Giles as *Strange Tales from a Chinese Studio*), compiled by the early Qing Dynasty writer Pu Songling. The book has remained a fruitful source for film adaptations including Tsui Hark's *A Chinese Ghost Story/Qiannü Youhun* (1987). Hu adds his own fictional coda to the short tale and radically rebuilds the story using the *Liaozhai* connection only to create atmosphere: there is a haunted fortress peopled by ghostly characters who in reality are political refugees hiding from the Dongchang. A painter, Gu Shengzhai (played by Shi Jun), pressured by his mother to find himself a bride, stumbles upon the ghostly fortress and is attracted to the girl (played by Xu Feng) who lives there. She appears to be a spirit-creature known as *huli* or fox-lady, but turns out to be the *xia nü* (the knight-lady) of the title. She persuades Gu to help the refugees. Once Hu has revealed the real identities of his pseudo-ghosts, he is not content simply to stick to an action-oriented martial arts picture using the Dao versus Mo formula. Instead, he delves into the realm of Buddhist metaphysics and introduces the character of the monk Hui Yuan who intervenes in worldly affairs by saving the refugees from the Dongchang. In the last section of the film, Hu proposes that Hui Yuan is a reincarnation of the Buddha: when Hui Yuan is stabbed by the treacherous Dongchang platoon-leader (Han Yingjie), he bleeds gold. The final image is of Hui Yuan sitting in the lotus position, silhouetted against the sun, one arm outstretched, pointing to the Way.

Hu has said of *Raining in the Mountain/Kong Shan Lingyu* that the film had little to do with Buddhism: 'I wanted to explore the question of power, whether it constituted the means or the end, and I let it all happen in a monastery.'[4] Esquire Wen (played by Sun Yue) and his companions Gold Lock (Wu Mingcai) and White Fox (Xu Feng) travel to the Sanbao monastery located in the mountains. Their hidden purpose is to steal a priceless sutra. Esquire Wen is the mastermind while Gold Lock and White Fox are the thieves who possess near mystical powers in the art of thievery as well as the martial arts. Upon their arrival, they waste no time in executing their plan: White Fox and Gold Lock set out, at dizzying pace and in broad daylight, to search for the vault where the sutra is placed. They cover the whole expanse of the monastery, moving like mice through its labyrinthine corridors, prowling, skulking and dodging clusters of monks who appear suddenly from corners. The thieves fail to steal the sutra in the first attempt – the sequence was purely designed to show off Hu's skill in camera choreography. The movement here is wholly sensual and almost abstract. For a moment one realises that in Hu's films, movement is an end in itself.

The main narrative of the film describes a power struggle between three monks for the position of abbot. The three thieves enter the political battle, Esquire Wen having been called as a layman to help settle the succession. Also entering the fray are other distinguished adherents of the faith including the Master Wu Wai who belongs to a sect that allows female companionship. Hu indeed succeeds in raising the question of power, and complicating the theme by setting the thieves among the monks, composing the whole piece as a lengthy fugue. The theme becomes a meditation on power and the relationship between materialism and spiritualism. As such, *Raining in the Mountain* is perhaps Hu's most accomplished film to date, its themes coalescing in a much more coherent way than in his other films.

Legend of the Mountain/ Shanzhong Chuanqi (1979), shot back to back with *Raining in the Mountain* on South Korean locations, is the first really unsatisfactory work in Hu's career, setting the stage for his decline in the 80s. For once, Hu's command of visual imagery deserts him. Landscapes, sunsets coloured by mixed orange and blue filters, empty space covered with smoke and mists, abound. While such images are always nice-looking, they nevertheless signify Hu's principal failure as a cinematic artist: his neglect of tight, coherent narratives in favour of pure style and picturesque imagery. The plot spurts out in between intervals of landscape shots. It deals with a group of unhappy spirits who seek a formula for true reincarnation contained in a sutra. A scholar, He Qingyun (played by Shi Jun), is commissioned to copy the sutra by the abbot of the monastery where the sutra has been placed for safekeeping. The scholar goes to the mountains to do his job and wanders into the abode of the spirits. He is seduced by two female spirits who do battle over him, their intent being to captivate his body in order to absorb his 'essence' as their first step towards becoming humans once more. The last-minute intervention of a Lamaist monk saves the scholar from transformation into a zombie.

The Juvenizer/ Zhongshen Dashi (1981) is Hu's only film with a contemporary setting. The story tells of a young Taipei bachelor, an advertising executive, who is given the job of marketing the 'Juvenizer', a health drink manufactured by a Japanese company. The client demands that the executive marry first before the contract can be signed. The search for a bride commences. First, the young executive meets a beautiful artist who is revealed to be a fake – her work is actually done by a ghost-painter. Next, he meets and marries a woman scientist who exposes the Juvenizer as a harmful body-pollutant. Congruent themes of art, fakery and cynicism are deployed with a heavy hand. The film was meant to be a light satire of modern materialism, but Hu was at least two decades behind the times, his perspective far removed from the world of Taipei in the 80s.

Hu's next Taiwan-based production, *All the King's Men/ Tianxia Diyi* (1983) is a period piece set at the end of the Tang Dynasty. It deals with the last Tang emperor and his descent into madness at the hands of a Daoist mystic. The prime minister employs the talents of a doctor, a painter and a thief to help save the emperor from falling further into the clutches of the Daoist, but to no avail. The emperor dies and the general of the imperial guard is elevated to the Dragon Throne, thus establishing the Song Dynasty. How a painter and thief got into the picture is yet another example of the incoherence marking Hu's later works.

One typical, fast-moving episode in the anthology film *The Wheel of Life/Dalun Hui* (1983), reaffirming Hu's fondness for the Ming period and the themes previously deployed in his 'inn films', was his only other work in the 80s. Hu started the 90s badly. Approaching sixty, he attempted to put his career on the right track by co-operating with Tsui Hark on a comeback martial arts epic, *Swordsman/Xiao'ao Jianghu* (1990). On paper at least, the film sounded right for Hu, with Tsui Hark producing. But Hu quit after a few weeks' work, complaining of Tsui's interference. The film was taken over by Tsui who, to his credit, went on to make the film in the style of an earlier Hu classic.

Hu's most recent film is *The Painted Skin/Hua Pi zhi Yinyang Fawang* (1992). Like *A Touch of Zen*, it draws on a story from Pu Songling's often filmed canon of ghosts, spirits and gremlins, *Liaozhai Zhiyi*. The result, however, is a disappointing conglomeration of old motifs and allusions to the special-effects packed ghost story-martial arts admixture familiar from *A Chinese Ghost Story* and its sequels made by the Tsui Hark and Ching Siu-tung team. The tale concerns a Master Wang who meets a listless, beautiful woman named You Feng in a Beijing alley, and persuades her to return home in order to become his concubine. Madam You is actually a 'painted skin', the human manifestation of a spirit who is neither in Yin nor Yang (that is, neither in Hell nor on Earth). Her soul is condemned to wander in the never-never land unable to undergo the transmigratory process for reincarnation. Her passage is blocked by a mutant who styles himself King of the Yin and Yang. The mutant comes from the depths of Hell itself, a pretender to King Yama, the Chinese Satan who guards the gates of Hell. A couple of Daoist itinerants and a 'high monk' (played by Sammo Hung) help You Feng to return to the Yin-world by taking on the King of Yin and Yang. Hu tries hard to recapture the old magic, but he evokes the wrong spirits: those of tired sophistry and anachronism. As an example of how Hu is unable to stave off unfavourable comparisons with Tsui Hark and Ching Siu-tung, it may suffice to point to the way he uses Joey Wong and Wu Ma, the stars of *A Chinese Ghost Story*, but elicits only routine performances from them and a bad one from his male lead, Adam Cheng, who plays one of the long line of scholar-dandies who appear in Hu's films stretching back to his apprentice work for Li Hanxiang in *The Love Eterne/Liang Shanbo yu Zhu Yingtai* (1963). The figure of the scholar appears to be Hu's alter ego. This means that when an actor under his direction cannot master such a characterisation, it is a sure indication that Hu himself has lost interest in his subject.

Hu's first major directorial achievement, *Sons of the Good Earth/Dadi Ernü* (1964), has been kept until last because of its atypicality. Not fully consonant with Hu's genre works or his mature themes, the film is a standard war epic made under contract to the Shaw Brothers where he was employed mainly as an actor. Hu himself took a key supporting role, playing the virtuous police chief of a provincial village who turns guerrilla leader to fight the Japanese. His portrayal of a whole community under pressure from a foreign enemy is notable for its keen observation of characters who could have stepped straight out of a novel by Lao She, the modern Chinese writer Hu admires most (and about whom he has written a treatise). If Hu's first and most recent films fall far short of his best work, they nevertheless prove him to be a compulsive film-maker, one who maintains a dogged approach to the craft, carefully composing his images with the exactitude of a painter. At his best, Hu is a film-maker able to surround his pictures with the aura of a great tradition. Watching his pictures, one sees classical China – its paintings, opera and music. Even dramatic structures are shaped with the symmetry of a Ming vase. Always an exuberant artist, his films either work or break apart like a splintered jar. But when they do work, they are strong and supremely crafted art objects.

NOTES
[1] 'Xingzhe de Guiji', *Film Biweekly*, no. 13, 1979 (translated by the author).
[2] *Sight and Sound*, Winter, 1975/76, pp. 8–13.
[3] 'Xingzhe de Guiji', *Film Biweekly*, no. 13, 1979 (translated by the author).
[4] Interview with author, 1984.

Chapter Seven

The Sword and the Fist

THE RISE OF THE *WUXIA* HERO

The death of the romantic hero in Hong Kong cinema came in the mid-60s when a rash of *wuxia*[1] movies appeared in the market. In 1965, the Shaw Brothers studio released *Temple of the Red Lotus/Jianghu Qixia* directed by Xu Zenghong, followed by Zhang Che's *Tiger Boy/Huxia Jianchou* and King Hu's *Come Drink With Me/Da Zui Xia* the following year. The left-wing Great Wall studio had released earlier in 1966 *The Jade Bow/Yunhai Yugong Yuan* which made an impact with its breakthrough action choreography directed by two young martial arts experts, Tang Jia and Lau Kar-leong. The picture itself was co-directed by Zhang Xinyan and its lead actor, Fu Qi. It tells the story of a young swordfighter (played by Fu Qi) who helps two women carry out their revenge on a villain who stole the secrets of a palm technique of martial arts and caused the deaths of their elders. The hero divides his affections between the two women, one of whom dies at the end to show her great love for the young man. Romanticism was a trait which endured into the martial arts genre, but what impressed audiences about *The Jade Bow* were its action scenes characterised by a fresh new style of action choreography. *The Jade Bow* was a transitional movie which seems somewhat stilted when compared to Tsui Hark's swordfighting movies today. Its action scenes still contain traces of pantomime and Chinese opera, though attempts were made to achieve more veracity. The film also introduced features such as swordspersons levitating during a duel or jumping fairy-like up and down roof tops. The figure of the acrobatic and levitating hero personified the energy of the rising martial arts genre.

The sudden interest of Hong Kong film-makers in the action genre can be seen as a reaction to changing times and tastes. If the effete romantic hero of the previous decades had been connected with the subordinate status of a colonised and dominated culture, the action hero may well be a cultural registration of an increasing sense of self-confidence expressed in the same mythical and historic narrative forms that had provided the generic framework for films such as Li Hanxiang's *The Love Eterne/Liang Shanbo* and *Zhu Yingtai* (1963). The *wuxia* or martial hero emerged in the mid-60s, when China was asserting its newly acquired superpower status and Hong Kong was becoming 'an Asian tiger' while the Japanese economic expansion into East and Southeast Asia was at its most aggressive.

The rise of Hong Kong's martial arts genre was also inspired by the popularity of imported Japanese samurai movies. The Zatoichi 'Blind Swordsman' series had been a particularly big hit. The two major studios, Shaw Brothers and MP and GI, seized the opportunity to produce their own brand of samurai movies in the form of the swordfighting *wuxia* picture. The release of movies such as *The Jade Bow, Tiger Boy* and *Come Drink With Me* in 1966 triggered a rash of other *wuxia* movies, and the genre came to dominate the popular imagination of overseas Chinese audiences for the rest of the decade and into the 70s, outgrossing and eventually replacing the Japanese samurai movies in the domestic market. The swordfighting *wuxia* movie had a few more years of popularity in the 70s before it was itself replaced by the kung fu movie. The crunch came in 1971 with the release of Bruce Lee's *The Big Boss/ Tang Shan Daxiong*.

Wuxia and kung fu can be considered two sides of the same coin, but their development actually progressed separately, though there were points of convergence. The difference, of course, was in their fighting styles: *wuxia* was swordfighting and kung fu was fist-fighting. In the 60s, cinema audiences saw these action pictures as markedly different formats and action styles. Kung fu and swordfighting *wuxia* pictures were clearly delineated. The Cantonese cinema produced a long series of kung fu movies featuring actor Kwan Tak-hing as the legendary kung fu hero Wong Fei-hung, and it seemed as if Cantonese cinema was the exclusive domain of the kung fu genre. In the late 60s, Mandarin *wuxia* pictures were so popular that it seemed as if *wuxia* pictures were exclusive to Mandarin cinema, although this was not strictly true.

The two directors usually credited for starting the *wuxia* trend are King Hu and Zhang Che. Both are Mandarin-speaking northerners, and northern cultural forms such as Peking opera were evoked by Hu in his *wuxia* pictures. The *wuxia* genre thus became associated with the northern style which audiences believed was more ancient and historical than the southern style. Novels and movies set their swordplay narratives in medieval dynasties and other mythical fantasies which, in turn, became stylistic conventions in the genre. For instance, the effortless facility of swordfighting heroes and heroines to leap, somersault and generally levitate in defiance of gravity generated a fairytale effect. This 'weightlessness' technique had its kung fu application too, but there it was less fantasy and more of an achievable skill gained through relentless training in techniques such as the *qigong* (breathing technique).

Kung fu thus emphasised the body and training rather than fantasy or the supernatural. Interestingly, Cantonese *wuxia* movies tended to feature special effects reminiscent of Méliès. Moreover, kung fu was thought of as a southern style of more recent historical vintage. It is a matter of historical record that kung fu masters, trained in the original Shaolin temple, dispersed to Guangdong Province after their temple was burned down by the Manchus, where they established their own schools. Subsequently, they produced new generations of skilled kung fu practitioners. Notwithstanding the eventual merging of both styles, the delineation of northern and southern action formats seems to have been accepted by audiences. Directors of both action styles also toed the line: northern directors such as Hu specialised in swordfighting movies, and southern directors, particularly Cantonese directors such as Lau Kar-leong, made kung fu movies.

When the *wuxia* movie started to wane as a result of the rise of kung fu movies, the martial arts picture became more comprehensive, mixing both forms of martial arts, albeit with a bias towards kung fu. Transitional devices were used to delineate and differentiate one action style from the other. For example, two protagonists would start to fight with swords, then lose their swords and resume the fight with fists. But this came later in the 70s. In the second half of the 60s, the *wuxia* hero was supreme, and swordfighting skills were considered the ultimate test of superiority, just as a skill with guns and a fast draw were the ultimate test for cowboys.

In their heyday (from 1966 to 1972), some of the best *wuxia* movies emphasised the skill of the swordfighter, male and female. The title of Zhang Che's *The One Armed Swordsman/Dubi Dao* (1967) refers to the character played by Wang Yu and also explains the hero's special skill as a swordsman. Wang was the obsessed hero of Pan Lei's *The Sword/Jian* (1972), a swordsman in search of the finest blade to match his skill. In Wang Tianlin's *Mad, Mad, Mad Sword/Shenjing Dao* (1969), the swordfighting hero was parodied as a bumbling, mediocre swordsman who passed as the master of his school. Swordswomen were the central characters of Tu Guangqi's *The First Sword/Diyi Jian* (1967) featuring actress Chen Manling; Wu Ma's *The Deaf and Mute Heroine/Longya Jian* (1971) starring Helen Ma; and in the films of King Hu featuring Zheng Peipei (*Come Drink With Me*, 1966), Shangguan Lingfeng (*Dragon Inn/Longmen Kezhan*, 1967) and Xu Feng (*A Touch of Zen/Xia Nü*, 1971).

Hu was the director who took the swordfighting movie into the realm of art-house respectability in the West. His movies were stylish, almost always set in his favourite period, the Ming Dynasty, and the films featured characters who became established types in the genre, particularly swordswomen and the eunuch super-villains who presided over the *dongchang*, the repressive organisation of Ming governments. Hu had a unique style which was often imitated, most successfully by Wang Xinglei in *Escorts Over Tiger Tills/Hu Shan Xing* (1969), an impressive swordfighting epic, and by Zhang Zengze in *From the Highway/Luke yu Daoke* (1970), a fine and rare example of a kung fu film with a northern Chinese setting.

ZHANG CHE, MASTER OF *WUXIA* VIOLENCE

While Hu's films are recognised as seminal works of the *wuxia* genre, he arguably did not make the best *wuxia* film. That honour goes to Zhang Che and his *The Golden Swallow/Jin Yanzi* (1968). Ostensibly a follow-up to Hu's *Come Drink With Me*, featuring the film's protagonist, Golden Swallow (played again by Zheng Peipei), Zhang's film is a baroque-poetic advance on Hu's achievement and is a narratively distinct, superior work. Golden Swallow is wooed by two men: the dashing knight Silver Roc (Wang Yu) who secretly loves her and goes to the extremes of killing villains in order to win her; and the rough-hewn hero Han Tao (Luo Lie) who hides his emotions for Golden Swallow but will, in a show of his real feelings, take action to protect her. In the climax, the two men fight a duel over Golden Swallow. Both men stick to their interpretations of chivalry, and the outcome is inevitably tragic.

Repressed desires and poetic flights of fancy are never good bedfellows in the action picture (they are seen as feminine traits more properly developed in romantic melodramas or the *wenyi pian*), but Zhang turns his *wuxia* picture into just such a study of conflicting personas, making *The Golden Swallow* the first psychological *wuxia* picture with *wenyi* elements. The character of Silver Roc, who dominates the film, is perhaps the most complex knight-hero ever seen in any action picture. He is a violent man with a martyrdom complex or death wish, a poet whose anarchic sensibility belies his longing for stability expressed as a monogamous longing for Golden Swallow. He is also a lover with clearly defined perspectives on women. They are, in his eyes, either saints or whores: he is torn between Golden Swallow and the courtesan-prostitute, Mei Niang.

Zhang devoted his entire career to making martial arts movies. A contract director to Shaw Brothers, he strengthened his position in the studio by carving out a niche for himself, first with the *wuxia* genre, then with kung fu. *The Golden Swallow* is one of Zhang's masterpieces, a film which lays out poetically his preoccupations with macho codes of conduct, the nature of heroism and the obligations of heroes. It is also gut-spillingly violent. Young audiences were captivated, seeing the new trend towards violence as a purging of repressed emotions. They were also attracted to a new kind of male hero. The character of Silver Roc was a prototype for many of Zhang's later male heroes. He stripped them of their romanticism and simplified them into one-dimensional characters, going to great lengths to make his movies more violent and more homogeneous (literally so, by using completely male casts) without diversions into romantic sub-plots. When the *wuxia* genre itself began to decline and Zhang abandoned it for kung fu, his pictures became even more male-centred. By then, Zhang had created the exemplary martial hero of the late 60s: a romantic who did not shirk from violence in the service of his principles.

Zhang's swordfighters in two of his best films, *The One Armed Swordsman* and *The Assassin/Da Cike* (1967), were, like Silver Roc, romantics who grappled with psychological conflicts. The protagonists of all three films were played by the same actor, Wang Yu, who would later, as director, lead the transition from swordfighting *wuxia* pictures to kung fu with *The Chinese Boxer/Long Hu Dou* (1970). But first he would flesh out the persona of a hero with psychological complexes resulting from either a physical maiming or a death-martyrdom wish. Fang Gang, the one-armed swords-man, is conscious of his working-class status and thinks himself unworthy of the attentions of his master, Qi Rufeng (played by Tian Feng). Fang is an orphan whose father died saving Qi's life. As a matter of obligation and charity, Qi took Fang as his disciple, rearing him to be his natural successor. However, Fang is taunted by his fellow pupils from a higher social class and by Qi's spoilt daughter, Qi Pei. They are jealous of Fang's standing as their master's best pupil. In a contest, Fang's arm is cut off by Qi Pei, the first explicit example of symbolic castration in Zhang's films where male heroes suffer physical maiming at the hands of jealous enemies. Fang Gang trains himself in one-armed swordfighting, using a sword with a broken blade, a fitting symbol to match Fang's own 'broken' physique. In the end, Fang saves his master and his whole family from impending massacre at the hands of a rival known as the 'Long-Armed Devil'. Fang Gang is a character who is visibly different from the weak-willed romantic heroes of the previous decade. This is borne out by his physical maiming and his subsequent forbearance in suffering and retraining himself to be a superb specimen of fighting manhood. Wang Yu's performance was a triumph of stoicism: he was good in imparting silent anguish and dogged perseverance.

Wang's next role, as the eponymous hero Nie Zheng in *The Assassin* gives him an even greater opportunity to paint his heroic persona with the brush of stoic masochism. A fatalistic mood accompanies Nie Zheng in his life as a young swordfighter waiting for his destiny to manifest itself. It comes when he is offered a job as an assassin by a statesman of the Han state. Nie's target is the emperor's uncle, an overly influential member of the court who wants his country to ally itself with an unfriendly neighbour. *The Assassin* is perhaps Zhang's most representative study of male heroism based on the principle of violence for a cause. Nie Zheng carries out the assassination and gives up his own life by disembowelling himself, an extreme show of heroism typical of Zhang's penchant for grisly death scenes. Nie Zheng is possibly the most individualistic of Zhang's heroes because of his willingness to die for a cause and his sense of manifest destiny. The destiny that is played out here concerns Nie's perception that his whole life was a preparation to kill the one person whose fate mattered to the future of the country and perhaps the world. Despite a long, plodding section where Nie Zheng takes leave of his lover on the eve of his departure to carry out the assassination, Zhang's mastery of narrative shows in his economic style, superb art direction and central performance of Wang Yu.

On losing the services of Wang Yu at the end of the 60s as the star became hugely popular and demanded the right to direct himself, Zhang employed a couple of male stars unknown at the time, Ti Lung and David Chiang, and groomed them into the next generation of Zhang Che heroes. The picture which pairs the two young actors and shows their naïvety to best advantage is *The New One Armed Swordsman/ Xin Dubi Dao* (1971). This was not a sequel to *The One Armed Swordsman*, but a completely new story featuring a one armed hero-protagonist, the prototype made famous by Wang Yu. Chiang played Lei Li, a young and arrogant swordfighter who cuts off his own right arm after losing a duel with an elderly master-swordsman, Long Yizhi (played by Gu Feng). Retired from swordfighting, Lei works as a waiter in a wayside inn, developing one-armed skills and becoming a kind of legend. He forms a relationship with the daughter of a blacksmith and an even more important relationship with a wandering swordsman, Feng Junjie (Ti Lung), who calls at the inn and inquires about the waiter. He is immediately impressed when told Lei's name.

As is the case in many of Zhang's later martial arts films centring on individualistic male protagonists – particularly the series starring David Chiang and Ti Lung – homosexual currents brew just below the surface whenever the hero meets another male hero. The heterosexual attraction between Lei and the blacksmith's daughter is, of course, more in line with convention. The one ingredient which signifies the homosexual passion between the two men is violence. When Feng is killed by Long Yizhi (Lei's old enemy), the one-armed Lei storms Long's fort and kills off his whole army before killing Long himself. The bloodletting and severing of limbs from bodies is extreme. Anyone familiar with the visceral violence in Zhang's pictures will recall abundant images of heroes spilling their guts, hatchets stuck in stomachs, swords up the backsides and bodies cut in half.

Among Hong Kong critics, there is consensus that Zhang did all his best work in the late 60s. By the early 70s, the *wuxia* trend was already giving way to kung fu. Accordingly, Zhang made the transition. He considered kung fu as falling within the domain of the martial arts genre. His real interest remained focused on the themes of male potency, individualism and fellowship, in short, on what Zhang preferred to call *yang gang* (male attributes). Unlike King Hu, Zhang easily made the transition from *wuxia* to kung fu precisely because the kung fu picture favoured male protagonists.

Zhang built up his own repertory company of actors and directing protégés including Wu Ma, John Woo and Bao Xueli. More importantly, he employed the talents of Lau Kar-leong as his martial arts director and action-choreographer. Lau and his partner Tang Jia had been head-hunted by Shaw Brothers after their success with *The Jade Bow*. Although Zhang generously shared credits with his co-directors, the consistency of his style made him the undisputed auteur of his films. Moreover, Zhang wrote his own scripts, usually in collaboration with Ni Kuang, who must also be considered as one of the director's stable-mates.

Zhang's first fully mature kung fu work and the first production in which he groomed a directorial protégé (Bao Xueli) was *The Boxer from Shantung/ Ma Yongzhen* (1972), with action choreography by Lau Kar-leong and Tang Jia. The title hero, Ma Yongzhen (Chen Guantai, making his debut) is a punk from Shandong who turns up in Shanghai looking for work, and quickly makes his mark in the city's underworld as a kung fu fighter. First he has a run-in with Tan (played by David Chiang), a young gangland boss who, even when he is humiliating Ma, seems also to inspire him. An unspoken bond immediately establishes itself between the two young men so that later, when Tan is killed by a rival boss, Ma avenges his death. The final blood-bath, set in a large tea-house, is staged in classic Zhang Che style where one man is pitted against practically an entire army. Wounded at the start with a hatchet stuck in his stomach, Ma successfully kills all his enemies before he himself dies. Ma Yongzhen is a typical Zhang Che character: a loner with a martyrdom complex, willing to sacrifice himself for an underworld code of justice. Ma evokes the archetypes portrayed by Wang Yu in the early Zhang Che classics, *The Assassin* and *The Golden Swallow.* The difference in the character and status of his heroes, inherent in the changeover from *wuxia* to kung fu, is obvious: Ma is a two-bit punk rather than a virtuous hero like Silver Roc and the assassin Nie Zheng, but, like them, Ma achieves apotheosis in death. *The Boxer from Shantung* is one of Zhang's best pictures, not least because the production values are so impressive (many of his latter productions tend to look slipshod and arbitrary). Perhaps spurred on by the presence of a co-director, Zhang paid careful attention to narrative pace and character.

At their best, Zhang's kung fu movies display a simplicity which distils the essence of movie-watching, allowing viewers to concentrate their full attention on his action sequences. Zhang's action scenes are choreographed as self-contained set-pieces commenting on the plot rather than it being advanced through the action. At their worst, Zhang's movies are simply routine productions. His later kung fu movies were increasingly mechanical, running like clockwork, with action sequences and characters being repeated in film after film, such as the ones he made in the second half of the 70s about the Shaolin temple and its kung fu alumni. By 1974, Zhang had formed his own production company to make the first film in the Shaolin series, *Heroes Two/Fang Shiyu yu Hong Xiguan.* The series is largely distinguished by the action choreography of Lau Kar-leong and Tang Jia, depicting the Shaolin fighting style. Lau went on to become a director in 1975 (as did Tang Jia) and made his own series of films portraying the original Shaolin heroes and their successors. *Heroes Two* is preceded by a short documentary about Shaolin kung fu styles, with Chen Guantai and Alexander Fu Sheng demonstrating various techniques based on movements of the stork and the tiger. It is the kind of self-contained film within a film which makes the kung fu movie appear disjointed and devoid of narrative. Zhang's kung fu films in this period seem like compendiums of short kung fu segments rather than whole movies.

THE KUNG FU BAND WAGON

When kung fu movies supplanted the swordfighting *wuxia* picture, actors who made their names in the latter genre had to make the shift as well. Wang Yu, the actor who rose to fame via Zhang Che's *wuxia* movies in the late 60s, typified the development when he starred in and directed *The Chinese Boxer/Longhu Dou* (1970). Along with Zhang, he was a contract employee of Shaw Brothers who had led the trend in *wuxia* pictures in the mid-60s. By 1970, Hong Kong was buzzing with rumours about kung fu and a new star from America, Bruce Lee, who would show the industry the way to glory. Shaw Brothers, the studio that first held negotiations with Lee but failed to secure his services, rushed *The Chinese Boxer* into production, pre-empting, if not actually igniting, the kung fu fever. As it turned out, *The*

Chinese Boxer was the first major movie to devote itself entirely to the art of kung fu. The studio also rush-produced a spate of kung fu movies which found distribution in the West, including Chor Yuen's *The Killer/Da Sha Shou* (1972) and Cheng Chang-ho's *King Boxer/Tianxia Diyi Quan* (1972). These films and *The Chinese Boxer* can be seen as a primer for the kung fu clichés and conventions which later found their way into the films of Bruce Lee. Examples are the classic confrontations between Japanese and Chinese martial arts, a lone hero versus the whole world, the reliance on revenge as a motive and a strong undercurrent of nationalist feeling. As directed by Wang Yu, *The Chinese Boxer* is full of rhetorical excess, the result of a perceived need to amplify violence and sex. It has more than its fair share of blood-gushing violence and coarse, zoomed images.

Wang Yu plays the kung fu student whose teacher was killed by Japanese karate fighters. After they knock him senseless, he resolves to train himself in the 'Iron Palm' technique (by washing his hands in a wok of burning gravel) and the art of gravity-defying leaps and somersaults. With his newly acquired skills, he dons a mask and starts to undo everything the Japanese have built up, including their control of gambling houses and protection rackets. Thus he riles the Japanese into combat: first he defeats samurai swordsmen hired to kill him in a bravura action sequence set amidst falling snow; and finally he meets karate fighters in a snowy field for a duel to the death. Although influenced by Japanese martial arts movies – as well as Zhang Che's – the film possesses its own stylish momentum, though marred by visual braggadocio.

Even with skimpy plots, kung fu movies continued to draw audiences on the strength of their action sequences which were a marvel to watch. Many of the stars were genuine practitioners of the art. They were required to execute the choreography, but many were also choreographers themselves, such as Bruce Lee, Sammo Hung and Jacky Chan. One of the best choreographers of kung fu action in the 70s was Lau Kar-leong. Lau's father, Lau Tsam, was a disciple of the legendary Cantonese kung fu master, Lam Sai-wing. A butcher by trade, Lam Sai-wing was in turn a disciple of Wong Fei-hung, the kung fu hero of Cantonese cinema and later of Tsui Hark's 90s movies. The young Lau Kar-leong came to Hong Kong from Guangdong and entered the film industry as a bit player in Wong Fei-hung movies starring Kwan Tak-hing. In 1966 he signed with Shaw Brothers as a martial arts director and worked with Zhang Che throughout the director's early career, choreographing both the *wuxia* swordplay and the kung fu in Zhang's pictures. On turning director in 1975, he attempted to integrate both swordplay and kung fu in his own movies. His action sequences were brilliantly choreographed and performed, mixing elaborate movements with a theatrical sense of posture, composure and discipline. There were two over-riding elements in Lau's movies: sexuality as a matter of balancing the yin and the yang elements of kung fu (so as to execute the art with greater efficacy), and the family (whether it be an extended community of fellow kung fu fighters or a close community of real kinsmen). Flowing from this theme of the family is a master and disciple relationship which

Lau often depicted as one separate from the family though not necessarily excluded from it.

Of all the martial arts figures, Lau has been the most consistent in utilising the theme of sexuality. While Bruce Lee is usually given credit for introducing kung fu to the West and became the favourite pin-up boy, it was Lau Kar-leong who explored the sexuality of kung fu more than Lee ever did. The sheer masculine presence of kung fu stars have led some Western critics to decipher homosexual motifs as an integral part of the genre. Zhang Che was, in his time, the most prominent director to deal with the homosexual undertones in the 'brotherhood' code of *yi*. In the case of Lau Kar-leong, it is in *Executioners from Shaolin/Hong Xiguan* (1977) that he gives the most graceful exposition of the links between kung fu and sexuality: how masculinity and femininity, strength and weakness, are all vital elements in the practice of kung fu, offering a more balanced approach to the martial arts.

Ostensibly a biography of the Shaolin hero Hong Xiguan (played by Chen Guantai), the plot deals with Hong's refuge in Guangdong after the burning of the Shaolin Temple. He travels on the 'red junks' which carry rebels disguised as Cantonese opera troupes to distant parts of the province to disseminate the anti-Qing message. Hong courts Yongchun (played by Lily Li), marries her and raises a son, Wending, while devoting most of his time to practising the Tiger technique in order to take revenge on Bai Mei, the renegade Shaolin monk who killed his master. Bai Mei (the name means 'white brows,' whiteness of facial hair being traditionally associated with eunuchs) is a master of the 'golden bell clasp' which utilises what is apparently the weakest part of one's body, the groin, as the strongest position to defeat attackers. This involves clamping one's legs together as enemies attack the genital area with their feet, so as to trap them. Hong Xiguan prepares to defeat Bai Mei by practising on a bronze figure which has pin balls running through its torso and coming out from the genitals. The balls mark the vital acupuncture points of the body so that Hong can recognise and use them to break down Bai Mei's defences. Lau prefigures the severe test of defeating Bai Mei in a scene showing Hong Xiguan forcing apart his bride's legs on his wedding night. His wife, Yongchun, is also a skilled kung fu artist specialising in the crane technique, which allows her to clamp her legs together, making it impossible for anyone to pull them apart. Hong's son, Wending, is taught the crane style of kung fu by his mother. When his father dies after failing to defeat Bai Mei, it is Wending who combines both the tiger and crane styles to defeat him. Wending's unorthodoxy extends to his effeminate appearance: he wears pinafores and ties his hair in two buns, a style only worn by girls in his village, clearly making him a symbol of ambivalent sexuality, shown here to triumph over the non-sexuality of the eunuch. Lau thus suggests that an understanding of sexuality is an important part of kung fu and its need for a balanced approach. Both strength and weakness, the latter being conventionally coded as feminine, must contribute to the implementation of the skills. In this respect, *Executioners from Shaolin* is Liu's most co-ordinated picture. It is both a tiger and a crane.

Lau's masterpiece – and possibly one of the all-time greats of Hong Kong cinema – is *Dirty Ho/Lantou He* (1979), a work which takes the breath away with its opulence of design and the complicity of its two main characters (a prince and a thief) in leading the audience in a devilish dance of delight. Enhancing the flavour of the film is the baroque choreography of the action sequences. Once again, there is a mutually interdependent relationship of 'opposite' forces, here presented in terms of class (or, at least, social status terms), embodied by the two male leads. Wang is a Manchu prince travelling incognito in the provinces who meets a thief named Ho. The prince is set upon by traitors who do not wish to see him succeed to the throne. He is assisted by the thief, on whose forehead the prince administers a poisonous wound which can only be countered by an antidote possessed by the prince alone (hence the title 'Dirty Ho' – the Chinese title translates more literally as 'Bad Head Ho').

The density of Lau's *mise en scène* is a feast to behold, particularly in the 'red junks' scene (brothel-boats in which prostitutes and courtesans entertain clients) where the prince first encounters the thief: the prince and the thief are seated face to face, framed by women in the background while a lantern hangs overhead. The prince and the thief are shown as dependent on each other in a relationship where, in keeping with the feudal setting, honour and merit count more than sexual attraction. The prince teaches the thief skills in kung fu, transforming him into a fully-fledged kung fu fighter as well as morally reforming him. On the other hand, the prince, wounded in the leg, must depend on the thief to carry him back on a wheel cart to the palace and win the final power struggle. The yin–yang theme of balance in the application of kung fu is also given play. In situations where survival is the goal, the kung fu fighter must be able to adapt one 'proclivity' to counteract another one, since strength and expertise in one particular skill do not necessarily lead to victory and survival. In fact, strength when exercised inappropriately is a weakness, and weakness, when appropriate, is strength. Lau shows in his movies that kung fu 'weaknesses' take the form of inferior kung fu styles, such as Drunken Kung Fu, and transsexual style of kung fu illustrated in *Executioners from Shaolin* and *Dirty Ho*, where the thief confronts an effeminate kung fu opponent. In the final analysis, what impresses in *Dirty Ho* and Lau's other pictures is the sheer geometry of his kung fu choreography. Two climactic action sequences in *Dirty Ho* (an ambush as the thief pushes the prince in his wheel-cart and the final duel within the palace) are genie-like in wonder and illusion. So too are the scenes where the prince encounters assassins disguised respectively as a wine connoisseur and an art dealer. They attempt to kill the prince through moves and actions under the guise of civilised manners as they sip wine and examine antiques, with the prince likewise defending himself by meticulously observing the same civilised protocols. The scenes are a prime example of the representation of supreme effort through seeming inaction or minimal gestures, a kind of inversion of the rhetoric of violence and excess. *Dirty Ho* is the one kung fu masterpiece – the other is possibly Wu Ma's *The Dead and the Deadly/ Ren Xia Ren* (1982) – which opens up a Pandora's Box of silk and velvet, exotic perfumes and Oriental verses to waft at the senses, permeate the mind and blunt the rough edges, all these in an action genre that normally banks on illiterate humour, fists and guts, blood and gore, grunts and thumps, to impress audiences.

Like Zhang Che, Lau similarly exhausted himself having to fulfil contractual obligations to his studio (Shaw Brothers). His work became routine, slotted in between worthier pictures. His films before *Executioners from Shaolin, The Spiritual Boxer/ Shen Da* (1975) and *Challenge of the Masters/ Lu Acai yu Huang Feihong* (1976) are among his best, as is his fourth film, *36th Chamber of Shaolin/ Shaolin Sanshiliu Fang* (1978). However, there is a sense of crudity about the way Lau sets out his main themes, particularly that of the master–disciple relationship. A few important films were to follow *Dirty Ho*, the best of which was *My Young Auntie/ Zhang Bei* (1980), a thrilling and funny study of gender politics, generational conflict and familial responsibilities revolving around a young widow asserting her rights to her late husband's estate.

Shaolin and Wu Tang/ Shaolin yu Wu Dang (1983) is a neglected work credited to Lau Kar-fai (Lau's adopted brother), but really directed by Lau himself under the pseudonym of 'Kung Fu Leong'. The plot deals with rival schools teaching the different disciplines of kung fu (Shaolin) and swordfighting (Wu Dang), and a conspiracy by the imperial court to obtain the secrets of these martial arts. The film has a derisive quality which recalls *Dirty Ho*, but its most fascinating theme is, once again, the role of the female in complementing the masculine features of the martial arts; indeed, it is no accident that the yin–yang symbol is used prominently in key scenes. The quest for a harmonic whole, the bringing together of the two schools in order to achieve the acme of martial arts, makes *Shaolin and Wu Tang* a significant work in Lau's oeuvre, despite his rather perfunctory credit in the film.

Lau's penultimate film for the Shaw Brothers studio – but really his swansong – was *The Eight Diagram Pole Fighter* aka *The Invincible Pole Fighter/ Wulang Bagua Gun* (1984). Here he adapted the story of the famous women warriors of the Yang clan (Song Dynasty loyalists during the period of the Mongol invasions) who were almost completely wiped out in a battle with a Mongol army because the Han General Pan Mei betrayed them. The story focuses on the seven sons of the Yang clan, five of whom are killed except for the fifth and sixth sons. The massacre opens the film as one of Lau's typically formal and theatrically staged kung fu showpieces. Lau's sense of theatre is seen to greatest effect in these scenes of martyrdom where the Yang heroes die, standing erect in postures of statuesque greatness. The surviving fifth and sixth sons are hunted by the Mongols. Sixth son goes mad with grief while fifth son – designated 'Wulang' in Chinese – takes shelter in a monastery where the techniques of pole fighting are taught. By converting his spear into a pole, Wulang learns the skills of pole fighting in order to take revenge on the traitor Pan Mei. The monks teach him to fight by using wooden models of wolves with sharp teeth. The trick is to de-fang the wolves and render them helpless but not to kill them, in accordance with Buddhist belief.

Lau dwells at some length on the theme of the Chinese family members' mutual obligations to each other, and the whole family's devotion to the state – perhaps his most incisive statement on that score. It is no accident that Lau's pictures were almost always performed by his own clan of relatives and disciples, and usually revolve around family groups and relationships, bolstered by an outer grid of the disciple–master relationship. Lau repeats the motif of having both disciple and master as cloistered monks, with the disciple harbouring a thirst for revenge, a plot device last used to good effect in *36th Chamber of Shaolin/Shaolin Sanshiliu Fang* (1978). In the final duel, the monks intervene to save Wulang and his sister who are trapped inside an inn by de-teething their enemies. They treat their opponents like wolves, sticking their poles into the mouths of the human 'predators' and jerking their teeth out – one of the most violent images Lau has created. In its own gross and macabre way, the sequence is not bereft of humour. It is also one of Lau's most exuberantly choreographed and exciting final set-pieces. *The Eight Diagram Pole Fighter* marks the end of the phase in Lau's career devoted to the exposition of kung fu in its most classical manifestation: the art being shown in its purely physical mode while the genre is still largely in an unadulterated form. As this classical aspect of the genre began to decline in the mid-80s, Lau's career was overtaken by new trends and new kung fu star-choreographers such as Jacky Chan, with whom he would work in the 90s.

While Lau's career as a kung fu director progressed to its peak in the late 70s, the swordfighting *wuxia* movie enjoyed a brief resurgence with director Chor Yuen's series of films based on the martial arts novels of Gu Long, the best of which was *The Magic Blade/Tianya, Mingyue, Dao* (1976). By then, a kind of esoteric new wavism had permeated the genre, as if anticipating a momentous avant-gardist happening: the rise of a Hong Kong new wave, which finally occurred in 1989. The *wuxia* genre did exert a hold on new wave directors, notably on Tsui Hark and Patrick Tam, whose first films, *The Butterfly Murders/Die Bian* (1979) by Tsui Hark and *The Sword/Ming Jian* (1980) by Patrick Tam, were conscious postmodern versions of the period swordplay movie. The artful, esoteric approaches to the genre led to its premature burial before it once again became a box-office trend in the 90s, triggered by the much less pretentious *Swordsman/Xiao'ao Jianghu* (1990) and its sequels made by Tsui Hark as producer and Ching Siu-tung as director.

The new wave films of Tsui and Tam are a far cry from the simple *wuxia* extravaganzas which the genre had become by the time kung fu challenged its predominance. Wang Yu's *Beach of the War Gods/Zhan Shen Tan* offers a kind of coda to the passing of the old genre. It was the swordfighting movie to end all swordfighting movies, accurately perceiving itself to be the last of its kind before the genre's demise with the rise of kung fu movies. Wang Yu

108

plays the lone swordfighter who mobilises a village against Japanese pirates. He recruits four other experts to act as his generals and to train the villagers in combat. The Japanese launch a massive attack and are beaten back, first by booby traps and then in battles at close quarters, with echoes of Kurosawa's *Seven Samurai/ Sinichin no Samurai* as well as the Hollywood and Italian versions of the story. The final section of the film is made up of scene after scene of nail-biting combat in which nearly all the standard sword-weapons ever seen in the genre – from broad swords to samurai swords to flying knives – are used. The final duel between the Japanese commander and Wang Yu's swordsman is set on the beach, then moves to a windmill where Wang clings to a sail like a bat while fending off his samurai opponent at every turn. The action then moves to a barnyard. The incongruous settings of both windmill and barnyard, conjuring up a vision of Don Quixote, reveal an eclectic imagination at work and convey a camp quality, more so than the turbulent scenes of sword-to-sword combat. But the image of Wang Yu on the sails of the windmill lingers on. He is the eternal swashbuckler calling all warriors to arms. More than any other cinema, the Hong Kong cinema takes to heart the adage that old warriors never die: they fade away and reappear, some taking the call to arms literally by using their fists as kung fu warriors. Others fence their way to a last moment of glory as expert swordsmen and women before the sword is sheathed and the scabbard hung up.

NOTES
[1] *Wuxia* means martial fighter, swordsman or knight-errant.

Chapter Eight

Bruce Lee: Narcissus and the Little Dragon

No other figure in Hong Kong cinema has done as much to bring East and West together in a common sharing of culture as Bruce Lee in his short lifetime. In him, Hong Kong cinema found its most forceful ambassador; an Asian role model espousing aspects of an Eastern culture who found receptive minds in the West. The only other examples of such a phenomenon that come to mind are figures from Japanese cinema such as Sessue Hayakawa or Toshiro Mifune, but they never enjoyed popular success on Lee's scale. Lee's success was based on the action choreography of his unique kung fu style – which he dubbed *Jeet Kune Do* or 'The Art of the Intercepting Fist'. However, his international success harboured aspects other than the purely physical dimensions of his art which cannot so readily be adopted by other cultures. His death in 1973 spawned a legend and the world-wide scale of the cult which developed suggests that there was something universal about his figure. Lee is all things to all men, but just what are these things?

The *mise en scène* of Lee's films is a superior example of what American reviewers dismissively call 'chop-socky' films, and there is a decidedly ironic side to his success in the West, since an anti-Western sentiment is more than apparent in his persona. In his short career, Bruce Lee stood for something that in the 90s is hardly deemed politically correct: Chinese nationalism as a way of feeling pride in one's identity. Lee had experienced his share of racial prejudice as an immigrant in the US and it was perhaps natural that he would incorporate the theme of pride and anti-racism in his movies. But he went further, overlaying what was essentially a humanist reaction against racism with a Chinese nationalist sentiment.

Nationalism is a potent theme in the work of both old and new Hong Kong directors, from social-realist Cantonese melodramas to Mandarin historical epics, and from martial arts films to new wave works. Bruce Lee's work accentuates it even more than usual, stirring the hearts of Chinese audiences everywhere while foreign critics talk of jingoism and chauvinism. Americans, though, may see in it the reaction of a Chinese immigrant struggling against racism and attempting to assert the right to be American. Lee, the ardent nationalist, was after all an American citizen. But the nationalistic theme in his films has nothing to do with his adoptive country.

110

Lee's Chinese nationalism cannot be easily dismissed if one wishes to appreciate fully his appeal to Chinese audiences. The nationalism Lee's films invoked is better understood as an abstract kind of cultural nationalism, manifesting itself as an emotional wish among Chinese people living outside China to identify with China and things Chinese, even though they may not have been born there or speak its national language or dialects. They wish to affirm themselves and fulfil their cultural aspirations by identifying with the 'mother culture', producing a rather abstract and apolitical type of nationalism. The historical formation of this rather exceptional form of nationalism is complex and deeply rooted. Briefly, and roughly, Chinese dynastic rule regarded China as the centre of the universe, the heart of the Heavenly Kingdom. In its terminology, *tianxia* signified both the Chinese Empire and the world as a whole, with its myriad people. Alongside this concept, the notion of *guo* designated a localised political unit, a specific part of the Empire or, in modern terminology, of the world. According to Confucian orthodoxy, *tianxia* designated a civilisational value, whereas *guo* referred to a regime of power, to what the West would regard as a state government or, since the Empire was also the world, with regional government. Chinese nationalism focuses on the moral and cultural aspects of Chinese civilisation, on *tianxia*. Questions of international relations and of political power structures related to the regulation of *guo*, including the specifics of the rise or fall of a particular ruling house, and to the regulation amongst different *guo*. It is with this dichotomy that Chinese nationalist thought entered the 20th century. It did not attach itself to any particular form of state government, partly because there was no effective state. Instead, Chinese nationalism remobilised seventeenth-century cultural philosophies relating to the achievement of the people's general well-being, and tried to combine that with the achievement of an economic modernity that would allow China to take its place as an equal amongst nation-states. It is this particular discourse which was formalised into a nationalist ideology by Sun Yat-sen and his chief ideologue, Dai Jitao, as well as by the founders of the Communist Party in China. The consequences of this intellectual and political history are still acutely present in contemporary forms of Chinese notions of identity and 'self-strengthening': a pride in a culturalist version of *tianxia* combined with a fairly sceptical attitude towards regimes of national state power. This ideology is particularly suited to a diasporic people since it allows them to remain distant from 'their' state while retaining pride in the cultural values allegedly embodied in their tradition which is, as all traditions are, highly portable.

The degree of multicultural tolerance in countries with sizeable Chinese minorities determines the interpretation and indeed the intensity of such a cultural nationalism. For instance, in certain Southeast Asian countries, this may amount to a 'cultural chauvinism' in the light of anti-Chinese discrimination. In this essay, cultural nationalism is understood as a culturally positive, politically abstract phenomenon emerging from *tianxia* and hitting Hong Kong cinema around the late 50s in the context of the

Cold War and its Yellow-Peril rhetoric rather than as a byproduct of the successful Communist Revolution (regarded with the scepticism befitting any *guo*).

Hong Kong film directors and writers readily delved into Chinese myths, legends and history to find themes and motifs on which to base their films and scripts. They were in a unique position to show abstract loyalty to China, unlike their counterparts in China itself or in Taiwan, which required its citizens to treat the island as the real China. Hong Kong is not a country, so that to speak of a Hong Kong nationalism would be a contradiction in terms. Its residents' dislike of communism and, in recent years, its distrust of Britain produced a nationalism based not on support for a particular regime or political ideology, but on a cultural ideal which, ironically, is rooted in *tianxia*, a residue of the Heavenly Kingdom.

One sign of Chinese communities expressing such an abstract nationalism is their ready identification with Chinese screen characters, especially when, as in some Southeast Asian countries, local political factors make it difficult for audiences to express their nationalistic feeling. In addition, the traditional apathy of overseas Chinese towards politics plays a key role in fostering this abstract nationalism. It has come to characterise the thinking of many overseas Chinese who do not call China their home, but view China as *zuguo* or motherland, the repository of one's cultural identity, the land of one's ancestors and the source of myths and legends which imbue the process of growing up, wherever. In later chapters, the abstract nationalism of contemporary Hong Kong directors such as Tsui Hark, Ann Hui and Yim Ho will be discussed in the context of the so-called new wave's 'China syndrome' in the mid-80s. Hong Kong's China syndrome belies the contemporary political equation of Chinese nationalism with the communist regime in China. On the contrary, it asserts Hong Kong's identity as a separate cultural, social and political entity not to be confused with China. However, this has not always been the case.

In the immediate post-war years, Hong Kong took in scores of Chinese refugees, including film-makers, fleeing the civil war and, later, the communist regime. Political feelings concerning the situation in China ran high. Hong Kong cinema was divided along left–right lines, with production companies being identified by their political affiliations to the Chinese Communist Party or to the KMT. Authorities in China and Taiwan wooed film-makers in Hong Kong and encouraged them to fight for Chinese hearts and minds. Whether any of these film-makers were card-carrying members of political parties was immaterial to the prevailing mood of partisan nationalism. Left-wing studios such as Great Wall, Fenghuang and Long Ma, were clearly oriented towards the communist regime. Other companies, such as Yonghua and the Asia Film Company, received financial aid from Taiwanese and American sources.[1]

Towards the late 50s, Shaw Brothers and the MP and GI studios consolidated their hold on the film market and initiated a more glamorous studio era. The competition between these two major studios, each with

112

their own roster of contract stars and directors, benefited both the industry and the audiences. The studio era coincided with the isolation from the world scene of a China that was also fast becoming a superpower, but the struggle between the left–right factions of the early 50s was abandoned in favour of the provision of glossy and escapist entertainment.

The two studios specialised in producing historical epics and romances, stories of concubines or emperors who either saved collapsing dynasties or wrecked them. Such films purveyed the notion of abstract nationalism (or cultural nationalism) to audiences in the region. In the 70s, the films of Bruce Lee inherited that tradition. Kung fu films were particularly conducive to nationalism of the abstract kind. Its martial heroes shared a Masonic-like background harking back to traditions laid down by venerable Shaolin monks and their disciples who make vows to fight the foreign Manchus and restore the Chinese Ming Dynasty. A kung fu fighter was seen as a person who fought for a cause, seeking to restore power and dignity to the Chinese race. The motto was that Chinese people should lift their heads rather than bow in shame and subjugation to foreigners (*ditou* in Chinese). The fact that China was for many years drawn, quartered and occupied by foreigners added to the Chinese inferiority complex. The anti-*ditou* syndrome informs Bruce Lee's nationalist spirit.

The case of Bruce Lee is of particular interest because his international appeal does not appear to contradict his forthright insistence on his Chineseness. Western admirers of Lee view him differently from his Eastern admirers, and the difference revolves around his nationalism. To many Western viewers, Lee's nationalism is a non-starter. American admirers of Lee's cult dwell in his art as a reaction against racism, as in Rob Cohen's appealing but over-simplified film biography of the actor, *Dragon: The Bruce Lee Story* (1993), where white racism against Asian migrants in America features as a strong motif. As for other details in the actor's philosophical make-up, Lee (played by Hawaiian actor Jason Scott Lee, no relation) is shown adhering to Chinese superstition, bound by some kind of fatal destiny which could be warded off by *bagua* emblems. Lee is consumed by nightmares in which he constantly battles an armour-clad knight obviously symbolising Death. In a climactic scene at the end, Lee fights the Death-knight in a Chinese cemetery (where his own grave is located), more as an attempt to divert the attention of Death from his son, Brandon, who died in an accident on a film set in 1993. Nationalism, where it features as part of the man's character-building framework, concerns Lee's struggle to win the public admission that Asians can be Americans too. But it is still Lee's kung fu style and methods which attract and make up the most important components of his philosophy, as seen in *Dragon*. Another component is Lee's sex appeal and magnetic personality, which draws Western audiences to him irrespective of the xenophobic streak in his Hong Kong films.

The English critic Tony Rayns has argued that Lee's narcissism is a trait which distinguishes him more than his nationalism.[2] To the West, Lee is a narcissistic hero who makes Asian culture more accessible. To the East, he is a nationalistic hero who has internationalised some aspects of Asian culture. Both views appear antithetical. Narcissism may well be one aspect of Lee's character through which an international audience gains access to eastern motives and behaviour, but it does not fully explain his appeal to a Chinese audience. For them, Lee's narcissism is a manifestation of the anti-*ditou* factor that galvanises characters into action in kung fu movies. Lee is literally putting his bravest face (and body) forward in order to show that the Chinese need no longer be weaklings. The physical art of kung fu entails the exertion of power and physique. Narcissism then ties in with Lee's urge to 'show face' (*biaomian*) as opposed to 'lose face' (*diaolian*).

Chinese audiences take pride in the image Lee projects as a superb fighting specimen of manhood who derives his status from 'traditional' skills. They are aware that his kung fu skills are not the result of supernatural strength or special effects. They know from versions and legends of Chinese history that this skill is achievable, a result of fitness and rigorous training. This principle of counting on one's own physical skills has been followed by other martial arts stars such as Jacky Chan. A scene in *The Way of the Dragon* illustrates the first principle of discipline and training in kung fu: before his gladiatorial bout with Chuck Norris in the Roman Coliseum, Lee warms up physically, stretches his muscles, creaks all his joints, reaches for his feet. Lee shows himself to be a specimen of thorough training, a true-to-life fighter and not the imaginary creation of an action movie director.

But Lee is more than a superb fighter, his kung fu skills more than physical brawn. His will to succeed, the philosophy of his kung fu, had to do with what influenced his return to Hong Kong from the United States to start his short but sensational career as a kung fu star. The legend of his return to Hong Kong (the story of his disappointment in losing the role of Kwai-chang/Caine in the Hollywood *Kung Fu* television series and the realisation that prejudice still ruled in the film capital) gave a special, classic status to the first three movies he made in the territory. Chinese audiences who see Lee in these films know that he has done all Chinese proud by using his skills in the service of a cause that inspires Chinese people to assert their identity and culture and never to bow their heads in shame (*ditou*) or lose face (*diaolian*).

The Big Boss/Tang Shan Daxiong (1971), Lee's first movie produced by a Hong Kong studio (Golden Harvest) after his failure to establish himself in Hollywood, is on the surface a simple and undemanding action picture. Lee plays Cheng Chiu-on, a new migrant in a Thai town who joins a group of other overseas Chinese workers employed in an ice factory. The plot develops around the disappearance of Cheng's buddies and his subsequent investigations. He comes into conflict with the factory's boss (Han Yingjie) who had in fact killed Cheng's buddies because they discovered his drug trafficking activities. Acting with a spontaneous but disciplined style, Lee etches out a character who is defined by action. However, Cheng is not a mere cypher for Lee's kung fu skills. He is a fully-rounded character who can evoke empathy in the audience's hearts with minimal interpretation

114

from Lee. Cheng resorts to action only through the trigger of conscience. He wears around his neck a jade amulet his mother had given him as a reminder that his kung fu skills should not be abused. Only when one of the thugs pulls off the chain and breaks the amulet does Cheng put his kung fu skills to use. Cheng is a character compelled to action for a reason. He fights for a cause. For better or worse, that cause is based on racial awareness, on the quest to make the Chinese character a dignified, respected and honoured figure. *The Big Boss* gains significance through Lee's propagation of such a cause.

In his next film, *Fist of Fury/Jingwu Men* (1972), Lee makes his strongest statement for the cause. It gives Lee his most substantial role, that of a young patriotic student named Chen Zhen who avenges the death of his master and redeems the honour of his martial arts school. The school is the Jingwu Men (or school of the most refined martial arts), located in the Japanese concession of Shanghai. Huo Yuanjia, the master, has been murdered by rival Japanese martial artists. During his memorial service, the Japanese launch a challenge to the Jingwu Men. Through a Chinese lackey-interpreter, they insult Huo's followers, brandishing a plaque with the words 'Sick Man of East Asia' and daring any member to fight them. Chen Zhen takes up the challenge, infiltrates the Japanese school and single-handedly defeats them.

In the role of Chen Zhen, Lee sheds the country bumpkin persona seen in *The Big Boss*. Chen Zhen has attained the rank of fifth disciple. With the death of his master, he alone among the school's students is willing to put his kung fu skills to work. In so doing, he risks abusing the ideals of the school which stresses that martial arts must only be put to the service of one's country and not for other bellicose reasons. The provocations of the Japanese prove too much for Chen and goad him into action. Part of the fascination of *Fist of Fury* lies in watching Chen harness his anger so as to release it in the form of powerful and deadly kung fu strokes, kicks, punches: a true marriage of action and intention executed with grace, simplicity and style. Chen's dilemma lies in the realisation that he could easily abuse his kung fu skills for the purpose of revenge, blood-letting and pure fun. Ironically, it is through such 'abuse' that Chen Zhen's sense of justice is satisfied. The film ends with Chen Zhen's arrest by the Shanghai police; but, taunted by the crowd of foreigners outside the gate who demand colonial justice, Chen runs towards them, leaping and flinging himself at the foreigners as they fire pistols at him. The image of the leap is frozen and Chen Zhen becomes a martyr, dying for a nationalistic cause. If evidence is needed to substantiate the nationalism which inspires Lee's characters, it is this final freeze-frame. Chen Zhen is also shown reacting against the semi-colonial subjugation of China: in addition to the 'Sick Man of East Asia' sign hurled at the Jingwu Men disciples, Chen Zhen takes issue with the 'No Dogs and Chinese' sign stuck in front of the gates of the city park. He destroys the sign after beating several Japanese who suggest that they would bring Chen into the park if he got down and crawled on all fours like a dog.

The anti-foreign bias in Lee's nationalism, most explicitly stated in *Fist of Fury*, can be dismissed as naked xenophobia, or acknowledged as the legitimate anger of a subjugated colonial and lowly Asian immigrant. Lee's feelings about his own experiences as an Asian immigrant in America undoubtedly seeped through. The nationalist motif in Lee's films is substantially a personal exorcism, a kind of retribution which Lee metes out to foreigners for their prejudices; it drives Lee's characters into action and puts Lee's kung fu talent to use. But it has been argued that such personal motivation diffuses the nationalist motif, leaving room for a psychological counter-argument in the form of Lee's narcissism.

Such a counter-argument is put forth by some critics in assessing *The Way of the Dragon*. It is, in their eyes, Lee's most narcissistic film. Lee's character, Tang Lung, goes to Rome to protect a Chinese restaurant threatened by a syndicate which has set its sights on the land on which the restaurant was built. After thwarting the first crude attempts to terrorise the owners into submission, Tang Lung must deal with professional fighter-killers hired by the syndicate. The film's biggest set-piece takes place in the Roman Coliseum where an American martial artist (played by Chuck Norris, Lee's sparring partner in the US) and Tang Lung fight to the death like the gladiators of ancient Rome.

The first work to be directed and scripted by Bruce Lee, *The Way of the Dragon* is, sadly, a flawed and transitional work which must now remain as Lee's testament, a reminder of themes which could have developed further and with more assurance and confidence had he lived. Up to this production, Bruce Lee had not only continuously espoused the art of Chinese kung fu, he had also dealt with the theme of the Chinese immigrant who must face discrimination and oppression: double blows to the pride and dignity of the Chinese character as they put roots in foreign lands. The character of Tang Lung is reprised from the immigrant persona previously seen in *The Big Boss*. The character is really part bumpkin, part martial arts master-philosopher. We see more of the former while the latter is relatively undeveloped. Unfortunately, the bumpkin persona takes over and transforms Lee's previous heroic figure into a parody. Signs of self-mockery can be detected in scenes such as those in the Roman Coliseum set-piece where Tang Lung rips body hair off the American's chest and blows it off the palm of his hand. Lee becomes a cult figure more at home in a cartoon comic. The parodic, almost camp, image of Lee probably originated from the famous scene in *The Big Boss* where a perfect image of a man is imprinted on a wooden wall after Lee has punched him through it.

Lee's indulgence in playing the bumpkin does not stand him in good stead with Western critics who will be put off by the grossness and crass naïvety of his character, because it strikes so close to home. This bumpkin easily reminds Westerners of the infamously rude Chinese waiters in Chinese restaurants all over Europe. On top of this negative image is Tang Lung's buffoonery. The first shot in *The Way of the Dragon* is a close-up of a tense and nervous Tang Lung. As the camera pulls back, we see why: he is in Rome's international airport surrounded by foreigners and stared at by a middle-aged European lady. Next, he goes to the restaurant and, unable to speak English or Italian, can only point to the menu, unaware of what he is ordering. Later, he is picked up by a prostitute. Not realising her real identity, he goes to her apartment. There, in front of a mirror, he practices kung fu (a scene held up by critics pushing the narcissistic line as a classic illustration of Lee's cinematic narcissism) before noticing the now naked prostitute, which is when he realises what her profession is.

The image of the bumpkin is emphasised at the expense of Lee's nationalism. We do not see much of Lee's master-fighter persona dealing with the cause. Tang Lung is a bumpkin who is skilled in kung fu rather than a kung fu master who comes from humble origins. The 'narcissism' scene of Tang Lung practising kung fu naked to the waist has become a major icon in Lee's myth. There is a camp quality to this scene which makes it memorable. But it forms only a brief segment in the whole film and actually ends with self-deprecating humour: as Tang Lung wraps up his exercise, he notices the poster of a naked couple embracing each other; quickly he puts palms together, shakes his head and closes his eyes as if to murmur a prayer. Other equally memorable scenes in *The Way of the Dragon* tend to be overlooked. One such is the mime scene where Tang Lung confronts the boss of the syndicate. His lack of English means that he cannot verbally warn the boss to lay off. He mimes it all out, with clenched fists, body movements, grunts and scowls, overcoming his verbal short-comings and conveying a clear message to the enemy. The fight scenes too are among Lee's most graceful. Although a flawed work, *The Way of the Dragon* crystallises all the important motifs seen in previous Lee films. His bumpkin-master fighter persona is a welded character which falls short of a new heroic persona because of the implicit caricature. Alas, Lee died before he could develop this persona further in more representative works.

Lee's last completed work was *Enter the Dragon* (1973), a co-production between Hollywood-based producers and Lee's Hong Kong backers, with guaranteed international distribution by Warner Brothers. This is surely an important work in Lee's career as it shows Lee at a certain disadvantage in the hands of Western film-makers. For precisely the same reason, not a few Western 'experts' on Lee consider it a minor work. Even when judged a superior work by the standards of the kung fu action genre, *Enter the Dragon* is really an uneasy amalgamation of antithetical East–West sentiments. It conveys the West's antipathy towards Lee's nationalism, and it shows a sullen and sulking Lee forced to submit to the West's perception of him as a mere action hero. Lee's strong personality still comes through as he performs a clichéd characterisation of the reserved, inscrutable and humourless Oriental hero so often seen in Hollywood movies. With the exception of an expository sequence before the opening credits introducing Lee's character (also called Lee), and putting his inheritance of the illustrious Shaolin kung fu tradition into perspective, the character has no significance beyond the purely mechanical. The theme of Chinese pride and honour *vis-à-vis* the prejudices and humiliations of foreigners, so starkly seen in Lee's Hong Kong productions, is only occasionally put forward. It is Lee's natural dignity and force of character which convey the message.

As the film opens, Lee is fighting in a practice session before a Shaolin high priest. Lee has reached the pinnacle of the Shaolin school of martial arts. The priest reminds him of the Shaolin precepts for mental preparedness: 'The enemy is only an illusion; the real enemy lies within oneself; he leaves and joins with the self.' Lee comprehends immediately: 'The self is abstract. To fight the enemy is a game; I play this game seriously.' Unlike Lee, the film-makers do not quite grasp the spiritual message. Whereas his Hong Kong movies such as *Fist of Fury* show Lee struggling with his inner self to exorcise the enemy within, all the better to fight a righteous cause without, *Enter the Dragon* only capitalises on the outer struggle. Together with Americans Roper and Williams (played by John Saxon and Jim Kelly, respectively), Lee goes to the island fortress ruled by an errant Shaolin disciple named Han (played by Cantonese villain Sek Kin). Nominally there to take part in a martial arts competition held once every three years, Lee is actually on a secret mission to collect evidence against Han's criminal operations and to bring him to task for betraying the Shaolin principles. Lee succeeds magnificently. With the help of Roper, he destroys the fortress. The compulsory duel scene between Han and Lee is set in a hall of mirrors. Lee is reminded of the principle that the 'enemy is an illusion'. With this in mind, he overcomes Han, who, in contrast, counted on gimmickry: his amputated right fist is armoured with weapons such as a talon and a steel hand.

Aesthetically, the Chineseness of *Enter the Dragon* does not integrate well with the Western sense of narrative decorum. From a Hong Kong perspective, the film moves slowly for a kung fu action movie, spending too much time on introducing characters. There is too much of a tendency to neatness. It is the kind of film-making that some critics may call 'literate' as opposed to the 'illiterate' slam-bang style of Hong Kong movies. But its literacy has nothing to do with a real understanding of the themes which Bruce Lee stood for.

The film does provide Lee with his only chance in any of his works to expound on the spiritual principles of kung fu: it briefly shows him inheriting the mantle of kung fu from a Shaolin high priest (played by Roy Chiao) who practises the illusory-self principle (a scene cut from most international release prints). He then passes on the inheritance to a younger disciple, to whom he intones: 'Emotional content, always remember, emotional content!' Lee's performance in *Enter the Dragon* is his least interesting, a casualty of the Western film-makers' demand for superficial decorum at the expense of character interpretation. Although the action sequences are finely choreographed by Lee, they appear academic. Seen today, Lee's presence in *Enter the Dragon* imparts a strange feeling. His 'serious' demeanour hints at a premonition of death. Clearly Lee could not fully express himself, finding satisfaction only in action – his shrieks, wails and cries are his most eloquent among all his movies.

Lee's improvised action choreography may have earned him the title of postmodern hero in Western eyes. But his kung fu, part of the generic tradition of Chinese action movies, is innovative and exotic compared to the fisticuffs and armaments of Western-style action scenes. So too is the element of narcissism if this is defined as the tendency of heroes to strike a pose in kung fu stance to evoke masculine sexuality. If narcissism is taken to mean homoeroticism, male bonding, *covert* homosexuality – then all these are part of the tradition of martial arts–kung fu films, particularly evident in the films of Zhang Che in the late 60s and 70s.

The West has tended to see an Eastern hero such as Lee as a camp figure who appeared in star vehicles designed to pander to the public's taste for action. Serious critics charge that Lee's movies do not amount to narrative wholes, and that they are only relevant or interesting because of the actor's presence and his skilful display of kung fu (a critical position which some critics also hold on Hong Kong cinema in general). What is not clear is whether some Western critics offer a thesis of narcissism as a counter argument to Hong Kong critics' focus on nationalism in Lee's movies, or whether their attempts to rationalise Eastern culture has brought forth a claim of narcissism to explain concepts such as nationalism and Lee's stand against racial prejudice.

The cult of Bruce Lee propagated after his death has resulted in blatant exploitation of his name and personality. Imitators sprung up sporting names like Bruce Le, Bruce Ly and Bruce Lai. Lee's own studio, Golden Harvest, was responsible for the travesty *Game of Death/Siwang Youxi* (1979), a film claimed to be Lee's last. The film credits Lee as lead actor, screenwriter and co-martial arts director, when in fact, these credits refer to only ten minutes of genuine Lee footage in the whole 102-minute running time of the film. The rest was directed by an American, Robert Clouse, Lee's director in *Enter the Dragon*, with new action sequences co-ordinated by Sammo Hung and choreographed by Yuan Biao. Clouse's film deals with a character named Billy Lo, a martial arts movie star who finds himself the target of an enlistment drive by an international crime syndicate. Billy Lo is played by a Bruce Lee lookalike, while his co-stars are grizzled Hollywood supporting actors Gig Young, Hugh O'Brian and Dean Jagger. The film cuts together out-takes, clips and inserts of the real Lee compiled from *The Way of the Dragon* and an undisclosed ten-minute sequence shot by Lee for his next production after *Enter the Dragon*. These incredible ten minutes show Lee entering a pagoda and on each level, encountering a protector whom he must subdue in order to continue up to the next level. On the second level, Lee's opponent is seven-foot tall Hakim, played by basketball star Kareem Abdul Jabbar, in line with Lee's practice of using former students and genuine martial arts professionals as actors in his pictures.

Both the Eastern and Western minders of Lee's cult showed their inability to understand Lee's legacy. *Game of Death* is a barely adequate action picture which hardly knows how to handle Lee's screen persona – whether to treat him as myth, common man hero, superhero or master

119

fighter. Needless to say, it gives no mention to Lee's real concerns and themes, not even in the film's most inspired moment: the allusion to the last shot of *Fist of Fury* in which Lee's character turns martyr for a nationalistic cause. During the shoot for a new movie, Lo is required to leap towards a hostile crowd aiming pistols at him. He is shot by a real bullet fired by an assassin planted among the extras, a scene which now assumes some poignancy since it is reminiscent of the circumstances surrounding the death of Lee's son, Brandon. Wounded in the face, Lo is taken to hospital and survives with nary a mark. He is persuaded by a journalist friend (Gig Young) to play dead. Lo's 'death' is reported in the press, giving the film-makers a chance to insert footage of Bruce Lee's actual funeral ceremony including a brief glimpse of him lying in the coffin.

The crucial freeze-frame image of the last leap in *Fist of Fury*, with its attendant philosophy, is squandered in the interest of a false tribute to Lee. The result is parody, exacerbated by the attempt to integrate his image into the narrative. One may well ask how Lee's admirers perceive the star after his death. Clouse obviously sees him in mechanical, stylistic terms, as an action star, and pays no heed to his nationalist consciousness or his spiritual kung fu philosophy. The cult worship of Lee seems unable to cope with all that, and more's the pity. With his death, Lee became an object, even a fetish.

This chapter which deals with nationalism as an important theme of Hong Kong cinema seeks to put the concept of nationalism in its right perspective. Lee's nationalism, and that of many other Hong Kong directors and actors, is of the popcorn variety, a lowbrow version of nationalism which appeals most to home-grown audiences. The common-man Chinese hero who is both physical and philosophical is unique in Hong Kong cinema and Bruce Lee was the only star who could have created the prototype. Furthermore, his films offer interesting subjects for analysis in terms of style versus content, demonstrating how the two either integrate or fall apart if one aspect is overemphasised.

To see Lee as a mere kung fu martial artist without taking into account his nationalist sentiments is to perceive Lee as Narcissus gazing in a mirror: the image reflected is an illusion without substance. It ignores the symbolism of the dragon in Lee's Chinese name, Li Xiaolong, which means Li, the Little Dragon. When the dragon looks in the mirror, it sees not Narcissus but the Chinese masses looking back. This is the substance behind the reflective theory of Hong Kong cinema – that it mirrors the aspirations of Hong Kong people, and reflects their psychological mind-set and behaviour. This is also the substance behind Lee's narcissism. With death, Lee achieved true mythic status, allowing him to be all things to all men: Narcissus gazing in the mirror or Little Dragon exhorting the Chinese to stand up and be counted. Lee achieved the distinction of being both Narcissus and Little Dragon, straddling East and West.

NOTES

[1] For left–right divide in the Hong Kong film industry and the rise of the two majors, Shaw Brothers and MP and GI, see Chapters 1 and 5 respectively.

[2] Tony Rayns, 'Bruce Lee: Narcissism and Nationalism', *A Study of the Hong Kong Martial Arts Film*, HKIFF catalogue, 1980.

Chapter Nine

Jacky Chan: The Other Kung Fu Dragon

Hong Kong actors tend to emphasise the physical art of performing and Jacky Chan is the one actor who best proves the rule. One need only look at his movies to get the sensation of images reaching out to strike, parry, turn, somersault and punch you in the face. Hailed as the successor to Bruce Lee, Jacky Chan is the star who most successfully continues the tradition of the kung fu action spectaculars which Bruce Lee brought to international prominence. Chan's Chinese name, Chenglong, which means 'to become a dragon', echoes Bruce Lee's Chinese name, Xiaolong, 'little dragon'. From Bruce Lee's heyday in the early 70s to Chan's box-office successes in the 80s, Hong Kong cinema was synonymous with the word kung fu.

Like Lee, Chan elevated the kung fu movie to new heights through his sheer bravado and skill in the martial arts, marking it with his own personal style. He abided by the tradition of the true kung fu artist by personally enacting the moves and undertaking dangerous stunts himself – an important principle observed by Bruce Lee and previous kung fu stars such as Kwan Tak-hing, the actor who portrayed Wong Fei-hung in the series of Cantonese kung fu adventures of the 50s and 60s. Chan's observance of this principle has propelled him into the realm of action-choreography, stunt co-ordination and, finally, the direction of his own pictures. He became the quintessential well-rounded kung fu star and artist. His pictures are still the best examples of physically achievable stunts executed via kung fu chor-eography rather than technical special effects. But like Bruce Lee, Chan is not a mere stunt man. He is a star of considerable creative prowess, pos-sessing a point of view that is more than the sum of its parts.

The success of Jacky Chan's martial arts movies in Hong Kong is commonly understood as a case of a popular actor adhering to a mainstream generic formula. This overlooks Chan's unique way of keeping the genre interesting and relevant to audiences. Chan's movies in the 80s were practically alone in preserving Bruce Lee's tradition of kung fu as an instinctive but disciplined art linked to a cultural and national identity. The overtones of nationalism in Lee's espousal of kung fu were picked up by Jacky Chan. However, whereas the late star possessed all the hallmarks of a kung fu master, being vigorous but solemn, strong but flexible, solid but mobile, Chan was basically an acrobatic character actor who emphasised versatility in play-acting, displaying facets of both clown and master.

As Chan became the number one box-office star of Hong Kong cinema, he acquired a small cult reputation among Western audiences through video releases of his films. Despite a couple of attempts to break into the US market, the actor has remained a specialised name with his own distinct cult among kung fu fans. Try as he might, Chan could not duplicate Lee's success in becoming a household name in America. But his influence and that of Hong Kong cinema's kung fu genre on certain contemporary action stars in America are not negligible, as can be seen in the performances of Jean-Claude Van Damme or Steven Seagal. In Asia, Chan's popularity was, and still is, phenomenal.

Chan's star began to shine in the late 70s though he had been a movie actor since the beginning of that decade. In the mid-70s, he was signed by director Luo Wei, who had directed Bruce Lee's first two films in Hong Kong. Luo featured him as a Bruce Lee clone in *New Fist of Fury/Xin Jingwu Men* (1976), *The Killer Meteors/Fengyu Shuangliu Xing* (1978), *To Kill With Intrigue/Jianhua Yanyu Jiangnan* (1977), *The Magnificent Bodyguard/Feidu Juanyun Shan* (1978), *Spiritual Kung Fu/Quan Jing* (1978) and *Dragon Fist/Long Quan* (1979). With the possible exception of *Dragon Fist*, these films were routine kung fu films. Chan was wooden in most of them, being required simply to go through the kung fu motions. One of his movies during this period was actually entitled *Shaolin Wooden Men/Shaolin Muren Xiang* (1976), which fortunately did not prove too prophetic.

Chan was at his animated best in two 1978 releases: Yuen Woo-ping's *Snake in the Eagle's Shadow/Shexing Diaoshou* and *Drunken Master/Zui Quan*. These two films were Chan's breakthrough into the big leagues. The actor created a character type that was a cross between a human livewire and a boy next door, mostly mischievous but also capable of sensitivity. The two films form a diptych through the presence of Chan and his co-star Yuan Xiaotian, a veteran king fu actor who, in both films, played the role of an old master to Chan's kung fu kid.

In *Snake in the Eagle's Shadow*, Chan's character, named Jianfu (to signify simple-mindedness and other characteristics of a sentimental fool), was finely balanced between comic and dramatic personae. Jianfu is an orphan employed as a menial servant in a kung fu school whose students use him as a punchbag. He meets an old beggar (Yuan Xiaotian) who teaches him the techniques of the snake fist. With his newly-learned skills, Jianfu teaches the bullies in his school a lesson but in the process attracts the attention of a passer-by, a master of the 'eagle's claw' dedicated to wiping out all disciples of the snake fist. The final duel sees Jianfu fighting the master of the eagle's claw, and securing victory through a combination of snake fist and cat's paw – the technique that gives the film its title. The scenes of kung fu practice and induction into the snake fist technique are the best things in the film, with their blend of slapstick, inventive acrobatics and sense of adventure. These scenes show Chan developing the masochistic style of his brand of kung fu, where a disciple undergoes tough training (equated with physical suffering) to master the art of a particular style of kung fu.

In *Drunken Master*, Chan plays the young Wong Fei-hung (the legendary character of old Cantonese movies and, more recently, Tsui Hark's *Once Upon a Time in China* series), nicknamed 'the naughty panther'. So naughty is Fei-hung that his father has summoned a grizzled old drunk named Sou Fa-zai (Yuan Xiaotian) to discipline his son. Sou teaches Wong the techniques of drunken kung fu, styled after the Eight Immortals, and it is through the comprehensive application of all styles that Wong defeats a mercenary hired to kill his father in the final duel. This time, Chan was encouraged to go overboard with his fool characterisation and he played it broad indeed, throwing away the mask of sensitivity that covered Jianfu in *Snake in the Eagle's Shadow*. So successful was the film and Chan's clown-like characterisation of Wong Fei-hung that the persona of the mischievous kung fu kid was to stay with him for several years.

At the end of 1978, Chan was firmly established as the new superstar in Hong Kong cinema. He was quick to capitalise on his success. After appearing in Luo Wei's *Dragon Fist* in 1979, he was freed of his contract with the director and embarked on an independent career, free to direct his own pictures and create his own screen personality. Before examining his career as a director, it is useful to refer to Luo Wei's *Dragon Fist* as a minor watershed film. It is an untypically serious Jacky Chan action picture. The dramatic tone is Jacobean in mood and it must be assumed that Chan wanted to show he was a capable dramatic performer along with his other talents. His willingness to tackle dramatic roles has been demonstrated in the course of his career in the 80s, sometimes in unexpected ways, by counterpointing light comedy with sudden bursts of serious 'dramatic' acting, as in *Police Story/Jingcha Gushi* (1985), but more often as tragedy sweetened with maudlin sentimentality, as in *Heart of the Dragon/Long de Xin* (1985), directed by Sammo Hung.

The story of *Dragon Fist* revolves around revenge. Chan plays Haoyun, the most outstanding disciple in a kung fu clan whose master is killed by the head of a rival clan, an expert of the Flying Kick. Haoyun seeks revenge but discovers that his enemy, in a fit of repentance, had cut off his own leg. By the end of the picture, Haoyun not only did not carry out his revenge but also helped his erstwhile enemy in a new vendetta against another clan. Of all of Chan's pictures, *Dragon Fist* is most involved with plot although action is not wanting. It features Chan in a dramatic, entirely humourless role which makes more of his ability as an actor than had previously been asked of him. It is the one film in his early career which gave him the best opportunity to display the conventional dramatic skills he had acquired in addition to kung fu training in an opera school during his childhood days.

Chan's first film as his own director is *The Fearless Hyena/Xiao Quan Guaizhao* (1979), the first chapter in a trilogy which includes his subsequent self-directed works, *The Young Master/Shidi Chuma* (1980) and *Dragon Lord/Long Shaoye* (1982). All three films are set in the countryside during the late Qing period and Chan's persona is that of the precocious kung fu kid who makes mischief but who is relied upon in dire situations to save the day – really the same character type that he portrayed in *Drunken Master*.

Chan's hero, also named Chan (the actor's real surname; most of his screen characters also adopt one or both parts of his professional Chinese name) is the youngest surviving member of the Xingyi School of kung fu which has been destroyed by a eunuch (played by Ren Shiguan). Chan lives with his grandfather (James Tien) in a countryside hide-out, practising kung fu under the grandfather's tutelage. After many years has passed, the eunuch catches up with them and kills the grandfather and another elderly Xingyi refugee known as the 'unicorn' (Chen Huilou). It is up to Chan to exact revenge. The plot structure which stresses pursuit, escape, training-in-hiding and the revenge motif is all too familiar. The film moves erratically from tragedy to comedy – one more indication that Chan was looking for ways of integrating drama and action – but it is Chan's style of comic kung fu which finally shapes the movie. Before his character 'matures' into a perfect fighting instrument, the audience is treated to several comedy sequences involving Chan as master of a martial arts school run by a buffoon (Li Kun). Chan has to fight off challengers and, in one scene, dresses up as a woman – this being the best way to feign off a macho challenger. Even the relatively serious business of carrying out his revenge in the climactic duel with the eunuchs is not without comic ingredients: Chan defeats his opponent by using a new technique which combines the elements of human emotions such as sorrow, anger, humour and happiness. Sorrow is used to fool, anger to attack, humour to evade, and happiness to tease and scare.

In 1980, Chan signed with Golden Harvest, the studio with which he would eventually establish a kind of partnership to make his own movies prior to setting up his own production company. Under the new deal, he made *The Young Master*, his second film as his own director. It was also the second film in the 'pastoral' trilogy and as such, *The Young Master* is a transitional work, though not a minor one. It provided Chan with his first real occasion to display the kind of choreographic skills that he would use to greater effect in his mature phase as a director.

The film opens with a festive sequence which places Chan, playing a character called Ah Loong (Cantonese for Dragon), in the context of tradition and martial arts discipline. Ah Loong is a student in a martial arts school run by Master Tian (played by Tian Feng). He is called upon to dance the part of the head in a lion dance contest with a rival team, replacing his more senior schoolmate Ah Keung, who has feigned injury in order to dance for the rival team. Ah Loong loses the contest, to the consternation of Master Tian who feels betrayed by his two best students. In a fit of pique, the master expels Ah Keung. Ah Loong makes an emotional atonement speech and the master agrees to reinstate Ah Keung. But he has already departed and Ah Loong is sent to look for him.

Here we see another glimpse of Chan indulging in the dramatic mode, perhaps in an attempt to break through the stereotype of the comic kung fu character he had created for himself. He was shaping a screen persona that would eventually develop into a character more heroic in tone but still with an ingenuous side. The balance in *The Young Master* was heavily skewed towards comedy rather than drama. Ah Loong sets out to search for Ah Keung and is caught in a series of picaresque misadventures. He meets a father and son team of law enforcers (played by Sek Kin and Yuan Biao) who mistake him for an outlaw. The outlaw they are really after is Ah Keung who has fallen into bad company and assisted the escape of a notorious kung fu bandit known as 'Big-Foot' Kim (played by Korean martial arts champion, Whong In-sik). Big Foot is so called because of his powerful left leg. After more humorous setbacks, Chan's kung fu clown goes into action to capture the bad guys. In the protracted finale, he must subdue Big Foot Kim. It is a remarkable action set-piece giving full rein to Chan's comprehensive kung fu skills which stress overall stamina and flexibility in tone-muscles over expertise and mastery in technique.

Dragon Lord completes the trilogy marking Chan's exercises in direction. He refines his screen persona of the irrepressible country kid whose derring-do and mischief-making hide an essentially shy and coy-romantic ego, distinct from the kung fu clown of the earlier phase of his career. His character here, also called Loong, is the son of a gentrified scholar who insists on instilling scholarly disciplines in his unruly boy. For the most part, *Dragon Lord* comes across as a pastoral comedy with Loong as a Chinese Huckleberry Finn, having fun with his childhood friend Ah Niu, and competing with him to woo the village beauty. The cornerstone of the film is a couple of set-pieces which are strong in festive atmosphere and village games: Loong and his mates feature as team-players in competitive matches rather like rugby and soccer. The former is played with a hardened Easter egg varnished in gold, the latter with a shuttlecock. A Masonic-type thriller involving a sinister one-eyed smuggler of antiques (played by Whong In-sik) intrudes into the light-hearted activities, justifying more orthodox kung fu action. In the finale, Loong defeats the villain through gumption rather than skill. This is in line with Chan's portrayal of characters who are not serious kung fu masters but comic buffoons whose abilities in the martial arts are nevertheless at the level of the masters. In *The Young Master*, Chan seems to be saying that specialising in technique will not be sufficient to master kung fu. Chan's whole screen persona testifies to the fact that kung fu must be based on character, that it must be flexibly applied to allow for genuine expression of one's character.

With *Project A/A Jihua* (1982), Chan moved into his mature phase as a multi-hyphenated film-maker (actor-stuntman-director-stunt co-ordinator-kung fu choreographer), coming up with one of his best constructed films. The kung fu sequences are better integrated with the narrative than had been the case in his previous films. Chan also appears less like a clown. Henceforth, the Chan persona would be that of an optimistic hero, restless and eager to play his part in Hong Kong's social development. In the film, Chan portrays Sergeant Ma Yu-loong of the Hong Kong Marine Police who wants his administration to be proactive in wiping out pirates active in Hong Kong's outlying islands. Before his regiment can set out on a search and destroy mission, the police vessels are blown up by an advance party of pirates protected by a local tycoon. Without boats and support from the government, the Marine Police is disbanded and regrouped as a unit of the ground force. The inter-force rivalry between the marine and land police is reminiscent of the army–navy rivalry in many a John Ford war film. The atmosphere is just as ingenuously patriotic and male-centred (there is even a bar-brawl scene between the two forces). So too is the final resolution: both sides join hands to destroy the pirates, with Chan leading a reconstituted marine police force. The other eminent Hollywood master brought to mind is Buster Keaton, whose name is most often mentioned by Western critics when describing the films of Jacky Chan. The Keatonesque influences are obvious in two superb sequences which rank among the most unforgettable in Chan's films. In the first one, Sergeant Ma is being pursued, cat and mouse fashion, by the pirates on bicycles. He evades them in a labyrinth of alleys and proceeds to knock them off their bikes, using his own bicycle as a weapon. The other sequence takes place inside a clock tower where Sergeant Ma is trapped together with his adversary. They engage in kung fu attack and defence, Ma dodging his opponent by jumping over the gears and meshing with the cogwheels of the giant clock which goes awry. The scene ends with Chan's sergeant hanging from the minute hand outside the tower. Finally, he drops to the ground with two canvas awnings acting as buffer. Jacky Chan earned his spurs, as Ford might say, with *Project A*.

Project A, Part II/ A Jihua Xuji (1987) is the lavish sequel continuing the adventures of Sergeant Ma Yu-loong. Ma is promoted to superintendent in charge of the Western District Police Department. His job is to wipe out crime and corruption in the police department. In many ways, this sequel is even more accomplished than the original, not only in the true-to-life recreation of Hong Kong in the Edwardian era (the production and wardrobe designers had a field day with exquisite renditions of sets and costumes of that era), but also as a narrative piece of work. Chan handles the ins and outs of a narrative cluttered with characters and incidents with a masterly sense of rhythm and tempo. The cast of characters is exceptionally colourful. Apart from the surviving remnants of the pirate force destroyed in the last picture, who vow to get even with Ma, there are pretty young women whose task in the picture is not just ornamental: they are patriotic revolutionaries out to collect funds in Hong Kong for the overthrow of the Qing Dynasty. They are stalked by agents of the Qing government who have hired a corrupt Hong Kong police inspector as their mole to stop the revolutionaries from using Hong Kong as their base. Amidst all these characters is Superintendent Ma, never failing in his duties and unswerving in his sworn allegiance to Hong Kong under His Majesty's Government, even when he is tempted by the girls, framed by a corrupt colleague or asked to join the revolutionary cause for the betterment of China (Ma declines, replying that politics is not his line). *Project A, Part II* is a work which provides the clearest perspective on Chan's own personality and his attachment to Hong Kong. The last action sequence in the film sees his screen character saving the revolutionaries from their Qing enemies. Although Chan's devotion is to Hong Kong (in a sense, *Project A*,

Part II is his love letter to the territory) he also knows enough to stand on the right side of history by having his character support the anti-Qing revolutionaries. On that level, *Project A, Part II* also works as an allegory of Hong Kong's 1997 dilemma. Like the majority of Hong Kong people, Chan's loyalty to Hong Kong is in no doubt, but he is also torn by an attachment to China.

The success of the *Project A* films firmly established Jacky Chan as the top box-office star of Hong Kong cinema in the 80s. More importantly, they demonstrated his skills as a director capable of handling narrative as well as action. He had also created a screen persona which showed the actor at his most confident, no longer having to resort to buffoonery to win audience approval. The new screen persona was more or less a straight version of the Fool character that he had been tagged with ever since the success of *Snake in the Eagle's Shadow* and *Drunken Master* – cheery and optimistic but with new-found virtues of honesty and loyalty in place of the vices of mischief and duplicity.

In his next film, *Police Story* (1985), Chan gave his most mature rendition of this new screen persona. He plays Sergeant Chan Ka-koey, a character almost inter-changeable with Sergeant Ma Yu-loong of *Project A*. Displaying a wider range of emotions expertly integrated into the narrative, so that the movie plays like light drama rather than an uneven spread of comedy and tragedy, the character has remained the one the actor would most like to be identified with. The film opens with a spectacular sequence in which a hillside squatter village is razed to the ground when drug dealers drive their cars through the village, plunging down the hill to escape a police dragnet. In the equally re-markable follow-up action sequence where Chan hangs from an umbrella hooked to the end of a hijacked bus containing the fugitives, the drug king-pin Chu To (played by director Chor Yuen) is finally apprehended. The plot centres on Sergeant Chan's protection of a state witness: Chu's secretary Salina Fong (played by Lin Ching-hsia), who at first refuses to co-operate but is brought around when Chu tries to have her killed. Freed by the court, Chu plots a successful frame-up against the sergeant who then becomes a fugitive wanted for the murder of a fellow police officer.

When not involved in a stunt, Chan's handling of the variety of emotions his character goes through is his most assured: from the sergeant's cocky optimism to the comedy of mistaken intentions when the sergeant's girlfriend, May (played by Maggie Cheung), finds him bringing Salina home, to the desperate pathos of his fall from grace as a wanted fugitive. The film comes to a satisfactory conclusion with yet another top-notch action sequence set inside a shopping mall. Chan takes on his enemies in a destructive orgy of violence, the aesthetic dimensions of which are worthy of comparison with Bruce Lee's incredible displays of kung fu anger in *Fist of Fury*. The action culminates in a breathtaking stunt in which Chan slides down a cable wired up with bulbs and light displays – which explode from the force of the slide. Chan lands many floors down to capture the chief villain. Needless to say, it is incumbent upon any critic to point out that Jacky Chan did all his own stunts.

In the sequel, *Police Story Part II/Jingcha Gushi Xuji* (1988), Chan botches his narrative somewhat by caricaturing his previous characters, including the villain Chu To (again played by Chor Yuen) who now appears as an invalid released from prison because he has only three months to live. Wasting no time to take revenge on Chan, he starts off by harassing Chan's girlfriend May (Maggie Cheung). Chan takes the law into his own hands and is sacked for his brutality against Chu's minions. But he is coaxed back into service just when he is set to fly away with May for a holiday in Bali. Chan is assigned to deal with a gang of terrorists extorting ransom money from a business syndicate by bombing its shopping complexes. The terrorists kidnap May and force Chan to be their bag-man, setting the stage for another fireworks finale. In the tradition of Chan's best movies, which include the two *Project A* films and *Police Story*, the climax is a brilliant action set-piece taking place in a giant warehouse designed to contain all sorts of platforms, traps, pitfalls and factory implements, which are used as weapons. The protagonists of the scene, the set, the props, are completely utilised in a self-sufficient way. Although the film does not attain the distinction of *Project A*, Chan discharges his directorial and other responsibilities more than adequately. An original touch in character-depiction was the portrayal of one of the terrorists as a mute kung fu fighter who is also an expert in fire-crackers.

Mr Canton and Lady Rose/Qiji (1989) is Jacky Chan's boisterous remake of a Damon Runyon story twice filmed by Frank Capra as *Lady for a Day* (1933) and *Pocketful of Miracles* (1961). The original plot and 30s atmosphere are faithfully observed. Chan plays Charlie Kuo, a naïve country lad from Guangdong who goes to Hong Kong to look for work but finds himself an innocent bystander in a gang war. Inducted on the spot to help a wounded gang boss, Kuo accidentally becomes his successor. Kuo slips into the role like an eel into water, helped by his extraordinary skills in kung fu. For luck, he buys a red rose every morning from 'Lady Rose', an old woman who writes to her daughter in Shanghai making believe that she is a high society lady. When the daughter decides to visit Hong Kong with her prospective bridegroom and rich father-in-law, Chan turns Lady Rose into the lady of her letters, and stages a masquerade to impress the visitors. In the meantime, he has to fend off the police and his rival, Tiger Lo (played by Taiwanese actor Ke Junxiong), who wants a piece of the action. Although action is really the key word in every Jacky Chan picture, it somehow recedes into the background in this one. Here, Chan seems even more determined to prove he is not just an action director. Hardly a routine production, *Mr Canton and Lady Rose* basks in the kind of glorious production values of old Hollywood as it existed under the studio system. This alone guarantees the picture top quality, with the added value of vintage action scenes which one continues to associate with Jacky Chan.

In between pictures produced domestically in Hong Kong (which show him at his best), Chan set out to break into the international market, particularly America, with appearances in co-productions which were deliberately designed to showcase his talents. The first was *Battle Creek Brawl* aka *The Big Brawl* (1980), which, as it turned out, was one of American director Robert Clouse's more adept efforts at synthesising Western and Eastern action. Chan stars as Jerry Kwan, whose father runs a restaurant in Chicago in the 30s. Local godfather Dominici (José Ferrer), demands protection money but uses a velvet glove to collect because he knows a better way to make money off the Kwans – by coercing Jerry into joining a Texas freestyle brawling contest. Chinese kung fu is thus contrasted with Western pugilism and wrestling. Jerry Kwan prevails of course but not before he has done away with gangsters who try to fix the contest. Chan's energetic presence lifts the picture above the average. Typically for Clouse, there is a hollowness to the non-action sequences despite the better than usual supporting cast.

The Protector (1985) was Chan's other international showcase. Cast alongside Chan was American actor Danny Aiello. Despite the presence of the co-star and the helming of an American director, James Glickenhaus, the film looks surprisingly like a made-to-order Hong Kong kung fu action movie. Chan is Billy Wong, a Chinese-American cop who is sent to Hong Kong to track down and rescue an American girl who has been kidnapped by a Hong Kong crime boss operating a 'heroin pipeline' to America. Partnered by Aiello's Danny Garoni, Wong is in his element in Hong Kong. The first ten minutes of the film showing Wong in action as a New York City cop, take some getting used to because the action is all guns and chases – which may be routine in Hollywood thrillers but indicate that Western directors still could not understand the premise of kung fu action. As usual with Chan, the do-it-yourself stunt work is remarkable. One sequence is particularly outstanding, featuring Chan chasing a bad guy attempting to get away in a sampan. Chan jumps from boat to boat moored in the harbour, pole-vaults over the water, scoots from deck to deck, getting through every hurdle to finally land on the sampan and catch the villain.

As his own director, Chan made *Armour of God/Long Xiong Hu Di* (1987) as a further foray into 'international' film-making. Shot in European locations with Chan as an Indiana Jones-type adventurer known as the 'Condor', the movie was nearly aborted by a case of bad luck when a stunt went badly wrong and Chan suffered a life-threatening injury (the accident is recorded in the out-takes shown at the end of the film under the credits). Possibly the weakest of Chan's self-directed works, the film is still a considerable visual display of stunt co-ordination. The sequel, *Armour of God, Part II: Operation Condor/Feiying Jihua* (1991) sees Chan back in his international mode, playing the Condor once again and roaming the globe (locations in Spain, Morocco and the Philippines) in search of gold. Reportedly the most expensive movie ever made by the Hong Kong film industry, costing about HK$100 million, or US$12 million, it is much better conceived and realised than its predecessor.

The Condor, accompanied by three women (one European blonde and two Hong Kong beauties), set out to search for gold which had been looted by the German Army during the last world war and hidden in the Sahara

Desert. The players try their best to keep things fresh and lively, no mean feat when half the movie is played out in the desert. The women have to endure lots of slaps and blows to the solar plexus, all in good fun. The climactic set-piece takes place inside a large set, a vaulted chamber with movable panels for walls and a giant fan operated by a control room. The Condor and his adversaries fight as the giant fan blows against them, plastering them against the wall like flies – they continue to fight nevertheless. The film's huge costs, desert setting and mindless burlesque evoke nothing less than the fiasco of Elaine May's *Ishtar*, but Chan just about manages to keep adverse comparisons at bay. He is the pivot around which interest revolves since the audience can always expect a good action sequence whenever the plot, the characters and the sets become too cumbersome.

Taking a breather from directing in the early 90s, Chan was content to appear as an actor in routine adventures directed by others. Chu Yen-ping's *Island of Fire/ Huo Shao Dao* (1991), was a made-in-Taiwan prison movie of interest only for its cast of stalwart action stars including Chan, Sammo Hung, Andy Lau and veteran Wang Yu. *Twin Dragons/ Shuanglong Hui* (1992), with direction credited to Tsui Hark and Ringo Lam, used the gimmick of casting Chan as twin brothers separated at birth but reunited in a modern-day adventure. Despite shoddy special effects the movie easily adjusts to Chan's personality, with a high quota of incredible stunts and death-defying antics. *City Hunter/ Chengshi Lieren* (1993), directed by Wong Jing, was a juvenile cartoon-like adventure, inspired by Japanese manga, and set on board a super-luxury liner with Chan foiling a hijack attempt by Western terrorists.

The actor's new policy of delegating direction, including stunt co-ordination, to younger protégés paid off spectacularly in the third edition of the *Police Story* series, *Police Story 3 – Super Cop/ Chaoji Jingcha* (1992). The film contains possibly the most daring stunts ever in a Jacky Chan movie, staged from moving trains, flying helicopters, speeding cars or motorcycles. Each and every stunt is co-ordinated with extraordinary precision, one following the other seemlessly. Thus, a car chase gives way to an escape on a train, followed by a helicopter attempt to rescue the villain riding on top of the train. Chan aborts the rescue by hanging from the helicopter's ladder; the ladder catches on the train and the helicopter literally makes a landing on top of it. As the protagonists continue to struggle, the train chugs along until the helicopter hits a bridge and explodes. None of this would have excited the viewer but for the sheer Keatonesque invention of its stunt co-ordinators and the panache of its performers.

With *Police Story 3*, action effects and stuntwork come of age in Hong Kong cinema. It is proof, if any were needed, that Hong Kong's action genre, in the right hands, is not only the most dynamic of all action genres in the world, it is also the most graceful, the most balletic. Chan reprises his role of Chan Ka-koey, assigned to infiltrate a drug warlord's operations in China, Thailand and Malaysia. In China, he helps the warlord's convicted associate, The Leopard, escape from prison. A hilarious episode follows in which Chinese police put on a masquerade in order to convince The Leopard that Chan is really a criminal. It recalls Chan's fondness for the kind of vaudeville-like showmanship, play-acting and camaraderie that were seen to greater effect in *Mr Canton and Lady Rose*. The story moves to Thailand where the warlord, Tsoi Ba (played by Tsang Kong), outwits his rivals in a drug deal, and finally to Malaysia where Tsoi Ba plans to rescue his wife who has been sentenced to death for drug trafficking. It is the Malaysian locations (Kuala Lumpur's Merdeka Square, the Railway Station and the Selangor Club) which provide the backdrop to Chan's spectacular action stunts.

Police Story 3 could be described as a contemporary kung fu classic, with Chan giving all his usual verve and aplomb, but offering no surprises in the interpretation of his old character. For the fourth edition of the series, however, Chan did surprise. *Crime Story/ Zhong An Zu* (1993) was a drastic departure from the series. Gone are the humour and fetching optimism of Sergeant Chan in the previous films. Promoted to inspector, we see him checking into a police psychiatrist's office in the film's opening minutes, suffering from the after-effects of a killing spree during a chase of gun-crazy criminals. Nevertheless, Chan is fit enough to be given a next assignment, protecting a property magnate, Wong Yat-fei, who has received kidnap threats, which Chan is eventually unable to prevent. The kidnap itself (apparently based on a real incident) is an audacious affair; the kidnappers jump from their own cars into Wong's Mercedes Benz while he is still driving and take over the car as their associates drive behind and keep a lookout. This is followed by an excitingly violent chase with Chan failing to catch the kidnappers and having to save a wounded policeman. The film develops at breakneck speed with classical Jacky Chan kung fu acrobatics and a spectacular finish in a typical Hong Kong tenement slum where Chan faces off his opponents including a corrupt colleague named Hung (played by the obese Kent Cheng), one of the masterminds of the kidnap.

The fundamental flaw in *Crime Story* is the contrast it provides of two action styles: one belonging to director Kirk Wong, a director with an abrasive bull-in-a-China-shop style, and the other to its star, Jacky Chan. Wong's approach to action is tuned towards the extreme: truculent, stubborn, unrelenting. The director is not known for martial arts choreography and neither is he known as a practitioner of kung fu. His best films were in the gangster genre, where somewhat clichéd material was distinguished by a heavy-handed personal style. Chan's style, on the other hand, is realistic but fundamentally graceful, almost ballet-like. Chan needed no direction (or perhaps could not brook any direction) in his martial arts scenes which thus came across as autonomous segments. At its best, the two styles are integrated into an exciting and well-made movie, but at times, Chan seems to be acting the matador to Wong's bull. *Crime Story* will be remembered for its presentation of a tougher, less sympathetic, screen persona for Chan. From the effervescent kung fu kid, Chan becomes a psychologically afflicted action hero unable to make sense of the violence around him and further disillusioned by the discovery that one of his role models is a corrupt cop.

Although Chan's own style and personality may be considered as unrelenting as Kirk Wong's, the appeal of Chan is based on the simplicity of his art rather than the intricacy of narrative structures or complex characterisations. This was a principle which Chan was prone to challenge occasionally by switching from comic to dramatic personae, mostly with mixed results. In offering audiences a far more complex, even psychopathic, character than they bargained for, *Crime Story* performed disappointingly at the box-office. Perhaps realising his mistake, Chan quickly reverted to type in *Drunken Master II/ Zui Quan II* (1994). Older but still hyper-kinetic (and masochistically inclined), Chan reprised the character of the young mischief-maker Wong Fei-hung, the part that had made him a superstar in Yuen Woo-ping's *Drunken Master* (1978). Fourteen years later, Chan offers no variations in his interpretation of young Wong Fei-hung, who seems not to have aged, at least not compared to other recent interpretations of the character, as in Jet Li's in the *Once Upon a Time in China* series. As in the original Yuen Woo-ping film, the sequel being directed by Lau Kar-leong, the focus is Wong Fei-hung's special skill in drunken kung fu fighting.

The story has Wong Fei-hung pitted against a group of kung fu thugs in collusion with foreign consular officials who abuse their privileges by smuggling antiques hidden in crates of steel products marked for export. Director Lau, himself a kung fu master, plays 'the last of the Manchu kung fu guardians', dispatched to retrieve one particular item of historical importance from the smugglers – the seal of the emperors. This item mistakenly falls into Wong Fei-hung's hands who must now prevent it from falling into the clutches of the foreigners and their Chinese thugs. The latter are shown as betraying their culture through their appearances: they wear Western suits and look clean-cut, the very models of distinguished Western gentlemanly appearance. Wong, wearing a Chinese robe, defeats the thugs by swilling alcohol to prompt his drunken kung fu skills into action. The final duel is set in a steel works where Chan displays his usual blend of masochism and ballet skills by rolling in a bed of burning coal.

After the commercially unsuccessful attempt to change his screen persona into a heavy-handed hero in Kirk Wong's *Crime Story* (1993), Chan plays Wong like the clown he was in the original, seemingly still fresh and less astute in his grasp of kung fu. In playing the clown, Chan may have resorted to playing it safe, but the formula of broad comedy, echoed in Anita Mui's performance as Chan's comic sidekick, and spectacular kung fu stunts have maintained Chan's star in Hong Kong cinema for nearly two decades. The formula may be, and indeed has been, disparaged by critics. However, Chan's personal style and his attempts at dramatic characterisations are mitigating factors distinguishing a genre all too often consigned to the trash bin of cinematic criticism.

Jacky Chan has had a good run of super-stardom and still shows no signs of burnout. The significance of a film such as *Police Story 3 – Super Cop* lies in Chan proving his staying power in the classical kung fu genre. He alone in the Hong Kong cinema of the 90s seems oblivious to fads. While his younger colleagues are entangling themselves in the postmodern phase of Hong Kong film-making in the 90s, Chan seems frozen in his own time. He is really showing that kung fu is timeless and that when practised with humour, charm and precision, it is a force unto itself. As a personification of that force, Chan is unsurpassed. He should be admired as one of the best of the purely physical performers in world cinema. His career is still on-going at the time of writing, but already in his best films, his combination of grace and derring-do have shown a face of Hong Kong cinema that is utterly irresistible.

PART THREE
Path Breakers

Chapter Ten

The New Wave

PERIOD OF TRANSITION AND THE PRECEDING WAVE
The kung fu genre made Hong Kong cinema internationally known, but its popularity unbalanced the perspectives of foreign audiences. They concluded that the Hong Kong film industry was capable only of producing kung fu films, and they were not too far wrong. In the first half of the 70s, kung fu movies so dominated film-making in Hong Kong that it overshadowed the other genres. In retrospect, one can see that this dominance laid the groundwork for the emergence of the Hong Kong new wave in the 80s. The kung fu genre's treatment of form, content and character accelerated the break with the kind of realism codified by the Cantonese family melodramas popular throughout the 50s and 60s; moreover, the notion of social relevance practised by kung fu films involved the mobilisation of more directly vernacular cultural elements such as 'vulgar' topical dialogue. Kung fu films served as an outlet for working-class audiences which may have identified with the archetypal kung fu heroes as underdog characters venting their pent-up frustrations and anger at the establishment (the international popularity of kung fu suggests that this was probably a reaction not limited to Hong Kong), and finally, the frenetic pace and dynamism of kung fu films also reflected both the economic boom and increasing sense of self-confidence among the Hong Kong Chinese in the 70s.

By the mid-70s, the once popular 'realist' melodramas had all but vanished from the big screens, being replaced by films of 'social relevance', such as those made by actor-director Lung Kong, where realism came coated with a degree of sensationalism. Realism now consisted of a cross between soap opera and exploitation film, tackling sensational topics such as prostitution, drug abuse and social hysteria. One feature of this new soap operatic realism was a boldness, particularly in relation to sexuality, never seen before in Hong Kong cinema. The 70s was the decade when the sexual revolution finally hit Hong Kong screens. Sex and nudity became acceptable, as exemplified by the series of sex comedies and soft-core entertainments directed by Li Hanxiang, Lui Kei and He Fan. The more successful of these films dealt with moral transgression which took in Christian notions of sin and accurately reflected the increasingly cynical attitudes and mores of the time. Moral transgression, or the notion of sin,

Hong Kong style, included sex, gambling and fraudulent business dealings. In contrast, the realism of the 50s and 60s had deployed a didactic approach to the need to observe morality and Confucianist family ethics.

Lung Kong's films bridged the didacticism of the 60s and the more exploitative 70s realism. In the late 60s, Lung's films were social exposés, as represented by *The Story of a Discharged Prisoner/ Yingxiong Bense* (1967) and *Teddy Girls/Feinü Zhengzhuan* (1969). In that sense, Lung was one of Hong Kong's most resilient film-makers in the 70s who refused to be influenced by the commercial trend of kung fu and martial arts. He did some of his best work in the early 70s, addressing serious subject matter which could pull in the crowds otherwise flocking to see kung fu movies. He was regarded by his fans as a quality director because of his serious themes. Like Stanley Kramer in America, Lung saw the cinema as an avenue for social propaganda. His movies were laced with liberal messages under a coating of sensationalism.

Yesterday, Today and Tomorrow/ Zuotian Jintian Mingtian (1970) is a Camus-like tale of a Hong Kong infested with the plague. Residents fall ill and die by the dozens. The whole city is declared a plague-stricken territory. Against this background, an overseas Chinese writer falls in love with a tour conductress; a television journalist tries to hide an extra-marital affair from his wife; families in the slums break down from the effects of the disease, a process exacerbated by drug abuse and emotional distress. The film offers a bleak, apocalyptic vision of a city seized with panic and fear. It was let down by poor acting and bad cutting (the film was drastically re-cut for general release before the censors would approve it). Another film, *The Call Girls/ Yingzhao Nülang* (1973), dealt with prostitution as experienced by five women. In theme and structure, the film was similar to Lung's earlier film, *Teddy Girls/ Feinü Zhengzhuan* (1969), which offered case-studies of female teenage delinquents.

Lung's most thematically ambitious work was probably *Hiroshima 28/ Guangdao Ershiba* (1974). It tells the story of a Japanese family (played by Hong Kong actors) affected by the atomic bombing of Hiroshima. The director's sympathy for his Japanese characters went against the grain of anti-Japanese feelings among the public at the time, but its anti-nuclear message and humanist sentiment are the film's most outstanding qualities. Lung Kong strove for significance, but, at the same time, sought to satisfy the audience's desire for sensational entertainment, which may explain why his critical stock has not risen as it should. However, Lung has not been overlooked: John Woo paid him a tribute by remaking *The Story of a Discharged Prisoner* as *A Better Tomorrow* (1986) following quite faithfully the original plot and its final dénouement in a gun battle with the police.

The most significant film of the early 70s came, not from Lung Kong, but from a woman director who has since faded from popular memory. For about a decade, Tang Shuxuan's *The Arch/ Dong Furen* (1970) was the standard-bearer of art films produced in the territory. *The Arch* is a wonderful, intricate movie suffused with subterranean emotions and indirect nuances. Madam Dong (played by Lu Yan, or Lisa Lu as she is known in Hollywood) is a middle-aged widow whose observance of celibacy since her husband's death is being honoured with the erection of an arch of chastity in her village, a standard practice in ancient China. She lives with her old, sickly mother-in-law, a young daughter and a loyal house servant. They are obliged to take in a house guest, a cavalry captain (Roy Chiao) on temporary duty in the village. Madam Dong finds herself struggling with new emotions as she becomes sexually attracted to him. The captain speaks and glances softly at Madam Dong; but fearing scandal and gossip, she stops herself from responding, preferring to mask her feelings with proper decorum. As such, Madam Dong is the quintessential good Chinese woman who exudes 'constant dignity', as the captain describes her in a poem. She is well respected not only as a chaste widow, but also as a school-teacher and a paramedic healer. She speaks in a sedate monotone, and keeps her face composed and devoid of emotion. Madam Dong's rejection of the captain's love and her own desires is to be expected of a woman caught in the web of feudal repression. In the circumstances of her enclosed world of propriety and form, that is the most realistic option. When the captain turns his attentions to the daughter, who, in contrast to the mother, is flirtatious, carefree and open to advances, the most immediate solution is to marry her, even though he has not completely abandoned his feelings towards the mother. Marriage is the honourable way since the situation may otherwise compromise Madam Dong's status as a virtuous woman. In return for her propriety, Madam Dong is rewarded with a piece of stone – the arch. The final scenes depict Madam Dong close to mental breakdown. Gripped in a witching spell of frustrated sexuality, she cuts off the head of a cockerel with a scythe in order to placate the demons haunting her. The film ends with a defeated, resigned Madam Dong accepting the honour of the arch now erect and standing high behind her, like the gallows awaiting a condemned prisoner.

Shot in black and white by Subrata Mitra, Satyajit Ray's cinematographer in *The Apu Trilogy* and *Charulata*, the film is almost certainly the first recognisable new wave work in Hong Kong cinema. There is a level of experimentation with impressive and expressive visual effects achieved by rhythmic editing, long dissolves and freeze frames that is startling in its effectiveness. As a debut work of a woman director working in a film industry wholly dedicated to commercialism and the exploration of male virtues, the conceptual and visual achievement of *The Arch* is all the more extraordinary and a cause for celebration.

Tang's talents were not fully utilised by Hong Kong cinema, nor were they recognised. She made only three more films before emigrating to America. Significantly, these films contained an attack on Hong Kong as an unliveable city bereft of humane qualities, a materialist jungle motivated by mercenary greed. Tang's reputation rests on *The Arch* and on her next major film, *China Behind* (1974), a truly outstanding work of political and artistic relevance. It was the first film to condemn the madness of the Cultural Revolution and to foreshadow Hong Kong people's apprehension over 1997 which surfaced more dramatically in the 80s. However, political censorship delayed the film's release until 1987.[1]

Tang Shuxuan's achievements stand as beacons for an artistic Hong Kong cinema in the 70s. Although in the case of *China Behind*, the beacon was dimmed by poor distribution and censorship, word of mouth ensured the reputation of the films. Tang's influence and status have grown as time passes. One sees in her work a strong feminist theme as well as a concern for political events in China which would later embellish the films of Ann Hui. In her short career, Tang was the first and last iconoclast of Hong Kong cinema, the forerunner of modernist trends in her attempts to integrate innovative technique and moral conscience. Unlike most of her colleagues, Tang resisted selling out to commercialism until the very end of her short film-making career, when she made a handful of distinctly commercial films before abandoning cinema altogether.

MICHAEL HUI: EVERYMAN, COMEDIAN

Tang's early 70s career has parallels with Li Hanxiang's. Li dabbled in commercial hack work after the failure of his venture to create a studio for like-minded artists, which forced him to resume work as a contract director for Shaw Brothers. Li was another representative figure of the decade who made his mark outside the martial arts genre. He pioneered the trend towards a new kind of comedy distinguished by cynicism, ribaldry and soft-core sex. In 1972, Li's *The Warlord/Da Junfa* was released, featuring the debut of Michael Hui, a popular Cantonese-speaking television sitcom performer and variety show host, guaranteeing box-office success for *The Warlord*, which launched his film career. The role was a character part: the actor sported a shaven head and a walrus moustache to impersonate a crude and bawdy northern warlord who spoke Mandarin with a thick regional accent. Hui played the part with panache, clearly enjoying himself.

After starring in three more films for Li, Hui established a production company and signed a deal with Golden Harvest to make his own films. He would not only star but produce, write and direct them as well. It was a turning point. His spectacular progress thereafter had important ramifications for the development of Hong Kong cinema from the mid-70s onwards. Hui was viewed as the first truly 'local' star from his generation to make it in the 70s, typifying the rise of a generation which had grown up in Hong Kong in the 50s and 60s. Hui was also instrumental in reviving the use of Cantonese in Hong Kong cinema at a point when Cantonese movies were thought to be moribund.

If the reason for the demise of Cantonese cinema is attributed to the rise of television, it is fitting that a television personality was responsible for its revival, dramatically displacing the Mandarin cinema and heralding the rise of a new generation. Unlike old Cantonese movies, generally regarded as parochial and exclusively of interest to Cantonese-speaking audiences, Hui's movies were culturally protean, attractive to both Mandarin and Cantonese-speakers, eroding the clear-cut division between Mandarin and Cantonese audiences to the point where this division no longer applied in the 80s. Cinema offered audiences in Southeast Asia the choice of seeing a

Hui film in either Cantonese or Mandarin. His popularity with audiences beyond Hong Kong was the first sign that Hong Kong cinema was gaining acceptance as it began to overcome its Shanghai-influenced past. A new generation was taking over, and it was recognised that the culture of this new generation was rooted in Cantonese.

Hui's popularity was embedded in his comic personality. His characters won the hearts of audiences because not only were they funny, they were common people striving to be uncommon. In his first film, *Games Gamblers Play/Guima Shuangxing* (1974), Hui perfected his comic persona playing a con-artist who is basically a decent, vulnerable man, a mixture of materialism and humanity that seemed to symbolise something of the Hong Kong lifestyle. When his efforts to make ends meet go awry, he touches the hearts of viewers with his proletarian decency and humour. The narrative is episodic, like a TV sitcom, with a plot centring on two inveterate gamblers, Man (Michael Hui) and Kit (played by Michael's brother, Samuel), who share a cell in prison and become buddies. After their release, they stay in Man's apartment together with his sister and wife, becoming a close-knit family. Man tries to press his sister upon Kit so that they can be proper relatives by marriage. Most of the time, the two men get into trouble as they hustle, trick or cheat their way into big money.

Games Gamblers Play broke the box-office record at the time and firmly established Hui as a Hong Kong celebrity. It cleared the way to a directorial career for Michael and set the Hui brothers on the road to a successful series of films before Samuel, who had his own independent career as a pop star and leading man, chose to go his own way. Third brother Ricky plays a small role in this first film but would later be incorporated as a staple member of the team. Gambling is a subject close to the hearts of Chinese all over the world and helps to explain the film's immense popularity. Gambling movies had developed into a genre of their own and Hui tried to parody them along with the oft-stated penchant of the Chinese for gambling. However, it was Michael Hui's comic persona as a Hong Kong Everyman which made his first comedy so memorable.

Hui's second film as his own director, *The Last Message/Tianchai yu Baichi* (1975), was narratively more coherent than *Games Gamblers Play*, but still fell short of being a total cinematic success. It takes place inside a mental hospital where Michael's character, Ah Tim, works as an orderly. Samuel plays a male nurse with innovative ways of treating patients. Hui veils his comedy with a wry attack on capitalism. All the characters, including the mental patients, are obsessed with money and sunken treasures. Ah Tim is once again the archetypal Hong Kong worker, just one foot away from country hickdom: he spends his free time pulling out facial hairs with a set of tweezers, and cannot resist picking his nose even in the company of others. He steals minor valuables from the patients and extracts gold teeth from fresh corpses in the mortuary. Ah Tim and Samuel's male nurse form a partnership to salvage sunken treasure, the secret location of which they learned from one of the patients. The treasure proves to be fake and, in the end, Ah Tim is consigned to the hospital as a patient himself.

141

Contributing to the box-office success of the film were Samuel Hui's hit songs (as musical sequences in the MTV style, performed by Samuel, and his band, The Lotus) which are integrated into the narrative. Samuel co-wrote the music (with Joseph Koo) but supplied his own lyrics decrying the general craze for money and materialism. *The Last Message* is one instance of a Hui Brothers movie where the title tune and other hit numbers performed by Samuel outshone the comic episodes. Samuel's songs were also representative of the rise of the 'Canto-Pop' phenomenon: popular songs sung in Cantonese with derisive, trenchant lyrics that spoke for a whole generation.

The screen partnership between Michael and Samuel must be put in the context of Cantonese cinema's buddy-buddy or *pak-dong* strain of comedies, focusing on the interplay of two characters who have fallen on hard times and who attempt to pick themselves up by becoming buddies or partners. One touts a simple but effective philosophy of life in a smart-assed way, the other is an honest fool. The classic of all *pak-dong* movies was Ch'un Kim's *Intimate Partners/Nanxiong Nandi* (1960) mentioned in Chapter 2. It established an audience-friendly style of comedy unabashedly evoked and transformed by Hui with variations of his own. Michael would often play the part of the smart-ass partner, but with much meaner characteristics than any of his cinematic predecessors; Samuel took the part of the honest fool who was smarter than he looked. Their *pak-dong* interplay was at its most effective in *The Private Eyes/Banjin Baliang* (1976), one of the best of the Hui Brothers movies. Perfect comedy timing is immediately apparent in the opening scene where Michael's private detective tails a woman wearing platform sandals. Michael himself is wearing a pair of dirt-cheap cloth shoes. The series of visual gags which follow are most effective: someone steps on Hui's heels, ripping off the sole of one shoe; with foot exposed, Hui steps on a beggar's bowl and a smouldering cigarette stub. But even more successful is Hui's characterisation of the parsimonious private eye. Brothers Samuel and Ricky play his hired hands: Samuel, a cocky apprentice who is good at kung fu, and Ricky, a stammering assistant wearing a neckbrace. Michael pays them subsistence wages but offers two meals a day and board in his own apartment. So mean is Michael that he carries a calculator to add up the costs of things that Samuel and Ricky have destroyed in the course of duty, subtracting the amount from their pay. Michael finally gets his comeuppance as Samuel receives all the kudos for catching a gang of thieves who robbed the patrons of a cinema during a film show (one of many successful original ideas in the film). In the end, Michael realises his weaknesses and accepts the strengths of others – the customary touch of human vulnerability in Hui's comedies. Unlike his two previous films, there is no social message in *The Private Eyes* save that which applies to character weaknesses and, possibly, employer–employee relations. The character of the private eye is the meanest Michael Hui has played so far in his career, but, despite this, Hui's persona, as the classic 'little man', evokes sympathy and mirth.

142

Michael Hui ended the decade with arguably his best film, *The Contract/Maishen Qi* (1978), a satire of the television industry. Hui obviously knew what he was dealing with, offering a biting caricature of television executives and their profiteering mentality in the ratings war which turns them into heartless morons. A dip in the ratings means an immediate sacking for the manager, and he or she literally takes the plunge from the top of the building. This suicide-plunge has become a kind of ritual: everybody gathers around the window to watch the fall, and bets are taken as to how long before the actual jump. Once it is over, a picture of the victim is hung up and the business of recruiting another manager, who is able to increase ratings by whatever means, proceeds. Hui portrays Sit Chi-man, a bit performer in search of a big break. He gets it from a rival station who asks him to host a game show with a difference: *Da Bosha* or 'The Big Kill'. Its gimmick is that participants must literally gamble away their lives on million-dollar stakes by answering questions. The show is a success, but Sit has already signed a contract with 'Mouse TV', now under the management of Miss Wong, a one-eyed *femme fatale* who goes about in a wheelchair with two henchmen at her side. Sit wants to steal his contract from Miss Wong's safe with the help of his brother, an inventor nicknamed Edison (Ricky Hui). He succeeds, but Edison is locked inside the safe. In order to rescue him, Sit enlists the help of a magician (Samuel Hui). Mayhem is let loose in the TV station as the manageress and her two goons try to stop them.

Hui's genius in comedy characterisations is evident in his creation of Miss Wong, ostensibly a black-hearted spider-woman who snares her victims with legal contracts. Even so, when she, a disabled person, takes the final suicide plunge for her failure to raise the ratings, one feels sympathy for her. In the character of Miss Wong, Hui displays his habitual feeling for the soft side of human behaviour, particularly when this is set against an apparent nastiness. Hui usually played the nasty role, but in *The Contract* he stressed the other side of his persona – the victim. While all his characters are lovable brutes, they are also eternal victims of the system.

Hui did not substantially vary this persona in his subsequent films. In *Security Unlimited/Modeng Baobiao* (1981), he plays a senior security guard, Chow Sai-cheung, employed by a private agency. Chow is both the butt of jokes and a sadistic jester. In his spare time, he teaches raw recruits the business of enforcing security. There are hilarious moments where he shows the tricks of his trade, such as sticking two fingers into the barrels of a robber's shotgun so that the gun will backfire (it works too). Hui's capacity for inventive humour has never been stronger. Samuel and Ricky play new recruits who are constantly berated and abused by Chow but who outshine him in the end, Samuel being promoted to sergeant at Chow's expense. Chow is again one of Hui's typical little-man creations: a boastful clown who aspires to be a hero but is consistently weak-kneed when confronting the bad guys (particularly when he is outnumbered) as his face drops into a mournful grimace, crying and reminding his assailants that 'I am only making a living, fellows.' Again typical of Hui's lovable brutes,

Chow makes the ultimate sacrifice in giving up his life's pension to save the career of Ricky who has stolen company funds in order to help a girl. The three brothers play well together, with third brother Ricky coming into his own. Michael, of course, continues to be the centre. This was the last film with all three Hui brothers, as Samuel left the team and did not co-star in any of Michael's subsequent movies until 1990, in *The Front Page/Xin Banjin Baliang*, a sequel to *The Private Eyes*.

Hui's screen persona of the 80s varied a little from that of the 70s. His characters became caricatures: without the straight-man presence of Samuel Hui, Michael's characters turned into fools with heroic pretensions. The portrayals were still funny, but Hui had become too established a personality to care about the social function of his characters. He directed one more film, *Teppanyaki/Tieban Shao* (1984), where he outlined the double-edged side of his new persona, both a fool and a hero, a cuckold and a philanderer. The film was one of the year's box-office hits. Thereafter, Hui delegated the direction of his films to others – notably director Clifton Ko – for star vehicles which he produced and wrote: *Happy Ding Dong/Huanle Dingdang* (1986), *Inspector Chocolate/Shentan Zhu Guli* (1986), *Chicken and Duck Talk/Ji Tong Ya Jiang* (1988) and *Mr Coconut/ Hejia Huan* (1989).

To accommodate the audiences of the 80s, Hui increasingly incorporated political jokes into these later films, poking fun at Chinese leaders, the 1997 issue and Hong Kong people's ambivalent attitudes towards their Mainland cousins. His personality brought the films box-office success, but none of his works in the 80s could rival his satires of the 70s with their anti-materialistic messages and memorable characterisations of working-class 'little people'. He returned to directing in *The Magic Touch/Shen Suan* (1992), but did not regain his earlier form, although his portrayal of a fortune teller who divines fortunes by stroking the fingers of clients was one of his more inspired characterisations.

INTO THE WAVE: CRIME AND CORRUPTION

The 70s comedies of Michael Hui are atypical examples of 'message films' which have stood up well in the 90s as Hong Kong continued to prosper. The revival of Cantonese played its part in raising the audience's level of interest, bringing the intimacy between the low-life characters on the screen closer to the mainly working-class audience. However, Hui's films were in fact preceded by Chor Yuen's *The House of 72 Tenants/Qishier Jia Fangke* (1973) in the use of Cantonese. Based on a play originally performed in Shanghai (and filmed once before in 1963 by Mainland Chinese artists), the film was readapted to a Hong Kong setting, utilising both Mandarin-speaking stars and well-known Cantonese TV performers. The film was a co-production between Shaw Brothers and the main television station, HK-TVB.

Although the characters were from different regional backgrounds (Shanghai, Shandong, Chaozhou), everyone spoke Cantonese – the non-native speakers speaking it with their regional accents. The characters were linked by their environment, a ramshackle apartment complex built around a courtyard, and a common language, suggesting the primacy of environment over culture. This was one of the first instances in Hong Kong cinema to show the territory as a Cantonese society able to assimilate Chinese people from different regions. The film broke the box-office record of the time, a feat which some critics attributed not to its aesthetic quality (the film is stagy and uncinematic), but to sociological and linguistic factors. Actually, fortunes in the Hong Kong film industry had turned around by the late 70s: Cantonese was reasserting itself as a legitimate force in cinema, not just as a special dialect used occasionally by film-makers to placate Hong Kong's Cantonese-speaking audiences. When the new wave broke in 1979, its directors signalled their preoccupation not just with personal identity, but with cinematic identity by readopting the use and nuances of the Cantonese dialect. In the 80s, almost every film released was in Cantonese. It was the turn of Mandarin cinema to face a drastic decline.

The 70s was also a time of socio-economic transition for Hong Kong. The territory was mired in social problems brought about by its rise as a manufacturing centre exploiting cheap labour. The housing problem was reflected in *House of 72 Tenants*. The problem of society's lower strata in making ends meet formed the content of Michael Hui's films. Other social problems such as drug abuse and prostitution were seen in Lung Kong's films. Police corruption, a major problem in the 70s, was addressed in a number of crime thrillers, most notably Ng See-yuen's 1975 *Anti Corruption/Lianzheng Fengbao*. Hong Kong as a base for international drug trafficking, and the complicity of big business in crime activities, were the subject-matter of *Jumping Ash/Tiao Hui* (1976), co-directed by Leong Po-chih (his first feature) and the actress Josephine Siao.

Jumping Ash was a thriller about a cop's determined efforts to nail a drug king who was in turn targeted by two assassins. The film has been called a pre-new wave work – the first Hong Kong film to feature a 'new look' based on free-style editing, realistic location photography and a faster than usual pace. The style might have been influenced by the French new wave but the plot, which had more than a passing resemblance to *The French Connection*, was derived from Hollywood thrillers making an impact at the time. Though it is common practice among Hong Kong film-makers to derive plots from Hollywood movies, the habit has marked director Leong's career in particular.

In *Jumping Ash*, the accent was on suspense rather than on action, contrary to the balance in kung fu pictures. However, there was another conceptual difference in its treatment of the action thriller: the movie was in a lighter vein, even during bursts of action. Comic moments pervaded the film, conferring a refreshing feeling of gleeful experimentation in an otherwise conventional, Hollywood-derived thriller. *Jumping Ash* was a transitional work pointing to new directions and preparing the way for other, younger directors to venture into more valid new wave aesthetics. Significantly, when the group of directors identified as belonging to the

145

Hong Kong New Wave (Ann Hui, Alex Cheung, Tsui Hark, Yim Ho, Peter Yung) burst onto the film-making scene between 1979–82, many chose to make their first films in the crime thriller genre.

The new wave film-makers started their careers in television in 1976–8, a period viewed by critic/film-maker Shu Kei as a 'golden age' of Hong Kong television. Many contributed episodes to series about crime and social problems produced by private commercial stations and the government owned RTHK (Radio Television Hong Kong). One such series, produced by HK-TVB, was entitled *C.I.D.* Another one was produced by the territory's Independent Commission Against Corruption (ICAC) which had its own film unit for propaganda work, simply entitled *ICAC.* Towards the end of 1979, this group of young directors, most of whom had attended film schools overseas and accumulated considerable experience in television, released their debut films. Not surprisingly, almost all of them dealt with subjects of crime and police work.

Alex Cheung's *Cops and Robbers/Dianzhi Bingbing* (1979) exemplified the crime–police–social problem syndrome of the first new wave films. A grittier work than *Jumping Ash,* the director brought his audience into the snakepit of marginal society, showing the workings of a criminal mind and the thin line dividing criminals and law enforcers. The film's criminal protagonist is a cross-eyed man whose application to join the police force was rejected because of his affliction. The film shows his evolution from an alienated young man to gun-crazed killer with a particular grouse against the police. The cops are the usual assortment of veterans and a young rookie. The latter is terrorised by the cross-eyed killer in a reversal of roles as the villain chases the cop. The movie has the realist look of a seedy alley in one of Hong Kong's tenement slums – a hallmark of new wave aesthetics.

Peter Yung brought a fresh, introspective approach to his under-rated *The System/Hang Gui* (1979). A senior narcotics inspector, Chan Cheuk (played by Taiwanese actor Bai Ying), leads a special unit to smash the operations of a drug king. He presses into service an informer, Tam (excellently played by Hong Kong cinema's perennial heavy, Sek Kin). Tam is a street-pusher and self-confessed drug addict employed by the drug king. Their efforts to nail him are obstructed by the existence of corrupt personnel within the police department. The relationship between Chan and Tam provides a moral focus to the story. Both men are inextricably linked in the pursuit of a criminal – but for Chan it is a private obsession where the means justify the end. The film states its theme of police corruption by way of the moral ruminations of a self-reflective individual who has premonitions of his own death but who nevertheless works hard to redeem a corrupt police force.

Ann Hui's *The Secret* (1979) is a bleak, psychological thriller which takes its cue from the Chinese title, *Feng Jie,* meaning 'to be gripped by madness'. Accordingly, it dwells on mental anguish and psychological disorder. It is a tale of murder told from the perspective of a nurse (played by Sylvia Chang) whose next-door neighbour, a girl engaged to a doctor, is supposedly murdered. The bodies of the couple (the girl's face is so bashed up as to be unrecognisable) are found not far from each other on a secluded hill. A madman living near the scene of the crime is the only suspect, but he eludes the police. The girl's 'ghost' returns as a figure clad in a red jacket and is seen foraging about in her grandmother's apartment. The nurse becomes obsessed with uncovering the truth about these strange occurrences, the 'secret' implied in the English title. A terse flashback narrative constructs the key events concerning the murdered couple. The nurse finally solves the mystery, at some risk to her own life.

Structurally, *The Secret* remains Ann Hui's most accomplished film. The flashbacks are cut together and integrated into the main narrative with such scissor-like precision that no time-change seems to have occurred. It skilfully inter-weaves motifs of ritual and superstition, inducing a mood leaden with the whiff of stale incense. The feeling it generates is intense claustrophobia and a sense of impending doom. This is not a thriller in the classic Hitchcock sense. Rather, it is more like something from Bergman, despite the obvious allusion to Nicolas Roeg's *Don't Look Now* (via the use of the figure in the red jacket and a protagonist's obsessive search for the truth about this mysterious figure). Hui covers her canvas with references to symbols and details associated with death, marriage and birth found in Chinese superstition. One of her themes concerns the deadweight of tradition which decays and changes into superstition, imposing a heavy burden on all within its grasp. Hui doesn't let up for one minute on her doomsday atmosphere and the movie ends as bleakly as it starts. As the murderer is revealed, Hui provides a startling conclusion, ending her film on a birth–death motif. The horror is palpable.

No less palpable is the horror in Yim Ho's *The Happenings/Ye Che* (1980), an expressionist work about disaffected youths driven to kill. After an evening spent in a disco, a gang of youths led by car-thief 'Cream' goes joy-riding. Their wild night of fun turns into a nightmare. Stopping at a gas station but having no money to pay, they provoke an attack by the attendants, one of whom is killed. The youths panic, rob the station and make their getaway. A series of misadventures befall the gang as they contrive to stay ahead of the law, leading to more deaths and assaults on innocent bystanders. As the youths become desperadoes hunted by the police, the action goes over the top. Still, it emphasises the shocking nature of the crimes and the hyper-excited state of the youths.

Yim and his writer, Shu Kei, painted Hong Kong society as contemptuous of youths marginalised by poverty, broken homes and unemployment. The innocent bystanders are far from sympathetic characters: too quick to prejudge the youths and no less responsible for causing the incidents which follow. Their actions are as relentless and their bigotry as irrational as the behaviour and attitudes of the marginalised youths. The film-makers thus place the burden of guilt on the adults. *The Happenings* is not a flattering portrait of youth culture, but neither does it offer a socially respectable perspective by seeing the problem through the eyes of a 'responsible' adult, as such films tend to do. Yim's film (his second) is a considerable achievement: it is contextually grounded in the new wave aspirations to make a cinema of social significance and is at the same time a stylistic breakthrough. *The Happenings* contains unforgettable visual moments which are expressionist in tone. The explosive scenes of violence are an indication of Yim's intentions to merge shocking subject matter with style. He is only let down by poor acting and misplaced moments of black humour – lapses which are, however, disguised by the fast pace and quirky inventiveness of the writer and director working in tandem.

Tsui Hark's *Dangerous Encounter – 1st Kind/Diyi Leixing Weixian* (1980) complements Yim Ho's film in etching out a portrait of disenchanted youth. The latter film is a more achieved piece in its placement of youth within a society that despises youth, building up a relentless momentum of emotion in the process. Both films concentrate their actions into one night. Tsui's youths, like Yim's, are caught in a whirlwind of violence when their brutish practical jokes misfire. The mystique of crime and male bondage took the thriller away from the subject of delinquent youths into the world of adult criminals in Kirk Wong's *The Club/Wu Ting* (1980). The Copacabana is a nightclub over which rival godfathers fight for territorial rights. Their protectors and henchmen engage in a war sparked off by the murder of the Copacabana's owner. His death leads to violent retribution: scores must be settled and the stuff of real heroes called into account. The action is meant to convey precepts of male bondage and the code of brotherhood or *yi* – areas which would be exploited to greater effect in the films of John Woo.

Kirk Wong is the erratic maverick in this context, a director who has slipped in and out of new wave status. A macho-minded film-maker who has no time for the nuances of characterisations, much less social conscience, Wong is nevertheless a capable stylist. The script and the characters of *The Club* are entirely at the service of action sequences strung together in a series of chases. Wong's hero conforms to the narcissistic type with subliminal homosexual sentiments like those found in the kung fu films of Zhang Che. Even the weapons used are knives and samurai swords rather than guns, harking back to the *wuxia* pictures of the late 60s. But the characters remain two-dimensional ciphers employed to display violence.

New wave crime thrillers produced between 1979 and 1982, the most intense period of new wave output, include Ronny Yu's *The Saviour/Jiushi Zhe* (1980), Alex Cheung's *Man on the Brink/Bianyuan Ren* (1981), Ann Hui's *The Story of Woo Viet/Hu Yue de Gushi* (1981), Patrick Tam's *Love Massacre/Ai Sha* (1981) and Terry Tong's *Coolie Killer/Shachu Xiying Pan* (1982). The fact that most of the new wave film-makers sought to debut with a crime thriller may be because of the genre's versatility. Young film-makers used a popular contemporary format and adapted it to accommodate their own personal preoccupations. Although a few works produced average results, on the whole, the new wave confirmed its vitality. Here, at last, was a group of local film-makers who had the ability and commitment to tackle the historical and social experiences of Hong Kong society.

The new tenet of social realism, accentuated by the emphasis on crime and corruption, formed part of the basis of new wave work; the other part concerned itself with stylistic experimentation. It was most important for film-makers to situate into the 'texts' of their films their own individual experiences. In fact, the work of the new wave directors suited the requirements of the commercial industry at a time when it was experiencing a generational change. Young film-makers were needed not because old film-makers were retiring but because the aspirations and preferences of young audiences had to be met. Professional standards were consequently upgraded, and variety in techniques and special effects was boosted by the fact that new wave directors tended to work in different genres. Indeed, the strength of the new wave directors was forged in genre cinema where established conventions and forms were critically and stylistically re-worked to suit the modern audiences of the 80s. The more skilful directors attempted at first to walk a tightrope between realism and genre conventions, but later naturally gravitated towards the latter. Their first successful works leaned towards realism, but genre conventions were exploited to realise personal visions, indeed to expound on the ills of society.

GENRE AND VISION: THE FILMS OF ANN HUI

Ann Hui, the most senior of the new wave directors, is also representative of the group in that she quickly expanded her range, although her style always was considerably more moderate than, for instance, that of her colleague Tsui Hark. Hui is a director with a self-imposed sense of discipline who knows precisely how to exploit the forms and conventions of long-established genres. A fine sense of style is, needless to say, imperative. While even Hui's minor works are distinguished by the mellowness of her style, she has been able to develop her own vision which becomes clearer with each film. Following *The Secret*, discussed earlier, Hui made *The Spooky Bunch/ Zhuang Dao Zheng* (1980). Although a comedy, it has the bleakness and nightmarish qualities of *The Secret* because of its preoccupation with the world of ghosts and the linking of a character's personal history with a broader, cultural past.

An opera company touring Cheung Chau Island has its feathers ruffled by the spirits of soldiers and a couple of harlots from two generations back. The spirits seek revenge on the descendants of those responsible for their deaths. Josephine Siao is Ah Chi, the *hua dan* (leading lady) of the company, one of the targets. She blithely makes friends with one of the spirits, a mischievous girl known as Catshit, who then possesses her. Ah Chi is wooed by Dick Ma (Kenny Bee), whose grandfather was the herbalist who had caused the death of a whole platoon of soldiers, its commander and the two prostitutes, one of whom is Catshit. Ah Chi's grandfather had been wrongly convicted for the deaths and executed. Before his death, he had put a curse on the Ma family damning it to childlessness for generations. In order to break the curse, Dick, the last of the Ma family, is ordered to marry Ah Chi. The comedy of situations involving the ghosts possessing members of the opera troupe is belied by a solemn theme that would soon become a motif in Hui's works: the examination of the kinds of legacy history leaves behind. In this film, the sins of a previous generation catch up with the descendants, and the past will settle accounts with the present. Hui explores history as a wellspring of a people's cultural memories and suggests that it is a decisive factor determining the psyches and events of the present. Hui continues this exploration in films as diverse as *The Boat People, Love in a Fallen City, Romance of Book and Sword* and *Song of the Exile,* all films which are closely allied to *The Spooky Bunch* through the director's vision of a tainted destiny.

Hui returned to her bleaker idiom in her next film, *The Story of Woo Viet/ Hu Yue de Gushi* (1981). In stylistic terms, the film is a pure thriller, free of any pretensions at social analysis. As a director working within the commercial constraints of Hong Kong cinema, Hui's works are marked by a unique blend of art and entertainment. Although she does not set out to purvey messages, her films are products of social conscience. Here, the political and social aspects of the problem of Vietnamese refugees and illegal migrants are not hidden in the entertainment – they stem from it.

The Story of Woo Viet is Hui's mature re-working of a subject and a theme which she had previously explored in her television work, *The Boy From Vietnam/ Lai Ke* (1978). The subject is Vietnamese refugees, the theme is displacement and exile. *The Story of Woo Viet* was followed by *The Boat People* (1984). The three works are regarded by Hong Kong critics as a trilogy about Vietnam and the boat people, a problem which troubled Hong Kong from the late 70s onwards. For Hui, Vietnam was a politically expedient subject as it allowed her to handle sensitive matters such as one's feelings towards China and the imponderables of its politics as they affected Hong Kong. *The Story of Woo Viet* opens with a boatload of Vietnamese refugees drifting into Hong Kong waters. On board is a young ex-soldier, Woo Viet (played by Chow Yun-fat). The refugees are sequestered in a camp, but Woo Viet is able to establish contact with a Hong Kong pen pal, Li Lap-kwan (played by Cora Miao). While inside the camp, Woo Viet becomes involved in a murderous tussle with Vietnamese secret agents, but he escapes and, with the help of Lap-kwan, plans to go to the United States with a forged passport. Instead, he ends up in the Philippines, a victim of foul play by the 'snake head', a euphemism for triad gangsters who operate in the illegal immigration rackets. The scenes in the Philippines evoke visions of a seamy, hellish 'other' world, and Woo Viet is forced to exist underground in Manila's Chinatown, where he is again caught in a quandary: while attempting to rescue a Vietnamese girl from sexual bondage, he comes into conflict with an underworld boss. If his escape from Vietnam was inspired by political will, his plight in a Manila hellhole has an existentialist overtone. *The Story of Woo Viet* becomes a stylish exercise in the thriller genre with echoes of Graham Greene and Joseph Conrad. Hui presents a claustrophobic vision of an environment suspended in a primal state of being which nevertheless exerts a seductive hold over its footloose adventurers and refugees who seek to escape from themselves as well as from political situations.

Hui reached a peak in her career with *The Boat People* (1982), the one work in the (unofficial) Vietnam trilogy that, in spite of its Cold War imagery, is the most allegorical treatment up to that time of the China syndrome haunting Hong Kong people in the early 80s. Thereafter, Hui became more openly preoccupied with the issue of 1997 and the wider context of the China question, leading to a series of flawed but ambitious works such as *Love in a Fallen City/Qingchen zhi Lian* (1984), *Romance of Book and Sword/Shujian Enchou Lu* (1987) and *Starry is the Night/Jinye Xingguang Canlan* (1988). Of these films, *Romance of Book and Sword*, released in two parts in Hong Kong, the second part being entitled *Princess Fragrance/Xiangxiang Gongzhu*, deals explicitly with the theme of China engulfed by discontent among its majority citizens of the Han ethnic variety.

Based on a novel by martial arts writer Jin Yong, the film proposes that the Emperor Qianlong, one of the Manchu Qing Dynasty's most successful emperors who reigned between 1735–96, was a Han Chinese and not of Manchu stock. The Red Flower Society, headed by a young Han named Chen Jialuo, captures the emperor and tries to persuade him to re-establish Han rule under a restored Ming Dynasty. To convince Qianlong that he is really a Han, Chen Jialuo discloses that he is his brother, offering proof in the shape of a letter written by their natural mother just before her death. Together, they discuss the premise of a Chinese society prospering under Manchu rule and the possibility that it might be foolhardy for the emperor to overthrow his own government to make way for the Hans. Chen Jialuo appears to agree, but a commitment to Han rule overpowers him and his Red Flower Society members. The theme of Han discontent brings up the issue of ethnic purity which lies behind Hui's treatment of history. She questions the thesis that China's historical tragedy for three hundred years stemmed from the Han's loss of power and offers the counter-thesis of a greater China, one encompassing different ethnic groups and cultures living together. Having overseen China's expansion to its Westernmost frontiers in Xinjiang and Central Asia, Qianlong's reign saw the first modern manifestation of a 'Great China' nationalism, sabotaged, it is suggested, by Han chauvinism. The notion of Chinese nationhood as comprising a wide range of ethnic identities gained a more intimate treatment in *Song of the Exile/Ketu Qiuhen* (1990),[2] an autobiographical work which addresses Hui's own mixed Sino-Japanese antecedence. The burden of the quest for ethnic purity was a theme never better treated by a Hong Kong director.

Even Hui's minor films were largely complementary to her personal themes. *Starry is the Night* deals with the love affairs of a woman social worker (played by Lin Ching-hsia) over twenty years, starting from her student days in 1967 when violent riots inspired by the Cultural Revolution rocked Hong Kong to 1987 when Hong Kong felt its way towards democratic reforms in the transition to 1997. The twenty years in the woman's life represent a period of change, reflected in the maturing of the character through different relationships, conveying Hui's theme that history and political events interact with personal lives. *My American Grandson/Shanghai Jiaqi* (1991) is a tale of a Chinese grandfather having to deal with his grandson from America. Hui accepted the assignment on the strength of its script, written by the Taiwanese writer Wu Nianzhen, the author of

Song of the Exile. There are familiar motifs from *Song of the Exile* and Hui's previous films dealing with the Hong Kong–China relationship and the quest for identity. Instead of a harmonious homecoming, the grandson experiences culture shock. The grandfather (a fine performance from Wu Ma), does all he can to ease the shock, but when he draws the line at national insults (the boy calls China an 'awful country' where people queue to go to toilets, and teachers teach their students 'stupid ideas' like selfless sacrifice), the grandson runs away to the countryside. There, the warmth of the peasants leads to his change of heart and wins the boy over to his ancestral land.

The Zodiac Killers/ Jidao Zhuizhong (1992) was a return to the thriller genre by way of the displaced characters of *The Story of Woo Viet*. The two films even share the same closing shot: an image of the hero on a ship looking at the ocean horizon. Set in Japan, the story deals with Mainland Chinese students working illegally in Tokyo and getting entangled with the Yakuza, Japan's version of the Chinese Triads. The narrative was muddled but Hui stayed the course with her usual sense of professionalism. In the 90s, as Hui settles into the status of a veteran director, she can look back with some satisfaction on her career in the 80s when her new wave credentials brought Hong Kong cinema greater recognition as a cinema of personal expression.

FROM REALISM TO MELODRAMA

Among the new wave directors, Allen Fong may well be the most personal, developing an approach combining documentary realism and melodrama, already exemplified in his work for television, such as the docu-drama *The Song of Yuen Chau Tsai/ Yuanzhou Zai zhi Ge* (1977) made for RTHK.

Fong's first film, *Father and Son/Fuzi Qing* (1981)[3] is somewhat atypical of this approach as a melodramatic autobiographical work, the first attempted by a new wave director consciously to recall Hong Kong's pre-kung fu cinematic past, the father and son subgenre of Cantonese melodrama. But although the film adheres to generic forms, the emotions it conveys and represents are real, because Hong Kong's rising generation did experience, while growing up, the same frustrations in communicating with one's parents, the pain and sacrifice of family members, the obsession with education, and the demand for absolute obedience to the patriarchy.

Fong's subsequent films *Ah Ying/ Banbian Ren* (1982), *Just Like Weather/ Meiguo Xin* (1986) and *Dancing Bull/ Wu Niu* (1990) are quasi-fictional works with aspects of investigative reportage. They revolve around central protagonists who find it hard to integrate personal aspirations with reality. In *Ah Ying*, a film-maker (played by Peter Wang) faces the difficulty of setting up a project in Hong Kong. He forms a friendship with a young girl, a fishmonger who wants to become an actress. The director conducts a series of interviews with the girl, her boyfriend and her family. Fong used amateurs who played themselves on screen, finding intimacy and meaning in these relationships with real people.

In *Just Like Weather*, a young couple faces the possibility of a breakdown in their marriage as they contemplate whether to stay in Hong Kong or to migrate to America. Fong himself appears in the movie as a film-maker, interviewer and interlocutor. Occasionally he appears to be shaping the lives of his subjects, even giving his central couple the opportunity to travel to America in order to record their emotions. In *Dancing Bull*, which is about a choreographer (played by Anthony Wong) and his disquiet over his marriage and career, reality is finally threatened by political repression as represented by the street demonstrations in Hong Kong against the Tiananmen massacre, forcing the artist to confront the creative process with the intricacies of an unpleasant reality.

Fong's docu-drama interpretation of new wave aesthetics has set him apart from his new wave colleagues. In the early years of the new wave, directors such as Yim Ho and Tsui Hark developed their aesthetics in the context of considerably less austere genres such as the thriller and comedy which seemed to offer greater scope for experimentation. Yim made his first film, *The Extras/Ka-le-fei* (1978) as a comedy, and Ann Hui followed her debut thriller with the comedy *The Spooky Bunch*. Yim and Tsui's move into comedy was significant, although, at the time, it was largely misunderstood. In fact, according to Hong Kong critics, the new wave avant-garde which introduced modern aesthetics to Hong Kong cinema in 1979, also ended with a comedy in 1981 when Tsui Hark made *All the Wrong Clues (for the Right Solution)*, a comedy of the crass and commercial school known as the 'Cinema City style'.

Cinema City was a production company founded in 1980 by comedians Karl Maka, Dean Shek and Raymond Wong. It became the most commercially successful film company in Hong Kong and prompted the industry to copy the Cinema City formula of comedies. The company emphasised collective effort (scripts were the results of brain-storming sessions between producers, directors and stars), big-budget packaging, stunt work and slapstick action. Representative films were *Chasing Girls/Zhui Nüzai* (1981) and *Aces Go Places/Zuijia Paidang* (1982), each generating a series of slapstick sequels which turned out to be the company's biggest hits. The fortunes of Cinema City rose together with the new wave; its commercial precepts threatened to overwhelm the new aesthetics. But when the company employed Tsui Hark, it was not immediately obvious that Tsui would infuse his new wave sensibility into the rather lowly but popular comedies. Tsui's own dynamic style of film-making initiated a level of structural experimentation which was to be highly influential. It provided a referential text for the postmodern comedies of the 90s. A look at *All the Wrong Clues* will bear this out: congested situations, fractured outlines, episodic sequences, a frenetic pace, the latter especially being a significant indication of how Hong Kong film-makers adapted Western aesthetics to its own local conditions. In fact, Tsui's films move with such breakneck speed that one is hard put to find a Western equivalent.

Yim Ho's *Wedding Bells, Wedding Belles/Gongzi Jiao* (1981), released a few months before Tsui Hark's *All the Wrong Clues*, shares the same sensibility of madcap excess. It is, however, more of a genuine oddity than Tsui's film. The film shows director Yim in command of his style, and is even more impressive when one considers that any allusions to Western screwball traditions are, in fact, not very relevant at all. Indeed, the film seems to have eschewed all classical allusions and styles, consciously offering a 'break' with both Western tradition and Hong Kong's own brand of comedy farces. It deals with a wealthy 78-year-old socialite's attempts to marry an 18-year-old beauty from Hong Kong's community of boat people. The marriage attempts go awry as the girl is kidnapped by two younger competitors: one is her lovestruck neighbour in the Yaumatei typhoon shelter, the other a media celebrity. The film is finally too oddball to be judged a genuine success. But the Cantonese dialogue and the satire of Hong Kong's boat people co-existing with wealthy yacht-owners make it an irrepressible comedy.

Yim's career, like Ann Hui's, took a more serious turn towards personal subject matter in the mid-80s, a time of anxiety as the Sino-British negotiations over Hong Kong's status after 1997 proceeded and China itself attracted the attention of Hong Kong film-makers as the implications of 1997 became clearer. *Homecoming/ Sishui Liunian* (1984) is an homage to China, albeit tempered by a city-sider's critical perspective. Its evocation of rural innocence strikes a bell with those Hong Kong people who still maintain links with their place of birth or with villages where their parents came from.

Rural China was again the setting of *Buddha's Lock/ Tian Pusa* (1987), which tells the story of an American pilot who crashlands in Yunnan Province during the Second World War and is adopted as a member of a minority tribe. He is virtually a prisoner at first, but finally learns to accept the merits of assimilation into the community. *Red Dust/ Gungun Hongchen* (1990) is a *wenyi* melodrama set in China during the tumultuous 30s (the film was shot in Taiwan). The romantic plot centres on a woman writer (played by Lin Ching-hsia) and her love affair with a man who collaborates with the Japanese. After the war, he goes into hiding and she goes in search of him, only to find him with another woman. The writer makes the ultimate sacrifice by saving her faithless lover on the eve of the communist takeover of China, giving him the ticket for a passage to Taiwan – and freedom. The film is florid and formulaic, signs of burnout as the director continues to search for themes to match a style which has matured too fast.

Although his films have ranged from raucous comedies to intimate melodramas and mock-epics (such as *Red Dust*), Yim's style has a consistency that is synchronised with an inner malaise which he locates within an historical scheme and the national context of China. His characters are confronted with social change and catastrophic events, making Chinese history the catalyst of personal agony. Perhaps the most representative film of Yim's, which treats modern Chinese history as a soul-searching endeavour, is *King of Chess/ Qi Wang* (1992). The film is set in both China and Taiwan, criss-crossing between the two countries in separate time periods: China during the Cultural Revolution and Taiwan in the contemporary 80s. The story deals with a 'chess king' who is sent to a labour camp during the Cultural Revolution and zig-zags to scenes in

Taiwan concerning a chess prodigy who is introduced as the latest sensation in a television ratings war. The two stories reflect on the vicissitudes of political history and their effects on the individual.

Yim began directing the film in 1988 with Tsui Hark as producer, but the project was shelved before it was given the Tsui Hark 'treatment' and finally released in 1992. As a project assigned to Yim Ho, it is clear that Tsui more than tampered with the film. However, the film brings both Yim and Tsui in line with their nationalistic concern for China, evident in the motifs of both directors' films. The core group of new wave directors (Ann Hui, Yim Ho and Tsui Hark) converged in their concerns stemming from the central motif of the China question: the 1997 syndrome, the affirmation of a Hong Kong identity *vis-à-vis* China combined with an abstract nationalism which takes into account Hong Kong people's kinship with Chinese culture, history and tradition.

The vexing questions of China–Hong Kong identity were dealt with by directors associated, in one form or another, with the new wave. Leong Po-chih, who made *Jumping Ash* (1976), the film which foreshadowed the new wave, deserves mention here for consciously tackling the theme of Hong Kong's identity crisis in the 80s. Leong, who is much older than his new wave colleagues, was born in London in 1939. He grew up there and trained as a film-maker, coming to Hong Kong in 1967 to work in television after employment at the BBC. He formed his own production company to make commercials before debuting with *Jumping Ash*. Subsequent works, such as *Banana Cop/Yinglun Pipa* (1984), *Hongkong 1941/Dengdai Liming* (1984, probably Leong's best film), *Welcome/Buhuo Yingxiong* (1985) and *Ping Pong* (1986, made in the UK), underline his view of Hong Kong as a bi-cultural entity. Leong constantly refers to himself as a 'banana' – yellow outside, white inside. His best films expound the 'banana' culture and dual identity of Hong Kong with a greater emphasis on the Anglo connection: thus *Banana Cop* is about an Anglicised Chinese cop who is sent to Hong Kong to solve a case; *Hong Kong 1941* is about the fall of Hong Kong to the Japanese – an allegory about Britain's implied betrayal of Hong Kong; *Welcome* is a satire about the early culture clash between East and West when Britain first took control of the New Territories bordering China. As an unofficial member of the new wave, Leong's films and his themes have enriched the periphery of the movement. The nucleus of the wave expanded in the first two years of the 80s to include many other young directors such as Clifford Choi, Stephen Shin, Rachel Zen and Patrick Tam. The new wave, of course, was a comprehensive movement taking in writers (a number of whom became directors, such as Shu Kei, Alfred Cheung, Clifton Ko), designers and cinematographers. Like the 1979 core group of directors, these film-makers all started out in television in the various departments of production, direction, scripting, photography and design, gaining substantial experience to pave the way for film careers, leading critic Law Kar to dub Hong Kong's television stations at the time, the 'Shaolin' school for film-makers.

155

RIDING THE WAVE

The debate over whether the new wave was ever a conscious movement with well-prescribed avant garde objectives now seems ill-conceived. The core group itself eventually showed that it was not a cohesive unit to begin with. Its members were too sectarian in their genres (Alex Cheung with gangster movies, for example) and some diverted into other fields (Peter Yung became a photographer). But there is no doubt that a movement defined by a 'new wave style' did exist in the early 80s, characterised by subject matter dealing with the problems of youth: school, sex, drugs and other travails of growing up in a materialistic society, misunderstood by parents and adults in authority. Representative films include those of Clifford Choi (*Teenage Dreamers/Ningmeng Kele*, 1982; *Grow Up in Anger/Qingchun Nuchao*, 1986); Shu Kei (*Sealed With a Kiss/Liang Xiao Wuzhi*, 1981); Stephen Shin (*Eclipse/Bohe Kafei*, 1982); David Lai (*Lonely 15/Liang Meizai*, 1982); Patrick Tam (*Nomad/Liehuo Qingchun*, 1982). In structural terms, these new wave youth films alternated between a free elliptical rhythm and a direct, quasi-documentary emphasis on style and content. The camera was relentlessly mobile, the performances naturalistic.

Patrick Tam was one of the most under-rated directors of the new wave as it dispersed in the mid-80s into individual careers of 'auteurs'. Tam shored up his new wave status with the psychological thriller *Love Massacre/Ai Sha* (1981) after his disappointing first film *The Sword/Ming Jian* (1980). An eclectic director who unabashedly draws on his fondness for things Japanese and for the films of Jean-Luc Godard, Tam is the most precocious auteur of the new wave: he designs his own sets, writes his own scripts (albeit usually in partnership with other writers), supervises the editing and composes his shots with a meticulous eye. In addition, his films are colour-composed: each film works according to a colour scheme of contrasting primary colours giving the viewer the impression of a completely structured edifice.

Nomad is his most representative work. Ostensibly a film about the 'youth problem', it shies away from more conventional treatments such as Clifford Choi's which deal with teenagers' growing-up pains, those of Johnny Mak's (the guiding spirit behind *Lonely 15*) which deals with drugs and prostitution, and Lawrence Ah Mon, who directed *Gangs/Tong Dang* about youths being pulled into triad-led gangs. Unlike these mainly topical films, *Nomad* is angst-ridden, style-conscious and somehow more representative of youthful transgressions and preoccupations in the 80s. Although his studied, new-wavish compositions appear a bit dated in the 90s, his characters continue to exert an appeal beyond the formalism of Tam's experimental inclinations.

The film tells of four youths who form overlapping relationships. Louis (Leslie Cheung) is a rich kid who is unable to get over the death of his mother and dreams of sailing a boat to Arabia. His girlfriend Kathy (Pat Ha) is a sexually-liberated Japanophile who has relationships with Shinsuke, a deserter from the Japanese Red Army hiding in Hong Kong, and Pong (Ken Tong), a lifeguard. Louis finds that he is more in tune with

'Tomato' (Cecilia Yip), a kooky girl who has just ended a relationship. These new alignments are confirmed by imaginative scenes of lovemaking (one such scene takes place on the top deck of a tram) as a listless, post-coital mood builds up: 'We don't seem to have anything to contribute to society,' complains Tomato. 'What society?' replies Louis, 'That's us … we are society!' The film ends in a sudden burst of violence: a beach assassination and an attack by Japanese Red Army terrorists pose stark, realistic choices for the youths, signalling the end of their somewhat depressive innocence.

Upon its release, *Nomad* sparked off a controversy among moral guardians in the territory decrying the 'negative' portrayal of youth, sexual amorality and ennui. The film's attempt at social analysis is overshadowed by Tam's attention to style, but it does, nevertheless, make a sharp comment on Hong Kong's consumerist society: Tam's youths are both disoriented and fascinated by affluence, avidly consuming popular culture from the West and Japan. They are the first youthful prototypes in Hong Kong cinema who convey the spiritual malaise of a post-industrial society.

The critical neglect of Patrick Tam in the 80s may partly be attributed to the perception that he is too 'experimental' for his own good; that his eye for formal design and pictorial composition is pretentious. In other words, while his new wave colleagues have grown out of 'experimenting', Tam continues to insist on maintaining it as the most important trait of new wave aesthetics. This is borne out by the formalism of some of his films, *Cherie/Xue'er* (1984), *Burning Snow/Xue Zai Shao* (1988). But in *Final Victory/Zui Hou Shengli* (1987), Tam's aestheticised approach is wholly at the service of an expressionism that works to convey the parlous state of his characters' feelings. *Final Victory* is perhaps Tam's most successfully realised work: a structural exercise that sets out to be a modern fairytale. It also marks Tam's first collaboration with a young protégé, Wong Kar-wai, who wrote the screenplay. Tam later supervised the editing of Wong's *Days of Being Wild/A Fei Zhengzhuan*.

The story is set in the sleazy, neon-lit milieu of Mongkok, the hub of Hong Kong's down-market sex industry and a gangland of mahjong parlours, bars and clubs, the natural home of Hong Kong's Triads. Gangster 'Big Bo' (played by new wave colleague Tsui Hark, excellent in his only substantial acting role to date) entrusts two girlfriends to the care of his wimpish brother, Hung (Eric Tsang), before going off to serve a jail sentence. Hung has to prevent the women from finding out that they are both Big Bo's girls. He falls in love with one of them, a love which is reciprocated. Big Bo views this as a betrayal of trust and vows to kill both his brother and ex-lover. As in *Nomad*, the final scene is a catharsis on the beach, a Japanese-like finale of death and sacrifice, but given a twist to comply with the convention of a happy ending in keeping with the film's fairytale overtones.

Tam's eclecticism, which contributes to his continuing poor standing among critics, is based on the extreme ends of the rainbow: the West and Japan. His allusions to European and Japanese aesthetics seem intellectu-

157

ally shallow in the circumstances of Hong Kong's 1997 fears and China syndrome – the themes which preoccupy Tam's colleagues. Consequently, Tam's movies are structural puzzles even when meticulously constructed. Their references stem from two dead ends which do not seem to converge. His best works, *Nomad* and *Final Victory*, give us some idea of Tam's destination: the no man's land of Hong Kong's cultural, spiritual and geographical dislocation.

The new wave operated in two distinct areas of concern from around the mid-80s onwards. One area was typified by Tam's predilection for style and form, the other sought social–political significance with new wave aesthetics, typified in films such as Clifford Choi's *Hong Kong, Hong Kong/Nan yu Nü* (1983), David King's *Home at Hong Kong/Jia Zai Xianggang* (1983) and the films of Allen Fong. One cannot speak of fixed borders between these two areas but they are broadly used here to differentiate one tendency from the other and to illustrate the theme of Hong Kong's predicament *vis-à-vis* China as political negotiations were concluded in 1984 to hand the territory back to China in 1997.

Style and significance were of course the by-words for a number of directors who wanted the best of both worlds. Kirk Wong's *Health Warning* (1983) was perhaps the classic indicator of this tendency: a rare hybrid of kung fu and science fiction containing a bizarre, not wholly satisfactory, allegory about Hong Kong's future. Johnny Mak, known as the 'creative producer' of teenage problem films (such as *Lonely 15*), made his directing debut with *Long Arm of the Law/Sheng Gang Qibing* (1984), a violent gangster thriller that graphically put the fear of China into Hong Kong audiences, being a story of Chinese gangsters from Guangzhou who illegally enter the territory to carry out a heist. Mak's style was cathartic and sensationalist, but so were the politics of the day. Alfred Cheung, who started as a scenarist working on the scripts of *Father and Son* and *The Story of Woo Viet*, graduated to directing comedies before he made *On the Run/Wangming Yuanyang* (1988), an excellent noir thriller with overtones of the 1997 syndrome. Cheung further explored the China–Hong Kong relationship in a series of satirical comedies following the success of *Her Fatal Ways/Biaojie Ni Haoye* (1990). The film and its sequels made fun of the system of Chinese law-enforcement and featured Carol Cheng Yuk-ling as the yokel Mainland policewoman seconded to the Hong Kong police department.

An unsung stylist of the late new wave is Tony Au. His association with the new wave was originally as production designer for Ann Hui's films, but he turned director for *The Last Affair/Hua Cheng* (1984), a fine melodrama-cum-psychological thriller containing a brilliant tragic performance by comedienne Carol Cheng Yuk-ling. The film starts as an idyllic romance in Paris. Cheng's character, Ha-ching, has a love affair with a struggling musician, played by Chow Yun-fat. The story develops into a tale of *amour fou* as Ha-ching discovers that her lover is a womaniser and she suffers a mental breakdown. Cheng's performance invests the film with a restless, languid tone reflecting her character's underlying discontent and her determination to resolve the emotional impasse building up within her. The lines 'Why Paris? Because it is Paris,' spoken by Ha-ching before the opening credits, pre-empts the film's mood and the lead character's slow descent to a flower-decked purgatory. The cinematography (by Bill Wong) is outstanding and the sense of style in the mellow, melodramatic mode of a Douglas Sirk, impeccable.

Au continued in this stylistic vein: *Dream Lovers/Meng Zhong Ren* (1986) is a superior ghost story starring superstars Chow Yun-fat and Lin Ching-hsia that was essentially re-made as *A Terra-Cotta Warrior/Qin Yong* (1990) by Ching Siu-tung; *Profiles of Pleasure/Qun Ying Luan Wu* (1988) is an irresistible piece of kitsch and soft-core eroticism; ending the series with the marvellous *I am Sorry/Shuo Huang de Nüren* (1989), in which Au, his cinematographer Christopher Doyle and his screenwriter Qiu-Dai Anping (the pseudonym of Qiu Gangjian), obviously share a deep sense of fellowship with the lead character, a kept woman named Cheung Ka-lok (played by Carina Lau). As the opening credits roll, Cheung Ka-lok is speaking on the phone – to herself. Through her monologue, we learn of her status as the mistress of a self-made tycoon and rising politician who is already married. Hers is the familiar story of a woman who loves an unworthy man. Ka-lok's free time – which is most of the day – is spent in the company of other 'kept' women. They chat about money and sex, exchanging tips about how to keep their lovers. Occasionally tacky but always stylish, *I Am Sorry* is arguably Tony Au's best film so far. A woman's movie, a melodrama, a romantic comedy – the movie is pitched at each level with ease and sophistication. It has the right sense of frivolity for its subject and allows its central character free rein to develop, and good solo scenes in which to do so. The part is a dream-role and Carina Lau rises to the occasion, giving an incredibly free-spirited interpretation. Au's next film, *Au Revoir Mon Amour/Heri Jun Zailai* (1991) featured another beautiful heroine: a nightclub singer (played by Anita Mui) courted by a young nationalist soldier (Tony Leung) and his nemesis, a Japanese secret agent in Shanghai in 1941. This time, the film is a little disappointing, beset by a sense of hollowness, but the film does provide a stunning showcase for Anita Mui.

In fact, Au's career may be seen as showcasing Hong Kong cinema at its most garish yet sophisticated. A superficial glance at any of Au's films – from *The Last Affair* to *Au Revoir, Mon Amour* – reveals the stylised nature and awareness of the craft of Hong Kong film-making. Because of Au's background as a designer, there is a greater emphasis on art direction, showing how the Hong Kong cinema of the 80s is consciously overhauling itself aesthetically as well as technically, and attaining standards of world-class production values, enhanced in large part by the rise of designers such as Au himself, William Chang, Eddy Ma and others who operated at the peak of their powers from the mid-80s onwards.

Hong Kong cinema developed in other areas as well: special effects, stunt co-ordination, cinematography – in fact, in most departments except possibly the scripting. The refrain in the 80s was that the screenplay was the weakest part in Hong Kong productions. The reason is obvious when one notes that Hong Kong cinema was not composed of the new wave alone. Even though the new wave produced a record number of young auteurs, Hong Kong cinema was still a commercial dream factory that depended on a star system, and unabashedly stuck to the principles of mass entertainment. Although the new wave brought greater quality control, its directors adhered for the most part to the same principles of commercial entertainment. In the 80s, Hong Kong cinema had reached a new peak in productivity and competitiveness as its movies drew top dollar in its own domestic market and dominated markets in Taiwan and Southeast Asia.

So, although the new wave provided new blood and aesthetic impetus, Hong Kong cinema continued to operate along the lines of the old studio system well after the big studios had gone. The studio system inculcated strong commercial principles of film-making that were the bread-and-butter of Hong Kong cinema. These principles were sustained throughout the 80s and were adopted by young film-makers who looked back fondly to the studio era. The kung fu films of Jacky Chan and Sammo Hung are representative of the entertainment-is-king principle, but so is the whole range of comedies stretching from Michael Hui's work to new-style 'moral' comedies such as Johnny To's *The Eighth Happiness/Baxing Baoxi* (1988), Stephen Shin's *Heart to Hearts/Sanren Shijie* (1988), and Gordon Chan's *The Yuppie Fantasia/Xiao Nanren Zhouji* (1989). Crime thrillers such as those by Ringo Lam (*City on Fire, Prison on Fire, Wild Search*) and John Woo; the gambling comedy-adventures of Wong Jing; and ghost story movies with their combo of kung fu and comedy – all propelled Hong Kong cinema to commercial high heaven. By the mid-80s, the new wave was so much a part of the Hong Kong film industry that there was never really any talk of it forming a separate, artistic entity. Yet, there is no doubt that there was a new wave which enriched Hong Kong cinema and pointed it in directions which are still being assessed. The 1979 movement initiated by a group of film-makers who entered the film industry through television culminated in a fresh, second wave during the mid-80s. This second wave did not appear too distinctive at first, but they soon made their mark. The film-makers of the second wave include Eddie Fong, Stanley Kwan, Wong Kar-wai, Clara Law, Jacob Cheung, Ching Siu-tung, Mabel Cheung, Alex Law and Lawrence Ah Mon. Again, like the first wave, these film-makers clocked up substantial television experience and most were trained in film schools overseas.

The films produced by the second wave from 1984 to 1990 have clarified certain developments in Hong Kong cinema which we will explore in the following chapter. To sum up, the second half of the 80s was possibly the most interesting period of Hong Kong cinema. The cautious optimism that greeted the 1984 Sino-British Agreement legalising the handover of Hong Kong to China changed into a mood of skepticism as the mechanics of the transition proved too complicated and unwieldy. In cinema, the second wave reflected this skeptical mood, but it did so with introspection rather than outright cynicism. In the process, it brought Hong Kong cinema to a new level of maturity.

NOTES

[1] See Chapter 13 for a critical analysis of *China Behind*.

[2] See Chapter 13 for detailed discussions of Hui's *Song of the Exile, The Boat People* and *Love in a Fallen City*, three of the director's most significant films which deal with the themes of identity and the China–Hong Kong equation.

[3] See Chapter 4 for a consideration of Allen Fong's film in relation to the 'father and son' theme in Hong Kong's cinema.

Chapter Eleven

The New Wave's Action Auteurs

Tsui Hark: NATIONALISM ON SPEED

As the Hong Kong cinema's one genuine prodigy, director and producer Tsui Hark does not mince images – he munches them. He is a primitive, even brutish, film-maker who provokes through a visual syntax of dazzling images which inundates the senses with movements and cutting rhythms that tend to shred the narrative to bits. To some, his movies are too fast and his narratives too cluttered to be easily digestible.

Digestion and, by implication, food provide appropriate metaphors for Tsui's style. He even used this imagery himself for his second film, *We're Going to Eat You/Diyu Wu Men* (1980). A film *maudit* with a rather exaggerated cult reputation (although not in Hong Kong), *We're Going to Eat You* is a daunting title on a tasteless subject, cannibalism. The film is played for laughs and purports to be a satire, but looks and feels like a decaying corpse. In this early phase of his career, Tsui clearly set out to provoke. From *We're Going to Eat You*, Tsui went on to make *Dangerous Encounter – 1st Kind/Diyi Leixing Weixian*, a fireball of a film (its alternative title was more incendiary and paradoxical *Don't Play With Fire*). Tsui's provocative period did not last long, however. He soon settled on being a commercial director, albeit one who continued to conjure up dazzling images.

Obsessed with gadgets and tricks, Tsui has developed into a special-effects whiz kid, but as a true artist, Tsui turns his obsessions into the tools of his craft to heighten the intensity of his work. His dazzling effects may have obscured the themes in some of his films, but they also impart to his more inspired works a marvellous sense of exuberance. *The Butterfly Murders/Die Bian*, his debut work which soon acquired a cult following, perfectly illustrates this paradox. It is an assured work that displays elements of his later action style, but, in contrast to the later films, the pace is slower and there are fewer action scenes, making it a disciplined and restrained, intricately constructed mystery and the 'talkiest' of Tsui's action films. Various martial arts experts are summoned to a medieval castle to investigate the appearance of killer butterflies. The experts include a writer named Fang Hongye; a taciturn hero named Tian Feng; and three fighters known as 'The Thunders', each with a special expertise revealed in their nicknames: 'Thousand Hands' (a skill with small weapons), 'Magic Fire' (a skill with dynamite) and 'Flying Cloud' (an ability to become invisible). Tian Feng is a New Age martial artist, one of the chiefs of a warring clan known as '72 trails of smoke' who mobilises two divisions of his White Flag and Red Flag army to solve the mystery of the butterflies. He is also accompanied in this task by a young girl known as 'Green Shadow'. These characters wander through the labyrinths beneath the castle to unravel the butterfly mystery, which deepens as the butterflies kill the lord of the castle. Secret chambers are discovered, including an arsenal of strange-looking weapons, and a man in armour appears suddenly to threaten the experts. He kills 'Thousand Hands' and the lord's wife.

In this film, we see the rudiments of a Chinese nationalism which runs through Tsui's films like a red thread. Its classic exposition can be seen in *Zu: Warriors of the Magic Mountain* and all three parts of *Once Upon a Time in China*. Tsui depicts the mythic world of the martial arts as a time when China's sciences and inventions were at their peak. This notion of Chinese science and military prowess, combined with the popular mythologising of the martial arts, form the substance of Tsui's nationalist theme. The theme seeps into *The Butterfly Murders* through the use of the cliché of the Dao (good) and the Mo (evil) as expressed in the maxim, 'If the Dao stands one feet tall, the Mo stands ten feet taller.'

Tsui may well have learned this well-worn cliché of the martial arts genre from the films of King Hu and, indeed, the film evokes the mood if not the style of Hu's *A Touch of Zen/Xia Nü*. In postulating the Dao–Mo struggle, Tsui writes into it the related theme of national loss. His view of Chinese history is that of a country that has failed to realise its potential due to the failure of talented individuals to unite, engaging instead in internecine struggles to the detriment of all. The bloody ending of *Butterfly Murders*, in which only the writer survives, demonstrates Tsui's essentially pessimistic view of Chinese history which belies the highly charged and hyperbolic presentation of his nationalistic theme.

We're Going to Eat You is a bizarre, outrageous farce which relates cannibalism to the workings of secret governmental agencies. The story focuses on a character known simply as '999' who professes to be an agent of 'Central Intelligence' and travels to an island to catch a thief known as 'Rolex'. The island is a cannibalistic community run by the 'Public Security Bureau' whose task it is to catch humans and slaughter them for meat. He and a sidekick try to avert the choppers of the Public Security butchers, but the community becomes alerted to their presence like hounds scenting wild game. If Tsui had possessed a surrealist frame of mind, he might have got somewhere with this subject. But he is too much into satirical point-scoring, taking it to extremes by giving characters specious names such as 'Rolex' and '999', and placing the human slaughterhouse under the rubric of the Public Security Bureau. Although meant as a farce with its black humour targeted at authoritarian centres of power, the movie is too black and the target too ambiguous to hit home, degenerating into a rollicking adventure story with sick jokes.

Tsui's third film (his fourth in order of release), *Dangerous Encounter – 1st Kind*, was the right sort of controversial movie to seal his 'provocative' reputation. As it turned out, it was the film that would be recognised as

Tsui's best and most representative work, affirming his status as a member of the New Wave before succumbing to mainstream, 'commercial' cinema. *Dangerous Encounter – 1st Kind* has to be described as a film made with extreme prejudice: it did not whitewash its nastiness or its vision of a miasmic social reality. As testimony of its power to shock, the first version of Tsui's film, screened at the Berlin Film Festival, was banned by the censors in Hong Kong.

From the start, Tsui pulls no punches with his images: a twitching white mouse with a pin stuck through it; some kids on top of a tenement building throw a bag of red paint down into the street, narrowly missing a female passer-by and exploding on impact, painting the screen a violent red. The noxious atmosphere is hard to stomach, alarmingly close to unacceptable levels. Tsui's main characters are four disoriented youths: three male high school students and an unemployed factory girl with a manic streak and a suicidal urge to play with fire. The young girl, Wan Chu (Lin Zhenqi), has witnessed a hit-and-run accident perpetrated by the three students and, challenging them, she draws them deeper and deeper into an abyss of reckless adventure and dangerous pranks. They begin by holding-up a tourist coach, a job botched by the boys but carried through by the girl; then they accidentally stumble onto the operations of an international gun and drug smuggling syndicate controlled by American Vietnam veterans. The four youths run up against an American driving a car, after having had an argument in which Wan Chu poured kerosene on the boys and tried to set them on fire. It is now the American who fires up their emotions when he insults them with an obscene sign. The three boys react by throwing stones at his car and returning the obscene sign – Tsui freezes the image at this point, underlining that the kids' sickeningly callous brutality is both an imitation of and a response to the truly infernal horrors perpetrated on a massive scale by superpowers such as the United States and its representatives in Asia. It is worth remembering that Tsui was born in Vietnam.

Wan Chu steals a box from the American's car and discovers a wad of bankable Japanese cheques which belong to the syndicate. The youths attempt to cash the cheques via the services of a black disc-jockey with links to the financial underworld. A web closes in on the four as the Americans try to retrieve the cheques; Wan Chu is killed by the foreigners as her brother, a police detective (Luo Lie), returns home and becomes entangled in the conflict. While *Tom and Jerry* commit unconscionable violence on each other on the television in her apartment, she is defenestrated and her head is speared, with a squashy sound, on the iron railings below. The film ends in a remarkable action sequence reminiscent of Fritz Lang's delirious ending of *The Indian Tomb*. The scene takes place in a cemetery, with endless rows of crosses and tombstones filling the Scope screen: the Americans stalk the three boys, killing two of them while the lone survivor, demented with fear, fires his machine gun wildly into the emptiness around him. The scene builds into an emotional climax of cosmic proportions worthy of Munch's *The Scream*. The first version then had a brief coda consisting of still photographs of the Hong Kong riots of 1967, but this coda disappeared after the censor's intervention.

Tsui carefully telegraphs his motifs with recurring images such as that of a decomposing dead cat impaled on a fence; a presentiment of Wan Chu's death, made all the more symbolic since it was hurled out of the window by Wan Chu herself. There is also the motif of playing with fire. In the first version of the film, called *Dangerous Encounter of the First Kind/Diyi Lei Weixian*, the three students were shown making explosive devices and placing them inside a cinema. Then there is the scene in which Wan Chu has an argument with the boys and tries to set them on fire after dousing them with kerosene. When the first version was submitted to the censors, objections were immediately raised about the anti-social attitudes of the students who placed bombs in public places, as well as their anti-foreign (anti-American?) sentiments. To a government whose memories about the 1967 anti-colonial riots inspired by the Cultural Revolution were still fresh and when bomb scares were common, these scenes struck too close to home. The film was banned. Tsui and the producers then re-edited the picture, shooting extra scenes and cutting out the original emphasis on the students as bombers. Entirely new scenes to do with the Hong Kong special branch police tracking down and keeping tabs on the gun smugglers were inserted. It is this second version that is now in general circulation while the negative of the more coherent and intense first version is rumoured to have been destroyed.

The tasks of re-shooting and re-editing *Dangerous Encounter* delayed its release until late 1981. In the meantime, Tsui had made and released *All the Wrong Clues (for the Right Solution)/Guima Zhiduo Xing* (1981), with which, it was said, he 'sold out' to commercial cinema. It was his first major commercial success and bolstered his standing in the industry after the somewhat disastrous reception to *Dangerous Encounters – 1st Kind*. It started the formula of entertaining comedies with stunts, special effects and cameo appearances by big-name stars which became known as the 'Cinema City style'[1] and launched Tsui both as director and producer of commercial hits. After staying with Cinema City for two more years, Tsui founded his own production company to produce and direct films such as *Peking Opera Blues*, *A Chinese Ghost Story* and its sequels, and *A Better Tomorrow*.

As an apprentice work of a kind, *All the Wrong Clues* displays the director's typical exuberance for fast pacing and flamboyant effects, but it appears to have been co-ordinated rather than directed by Tsui, subordinating his style to that of his star and producer, Karl Maka, who plays a big-time mobster just released from jail and pursuing a vendetta against the private detective (played by George Lam) who had put him in prison. A police inspector (Teddy Robin) is assigned to protect the detective and becomes his sidekick in the battle against organised crime. The movie plays like an arbitrary, playful entertainment effort emanating from a well-equipped film school. However, Tsui reconfirmed his talent with his next release *Zu: Warriors from the Magic Mountain/Xin Shu Shan Jian Xia* (1983), a high-budget production for Golden Harvest. It was the first time Tsui resorted to his battery of classic 80s special effects to deploy his rather Wagnerian thesis that a nation's fate and identity are tied up with the deeds and adventures of its mythical heroes and heroines. In Tsui's film, heroes with superpowers are mobilised to help China rid itself of civil strife before the real apocalypse threatens in the form of a giant, multi-horned demon about to emerge from its cocoon. The super-heroes are Ding Yin, a swordsman dressed entirely in white (played by Adam Cheng) and Xiao Yue, a Zen Buddhist monk (played by Liu Songren). They are accompanied by their respective disciples, Di Mingqi (Yuan Biao) and Yi Zhen (Meng Hai), both equally invested with superpowers. At first, they are unable to subjugate the evil forces within the realm of the Magic Mountain because they bicker among themselves and cannot come up with a common strategy. The monk is possessed by an evil force manifested earlier in the film by special-effect light rays, humanoids and a heretical sect of anti-heroes. The unscathed heroes bring the monk to a castle of female 'celestials' headed by a princess (played by Lin Ching-hsia) who has the power to save the monk. The heroes continue to search for a pair of swords, one coloured purple, the other green, the only weapons capable of destroying the demon. To be effective, the two swords must be joined together and wielded in unison.

The message is clear: for peace to be achieved and the nation to recover its prosperity, the union of diverse forces must first be attained. Not that this message gets in the way of the entertainment. Tsui's film is a wondrous farrago of special effects achieving a seemingly endless succession of stunning, comic-strip imagery, at times even overwhelming the narrative which disintegrates into a montage of 'attractions'. Elaborate choreography of flying stunts and martial arts action complement the special effects of Hollywood experts brought to Hong Kong – an instance where Hollywood special-effects men and Hong Kong stunt professionals blended their efforts harmoniously. Tsui would resort again to special effects but only as producer and for the series of ghost films initiated by *A Chinese Ghost Story* (1987).

After churning out one more potboiler for Cinema City (yet another sequel to the *Aces Go Places* series), Tsui embarked on the most significant phase of his career in 1984. He became an independent film-maker operating through his own production company, Film Workshop. The first film under his own banner was *Shanghai Blues/Shanghai zhi Ye* (1984), a romance-comedy set in Shanghai before and after the anti-Japanese war. Tung Kwok-man (played by Kenny Bee) bumps into Shu Pui-lam (played by Sylvia Chang) during an air raid by Japanese bombers in 1937. They take cover under the Soochow Bridge and because it is dark, they cannot see each other's faces. They fall in love nevertheless and vow to meet under the bridge after the war. The narrative jumps to 1947. Tung is discharged from the army and becomes a struggling composer while Shu finds work as a dancer in a nightclub. Shanghai is invaded by new migrants from the countryside attracted to the city's bright lights and prospects for work. Enter 'Stool' (played by Sally Yeh), the nickname of a virginal country girl who is a new migrant to the city. 'Stool' and Shu become friends through an accidental meeting. Shu brings 'Stool' back to her apartment, where, coincidentally and unbeknownst to Shu, Tung is also staying – on the rooftop. A triangular relationship develops between them, before Tung and Shu realise they were the sweethearts under the bridge.

The allusion to the Shanghai classic *Crossroads/ Shizi Jietou* (1937) and the depiction of Shanghai as a magical metropolis, is Tsui's way of paying tribute to the golden era of Chinese cinema. Like its companion piece, *Peking Opera Blues/Dao Ma Dan* (1986), the beautifully designed and elaborate sets, with bright colour schemes and dazzling movements enhance an intricately choreographed, exquisitely timed, crazy comedy that effortlessly segues into dramatic scenes. Tsui seems to have taken to evoking and parodying the classic movies of the Shanghai cinema in order to make a point about the artistic status of Hong Kong cinema itself. He is looking fondly back to the depictions of Shanghai, its skyline and environs as well as to the style and conventions of the old Shanghai cinema of the 30s. Here, it is their interpretation of social comedy and realism which Tsui seeks to develop. He parodies their sense of realism via the sets and design while emphasising the craftsmanship and expertise of movie-making achieved by Hong Kong cinema. *Shanghai Blues* is the first explicit indication of Tsui's status as a true 'movie brat',[2] conscious of Chinese film history and its links with Hong Kong cinema.

Before making *Beijing Opera Blues*, Tsui completed *Working Class/Dagong Huangdi* (1985), a minor but interesting work. Set in a factory manufacturing instant noodles, the story revolves around a trio of labouring buddies. In common with movies in which the factory is the stage and the workers are heroes, management is made the villain of the piece. The film possesses genuine charm and a proletarian dynamism which social realism unsuccessfully sought to achieve in the days of Stalin and Mao. Much of the film's interest stems not only from the bouncing narrative but also in Tsui's decision to give the whole thing a bright, crystalline look – not for Hong Kong workers the realist nonsense of dreary factories, drab working conditions and smog-polluted atmosphere.

Peking Opera Blues is set in Beijing two years after the 1911 revolution which toppled the Qing Dynasty, dubbed the 'democratic revolution' by the film's writers. One of its lead characters is a nationalist revolutionary fighting for 'democracy', seeking to undermine the warlords and secret police working for the regime of Yuan Shikai, the fledgling republic's first president who later sold out the Nationalist Party's ideals so as to proclaim himself emperor. Cao Yun (played by Lin Ching-hsia) is the revolutionary whose father is a warlord acting as the president's intermediary with foreign bankers in order to raise an army for a planned invasion against the nationalist government in the south. Cao successfully hides her identity from her father and is assigned to steal the contracts for the foreign loan. 'Understudied' by a male colleague, Ling (played by Mark Cheng), the two revolutionaries find their task complicated by the intrusions of other characters with whom they become entangled. There is Xiang Hong

(Cherie Chung), a sing-song girl with a taste for gold and jewellery, and Bai Niu (Sally Yeh), a performer in a Beijing Opera troupe. The revolutionaries and the entertainers join forces to steal the key to the safe hiding the documents. The revolutionaries are captured by the secret police but are rescued by Xiang Hong and Bai Niu, more out of a sense of adventure than lofty conviction for the revolutionary cause.

Tsui's marvellous *mise en scène* and the pure exuberance of the action are the highlights of the movie. All the sensory elements seem perfectly designed and, for once, the viewer feels that the director has achieved a fine balance. The colour, movement, action and the relationships between characters are purely stylistic rather than dynamic in terms of the plot. The interplay in the relationships between the three female leads provide only a momentary focus to a picture otherwise preoccupied with pure movement and action. Nevertheless, the characters are endearing, with Cherie Chung's kooky and materialistic sing-song girl coming across as the most memorable of the trio. Hence, despite the overall exuberance and the achievement of his production designers, neither *Peking Opera Blues* nor *Shanghai Blues* resonate as works which enrich one's understanding of Tsui's motifs and themes; instead, both films may be viewed as by no means overly reverent tributes to the old classics of Chinese cinema and the benign influence of Chinese theatre on the movies, although Western audiences may also detect the impact of, for instance, Frank Tashlin's cartoon-inspired Hollywood comedies.

The success of *Peking Opera Blues* opened doors for Tsui Hark and Film Workshop to expand its base. The first film he produced as a *bona fide* production executive was John Woo's hit, *A Better Tomorrow/ Yingxiong Bense* (1986). Woo and Tsui had been colleagues at Cinema City, both eager to become their own bosses and to shine in their own individual ways while Cinema City confined them mostly to making comedies. While both directors share certain traits, not least the emphasis on fast pacing and a fondness for action genres, they developed very distinctive individual styles. *A Better Tomorrow* is undoubtedly a Woo film. In its own unique way, it is an introspective thriller examining moral values binding gangsters and killers. The quality of introspection rarely exerts itself in Tsui's own work, a fact borne out by *A Better Tomorrow III/ Yingxiong Bense III – Xiyang zhi Ge* (1989), Tsui's own contribution to the series. Tsui's *Part Three* is wholly devoted to Mark, the character played by Chow Yun-fat, who was killed in *Part One*. Hence, it offers a 'pre-history' of a key character which, by then, was familiar to the audience. The story sees Mark going to Saigon during the last days of the South Vietnamese regime to help his cousin and uncle get out of the country. They receive help from an unexpected quarter – a mysterious lady of the underworld (played by Anita Mui) whose connections with the corrupted bureaucracy greatly facilitate the process of evacuating Mark and his relatives from Vietnam. The unusual decision to locate a Hong Kong heroic prototype against the background of Vietnam, Tsui's native country, probably carries more than a tinge of allegory about Hong Kong's dilemma with China over the 1997 issue. But the highly strung melodrama format has too many insertions of sentimental kitsch, as demonstrated by the film's ending. The evocation of *yi*, a vital concept in the series, is done through Mui's character, a woman called Chow Ying-kit, rather than through the male character Mark, which skews the film's focus away from him. It is Chow Ying-kit who bears the mark of the true 'hero', the masculine term being appropriate in the light of the genre's conventional emphasis on male bonding. She is a genuine underworld figure, reminiscent of Howard Hawks's films, able to deal with tough guys on equal terms. In comparison, Mark is a novice. Even Tsui seems intimidated by Mui's character, as she inhabits a world which is not Tsui's natural habitat in cinema, although it is John Woo's.

Tsui's association with John Woo was short, lasting only for the production of *A Better Tomorrow* and its immediate sequel. As a producer, his most creative partnership with a director has been with Ching Siu-tung, who directed *A Chinese Ghost Story/Qiannü Youhun* (1987). Spectacular special effects were used to update the ghost story genre and the success of *A Chinese Ghost Story* led to two more sequels, all directed by Ching. The Tsui–Ching partnership was also responsible for *Swordsman/Xiao'ao Jianghu* (1990) and its sequels. Tsui is credited as one of the co-directors of *Swordsman*, which was meant to be directed by King Hu, who retains credit, but who was taken off the production. The resulting film is a unique hybrid, containing virtually all of Tsui Hark's trademarks in addition to some of King Hu's. Thus began the legend of Tsui as an interfering producer not content merely to facilitate and oversee the process of creation.

The fact of the matter is that Tsui has the mentality of an auteur, someone who is able to orchestrate all aspects of narrative film-making, including the scripts. This implies that Tsui has his own thematic preoccupations, his own philosophical niche. He may draw on Western influences (Tashlin or, for instance, Spielberg, with whom he shares an affinity for special effects and fast pacing), but it is obvious too that Tsui, like Hu, has drawn on Beijing opera in generating rollicking action sequences. Another influential cinematic figure would be Bruce Lee, especially when one considers Lee's evocation of Chinese nationalism as a requisite philosophy of martial arts.

The nationalistic current in most of Tsui' work is also evident in *Once Upon a Time in China/Huang Feihong* (1991). Tsui's vision of a mythical China, where heroic citizens possess extraordinary powers and self-sufficiency, is based on the realisation that it is a country the potential strength of which remains curbed by tradition and the refusal of talented individuals to come to terms with a new world. Accordingly, the China of *Once Upon a Time in China* is subjugated to and bullied by Western powers. In the latter half of the 19th century, China has lost the Opium Wars of 1840–1 and 1856–60, trying to stop the British from flooding China with drugs. China's defeat led to the foundation of Hong Kong as a British colony. Heroic patriots such as the young Wong Fei-hung from Guangdong, a genuine historical figure and an expert in martial arts, are required to do their bit to save China.

Wong had always been depicted as a patriot who does not need to be motivated by governments or political movements. In the 50s and 60s, the Cantonese cinema produced a long-running series featuring the character, portrayed by Cantonese actor Kwan Tak-hing, whose characterisation has lingered in popular memory through a long series of Cantonese-dialect kung fu adventures in the 50s. Kwan played the role in several more kung fu movies in the 70s. So stereotyped in the role was Kwan that the public virtually identified him as Wong Fei-hung. Tsui's Wong Fei-hung (portrayed by Jet Li or Li Lianjie, a Mainland Chinese kung fu actor) is in many respects a different figure altogether: a much more naïve, somewhat coy and school-boyish figure, but also more modern in a peculiar kind of way. He is associated with the Westernisation movement within China through his admiration of 'Aunt' Yee (played by Rosamund Kwan), a Westernised distant relative who is his follower, intimate companion and adviser on Western ways. But Wong is no real connoisseur of Western culture. He views the movement as a necessary step to rejuvenate the nation so that it may deal with Western intruders and rise up to face the world on equal terms. Wong Fei-hung, as portrayed by Kwan Tak-hing, was a patriarchal icon, a benevolent autocrat with smatterings of do-good liberalism. Tsui's Wong Fei-hung shares one trait with Kwan's Wong Fei-hung – they are both conservatives at heart, practitioners of Chinese martial arts who lament the fact that Western technology has overtaken the usefulness of kung fu as a traditional art of defence. Wong's disciples, including a fat butcher and a gangly Western-educated young man, are organised into a civilian militia. They are expected to learn the precepts and techniques of kung fu and the political truths concerning the fate of the nation so that they can put their skills to use in defending the country. Wong's enemies are not only Westerners but also local rivals who envy his eminence in kung fu, and bureaucrats in the provincial government who do not look kindly on his private militia, seeing it as a political threat. The Westerners are depicted as rapacious colonialists and slave traders who kidnap young men and women and ship them off to the 'Gold Mountain' (America).

Tsui's characters, both Chinese and Westerners, have a chauvinistic bent – moderates they certainly are not, with the exception of Aunt Yee, whose function in life is apparently to exert a moderating influence on Wong Fei-hung. The director goes as far as he can to depict arrogant, uncouth and bellicose Westerners, stereotypical 'foreign devils' or *gweilos*. Here he contrasts the negative image of Westerners with the depiction of Wong Fei-hung as the personification of *ren* (a mixture of nobility and benevolence). *Ren* is pronounced in the same way as the Chinese word for human being. All Chinese are *ren* while all foreigners are *gui* (devils; *gwei-los* is the Cantonese term for 'foreign devils').

Wong Fei-hung is both country boy and gentleman of the Chinese gentry. In addition to his kung fu skills, he is also a doctor of traditional medicine. He symbolises the two aspects of the nation, one which is characterised by a peasant tradition, one which aspires to become a member of the modern civilised world. The country's predicament is its inability to reconcile these two aspects, remaining in the grip of a peasant tradition unwilling or unable to adapt to modern ways. To aggravate the situation, Western powers have gained a foothold in China; their representatives are jingoists masquerading as missionaries, merchants and consular officials. The Chinese government, on the other hand, is staffed by ineffective officials easily corrupted or fooled by the Westerners. Wong Fei-hung is the only person who personifies *ren*; he alone is a man among wolves, one man against the world.

Once Upon a Time in China can be seen as an inversion of a work such as Kipling's Gunga Din. The bad guys are Britons and Americans while Jesuit missionaries barely pass muster in the Gunga Din role of intermediaries between Asians and Westerners. Tsui's work seems to play back, mischievously, the negative Asian stereotypes of Hollywood movies, answering with negative Western stereotypes of his own. However, Tsui's sensibility for movement and action over-rides all feelings of malice. The film has many well-choreographed action scenes. The one most people will remember is Wong Fei-hung's duel with a hot-headed rival kung fu master: in a warehouse, the two men scuttle to the top of long bamboo ladders, dodging each other's blows as they jump and leap from one ladder to the next. The rival is finally shot down by the Westerner's guns, and from being his deadly enemy, Wong immediately becomes his comforter in death. In his dying gasp, the rival master utters the film's most meaningful line, affirming that kung fu cannot withstand the guns and bullets of the West, underlining Tsui's theme of China as a country of lost opportunities. The film brings Tsui into focus as a mature artist, confirmed in the next edition of the Wong Fei-hung saga, *Once Upon a Time in China, Part II/ Feihong zhi Nan'er Dang Ziqiang* (1992).

Wong Fei-hung goes to Canton, accompanied by Aunt Yee and Leung Foon, to give a lecture on acupuncture, encountering a rebellion in progress. China has just signed the Shimonoseki Treaty giving away Taiwan to Japan, triggering student demonstrations in the streets of China's cities. The year is 1895. Western powers have entrenched themselves in China with consulates and trading companies – one more sign of China's weakness in the face of foreign intrusion. Xenophobic followers of a sect known as the White Lotus, under the control of a martial arts mystic, Master Kung, is running amok in Canton killing foreigners and laying siege to the British Consulate. Even as the provincial authorities mobilise troops to protect the foreigners, they are alerted to a far greater threat than the White Lotus xenophobes: a young doctor, Sun Yat-sen, is in Canton organising revolution against the Qing Dynasty. Rather than stem the tide of xenophobia, they are more eager to nip the flower of revolution in the bud.

Wong Fei-hung becomes acquainted with Sun while giving his lecture. Later, they find themselves sheltering in the British Consulate, caring for some orphans while the White Lotus xenophobes are making chaos outside. The Manchu commander of the provincial forces is ordered to

171

arrest Sun and his follower, Luk Hao-tung (played by David Chiang), in the consulate, but are rebuffed by the consul. In order to arrest the revolutionaries, the Manchus make a pact with the White Lotus allowing them to invade the consulate. Wong Fei-hung fights off the White Lotus thugs, going straight to their lair to defeat Master Kung and exposing him as a false god. He then tackles the Manchu commander who uses a long cloth whip as his special weapon. Their duel is set in an alley that is walled on both sides, with no avenues of escape. It is a superb sequence using a longitudinal space to emphasise the action generated by the adversary's method of wielding his whip. Wong's defensive tactics and weapon are surprisingly simple but nevertheless deadly. Sun's revolution is saved for the time being (he would suffer more setbacks before succeeding in 1911). The fact that it is saved by Wong Fei-hung seems to put our hero firmly into the ranks of progressive Chinese. But Wong's status is much more than that: it transcends the progressive politics of the day. He is first and foremost a classicist, a position that Tsui himself takes pains to emphasise in the Chinese title (*Nan'er Dang Zi Qiang*), which resists easy translation. Roughly, it points to Wong as a strong individual who is his own master, a man who is a paragon of strength amidst chaos. It could also refer to Sun Yat-sen, a hero who uses political means to heal the nation, but it is the figure of Wong as a paragon of classicism that endures. A certain irony thus comes into the interpretation of Wong as a classical Chinese martial artist who is allied to forces of Westernisation and modernisation.

Once Upon a Time in China, Part II, is one of Tsui's most finely crafted movies, a fact that is also apparent in its relatively straightforward narrative structure. The action is finely honed, with a sense of purpose to distinguish the usual élan, precision and elaboration of the choreography. One reason for this is that Tsui seems much more mindful of tempo than he has ever been, a trait underlined in the narrative by having his revolutionary characters, Sun and Luk, always check their time-pieces. Previously, Tsui's action sequences tended to be expansive, to say the least. The two action sequences which form the core of this movie, the duel with Master Kung and the final showdown with the Manchu Commander, are among Tsui's most direct and concise set-pieces. Credit should be given to Yuen Woo-ping, Tsui's action choreographer and himself a director of many kung fu classics, but the temporal finesse and the utilisation of time as a motif in the narrative are surely an outcome of Tsui's design (the director's credit as one of the scriptwriters in not there by accident).

In *Once Upon a Time in China, Part III* (1993), Wong Fei-hung continues his adventures with Aunt Yee and disciple Leung Foon against a background of China falling prey to Western predators trying to grab concessions in Beijing and China's other major cities. The Empress Dowager has called on all martial artists to unite and rid China of the foreigners. To prove that martial arts is the answer to the problem, she exhorts her officials to organise a lion dance tournament bringing together the best of China's martial artists. This time, it is the Russians who are the imperialist bogeymen. They plan to assassinate Premier Li Hongzhang who is about to sign a treaty ceding the Liaodong Peninsula to Japan, thus giving it a strategic advantage in its war plans against Russia. The occasion for the assassination is the lion dance tournament presided over by the premier.

Wong's agitated state when face to face with Westerners is much more pronounced in this third edition. He is particularly miffed at the Russians because of Aunt Yee's more than friendly relations with a young Chinese-speaking officer. Wong is in Beijing to participate in the tournament under the banner of the Guangdong Association, the famous martial arts club established by his father, who will enter the contest with his southern lions. The Cantonese, however, are threatened by members of the Taiping Club, led by a northern lout, Chiu Tin-ba, who is not above using dirty tricks to eliminate rivals. Chiu employs thugs, such as 'Club Foot' Seven, to deal with Wong Fei-hung. But when Club Foot is wounded, he is dropped like a stone and humiliated. Wong Fei-hung, ever the upright and righteous martial artist-cum-medial healer, tends to Club Foot and brings him around. In the tournament, Club Foot dances for the Guangdong Association, covering for Wong Fei-hung who has not only to win the contest but also to foil the Russians in their dastardly plan to assassinate the premier.

The narrative roller-coasts from one action sequence to the next, climaxing in the excellent lion dance tournament in the Forbidden City. The exhilarating lion dance choreography brings this edition of the Wong Fei-hung series as close to pure dance as is possible in kung fu movies. The lion dance is, of course, the showpiece in all Chinese festivities. To the Chinese, it is culture in its most popular form, and as a mascot for unity, it brings the masses together. The lion dance was featured in Wong Fei-hung movies starring Kwan Tak-hing (as in Yuen Woo-ping's 1981 *Dreadnaught/ Yongzhe Wu Ju*, which still contains the best lion dance sequence ever choreographed in front of the camera). The lion is thus regarded as a unity-mascot or symbol closely associated with the figure of Wong Fei-hung. Of all Chinese folk heroes, Wong is seen not only as the pre-eminent gentleman martial artist who practises kung fu as culture, he is also considered the best lion dancer of his time. When the master dances the lion, physical and mental powers are welded with mime to give the impression that he is the lion, a symbol come to life.

Tsui has achieved a similar fusion of style and content with his Wong Fei-hung series – one could say that he is a Chinese lion dancer among film directors. He has certainly achieved a place as a mascot among Hong Kong directors, one of the most commercially successful directors who is still a fundamental pillar of the new wave. Tsui has not stumbled in his career as a film-maker who is always conscious of achieving choreographed precision in action and movement, although one may criticise him for making wrong moves or turns. Tsui shares with all his new wave colleagues a concern for China. His interpretation of the China question, whether as an allegory for 1997 or as emotional affiliation for one's ancestral country and source of cultural identity, is his stock-in-trade. Tsui is an artist who deals in nationalism, a subject easily misconstrued. Fortunately, Tsui is too restless and mobile an artist to let his subject congeal into jingoism.

A BETTER TOMORROW – JOHN WOO'S MORAL DIMENSION

John Woo is a paradox: a gentle man who makes violent movies, as many critics who have met him will confirm. The paradox is not immediately apparent from Woo's movies which show him as an action director, pure and simple. The paradox lies in the combination of the man and his images. Woo is a director with a religious conscience whose early childhood was spent in a rough-and-tumble environment. His family were poor slum-dwellers and he grew up in a neighbourhood where kids often ended up in gangs. With such a background, it seems surprising that religious symbolism found its way into his films, although perhaps superficial resemblances with New York-based gangster films, as in Scorsese's work, may come to mind. In *The Killer/Diexie Shuangxiong* (1989), the final duel takes place in an empty church filled with lighted candles and flying pigeons. A statue of the Virgin Mary is blown up by a missile to the accompaniment of baroque music from a requiem mass; a priest appears to find out what is going on and, seeing the carnage, makes the sign of the cross. Meanwhile, the two heroes continue to mow down the bad guys with their rapid-fire automatic pistols and machine guns. The dance of death, the requiem mass, the day of wrath – these are the interlocking motifs played out before a breathless audience.

Woo's family was too poor to give him an education and it was only under the sponsorship of an American family, through the Lutheran Church, that Woo was put to school. His junior high school education was undertaken at a strict, puritanical school run by Lutherans. Their intention, Woo says, 'was to make decent young men and women out of us slum-dwellers. And, I must say, the school achieved its aim.' In his own words, Woo ended up 'a fervent Christian' and wanted to become a minister because 'I wanted to return the favour – to help people as I had been helped. I was deeply impressed with the altruism of the American family who paid for my education that my family valued but was simply unable to supply.'[3] However, Woo performed badly in school and constantly skipped classes to go to the cinema, art museums and libraries. In this way he managed to get a well-rounded education in the arts. He finished high school education at a Catholic school named after the Jesuit missionary, Matteo Ricci, and began making experimental films. He wanted to go to film school, but his family could not afford it. Instead, he worked for the Lutheran Church to support his film-making activities. He developed his writing skills and was exposed to foreign ideas. In 1969, he was hired by the now defunct Cathay Studio where he worked his way up from stage hand to assistant director. He switched studios, joining Shaw Brothers in 1971, where he worked as an assistant to action maestro Zhang Che. His debt to Zhang Che is evident from the themes and characters in his films. Woo would later dedicate a film to Zhang Che, *Just Heroes/Yidan Qunying* (1989), which he co-directed with Wu Ma.

Woo started his directing career in 1973 when the kung fu genre was at the height of its popularity. His first films were excursions into the genre, although kung fu did not hold Woo's interest for long. Of these early films, Woo said he is fond of *Princess Cheung Ping/Dinü Hua*, a Cantonese opera film and a re-make of a classic of the genre released in 1959. The more or less straight version of the original opera was an attempt to revitalise an old genre which had gone out of fashion in the 70s, and the theatrical trappings gave Woo little leeway to 'open up' the action. The film differed little from the 1959 film version, *Tragedy of the Emperor's Daughter* directed by Tso Kei, and was distinguished only by the showcasing of the two leads as protégés of the famous operatic couple, Yam Kim-fai and Pak Suet-sin, who had starred in the 1959 film. Nevertheless, Woo recalls having a lot of fun making the movie, which was a huge box-office success.

He was offered a bigger budget to make a swordplay movie, *Last Hurrah for Chivalry/Hao Xia*, released in 1978. As with *Princess Cheung Ping*, it was another attempt to revive an outdated genre, the *wuxia* movie, into which Woo injected his own brand of modern pastiche: his characters had nicknames such as 'Magic Sword', 'Green Shirt' and 'Sleeping Wizard'. The film added little to Woo and the genre's fortunes, but did suggest that the director had an abiding interest in conventional forms, stylistic effects and thematic concerns specific to action genres. If he sought to break new ground with old genres, he did not manage it in these two films. Nevertheless, *Last Hurrah in Chivalry* is interesting for the sign-posting of themes that Woo would explore more successfully in his later films. Woo himself calls *Last Hurrah* a 'prequel' to *A Better Tomorrow/Yingxiong Bense* (1986), both films dealing with chivalry and loyalty.

Like his screen heroes, Woo tended to be a loner, standing apart from current trends in artistic development. The 1979 emergence of a new wave passed him by. When younger directors were making ground-breaking films, Woo was indulging his fondness for silent comedians such as Keaton and Chaplin in largely inane comedies such as *Follow the Star/Da Shaxing yu Xiao Meitou* (1978) and *Laughing Times/Huaji Shidai* (1981). In other comedies, he tackled the Faust legend: *To Hell With the Devil/Modeng Tianshi* (1982); and Mark Twain: *Run, Tiger, Run/Liangzhi Laohu* (1985), which was a version of *The Prince and the Pauper*, made in Taiwan. These comedies were barely successful. It was not until *A Better Tomorrow/Yingxiong Bense* that Woo was able to fuse the old and the new.

A Better Tomorrow struck a nerve in the development of genres in Hong Kong cinema. Woo became recognised as a new kind of action director. In purely conceptual terms, he had not done anything new. He had simply redefined old concepts which held the action genre together from the 60s, reinterpreting them through a modern looking glass. The film was a remake of Cantonese director Lung Kong's *The Story of a Discharged Prisoner/Yingxiong Bense* (1967), following its basic plot but expanding further on the Chinese concept of *yi*. A major part of Woo's success lay in his re-examination of this concept, usually expounded in martial arts novels, comics and films. Western audiences may recognise the term from its deployment in Japanese *Yakuza* pictures, where it functions as '*giri*', translated as 'duty' or 'obligation'. *Giri* stems from the Chinese word *yi*, signifying justice or righteousness. As in Chinese *wuxia* and gangster films, the Japanese counterparts expounded on *yi* as an unwritten code originating from the ancient practice of knight-errantry in China.

Yi postulates a system of brotherhood, honour and justice binding all who operate within a (class- and caste-defined) fraternity, whether criminal or otherwise. More specifically, individual characters talk of *yiqi* (literally, 'breath of *yi*') as a system of personal loyalty. Anyone who transgresses is considered to be without *yiqi* and thus a traitor to *yi*. In addition to rejuvenating *yi* as a life force still relevant in our modern times, the new elements in Woo's film are mainly stylistic. His blend of balletic violence and male-bonding heroism mark him as a new wave innovator. In addition to the actors' intuitive performances, Woo's choreographic style for stunts is characterised by multiple shootouts, explosions and slow-motion shots of protagonists ducking or taking cover when they are not throwing explosive devices or firing guns. The single most representative, most classically perfect Woo picture is, to my mind, *A Better Tomorrow*. The story is all about keeping faith and observing the code of *yi*. Sung Chi-ho (portrayed by Ti Lung) and Mark Lee (Chow Yun-fat) are delivery boys for a syndicate dealing in counterfeit notes. When they try to smuggle notes into Taiwan, Sung is betrayed, captured and goes to prison, leaving Mark alone to square up to his betrayers. In the splendidly-staged gun duel which follows, Mark kills all his enemies but is himself shot in the leg and crippled for life. Three years later in Hong Kong, Mark goes through life as a bum, humiliated by the new boss of the syndicate, Shing, the man who betrayed them. The final showdown is, in essence, a battle between the traitors and loyalists of the code of *yi*. The blood-bath would be tragic if not for the protagonists' grotesque refusals to die and their florid gestures toward martyrdom when they actually do die.

The thin line between the grotesque and tragedy was more finely balanced in *A Better Tomorrow* than in the sequel. *A Better Tomorrow Part II/Yingiong Bense Xuji* (1987) is an irresistible serio-comic reinterpretation of events and characters from the previous edition. Seemingly unable to surmount a tendency towards pastiche, Woo produced a work containing an astonishing, almost Catholic death-and-resurrection theme. But, as he is prone to do, Woo subverts his own themes with touches of absurdity which end up as irregular though hugely enjoyable patches in his narratives. According to Woo, it is his least favourite film. He delivered an original cut of 2 hours and 40 minutes, but was given a week to cut it down to under two hours: 'Tsui Hark (the film's producer) took half and I took half and we cut our parts separately. I didn't get to see the whole picture until its opening night. Naturally, the result was uneven and unsatisfying.'[4]

The death of the dauntless Mark (Chow Yun-fat) in *Part One* poses no obstacle to *Part Two's* narrative continuity. Mark is simply 'resurrected' in the person of an identical twin brother, Ken, who works in New York City as a cook. He is conveniently called upon to fit into the hero's shoes vacated by Mark. He even wears Mark's bullet-hole ridden overcoat, stuffing it with grenades and explosive devices for the final duel. With the theme of death and resurrection so much to the forefront, ancillary themes of suffering, loss and recovery brim over to the surface. The plot centres around a retired godfather (an impressive dramatic performance by comedian Dean Shek), who is framed for the murder of a rival gang boss. This old, retired and shell-shocked gangster is packed off to New York City for his own security. But further attempts on his life cause him to have a mental breakdown. It is left to Ken to nurse the old man back to health from a near-vegetable state. The turning point comes when both men are pursued by hired killers; when Ken is wounded, the old man is jolted back into action (and reality) with gunplay that puts younger men to shame. The scenes between the old man and Ken are the nearest thing to a father and son relationship in Woo's modern action thrillers, a generational variant on the theme of male bonding. Shek's performance is the best thing in the film. He portrays the father as a tragic and remorseful Lear-figure, repelled by violence but also revived by it at the moment he realises that a son's life is in danger. Back in Hong Kong, the rejuvenated godfather and Ken are joined in a plan of revenge by other surrogate sons: Sung Chi-ho and his brother Kit (played, as in the first edition, by Ti Lung and Leslie Cheung). The final death-duel is like a ritual, filmed in slow-motion as people are mown down by automatic gunfire; blood spurting through the edges of the frame; explosions, with the hero in the foreground reeling only slightly from the effects; the hero facing up to the silent killer (redolent of the final gunfight in classic Westerns); the confrontation between avenger and villain. In this picture, parody as an antidote to violence is never far away. In the end, the heroes are the only ones alive, but only just. It is an indication of the serio-comic vein running through the film that the penultimate line spoken by Ken is a kind of put-down of the cliché that heroes never die: 'We're dying, can we leave now?'

Woo's next film *The Killer/Diexie Shuangxiong*, dedicated to Martin Scorsese and evocative of Jean-Pierre Melville's super-cool thrillers (particularly *Le Samourai*), is really his most Leone-esque movie,[5] full of languidly intense moments when the camera lingers on faces in extreme close-ups, complemented by an adagio on the soundtrack. These moments are plentiful and occur in between Woo's typically baroque action scenes. The sum total of balletic violence and poetic meditations of killer and cop as they size each other up in almost transcendental terms, gives the impression that *The Killer* is more about sentiment and feeling. For Woo, it is a kind of *New Testament* film, heralding the advent of a neo-romantic artist. It starts rather like a conventional love story between a man and a woman, but is later complicated by the extraordinary emotions of the killer and his affections for another man, the cop, in one more variation on the theme of male bonding. Chow Yun-fat's Jeff (the name of Alain Delon's character in *Le Samourai*) is a professional killer, but he is also a compassionate man.[6] On the verge of retirement, he accidentally causes the blindness of a singer, Jennie (Sally Yeh). As a sign of his honour, Jeff takes on one more job so that he can finance a cornea transplant for her. Li (Danny Lee) is the police inspector on his tail who is really a fan of Jeff's style, initially impressed by the fact that Jeff had saved the life of a little girl hurt during a shoot-out after he has been betrayed by his partner Sidney Fung (Chu Kong). The cop's pursuit converges with these attempts to get rid of Jeff. Still unpaid for his last job, Jeff attempts to kill his employer, Wang, but fails. Wang, in turn, hires other professionals to kill Jeff.

The movie is at its most elegiac in dealing with the conflict of interests between the two erstwhile partners, Jeff and Fung. Fung's life is spared by Jeff for old times' sake. In return, Fung risks his own life in asking Wang for Jeff's money. He does it as 'a last tribute to a friend' but he must also prove his own worth in terms of a professional code which binds the two killers – evidence yet again of Woo's preoccupation with *yi* and *yiqi* as a private loyalty between his characters. It is also *yiqi* which brings Jeff, the killer, and Li, the cop, together and reinforces their feeling of deep loss when betrayal of *yi* entails sacrifice to prove one's personal worth and friendship. *The Killer* is an elegy to the past, filled with the sort of ethical norms that Woo clearly feels have no modern-day substitutes. It may be ironic that Woo's heroes are models of modern-day styles, fashion and behaviour. However, Woo was less concerned here with irony than with feelings and emotions, to the point of excess. His flamboyant finale in the church sees Woo at his most hysterically excessive, bar the final scenes in *Hardboiled/Lashou Shentan* (1992) set in a hospital, with babies used as hostages.

Yet, in between excesses of this nature, *The Killer* is terse and laconic in a poetic sort of way, setting out to be a paean both to Western masters (Melville, Scorsese, Leone, Peckinpah) and to classics of the swordfighting martial arts genre in Hong Kong which Woo evokes and transforms through his own 'hero movies', a term derived from the word *yingxiong* (meaning hero), as in *Yinxiong Bense*, the Chinese title of Woo's *A Better Tomorrow* (meaning 'The Essence of Heroes'). If only because it gave a name to a new type of action thriller, *A Better Tomorrow* is arguably Woo's most significant film, crystallising his concerns with the genre's motifs of male bonding based on the code of *yi* and its betrayal. It also was the film which gave full play to Woo's modern action version of swordplay and kung fu films, replacing them with balletic gunplay and shoot-outs. *The Killer*, on the other hand, is too full of florid gestures and introspective melancholy to be taken as an elementary thriller.

The Vietnam War is the setting for *Bullet in the Head/Diexie Jietou* (1990), John Woo's most extreme statement yet on the theme of male bonding and Hong Kong people's capacity for courage, cowardice and greed. Behind all this lurks 1997. Woo's protagonists, Ben, Frank and Paul, are typical *feizai* (teenage rebels and gangsters). On his wedding night, Ben kills a rival *feizai*. It is 1967 – not a good year for the territory. For perhaps the first time in its history, Hong Kong is shaken by violent political riots instigated by local followers of Mao's Cultural Revolution. The three buddies leave for Vietnam and are quickly overcome by events there. On the day of their

178

arrival, they witness the assassination of an army general and are arrested as suspects in the resulting melée. Unflustered by the experience, they stay on and, together with a soldier of fortune named Luke, stick up a local big-time gangster, getting away with a casket of gold along with a Hong Kong girl whom they have rescued from prostitution. At times, the Hong Kong visitors appear to be waging their own private war, reducing the real war in Vietnam to a sideshow. At other times, they appear as out-of-place innocents, wading through the rice fields which happen also to be battlegrounds. Ben, the most rational of the three, which isn't saying much, keeps the group together. Frank is brittle, and Paul goes completely gold crazy. In their getaway, they are captured by Vietcong soldiers and submit to the most grievous mental torture – being forced to kill fellow prisoners. Ensuing scenes make *The Deer Hunter* look like a garden party. Miraculously, all three buddies survive the ordeal, saved by the timely attack of American forces on the Vietcong camp. Frank survives but has a bullet in his head, put there by a crazed Paul thinking only of dragging his gold out of harm's way.

Woo heavy-handedly hammers in his themes and allusions to Vietnam War movies in order to make a statement about Hong Kong. The film was released one year after the Tiananmen massacre. Woo says he 'poured a lot of emotion' into the film because of his feelings about the massacre: 'What I really wanted to do was to make a film about how people behave in wartime or in times of chaos. Friendship is important to me because I have seen this is one of the first things that is lost during wartime. People become selfish when their survival is threatened, allowing evil the chance to grow. And this is a real tragedy; it is the way we become spiritually defeated, by abandoning our trust in one another. In this film I wanted to address something that was happening in Hong Kong or will happen in Hong Kong. Wartime Vietnam was a metaphor for all this.'[7]

Bullet in the Head explores the fundamentally shaky, explosive nature of the Hong Kong character and its reliance on violent stereotypes and emotional tokens designed to counter the suggestion that Chinese people are unemotional. The substance of male bonding lies in this need for emotional tokens as much as in the code of *yi* with its associations of honour, duty, decency and loyalty. The loss of friendship means the ultimate betrayal of the code of *yi*: 'The way I see it, it is only by bonding together and trusting each other that we will survive,' Woo said.[8] But the film is too grotesque, too precariously perched on the edge, to be accepted at face value. Woo was confronting Hong Kong audiences with an un-flattering picture of themselves and they did not like it: *Bullet in the Head* was a box-office failure and may not even have recouped its substantial costs on first release (US $4 million, double its original budget). Woo pointed out that the film had a tragic tone and was utterly devoid of heroes, while audiences could sense that wartime Vietnam functioned as a metaphor for their own predicament, having filled their spiritual void with materialistic greed. On top of that, people had experienced the pain of the Tiananmen massacre the year before. But Woo stuck to his guns: 'I don't think anyone in Hong Kong was in the mood to see the picture more than once, which is necessary in a small market like Hong Kong to make money on a picture, and so, they stayed away. But I still consider this my favourite movie because of how much I poured into it.'[9]

In *Once a Thief/Zongheng Sihai* (1991), Woo shows that his label as an exuberant, over-the-top director is really a pretext for an extravagant stylistic unevenness encompassing wild swings in dramatic moods. Starting life as a comedy with Chow Yung-fat indulging in his throw-away lines, *Once a Thief* shifts gears like an automatic transmission gone haywire. In both style and content, it is close to Woo's *A Better Tomorrow, Part II*, which is a self-parody disguised as a sequel to a pathbreaking work. Yet, both films exert some kind of fascination, not least because they are about fathers and sons – a standard relationship in Cantonese social-realist family melodramas of the 50s. With *Once a Thief*, Woo goes even further in breaking through the limits of the comedy and action film by making it a fairytale about the father and son relationship. This urge to test the limits and to breach the barriers of genres is one of Woo's hallmarks, shown at its most breathtaking and pop-eyed manner in the hospital shoot-out scenes of *Hardboiled*.

In *Once a Thief*, Joe (Chow), Jim (Leslie Cheung) and Cherie (Cherie Chung) are orphans who have grown up together under an adopted father, a Fagin-like criminal who taught them the art of thievery. Abused and half-abandoned by the bad father, they found an alternative good father in the person of a police detective who had come upon the delinquent children. In France to steal a painting, Joe and Jim become victims of a set-up after their successful heist. In the ensuing gun battle, Jim escapes while Joe supposedly dies in a crash. From this *Hudson Hawk* beginning, the narrative moves to Hong Kong two years later. Joe returns from the dead (a restatement of the resurrection theme), a cripple on a wheelchair, to find Jim and Cherie married. The plot thickens with the two 'fathers' vying for the affections of the sons, the bad father drawing Joe and Jim into another heist, while the good father stays in the background providing a moral conscience. The father–son theme becomes flimsy once Woo gets to the action. The final gun-play is a hodgepodge of comedy and dramatic action staged with typical exuberance. It turns out that Joe is not a cripple after all, and had carried out the masquerade only to deceive the bad father and lure him into a trap in order to finish him off once and for all. With his usual dash, Joe shoots down everyone in sight – stopping short of patricide, however. Here again, the code of *yi*, which also operates between family members, determines the behaviour of an individual.

When thieving fathers and sons fall out, John Woo gives the sons a choice of two fathers – one good, one bad. As a filial member of the Chinese family, Woo is bound by *yi* at least to offer that choice. This is the first overt indication in Woo's films that there is a moral dimension to his violence and that his expressive style is not pure bombast. In all his previous films, from *A Better Tomorrow* onwards, one can argue that Woo was hard put to state a clearly defined moral choice between good and bad.

Cop and killer were never clearly set apart enough for audiences to be able to take sides. Not so in *Once a Thief*. Perhaps it took a comparatively light-hearted romp to bring out what is after all a cliché of all action genres.

With *Hardboiled*, Woo reverts to the hard ground of the violent action thriller. So far, *yi* established the rules of the game in which even the bad guys know the limits of their wrongdoing. To a bad guy versed in *yi*, the cops may be the mortal enemy, but in battle one tries not to involve innocent bystanders and certainly to leave the sick and disabled, not to mention babies, out of harm's way. *Hardboiled* blows this professional rule to smithereens. Woo comes up with the following thesis: there are no standards of morality which underlie the art of killing by bad men. Woo appears to abandon his concept of *yi* as the only arbiter of morality in the action genre. He acknowledges that there is a social morality to contend with.

Woo had clearly intended to seek the truth from movie convention, to ground the deeds of movie gangsters in the real context of modern Hong Kong. The territory had become a hot target for criminals. Shoot-outs on the streets were common occurrences; passers-by were killed. The intention is signalled in the title 'Hardboiled' and the groundwork for a revisionist treatment of the action thriller laid in the very first action scene. Chow Yun-fat's cop (called 'Tequila') intercepts a gang of gun-smugglers in a public tea-house. As they try to escape, the bad guys routinely shoot innocent clients in the tea-house. Tequila kills one of the gangsters in the confusion but is told that his victim is an undercover cop. As his nickname implies, Tequila is an obsessive, volatile man intent on becoming the nemesis of the chief gun-runner, Johnny, and in so doing, nearly ruins the plans of another undercover cop, Tony (Tony Leung Chiu-wai), who has infiltrated Johnny's organisation. The relationship between Tequila and Tony is more conventional than the film's treatment of its bad guys, who are no longer seen as romantic sub-heroes because *yi* makes them so. The bad guys really are very bad guys. Even Tony is seen as an inveterate, if also introspective, killer. Tequila and Tony are but variations of Jeff and Li of *The Killer*, repeating the borderline relationship between cop and killer, good guy and bad guy. This time, both Tony and Tequila are tragic heroes who know that action and violence somehow bring out their worth as human beings. We begin to see the nature-of-the-beast quality of Woo's heroes. Killing and violence are so much a part of their characters that they must make something meaningful out of them. In Woo's films, it is the code of *yi* which helps to confer meaning and moral justification, changing the beast's fundamental nature into one of knightly gallantry.

Ironically, Tequila and Tony are on the right side of the law, though they do not subscribe to Queen's rules and regulations – the underground code of *yi* is more binding. But there is now a difference, a clearer delineation of right and wrong. Put in another way, the wrong side has no more recourse to moral strength. That it did so previously was all along an old-fashioned ideal. Modern precepts of law and morality had at last caught up with John Woo. He now portrayed his villains as neo-savages, modern barbarians who appear to have inherited the tradition of Attila the Hun and his baby-eating hordes. Just as the first action sequence sets the mirror-shattering pace in which a genre's conventions are broken, the grand finale grips audiences in heart-of-darkness horror as they stare into the reality of the criminal underworld. Johnny and his gang invade a hospital using the sick, the infirm, the old, women, children and babies as shields and hostages. The excess of the sequence, rather than its imagined atrocities, is what blows the mind. Even though the babies survive the sequence, the audience's sympathies with the film may not.

Shocking as it is, the whole sequence does once again reveal Woo's penchant for the absurd, his liking for the grotesque. In both a negative and positive way, Woo does not flinch from showing what is elemental or crude in his own society, for Hong Kong, like most developing Asian societies, is a place of extremes. Though appearing to be sophisticated, Hong Kong actually relies largely on stereotypes for character assessments: bad guys and good guys are not hackneyed descriptions. Without the softening effect of middle-class placidity, venality and vanity are the norm. Woo's florid style or his tendency for excess cannot therefore be dismissed as mere indulgence. Hong Kong's residents can be grotesquely rude, temperamental and crude; hence actors overact and Woo makes his pictures accordingly. He is not the only director to reflect the basic nature of Hong Kong society in the movies. But he is one who has won the admiration of cineastes all over the world for essentially showing man rising just above his baser instincts. The irony that Woo's movies are shown in art-houses in the West cannot be lost on him. Base emotions and vulgarity, the sort that makes an ordinary man queasy, have won Woo a new respectability.

That Woo's elemental rawness does not work against him is due to the incredible array of themes and stylistic conceits with which he bombards his audience. Religion and morality, with the attendant rituals, rules of behaviour and dangers of transgressions, add an unexpected and universal dimension to Woo's pictures. In spite of the intermingling of violence and religious symbolism in films such as *The Killer*, Woo cannot be called a sacrilegious artist. He challenges the conscience of the establishment and attacks its power and hypocrisy. His heroes are vain and revengeful but they hold honour, truth and integrity in high esteem. Morality as a wholistic concept does not concern Woo as much as the question of ethics – that dimension which claims that morality by itself has no foundation unless backed by an individual's ethical decision. Ethics is inferred by the fact that his characters are professionals doing their job. The central theme of religion and ethics binding characters together permeates *Hard Target* (1993), Woo's first Hollywood film in a career move taking him away from Hong Kong to America where violence is second-nature to screen heroes. Lacking a complex hero (his star being Jean-Claude Van Damme instead of Chow Yun-fat), Woo plied his audience with neatly-choreographed action sequences, but the film is a virtual textbook of classic Woo symbols for anyone who wants to discern them.

Woo presents violence as something both real and unreal. There are good guys and bad guys. Within the circle of bad guys, there is a further moral division of right and wrong. There is that moral choice between adherence or non-adherence to *yi*. Adherence implies hope and salvation, important elements to Hong Kong people torn by doubt over their future. The title, *A Better Tomorrow*, offers not a false hope but a real one. There is a yearning for redemption, almost as if Hong Kong people were mired in a sinful past and no less sinful present. To an audience, the choice is whether to take Woo's message seriously.

NOTES

[1] Cinema City was the production company founded by stars Karl Maka, Dean Shek and Raymond Wong. The style was also sustained by subsequent box-office hits such as *Aces Go Places/ Zui Jia Paidang* and its sequels.

[2] A 'movie brat' being defined as a director who always evokes or quotes the classics of bygone eras.

[3] Interview with author.

[4] Interview with author.

[5] Leone's influence was seminal and stems not so much from his Westerns but from his one gangster movie, *Once Upon a Time in America* (1984), particularly in its theme of loyalty and betrayal which understandably evokes a great sense of empathy with Hong Kong film-makers who saw in the theme parallels with the code of *yi*. It is not too far-fetched to say that it was really Leone's film which provoked the production of a rash of gangster movies in the mid-80s centred on male bondage and gang loyalty, such as Stephen Shin's *Brotherhood/ Xiong Di* (1986), Woo's own *A Better Tomorrow* (1987) and Ringo Lam's *City on Fire/ Longhu Fengyun* (1987).

[6] The laser disc version of *The Killer* released in the US reverts to the original name intended for Chow's character: John.

[7] Interview with author.

[8] Interview with author.

[9] Interview with author.

Chapter Twelve

The Second Wave

The rise of the new wave in Hong Kong was a result of the confluence of events and geography. As a strategic Western outpost on the East Asian Pacific rim, Hong Kong is the region's most liberal society and an important manufacturing and financial centre, qualities which are reflected and elaborated in Hong Kong movies. Its impact on popular culture in the whole East Asian region cannot be underestimated. The rapid generational turnover in Hong Kong cinema in the late 70s was an inevitable outcome of the coming of age of the territory's own 'baby-boomers' – those born in the 50s who grew up with the Western lifestyle and education that had become integral parts of the system. In the early 80s, there were more young directors in their late 20s and early 30s making debut films in Hong Kong than probably anywhere else in the world. As the new wave pushed the talented into the forefront, many other young directors were waiting to join their ranks. Aspiring film-makers were complemented by young entrepreneurs eager to get into the business who set up independent production companies, though many did not last long. Some young directors have been characterised as a 'second wave' in Chapter 10. In truth, they are a delayed part of the first new wave; many of the directors, such as Stanley Kwan, Eddie Fong, Ching Siu-tung and Wong Kar-wai had worked as assistants or writers to Ann Hui, Tsui Hark or Patrick Tam. The benefit of hindsight has shown that the wave did not come to an end as its directors were co-opted and became established in the industry. It went on and the achievements of the younger directors consolidated the aesthetics introduced by their elders. Indeed, the second phase ushered in a more mature kind of experimentation which ultimately brought greater international recognition to Hong Kong cinema in the late 80s. The first film to show signs that the new wave had not abated was Eddie Fong's *An Amorous Woman of the Tang Dynasty/ Tang Chao Haofang Nü* (1984). It is an extraordinary first film by Fong, who began his cinema career as a screenwriter in 1982. The film is centred around a liberated woman known as Xuan Ji (superbly performed by Pat Ha), whose promiscuity and moral ambivalence, based on Daoist existentialist attitudes, symbolised an age of poetic glory in Chinese history. The fact that she is 'an amorous woman of the Tang Dynasty' speaks volumes about Fong's view of Chinese history as the proper point of reference for modernism in Chinese culture, a perspective which reacts against the equation of modernism with Westernisation.

Sex and existentialism, Daoist style, in China's most creative period, the Tang, was an advance on contemporary mores where moral concerns had overcome the creative instinct. Xuan Ji aspires to the secrets of Daoist existentialism in which the purpose of life is to surrender oneself to physical and sensual pleasures. Xuan Ji is a poet, a well-known practitioner of the arts and an all-round cultural savant. But it is in matters of love that Xuan Ji strives to reach the Daoist goal of immortality. She leaves an old tea merchant whose concubine she had been, to become a Daoist priestess. Xuan Ji is accepted into the religious order only if she can give up worldly and sensual pleasures. This she is not able to do. She meets a wandering swordsman and falls in love with him, but she is desired by others just as she desires a young Daoist priest and her own maid with whom she consummates a lesbian affair. It is Xuan Ji's indulgence in physical desires that poses the dialectic between the mind and the body. The message seems to be that the abandonment of the body to desire is the avenue to true liberation and spirituality. It is a sexual-libertarian interpretation of Chinese existentialism where the Daoist aspiration to immortality begins not with the soul but with the body. Fong may, of course, be criticised for this thesis, but if it is a flaw, it is a chosen one. Xuan Ji is presented as a typical existentialist in that her desires and affairs are the consequences of her own choice, as is her death by execution at the end. The mood of the film is both contemplative and sensual. The sensuality is cool but no less scintillating, with some of the most sensual sex scenes ever seen in Hong Kong cinema.

Fong's subsequent films did not extend the remarkable aesthetic and moral incisiveness of his first work, but they are by no means negligible. Like Patrick Tam (on whose film *Nomad* he worked as a writer), Fong has a fondness for things Japanese, reflecting the impact which Japanese culture exerted on the minds of young people in Hong Kong, particularly in the fields of fashion, cinema, music and pop art. Japanese allusions may be noted in *Amorous Woman of the Tang Dynasty*, but in his next two films, Fong brought Japan directly into focus. *Cherry Blossoms/Yu Dafu Chuanqi* (1987) offers a lustrous evocation of Japan in the period 1910–20. Japan was then a haven for Chinese students and intellectuals concerned about their country's status as the 'sick man of Asia'. Japanese intellectuals, on the other hand, were rediscovering themselves in the light of Japan's rise as a major world power. The film deals with the teenage years of Chinese writer Yu Dafu as a student in Japan, and his relationship with a Japanese student and a Chinese girl brought up by her father to assimilate into Japanese culture and forget her Chineseness. The film seethes with an atmosphere of repressed desire, its characters having just reached an age of sexual discovery but holding themselves back because of a restless need to clarify their national identity and personal situation. The clash of national identity and individual feelings infuses the film with a mesmerising quality while enriching it with political themes.

The Last Princess of Manchuria aka *Kawashima Yoshiko/Chuandao Fangzi* (1990) continues the Japan–China love–hate affair. It is a handsomely mounted biography of the checkered career of China's own Mata Hari who was executed in 1945 as a spy, collaborator and empire-builder for the Japanese. Anita Mui portrays Kam Bik-fai alias Kawashima Yoshiko, actually Princess Hin-Tsee, fourteenth daughter of Prince Su, a member of the Manchurian royal family. Two years after the overthrow of the Qing Dynasty, the young princess was sent to Japan where she grew up as the adopted daughter of a Japanese empire-plotter. She is forced into a marriage with a Mongolian prince and becomes part of a Japanese scheme to interfere in Chinese affairs. The cornerstone of the scheme is to set up Mongolia and Manchuria as independent states. The marriage fails and Kawashima moves to China in the 30s, a period of unrestrained Japanese expansion into China. Kawashima Yoshiko matures into womanhood and continues to work for the Japanese. The film details her affairs with men and women – Japanese, Manchurian and Chinese.

Fong's preoccupation with sex is obvious in all his films. Sex is viewed as a force which drives and shapes people, but it is not presented as all-consuming: it loses its lustre and life has other meanings, usually political in nature. This side of Fong's perspective on the power of sex in one's lives and its eventual refutation by greater events of political and social significance is more incisively tackled in his scripts for other directors. Particularly noteworthy are *Nomad*, written for Patrick Tam, and the three which he wrote for his wife, director Clara Law, *Farewell, China/Ai Zai Biexiang de Jijie* (1990), *Autumn Moon/Qiu Yue* (1992) and *Temptations of a Monk/You Seng* (1993).

Fong had collaborated with Law on her first work, *The Other Half and the Other Half/Wo Ai Taikong Ren* (1988), a flat marital comedy about immigration to Canada and its effect on the marriages of two typical yuppies. Immigration and its effect on people's lives is developed to greater effect in *Farewell China* and *Autumn Moon*. *Farewell China* is Law's depiction of the Chinese Diaspora as a Dantesque descent into an American Inferno (New York City). Although much maligned by critics at the time, it is a key work in Law's career, audaciously spelling out the director's obsessions with personal identity and Hong Kong's China syndrome.[1] In a breathtakingly melodramatic style, Law also attacks the persisting myth of the American Dream harboured by Chinese emigrants. *Autumn Moon*, the next Clara Law–Eddie Fong collaboration tells the story of Tokio (Masatoshi Nagase, later seen in Jim Jarmusch's *Mystery Train*), a young Japanese tourist in Hong Kong.[2] He carries a Super 8 video camera like a notebook, recording images wherever he goes. Tokio makes friends with Wai, a 15-year-old schoolgirl whose parents went to Canada with her older brother, leaving her alone with her grandmother in Hong Kong. Old grandma will soon be abandoned as Wai is expected to join her parents in Canada – an event she does not look forward to. Both Tokio and Wai are provided with monologues which they deliver with warm intelligence. Wai does not speak Japanese and Tokio does not speak Chinese. Paradoxically, their halting

English forces them to speak with candour. The film seems to suggest that there is no real communication gap when the heart is true.

Not surprisingly for an Eddie Fong script, sex has a role to play in a story that is seemingly about innocent youth. Tokio accidentally meets Mikio, an old girlfriend from his neighbourhood in Tokyo. In a rather crude scene they have sex in his hotel, but Law contrasts this with a gentler lovemaking scene later in the film, after Tokio confesses to the meaninglessness of his life. Law staunchly defends these sex scenes as 'very important',[3] revealing 'many things about Tokio .... Modern man does not see linkages or connections,' a statement she illustrates with the scene where Wai and her boyfriend spend a night together on one of Hong Kong's outlying islands. He lies in bed planning his future as a nuclear physicist while she sits by the bed, waiting for affection. One may draw a superficial parallel between Tokio having sex without love and Wai being deprived of love and attention. In this context, Law speaks of the 'cumulative effect' of personal experiences, as in the postmodern age things and relationships are seen to be without cause and effect, but 'the body has memories'. The role of sex is the body's way of re-living these memories.

Law's characters are both 'modern nomads' who must try to deal with their sense of desolation and lack of identity. She shows how Hong Kong people's obsession with education and migration has obscured true human values. Similarly, their preoccupation with objects and technology has taken the place of real communication between people. There are recurring helicopter shots of high-rise apartment buildings and architectural structures, showing how impersonal Hong Kong can be. Wai's isolation is emphasised by the plethora of technical gadgets in her apartment, such as computers and karaoke machines; Tokio's preoccupation with his video camera also bespeaks the same alienation. Law creates out of ordinary material a story about rootlessness and loss of tradition, nurturing her characters and eliciting charming performances from the actors – no mean feat when one considers how mundane the characters and the settings really are.

Temptations of a Monk, the third Law–Fong collaboration, is based on a story by Lilian Lee (of *Rouge* and *Farewell My Concubine* fame), and shows Law developing into a virtuoso stylist. A period piece set in the Tang Dynasty, the film makes use of an astonishing range of eclectic allusions from East and West – astonishing even by the standards of Hong Kong cinema: allusions to Fong's own *Amorous Woman of the Tang Dynasty* and references to Chinese literature (particularly martial arts and romantic stories), with echoes of Japanese period dramas and samurai epics (Kurosawa and Mizoguchi movies come to mind), and, finally, allusions to baroque Italian cinema (a Fellini-like bacchanale and, in the episode involving the seduction of the monk by a beautiful passer-by, touches of the Taviani Brothers' *Night Sun*). Law's sheer bravado and technical mastery make the whole thing work, although the director confesses to having had to compromise on many things in the production, and asserts that it was her most difficult project: shot on location in China in a co-production deal utilising Chinese crews and studios, with funds wholly provided by the Hong Kong production company.

Wu Xingguo (a Taiwanese actor trained in Peking opera) plays General Shi Yansheng, who betrays the crown prince whom he was serving, for the sake of reforms promised by General Huo Da (Zhang Fengyi), a loyalist to the crown prince's bother. Huo Da reneges on his pledge to Shi when the crown prince is killed and his pretender rises to the throne, eventually to become the dynasty's most popular emperor. Devastated more by his own treachery than by Huo Da's betrayal, and spurred by his mother (Lisa Lu, remarkable in a brief appearance), Shi swears before the family altar never to serve the new emperor. The general and remnants of his regiment become monks, with the aim of re-grouping and rising up again. The story slowly assumes the force of a moral tale hinging on a puzzle: will Shi, who has assumed the name of Jing Yi, adhere to his monk's vows not to take revenge and kill Huo Da, or will he strip away the pretence of honouring his pledge, return to secular life as a dissident general and fulfil his violent destiny? Shi wrestles with moral and physical conflicts, and these struggles form the tantalising narrative of the second half of the film. He must face up to seductions by beautiful women, including Scarlet, the 19th princess of the Tang royal family (played by Joan Chen), and a female assassin dispatched to seduce and kill him, as well as the final violence which he must commit against Huo Da. Law displays a mature grasp of character and Shi Yansheng is the most convincing of Law's characters, all of whom have to struggle with themselves over the nature of ethical codes. The film is a very fine achievement with excellent production design and action choreography, enhanced by Law's *mise en scène*, superbly recreating the fine details of Fong's screenplay.

Clara Law is, along with Mabel Cheung, Ann Hui and Tang Shuxuan, one of Hong Kong's few women directors who has successfully carved out careers with personal works in Hong Kong's commercially-minded industry. Mabel Cheung is Clara Law's contemporary in the late second wave. Like Law's partnership with Eddie Fong, Cheung has worked as part of a two-person team, the other part being Alex Law. Cheung and Law's films are more oriented to the commercial end of the market, but they also represent the collective need among Hong Kong intellectuals to tackle concerns about immigration and rootlessness. In each successive film, Cheung and Law alternate in handling the creative jobs such as direction, writing and overseeing the production.

Their first film, *Illegal Immigrant/Feifa Yimin* (1984), sponsored and released by Shaw Brothers, was set and shot in New York as a student work, with Cheung directing and Law writing the script. It is an amateurish version of situations which have since been handled more glamorously by Hollywood itself (in Peter Weir's *Green Card*, for example). Cheung next directed *An Autumn's Tale/Qiu Tian de Tonghua* (1987), a big commercial hit with superstars Chow Yun-fat doing his Hong Kong native-son act as an immigrant cook in New York, and Cherie Chung as the student Chow meets and falls in love with. Cheung and Law then tackled the theme of homecoming in *Painted Faces/Qi Xiao Fu* (1988, directed by Law), *Eight Taels of Gold/Ba Liang Jin* (1989) and *Now You See Love, Now You Don't/Wo Ai Niu Wencai* (1992, directed by Law). In these films, Cheung and Law recreate a vision of Eden based on the rustic, agrarian community of southern Chinese villages. The film-makers' strong suit lies not so much in evoking the lost innocence of country life as in conveying the ingenuous innocence of rural characters confronted with the sophisticated ways of the city. The urge for immigration – from country to city, from China/Hong Kong to America – marks the psychology of the characters. Cheung and Law's films certainly are consistent. So far, they have been set either in the rural countryside (*Eight Taels of Gold*) or they are peopled by rustic characters, with all that this implies in speech, custom and manners (*An Autumn's Tale, Painted Faces, Now You See Love, Now You Don't*). These characters have tended to be very similar: the incorrigible rustic, portrayed either by Chow Yun-fat or Sammo Hung, who act their characters as strong, honourable men possessing large feelings and sentiments springing from their rural roots and attachment to home.

Sentimentality and the theme of Hong Kong-as-home also prevail in the works of Jacob Cheung, Stanley Kwan and Wong Kar-wai, three directors in the second wave who have made the strongest impact in the late 80s and early 90s. Cheung's *Beyond the Sunset/Feiyue Huanghun* (1989) evokes classic Cantonese family dramas. This tale of a mother and daughter stars Fung Bo-bo, a child star in Cantonese cinema's golden days (the 50s and 60s), as a grandmother living alone in Hong Kong because her only child, a daughter (Cecilia Yip), has emigrated. Cheung clearly has an affinity for the old, as proven by *Cageman/Long Min* (1992), an earnest film about a social problem that has long been one of Hong Kong's bugbears: how to provide adequate housing for the territory's six million inhabitants. In the 50s, a whole genre developed around this housing theme, which continues into the 90s, along with the problem it addresses. Cheung filled his cast with veteran actors from the 50s and 60s giving the film a genial, humanistic though geriatric atmosphere. *Cageman* revolves around a core group of garrulous characters who are tenants in a run-down apartment used as a hostel by grizzled and seedy city-dwellers. Known as 'cagemen' because they live in wired bunks which serve as bed and board for a small rent, the tenants face the threat of eviction when property developers move into the area. Opportunistic politicians help to fight their cause but to no avail. The film is as much about group loyalty and peer pressure as it is about corrupt businessmen, politicians and ineffective government. Cheung's adept handling of his actors sustains interest throughout the lengthy film which works more as a character study than a social analysis. The central situations in which two rival politicians stay for three nights among the cagemen in order to win their support and kindle public interest in the issue, are amusingly done.

Characters as individuals – people with soul and feelings other than greed – are the subject of Stanley Kwan's films. Kwan has focused on women in all his films: *Women/Nüren Xin* (1984), *Love Unto Waste/Dixia*

Qing (1986), *Rouge/Yanzhi Kou* (1989), *Full Moon in New York/Ren Zai Niuyue* (1989) and *Actress/Ruan Lingyu* (1992). His female protagonists face the uncertainty of romantic love and strive to assert their individuality as they struggle with the restrictions imposed upon them by their stifling surroundings. Hence, Kwan deals with environment and place as much as he deals with human characters. Kwan's masterpiece, *Rouge*, is about the paradox of human existence in a city which has no history. In this respect, it imparts a sense of Hong Kong as an ideal locality as no other film has done satisfactorily before or since. Hong Kong evokes different emotions in different film-makers, but no film-maker has seen Hong Kong in purely aesthetic terms – with the exception perhaps of foreign directors who treated Hong Kong as a vast movie set (Hollywood's Richard Quine offered the best paradigm of this tendency among foreign film-makers in *The World of Suzy Wong*). Kwan sees Hong Kong as homeland, a place where the heart is. His central character is literally a spirit of old Hong Kong who returns to haunt modern Hong Kong.

There are a number of paradoxical layers in *Rouge*. It is a ghost story with a conventional reincarnation theme in the contemporary setting of a city that is ever changing, so that even ghosts cannot recognise it. A modern couple befriend the ghost of a woman named Fleur (played by Anita Mui) who has been dead for fifty years: she was a high class lady of 'dubious morals' living in the 30s who committed suicide with her lover (played by Leslie Cheung) in a double suicide pact; when the lover does not turn up in the nether world, Fleur returns to the mortal world to search for him. The film attempts to contrast the old world values of Fleur with contemporary moral values represented by the couple. The outcome is melancholic: through their characters, the film's creators acknowledge that the values of the old world are irretrievably lost, to the detriment of the modern one. *Rouge* beats with an introspective pulse: it is the heartbeat of an audience who must face uncertain changes as Hong Kong experiences the 1997 changeover and reviews what history it possesses. *Rouge* is almost neatly divided into two sections which contrast the past and the present. The past is evoked through the theme of love and the conduct of a romantic, erotic courtship. The present is seen as an age of materialistic change where time does not stand still to allow for any reflection of the past. It is in the present that Fleur, the romantic ghost, must look for signs of the past in order to be re-united with the lover who represents her lost ideals.

In *Full Moon in New York* (1989), his next film, it is the city of New York which imprints itself in the minds of the three central female characters. Essentially a tale of three Chinese women in a foreign city who meet and find common cause in being Chinese, the film attempts to define 'Chineseness' as comprised by the 'three Chinas': Hong Kong, Taiwan and China. The three women meet occasionally in the Chinese restaurant owned by one of them (the Hong Kong woman, played by Maggie Cheung) and in drunken binges, lament their state of exile. However, the film's real subject is the tragedy of China – the plight and disunity of an agrarian society striving to be modern. At best, *Full Moon in New York* is a promising woman's film with a classic plot of women meeting, falling out, making up, indulging in togetherness. At worst, it is a pretentious work underscored by the wretched acting of at least two of its principals (Sylvia Chang and Siqin Gaowa), and the tendency of the director and writers (Qiu Dai Anping and Mainland Chinese writer Zhong Acheng) to understate their themes. The film-makers hold to a vision of China which means more to them than to the characters. New York is perhaps too foreign a setting for a Chinese story dealing with Chineseness. As implied in one scene, New York contains bad *feng shui*, literally, Wind and Water, the Chinese 'science' of geomancy which plays an inordinate part in everyday Chinese life.

A note of awkwardness is struck in the very first scene: at her wedding, Zhao Hong, the character from China (played by Siqin Gaowa), appears as the very picture of a bashful Chinese bride marrying an American businessman. Her coyness betrays a cultural vacuum which probably has more to do with the film-makers' own sense of awkwardness as they confront a foreign culture, depicting New York as if it were a moonscape: the film's last pan shot of lower Manhattan seems to etch out a cheese-holed moonscape as the symbol of an airless and alien land.

Actress/Ruan Lingyu (1992) is a biography of China's greatest silent screen actress, Ruan Lingyu, who reached the peak of her career in the early 30s and committed suicide in 1935, hounded by the malicious gossip about her private life in Shanghai's yellow press, leaving a note which included the famous line much quoted by historians as a sort of epitaph, *renyan kewei*, 'the words of people are fearful'. As befitted a silent actress whose performances came from deep within her, *renyan kewei* demonstrated her fear of words.

Actress offers more than a mere reconstruction of Ruan's on-screen and off-screen life: it is a film about history at perhaps the most interesting period in Chinese cinema (not to mention Chinese national politics) and its lasting impact on Hong Kong artists. Kwan conducts an interview with his leading actress, Maggie Cheung, about playing Ruan Lingyu, the Chinese Garbo, and this 'documentary' is inserted into key points of the narrative, together with other interviews with critics and biographers of Ruan. For perhaps the first time, a Hong Kong director shows a mature grasp of Hong Kong's role in the wider national context of China and the spiritual solidarity with fellow Chinese for a common good. Although the film is not about Hong Kong *per se*, it deals with issues and questions about the impact of art on Hong Kong. The point is that Hong Kong's culture originated from a source that has always been presented as the motherland through the concept of *zuguo* or the land of one's ancestors. *Actress* is an uncommon rendition of the *zuguo* theme – a nationalistic theme which Hong Kong cinema has constantly drawn on and refined.

Ruan typifies the modern Chinese woman caught in the web of tradition, unable to make the choice between happiness and tragedy. The archetypal Ruan image is a big close-up of her face (in *The Goddess*, there are many), her eyes gazing out over vistas of the city or staring at bare walls, questioning the materialism that lay at the basis of her existence. With the stylistics of Garbo-like acting, Ruan Lingyu went against the grain of social realism then rearing its head in Chinese cinema with left-oriented film-makers such as Cai Chusheng and Wu Yonggang coming to the fore. Nevertheless, these directors knew how to utilise Ruan's talents to reach the spiritual core, a desire for full gender equality and sexual liberation that lay beyond her formal style. Inserting clips from Ruan Lingyu's extant pictures into the narrative, Kwan achieved a daring concept of a documentary inserted within a *wenyi* narrative, generating a dialectical, self-critical text in an attempt to 'write' film criticism within the context of his own work, while at the same time providing a historical pre-1949 or pre-communist view of Chinese cinema.

The film depicts Ruan Lingyu's success as a star who achieved pure grace in her portrayal of tragic characters on the silent screen. Her famous portrayal of the prostitute in *The Goddess* and other roles are recreated with Maggie Cheung giving the most remarkable performance of her career to date. Also treated were the circumstances leading to her suicide: the scandal that broke as a result of her weak husband's attempt to cash in on her adulterous relationship with a Shanghai businessman. The film assesses the impact of Ruan's death on Chinese cinema and comes to the conclusion that her career was not only crucial to an understanding of Chinese silent pictures, it also represented one aspect of drama which Chinese cinema never really developed until recently: an intellectual approach which Ruan presented as a form of grace, melancholic in substance and pose. The realism implied in her work with directors Cai Chusheng, Wu Yonggang, Sun Yu and Fei Mu, all of whom are depicted in the film, showed that style and form were indivisible yet somehow contradictory concepts. The contradictions between style and formalism, realism and content, are also written into the overall conception of Kwan's film.

With the modest international success of *Actress*, Kwan embarked on a phase of growth and experimentation, seemingly reverting to the status of a fledgeling director. He made two short films: *Too Happy for Words* (1993) and an episode for a television series produced by RTHK entitled *Two Sisters/Yi Shiren Liang Zimei* (1993). Both focus on a female duo who engage in end-of-relationship ruminations about love, sex, marriage and womanhood. Although apparently perplexed and disturbed by their relationships with men, the protagonists also appear to be taking each other's measure, sizing each other up. *Too Happy for Words* and *Two Sisters* both serve as dry runs for Kwan's next major work, *Red Rose, White Rose*, a lush adaptation of a Shanghai story by Eileen Chang, whose *Love in a Fallen City/Qingcheng zhi Lian* had previously been filmed by Ann Hui.

In all three works, a literary text threatens to overcome the visual style (titles quoting whole sentences from Eileen Chang's book appear liberally throughout *Red Rose, White Rose*, like chapter headings). This literary phase of Kwan's cinema has come about through a new partnership with scenarist Edward Lam, who wrote all Kwan's films since *Too Happy for Words* (Kwan's previous screenwriter was Qiu Gangjian, who wrote all the director's films up to *Centre Stage*).

Red Rose, White Rose begins with a prologue introducing Tong Zhenbao as a student in Europe in the 30s; Tong initiates himself into sex by sleeping with a Parisian prostitute, then making advances to a Chinese girl in the back of a car. Zhenbao (Winston Chao) is a handsome figure, the very model of a Chinese man who indulges in Western ways while acknowledging the primacy of his Eastern values. Returning to Shanghai, he lodges in the house of a classmate and falls in love with Wang Jiaorui (Joan Chen), his friend's wife. Dubbed 'Red Rose', Jiaorui also falls in love with Zhenbao, but when she proposes that she divorce her husband and marry Zhenbao, he takes fright and runs away. The 'White Rose' second half involves the marriage of Zhenbao to Meng Yanli (Veronica Yip), a woman supposedly the opposite of Jiaorui as indicated by the emotional symbolism of the different colours (white equals frigidity, red equals warmth). Here, Kwan and his writer, Edward Lam, evoke the standard themes of an Eileen Chang melodrama much more succinctly by relying on the female character's state of mind rather than on dialogue (ironically, this is also the section where Lam has purportedly made most of his original contributions). Exasperated by her husband's callous coldness and infidelities, the wife turns her bitterness and anger against herself and becomes neurotic, closeting herself in the bathroom.

Chang addresses the plight of the independent woman who faces family pressures to conform to traditional customs and values. The man works hard to realise his desire to be a 'respectable' member of society, but thus loses his ability to love. The woman is like a Tower of Pisa that refuses to collapse: she is self-sacrificing, considerate of the husband's status, but utterly vulnerable beneath the surface. In this regard, the film's 'quotation' of *Long Live the Missus/Taitai Wansui*, a 1947 Shanghai screwball comedy classic scripted by Eileen Chang, serves as an apt reminder of the author's thematic preoccupations. Eileen Chang's novels, which are fast gaining a cult following, are marvels of subterranean narratives representing the stresses experienced by women in the turbulent modernising Shanghai in the 30s. It is a daring, ambitious director who takes up the challenge to adapt her works to the screen, and, generally speaking, Kwan is up to the challenge. However, at one point, the camera gazes at Meng Yanli's navel in close-up as she does her toilet – a voyeuristic shot that illustrates how self-indulgent Kwan can be.

The very latest auteur produced by the second wave, Wong Kar-wai, focuses on the problem of identity in Hong Kong. Almost at a stroke, Wong proved himself to be Hong Kong's most uncompromising artist with *Days of Being Wild/A Fei Zhengzhuan* (1990), a highly personal 'chamber' film that is both nostalgic and contemporary, presenting lost youths as an allegory for the plight of Hong Kong's people as they prepare for the transition to 1997. The time is the 60s when 'A Fei' was a common euphemism for vaseline-haired and rock-loving delinquents and unsavoury teenagers with gangland connections. Wong's hero is an archetypal 60s A

Fei, but with an ageless sensibility for self-destruction. In Leslie Cheung's interpretation, the A Fei character is both macho and vulnerable, sensitive and insensitive. The dialectic between the conventional 'A Fei type' (a ruffian given to macho posturing) and the tortured soul evokes the James Dean of *Rebel Without a Cause*. In *Days of Being Wild*, however, Leslie Cheung's A Fei (named 'Yuddy') is an abstract everyman, the undefined soul of Hong Kong who seeks to find himself an identity he can respect.

Yuddy is in many respects a meaner alter ego of Jim Stark, the James Dean character in *Rebel Without a Cause*. Yuddy seduces a girl (Maggie Cheung) who works in a soft-drinks kiosk in a soccer stadium. But he then rejects her in a way that reflects his enigmatic personality: he affects a callous indifference to her feelings while secretly longing for her. He is less enigmatic with the showgirl, Mimi (Carina Lau), although she is similarly smitten and vexed by Yuddy. His life obsession actually centres around one particular woman: he wants to meet his real mother, a Filipino woman who has disowned him. This obsession drives him to torment his surrogate mother, a Shanghainese lady of dubious means (played by Rebecca Pan). Other relationships are woven into the story: Yuddy's pal, the Sal Mineo-like character, played by Jacky Cheung, who really loves Mimi, and a sympathetic policeman (played by Andy Lau) who really loves the kiosk girl. In this enigmatic A Fei personality, Wong has created a pillar of salt from which all the other characters attempt to derive some sustenance: each flinches at the unsavoury taste.

The associations of the characters are built up through a kind of narrative puzzle: each character is a connective piece. However, each character also exists in a capsule, unable to strike up lasting relationships. The connections between them are literary: mind-dialogues rather than actual conversations, making *Days of Being Wild* possibly the most literary of Hong Kong films. It is a film full of marvellous stories evoked by one character's association with another. Such a literary device has fallen out of fashion, being considered theatrical even when it was used widely in the 50s, the master practitioner being Joseph L. Mankiewicz who pioneered it in *A Letter to Three Wives* (1949), *All About Eve* (1950) and *The Barefoot Contessa* (1954). Like Mankiewicz, Wong's utilisation of the literary narrative is intended as a psychoanalytical trigger for an outpouring of loss and melancholy; evoking at the same time a nostalgia for the 60s, when the new wave generation was growing up. It is ultimately in the literary vein that one must take the film's enigmatic ending: the appearance of a new character (played by Tony Leung Chiu-wai), unrelated to any of the previous characters. From his appearance, he is another typical A Fei, instantly recognisable by his vanity: the scene shows him sitting on a bed, manicuring his nails and then getting up to comb his hair. He is the next connective piece in the puzzle, containing a story inside his own capsule.

Its literary qualities notwithstanding, *Days of Being Wild* is a handsome film, with outstanding photography by Christopher Doyle and sets by William Chang. Wong Kar-wai's visual style is intricate and complex as well as relentless, using a ticking clock as its central metaphor. The clock, of course, ticks back to the sixties, but it is an obvious allusion to the 1997 syndrome yet again. However, Wong does not push this allusion too far; he does not offer a banal interpretation of time. Instead, he turns it into a productive principle. Note the marvellous piece of business with time in the scene where Yuddy seduces Maggie Cheung: 'Let's be friends for one minute,' Yuddy says to her. If time slips away, so does a relationship. Clocks appear throughout the movie reminding characters of what they are losing and of the urgency of their fleeting, uncertain relationships. Time is the real subject of *Days of Being Wild*. Wong's achievement is to have produced a genuinely abstract art film in Hong Kong, completely dedicated to its characters and their feelings rather than to plot and situations.

Days of Being Wild was Wong's second film. His first film, *As Tears Go By/Wangjiao Kamen* (1988) was an accomplished but comparatively slight work that gave some pointers to Wong's visual style and his affinity for *feizai* (the plural of A Fei). By this time in the 80s, the *feizai* had grown beyond being mere rebels: they had become immersed in the mythology of gangster brotherhood, observing codes of undying fraternal loyalty and male bondage. Wah (Andy Lau) is 'Big Brother' to his junior henchman Fly (Jacky Cheung), a young man eager to make good in Mongkok's gangsterland, but going spectacularly off the rails. He is reproached for his errant behaviour and eventually put to work as an illegal street hawker selling fishballs. Fly's frustration is exacerbated by taunts from Tony (Alex Man), the protector of a mahjong joint, from whom Fly borrows money. Tony demands his principal and interest leading to a stand-off between him and Wah, who, as Fly's big brother, is required to pay up. Their violent one-upmanship results in the humiliating beatings of Wah and Fly. The latter is now honour-bound to prove himself to his Big Brother, while Big Brother is even more compelled to stand by his junior to protect him. The last scenes testify to the apotheosis of gangster brotherhood: the final test of loyalty where Big Brother dies for Junior Brother in the course of doing their duty, that is to say, when assassinating an informer.

As Tears Go By stands on its own as a stylish genre piece that supports the conventions and mythology of the Brotherhood syndrome in gangster movies, a subject portrayed to more startling effect in John Woo's movies, particularly *Bullet in the Head*. Fragments of the doomed romance between Wah and Ngor, the straight, sickly girl (played by Maggie Cheung) who convalesces in Wah's house on Lantau Island, recall Cheung's heartbroken girl and Lau's policeman in *Days of Being Wild*, but none of the rich complexity of that relationship. The swanky MTV images that underline the Lantau romance are off-set by the visceral violence of the Mongkok scenes, attesting to Wong's use of genre stereotypes. In contrast, *Days of Being Wild* was an ambiguous character piece.

Days of Being Wild, originally planned in two parts, had failed at the box-office; the second part was cancelled by the producers and Wong's future was in some doubt. He was criticised by the industry for his meticulous methods and demands which inflated the budget and the shooting schedule. However, the film's artistic success served at the same time to increase Wong's prestige. It was a sign of the film industry's maturity that a director who had flouted Hong Kong's commercial tenets of film-making, could still survive. Moreover, Wong had opened a new chapter in the development of the new wave in Hong Kong cinema. As the latest new wave auteur, Wong may be said to have brought the Hong Kong new wave into the 90s by combining postmodern themes with new wave stylistics.

Wong's next film *Chungking Express/ Chongqing Senlin* (1994), looks and plays like a revitalised Godard movie. When Hong Kong's own new wave broke in 1979, its aesthetics were overtaken by a kind of moral compunction based on a search for identity and nationality: crime thrillers and social dramas about rejected youth made up the bulk of the first new wave films. Technically, the directors of the new wave (Ann Hui, Tsui Hark, Yim Ho, *et al.*) were certainly aware of style, but style was largely subordinated to function, seen as an effective means to a conventional narrative end. Only one director in this first period, Patrick Tam, adopted the kind of aesthetics that one would normally associate with avant-gardist experimentation in structure and narrative. Wong Kar-wai served a kind of apprenticeship with Patrick Tam, writing the script for Tam's *Final Victory*, while Tam was supervising editor on Wong's *Days of Being Wild* and *Ashes of Time*.

The sensual slow motion shots which open *Chungking Express*, showing a cop in plain clothes chasing a drug suspect in Hong Kong's lively hub of Asian multiculturalism – the Chungking Mansion building – signal a slow recognition that the Hong Kong new wave is coming full circle. *Chungking Express* is an expression of the convergence of Hong Kong's postmodern aesthetics and a curiously old-fashioned, but not outmoded, romanticism. Wong's work to date sums up the circuitous development of the Hong Kong new wave. However, the film doesn't look back as much as it attempts to push forward. Indeed, at times Wong even seems to be shoving a new genre at his audience – a postmodern romance, a new wave editing style, on-location realism and narrative dissonance. It may well be a slight work, but it is by no means an impersonal one. Half the fun lies in working out the interlocking motifs between the film and Wong's previous *Days of Being Wild*.

The film is made up of two separate, unrelated but somehow interlocking stories, both featuring cops. The cop in the first story is Taiwanese He Zhiwu (played by the new star Takeshi Kaneshiro, of mixed Taiwanese–Japanese parentage) who collides with an unnamed mysterious woman wearing a blonde wig (played by Lin Ching-hsia) while chasing a suspect in Chungking Mansion. She is a drug dealer left high and dry when would-be couriers run off with her goods. He is reeling from a broken affair with a girl named May. Both meet by chance in a bar and end up spending the night together, but not in bed. Their affair remains desultory, unconsummated, unresolved. The story ends nonchalantly, with the woman killing the foreigner who has betrayed her in the drug deal and walking off minus her wig. This theme of a man abandoned by a former lover who has a chance meeting with another woman who then becomes his surrogate lover for a short while, is re-played (with variations) in the second episode. Here a cop (played by Tony Leung Chiu-wai) has an affair with an air stewardess. Their usual meeting place is a streetside takeaway restaurant where a girl (unnamed until the end when we learn that she is called May) works behind the counter. The airline stewardess walks out of the cop's life, putting the key to the cop's apartment in an envelope and leaving it at the restaurant. Leung doesn't bother to open the envelope. Instead he forms a budding but uncertain relationship with May (played by pop star Faye Wong), who serves him in the restaurant. May steals into the cop's apartment by opening the letter to the jilted cop and using the key. She lies in his bed and generally makes her presence felt. In short, she becomes a surrogate replacement for Leung's departed lover. She even quits her job to become an air hostess, realising her dream to go to California. Back in Hong Kong, she goes to the restaurant only to discover that Leung has bought the place. The identities of the characters have shifted and it is not clear whether their affair will take off.

As in *Days of Being Wild*, plot is secondary to character as Wong develops motifs from his previous film. There is the same preoccupation with time, dates and memory: because May loves to eat pineapples, He Zhiwu is eccentrically obsessed with buying cans of pineapples that have a use-by date on 1 May, his birthday, believing that this will bring May back to him. The motif of the uniformed cop pursuing a relationship with an emotionally unstable woman is given a lighter treatment while conforming to the themes of loneliness and unrequited love. Above all, Wong is consistent in adopting a free-flowing, transitional approach to narrative construction that is further strengthened by a literary quality in the dialogue (spoken in voice-over monologues) with each character given their own space to tell their stories. Although the stories here may not be as affecting, the accent on style conveys a feeling of sharp-edged excitement and a sense of high-octane elation recalling the impact of the French new wave in Europe. However, despite the pyrotechnics of his style, Wong's approach is highly impressionistic, largely because his narratives give way to the characters' intensity. Whether it is they who determine the style and outlook of the narrative, or whether Wong manipulates the different planes of narrative style and character in order to play them off against each other, is not always clear. In so far as he is a poet who relies on words but knows that they must be translated into a visual medium, Wong clearly favours an abstract reading of his films.

Chungking Express was made in a spontaneous burst of energy in the midst of the production of *Ashes of Time/ Dongie Xidu*, which promised to be the director's most rigorous and abstract work. When it opened two months after *Chungking Express*, it was both condemned and praised in equal measure for its apparent inaccessibility. The narrative re-works the popular martial arts novel *The Eagle Shooting Heroes/ Shediao Yingiong Zhuan* by Jin Yong, filmed many times before in conventional genre terms. Wong dispenses with the plot of the original story. The characters form brief relationships, drift apart and tell of their pain and remorse while separated. An off-screen monologue provides a way through the narrative. As in Wong's other films, the characters only seem to carry the plot. They spend much of their time lamenting or recalling the ephemerality of experiences and connections made during their lives. Accordingly, the film is made up of themes and meditations. Wong's is a freestyle approach that works against Hong Kong cinema's wholly commercialised styles which demand conventional narratives – it confirms Wong as an uncompromising artist who is nevertheless able to command respect in the industry, as is evident from the director's ability to assemble all-star casts for his films and to command big budgets.

The film's Chinese title, *Dongxie Xidu*, refers to the characters played by Tony Leung Kar-fai (Dongxie) and Leslie Cheung (Xidu). Although inspired by Jin Yong's book, Wong has practically created his own original characters, with both Leslie Cheung and Tony Leung offering 'backstory' interpretations of the two eponymous heroes. Cheung's 'Xidu' – translated in the subtitles as 'Malicious West' – is a swordsman named Ouyang Feng who lives in a way-station in the desert and whose services as a killer are for sale. Characters stop by, some to hire Ouyang's services, others are rival swordsmen (such as Tony Leung Ka-fai's 'Dongxie' or 'Evil East') who are drinking partners and soulmates in the best tradition of the male-bonding heroes of the American Western. Although Leung's 'Dongxie' is prominently featured in the Chinese title, it is 'Xidu' (Cheung's character) who acts as the pivot of the film – all other characters revolve around him and meet each other fortuitously as a result. Each character is then given his or her own narrative space. Dongxie (whose real name is Huang Yaoshi) meets a gender-bending swordswoman (Brigitte Lin) whose dual personalities literally call themselves Yin and Yang (in the English subtitles; the original Cantonese dialogue is not so clear-cut). Yin hires Ouyang Feng to kill Huang Yaoshi because he had failed to keep an appointment with her, but Ouyang is perturbed by his client's gender switching. This plot strand ends with a stunning coda showing Yin/Yang practising swordplay with her own reflection in a pond.

The narrative effortlessly connects one strand with the next strand as each new character, via perfunctory links, comes into focus, including a swordsman who is slowly going blind (played by Tony Leung Chiu-wai) and a beggar-swordsman (played by Jacky Cheung), both pursuing vendettas against a gang of horse thieves. These various figures with their individual stories are threaded together as they meet with Ouyang in the desert and talk about their lives and loves. Women appear seeking vengeance more with sorrow than hatred, while heroes pontificate about their women and unrequited love: Ouyang, for example, yearns for the woman who married his brother, a plot development that recalls Ethan Edwards' silent yearning for his brother's wife in *The Searchers*. Instead of the stories, however, it is the notions of time, space and memory which converge and tie the narrative together in a kaleidoscopic manner. The cohesiveness of *Ashes of Time* also stems from the film's remarkable look, which is nothing short of ravishing. Christopher Doyle's grainy colour photography imparts an impressionist quality, while the pastel lighting recalls motifs from Chinese painting, pointed up appropriately by the desert location and other more temperate landscapes (creeks, ponds). The slow-motion action scenes convey a feeling of an artist daubing paint freely on a canvas. Using a Chinese phrase, the genre is 'a heavenly steed soaring across the skies' (*tianma xingkong*) and Wong has goaded it to a distant heaven, which explains why the film, for all its cohesiveness, is emotionally rather distant from its audience.

Wong's adventurous spirit does the second wave credit, but it also epitomises the dilemma faced by young film-makers who wish to experiment with narrative structures in Hong Kong. How far can they go in eschewing narratives laid down in the popular genres? The answer most of the new wave directors seem to have found is to focus on characterisations while at the same time nurturing a sense of style. Directors such as Lawrence Ah Mon and Ching Siu-tung exemplify both ends of this tendency: Ah Mon (or Lau Kwok-cheung, to call the director by his full Chinese name) has focused on low-life characters and social outcasts (prostitutes, gangsters), while Ching, who has worked closely with Tsui Hark, delved into the area of special effects and action stunts as the most effective means of stylistic expression.

The films of Lawrence Ah Mon hark back to the days of the 50s 'social-realist' Cantonese cinema, a genre often put forward as a worthy example of 'prestige cinema'. A feature of this genre, shared by its capitalist twin, neo-realism, is its melodramatic idiom. Ah Mon has continued this idiom in his films: *Gangs/Tong Dang* (1986), *Queen of Temple Street/Miaojie Huanghou* (1990), *Lee Rock/Leiluo Zhuan* (1991) and *Three Summers/San Ge Xia Tian* (1992). Ching Siu-tung, on the other hand, evokes a different tradition, that of martial arts cinema, particularly the Mandarin cinema's swordfighting films.

The films of Ching Siu-tung are at the edge of the commercial market, but Ching is an astute director capable of combining modernist expression with traditionalist convention. His association with Tsui Hark was a seminal factor in his development. The two film-makers share a love for action genres and a desire to transform Hong Kong cinema into a truly unique institution by the most eclectic means possible. Their partnership began with the successful series initiated by *A Chinese Ghost Story/Qiannü Youhun* (1987) and has yielded early 90s films such as *Swordsman/Xiao'ao Jianghu* (1990) and *Swordsman II/Xiao'ao Jianghu II Dongfang Bubai* (1992), which have pushed Hong Kong cinema into postmodernism with their portrayal of a new type of gender-bending hero/heroine.

Swordsman is a mad, muddled and marvellous 90s update of *wuxia* films, originally intended to be directed by King Hu but turned into a tribute to his style, motifs and favourite dynastic period (the Ming), Hu retains a credit as director, but the film was really made by Tsui Hark and Ching Siu-tung (another director, Raymond Lee, also shares the director's credit). Followers of Hu will find familiar plot details such as the classic Hu McGuffin: a precious scroll supposedly containing secrets of martial arts is stolen from the Imperial Library of the Ming Court; the eunuch with superhuman powers who heads the Ming Court's secret service, the Dongchang; the family of a loyal Ming official who hides in an inn waiting to be rescued by virtuous knights. All these motifs are handled confidently, but with minor variations, by the young self-professed 'disciples' of the older master. Based on a novel by one of the genre's veteran writers, Jin Yong, the film is populated by an assortment of martial arts characters headed by a laidback swordsman named Lingwu Chong (played by Sam Hui). Lingwu is the only person who knows the whereabouts of the 'sacred scroll' sought by the eunuch and the members of a minority tribe. While hiding from the searchers for the scroll, the handsome hero is wooed by three women: his master's daughter who poses as his sidekick disguised as a boy (Cecilia Yip), and two Miao tribeswomen. The tribal women seek retribution for their tribe framed by the eunuch for the murder of the official who owned the scroll. Lingwu's adventures on the run, accompanied by his sidekick, are marked by encounters with memorable eccentrics, including an old mystic who imparts rare swordfighting skills to the swordsman. The action is fast and furious, the first mature exposition of the stunt co-ordinating skills of Ching Siu-tung, who evolved into a director from an early career as a stuntman and martial arts director. The film works as a genuine spectacle, choreographed and directed with unclassical speed and flurried movements too quick for the eye to catch. It evokes the classics of King Hu, but is recognisably different from Hu's style in the tempo and the execution of the stunts. Ching shows that he is the 90s successor to Hu. With *Swordsman II*, however, Ching comes into his own as a new wave film-maker, substantially boosted by his association with new wave master Tsui Hark.

Although the hero of *Swordsman II* continues to be Lingwu Chong, now portrayed by Jet Li, the film presents a telling attack on the stereotype of the male hero. Lingwu's leading man is subsidiary to a gender-bending character with an operatic-sounding name, 'Asia the Invincible' (played by Lin Ching-hsia). Asia was previously the male chief of the Sun-Moon sect of the Miao tribe who castrated himself in order to master the arts and powers contained in the Sacred Scroll (from the previous edition). Now an androgyne on her way to a full sex change, Asia's plan is to dominate China, thus the world, by first encouraging the Miaos, whose chief she has imprisoned, to rebel against the emperor. She enlists Japanese mercenaries to help in this task. However, the plan is not foolproof. The daughter of the Miao chief, Ren Yingying, is mobilising loyalists to rescue her father. Along comes Lingwu Chong, who is seduced by Asia's beauty in a scene by a lake. Not knowing Asia's real identity, he is immediately besotted, a process helped along by the wine Asia gives him to drink. He is fooled by a stand-in, a female retainer who is also Asia's lover, into believing that he is making love to Asia. In the final battle, Asia reveals that she *is* in love with Lingwu and holds back from administering the fatal stroke. As a result, she falls down a cliff to her death – but then, nothing in this film is for certain. Lingwu survives with a broken heart.

Like the good trend-followers that they are, Hong Kong film-makers have created a rash of martial arts movies in the 90s on the back of the success of the *Swordsman* films. The character of Asia the Invincible has also given them a new type of hero/heroine, a gender-bending character so malleable that he or she bends not only genders, but all character types: Asia is a villainess, a romantic protagonist, and ultimately a character who wins the sympathy of the hero – and the audience. A follower as well as a trend-setter, Ching himself continued the saga of Asia the Invincible in a third instalment of *Swordsman* entitled *The East is Red/Dongfang Bubai Fengyun Zaiqi* (1993), a wonderfully exotic sequel to *Swordsman II* with Asia (played again by Lin Ching-hsia) coming back from the dead to fight off Spanish conquistadors in search of the Sacred Scroll guided by Ming palace officials. The Spaniards ask their guides questions such as 'What is *Wulin?*', 'What is *Jianghu?*'. These are the Chinese terms for the world of martial arts and the never-never land of Chinese knight-errants, now in a state of frenzy because false Asia the Invincibles have appeared to whip up religious fervour and cult worship in order to unite the *jianghu* and rule over all martial artists. Asia goes back to the *jianghu* to investigate the cult worship built around her myth and to destroy the imposters, one of whom is Snow (played by Joey Wong), an ex-lover of Asia. Snow assumes Asia's identity to hold a rendezvous in the sea with a Japanese mercenary samurai who is after bigger things. The film fits in a wonderful mélange of Spanish galleons and conquistadors, a Japanese warjunk which is also a transposable submarine, a Japanese Ninja made up like a *butoh* dancer, and two Asia the Invincibles spinning marvellous webs of needles and threads around their enemies.

The female as a dangerous, elusive, creature is a theme embellished by the action choreography of Asia's specialised skill in throwing needles and spinning threads from her fingers to pin down her opponents. Like Asia's threads, the theme of sexual ambiguity is spun around her novel character to underline the threat that the character poses to male heroes, and also as an appropriate device to reflect the growing power of women. Gender-bending has been taken up as an important 90s motif in the development of a postmodern Hong Kong cinema, a device that reflects changing sexual mores and attitudes towards women and homosexuals (homosexuality was decriminalised in 1989). In fact, gender-bending, adopted as a fashionable theme in the 90s, stems from the tradition in Chinese theatre (as in Peking opera) of having male actors play female roles. Ching used it in *A Chinese Ghost Story*, released in 1987, where a gender-bending demon (played by a male actor) rip-snorted its way through the narrative.

Gender-bending may also be seen as a 90s rationalisation of a villainous stereotype long employed in the genre: that of silver-haired eunuchs who, even when seriously impaired, possess transcendental powers (a stereotype first used effectively by King Hu in his 1966 film *Dragon Inn/Longmen Kezhan* and invoked by Ching in his 1992 remake of Hu's film, *New Dragon Gate Inn/Xin Longmen Kezhan*). The kung fu movie has now jumped on the bandwagon with the release of Yuen Kwai's *Fong Sai-yuk/Fang Shiyu* (1993), about the eponymous kung fu hero who fights a duel to win the right to

201

marry the girl he loves. Fong Sai-yuk was featured in Cantonese movies of the 60s and in Zhang Che's 70s cycle of Shaolin heroes, which typically featured him as a somewhat asexual young kung fu fighter played by Alexander Fu Sheng. The duel is arranged by the girl's father and contenders must fight her mother, who is well versed in kung fu martial arts. Fong's mother (played by Josephine Siao) poses as a man to fight the girl's mother, but the latter is immediately attracted to her androgynous disguise.

These new developments regarding the representation of gender have to some degree deflected the criticism often made of Hong Kong films that they are fearful of and hostile to women. It is perhaps the most popular manifestation of the new thinking which takes into account the growing role women play in Hong Kong affairs, not least in the film industry. That women's role is emphasised in the male-dominated genre of martial arts films is the clearest sign yet of the more mature direction taken by Hong Kong cinema from the late 80s onwards, mainly by the second wave of young film-makers. Hong Kong is defined and felt through the heartbeat and perspectives of women in the films of Stanley Kwan and others as diverse as Kam Kwok-leong's *Wonder Women/Shenqi Liang Nüxia* (1988), an interesting rendition of Hollywood comedies featuring dumb blondes and smart brunettes, and the independent feature *To Liv(e)/Fushi Jian* (1992) made by critic-turned-director Evans Chan, who structured his film as a love-letter to Hong Kong written by a Eurasian Hong Kong woman aghast at the criticisms of actress Liv Ullmann directed against the territory's policy of repatriating Vietnamese refugees. Actress Sylvia Chang also directed characteristically 'women's films' such as *Passion/Zui Ai* (1986) and *Mary From Beijing/Mengxing Shifen* (1992). The surprising box-office success of Yee Tung-shing's *C'est la vie, Mon Chérie/Xin Bu Liao Qing* (1993) further confirms the trend. A re-make of Tao Qin's Mandarin love story *Love Without End/Bu Liao Qing*, Yee's film presents the 90s as a gentle, romantic age, with a dying heroine at its centre, and Jazz (the Canto-pop variation) and Cantonese opera resounding at its periphery.

Hong Kong cinema in the 90s gives the impression that it is on its way to achieving a new kind of maturity, able to integrate feminist perspectives as well as facing up to the city's postmodern phase. That impression is largely the result of the consolidation of second wave talent in the latter half of the 80s, young people who view Hong Kong as their home city and who express their affection for it. They are the true believers: film-makers who invest their heart and soul in a place that is, more often than not, merely a transit point. The new wave, with its first and second phase directors, gives meaning to Hong Kong's transient destiny by exploring its history, its cinema, its politics in relation to China, and, above all, the loves and hates of its citizens. In the process, Hong Kong is affirmed, though its destiny remains transient.

NOTES

[1] For a full discussion of *Farewell China*, see Chapter 13.

[2] The film was the Hong Kong contribution to the series named 'Asian Beat', conceived and produced by a Japanese company and featuring the same Japanese character played by Masatoshi Nagase.

[3] Quotes are from a personal interview with author.

Part Four

Characters on the Edge

Chapter Thirteen

Reverence and Fear: Hong Kong's China Syndrome

In the early 80s, when Britain and China began negotiating the return of Hong Kong to China, a 'China syndrome' began to develop in the territory, colouring perceptions of kinship and cultural affinity with undertones of political anxiety and fear. In cinema, the complex relationship between Hong Kong and China has been explored by contemporary film-makers with a sense of both intimacy and unease. The directors of the new wave mooted questions of identity, nationality and ethnicity in their works. These were sensitive questions never asked before, but as Hong Kong cinema renewed itself in the 80s, artists also started looking back into their own history, tracing the roots of Hong Kong cinema in the Shanghai films of the 30s, the heyday of Chinese cinema and an era when the linkage between Hong Kong and China was not so clearly marked by political divisions. Young Hong Kong film-makers related as closely, if not more so, to Chinese cinema as they did to the West's cinematic traditions. The transformation of styles and techniques which occurred with the rise of the new wave implied roots in both film histories simultaneously.

The Chinese influence began to manifest itself as an identification with China as the source of one's culture and language, a kind of abstract nationalism[1] that while registering it, bypassed fear and loathing for the communist regime as well as for aspects of the colonial, *laissez-faire* capitalism which ruled Hong Kong and Taiwan. Tsui Hark paid tribute to pre-Liberation Chinese cinema by evoking Shen Xiling's much loved 1937 classic *Crossroads/Shizi Jietou* in *Shanghai Blues/Shanghai zhi Ye* (1984), and in subsequent works, built upon a sense of Chinese nationalism to evoke the concept of a genuinely 'Chinese' cinema that would unite all Chinese. Ann Hui invoked the martial arts serials in her two-part opus *Romance of the Book and Sword/Shu Jian Enchou Lu* (1987), which attempted to analyse Chinese nationalism and its flimsy foundations, a theme which she developed in subsequent works. Stanley Kwan paid an extraordinary homage to the greatest of all Chinese silent film stars, Ruan Lingyu, in *Actress* aka *Centre Stage/Ruan Lingyu* (1991), a film virtually encompassing the history of Chinese cinema in several textual layers and featuring some of the great names of the period: Ruan Lingyu, Fei Mu, Wu Yonggang, Sun Yu, Cai Chusheng and Li Lili, among others. The impact of the tradition of *wenyi* melodrama, a staple of sound cinema, pervades the Hong Kong cinema, suggesting that the *wenyi* genre was one of the many umbilical cords linking Chinese cinema with its counterparts in Hong Kong and Taiwan.

The term *wenyi*, an abbreviation of *wenxue* (literature) and *yishu* (art), can be amplified further by taking the words *wen* and *yi* on their own: the former implies refinement and civilisation, the latter craft and technique. The *wenyi* melodrama is, of all Chinese genres, conceptually the closest to Western modern theatre. It represents a modern branch of drama, with psychological underpinnings which are not found in other traditional genres such as the martial arts and the opera film. Cinematically, *wenyi* has affinities with Frank Borzage's romances of the late silent era, such as *Seventh Heaven* (1927) and *Street Angel* (1928) – the latter was even re-made, after a fashion, by Yuan Muzhi in 1933, with Zhao Dan and Zhou Xuan in the roles played by Charles Farrell and Janet Gaynor. Borzage's classic dramas of modernisation featured couples who, in the face of a rising, urban commodity culture, asserted a romantic notion of love heavily influenced by the pre-capitalist notion of the inextricable fusion between sacred and profane love. As such, Borzage's films offered a powerfully complex way of dramatising the dissonances between two sets of ideologies: one which requires the legitimacy of desiring relationships to be sanctioned by traditional institutions, the other affirming the autonomy of the individual from prevailing institutional arrangements. Borzage resolved this conflict by way of deliriously neurotic love stories in which individual desire transcends history altogether, breaking all boundaries to reach quasi-mystical levels. This approach underwent variations in the *wenyi* romance to incorporate love triangles inter-woven with the theme of transcendence and redemption.

The masterpiece of the *wenyi* films and one of the greatest Chinese films of all time is Fei Mu's *Spring in a Small City/Xiao Cheng zhi Chun* (1948).[2] Made one year before the communist victory in 1949, *Spring in a Small City* is essentially a chamber work with a quintet of players. It centres around the triangle of a sick husband, his bored wife and a doctor who is an intimate friend of the husband and also the wife's ex-lover. Two other characters, an old servant and the young sister of the husband, complete the pentagraphic poem in the metrical style of *jintishi*, a form of Tang poetry then thought of as 'the modern style'. The film deploys a strict, formal code of presentation, the prime element of which is rhythm, with pauses and timing as crucial dramaturgical elements. This metrical structure gives the impression of a finely-sculpted film, rarely seen in Chinese cinema before or since. Like most socially conscious Chinese films of the post-war period, it incorporates a subtle message of recovery and reconstruction, and hints at political leftism as the way out. Despite this, *Spring in a Small City* remains a self-contained work of *wenyi* themes. The story is narrated as a recollection in the first-person by the wife, Zhou Yuwen (a sensational performance by Wei Wei): after the war, Dr Zhang decides one spring day to visit his sick friend Dai Liyan, who lives in a bungalow on the grounds of his ruined mansion (the 'small city' of the title) with his wife, sister and servant, thus unexpectedly reuniting Dr Zhang with his former lover, Zhou Yuwen. Old passions are rekindled, but the doctor and the wife fall short of consummating their affair, affirming the *wenyi* convention summarised in the adage 'begin from emotion, end in humility' (*fahu qing, zhihu li*). In other words, desire should be bound by ethics. However, this subordination to a particular ethical code is experienced as tragedy and loss, making the submission rather double-edged. Desire retrained by one's sense of moral duty is fully expressed in the scene where Zhou Yuwen meets her ex-lover alone in his room for the first time in ten years. Passion seeps through repressed feelings and Yuwen veils her face intermittently with her silk scarf, but silk is also a sig-nifier of seduction. The paradox of abandonment and restraint is nowhere more profoundly stated in Chinese cinema than in this scene with the silk scarf.[3] Zhou Yuwen does battle with her traditional, sanc-tioned desiring relationship, represented by her sick husband, struggling to liberate herself from it and thus from tradition. However, it is an indi-cation of the differences between the urban China of the 40s and the US of the 20s and 30s, Borzage's world, that Zhou Yuwen and her beloved do not quite have the strength to overcome the traditional-historical arrange-ments which prevent their union, even though the old social conventions are reduced to the condition of a 'ruined city'. Fei Mu's great achieve-ment is to portray this understanding without resorting to overt political propaganda.

The standard reference work on the history of Chinese cinema published by the communist regime, the two-volume *History of the Development of Chinese Cinema* edited by Cheng Jihua, describes *Spring in a Small City* as a 'negative film which plays up the decadent emotions of a declining bourgeois class'. The film's detractors poured scorn on the character of the sick husband as a metaphorical figure representing sick China, repressive tradition and the ill wind of history. The *wenyi* tradition was thus condemned even though it was the same tradition which graced Wu Yonggang's *The Goddess/ Shen Nü* (1934), much praised by leftist critics. Wei Wei's performance in *Spring in a Small City* was to a large extent influenced by silent actress Ruan Lingyu's style.

Stanley Kwan may well be the *wenyi* master of current Hong Kong cinema, the true inheritor of the *wenyi* tradition found in a long line of Chinese classics, from *The Goddess* and *Spring in a Small City* to Li Hanxiang's *The Winter*. Kwan's reverential treatment of the *wenyi* tradition in his master works, *Rouge/ Yanzhi Kou* (1989) and *Actress*, were tributes to Chinese cinema classics and to a great Chinese star, but he was also following Hong Kong's own *wenyi* tradition. *Spring in a Small City* was probably the last great *wenyi* melodrama filmed in China, but the genre had found receptive hearts and minds among both Cantonese- and Mandarin-speaking film-makers in Hong Kong, who carried its tradition forward and developed it further by incorporating attacks on feudal morality and calls for the adoption of progressive ideas.

Cantonese cinema was particularly sensitive to this development: Ch'un Kim's *The Spirit of Azalea/Du Juan Hun* (1954) and *Autumn Comes to Purple Rose Garden/Ziwei Yuan de Qiu Tian* (1958) are superior examples of the *wenyi* strain, recalled today as emotional tales of star-crossed lovers or women's films containing memorable performances from both the female and the male leads such as Ng Cho-fan and Pak Yin, the archetypal *wenyi* couple with Ng as the weak husband or lover and Pak as his suffering but stoic beloved, as in Lei San-fung's *Cold Nights/Han Ye*. Ng Cho-fan was paired with Siu-yin Fei (memorable as the servant girl Azalea) in *The Spirit of Azalea*. She is forced to marry an old autocrat though she loves his grandson (played by Cheung Wood-yau). As war ensues, she loses everything, including her five-year-old daughter, but finds sympathy and love in the person of a fellow war refugee, Ng Cho-fan. The *wenyi* formula has Azalea re-unite with ex-lover Cheung Wood-yau, now a doctor, and a love triangle comes inexorably into play. In *Autumn Comes to Purple Rose Garden*, Ng Cho-fan was again the weak character with Pak Yin as the strong-minded woman who stirs things up in a family dominated by a feudal matriarch.

Ch'un Kim was the leading *wenyi* melodramatist of his time. He made a few more *wenyi* classics in both Cantonese and Mandarin cinemas before his death in 1969: the Cantonese-speaking *Moon Under the Palm Grove/Yelin Yue* (1959) was set in Singapore and Malaysia, and varied the formula with the story of a man (played by Tse Yin) torn between careers in education or in business and between the love of two women, each associated with one of the possible careers; the Mandarin-speaking *Till the End of Time/Heri Jun Zailai* (1966) was Ch'un's *wenyi* testament, a near-tragic tale of sacrifice as a man (Peter Chen Hou) battles to overcome his feelings of ineptitude and jealousy in order to keep his marriage intact.

Ch'un Kim, along with Lee Sun-fung and Chor Yuen (who was Ch'un's protégé) were the foremost stylists of *wenyi* in Cantonese cinema. In Mandarin cinema, Yi Wen's *Fire of Passion/Lian zhi Huo* (1955) was a good example of how the influence of Shanghai's *Spring in a Small City* carried over into Hong Kong. The plot is almost a carbon copy of *Spring in a Small City* with a more hyperbolic tone. Li Lihua occupies the central role in the triangular affair, playing the wife whose husband is impotent and who falls in love with her brother-in-law; the husband commits suicide, which brings the wife under suspicion of murder.

The Mandarin cinema emphasised the literary antecedents of the *wenyi* genre, adapting popular novelists such as Zhang Henshui (whose novel *The Story of Three Loves/Tixiao Yinyuan* was filmed numerous times), Eileen Chang, who began her career in Shanghai and then emigrated to Hong Kong before going to the US, and the Taiwanese writer, Qiong Yao. Their books were a rich source of *wenyi* material in the 60s and 70s. It is basically writers like Chang and Qiong who have carried on the *wenyi* line in the Mandarin-speaking cinemas of Hong Kong and Taiwan. In the 80s, *wenyi* material acquired a tinge of apocalyptic foreboding which betrayed the anxiety of Hong Kong people as they faced up to the reality of 1997.

Eileen Chang's *Love in a Fallen City/Qingcheng zhi Lian* was made into a film by Ann Hui in 1984, keeping the romantic strand of *wenyi* intact, as were concomitant themes about tradition and the past. The story is set both in Shanghai and Hong Kong and ends in Hong Kong as it falls to the Japanese in 1941. Hong Kong critics have preferred to see the film as an allegory, linking the Japanese conquest of Hong Kong in 1941 to the impending takeover of the territory by the Chinese in 1997. Whatever the merits of the original story by Eileen Chang, Hui's film is too unemotional a romantic saga for the allegory to work. The *wenyi* style romance between the wealthy, Gatsbyesque socialite, Fan Liuyuan (played by Chow Yun-fat) and Shanghai divorcee, Bai Liusu (played by Cora Miao), hardly transcends the level of high-society gossip: will Fan Liuyuan marry Bai Liusu or make her his mistress? Fan, who moves with ease among the territory's high-society types and is involved with an Indian woman of royal blood, explains to Liusu that he is attracted to her because her manner suggests she is '100% Chinese'. She personifies the Chineseness that he, a Westernised overseas Chinese, yearns for. However, it isn't until the Japanese invade Hong Kong that he makes up his mind to take Liusu for his wife. As the Japanese bomb Hong Kong, Fan brings Liusu to shelter in the fashionable Repulse Bay Hotel (an old colonial relic which was thus fortunately preserved on celluloid before it was demolished) in the belief that the Japanese would not dare attack the respectable hive of expatriates and foreign dandies. Fan and Liusu see their world crumble around them as the Japanese do in fact mercilessly attack and break through the British defence.

Hui missed the chance fully to realise the potential of the material, in spite (or because) of the opportunities provided her by the support of a major studio such as Shaw Brothers and the talent of a major star such as Chow Yun-fat. It remains an interesting though ultimately disappointing work. Bai Liusu is the archetypal 'hurt' woman in Chinese literature. Like Zhou Yuwen in *Spring in a Small City* and Ruan Lingyu in *Actress*, Bai Liusu is a traditionalist seeking sexual liberation. Even though there is the happy resolution of marriage, her character is essentially traditional. Fan Liuyuan, after all, finds this attractive and it is probably why he can be seen to marry her. The Bai household dominated by Liusu's elder brother is also archetypal. The extended family and its social network of friends, matchmakers and distant relatives are depicted with penetrating detail. One such detail is the manner in which Liusu's younger sister-in-law (the character played by Jiao Jiao) goes about berating, insulting and taunting Liusu. Such a character may well be a stereotype, but it is one which sparks instant recognition in anyone who has lived in an extended Chinese household. The style of bitching about someone else within the family is marked by innuendo, an indirect style of confrontation usually done behind closed doors, but it can also be carried out in an open forum such as the dinner table, availing oneself of the tradition that someone younger, particularly a woman, may not answer back even when being openly criticised. Such scenes in *Love in a Fallen City* are in line with the central antithesis of the *wenyi* genre: sexuality versus tradition. The sister-in-law is appropriately bitchy. When she speaks ill of someone who remains unnamed, everybody knows who is being criticised. Once again, the *wenyi* genre shows that art imitates life and that in *wenyi* films, of which the family melodrama forms one component, the viewer can identify conventions which link cinema with society. In truth, the Chinese art of bitching permeates relationships within family members and is not just a prerogative of the in-laws. Fathers, mothers and elder siblings frequently indulge in the practice, with the style of confrontation being determined by one's place in the family hierarchy. However, in the *wenyi* melodramas, the spotlight tends to be on women who seek to break out of the feudal straitjacket.

Hui's films, including *The Secret/Feng Jie* (1979) and *Song of the Exile/Ketu Qiuhen* (1990), are about women who must live up to and justify their roles in a system wrought by tradition. In *The Spooky Bunch/Zhuang Dao Zheng* (1980), Hui looks at how the sins of a previous generation confront the next. History is viewed as the wellspring of a people's cultural roots, and Hui suggests that it decisively affects the psyches and events of the present. This view is further explored in films such as *The Boat People/Touben Nuhai* (1982), which is as much about China as Vietnam, and *Love in a Fallen City*, which is about Hong Kong and China. The theme of personal identity is most explicit in *Song of the Exile* which questions the idea of 'Chineseness'. The film suggests that the predominantly Chinese inhabitants of Hong Kong may not be as homogeneous as they appear. The ambivalence of Chinese identity is, in fact, its central theme. Although marred by the inability of Hui's actors to deliver the right nuances, the film states that the separateness of Hong Kong lies in this very ambivalence, despite the fact that its residents speak mostly Cantonese and adhere to Chinese customs. In *Love in a Fallen City*, Fan Liuyuan's description of Bai Liusu as '100% Chinese' is ironic, coming as it does from the Ann Hui who also made *Song of the Exile.*

The film focuses on a mother and daughter relationship. The ambivalence of the mother's identity affects her behaviour and explains her estrangement from her daughter and in-laws. Her tale, and the reasons for her growing estrangement, is told in a flashback to the 50s in Macao where Cheung Hueyin, the daughter, is adored by grandparents who instil in her the seeds of distrust towards her mother. The grandfather is the very essence of a Chinese gentleman; we see him, with a Chinese brush, writing calligraphy and listening to poetry. The mother loses the battle for her daughter's emotions, and it is not until the family moves to Hong Kong where Hueyin's father works, that we understand why: the mother is Japanese. Hueyin, increasingly hostile to her mother, learns this through her father.

The bulk of the film is given to the reconciliation between mother and daughter during a journey to the mother's birthplace in Japan. Aiko, the mother's real name, takes centre stage. The viewer feels her relief in being in her home environment. We also see Hueyin's predicament in not being

212

able to speak Japanese and understand the customs of another culture. The parallel is drawn between Hueyin's predicament in Japan and Aiko's in China, Macao and Hong Kong. Once back in Japan, Aiko can barely hide her contempt for Chinese assertions of superiority in matters of culture and food which she has had to endure. But neither is everything rosy in Japan. Aiko's past connections with her country catch up with her as she picks up the threads of previous relationships, and people recollect their impressions of her as a young girl. In these scenes, Hui reprises the theme of history interacting with the personal lives of people who must bear its consequences. The film ends with Hueyin in a China engulfed in the Cultural Revolution. She goes to Guangzhou to visit her ailing grandfather who has been criticised by Red Guards for sending a book of Song Dynasty poetry to his granddaughter. We see in the figure of the grandfather a patriarch who has submitted himself to the greater patriarchy of the state. He persists in imparting one final word of wisdom: 'China still has hope.'

A film which sees China in a nostalgic and sentimental light is Yim Ho's *Homecoming/Sishui Liunian* (1984). It is another unique work in the *wenyi* genre characterised by realism and the usual stock of characters struggling with repressed feelings. Accordingly, China is not portrayed as a lush, Technicolored land but as a seedy rural locality. A sensitive and sincere work dedicated to the memory of Yim Ho's father whose passing inspired the making of the film, the narrative centres on a Hong Kong woman's return to her home village in Fujian province to visit the grave of her grandmother, recently deceased. San San (played by Josephine Koo) is a far cry from the repressed characters of Zhou Yuwen, Ruan Lingyu and Bai Liusu. She is a typical modern woman, urban, fashionable and liberated to the point of promiscuity, although the fact that she has suffered two abortions suggests that her sexual individualism is marred by an inadequate awareness of or a rejection of modern contraceptive methods. She leaves Hong Kong to set her mind free for a while from her failed business and a nasty legal wrangle with her younger sister over property.

Her stay in her grandmother's home brings back memories of childhood, as does the reunion with her friend, A Zhen (played by Siqin Gaowa), a schoolteacher married to another childhood friend, the farmer Song (Xie Weixiong). San San's relationship with this couple is described in the innocent phraseology of *qingmei zhuma* ('green plum and bamboo horse'), which implies a close intimacy established from childhood. The presence of San San is, however, the thin edge of the wedge leading to marital discord between A Zhen and Song. As an overseas Chinese from a sophisticated city, San San is perceived as a source of passion missing in the mundane lives of her childhood friends. A visit to Guangzhou organised for the schoolchildren and paid for by San San, reveals the rift in living standards between the city and the countryside. A Zhen's brief indulgence in a materialistic lifestyle, helped by San San, shows how much she, and by implication China, has really missed. The homecoming of overseas Chinese brings out subliminal feelings (especially materialistic greed) in the natives while it reinforces nostalgia in those who have returned. The 'spiritual homecoming' motif is further illustrated by San San's fellow overseas Chinese, Mr Zhuang, and a pair of elderly twin brothers who have come back from Australia. These characters are shown to revel in spiritual and physical contentment. The optimism of *Homecoming* is not accidental, however. Co-produced by Mainland Chinese companies, it was intended to be a positive picture with a 'you can come home again' message targeted at Hong Kong audiences which stubbornly remain worried about their future. The year 1984 was the most optimistic period in the Sino-British negotiations over 1997.

Yim Ho showed that he did not intend to convey the 'United Front' propaganda of his Chinese backers. It is the subtleties in the narrative which cast a delicate spell, such as Song pausing over a kite hidden away in the attic, and the lovely moment when A Zhen puts her daughter to bed and begins to tell her a story, but stops when she hears Song's voice in the next room telling San San, 'Since you are unhappy in Hong Kong, you are welcome to stay here, our house is your house.'

There are films, of course, where the reverse is true. Ann Hui's *The Boat People*[4] is a bitter epic, ostensibly about post-liberation Vietnam. Like *Homecoming*, it was produced by former actress Xia Meng (who appeared in several films by Zhu Shilin) as a co-production with China, with Hainan Island standing in for the Vietnamese port of Danang. The film was meant as a criticism of Vietnam, China's southern communist rival with whom it had fought a short border war in 1979. When the film was released in Hong Kong in 1982, audiences saw it instead as an attack on the communist system itself. What drew audiences was the allegory of Hong Kong turned into a communist 'new economic zone', in reality a forced labour camp where inmates got to farm the land if they were lucky, and were forced to dig for landmines if they were not. Thus Hui's work is now seen as the first Hong Kong picture to address the phobia and anxiety of Hong Kong people about 1997. Hong Kong critics saw it as the last chapter in Hui's trilogy about Vietnam with *The Boy From Vietnam/Lai Ke* (1978, for television) and *The Story of Woo Viet/Hu Yue de Gushi* (1981). *The Boat People* is set right in Vietnam, three years after the communist victory, when a Japanese photographer, Akutagawa (played by George Lam), who took pictures of the victorious North Vietnamese troops entering Danang in 1975, is invited back as a 'foreign friend'. He is given free access to ordinary Vietnamese and even allowed to take pictures of the most sensitive areas. Soon, he makes friends with a 14-year-old girl, Cam Nuong (played by Season Ma) and comes to know her family: her mother is a prostitute, her brother scavenges for scrap iron, and both scavenge the bodies of corpses in 'chicken farms': back alleys where people are executed. The Japanese visitor begins to see the 'reality' of Vietnam and, as befits a Cold War genre picture, he begins to have his doubts about Vietnamese communism, a feeling shared by a senior communist cadre. Comrade Nguyen (played by Chinese actor Qimeng Shi), a Sorbonne graduate, comments: 'Vietnam has won its revolution, but I have lost mine.' He hankers for French wine, food and women and is a regular customer at a bistro run by a Chinese Mama-san, known simply as 'Madame' (played by Cora Miao) where he gets vintage wine and the best French food in Danang. In this Bohemian, not to say decadent, setting, the comrade quotes Baudelaire: 'There are scents as fresh as the flesh of children/And others, rich and triumphant, that reek of decay' (according to the subtitles). Akutagawa's visit to Vietnam ends in tragedy when he is shot and devoured by flames sparked off by the gas tank he is carrying to help Cam Nuong leave Vietnam illegally by boat.

Hui has a particular flair for nicely understated action scenes. The success of *The Boat People* is due as much to Hui's emotive direction as to its allegorical impact, widely, and with considerable justification,[5] accepted as an anti-communist film even though it was intended as a plea addressed to Hong Kong's population to understand and accept the boat people in the territory, rather than to resent and attack their presence. Hui need not have intended the allegory to be about Chinese politics as well as about Vietnam, but the audience knew at once. The success of *The Boat People* was the only instance in which a Hong Kong film dealing with sensitive politics did not immediately fall victim to censorship within the territory. The Chinese authorities banned the film in China, citing it as an 'anti-communist' work. For ten years after its initial public release, the film was never revived in Hong Kong; distributors were well aware of China's dislike of the film.

A rule in the territory's censorship regulations allows for the banning of a film deemed 'prejudicial to good relations' with other countries. This clause has been used in the past to justify the banning of films deemed to be critical of China. While not exercised in the case of *The Boat People*, the Hong Kong government did invoke the ruling to ban two Taiwanese productions: *If I Were Real/Jiaru Wo Shi Zhen De* (1980) and *The Coldest Winter in Beijing/Huang Tina Hou Tu* (1981) which dealt with the devastating effects of the Cultural Revolution on the lives of young people and their families. The films were eventually released with the relaxation of politically influenced censorship in the late 80s, even though the 'good relations' ruling remained in a new censorship ordinance passed in 1987. The ordinance clearly provides future administrations with the power to exercise political censorship if they so wish. A third movie, *China Behind/Zaijian Zhongguo*, a Hong Kong production shot in Taiwan in 1974 and kept off the distribution circuit until 1987, was perhaps the most prominent victim of censorship in the territory. Director Tang Shuxuan's realistic work about four college students escaping to Hong Kong from Guangzhou during the Cultural Revolution is one of Hong Kong cinema's most outstanding features, the first to criticise its madness and to see it as having catastrophic implications for a whole generation of young people. The narrative imparts an unrelenting sense of desperation and fear. The four young protagonists (plus a doctor who drops out half-way) make the choice for freedom in the belief that they are unwanted in a 'socialist' system about to go haywire. Setting out from Guangzhou under the pretext of engaging in Red Guard activity, they reach the coast near Hong Kong in order to swim across to another, supposedly freer, society. Their trek is harrowingly vivid. As they pass through villages with megaphones blaring Mao's revolutionary doctrine, farmers and children within earshot of their whereabouts become their victims. Only three make it to Hong Kong, but director Tang offers her escapees no relief: they are shown struggling 'between two worlds' (a line uttered by one of the characters) amidst the cathedrals of materialism (a stockmarket) and exploitation (a factory). They find a society that is indifferent to their plight; solace is found only in a church. The movie is unforgettably stark with indelible images of life under Mao and life under capitalism. The film ends with two of the escapees gazing out of a window into the void. The existential pessimism makes this one of the most uncompromising social-political works from a Hong Kong film director.

Director Tang Shuxuan acquired a reputation as an iconoclastic artist with her first feature, *The Arch/Dong Furen* (1970), which had extremely limited distribution in Taiwan and Hong Kong. *China Behind*'s refusal to be clear-cut in its commendation of Hong Kong as a brighter alternative to China is a typical manifestation of this iconoclasm. In *China Behind*, her anti-communist stance is self-evident while in *The Arch*, primitive feudalism is shown to oppress Chinese women. Her politics can perhaps best be summed up as committed to individualist humanism with a strong sense of existential doubt marking the fact that even humanism has its darker sides.

The acute pessimism of *China Behind* lifts the picture above trite anti-communist propaganda and stamps it with complexity. Though not a masterpiece, it improves with age and impresses as a prophetic work – both in its verdict over the Cultural Revolution and its depiction of Hong Kong's callous indifference to people's lives. The title alone contains a mountain of irony. Its protagonists leave *China Behind*. Once in Hong Kong, they are filled with doubt, insecurity and paranoia. Perhaps in their heart of hearts, they really need China. In the 80s, the tide reversed: Hong Kong turned to face the reality of China, acknowledging the inexorable fact that China is not behind, but right in front. As Hong Kong came face to face with China, director Clara Law, a generation younger than Tang Shuxuan and belonging to the generation that probably has the most to lose in terms of a bona fide 'Hong Kong identity' as a result of the Chinese take-over in 1997, responded with her own variation of the 'China behind' syndrome. The English title of Law's film is even more apposite: *Farewell China/Ai Zai Bieiang de Jijie* (1990). The film deals with the latent desire of Chinese to leave China. More precisely, it deals with every prospective Chinese emigrant's belief in the myth of the American Dream.

Law sees America in symbolic terms, more as the land of liberty (the better to shatter this image), than the land of milk and honey. A telling bit of symbolism at the end, involving a replica of the Goddess of Liberty statue built by students in Tiananmen Square, and a few lines of dialogue about freedom, reveal this to be the case. The story starts off as a typical tale of a Chinese woman, Li Hong (played by Maggie Cheung), trying desperately to get to America. To ensure that she gets a visa, she becomes pregnant and gives birth to a baby so that she looks plain and less pretty (her previous applications were rejected because she looked too pretty). She is given a visa and goes to America, leaving behind her husband, Zhao Nansheng (Tony Leung) and their baby boy. When his letters to his wife are returned, Nansheng decides to look for her in New York, entering the country illegally through Panama. Thus begins his nightmarish odyssey into the diaspora. The characters Nansheng encounters are mostly Chinese, including Jane, a wayward teenage girl who helps him find Li Hong. The film exposes the ugly side of the Chinese community in America, showing its characters as heartless, hypocritical, self-centred individuals. The story of the wife's progress from an aspiring Chinese emigrant to her final descent into madness in America, recounted in flashbacks by people she has known, including a man whom she marries in order to get a green card, is equally bleak. In the end, Nansheng finds her, but the outcome is desperately tragic. Their tragedy is the tragedy of China, which is the real theme of the film. Li Hong is presented as a schizoid personality: one side of her is Chinese, the other side despises the Chinese, even refusing to speak Chinese. Law offers not so much a distorted vision of the American Dream as a comment about the spiritual malaise gripping Chinese people. However, Law's solution seems equally problematic, hanging on to an idealised notion of the Chinese homeland represented repeatedly in the form of a folk-like ballad sung, unaccountably, in Fujianese. Yet, there is no denying the intrinsic power of Law's treatment of her great theme of a China prone to tragedy, a China that is literally driving her people away.

NOTES

[1] For a discussion of 'abstract nationalism', see Chapter 8.
[2] Suppressed for many years, it was shown in Hong Kong in 1983, the first such showing outside China, in a retrospective of Chinese classics organised with the co-operation of the Beijing Film Archive.
[3] Perhaps only Stanley Kwan has managed to capture a similarly fine sense of repressed desire in *Rouge*.
[4] See Chapter 10 for a discussion of Ann Hui's other works.
[5] In the West, a negative portrayal of Vietnam's communism merely confirmed expectations programmed by four decades of Cold War propaganda about communism wherever it gained power; some of Hui's imagery, such as the final dash to the boat, at night through rain-drenched passageways between warehouses, dodging searchlights, closely approximates dozens of 'escape from communism' movies, usually set at the Berlin wall; moreover, Hui's film withholds crucial information which might inflect the anti-communist message, such as the fact that de-mining work was forced, not on the population in general, but on the former South Vietnamese soldiers, who had laid the mines in the first place, indiscriminately killing and maiming hundreds of men, women and children. By withholding this information, these most harrowing of sequences suggest that the Vietnamese communists exercised a gruesome, Pol Pot-type of terror against the entire population. If this were true, they could hardly have defeated the US and its local collaborators. In order to solicit sympathy for the victims of Hong Kong

people's anti-Vietnamese racism, Hui ended up legitimating the US's aggression along with the Chinese invasion of Vietnam in 1978 in pursuit of its own imperial foreign policy.

Chapter Fourteen

Ghosts, Cadavers, Demons and Other Hybrids

Hong Kong cinema's hybridity, freely mixing elements from East and West, is perhaps seen to best effect in the horror genre, combining aspects of Western vampire movies, Chinese ghost stories and Hong Kong's own kung fu and comedy genres. The vampire motif is a variation on the Western form which Hong Kong cinema assimilated with the release of *Mr Vampire/Jiangshi Xiansheng* (1985). The movie's box-office success started a trend of 'vampire movies', Hong Kong-style. The term is somewhat misleading. In Chinese, the new genre is known as *jiangshi dianying* or 'cadaver movies'. The label 'vampire movies' was introduced by Hong Kong film publicists. Scholars may wish to note that Chinese cadavers cannot change their shapes and fly away into the night as bats. Transsubstantiation is unthinkable in Chinese culture since the rule of pragmatism which guides Chinese thinking in matters of the afterlife requires that one's physical, human shape be kept intact for reincarnation and for the wheel of life to keep on revolving. The Chinese preference for cutting off one's head as the ultimate form of capital punishment takes this thinking into account. When one's head is cut off, reincarnation is not possible and one is condemned to eternal punishment as a lost soul wandering in hell. The fact that Chinese vampire movies draw on the Chinese tradition of ghostlore and supernatural stories has not been properly acknowledged. While foreign audiences may recognise Western motifs, the Chinese vampire movies merely allude to Western horror movies, and to much else besides. They offer the best examples of Hong Kong cinema's pragmatic exploitation of Chinese literary tradition to produce popular works which find relevance to and affinity with its modern audiences.

The title of *A Chinese Ghost Story/Qiannü Youhun* (1987) produced by Tsui Hark and directed by Ching Siu-tung, puts Hong Kong cinema's horror genre in its proper place within the Chinese literary tradition. A costumed adventure, a Hollywood-style special-effects extravaganza, a Chinese ghost story with the requisite ghosts and demons kitted out in traditional fashion – these descriptions all apply. Special-effects wizardry conveys the modern, Western idiom of Hong Kong's cinematic storytelling while the fragmented cutting style within sequences recalls a *manga* kind of comic strip narration. The period setting and costumes convey an updated ghost story-adventure rather than the rarefied world of a historical epic. Tsui Hark and Ching Siu-tung have adapted the old to suit the modern, and done it with a sense of sublime confidence.

The film was based on a story taken from a voluminous anthology of ghost stories collected by Pu Songling (1640–1715), a writer and chronicler of strange tales known as 'Master Liaozhai' after the title of his masterpiece *Liaozhai Zhiyi* (translated as *Strange Stories from a Chinese Studio*). Pu was a failed scholar whose one claim to literary fame was the *Liaozhai*, as it is usually abbreviated. It consists of several volumes of stories written in a terse, melodramatic style known as *chuanqi*, which was current during the Tang Dynasty. Although melodramatic in tone, readers of Liaozhai will perceive touches of a 'documentary' approach. The terse and laconic formats of the stories proved to be eminently suited for adaptation into screenplays. Movie writers and directors often broadened and embellished the stories, as King Hu did for *A Touch of Zen/Xia Nü*. From Liaozhai, therefore, springs the Chinese cinema's horror tradition. In fact, one speaks of the atmosphere of a ghost story as *hen liaozhai* or 'very liaozhai'.

It is doubtful, however, whether *A Chinese Ghost Story* would be described as 'very liaozhai'. It is quite faithful to the original plot: a scholar-cum-tax collector (played by Leslie Cheung) takes shelter in a dilapidated temple. There he comes across the beautiful Xiaoqian and falls in love with her, not knowing at first that she is a ghost (Xiaoqian was played by Joey Wong, now typecast as ghost-seductresses). Master Yan, a reclusive Daoist swordsman (played by Wu Ma, in rapturous style) saves the bewitched scholar by confronting and exorcising the ghost and other demons. These characters and situations are all standard in Liaozhai. However, the atmosphere of antiquarian ghosts is compromised by the razzle-dazzle of modern special effects. The pace is closer to that of a martial arts action picture, to which *A Chinese Ghost Story* is rather similar.

The story was filmed once before in 1960 by Li Hanxiang as *The Enchanting Shadow*, without special effects, but making full use of artificial smoke and shadowy lighting to convey a haunting, poetic atmosphere. Seen today, the contrast in styles between Li's film and Tsui and Ching's version signifies also the different aesthetic as well as technological emphases of Hong Kong cinema. In fact, by not overly respecting their source, Tsui and Ching have transformed Liaozhai into a modern and relevant text. The Liaozhai stories deal with age-old human phobias about death, the afterlife, strange occurrences and other-worldly demons and spirits. The emphasis is on the mind/body dichotomy and Liaozhai's work is redolent with what now could be described as surreal imagery, although Pu Songling was a secular writer who told macabre and incredible tales in order to convey a moral code, like a fabulist. He declared that the most precious thing on earth was the human body and went on to document numerous cases of ghosts and spirits seeking human bodies to possess for reincarnation. The dead take the form of abstract spirits (usually manifested in Pu's literature as *huli* or fox creatures), but can also assume human shape by imbibing life 'essence' through sexual encounters. In Pu's world, death is a supernatural realm populated by spirits and ghosts who seek rebirth. Once rebirth is achieved through reincarnation, peace and harmony are restored between the real and the nether worlds: the dead are truly dead. When the dead are not dead, there is no harmony between the soul and the body and reincarnation is not able to take its course. Xiaoqian, the beautiful ghost in *A Chinese Ghost Story*, is a typical haunted soul unable to reincarnate and therefore condemned to haunt the living. She lures men into a trap where their life force is sucked away by a tree demon in the form of a gender-bending human. The demon is able to change sex and shape – from tree to androgynous human – with great ease, a sign of great evil. Xiaoqian's destiny and her ultimate path to reincarnation are controlled by the tree-demon because her grave is located under the tree, and it is her love for the scholar which finally redeems her. After subduing the demon and a guardian of hell who wants Xiaoqian's spirit in marriage, the scholar brings her ashes to her family grave so that she can fulfil the process of reincarnation and become human again.

The reincarnation theme is the backbone in all ghost stories, and it is the ghost story which defines Hong Kong's horror genre, which may also include films such as Tsui Hark's *We're Going to Eat You* (1980) and whodunits like Ann Hui's *The Secret* (1979), which can be seen as a pseudo-ghost story. However, it is the Chinese ghost story genre involving reincarnation which remains the central reference point in relation to which elements from the Western horror genre are incorporated. The ghost story is one strand of the Chinese horror tradition represented in films as different as *A Chinese Ghost Story* and Stanley Kwan's *Rouge*. It is also the oldest strand in the horror cinema, stretching back to the inception of Chinese film-making and drawing inspiration from a long oral and literary tradition.

One of the earliest ghost story movies in Cantonese cinema is *Ghost Woman of the Old Mansion/ Guyuan Yaoji*, released in 1949. Directed by Chiu Shu-ken and Lau Fong, the film is a richly evocative thriller that shows Cantonese cinema absorbing the influences of classic Hollywood horror movies and Chinese cinema's own traditions of grand guignol. It bears comparison with Ma-Xu Weibang's Hong Kong horror classic *A Maid's Bitter Story/ Qionglou Hen*, released the same year. As one of the first ghost stories to hit the screen in the immediate post-war period, *Ghost Woman* is startling for its portrayal of necrophiliac desire. Ng Cho-fan plays a property agent who goes to an old mansion to clinch a deal. There he meets the ghost of a woman who is the spitting image of his dead wife, and he falls in love with her.

Cantonese and Mandarin cinemas of the 50s and 60s were replete with ghost films displaying overtones of necrophilia, one of the best being Lee Sun-fung's *Beauty Raised From the Dead/ Yanshi Huanhun Ji* (1956). Lee's film is typical of ghost stories, the ghost invariably being a woman, usually one who has died as a victim of injustice. The fact that the ghost is always

221

beautiful (in Lee's film, Pak Yin played the ghost) usually implies that she was a victim of a love that went wrong. However, Cantonese ghost movies also followed the traditional Radcliffian gothic model, indulging in the full panoply of supernatural thrills only to insist, in the end, on a rational explanation for the proceedings. In Ch'un Kim's *Nightly Cry of the Ghost/Gui Yeku* (1957) and *The Haunted Night/Huihun Ye* (1962), directed by Cheung Ying and Choi Cheung, as well as in Chor Yuen's *A Mad Woman/Feng Fu* (1964), the ghost is exposed as a hoax, a criminal scheme or a mad woman misunderstood and mistreated by society.

In Mandarin cinema, Ma-Xu Weibang's *A Maid's Bitter Story* (1949) was his only major work in the genre after emigrating from Shanghai to Hong Kong. It combined elements of the haunted house story with aspects of the thriller, closer in atmosphere to James Whale's *The Old Dark House* (1932) or a Daphne du Maurier story than Liaozhai. Ma-Xu was something of an iconoclast who virtually created the modern horror genre in Chinese cinema with *Song at Midnight/Yeban Gesheng* (1937), a version of *Phantom of the Opera* carrying a statement about China's lamentable condition under the yoke of feudalism and oppressive warlords. He was influenced more by Western gothic than the Chinese horror tradition. This was in line with his progressive thinking and strong espousal of revolution (of the bourgeois democratic sort) as the only way China could overcome oppressive feudal elements.

Apart from Ma-Xu, the Mandarin cinema in Hong Kong in the 50s, the period of post-war recovery, did not develop an overt fondness for horror movies. Even Ma-Xu's horror films were few and far between as he was forced to make musicals and comedies, and other Mandarin directors who did work in the genre tended to use Liaozhai as their source. Moreover, while Cantonese cinema mixed fantasy with didactic melodrama arguing against superstition and injustice, Mandarin directors preferred the classical values of Chinese tradition: the poetry, music, dance and atmosphere of a bygone era.

Liaozhai-type ghost films were produced intermittently in the 50s and 60s, the best known being Li Hanxiang's *The Enchanting Shadow* (1960), Tang Huang's *Fairy, Ghost, Vixen/Liaozhai Zhiyi* (1965), Ding Shanxi's *Blood Reincarnation/Yinyang Jie* (1974) and King Hu's re-working of a Liaozhai tale as the martial arts epic *A Touch of Zen* (1971). Hu's *Legend of the Mountain/Shanzhong Chuanqi* (1979) was a more conventional ghost story with Liaozhai influences. These films featured beautiful female ghosts (as *huli*, seductresses or 'vixens') and their love object, the effete male scholar. A variation of the female ghost was the *xian* or fairy, an immortal from heaven who longs for the love and companionship of humans.

The ghost movies of the 80s invoked the Chinese pantheon of gods and demons more freely, extending this to archaeological artifacts such as the famous terra-cotta warriors unearthed from Emperor Qin's tomb in 1974. The central figure of the beautiful ghost attracts ferocious guardians of hell and heroic terra-cotta warriors as much as she attracts vulnerable humans. She is coveted in flesh and in spirit, as in *A Chinese Ghost Story*, Ringo Lam's

Esprit d'Amour/Yinyang Cuo (1983) and David Lai's *Spiritual Love/Gui Xinniang* (1987). The ghost story featuring the female ghost underwent variations in the mid-80s when the focus turned to human beings and special effects rather than spirits, while, of course, beautiful ghosts continued to provide sex appeal. Films such as Fok Yiu-leung's *The Iceman Cometh/Jidong Qixia* (1989) and Ching Siu-tung's *A Terra-Cotta Warrior/Qin Yong* (1990) blend the reincarnation theme with that of time travel: terra-cotta warriors buried in Emperor Qin's tomb are reincarnated and transported through time from the 2nd century BC to the 20th century. Tony Au first introduced a terra-cotta warrior to Hong Kong cinema in *Dream Lovers/Mengzhong Ren* (1986), a ghost story with a difference: there are really no ghosts as such, but the spirits of two dead lovers from the Qin Dynasty which have reincarnated after two thousand years as Chow Yun-fat and Lin Ching-hsia, two modern professionals. He is a music conductor, she an interior decorator, brought together by shared hallucinations and a chance meeting during an exhibition of the terra-cotta warriors in Hong Kong.

The reincarnation theme inter-woven with an allegory about Chinese history was the agenda behind Clara Law's ghost story, *The Reincarnation of Golden Lotus/Pan Jialian zhi Qian Shi Jin Sheng* (1989), a re-telling of the Ming Dynasty erotic classic *Jin Ping Mei* (translated as *The Golden Lotus*), starring Joey Wong as Pan Jinlian, the object of men's desire, reincarnated from Ming China to Maoist China during the Cultural Revolution. Pan eventually comes to Hong Kong as a refugee where she renews acquaintances with several men, all reincarnations of previous lovers.

Although indebted to Hollywood and to Britain's Hammer films, the cadavers which contributed to the success of the series were a venerable part of Chinese folklore, recounted not only in Liaozhai but in other literary sources as well. The ghost story format and its reincarnation theme allow for an allegorical tale of betrayal and fate, transporting characters on a journey through a psychic realm where the past determines the future. Variations on the theme led to the so-called vampire movies which form a distinct subgenre that became popular with the success of *Mr Vampire* (1985). A hugely entertaining comedy, *Mr Vampire* tells the story of a Daoist fat-si (in pinyin, *fashi*), a priest or shaman with special spells and magical powers to deal with spirits and ghosts. The fat-si is hired to disinter a corpse because of the grave's bad *feng shui* and to re-bury it in a distant part of town. The fat-si, assisted by two bumbling disciples, transports the corpse by making it hop all the way with its arms out-stretched, a practice also known as 'corpse driving'. Thus, the cadaver is to all intents and purposes 'alive'. It is able to sense and imbibe human breath, literally inhaling the essence of life into its own body and become a living being again at the expense of the one whose breath has been sucked out. The fat-si restrains the cadaver's impulse to attack human beings by glueing on its forehead a yellow scroll containing Daoist or Buddhist invocations. The fat-si walks in front of the cadaver shouting warnings to humans to get out of the way or risk being chased by the hopping cadaver. The fat-si differentiates between a *jiangshi* (cadaver or vampire) and a *sishi* (a corpse). A *jiangshi* possesses an 'extra breath' of life; a *sishi* is merely dead. When one does not die an auspicious death, an extra breath is retained in the body and the cadaver awaits an opportune moment to reactivate itself, searching for life forces to absorb. This explanation makes *Mr Vampire* something of a seminal work which spawned a series of sequels and imitations under the label of 'vampire films' in the second half of the 80s, but in fact the fat-si and hopping cadavers had already been featured in films of the late 70s and early 80s, fusing Chinese ghostlore with kung fu.

Kung fu maestro Lau Kar-leong had introduced the fat-si and hopping cadavers to Hong Kong cinema in *The Spiritual Boxer, Part II/Mao Shan Jianshi Quan* (1979). Although it was not one of Lau's most inspired works, the film injected comedy into a flagging kung fu genre. Lau introduced ingredients from other genres such as comedy and, later, horror, to revive the action genre, including the prototypes for the fat-si and hopping cadavers: the fat-si being a Daoist master from the Mao Shan school[1] while the hopping cadavers are recognised by their long Qing-Dynasty robes, Mandarin caps and yellow scrolls pasted on their foreheads. These prototypes were immediately taken up and expanded in Sammo Hung's *Encounters of the Spooky Kind/Gui Da Gui* (1980), a near-class kung fu-horror comedy featuring Sammo as 'Brave' Cheung, a town braggart who boasts that he is not afraid of spending a night in a haunted house. Cheung is lured into doing just that by his unfaithful wife; her lover hires a fat-si to awaken human cadavers in the house to scare Cheung to death. However, a rival fat-si discovers the plan and helps Sammo to defeat the cadavers and the bad fat-si.

The fat-si's power to deal with the dead has its moral dimension. He is not only an intermediary between life and death, he is also capable of casting spells on humans and manipulating them like puppets, as seen in the last sequence of *Encounters of the Spooky Kind* where Cheung fights a last-ditch battle with the cadavers: Cheung, the film's nominal hero, is putty in the hands of the two fat-si, just as the cadavers are. The fat-si is the most extraordinary character in the Chinese horror tradition because he represents forces of genuinely metaphysical dimensions. Unlike the mad scientists in Western horror, the fat-si takes on spiritual tasks as well as physical ones, refusing the modern Western distinction between religion and science, belief and knowledge, relying on revelatory texts which themselves have the status of absolute, irresistible truth, rather analogous to the premodern status of the scriptures in Western societies. In this respect, the presence, even the centrality, of a Daoist priest in both the horror and the kung fu genres indicates something of the values and ideologies which modern, even postmodern Hong Kong cinema seeks to renegotiate, betraying the stubborn survival of premodern ways of thinking beyond the historical moment when they ought to have died, just like the cadavers. Seen in this light, the theme of reincarnation also takes on a somewhat different hue. Reincarnation involves the recognition of a fundamental contradiction between continuity and transience, a contradiction which religion tries to resolve by inventing the notion of reincarnation. However, this notion may also serve as a metaphor for dealing with the awkward fact that all manner of cultural and social values which belong to a bygone era are still very much with us, and are by no means all to be discarded. In this sense, the theme of reincarnation in Hong Kong's cinema may be read also as a way of dealing with the fundamental hybridity of Hong Kong's situation, caught between the modern worlds of both Western capitalism and Chinese 'communism' on the one hand, and the abstract nationalism invoking an older, vaguer notion of Chineseness on the other. One way of dealing with these tensions, so the horror films and their emphasis on reincarnation suggest, is to recognise that the old persists in what seem to be new forms.

Yuen Woo-ping's exhilarating *The Miracle Fighters/Qimen Dunjia* (1982), is entirely devoted to the fat-si. The title refers to them and the fact that they possess martial skills as well as an ability to perform miracles such as raising the dead. As in *Encounters of the Spooky Kind,* the film features more than one fat-si, divided accordingly to classically Manichaean lines of good and bad. A young disciple of some elderly 'miracle fighters' is trained in *fashu* (the arts of the fat-si) as well as *wushu* (martial arts). He is mistaken for the crown prince who has gone missing since childhood. The emperor dispatches a eunuch who has the powers of a fat-si to apprehend the young man, but he must first get rid of the supposed prince's elderly guardians and protectors. The climactic action set-piece takes place in hell. The eunuch and the young disciple are forced into a contest to determine who is more powerful, a remarkable sequence of pure kung fu action, recalling the best films of Lau Kar-leong, such as *36th Chamber of Shaolin/Shaolin Sanshiliu Fang,* which deals with the overcoming of physical tests to determine whether or not one has achieved true kung fu skills. The stylised action is choreographed in the fashion of Peking opera. Indeed, the film has many operatic moments and delightfully eccentric characters, such as a guard in the imperial palace whose head pops out of a jar and, like a Ninja turtle, engages the hero in a duel, with the jar acting like an armour.

In Dennis Yu's *The Imp/Xiongbang* (1981), a horror film with a contemporary setting, a fat-si presides over the rituals of exorcism. Tools of the trade include the familiar yellow scrolls which, when burned, have the power to expel spirits. In many other films, rice is used not only to expel but also to summon spirits. Other methods entail the use of babies and dogs: having a baby piss on the head of a person possessed by a spirit exorcises the spirit; an invisible spirit is made visible when one sprinkles dog's blood over it.

The fat-si in *Mr Vampire* explains that spirits are motivated to possess human bodies because they were human beings once. So they not only feel the urge to be human, they also retain human characteristics such as vanity, vulnerability and other foibles. This is the tongue-in-cheek theme of Ann Hui's *The Spooky Bunch/Zhuang Dao Zheng* (1980), where feuding ghosts from a previous era try to settle scores with the children of succeeding generations because of past errors. The comic potential of such religious beliefs (or tall tales, depending on one's historical consciousness) is borne out by Hui's exuberant comedy as well as by *Encounters of the Spooky Kind, The Miracle Fighters* and *Mr Vampire*.

By far the best of the kung fu–horror comedies is *The Dead and the Deadly/Ren Xia Ren* (1982), the masterpiece of the genre directed by Wu Ma. It works as an unassailable, macabre, funny and ultimately wonderful fusion of kung fu and horror. Wu Ma, best known for martial arts movies such as *Deaf and Mute Heroine/Longya Jian*, has a leading role as Ma Linxiang, a sexually impotent gnome of a man with an ugly pug nose. In order to swindle an inheritance from his father, Ma hatches a scheme with unscrupulous cohorts. Ma pretends to be dead while a pregnant woman masquerading as his wife escorts him back to his family home to claim the inheritance. Ma is double-crossed and killed, and his ghost turns to his best friend, Zhu Hongli (played by Sammo Hung), for help, borrowing Zhu's body to exact revenge on his killers. The film makes light of a person's physical endowments as well as of death itself. Ma is small, ugly and pug-nosed, while Zhu is fat but agile. Ma possesses Zhu's body and, having taken care of his enemies, he inadvertently leaves Zhu's body behind in the nether world, so that Zhu is now without a body. As Zhu's spirit slowly evaporates, it is up to his sweetheart (played by Cherie Chung) to retrieve his body with the help of a fat-si. Here, a woman plays the crucial role in determining the hero's fate, a role usually reserved for the fat-si. Hung's everyman and buffoon persona is finally saved by a woman. The action springs from the motivations of its characters who are delineated with layers of emotion: greed, terror, revenge, loyalty, friendship. The audience gets completely caught up in the interplay of these emotions as in a Grimm-like atmosphere of ghouls and creatures from the nether world.

Since that success, actor-director Wu Ma has been an ubiquitous presence in the genre, proving himself an old hand in crossing from kung fu to horror, becoming equally adept at both as well as at comedy. In *My Cousin the Ghost/Biaoge Dao* (1987), Wu Ma constructs a blithe and mellow variation of the ghost/cadaver theme. A cook returns to Hong Kong from London and puts up with four other cousins, including Wu Ma, who has long been at odds with the cook. The Hong Kong cousins receive a cable telling them that their London cousin has gone missing and is believed dead; only then are they made aware that this cousin is a ghost. The cousin, however, is blissfully unaware that he is a ghost and continues daily life as a supposedly normal human being. He even falls in love with a woman in the next apartment. As Wu Ma's irascible cousin explains: 'It's a case of a corpse which refuses to rot.' The woman next door also turns out to be a ghost, giving the story a happy ending, the cousin realising his true ghostly status and able to form a union with his lover in the afterlife.

Other Wu Ma-directed ghost stories include a Liaozhai adaptation, *Picture of a Nymph/Hua Zhong Xian* (1988), in which Wu essentially repeats his role of *A Chinese Ghost Story* as a Daoist master and ghost-fighter trying to separate a scholar and his beautiful woman ghost-lover – who emerges from a painting; and *Burning Sensation/Huozhuo Gui* (1989), a modern ghost story featuring a romance between a fireman and a lady ghost. However, it is as an actor in kung fu-horror movies that Wu will probably be remembered. His contribution to the ghost story movies as distinct from the vampire-cadaver movies is his definitive characterisations of Daoist eccentrics: reclusive hermits or *daoshi* who have attained the status of master and take on younger disciples in order to train them to be fat-si.

In *A Chinese Ghost Story*, Wu's Daoist swordsman–eccentric had wilfully withdrawn from the outside world to agonise over the human condition. Although his avowed task as a Daoist master is to maintain the separation of the *yin* (the world of the ghosts) and the *yang* (the world of humans), Wu agrees to help the female ghost by easing her path towards reincarnation. The ghost will become human again and perhaps unite with her love, the scholar. Such a possibility forms the storyline of the sequel, *A Chinese Ghost Story, Part II: Qiannü Youhun – Renjian Dao* (1990), again produced by Tsui Hark and directed by Ching Siu-tung, where Joey Wong's ghost in the first edition is reincarnated as the daughter of an upright official trying to rescue her father, a political prisoner. She meets up with Leslie Cheung's scholar but, in her new personality, does not recognise him.

Wu Ma's Daoist swordsman-eccentric features only in the film's incredible finale: a battle with a demon manifesting itself as a false Buddha who steals the personality of the emperor's official monk in order to wreak havoc throughout the empire. Thus *A Chinese Ghost Story, Part II* further develops, and indeed modernises the themes of the horror genre by presenting a buddha as a false idol and a dangerous demon. It is Wu's Daoist master who saves the day with the help of a young fat-si (played by Jacky Cheung), but not before he has made a comment about the increasing complexity of a world where one must battle ghosts as well as all sorts of ghouls and demons. Demons are a particularly bad portent because they only surface when a country is close to collapse, when the end of the world is nigh.

The film's auteurs, Tsui Hark and Ching Siu-tung, but primarily the former, have underscored with a tint of allegory the point about demons surfacing from hell when a country or dynasty is near collapse. As the demon turns into the image of the golden buddha, the opening bars of the Internationale are hard as a short pastiche in the score. The allusion is, of course, to the collapse of communism. In the Hong Kong context, such an allusion has added significance. It is further evidence of Tsui Hark's knack for using symbols to illustrate his disquiet over Hong Kong's 1997 dilemma and the China syndrome.

Tsui Hark has since developed this theme of apocalyptic demons foreshadowing the end of the world with even greater panache in *The Wicked City* (1992), a sci-fi movie crossed with another important strand of the Chinese horror tradition, that of *yaoguai* or demons. *A Chinese Ghost Story, Part II* is a good example of a *yaoguai* movie. The central demon is memorable for its ability to manifest itself as a false buddha and high priest who recites a hypnotic and deadly mantra exhorting humans to lay down their arms and kneel before buddha; the power of this deceptive mantra destroys anyone who recites it long enough. The demon, in the image of a golden buddha, asks Wu Ma's Daoist master why he does not kneel and humble himself before it like all other humans. The Daoist, being above it all, says that humans are ignorant and easily fooled, thus the power of a false god is all the greater. The demon is therefore one of Tsui Hark's most potent symbols, imparting a political message about rising above the need to pay allegiance or homage to a false god, and the importance of staying vigilant as one's country experiences a turning point in history.

Tsui Hark's role as a Hong Kong film-maker may be likened to that of the character of Wu Ma's Daoist master in parts one and two of *A Chinese Ghost Story*. Although he is not the hero, the Daoist plays the role of a *deus ex machina* in putting things right and making sure that the natural order is not disturbed. That this order may be abused, and the *yin* and *yang* turned topsy-turvy by false priests, is a theme taken up spectacularly in *A Chinese Ghost Story, Part II*. In the third edition, *A Chinese Ghost Story, Part III/Qiannü Youhun III: Dao Dao Dao* (1991), two Buddhist monks, an old master and his young disciple, take the leading roles in battling the androgynous tree demon of the first edition and its bevy of beautiful woman ghosts, one of which attempts to seduce the young monk (played by Tony Leung Chiu-wai). The conflict is more decisively Manichaean. Good being represented by the monks (who this time do not need to act on behalf of an effete human hero, although human vulnerability is represented by Tony Leung's young, inexperienced monk). Evil, of course, is represented by the demon.

One of Tsui's most impressive symbols appears in *A Chinese Ghost Story* as one of the film's most memorable special effects. It is a giant, elongating tongue stretching out from the androgynous tree-demon, rolling over everything in its path. The tongue is used as a weapon by the demon to catch victims and swallow them. The tongue sticking out in death is a popular motif in horror movies, so it is an appropriate symbol which binds ghosts, cadavers and demons, all of whom share the condition of living when they ought to be dead. It unifies the various strands of Hong Kong's horror genre and even crosses over into kung fu, comedy and science fiction. The elongating, rolling tongue seen in *A Chinese Ghost Story* illustrates the point admirably: it is horror and high camp, kung fu and special-effects fantasy, it is hyperactive, pathological and multi-dimensional. It lashes out, moving in waves to unbalance nature and man; it penetrates right into one's stomach to tear out the liver; it divides into two crocodile beaks to swallow a man; it sticks out further little tongues to cover one's face with goo. At the base of the throat, the horrifying human face of the demon shrieks with laughter. The tongue is also the main attraction in *A Chinese Ghost Story, Part III*, where the tree-demon returns, one hundred years after its appearance in the first edition, to deal with a couple of monks who try to destroy it. The tongue is only one part of the facial features which are developed as important props in the third edition. The elderly monk, one of the film's heroes, is kept prisoner by the tree-demon after having been blinded by a yellow light thrown by the demon. The monk develops extra-sensory auditory powers activated by his earlobes which elongate and vibrate, flicking feverishly as they sense evil approaching. When the monk is blinded, his earlobes stretch out to cover and protect his eyes. Hence, all the sensory perceptions act to protect and heal the body, whereas a demon abuses the proper function of the senses.

Tsui Hark's ability to make something incredible and outlandish out of ordinary facial features such as eyes, ears and tongue must mark him as a unique film-maker. In spite of the incessant action and movement in his pictures (which hardly encourage reflection), and the seemingly cavalier way in which he dispatches animals and human beings alike in his narratives, Tsui shows in the three editions of *A Chinese Ghost Story* that he is an artist with a humanist sensibility.

This is also the tradition of Pu Songling's *Liaozhai Zhiyi*, on the surface a collection of fantastic tales. Pu was not above moralising, but in *Liaozhai*, one can find traces of a regard for spirituality as a necessary component of human life. Ironically, perhaps, there is a pragmatic emphasis on the body and material being as the basis for life. Bringing a modern interpretation of the fantasy genre, Tsui Hark extends that pragmatic tradition and expands on Ma-Xu's penchant for allegory about China's tragedy and future pain. To be fair, most of Tsui's contemporaries working in the genre have done the same thing. Wu Ma's *The Dead and the Deadly* is arguably a finer film than any of the three editions of *A Chinese Ghost Story*, but Tsui and Ching's films have gone a step further with their freewheeling allegory of the spiritual plight of contemporary Man ruled by materialism and greed, highlighting also the present predicament of Hong Kong. All three editions of *A Chinese Ghost Story* and *The Wicked City* summarise the feeling of impending doom as Hong Kong faces up to its destiny. *Yaoshou Dushi*, the Chinese title of *The Wicked City*, underlines the doomsday mood with greater intensity. It translates literally as 'City of Demons', but the emphasis is on the word *shou*, to denote demons, creatures and half-human animals which awake as one century closes and a new era begins. They are apocalyptic portents of disaster containing, nevertheless, a positive element for the future: a belief in the intrinsic value of hybridity, as demonstrated by the central characters of *The Wicked City* who are products of cross-breeding between different species or whose love story suggests the desirability of cross-breeding.

NOTES

[1] Mao Shan is the name of a mountain in Jiangsu Province where three brothers became Daoist mystics and initiated the art of dealing with the supernatural.

Chapter Fifteen

Bad Customers and Big Timers

Touch-down at Hong Kong's Kaitak Airport is a sensation. It is the only airport in the world located within a stone's throw of the inner city of an international metropolis. As the plane approaches the runway, one can almost reach out and touch a neon light, a television antenna or laundry poles sticking out from tenement windows. The lights of neon-lit buildings dazzle the eyes while the nose is assaulted by the pungent smell of the adjacent waters around the Kaitak 'nullah' (as Hong Kong's expatriate Britons like to call the waters surrounding the runway jutting out into Kowloon Bay), bringing to mind the irony that in Chinese, Hong Kong means 'Fragrant Harbour'. The scent reminds the traveller that a dark side exists behind the glittering façade.

If one were to fall out of the plane as it aims for the runway, one would land where the Kowloon Walled City used to be before it was razed to the ground in 1993. Originally built in 1847 by the Qing government to strengthen its coastal defence and used as a *yamen* (administrative office), the Walled City evolved into a patchwork of high-rise buildings without proper electricity, water and sanitation, an administrative anomaly due to a lapse in the original agreement leasing the New Territories to Britain in 1898. Consequently, the Hong Kong government could not provide normal services to its residents since it was technically outside of Hong Kong's jurisdiction. Over time, it became a convenient launching pad for criminal activities by Hong Kong's infamous Triads and other hardened criminals such as the notorious Big Circle gangs whose members originated from the Mainland. It was a refuge for criminals, a convenient hideout for outlaws after a robbery or a shootout, since the police could not follow them into the city.

The Walled City was Hong Kong's asphalt jungle. Hong Kong's shopping malls may glisten and beckon, but to the citizens of the Walled City, crime seemed the only way to achieve the high-life. The Walled City was featured in Johnny Mak's *Long Arm of the Law/Sheng Gang Qibing* (1984), the first, and arguably, the best film in a trilogy about 'Big Circle' gangs who are, next to the Triads, Hong Kong's most notorious criminals. '90% of all crimes in Hong Kong are committed by Big Circle gangs,' a police inspector observed in part two of the trilogy. 'These gangs are united, loyal to each other and exclusivist.' Membership in Big Circle gangs is open only to people who come from the Mainland, usually illegally, having received training in the army or as Red Guards during the Cultural Revolution. In Hong Kong, they are well known for carrying out desperate and violent acts of robbery.

The leader of the gang in part one, the only film directed by Johnny Mak, is Ho Yiu-tung (Lam Wai), ex-Red Guard and one of 'ten most wanted criminals' in the territory – information gleaned from computer-titles flashed on the screen as Ho, nicknamed Tai Tung (meaning 'Big' Tung), sits in a train bound for Guangzhou. Tai Tung is on his way to organise his gang of five disaffected men who steal into Hong Kong (only four make it) with the intention of carrying out a heist and returning to China loaded with money. Once in Hong Kong, the would-be criminals show their inexperience by circling around a jewel shop filled with police investigating a failed robbery. The police immediately spot their car and rightly conclude it as suspicious: a violent chase ensues with the gang making a break for it by firing guns and lobbing grenades into the heart of Tsimshatsui.

The criminals from Guangzhou are babes in the concrete woods of Kowloon and they are soon out-matched by the police and their underworld contacts. There is tension between them and a group of small-time Hong Kong mobsters led by Ah Tai, who runs a video-parlour and is also a police informer. The Big Circle gang is betrayed by Ah Tai after their robbery and falls into an ambush in a scene where a police helicopter suddenly ascends to confront the gang as they are about to shoot Ah Tai (a scene which may have provided the inspiration for the helicopter-ambush scene in Coppola's *Godfather III*). During the shoot-out, the gang escapes into the Walled City. The Hong Kong police enter the City after a tip-off and finally corner the gang, who are wiped out in a gun battle. In real life, there is no record of the Hong Kong police ever arresting a criminal inside the Walled City, much less eliminating a whole gang. The climactic scene, therefore, is more in line with generic convention and wish fulfilment. In the context of the film, the deaths of the gangsters are a logical conclusion because of their inexperience in the Hong Kong criminal underworld. Their violence and desperate behaviour are explained in part by their alienation. They view the territory simply as a robber's playing field.

The network of loyalty linking the gang members is reminiscent of Peckinpah's *The Wild Bunch*. The Big Circle bunch are similarly seen as the last primitives in a modern world where gadgets and machines have taken over. Johnny Mak depicts his gangsters with humour. In one telling scene, the gang members set up a tablet in memory of their fallen comrade who did not make it across the border. In accordance with Chinese custom, they place food in front of his photograph, the picture from his Chinese identity card; the food consists of Big Macs and Pizzas instead of the traditional pig's head and rice. The scene is funny because it underlines a certain truth about Mainland Chinese in Hong Kong. Often derided as country bumpkins, Mainlanders share the same dream about the good life as their

Hong Kong cousins, but they cannot partake of it without first learning the ropes.

Apart from these touches of humour, Mak displays his usual affinity for cynical, gritty realism when portraying the milieu of his criminals. One senses that he knows his characters to the marrow of their bones. The film clearly stands on their side through its minute observations of the characters of gang members: a farewell scene in Guangzhou with wife and baby; a reunion scene in Hong Kong with a former girlfriend now working as a dancehall girl; a whore demanding more money from the simplest member of the bunch and then refusing to sleep with him. It evokes a sense of tragedy as this wild bunch from Guangzhou forfeit their lives in chasing after a materialistic dream. The next two films in the series similarly showed Mainlanders in a disadvantaged light, but without the black humour or touches of irony.

Long Arm of the Law, Part Two/Sheng Gang Qibing Xuji (1987) and *Long Arm of the Law, Part Three/Sheng Gang Qibing Disanji* (1989), both directed by Michael Mak (Johnny's younger brother), had more exploitative, sensational violence. In contrast with part one, where the inexperience of the protagonists is an important factor in the characterisations, the gang members of the sequels are portrayed as neo-savages in an urban wilderness. Part two has a trio of illegal immigrants from the Mainland being forced to infiltrate the Big Circle gang. They are supervised by a local undercover cop who is waylaid by members of the gang and tortured: he is hung upside down, his head covered in a gunny sack filled with screeching rats (a form of torture apparently reserved for stool pigeons in the cinema mythology of crime films featuring Triad gangs). When he refuses to talk, his sack-covered head is chopped off. The virtue of the first edition was its straightforward depiction of the basic desires and frustrations of Mainland transients who come to the territory for the first time and resort to crime to obtain its capitalist riches. Part two tended to underscore the worst prejudices of Hong Kong people regarding Mainland Chinese: they are seen as misfits, outsiders and worse of all, murderous criminals.

The violence and intense low-life cynicism of the first two editions are upheld in part three. An ex-People's Liberation Army soldier (played by Andy Lau) falls victim to the judiciary system in the Mainland and escapes to Hong Kong where he is recruited by the Big Circle gang. An officer of the Public Security Bureau (China's police department) is sent to Hong Kong to apprehend him. The characters seem to have barely emerged from a primitive cave society. Hong Kong is nothing more than an urban variation of the cave occupied by Big Circle cavemen (the symbol of the big circle used by the gang is thus quite apt – Hong Kong is equated with the Big Circle cave). The social references of the hero are limited within the cave and he must fight for every inch of space and for the woman he desires – a fellow Mainlander brought to Hong Kong for the purpose of prostitution.

Proceeding from the premise that Big Circle gangsters are savages, exploitation was mixed with an element of social criticism aimed in particular at Hong Kong residents' prejudices and suspicions against outsiders. Thus the series made a point about the uncaring, essentially intolerant nature of Hong Kong society. Furthermore, the main characters possessed redeeming features because of a factor mythologising their behaviour: savages too have their own code of honour. Protagonists were bound by this unspoken code even when on opposite sides. Admirers of John Woo's action films know the code as *yi*, where personal loyalties count more than any law.

As the series progressed, there was a tendency to feature more inner conflict within the Big Circle gang, reflecting the internal contradictions within Mainland society. Public Security officers became protagonists hunting down their fellow Mainlanders in Hong Kong. Savage was pitted against savage, but a code of honour could still be depended upon to ensure that human decency was not irretrievably lost. *Yi* offers a way out for humans too steeped in crime to consider themselves remediable, and therefore justifies their savagery. As the Chinese saying goes: they are like cracked pots that cannot be mended, so they smash themselves to pieces. Ultimately, it was not always clear how a code of honour could prevail in the ensuing violence. The power of the series lies in its questioning of the notion of Chinese civilisation when it is being threatened from within. And the battleground was Hong Kong.

It is perhaps too big a claim to say that the crime or gangster thriller provided Hong Kong cinema with its most incisive analysis of the nature of modern Chinese civilisation. However, in terms of their description of human behaviour *in extremis*, the thin line dividing enforcers of the law and criminals, together with the unwritten code that binds them together, gangster movies have constantly pushed Hong Kong cinema over the edge. They are tough, raw and jagged – often frighteningly so. A Hong Kong gangster movie can make viewers feel that civilisation is indeed at risk and that Hong Kong is the last place on earth they would want to be.

One of the toughest hardboiled films to explore the *doppelgänger* theme of cop and robber is Ringo Lam's *City on Fire/ Longhu Fengyun* (1987). Its hero is an undercover cop, Ko Chow (played by Chow Yun-fat) who infiltrates a gang of robbers. Although not so named, the gang members are Big Circle types; their leader is Zhou Nan,[1] whose accent gives him away: he speaks Cantonese with a Mainland accent. The rest of the gang members could well have come straight from *Long Arm of the Law*. As Ko is inducted into the gang (selling them small arms and finally joining them in a heist so as to set them up for their arrest), he finds his alter ego in the person of one of the gangsters, the illiterate but stylish Fu (played by Danny Lee). Both men fast become friends. As the robbery goes wrong, Ko is confronted by the boss, but Fu defends Ko against accusations of betrayal in a tense stand-off as each character points guns at the other's temple – long before *Reservoir Dogs*.[2] In the end, as Ko lies dying from gunshot wounds, he reveals that he is really a cop, but Fu cannot bring himself to kill his friend. The relationship between the two men is conducted in the grey area where crime-buster and criminal stand on common ground and recognise each other as soul brothers – an area since explored most spectacularly in John Woo's *The Killer* (1989), also starring Chow Yun-fat and Danny Lee. Director Lam presents his cop and gangster in more simplified, if somewhat hysterical, terms. Indeed, the film may be seen as a dry run for the more complex characterisations of the same cop and gangster types in Woo's film. Unlike *The Killer*, Lam's two central protagonists are much less given to brooding about betrayal and the nature of friendship (until the very end, where Fu only has a brief moment to let the betrayal sink in); the word *yi* is never mentioned although it must surely lie at the back of the tongues of all the characters, including the police, who are seen as internally divided, with a veteran cop at loggerheads with a ruthlessly ambitious younger rival.

Chow Yun-fat's cop is a character very much on the brink: he has been undercover far too long. He wants to retire, but is persuaded by his superior, Inspector Lau (played by Taiwanese actor Sun Yue), to do one last job. Ko has strayed into the minefield of emotional instability via his volatile relationship with a nightclub escort girl who runs away to Canada with another man when she realises he won't marry her. His status in the police department is so murky that even his own superior cannot adequately protect him (he is picked up by the young inspector and beaten up). In short, Ko is as good as a criminal.

Chow gives a splendid performance, portraying a man with innate charm, sensitive but tough. He is trapped in an environment where his only friend is a criminal; on the verge of losing perspective, he is unable to make out the line separating himself from a criminal. In revealing his true identity to Fu, Ko underlines the superficiality of such a division, surrendering himself to the outlaw code of loyalty, which, ironically, gains more significance in the light of his betrayal. The relationship between the two men may be seen as one more metaphor of the China–Hong Kong relationship which really lies at the heart of the gangster thrillers mentioned so far: the *Long Arm of the Law* series and *City on Fire*.

Lam further expounded on this metaphor, with lesser success, in *Prison on Fire, Part II/ Jianyu Fengyun zhi Tao Fan* (1991). Hong Kong convicts come into conflict with China-born convicts led by a Big Circle gang leader known as 'Dragon'. Caught in the melée is convict 41671, Chung Tin-ching (played by Chow Yun-fat), set up by the warden as an informer within the Big Circle in order to implicate Dragon in a conspiracy. Chung and Dragon come to terms with each other; the former proves his honour and decency, and they both escape, Chung to find his son who ran away from an orphanage; in the end, he faces up to the task of confessing to the boy that he had killed his mother, having caught her *in flagrante delicto* as a prostitute.

Overwrought and implausible, *Prison on Fire, Part II* lacked the conviction of its predecessor *Prison on Fire/ Jianyu Fengyun* (1988), an exposé of prison conditions, particularly in its insider's view of inmates being bullied and threatened by convicts with Triad connections. *Prison on Fire* also starred Chow Yun-fat (next to John Woo, Lam is the director who has most often used Chow's star persona as the director's alter ego) as the smooth-talking convict who comes between the Triads and a first-time inmate with no background in crime (played by Tony Leung Ka-fai). Inmates are organised into Triad 'units', each headed by a 'big brother' from one or more of the Triad organisations (in the opening scenes, one such big brother approaches new inmates, asking whether anyone comes from the 14K or a Chiuchow gang, referring to the two most notorious Triad groups). Leung's character is a middle-class Hong Kong male serving a three-year term for manslaughter. His prison experience is a baptism of fire: much of the film shows Leung (who typically personifies the ingenuous Hong Kong middle-class male) being framed, undergoing brutal treatment by both prison authorities, in the person of a corrupt warden, and the Triad big brothers. His only friend is the character played by Chow Yun-fat.

Triad personalities featured prominently in Hong Kong films from the mid-80s to the early 90s. Although not new, the interest in Triad criminals and godfathers during this period reflected increasing Triad involvement in the film industry. From protection rackets to the harassment of stars and directors forced to make films against their will, Triad involvement also took a more respectable form, with figures connected to big Triad organisations emerging as producers, agents and distributors.[3] (Triad figures also play a role in Hong Kong's newspaper industry.) Most prominent are two brothers of Heung Wah-yim, the 'Dragon Head' (a synonym for 'boss') of the Sun Yee On, one of the biggest Triad societies, who was arrested in 1988 during a police crackdown on Triads. The Heung brothers, Wah-sing and Wah-keung, are major players in the film industry (the latter is also an actor), producing some of the biggest-grossing films in the past several years, particularly the films of Stephen Chiau. Many other figures in the film industry, including actors and other behind-the-scenes workers, are widely rumoured to have Triad connections. Against this background of Triad involvement, one can perhaps see where the graphic, realistic, even authentic, nature of Hong Kong's gangster thrillers comes from. On the other hand, Hong Kong's police force and the government's anti-corruption body, the Independent Commission Against Corruption, have also obtained their own foothold in the film industry. The ICAC has its own film production unit, largely making public-relations exercises and short films with anti-corruption themes using professional actors and directors. Although not active players, the police authorities have their 'representatives' in the industry. Actor-director Philip Chan, an ex-policeman, wrote the script for *Long Arm of the Law* and later directed the creditable *Tongs, a Chinatown Story/Tangkou Gushi* (1986), about Chinese gangs in New York City's Chinatown. Chan often acted as the film industry's adviser and front-man on police matters as well as a source for crime stories.

The sensational realism of crime thrillers therefore stemmed from the input of film-makers who had the benefit of personal experience on both sides of the law. It is, of course, true to say that the hard-hitting realism of these thrillers also betrays a clearer understanding on the part of the younger film-makers of the very nature of contemporary Hong Kong. Crime as a social problem was a major theme of the new wave directors in the late 70s.[4] The crime thriller provided the contemporary background for new wave directors to tackle social issues and make allegorical statements about Hong Kong. Kirk Wong's *The Club/ Wu Ting* (1981), Ann Hui's *The Story of Woo Viet/ Hu Yue de Gushi* (1981), Terry Tong's *Coolie Killer/ Sha Chu Xiying Pan* (1982) were the most outstanding examples of this fascination with the criminal milieu in the early 80s. The underworld was, needless to say, a murky, dark underworld in line with the *film noir* aspirations of the new wave film-makers. Their heroes were introspective, fatalistically inclined and, more often than not, seen with detachment from a distance.

In the mid-80s, the genre received a boost with the success of John Woo's *A Better Tomorrow/ Yingxiong Bense* (1986) and its pathbreaking emphasis on the code of *yi* as the 'essence of heroes'. Audiences were dazzled by the designer chic of the underworld characters, bound by *yi* and obliged to give their lives for honour and loyalty, dressed in Armani suits. A new genre of 'hero' films, or *yingxiong pian*, sprang up. However, hero films (usually featuring Chow Yun-fat and Danny Lee) were soon off-set by the realism of gangster and prison movies such as Johnny Mak's *Long Arm of the Law* series and Ringo Lam's *City on Fire* and *Prison on Fire*. A subgenre of 'hero' films – known in Chinese as the *xiaoxiong pian* or 'Big Timer' films[5] – straddled the realism of a Johnny Mak and the glamour-style of John Woo. The term *xiaoxiong* puts an emphasis on the hero as a leader, a general, a first among equals. Hence, *xiaoxiong* was not a mere hero, but a genuine *führer* in a business suit, more a corporate leader in a firm of executives managing the 'left-handed form of human endeavour', as it is put in John Huston's *Asphalt Jungle* (1950). The firm was the Triad. However, the Big Timer films adopted a moral ambivalence towards its heroes. According to the Chinese term *xiaoxiong pian*, ambivalence doesn't even apply: the genre is downright hagiographic.

The first of the Big Timer films is Johnny Mak's *To Be Number One/ Bie Hao* (1991). Mak produced the film in association with Raymond Chow, but his standing as a 'creative producer' is such that his signature – like that of Tsui Hark's in his capacity as producer – seems to surpass that of the directors of the films he has produced: Poon Man-kit directed this one. A biography of the real-life Triad godfather and drug baron Ng Sik-ho, nicknamed 'Limpy' Ho after he was crippled during an attempt on his life, the film begins with a contrite Ng inside a prison chapel (Ng received a thirty-year jail sentence in 1975; he was released in 1991 not long after the film was released, and died from cancer a few months later). Ng ponders on the parable of the prodigal son and traces the events of his life of crime from his low-life beginnings as a Chiuchow-speaking refugee from China in 1962, to his arrest in the early 70s as the linchpin of the illegal drug trafficking network linking Triad gangsters with corrupt police officials. The film is crude and sensationalist, but it has production values to burn: the glamorous production design (by Virginia Lok) and wide-screen photography (by Peter Pau) give the movie a sense of sophistication it does not deserve. In short, the picture is an overdone tribute to Ng Sik-ho. Uneducated, semi-literate and mired in poverty, Ng made it to the top purely with guts and gumption – the path of many a ruthless semi-literate tycoon in East Asia. Hence, the virtue of Ng and his appeal are that he is a straightforward hero-villain. The film makes no pretensions to be a character study with complex moral or ethical insights. Ng's contrition in the film's opening is given short shrift as we see him rise to the top of the criminal ladder through the 60s, cleverly and ruthlessly exploiting his Chiuchow clan of relatives and loyalists, including his wife. The film makes the sociological point that the 60s and 70s were the era of big-time Chiuchow criminals who had come to Hong Kong as refugees in 1949, while the 80s, of course, were dominated by small-time Mainland Chinese criminals who came to Hong Kong as illegal immigrants. The narrative piles up scenes of violence and soft-core sexual titillation (provided by soft-porn star Amy Yip), but exerts some kind of morbid appeal through the performances: Ray Lui's Ng Sik-ho is a permanently scowling Richard III, and heavyweight character actor Kent Cheng offers a Falstaff-like villain, perhaps less likeable but possessing the same crude sense of humour (in one scene he compares his round head with the breasts of his co-star, Amy Yip). *To Be Number One* was among the top ten box-office successes of 1991, spawning a rash of imitations, mostly starring Ray Lui and Kent Cheng, as well as another, even more ambitious attempt at a *Godfather*-like epic from the same production team, *Lord of the East China Sea/Shanghai Huangdi* (1993), which told the story of Du Yuesheng, the most powerful criminal godfather of all time.

Du Yuesheng (the film substitutes his surname with 'Lu') was the leader of the notorious Green Gang which dominated Shanghai in the 20s and 30s. The film is an overlong, glorified biography of Du depicting his rise from lowly fruit peddler and organiser of petty criminals to the top of Shanghai's underworld. Like the saga of Limpy Ho, this film biography is both trashy and camp. There is no real attempt to flesh out the character of an obviously fascinating man who was both evil and charismatic. Consequently, we only see the bare outlines of events: the narrative is muddled, spending too much time on irrelevancies and supporting characters. We are treated to a rather simple hero whom we are asked to consider in a sympathetic light – a much more difficult proposition when the hero is one-dimensional. As produced by Johnny Mak and Raymond Chow, the production values are superb, and Du Yuesheng certainly had an interesting and colourful life, good material for a film. Having amassed a fortune from opium trading, vice and gambling, Du Yuesheng together with two other underworld figures made an indelible mark on the economic and political life of Shanghai. Du, in real life, undertook orders from the KMT to eliminate communist workers, their leaders and sympathisers. He clearly was a man who knew which side his bread was buttered. Instead of including such elements, the film glosses over Du's political hooliganism and supports the legend that the Triad godfather was a key patriotic figure during the dark days of the Japanese occupation of Shanghai and the civil war.

The narrative spans a period of over forty years: from 1910 to Du's death in Hong Kong in the 50s, rigorously avoiding any perspective which might be construed as critical. Released in two parts, the first part deals with Du's (played by Ray Lui) induction into the Red Gang, led by the obese Wong (played by Kent Cheng) who holds the post of chief detective in the French concession, and Du's rise through the ranks as Wong's chief henchman with his own followers (the core of the Green Gang). Du convinces Wong to join Yuen, an opium smuggler and leader of the Blue Gang. Du, Wong and Yuen became known as Shanghai's 'three big bosses'; controlling the city's underworld activities and much of its legitimate ones as well, with Du emerging as the most influential of the troika.

Part two sees Du seeking social respectability through his entry into financial markets and his complicity in political events. As Shanghai falls to the Japanese, he flees to Hong Kong while his two cronies stay behind. Yuen collaborates with the Japanese and is eventually assassinated by one of Du's loyal henchmen, an alcoholic killer. After the war, Du attempts to enter politics, but is talked out of it by the KMT. The film ends mawkishly as a bitter Du, disappointed because he was not accorded official recognition by the KMT for his political services, dies in Hong Kong, surrounded by his extended family of concubines, wives and loyal henchmen.

To Be Number One and *Lord of the East China Sea* were made by a major studio, Golden Harvest, which openly mythologised the Triads. Producers Johnny Mak and Raymond Chow are respected figures in the Hong Kong film industry and their motives for producing the films may be attributed to their shrewd judgments regarding the film-going public's curiosity about Ng Sik-ho and Du Yuesheng. On the other hand, it is not difficult to discern a vanity-press quality to Triad involvement in the film industry in general. One representative example was *Shanghai 1920* (1991), produced by Choi Tzi-ming, a secretive figure thought to have Triad connections, with international interests extending to the Netherlands, one of the key centres of the international Triad network. Choi was gunned down in April 1992 in his Tsimshatsui office in circumstances smacking of a gangland killing. *Shanghai 1920* (the year of the title is puzzling since much of the film takes place in the 30s) recycled the cliché of the rags-to-riches rise of a Shanghai petty hoodlum (played by the glamorous John Lone) and his eventual control of the city's underworld by ruthlessly eliminating all rivals. Lone's character kills off the 'three big bosses', presented as fictionalised caricatures of the real figures. A vanity-production from a producer with Triad connections, the film was shot in Shanghai with a budget reported to be one of the highest on record for a Hong Kong production. As directed by Leong Po-chih, the staunchest of Hong Kong cinema's bi-cultural representatives, the film featured a bi-cultural relationship between Lone and an American who becomes the former's reluctant partner-in-crime. The key element in the film was Lone's performance, characterised by homoerotic body language, as in the scene when Lone first appears: he lies face down, completely naked, in Shanghai's famous steam bath, as the camera cautiously approaches from the audience's point of view.

Vanity (or the Chinese preoccupation with 'face') was really the biggest factor in movies about Triad personalities, a factor akin to sex in movies about spies and secret agents. One of the most interesting recent films in the genre is Andy Chin's *Love Among the Triads/Ai Zai Hei Shehui de Rizi* (1993), a melodrama subverting the motif of vanity, poking subtle fun at the sex lives and love affairs of Triad 'big brothers'. Tong (played by Wan Yeung-ming) is a typical hot-headed big brother married to a beautiful wife (played by Veronica Yip), but he has an affair with a singer (played by Cecilia Yip). In the company of his mistress, Tong appears vulnerable and even sensible, although in one scene he beats up her brother after mistaking him for her lover. However, Tong is unwilling to give up his wife and the couple does seem to have a genuine regard for each other, even though the marriage is due to a business alliance linking Tong's Triad group with that of another led by his brother-in-law (played by Simon Yam), who has his own problems with his girlfriend (played by Rosamund Kwan). The Triad linkages are perhaps incidental to the melodrama: the movie is surprisingly affective as a romance-cum-comedy of manners with inter-related characters. But its portrait of beautiful, successful people is in line with the modern romantic myth of Triad vanity (the wry humour countervailing the myth). In the final analysis, *Love Among the Triads* is a rare movie featuring Triad characters who come across, for the first time, as human and somewhat silly.

A similar notion of vanity and awe towards wealthy people[6] is also behind films that put a different spin to the notion of the Big Timer, in which the heroes are not powerful Triad figures but corrupt cops (who may be regarded as *de facto* Triad bosses). Lawrence Ah Mon's *Lee Rock/Lei Luo Zhuan* (1991), produced by Heung Wah-keung and released in two parts, was the first of the Big Timer spin-offs that treated Triad mythology from the perspective of how it affected and corrupted the Royal Hong Kong Police Force, thus confirming that Triads have infiltrated all important sectors in society. Like the Big Timer heroes, the central figure here is based on a real-life figure – the corrupt policeman Lee Rock, who rose from constable to the top post of chief Chinese officer in the police force. Lee accumulated a vast fortune through his collusion with Triad gangs, devising an ingenious system of pay-offs in which 90 per cent of the police force was on the take. The real-life Lee retired from the force in 1969. In 1974, the newly-established Independent Commission Against Corruption instituted legal proceedings against Lee who had emigrated to Canada. He took off for Taiwan, a country treated as a safe haven by Triad bosses, where he apparently still resides.

The film, released in the customary two parts typical of epic film-biographies of criminal figures, entirely romanticises the early career of Lee Rock (played by Andy Lau). In the first part he is shown as a virtuous rookie cop. His eventual rise to key man in the system of corruption is told in familiar clichés. The production is impressive, but still fails in the final analysis for the same reason that the Big Timer films did: the one-dimensionality of the lead character. Once again, it is possible for the viewer to see a certain vested interest at work. The success of *Lee Rock* propelled the corrupt cop to commercial respectability.

The corrupt-cop genre may well have been precipitated by a film such as Eric Tsang's overblown *The Tigers/Wu Hu Jiang zhi Juelie* (1991), which was even more morally ambivalent about police corruption than *Lee Rock*. Five CID buddies slowly sink into a morass of corruption after receiving drug money. They are picked up by the ICAC, but they stick to their guns. The two lead heroes (played by Andy Lau and Tony Leung Chiu-wai) adopt implausibly flippant (or pragmatic, depending on one's point of view) attitudes about taking dirty money. To round off the morally ambivalent tone of the film, the ICAC comes off worse than the drug dealers. No doubt, part of the Triad mythology hinges on the convention of good guys (corrupt cops) versus bad guys (the ICAC), but *The Tigers* is the most hysterical example to date in the genre that presents corruption as hard-nosed heroism.

Moral ambivalence is the bedrock of the crime thriller and its various streams of gangster, police and corrupt-cop movies of the 90s. The law-and-order situation in Hong Kong is a serious public issue; as people generally felt a loss of confidence in the colonial government's ability to defend Hong Kong's interests, cynicism towards the rule of law now that China has taken over has crept into the public psyche. The Big Timer films reflect in no small part the perception of the Hong Kong public that the concept of the rule of law will collapse. Replacing the rule of law would be the concept of 'family law' (in Chinese, *jia fa*): the law invoked by Triad bosses and other family-like cliques or societies operating within Chinese-speaking communities. The biggest such cliques, of course, are the ruling elites themselves running the governments in Beijing and Taipei.

Cynicism about the state of Hong Kong and the growing *jia fa* mentality, a belief in the sanctity and efficacy of family law as opposed to the common law of the land, are themes in Wayne Wang's *Life is Cheap . . . but Toilet Paper is Expensive* (1990), a quintessential film about Hong Kong as it trundles towards 1997. Proceeding on the barest of plots – an American of mixed Chinese-Japanese parentage goes to Hong Kong, handcuffed to a briefcase which he is to hand over to a Triad big boss – the film presents a series of cameos (performed mainly by veterans of Hong Kong's Mandarin cinema) which show a culture losing its soul. The cameos have some narrative purport, but seem otherwise to exist in their own right as experimental documentaries reflecting the main character's subjective experience of Hong Kong. Actress Cora Miao's (the director's wife) cameo advances the plot significantly. She plays 'Money', ex-good-time girl and current mistress of the Triad boss (played by actor-director Luo Wei). Money has acquired the deadly reputation of being a 'chopping block': as she tells it, two big-time lovers who paid for her favours died from heart failure 'the moment I spread my legs'. Money's current relationship with the Triad boss thus earns him the reputation of 'Super Cock', although he too is impotent. Money's 'chopping block' nickname lends the film its choppy narrative and editing style. The film is punctuated by chopping block symbolisms – in particular a hand being chopped off – and the concomitant blood that spills forth.

A part-Hong Kong production, *Life is Cheap* was thought to be unreleasable in Hong Kong, mainly due, it was said, to the preponderance of foul language. But the reason probably lies in the film-maker's adoption of a heavily ambivalent attitude towards the territory. Its outsider's perceptive is revealed through the cameos which show Hong Kong residents gone to seed or grown too cynical to care about the quality of life. A film about Hong Kong that treats its characters with a degree of misanthropic licence is not guaranteed to find an audience in Hong Kong. From this outsider's perspective, Hong Kong is shown to be virtually ruled by mobsters who force the hero to eat human faeces in order to save the face of the biggest of the big bosses: he had discovered that Mr Big was impotent.

Life in Hong Kong may indeed be cheapened by the rule of the Triads whose bosses are vain and ruthless villains, but who, in cinema mythology, appear as awe-inspiring heroes to be worshipped by the rest of us, small timers all. Somewhere along the way, Wayne Wang throws in the implication that the biggest Triad is the one that is around the corner: the State that will take over in 1997. Will Hong Kong ever be the same again? Watching the Big Timer films, the corrupt-cop films and the films featuring the Big Circle gangs, we may well see history repeating itself as the cycle of corruption and crime comes full circle.

NOTES

[1] Curiously, also the name of the current Head of the New China News Agency in the territory, a post which functions practically as the ambassador from China to Hong Kong. Zhou Nan was also the leader of the Chinese negotiating team handling the handover of Hong Kong to China in 1997 prior to the signing of the Sino-British Agreement in 1984. Such allegorical references to real personalities linked to the 1997 negotiations or other political matters concerning Hong Kong were quite common in Hong Kong films.

[2] *Reservoir Dogs* is in some respects a virtual remake of *City on Fire*, a similar scene occurs in Johnny Mak's earlier *Long Arm of the Law*, and it is not improbable that Lam copied it from Mak; later on, John Woo also used the gesture of adversaries pointing guns at each other's heads as a signature shot, particularly in *The Killer*. For a discussion of the resemblance between *Reservoir Dogs* and *City on Fire*, see David E. Williams' essay 'Gone to the Dogs', *Film Threat*, no. 17 (August 1994), pp. 9–11; and David Bourgeois' follow-up article, 'Stalking the Dog', *Film Threat*, no. 18 (October 1994), pp. 18–23.

[3] Under the banner heading of 'Show Business Against Violence', a demonstration against Triad extortions and threats was held by stars and directors on 15 January 1992.

[4] See Chapter 10, concerning the new wave directors' treatment of crime and other social problems in their first feature films.

241

⁵ A translation first used by critic Li Cheuk-to (see Li's article 'The Rise of the Big Timer', HKIFF catalogue, 1992) and retained here for its aptness.

⁶ Like the theme of reincarnation discussed in Chapter 14, the glorification of wealthy gangsters also carries a whiff of premodern mentality in which virtue, status and wealth were seen as equivalents. The notion that a wealthy and powerful person can also be, and mostly is, a villainous parasite, presents a status inconsistency which other, more modern-minded Hong Kong thrillers and fantasy films address.

Chapter Sixteen

Postmodernism and the End of Hong Kong Cinema

For the last few years Hong Kong cinema has been keeping pace with people's feverish attempts to prepare themselves for the 1997 transition. The general feeling has been of an era coming to a close. But before dynasties change, there is one last great social surge forward, like the frantic rush of a crowd at an end of year sale. The unanimous goal is to earn as much and as quickly as possible. Those who can will migrate and invest their money overseas; those who cannot will save their money in case of an emergency. Others indulge in a consumerist binge with a sense of *fin de siècle* fatalism.

With the prospect of a future over which it will have little or no say, Hong Kong's sense of the past has undergone major changes. Instead of, as Fredric Jameson puts it, mobilising a 'retrospective dimension indispensable to any vital reorientation of our collective future', the relation to the past has become historicist[1] in the words of postmodern architectural historians. The loss of a sense of the future together with the near-hysterical stress on the accumulation of and speculation in exchange values have triggered the current spirit of postmodernism and 'the random cannibalization of all the styles of the past', reducing that past to 'little more than a set of dusty spectacles ... leaving us with nothing but texts to be consumed as a 'tangible symptom of an omnipresent, omnivorous and well-nigh libidinal historicism'.[2] In the 90s, denizens of Hong Kong gobble up fads and gimmicks like fast food, moving images being no exception. Although Hong Kong confirms Linda Hutcheon's proposition that postmodernism is 'a contradictory phenomenon which uses and abuses, installs and then subverts, the very concepts it challenges',[3] it also gives the lie to postmodernism as a Western theory of development and historical periodisation. Given what has been Hong Kong's pre-determined scenario of time running out and its eventual assimilation into a vastly different political culture, it is important to understand the role of what may look like postmodernism and the context from which it developed. One need only look back to the 70s and the popularity of martial arts kung fu films to see how fast Hong Kong cinema evolved. The martial arts genre was full of vigour: shots were put together with a zest that matched the actions of its characters. The 70s were the dynamic decade in Hong Kong, and this was reflected in the energy and fevered pace of its kung fu films.

In previous chapters the point was made that the aesthetics of kung fu movies also provided the conditions for the birth of a new wave in 1979, implemented by directors born in the late 40s and early 50s who combined American style gusto and know-how with European aesthetics. They were followed by a second group of even younger directors who began to establish their careers in the mid-80s, producing work of uncharacteristic maturity. One can argue over when the new wave really came of age. There was more than one possible turning point: in 1981 Tsui Hark made *All the Wrong Clues (For the Right Solution)*, or much later, with works produced by the second wave such as Stanley Kwan's *Rouge* and *Actress* or Wong Kar-wai's *Days of Being Wild*. Rather than determine a cut-off date, it is more productive to think of the new wave as an ongoing movement. The trend towards a cinema that could more easily be discussed in terms of postmodernism was first glimpsed in the mid-80s with the increased application of special effects in the work of Tsui Hark. Content-wise, the new wave directors evolved a preoccupation with 1997 and the wider question of China and its relations with Hong Kong, Hong Kong's own 'China syndrome'. The 1997 issue was at first dealt with allegorically, but it became an open secret as film-makers faced up to China in personal attempts to examine Hong Kong's own identity. Towards the late 80s, Hong Kong critics were already referring to a 'post-1997' sentiment. The best films at the time exerted a double impact: film-makers asserted their identity in terms of its difference from what they presented as China's, but they at the same time attempted to come to terms with China. There was an inherent contradiction in wanting to be different and yet feeling a nationalist empathy with China, a tension which increasingly became the point of reference for identity questions. Although Hong Kong is not a country, its residents possessed a form of national identity increasingly identified as Chinese even though artists expressed their Chineseness in ways that were certainly different from the way artists in China negotiated theirs.

For Hong Kong cinema, the late 80s was also a period of social change signalled by more liberal attitudes towards film censorship and the decriminalisation of homosexuality, confirmed in 1990 through a majority vote in the legislative council. The new censorship ordinance was passed in 1988 and introduced, for the first time in the territory, a ratings system. It was organised in three tiers, resulting in the rise of a new genre of soft-core pornographic films known as 'Category III films', the category reserved for those over eighteen years of age (the equivalent of the Restricted ['R'] category in Western countries). Category III films have now become such a commercial proposition that producers, distributors and exhibitors have chosen to specialise in them as a genre. Actresses such as Veronica Yip have come up through the ranks of Category III films to mainstream respectability. In political terms, however, the new censorship ordinance retained a clause to ban films that were judged to be politically sensitive and 'prejudicial to good relations with neighbouring countries'.

244

In the transition period to 1997, Hong Kong's relations with its future rulers remained marked by caution. In 1989, the initial outlook was one of hope and optimism, soon to be dashed by the Tiananmen massacre on 4 June. Hong Kong cinema became filled with despair and frustration, qualities expressed in John Woo's *Bullet in the Head*, released in the fall of that year. The post-Tiananmen blues also pervaded Shu Kei's documentary, *Sunless Days/Meiyou Taiyang de Rizi* (1990), which showed the film-maker's own family in transition as mother is left behind by sons who have migrated overseas. The tone was confessional, never a popular form among Hong Kong film-makers. *Bullet in the Head* failed at the box-office. *Sunless Days*, originally made for Japanese TV, was hardly shown on movie screens in the territory.

As the 90s proceeded, a renewed optimism surfaced, tempered only by another wave of anxiety caused by Governor Chris Patten's injudicious but nevertheless popular attempts to democratise Hong Kong in the teeth of China's objections. Along with the new optimism, a new mood engulfed Hong Kong cinema in the early 90s, characterised by local critics as postmodernism, in spite of the notorious meaninglessness of that epithet. One concrete example of 'postmodernist' restructuring in the 90s is the virtual disappearance of the old picture palaces in the territory to make way for multiplexes and mini-theatres. In their own way, the rise of the new multiplexes shows Hong Kong succumbing to the pressure of Western-style 'uniformity'. But, as we shall see, postmodernism in Hong Kong cinema shows quite another proposition: Hong Kong society reacting against cultural uniformity, a postmodernism that is also profoundly anti-postmodernist (or post-modern).

The reason for the new optimism in the early 90s may be found in China's own post-Tiananmen booming economy. Hong Kong film-makers seem to have outgrown the China syndrome of the mid-80s; the easiest way Hong Kong can identify itself with China is through a booming economy. The China boom recalls Hong Kong's own experience of economic developments: it essentially leapfrogged from pre-industrial trading post to wealthy exporting, financial centre within a generation. The shift towards an economy dominated by financial speculation, skipping to a large extent the 'industrial production' phase of capitalist development, meant that Hong Kong cinema too could leap into a 'postmodern' phase without ever having been fully modern. Hong Kong's cinematic past is generally regarded as being composed of *tsaan pin*, a Cantonese term referring to dilapidated movies that are rotting away, only to be revived on TV in the graveyard hours. Cantonese opera films, melodramas, comedies, Mandarin soaps, musicals and historical epics, all these genres seeking to negotiate ways of transiting to modernism were short-circuited and prematurely relegated to the graveyard.

Most of the new wave directors were educated in film schools in the West, but they were conscious of a Chinese past. While holding the torch of an avant garde by introducing modern aesthetics into Hong Kong cinema, they had to make themselves credible directors in the eyes of the

245

commercial industry. They made films of a personal nature, but alternated these with commercial works; they were keen to inject generic conventions and principles of entertainment. This practice allowed them to explore the legacy of the Cantonese and Mandarin cinemas of the 50s and 60s and thus the history of Hong Kong itself. The one key work which, when first released, was both condemned as a sell-out and praised as an amalgamation of old and new styles was, of course, Tsui Hark's *All the Wrong Clues.*

Tsui held the key then, and holds the key now, to the new epochal shift, this time to a notion of postmodernism which can be seen as a natural outcome of the maturation of the new wave and its absorption of commercial precepts. Using Tsui as a yardstick, the postmodern phenomenon grew from a ragbag of causes and effects: new wave aesthetics mixed with Cinema City-style slapstick, anxiety over 1997 and the China syndrome, the assertion of Hong Kong's own identity as different from China, and a new sexual awakening arising from an increasing awareness of women's human rights and the decriminalisation of homosexuality. But Tsui was not the only proponent of postmodernism in the 90s. Hong Kong was also ushered into the postmodernist age by a young actor with the look of a bemused clown.[4]

Stephen Chiau Sing-chi is the ubiquitous star of the new genre of 'nonsense comedies', one manifestation in the multi-faceted grid of the postmodernist edifice. At first, he may seem a most unlikely proponent of postmodernism. In fact, he is its perfect embodiment. His screen persona mirrors the paradox that is inherent in Hong Kong's postmodernism: Chiau's characters are presented as premoderns, usually bumpkins from a Chinese village somewhere in Guangdong, who accidentally find themselves in the big city. Inevitably, these bumpkins confound everybody's lowly expectations by making big successes of themselves. Chiau's characters carry the vice of ignorance like a shining virtue and turn vulgarity into the stuff of humour. Furthermore, they are heroes of irrationality. Chiau's clowns have loose, gaping mouths whose speech patterns and dialogue are Cantonese versions of nonsense verse. In Cantonese, Chiau's brand of humour is known as *mou lei-tau* (literally, nonsense).

There is in Chiau's performances, a tone of witty self-criticism of Hong Kong people's latent prejudices against Mainlanders. His characters reflect Hong Kong's Chinese migrants as emerging from the premodern agrarian society of China into (pre/post)modern Hong Kong and, somewhat im-probably, becoming an overnight success. Chiau's is, of course, a parody not only of the rags-to-riches story of Hong Kong's economic development, but also of the can-do attitudes of its entrepreneurial and gambling resi-dents. Chiau is the archetypal postmodern (con)man, his screen persona conveying that a society has successfully side-stepped or leapt over stages of orthodox development and a new generation has come of age faster and smarter.

Chiau's rise to stardom was meteoric. A television performer who hosted a children's show and then turned to acting in drama series in the late 80s, he first made an impact in cinema in a rather nondescript police thriller, *Final Justice/Pili Xianfeng* (1988), where he played a quick-witted, street-wise kid who would go far in life while running foul of the law. Chiau repeated this characterisation, with increasingly comic variations, in films such as *My Hero/Yiben Manhua Chuang Tianya* (1990) and *Curry and Pepper/Jiali Lajiao* (1990), announcing the wild and wacky heroes that would later characterise his screen image. In the summer of 1990 Chiau became 'red', as the Hong Kong saying goes, meaning 'all the rage', a household sensation. The vehicle carrying Chiau to overnight success was *All for the Winner/Du Sheng*, as Shing, a green kid from Guangzhou who comes to Hong Kong to visit his uncle (played by Ng Mang-tat, who appeared in virtually all of Chiau's movies as his sidekick). Shing possesses X-ray vision, which makes him a natural gambler. In no time, he becomes known as the 'Saint of Gamblers' and takes part in an international gambling tournament for the title King of Gamblers. He loses his X-ray vision at this crucial point because the girl he loves has been kidnapped by his opponent, only regaining his special ability when his uncle hits on the brainwave of hiring a girl to become Shing's substitute lover. That the plan works is due to Shing's discovery that the proxy lover shares one thing in common with the real one: a mole in her armpit.

All for the Winner grossed over HK $40 million, putting it among the highest-grossing movies of all time in Hong Kong cinema. Since then, four of Chiau's subsequent movies have grossed more than the magical 40 million dollar mark. Three other Chiau movies are more moderate grossers, but still substantial box-office winners, bringing in over 30 million dollars each. Clearly, Chiau's movies are big money-spinners, all the more phenomenal when one considers that these earnings are from Hong Kong's domestic market alone.

Western critics who have had a taste of Chiau's humour say that it will not 'translate'. Much of the humour is vulgar (toilet jokes abound in all of Chiau's films) and based on a peculiar Cantonese argot which presupposes Hong Kong residents to fully enjoy the insinuations, slang and in-jokes. The truth is that native humorists anywhere rarely do 'translate'. If they do, they have hit some kind of a nerve that transcends language. But Chiau has not confined himself to linguistic humour. One of his best films is the distinctly un-Shakespearean *All's Well, End's Well/Jia You Xi Shi* (1992, directed by Clifton Ko), a deliciously hare-brained comedy which gives the impression that Hong Kong cinema can virtually invent anything on the spot. The movie conforms to a formula of literate Cantonese humour and visual tomfoolery, with the cast (including Leslie Cheung and Maggie Cheung) sending themselves up and having great fun doing so.

Sophistication is, of course, a relative term when applied to Stephen Chiau. His next big hit, *Fight Back to School/Tao Xue Wei Long* (1992, directed by Gordon Chan), is not as unremittingly boorish or vulgar as most of Chiau's films. He plays a policeman who disguises himself as an eighteen-year-old juvenile and goes undercover as a student in a school in order to recover a pistol stolen from his superior. Although not departing from his standard oafish characterisations, including that of Ng Man-tat, Chiau's perennial sidekick, of more interest is the interplay between Chiau and his teachers, who are given to hurling the blackboard duster at our hero everytime he is remiss, and that between Chiau and his fellow students, who call him 'Grandpa' after he has defeated the school bully linked to the Triads.

Chiau's next mega-success, *Justice, My Foot/Shensi Guan* (which grossed just short of 50 million dollars) is filled, as usual, with vulgar jokes and episodic sketches that are barely related to each other. The premise for the movie lies in a sick joke: Chiau, a successful and unscrupulous lawyer in the last century is hit by bad luck – he remains childless even though his wife (played by Anita Mui) gives birth to thirteen baby boys, all of whom die at birth. Both husband and wife are distraught, but you wouldn't know it from the feckless tone of the movie. Chiau goes on defending hopeless cases which he wins by sleight-of-mouth, and his wife, when she's not giving birth, is a part-time swordswoman fighting on the side of the oppressed.

At last count, another comedy, *Royal Tramp/Lu Ding Ji* (1992), released in two parts, took in a combined gross of 77 million dollars (US $10 million), a new record. Chiau's movies prepared audiences for *mou lei-tau* parody and farce, but it is the latest 'postmoden' hits not starring Chiau which give new meaning to parody and pastiche. Improbable as it may seem, these movies with the somewhat arcane titles, *92 Legendary La Rose Noire* (1992) and *Dongcheng Xijiu* (1993), have added substance to the idea that there is a postmodernism unique to Hong Kong in the last decade of the century, before reverting to Chinese rule.

The uniqueness of Hong Kong in this respect was its existence in the modern world as a colonial outpost of the British Empire in the heart of East Asia. However, since the British Empire is itself defunct, Hong Kong, while it remained subaltern in many ways, also outstripped the Imperial power as a crucial meeting ground of East and West and, more importantly, as the base for Western capitalism's attempts to 'crack' the Chinese market. Hong Kong is both East (from a Western point of view) and West (from a Chinese point of view), both subaltern and hegemonic as a dynamic financial and trading centre, both premodern and postmodern. The Chinese have, on the whole, looked upon this blending in mock-heroic terms. Indeed, it is the very essence of parody to address such mixtures. Hong Kong film-makers in the 90s have shown that the encounter produces strange outcomes which take the form of a kind of postmodernist high jinks which is nothing like what, for instance, American or Japanese postmodernism is supposed to be.

Hong Kong's postmodernist farces have underscored the derision in the mixing of East and West. The result is possibly to increase self-awareness – not only of what is unique about Hong Kong, but also that aspect of identity which persists in spite of the blending of cultures. Even as they join in the merry-making of mixing East and West, Hong Kong film-makers have looked increasingly into the celluloid dustbin of *tsaan pin* or 'dilapidated' cinema, which is as much a documented history of Hong Kong as any history book can be. It is a 'putative past' which belongs to Hong Kong people themselves and is the least understood and known by outsiders. This looking back into the celluloid past is best illustrated by *92 Legendary La Rose Noire*, the unexpected hit of its year which has since won a cult following among critics and audiences alike.

An off-beat pastiche of Cantonese comedy thrillers of the 60s, the film deliberately recalls a kind of nostalgia for the pre-high tech 60s. Outsiders may be left in the dark about its generic pedigree, but Cantonese movie buffs will pick up the nuances of the actors' speech and gestures: the jokey but not unkind allusions to *The Black Rose/Hei Meigui* (1965) directed by Chor Yuen, a black and white classic *tsaan pin* whose title character, a masked cat burglar dressed in black who steals from the rich to help the poor, re-emerges in postmodern form as the legendary *La Rose Noire. 92 Legendary La Rose Noire* recalls Hong Kong cinema's history and analyses its shape and form. It breaks the myth that Hong Kong cinema has no history, only images. On the other hand, it suggests that Hong Kong cinema presumes to be postmodern without having been modern, implying that the 60s was the period Hong Kong cinema should have modernised, but did not.

The trend towards pastiche has built up momentum with each new postmodern film released in the past few years. *Rose, Rose I Love* You/ *Meigui Meigui Wo Ai Ni* (1993), the sequel to *Legendary La Rose Noire*, contains much the same zany humour as the original and similarly purports to send up (or pay tribute to) old Cantonese movies and movie stars. All the characters are named after Cantonese movie stars of the 50s and 60s. It tries to trump its predecessor by sending up the pop songs, styles and behaviour of the period as well. The quaintness of the old days is stressed and contrasted with changing contemporary fads and mores (karaoke and gay liberation, for instance). Erratic and eccentric like its predecessor, the parody is less fresh a second time around, but no less enjoyable.

Comedy and parody (or rather, self-parody) have always been looked upon by Hong Kong film-makers as somewhere near the summit of entertainment. In their eyes, the art of pastiche is a refinement of parody. *Dongcheng Xijiu*, a title which may literally be translated as 'The East Achieves, the West Follows', provides a summary of Hong Kong postmodernism as an exercise in the pastiching of form. Perhaps inadvertently, it has let loose formalist demons in the form of vexing questions about the real shape of Hong Kong cinema. The film is a pastiche of epic narratives inspired by the serialised martial arts novels of Jin Yong, the most popular writer in the genre whose books have been recycled into long-running TV series and movie-plus-sequels (in real life, the writer is Louis Cha, one of Hong Kong's press czars, the boss of the *Ming Pao Daily*). The actual novel parodied by the film is *The Eagle Shooting Heroes/Shediao Yingxiong Zhuan*, which features heroes with mythic powers and provided the basis for straight productions of several film versions and a TV series. The film's full title, *Shediao Yingxion Zhuan zhi Dongcheng Xijiu*, refers to a zany episode in the novel where the heroes experience adventures while saving a princess from a wicked usurper of the throne. The cast of characters includes a wicked prince, a beautiful princess, naïve young swordsmen and swordswomen, Taoist acolytes and, most memorable of all, a Buddhist devotee (played by Tony Leung Ka-fai) seeking Nirvana and reaching it only after he finds a lover who must say 'I Love You' three times. Characters are paired off and required to perform two-handed skits that recall televisual sitcoms. They congregate in an inn where the comedy becomes ever more farcical before climaxing in a Middle-Eastern palace. The incongruous set parodies *Arabian Nights* fantasies with flying boots appearing instead of flying carpets. The form is a hodgepodge, evoking Cinema City slapstick, high camp Maria Montez-Carmen Miranda comedies, Chinese episodic novels and Vaudeville sketches from Chinese opera. Eschewing linear narrative modes, the free-form has evolved not just from new wave aesthetics, but from Chinese literary and theatrical conventions as well. The title may puzzle, but the film itself should translate as postmodernist humour, Hong Kong style.

The eagerness of Hong Kong film-makers to delve into the past seems to confirm the historicist approach characterised by Jameson as one in which 'intertextuality' is the 'operator of a new connotation of "pastness" and pseudo-historical depth, in which the history of aesthetic style displaces "real" history'.[5] Nevertheless, I would argue that, contrary to the postmodern use of intertextuality as a random practice of stylistic allusions designed to efface history, there is a genuine attempt to explore history and to acknowledge, even if only grudgingly, Hong Kong's kinship with China's history, both in its glorious and tragic manifestations, while at the same time inscribing a wish to stick one's head in the sand and to efface the history that looms on the horizon by effacing the 'real' history of the past. The eclecticism that underpins Hong Kong's type of postmodernism can thus be seen as a sign of a culture caught in the tension between a desire to construct a non-colonial identity by mobilising a sense of the past, and a profound anxiety about the possibility of that very identity being imposed rather than being constructed autonomously.

Gender-bending may be a surprising manifestation of the search for sexual identity, but it has electrified the imaginations of Hong Kong film-makers in their turn towards postmodernism. Taking its cue from older Chinese traditions of gender-bending, the Tsui Hark-produced *Swordsman II/Xiao'ao Jianghu II Dongfang Bubai* (1992) started the trend, since followed by other martial arts pictures with remote period settings, with the beautiful Dongfang Bubai or 'Asia the Invincible', the former South China tribal chief who castrated himself in order to master the arts and powers contained in a sacred scroll. The eunuch is transformed into an androgyne, a sexual state half-way towards a full sex change. Asian's plan is to dominate China, thus the world, but she fails to take into account that a woman may love a man. Asia's love object, and opponent, is the male swordsman of the title. The theme of sexual ambiguity or non-gender masks a wider sentiment of feminism and gay liberation. On the evidence of *Swordsman II* and its follow-up, *Swordsman III: The East is Red*, Tsui Hark must be considered the master of gender-bending films (although Ching Siu-tung is the actual director). Asia the Invincible is not Tsui's first character of this type: there is also the demon in *A Chinese Ghost Story*. Then as now, the motif proposes that ancient China had more liberal views towards sexuality. The central paradox of Hong Kong's postmodernism is seen working once again: the suggestion that values or attitudes to be achieved in fact stem from somewhere in the very distant past. This theme has marked other new wave works such as Eddie Fong's *An Amorous Woman of the Tang Dynasty*, a genuinely erotic work that seduces with its existentialist view of sex and liberty, perhaps Hong Kong's first mature work to offer sex as a route to existential Nirvana.

Hong Kong's postmodernism has a time dimension skewed in favour of the past and the future, skipping the present, as illustrated by the use of clocks in Wong Kar-wai's *Days of Being Wild*. It asserts that Hong Kong is what it is until a certain moment (1997), though it is anybody's guess how long after 1997 'Hong Kong' will continue to survive, not merely as an entity, but as an idea. Film-makers and other intellectuals are becoming increasingly aware that Hong Kong tradition, such as it is, will be lost and will become diluted. A fundamental contradiction arises from the adoption of a postmodern perspective. While Hong Kong intellectuals wish to ascribe Hong Kong's achievements to Chinese cultural-religious values (such as the idea that a Confucianist work ethic produced the economic miracles of East Asian countries), there is the danger that the return of 'China' may obliterate the very notion of Chineseness elaborated by the territory's artists. The loss of values which Hong Kong holds dear will correspond with its gradual assimilation into Mainland Chinese culture (more optimist pundits think that it will be the other way around). The fear is that Hong Kong's modern, unique culture which evolved from its life as a treaty port, which popular writers characterised in terms of comprador capitalism, tai-pans, coolies, sing-song girls, rickshaw pullers and the like, will die off. Such a fear is reflected in the postmodern cinema of the early 90s. It acknowledges that Hong Kong culture is *also* Western and makes a last-ditch effort to assert it.

Tsui Hark's *The Wicked City/ Yaoshou Dushi* (1992) conveys this post-1997 fear (the movie itself takes place after 1997). Although it is not directed by Tsui, it bears his unmistakeable stamp, being produced and scripted by him. It is an extraordinary extension of his *Once Upon a Time in China* and *Swordsman* series, all of which explore the question of East Asian malaise and rejuvenation. *The Wicked City* brings the issue home. Adapted from a Japanese animated *manga* feature of the same name, *The Wicked City* cleverly uses Hong Kong's skyline to provide a setting for an allegory about its political fate: Tsui has invoked the superstitious idea, expounded in the previous chapter, that as Hong Kong races to keep its date with destiny, demons will rise up from the nether world to control the future. The plot concerns the attempts of humans to control the activities of half-human creatures called 'Rapters' who mingle with humans in the Hong Kong (and

251

Tokyo) of the future. Although the setting is futuristic, the mood is inescapably 'now', integrating the new Japanese-Western subculture of cyberpunk and attendant concepts such as dystopia and smart drugs: the Rapters purvey 'Happiness' potions, the basis of a new drug culture. The half-man half-monster villain climbs up to the top of Hong Kong's tallest building, the Bank of China headquarters, to drug the territory by releasing a Happiness gas in a finale unmatched since King Kong climbed the Empire State Building. The villain's father attempts to put down his son from the cockpit of a jumbo jet flying over the building. There is also a battle with a clock, signifying Hong Kong's fight against time, with the hero commenting that 'Time is a pain in the arse'. *The Wicked City* is a classic by all the standards of postmodernism: irony, parody, critical re-working of history, politics and the future. It could properly mark the end of Hong Kong cinema.

POSTSCRIPT

The surge of postmodernism in Hong Kong cinema in the early 90s coincided perfectly with the feeling that Hong Kong was pressed for time; that it was imperative for everyone to chase time in order to get the most out of their lives. Hong Kong cinema was appropriately defined by the consciousness of the impatient momentum of modern living, not to mention the consciousness of 1997 and the edgy feeling of there being no time left. However, in the two-and-a-half years since the release of *The Wicked City* and the postmodern comedies, Hong Kong cinema appears to have reacted against postmodern freneticism and the pressed-for-time mentality. It has seemed to settle down into a state of almost sublime self-reflection. The box-office 'sleeper' of 1993 was a contemporary, nostalgia-tinged re-make of the old Shaw Brothers classic *Love Without End/Bu Liao Qing* entitled *C'est la Vie, Mon Cherie/Xin Bu Liao Qing*. The film quietly reaffirmed old-fashioned virtues as its leading man, new star Lau Ching-wan, romanced a dying Anita Yuen against a background of street-singing opera troupes. Lau and Yuen are the new icons of an intermediate generation that will bridge the 1997 transition. Similarly, the sleeper hit of 1994 was another journey into nostalgia featuring complete new stars: Clifton Ko's *I Have a Date With Spring/Wo He Chun Tian You Ge Yue Hui*. Retired singer Butterfly Yiu stages a comeback in her old Kowloon nightclub and, through flashbacks, reminisces about her life with three other female singers and her unrequited love for a saxophone player. Ko successfully adapted the long-running stage play To Kowk-wai, which earned a cult following through the Urban Council theatre circuit. The film evokes a Hong Kong experiencing political instability, the action flashing back to 1967, the year of political riots inspired by China's Cultural Revolution, reflected in the uncertainty of the lives of its protagonists. Equally a backstage comedy and a sentimental but evocative melodrama, *I Have a Date With Spring* required a mature use of actors and dialogue that militated against the anarchy of postmodernism which Clifton Ko himself had previously practised in his 90s comedies.

Gordon Chan's *The Long and Winding Road/Jinxiu Qiancheng* (1994) was perhaps the best example of the move towards a low-key restatement of humanist sentiments. A charming buddy-buddy comedy, it features Leslie Cheung as an endearing rogue, the personification of Hong Kong professionals in the 90s with little regard for scruples and friendships in their headlong rush towards making as much money as possible. Tony Leung plays his nemesis, a drummer who works in an old folks' home. The movie deals with the ability of friendship to endure in a materialistic money-minded environment: Cheung betrays his friends by buying over the old folks home in order to earn a hefty commission, but does the right thing by his conscience in the end. Gordon Chan directs in a deliberately flat and nonchalant style that complements the two key, beautifully under-stated performances of Cheung and Leung.

C'est la Vie, Mon Cheri, I Have a Date With Spring and *The Long and Winding Road* encapsulated qualities of a more sedate, middle-ground consciousness tempered by a respect for old virtues while paying more than mere lip service to contemporary counter-culture conceits. The post-postmodernist films reaffirmed Hong Kong cinema's penchant for the cross-fertilisation of genres, as shown by the films of the United Film-makers Organisation (UFO), a new production company founded in 1993 by director Peter Chan. In *Twenty Something/Wan Jiu Zhao Wu* and *He's a Woman, She's a Man/Jin Zhi Yu Ye*, both 1994 releases, uninhibited sex drives and cross-dressing were central to the plots. Although they appear consciously to discard the mantle of postmodernism, they were postmod-ernist in all but style. Sections of documentary-format interviews inter-spersed into the narratives of both films suggest that the configuration of postmodern and new wave styles was not completely obliterated. Derivative and hackneyed as they may be, they were nevertheless engag-ing, hugely entertaining studies of yet another generational change taking place in Hong Kong cinema.

However, even as it heads towards another chapter of generational change, all is not well within the film industry. A sense of crisis has pervaded the industry for the past two years as cinema attendances steadily fell from record levels in the late 80s, due in large part to the rise of admission prices as cinemas upgraded facilities and transformed into multiplexes. Higher prices and more sophisticated, albeit smaller, auditoriums raised the level of expectations for quality products which were met by imported Hollywood films. For the first time, Hong Kong cinema felt threatened by Hollywood as audiences flocked to the likes of *Jurassic Park, Speed* and other foreign blockbusters. Local budgets soared accordingly, but the shrinking market, both in Hong Kong and Southeast Asia has compounded the crisis of decreased capital returns. Ironically, companies such as UFO appear to have done well by producing low-budget, quirky and personal but also commercially viable films that de-note some kind of progressive momentum towards the future.

In the mid-90s, Hong Kong was wobbling as a result of the combined effects of the bursting of economic bubbles fuelled by rising inflation rates bordering on double digits, a shrinking manufacturing sector and rising unemployment. Old Hong Kongers were starting to desert the territory, defeated by impossible rents and overcome by a conviction that standards of living have irretrievably gone down. Anxiety over 1997 and the attendant political uncertainties have undoubtedly contributed to the general sense of malaise.

Like its society, Hong Kong cinema is in a state of flux. Its present travails are the results of pondering over how to adapt to integration with China. As its transitional markets begin to shrink, the Hong Kong film industry is once again eyeing the Chinese mainland as its next great frontier. Joint ventures and co-productions with Chinese film-makers and studios are becoming the norm. It may well be that Hong Kong cinema is coming full circle. As the Shanghai cinema indisputably gave form to the Hong Kong cinema, it is now set to return to the fold of the industry in the Mainland and perhaps be brought back to the cradle of Shanghai, the original Hollywood of the East. When or if that happens, Hong Kong cinema will never be the same again.

The 80s may well prove to be the decade in which Hong Kong achieved a full-flowering native cinema where a generation that was born and grew up in the territory came of age and took over the industry. The challenge of the future is how this generation, and the intermediate one, will adapt to integration with China and still assert the separate identity that was, briefly, theirs. In the long term, it is not even certain whether Hong Kong will be able to continue making movies in Cantonese, the dialect that has made Hong Kong cinema unique and given it its identity. As Hong Kong directors turn to making more and more films with the Mainland market in mind, Mandarin will clearly replace Cantonese as the preferred screen language, although dubbing into Cantonese may remain an option to secure Hong Kong's domestic market. The rise of Mandarin films will recall the days when Cantonese-speaking audiences flocked to see Mandarin films. Then, Cantonese films faced a crisis of outmoded standards, poor quality, and a perception that Cantonese was not the language of the future. The rise of younger generations bred and born in a Hong Kong that was free to develop on its own brought Cantonese back to the screen. The conditions pertaining after 1997 will be different. Younger generations will have to live with the fact that Hong Kong is, after all, part of Mandarin-speaking China.

What will transpire now remains to be seen, but the present economic crisis faced by Hong Kong cinema as it approaches a new century appears to signal the closing of an era and the beginning of the age of uncertainty. Hong Kong post-1997 will strive to find new cinematic paradigms as it gropes all over again to find another identity within the embrace of the great Chinese dragon.

NOTES

[1] Fredric Jameson, 'Postmodernism, or the Cultural Logic of Late Capitalism', *New Left Review*, no. 146, 1984, p. 66. It is worth noting that this sense of historicism is rather eccentric, since it in effect evacuates any notion of history rather than overemphasising linear historical genealogies, which is the usual implication of the term.

[2] Jameson, 'Postmodernism, or the Cultural Logic of Late Capitalism', pp. 65–6.

[3] Linda Hutcheon, *A Poetics of Postmodernism* (London: Routledge, 1988), p. 3.

[4] The look of a bemused clown could also be read as a fitting definition of or reaction to the way terms like postmodernism are bandied about, in which case Stephen Chiau Sing-chi's face represents an example of the way Hong Kong cinema simultaneously confirms and belies any notion of the postmodern.

[5] Jameson, 'Postmodernism, or the Cultural Logic of Late Capitalism', p. 67.

Bio-filmographies

Abbreviations:
act. – actor   art. dir. – art director   ed. – editor   exec. prod. – executive producer
MAD – martial arts director   photog. – photography   prod. – producer
prod. design – production design   scr. – screenplay

Lawrence Ah Mon (name in pinyin: Liu Guochang; name in Cantonese: Lau Kwok-cheong), b. 1949, Pretoria, South Africa. Director. USC graduate. TV work in RTHK led to film debut in 1986 with study of juvenile gangs, titled *Gangs/Tong Dang*.

FILMS: *Gangs/Tong Dang* **1986**; *Queen of Temple Street/Miao Jie Huanghou* **1990**; *Lee Rock, Parts One and Two/Lei Luo Zhuan, Dreams of Glory: A Boxer's Story/Quan Wang* **1991**; *Arrest the Restless/Lan Jiang Zhuan zhi Fanfei Zu Fengyun* **1992**; *Three Summers/Gege de Qingren, When Mountains Meet/Qingtian Pili zhi Xiaji Da Jieju* **1993**.

Tony Au (name in pinyin: Ou Dingping; name in Cantonese: Au Ting-ping), b. 1954, Guangdong Province. Director, art director. Studied at the London Film School but took up fashion design in Hong Kong before he was enticed into the film industry, by director Dennis Yu, as art director (as production designers are known in Hong Kong's film industry). He made an auspicious directing debut with *The Last Affair/Hua Cheng* in 1983. Subsequent works have established Au as a superb stylist though he remains a critically neglected director.

FILMS: *The Last Affair/Hua Cheng* **1983**; *Dream Lovers/Meng Zhong Ren* **1986**; *Profiles of Pleasure/Qun Ying Luan Wu* **1988**; *I Am Sorry/Shuohuang de Nüren* **1989**; *Au Revoir, Mon Amour/Heri Jun Zailai* **1991**; *A Roof With a View/Tiantai de Yueguang* **1993**; *A Touch of Evil/Kuangye Shengsi Lian, The Christ of Nanjing/Nanjing de Jidu* **1995**.
AS ART DIRECTOR: *See-Bar/Shi Ba, Dangerous Encounter – 1st Kind/Diyi Lei Xing Weixian* **1980**; *The Story of Woo Viet/Hu Yue de Gushi* **1981**; *Teenage Dreamers/Ningmeng Kele, The Postman Strikes Back/Xuncheng Ma, The Boat People/Touben Nuhai* **1982**; *Love in a Fallen City/Qingcheng zhi Lian* **1984**; *Women/Nüren Xin* **1985**; *The Millionaires' Express/Fugui Lieche* (co-art dir.), *Where's Officer Tuba?/Pili Da Laba* (co-art dir.), *Rosa/Shenyong Shuang Xiang Pao Xuji* (co- art dir.), *Soul/Laoniang*

Gou Sao, Legacy of Rage/Long Zai Jianghu **1986**; *Sworn Brothers/Gandan Xiangzhao* **1987**; *Blonde Fury/Shijie Da Sai* **1989**; *The Last Hero in China/Huang Feihong Tieji Dou Wusong* (as costume designer only), *Flying Dagger/Shenjing Dao yu Feitian Mao* (co-art dir.), *Crime Story/Zhong An Zu* (co-art dir.) **1993**.

Bu Wancang, b. 1903, Anhui Province; d. 1974. Director, a veteran from the early Shanghai cinema. Began as cinematographer from 1921–1925; directed his first picture in 1926. Directed Ruan Lingyu (China's Garbo) in several movies. Collaboration with left-wing scenarist Tian Han in the 1930s marks his most critically successful period as director. Stays on in Shanghai during the anti-Japanese war (1937-45), as 'Orphan Island' director, later co-opted into working for 'Huaying'. In Hong Kong in 1948, directing Yonghua epic *Soul of China/Guo Hun*. Founded his own Taishan company 1951. Has directed for various independent companies as well as MP and GI and Shaw Brothers.

FILMS: (IN SHANGHAI) *Pure as Jade, Clear as Ice/Yujie Bingqing, Fiancée/Weihun Qi* (also scr.), *Repentance/Liangxin Fuhuo* **1926**; *The False Couple/Guaming de Fuqi, Spring Dream by the Lake/Hubian Chun Meng* **1927**; *The Pass of Beauties/Meiren Guan, The Little Detective/Xiao Zhentan* **1928**; *The Short Family/Ai Qinjia, Two Shorts in Rivalry/Liang Ai Zheng Feng, Blind Love/Nuling Fuchou Ji, Tying the Knot/Tongxin Jie* (also act.) **1929**; *Two Generations of Heroes/Fuzi Yingxiong, The Tragedy of the Songstress/Genü Hen, Eternal Revenge/Haitian Qingchou* **1930**; *Love and Duty/Lian'ai yu Yiwu, A Branch of Plum Blossoms/Yi Jian Mei, Peach Blossom Weeps Tears of Blood/Taohua Qixue Ji* **1931**; *Humanity/Rendao, Spring Dream in the Old Capital, Part Two/Xu Gudu Chunmeng* **1932**; *Three Modern Women/Sange Modeng Nüxing, Light of Motherhood/Muxing zhi Guang* **1933**; *The Golden Age/Huangjin Shidai* **1934**; *Victory Song/Kaige* **1935**; *Humanity/Xin Rendao* (sound remake of 1932 film) **1937**; *The*

Beggar's Daughter/Qigai Qianjin, Diao Chan **1938**; Mulan Joins the Army aka Maiden in Armour/Mulan Congjun **1939**; The Jade Hairpiece/Biyu Zan, Night Rain on the Xiang River/Xiaoxiang Yeyu, Xi Shi **1940**; Family/Jia (co-dir. with several others), Ningwu Pass (short) **1941**; The Standard Woman/Biaozhun Furen, Marital Love/Bo Ai (co-dir. with several others), Eternal Fame/Wan Gu Liufang (co-dir. with several others) **1942**; Dream of the Red Chamber/Honglou Meng **1945**; (IN HONG KONG) Soul of China/Guo Hun **1948**; Sins of Our Father/Da Liang Shan Enchou Ji **1949**; The Affair of Diana/Nüren yu Laohu **1951**; A Woman's Heart/Furen Xin (also scr.), Portrait of a Lady/Shu Nü Tu, Sweet Memories/Man Yuan Chun Se (dir. with several others), Destroy/Huimie **1952**; Beauty in Disguise/Huashen Yanying (also scr., prod.), Seven Sisters/Qi Zimei (also scr., prod.) **1953**; Blood-Stained Flowers aka The 72 Martyrs of Canton/Bixue Huanghua (dir. with several others), It Blossoms Again/Zai Chun Hua (co-dir. with Wu Jingping) **1954**; Fisherman's Daughter/Yu Ge (also scr.), The Ingenious Seduction aka Three Laughs/Tang Bohu yu Qiu Xiang (co-dir. with Li Ying, also scr.), The Long Lane/Chang Xiang **1956**; Sisters Three/San Zimei, Miss Evening Sweet/Ye Laixiang **1957**; The Unforgettable Night/Yi Ye Fengliu **1958**; Stolen Love/Touqing Ji, Bean-curd Queen/Doufu Xi Shi **1959**; Eve of the Wedding/Daijia Chunxin, Nobody's Child/Kuer Liulang Ji, My Daughter, My Daughter/Liang Dai Nüxing (also scr.), The Bedside Story/Tongchuang Yimeng, Dreams Come True/Xi Xiang Feng, Kiss Me Again/Di Er Wen **1960**; The Lost Love/Mangmu de Aiqing **1961**; Lady With the Lute/Zhao Wu Niang **1963**.

Jackie Chan (name in pinyin: Cheng Long; name in Cantonese: Sing Lung), b. 1954, Hong Kong, credited in the early 70s as Chen Yuanlong. Kung fu superstar. At age six, studied in opera school and appeared on stage as one of the 'Seven Little Fortunes'. The movies beckoned as Chan grew into adulthood. He entered the industry as an actor, then in 1973, as martial arts director (on The Heroine/Nü Jingcha). Was groomed as a kung fu star by director Luo Wei in mid-70s but did not become a superstar until Snake in the Eagle's Shadow/Shexing Diaoshou (1978), directed by Yuen Woo-ping. His own directing debut came in 1979. Several forays into American films did not make him an international name but his self-directed Hong Kong films (Project A/A Jihua and Police Story/Jingcha

Gushi series) have made him a cult success in international niche markets. He does all his own stunts and has his own stunt team (known in Cantonese as 'Sing Kar Ban') which co-ordinates stunt choreography in all his movies.

FILMS (all also act. and martial arts dir. (MAD)): The Fearless Hyena/Xiao Quan Guaizhao (also scr.) **1979**; The Young Master/Shidi Chu Ma (also co-scr.) **1980**; Dragon Lord/Long Shaoye (also co-scr.) **1982**; Project A/A Jihua (also co-scr.) **1983**; Police Story/Jingcha Gushi (also co-scr.) **1985**; Armour of God/Longxiong Hudi, Project A, Part II/A Jihua Xuji (also co-scr.) **1987**; Police Story, Part II/Jingcha Gushi Xuji (also co-scr.) 1988; Mr. Canton and Lady Rose/Qi Ji (also co-scr.) **1989**; Armour of God II: Operation Condor/Feiying Jihua (also co-scr.) **1991**.
AS ACTOR: Not Scared to Die/Dingtian Lidi, The Heroine/Nü Jingcha (also MAD) **1973**; The Golden Lotus/Jin Ping Shuang Yan, Supermen Against the Orient/Siwang Yihou **1974**; All in the Family/Huafei Mancheng Chun, No End of Surprises/Pai'an Jingqi 1975; New Fist of Fury/Xin Jingwu Men, Hand of Death aka Countdown in Kung Fu/Shaolin Men, Shaolin Wooden Men/Shaolin Muren Xiang, The Killer Meteors/Fengyu Shuangliu Xing (Taiwan) **1976**; To Kill With Intrigue/Jianhua Yanyu Jiangnan (Taiwan) **1977**; Snake in the Eagle's Shadow/Shexing Diao Shou, Snake and Crane Arts of Shaolin/She He Babu, The Magnificent Bodyguard/Feidu Juanyun Shan, Drunken Master/Zui Quan, Spiritual Kung Fu/Quan Jing **1978**; Dragon Fist/Long Quan (also MAD) **1979**; Battle Creek Brawl aka The Big Brawl (US) **1980**; Cannonball Run (US) **1981**; Cannonball Run II (US), Winners and Sinners/Qimou Miaoji Wu Fuxing **1983**; Wheels on Meals/Kuaican Che **1984**; My Lucky Stars/Fuxing Gaozhao, Twinkle Twinkle Little Star/Xiari Fuxing, The Protector (US/Hong Kong), Heart of the Dragon/Long de Xin **1985**; Island of Fire/Huo Shao Dao (Taiwan) **1991**; Twin Dragons/Shuanglong Hui, Police Story 3 – Super Cop/Chaoji Jingcha **1992**; City Hunter/Chengshi Lieren, Crime Story/Zhong An Zu **1993**; Drunken Master II/Zui Quan II **1994**; Rumble in the Bronx/Hongfan Qu, Thunderbolt/Pili Huo **1995**; First Strike/Jingcha Gushi 4 zhi Jiandan Renwu **1996**; Mr. Nice Guy/Yige Hao Ren **1997**.

Peter Chan (name in pinyin: Chen Kexin; name in Cantonese: Chan Ho-sun), b. 1962, Hong Kong.

Director, producer. Raised in Bangkok, Thailand, Chan went to America for his tertiary education before returning to Hong Kong in the early 80s as a production assistant and assistant director in Golden Harvest. Debuted as a director in 1991; founded the United Filmmakers Organisation (UFO) the same year. Achieved great success with *He's a Woman, She's a Man* (1994) and *Comrades, Almost a Love Story* (1996).

FILMS: *Alan and Eric: Between Hello and Goodbye/Shuangcheng Gushi* **1991**; *Tom, Dick and Hairy/Fengchen San Xia* (co-dir.) **1993**; *He Ain't Heavy, He's My Father/Xin Nan Xiong Nan Di* (co-dir.), *He's a Woman, She's a Man/Jinzhi Yuye* **1994**; *The Age of Miracles/Mama Fanfan* **1995**; *Who's the Woman, Who's the Man?/Jinzhi Yuye 2; Comrades, Almost a Love Story/Tian Mimi* **1996**.

Sylvia Chang (name in pinyin: Zhang Aijia; name in Cantonese: Cheung Ngai-kar). b. 1953, Taiwan. Actor-director. She was a teenage TV performer in Taiwan before being signed on by Hong Kong's Golden Harvest studio in the early 70s. She returned to Taiwan to star in a spate of melodramas, winning a Golden Horse award in 1976 for Best Supporting Actress in Li Xing's *Posterity and Perplexity/Biyun Tian*, winning again in the same category in 1981 for Ke Junxiong's *My Grandfather/Wo De Yeye*. In the 1980s, her career developed mostly in Hong Kong although she continues to commute to Taiwan for some of her best roles, e.g. Edward Yang's *That Day on the Beach/Haitan de Yi Tian* (1983). Directing debut in 1981.

FILMS: *Once Upon a Time/Jiumeng Bu Xu Ji* (also co-scr.) **1981**; *Passion/Zui Ai* (also scr. and act.) **1986**; *The Game They Call Sex/Huangse Gushi* (dir. episode only) **1988**; *Mary From Beijing/Mengxing Shifen* (also scr.) **1992**; *Conjugal Affair* aka *In Between/Xin Tongju Shidai* (dir. episode only, also act. and co-scr.), *Siao Yu/Xiao Nü Xiao Yu* (also co-scr., Taiwan) **1994**; *Nobody Wants to Go Home/Jintian Bu Hui Jia* (also co-scr.) **1996**.
AS ACTOR: *The Chinese Enforcers/Xiao Yingxiong Da Nao Tangren Jie, Yellow-Faced Tiger/Huangmian Laohu,* (IN TAIWAN) *Seventeen, Seventeen, Eighteen/Shiqi, Shiqi, Shiba* **1974**; *Inside and Outside/Menli Menwai* **1975**; *The Victory/Mei Hua, Confused Love/Bianse de Taiyang, Warmth in Autumn/Wennuan Zai Qiutian, Posterity and*

Perplexity/Biyun Tian, Flight of Fallen Leaves/Luo Ye Piao Piao, Autumn Affair/Qiu Chan, Blown Spray/Lang Hua, Star Talk/Xing Yu **1976**; *Mitra/Bosi Xiyang Qing, Taipei 66/Taibei Liushi Liu, Pirate Ship of Love/Ai de Zei Quan, Yesterday in a Hurry/Zuori Chongchong, Green Mountains/Qingse Shanmai, I've Found Love/Aiqing Wo Zhao Dao Le, The Golden Age/Shanliang de Rizi* **1977**; *Dream of the Red Chamber/Jinyu Liangyuan Houlou Meng* (HK) **1978**; *Legend of the Mountain/Shanzhong Chuanqi, The Mad Woman/Mafeng Nü, Gold Branch Jade Leaf/Jinzhi Yuye, The Secret/Feng Jie* (HK) **1979**; *White Jasmine/Moli Hua, Great Laughter on Earth/Tianxia Yi Da Xiao, Mission Over the Eagle Castle/Xue Jian Leng Ying Bao* **1980**; *The Comedy General/Daxiao Jiangjun, Attack Force Z* (Australia/Taiwan), *The Juvenizer/Zhongshen Dashi, My Grandfather/Wo De Yeye, Heroes of the Sky/Kongzhong Wushi* **1981**; (IN HONG KONG) *Aces Go Places/Zuijia Paidang, He Lives By Night/Ye Jing Hun, In Our Time/Guangyin de Gushi* (episode, Taiwan) **1982**; *Aces Go Places, Part Two/Zuijia Paidang Daxian Shentong, That Day on the Beach/Haitan de Yitian* (Taiwan) **1983**; *Aces Go Places: Our Man From Bond Street/Zuijia Paidang Nühuang Miling, Double Trouble/Daxiao Buliang, Shanghai Blues/Shanghai zhi Ye* **1984**; *Crazy Romance/Qiu Ai Fan Douxing* **1985**; *Aces Go Places, Part Four/Zuijia Paidang Qianli Jiu Chaipo, Lucky Stars Go Places/Zuijia Fuxing, Immortal Story/Haishang Hua* **1986**; *The Seven-Year Itch/Qi Nian zhi Yang* **1987**; *Soursweet* (UK), *Chicken and Duck Talk/Ji Tong Ya Jiang, King of Stanley Market/Ku Jia Tianxia* **1988**; *All About Ah Long/A Lang de Gushi* (also co-scr.), *Eight Taels of Gold/Ba Liang Jin* **1989**; *The Fun, The Luck, and the Tycoon/Jixing Gongzhao, Full Moon in New York/Ren Zai Niuyue, Queen of Temple Street/Miaojie Huanghou, My Mother's Teahouse/Chunqiu Chashi* (Taiwan) **1990**; *A Rascal's Tale/Baofeng Shaonian, Sisters of the World Unite!/Shasha Jiajia Zhan Qi Lai* (also prod., co-scr.) **1991**; *Shadow of Dreams/Huan Ying* (Taiwan/China) **1993**; *Eat Drink Man Woman/Yin Shi Nan Nü* (Taiwan) **1994**; *I Want to Go On Living/Wo Yao Huo Xia Qu* (also co-scr.) **1995**.

Cheng Bugao, b. 1906, Zhejiang Province; d. 1966, Hong Kong. Veteran director from the Shanghai cinema. A film critic in his student days; formed his own company to direct first film in 1924. Best remembered for his 1930s classics, *Wild Torrent/Kuang*

Liu and *Spring Silkworms/Chun Can*, both written by Xia Yan. In Hong Kong in 1947, directing mainly for Great Wall.

FILMS: (IN SHANGHAI) *The Mismatched Couple/Shuihuo Yuanyang, Tears in the Battleground/Shachang Lei* (also scr.) **1925**; *The Virtuous Wife/Kongmen Xianxi* **1927**; *Lady with the Flying Sword/Feijian Nüxia, Black-Clad Lady Knight/Heiyi Nüxia* (co-dir. with Zheng Zhengqiu), *Tears of Blood on the Yellow Flower/Xuelei Huanghua, Part One and Two* (co-dir. with Zheng Zhengqiu), *The Marriage Struggle/Fendou Hunyin, Divorce/Lihun* **1928**; *A Rich Man's Life/Furen de Shenghuo, The Little Hero/Xiao Yingxiong Liu Jin, Lover's Blood/Ai Ren de Xue, Papa Loves Mama/Baba Ai Mama* **1929**; *Journey to the West, Part Three/Xin Xiyou Ji, Disan Ji* (co-dir. with Zhang Shichuan), *The Golden Road/Huangjin zhi Lu, One Red Egg/Yige Hong Dan, The Romantic Girl/Langman Nüzi, Whore and Mother/Changmen Xianmu* **1930**; *Sing Song Girl Red Peony/Genü Hong Mudan* (assisted Zhang Shichuan), *Screen Love Stories, Part One and Two/Yinmu Yanshi, Shadow on the Window/Chuangshang Ren Ying, A Shanghai Miss/Yige Shanghai Xiaojie, Unlucky To Be a Woman/Buxing Sheng Wei Nüer Shen* **1931**; *A Lonely Duck After Sunset/Luoxia Guwu, Love and Death/Ai yu Si, War at Shanghai/Shanghai zhi Zhan* (documentary), *The Lovable Foe/Keai de Choudi* **1932**; *Wild Torrent/Kuang Liu, Prospects/Qiancheng* (co-dir. with Zhang Shichuan), *Sunset On the River/Man Jiang Hong, Spring Silkworms/Chun Can* **1933**; *The Common Enemy/Tong Chou, Romance of Mount Hua/Hua Shan Yanshi, To the Northwest/Dao Xibei Qu, A Bible for Women/Nüer Jing* (episode) **1934**; *The Brothers/Xiongdi Xing, Ye Laixiang* **1935**; *New and Old Shanghai/Xin Jiu Shanghai, Little Lingzi/Xiao Lingzi* **1936**; *Dream World/Mengli Qiankun, Elopement/Yeben* **1937**; (IN HONG KONG) *Sons of Warfare/Luanshi Ernü* **1947**; *Lovers of Spite/Yuan'ou Qingshen* **1948**; *Virtue in the Dust/Chun Cheng Hua Luo, Heavenly Souls/Jinxiu Tiantang, A Fisherman's Honour/Hai Shi* **1949**; *Celestial Lovers/Yaochi Yuanyang* **1951**; *Old and New Loves/Jiu Ai Xin Huan, Merry-Go-Round/Huanxi Yuanjia, Till We Meet Again/Shen Gui Mengli Ren* **1954**; *The Wayward Love/Mitu de Aiqing, Irreparable/Shaonü de Fannao* **1955**; *Rose Cliff/Meigui Dang* **1956**; *The Fairy Dove/Xiao Gezi Guniang, Ming Phoon/Ming Feng* **1957**; *When You Were Not With Me/Lan Huahua, Street Boy/Cimu Wan'er, The Nature of*

Spring/You Nü Huai Chun (co-dir. with Lin Huan) **1958**; *Wonderful Thoughts/Jiling Gui yu Xiao Laimao* **1959**; *Comedy of 100 Girls/Zhifen Xiao Bawang* **1960**; *The Lady Racketeer/Meiren Ji* **1961**.

Cheng Gang (name in Cantonese: Ching Kong) b. 1924, Anhui Province. Director-writer. A wandering child performer during the anti-Japanese war, joining different troupes from Guilin to Chongqing. In Shanghai after the war, studying production design. In Hong Kong in 1949, entered film industry as writer on Cantonese, Mandarin and other dialect films (mainly Chaozhou and Amoy). Started directing Cantonese films in 1951. Employed as second-unit director by Shaw Brothers in mid-60s, turning full director in 1967. Father of director Ching Siu-tung.

CANTONESE FILMS: *Mother and Son in Grief/Changduan Muzi Xin, Song of a Mother/Chun Dao Renjian* **1951**; *Sweet Love Lingers On/Ernü Qingchang* (co-dir. with Ng Wui) **1952**; *Bright Nights/Huoshu Yinhua Xiangying Hong* (co-dir. with Ng Wui and Chu Kea, also co-scr.) **1953**. (MANDARIN FILMS) *Kiss and Kill/Fengliu Tiehan* (co-dir.) **1967**; *Gun Brothers/Qianmian Dadao* (co-dir. with Wu Jiaxiang), *The Magnificent Swordsman/Guai Xia* (co-dir. with Yue Feng), *The Sword of Swords/Shen Dao* **1968**; *Killers/Haoxia Zhuan* (also scr.) **1969**; *The Twelve Gold Medallions/Shier Jinpai* (also scr.) 1970; *Trilogy of Swordsmanship* (episode, also scr.), *Pursuit/Lin Chong Yeben* (also scr.), *The Fourteen Amazons/Shisi Nü Yinghao* (also scr.) **1972**; *Kidnap/Tianwang* (also scr.) **1974**; *Temperament of Life/Xixiao Numa* (also scr., act.) **1975**; *The Criminals/Xianggang Qi An* (episode, also scr.), *King Gambler/Duwang Da Pianju* (also scr.) **1976**; *The Call Girls/Yingzhao Mingche* **1977**; *The Flying Guillotine, Part Two/Canku Da Cisha* (co-dir. with Hua Shan) **1978**; *The Invincible Enforcer/Bawan Zuiren* **1979**; *The King of Gamblers/Duwang Qunying Hui, Gambler's Delight/Liumang Qianwang* **1981**.

Alex Cheung (name in pinyin: Zhang Guoming name in Cantonese: Cheung Kwok-ming), b. 1951, Hong Kong. New wave director. Got into films through experimental film-making. TV employment followed. Feature debut in 1979 with *Cops and Robbers/Dianzhi Bingbing*, one of the first films that broke the new wave.

FEATURE FILMS: *Cops and Robbers/Dianzhi Bing Bing* (also co-scr.) **1979**; *Man on the Brink/Bianyuan Ren* (also scr., dir. of photog.) **1981**; *Twinkle Twinkle Little Star/Xingji Duntai* **1983**; *Danger Has Two Faces/Huangjia Da Zei* **1985**; *Legend of Wisely/Weisili Chuanshuo* (special effects dir. only) **1987**; *Imaginary Suspects/Dianzhi Zei Zei* **1988**; *Framed/Chendi E* **1989**; *Midnight Caller/Lang Wen Ye Jinghun* (co-dir.) **1995**.

Alfred Cheung (name in pinyin: Zhang Jianting name in Cantonese: Cheung Kin-ting), b. 1955, Guangzhou. Writer-director-actor. Studied at Columbia University. Much TV work (research and writing) in the 1970s. First feature film script in 1980 for Ronny Yu's *The Saviour/Jiushi Zhe*.; he also contributed to the screenplays of Allen Fong's *Father and Son/Fu yu Zi* (1981) and Ann Hui's *The Story of Woo Viet/Hu Yue de Gushi* (1981). Directing debut in 1982; has mostly specialised in comedies although his *On the Run/Wangming Yuanyang* (1988) is an excellent noir thriller.

FILMS: *Monkey Business/Maliu Guohai* **1982**; *Let's Make Laugh/Biao Cuo Qiri Qing* (also scr.) **1983**; *Family Light Affair/Chengshi zhi Guang* (also scr.) **1984**; *Let's Make Laugh, Part Two/Zai Jian Qiren Qing* (also scr.) **1985**; *Strange Bedfellows/Liang Gongbo Ba Tiao Xin* (episode only, also scr., act.) **1986**; *To Err is Humane/Biao Cuo Shen* (also co-scr.) **1987**; *Paper Marriage/Guofu Xinniang* (also act.), *On the Run/Wangming Yuanyang* (also co-scr.) **1988**; *Her Fatal Ways/Biaojie Ni Hao Ye!* (also co-scr., act.), *Queen's Bench, Part Three/Guhuo Da Lüshi* (also co-scr., act.) **1990**; *Her Fatal Ways, Part Two/Biaojie, Ni Hao Ye! Xuji* (also co-scr., act.), *The Banquet/Haomen Yeyan* (co-dir.) **1991**; *Her Fatal Ways, Part Three/Biaojie, Ni Hao Ye! 3 zhi Da Ren Ma Dao* (also co-scr., act.), *Talk to Me Dicky/Xilao Shi Jiang Ye* (also scr., act.) **1992**; *Her Fatal Ways, Part Four/Biaojie Ni Hao Ye!4 zhi Qing Bu Zi Jin* (also act.) **1994**; *Green Hat/Dai Lü Mao de Nüren* (also co-scr.) **1995**; *The Bodyguard of the Last Governor/Gang Du Zuihou Yige Baobiao* (also co-scr.) **1996**; *All's Well Ends Well 1997/97 Jia You Xishi* **1997**.

Jacob Cheung (name in pinyin: Zhang Zhiliang; name in Cantonese: Cheung Chi-leung), b. 1959, Hong Kong. Director, producer. Entered HK-TVB after high school, then switched to film industry in 1983, joining Cinema City, Golden Harvest,

and Bo Ho Films in succession, working as line producer on several films. First feature film as director released in 1988; breakthrough work as director, *Cageman/Long Min* (1992), putting him in the ranks of Second Wave directors. Founded Simpson Productions Co. in 1993 to produce independent works mainly in collaboration with Mainland and Taiwanese directors.

FILMS: *Lai Shi, China's Last Eunuch/Zhongguo Zuihou Yige Taijian* **1988**; *Beyond the Sunset/Feiyue Huanghun* (also co-scr.) **1989**; *Goodbye Hero/Wanming Yingxiong* (also scr.) **1990**; *Lover's Tear/Shi Bu Wang Qing* (also co-scr.), *Cageman/Long Min* (also co-scr., act.) **1992**; *Always on My Mind/Qiang Qian Fuqi* **1993**; *The Returning/Dengzhe Ni Huilai* **1994**; *Whatever Will Be, Will Be/Xianle Piaopiao* **1995**.
AS PRODUCER: *This Thing Called Love/Hunyin Wuyu* **1991**; *Back to Back, Face to Face/Bei Dui Bei, Lian Dui Lian* (HK/China), *Sparkling Fox/Huo Hu* (HK/China), *Mr. Sardine/Guoqi Shadin Yu*, *Midnight Revenge/Anye Qiangsheng* (HK/Taiwan) **1994**.

Mable Cheung (name in pinyin: Zhang Wanting; name in Cantonese: Cheung Yuen-ting) Director. Graduated from Hong Kong University and Bristol University, UK. Worked in RTHK 1978–80 before enrolling for a film-making course in New York University. While in New York, Shaw Brothers gave her a chance to make *The Illegal Immigrants* in 1984. Has made most of her films in partnership with Alex Law.

FILMS: *The Illegal Immigrants/Feifa Yimin* **1985**; *An Autumn's Tale/Qiu Tian de Tonghua* **1987**; *Painted Faces/Qi Xiao Fu* **1988**; *Eight Taels of Gold/Ba Liang Jin* **1989**; *Now You See Love, Now You Don't/ Wo Ai Niu Wencai* **1992**; *The Soong Sisters/Song Jia Huangchao* **1997**.

Ching Siu-tung (name in pinyin: Cheng Xiaodong), b. 1953, Hong Kong. Director and martial arts choreographer. Son of director Cheng Gang, he grew up on film sets. Received seven years' training in martial arts, and was employed by TV stations and film companies as martial arts director. Directing debut in **1983**; breakthrough film: *A Chinese Ghost Story/Qiannü Youhun* (1987). Best films so far made in collaboration with Tsui Hark (as producer).

FILMS (as director, all films also MAD): *Duel to the Death/Shengsi Jue* (also co-scr.) **1983**; *Nepal Affair* aka *Witch From Nepal/Qiyuan* **1986**; *A Chinese Ghost Story/Qiannü Youhun* **1987**; *Swordsman/Xiao'ao Jianghu* (co-dir. with King Hu, Tsui Hark, Raymond Lee), *A Terra-Cotta Warrior/Qin Yong, A Chinese Ghost Story, Part Two/Qiannü Youhun II Renjian Dao* **1990**; *The Raid/Cai Shu zhi Hengsao Qianjun* (co-dir. with Tsui Hark), *A Chinese Ghost Story, Part Three/Qiannü Youhun III Dao Dao Dao* **1991**; *Swordsman, Part Two/Xiao'ao Jianghu II Dongfang Bubai* **1992**; *Swordsman, Part Three: The East is Red/Dongfang Bubai Fengyun Zai Qi* (co-dir. with Raymond Lee), *Executioners/Xiandai Haoxia Zhuan* (co-dir. with Johnny To) **1993**; *Wonder Seven/Qi Jin Gang* **1994**; *Dr Wai in The Scripture With No Words/Maoxian Wang* **1996**.

AS MARTIAL ARTS DIRECTOR (selected films): *The Fourteen Amazons/Shisi Nü Yinghao* **1972**; *The Sword/Ming Jian, Dangerous Encounter – 1st Kind/Diyi Leixing Weixian, The Spooky Bunch/Zhuang Dao Zheng* **1980**; *Zu: Warriors From the Sacred Mountain//Xin Shushan Jianxia* **1983**; *Peking Opera Blues/Dao Ma Dan* **1986**; *A Better Tomorrow, Part Two/Yingxiong Bense Xuji* **1987**; *The Killer/Diexue Shuangxiong* 1989; *The Fun, the Luck and the Tycoon/Jixing Gongzhao* **1990**; *Justice My Foot/Shensi Guan, Royal Tramp, Parts One and Two/Luding Ji, Dragon Inn/Xin Longmen Kezhan, The Moon Warriors/Zhanshen Chuanshuo* **1992**; *City Hunter/Chengshi Lieren, The Heroic Trio/Dongfang San Xia, Future Cops/Chaoji Xuexiao Bawang, The Mad Monk/Ji Gong* **1993**; *Love on Delivery/Pohuai zhi Wang* **1994**; *Ah Kam/A Jin* **1996**.

Chor Yuen (name in pinyin: Chu Yuan), b. 1934, Guangzhou. Cantonese director (also Mandarin films in early 70s). A chemistry student at Sun Yat-sen University in Guangzhou, he entered Cantonese films in Hong Kong as a scriptwriter in 1956. Assisted director Ch'un Kim, and debuted as director in 1958. Very prolific output (mostly melodramas, comedies, parodies of spy thrillers). 1972, signed on by Shaw Brothers where he tended to specialise in martial arts flicks, making one of the best in the genre, *The Magic Blade/Tianya Mingyue Dao* (1976). Also actor, notably in Patrick Tam's *Cherie/Xue'er* (1984) and Jacky Chan's *Police Story/Jingcha Gushi*

(1985). Son of Cantonese actor Cheung Wood-yau.

FILMS (most films also scr.): *Grass by the Lake/Hupan Cao, Orchid in the Storm/Fengyu Youlan* **1959**; *Autumn Leaf/Qiufeng Canye, Parents' Love/Kelian Tianxia Fumu Xin* **1960**; *Forever Beloved/Qingtian Weilao, The Ghost That Was Not/Yeban Youling* **1961**; *True Love/Huannan Zhenqing, Eternal Regret/Niehai Yihen, A Time for Mourning/Qingming Shijie* **1962**; *My Only Love/Qing zhi Suo Zhong, The Tear Laden Rose/Hanlei de Meigui, In My Dream Last Night/Zuoye Menghun Zhong* **1963**; *Too High to Touch/Gaochu Bu Sheng Han, Diary of a Husband, Parts One and Two/Da Zhangfu Riji, A Blundering Wife/Hutu Taitai, A Secluded Orchid/Qinghai Youlan, A Deadly Night/Siwang Jiao zhi Ye, Their Lost Romance/Hun Duan Naihe Tian, A Mad Woman/Feng Fu* **1964**; *The Black Rose/Hei Meigui, Lover in Disguise/Hua Shen Qingren, Love Has Many Faces/Chun Yuan, The Sinner, Part One/Zhui Ren, Honeymoon/Miyue, Secrets of a Husband/Zhangfu de Mimi, Remorse/Yuanlai Wo Fuqing, Lost in Love/Qing Hai Mangmang, An Ocean of Love/Qing Hai Jin Zhi, Love Never Fades/Chun Can Hua Wei Luo, Doomed Love/Qing Tian Jie, Silent Love/Xiangsi Hupan* **1965**; *Affection/Qin Qing Shen Si Hai, Running Tears/Can Hua Lei, A Million Dollar Inheritance* aka *Legacy/Yichan Yibai Wan, Spy With My Face/Hei Meigui yu Hei Meigui, The Thief With the Baby Face/Zei Meiren, A Fatal Adventure/Shenmi de Xue An, Violet Girl* aka *I Love Violet/Wo Ai Zi Luolan, Little Foursome Family/Xiao Kang zhi Jia* **1966**; *The Man From Interpol/Lanse Ye Zonghui, Romance of a Teenage Girl/Shaonü Qing, Diamond Robbery/Zuanshi Da Jie An, My Darling Wife/Jiao Qi* **1967**; *Winter Love* aka *Be My Love/Dong Lian, Purple Night/Zise Fengyu Meng, Rhapsody/Qingchun Liange* **1968**; *Joys and Sorrows of Youth/Lengnuan Qingchun* (also appears to introduce film), *Wise Wives and Foolish Husbands/Congming Taitai Ben Zhangfu, The Prodigal/Langzi* **1969**; *Violet Clove and Firebird/Huoniao Diyi Hao, Dial for Murder/Luyin Ji Qingsha An, The Lost Spring/Yu Lou Chun Meng, Cold Blade/Longmu Xiang* **1970**; *Duel for Gold/Huo Ping* **1971**; *The Killer/Da Sha Shou, Intimate Confessions of a Chinese Courtesan/Ai Nu, The Lizard/Bi Hu* **1972**; *The Villains/Tu Fei, The House of 72 Tenants/Qishier Jia Fangke* **1973**, *Sex, Love and Hate/Wuyi, Hong Kong 73/Xianggang Qishisan, Sorrow of the*

Gentry/Zhumen Yuan **1974**; Lover's Destiny/Xin Tixiao Yinyuan, The Big Holdup/Da Jie An **1975**; The Forbidden Past/Xiaolou Canmeng, Killer Clans/Liuxing Hudie Jian, The Magic Blade/Tianya Mingyue Dao, The Web of Death/Wudu Tianluo, Farewell to a Warrior/Cilang Zhou **1976**; Clans of Intrigue/Chu Liuxiang, Jade Tiger/Baiyu Laohu, The Sentimental Swordsman/Duoqing Jianke Wuqing Jian **1977**; Legend of the Bat/Bianfu Chuanqi, Heaven Sword and Dragon Sabre, Parts One and Two/Yitian Tulong Ji, Swordsman and Enchantress/Xiao Shiyi Lang **1978**; Full Moon Scimitar/Yuan Yue Wan Dao, Murder Plot/Kongque Wang Chao **1979**; The Convict Killer/Chachi Nanfei, Haunted Tales/Die Xian, Bat Without Wings/Wu Yi Bianfu **1980**; Return of the Sentimental Swordsman/Mojian Xiaqing, The Emperor and His Brother/Shujian Enchou Lu, Duel of the Century/Jue Zhan Qianhou, The Black Lizard/Hei Xiyi **1981**; Perils of the Sentimental Swordsman/Youling Shanzhuang, The Spirit of the Sword/Huanhua Xijian **1982**; The Roving Swordsman/Da Xia Shen Shengyi, Descendant of the Sun/Ri Jie **1983**; Lust for Love of a Chinese Courtesan/Ai Nu Xinzhuan **1984**; Fascinating Affairs/Huaxin Hongxing, Let's Have a Baby/Tiqing Laodou **1985**; Last Song in Paris/Ouran **1986**; The Enchanting Night/Liangxiao Hua Nong Yue **1987**; The Diary of a Big Man/Da Zhangfu Riji **1988**; The Legend of Lee Heung Kwan/Li Xiangjun, Blood Stained Tradewinds/Xue Zai Feng Shang **1990**.

Chiu Shu-sun (name in pinyin: Zhao Shushen; also known as Joseph Sunn), b. 1904, in America; d. 1990. Director, producer, cinematographer. He was fond of the movies since childhood and worked as an assistant in cartoon animation films as well as a set designer. He was the founding partner of the Grandview (Daguan) Film Company in 1933 (established in San Francisco) and directed Romance of the Songsters/Gelü Qingchao starring Kwan Tak-hing (who was then touring in America) as Grandview's first production. He went to Hong Kong the following year to establish Grandview in the territory and stayed to become a key figure in the development of Hong Kong cinema in the 30s and in the post-war period (he made Hong Kong's first colour film, first 3-D film, and the first CinemaScope film). Chiu retired to America in the late 50s.

FILMS: Romance of the Songsters/Gelü Qingchao,

Fellow Sufferer/Nan Xiong (also scr.), Spoondrift Village/Langhua Cun (also scr.), Black Heart Symbol/Heixin Fu (also scr.) **1934**; Yesterday's Song/Zuori zhi Ge (also scr.), The Broken Song/Can Ge, The Fool Goes to the City/Da Sha Chu Cheng (also scr.) **1935**; The Bumbling Detective/Sha Zhentian (also scr.), Tears of the Reed Catkins/Luhua Lei, Pear Flowers Drop/Lihua Luo **1936**; The Village Woman Joins the Army/Xiangxia Po Congjun, Strange Shadows of the Deserted Village/Huangchun Guaiying, Hand-to-Hand Combat/Rou Bo, Song of Parting/Lihen Qu, Recreating the Family/Chongzuo Tianlun, 48 Hours/Sishiba Xiaoshi **1937**; Joy in the World/Putian Tongqing (also scr.), At This Crucial Moment!/Zuihou Guantou (episode only), Tears of a Mother/Cimu Lei, Four Sons Join the Army, The Wandering Father, Seven Roses/Qiduo Xian Meigui **1938**; Seven Roses, Part Two/Xu Qiduo Xian Meigui, The Coquettish Professor/Fengsao Boshi, The Big Landlord/Da Dizhu **1939**; Light of the Overseas Chinese/Huaqiao zhi Guang **1940**; The Entangling Ones/Kuangfeng Langdie (also scr.) **1946**; White Powder and Neon Lights/Jinfen Nishang (Hong Kong's first colour film), The Perfect Couple/Jiaou Tiancheng, The Great Lover/Qinghai Yingxiong (also scr.) **1947**; Romance of the Golden Country/Jinguo Qingyuan (also scr.) **1948**; Honeymoon for Two/Dongfang Yi Zuo Liang Jia Chun, Two Women After One Man/Shuang Feng Qiu Huang **1949**; The Golden Chain/Jinsuo Ji, Kaleidoscope/Renhai Wanhua Tong (episode 'Complaints/Yuantian Youren'), A Small Gift From Afar/Qianli Song Jimao **1950**; Phantom in the Limelight/Yindeng Moying **1951**; Sweet Girl and Good Car/Xiangche Meiren **1952**; Rich and Happy/Fugui Huakai Bing Dilian, Due Sim/Diao Chan (co-dir. with Chen Huanwen) **1953**; The Princess is Kidnapped/Hu Jiang Duo Huang Fei, Chang E's Flight to the Moon/Chang E Ben Yue (co-dir. with Wong Hok-sing), General Kwan Seduced by Due Sim under Moonlight (also prod., photog.) **1956**; The Eight Immortals in Jiangnan/Ba Xian Nao Jiangnan, The Hidden Dagger/Yuchang Jian (co-dir. with Wong Hok-sing, also co-scr.), General Kwan Escorts His Brother's Wife (co-dir. with Kwan Man-ching), The Goddess Who Came to Prince Xiang/Shen Nü Hui Xiang Wang **1957**; A Filial Son Meets a Fairy/Qicai Xiaozi Yu Xian Ji **1958**.

MANDARIN FILMS: Burning of the Chained Barges/Huoshao Lianhuan Chuan **1950**; A

Woman's Revenge/Yunü Qingchou (co-dir. with Chiu Shu-kin, also co-scr., Hong Kong's first 3-D movie) **1953**; *Returning the Pearl/Huan Zhu Ji, New Yu Tangchun* (Hong Kong's first CinemaScope movie), *Strayed Beauty/Liu Ying Qiu, The Long Yearning/Chang Xiangsi* **1954**; *The Life, Love and Death of Ta Chee/Da Ji, The Life, Love and Death of Yang Kwei Fei/Yang Guifei* **1955**.

Ch'un Kim (name in pinyin: Qin Jian), b. 1926, Guangdong Province, d. 1969, Hong Kong. Director, of Cantonese and Mandarin films. Entered the Cantonese film industry in 1944 as an assistant to director Wu Pang (name in pinyin: Hu Peng). Wrote first screenplay *Two Dragons Fighting For a Pearl/Erlong Zheng Zhu* in 1948 and directed his first feature the same year. A romantic artist, Ch'un was very much at home in the melodrama, some of his finest films being classic examples of the genre (*The Spirit of Azalea/Dujuan Hun, Parents' Hearts/Fumu Xin, Till the End of Time/Heri Jun Zailai*). One of the founders of the Chung-luen company, he also founded the Kwong Ngai company in 1956. He switched almost exclusively to Mandarin features in 1964, joining Shaw Brothers in 1965. Married actress Lin Cui in 1959, later divorced. Committed suicide in 1969.

CANTONESE FILMS: *Love is Severed Before Beauty Withers/Hongyan Weilao En Xian Duan* (co-dir. with Ng Wui, also co-scr.) **1948**; *Red-Brimmed River/Man Jiang Hong* (also scr.) **1949**; *Abandoned Woman of a Rich Family/Haomen Qi Fu, Girl Minstrel/Tianya Genü, Fishermen's Song of Nanhai/Nanhai Yu Ge* **1950**; *Weep for the Fallen Petals/Qi Can Hong, Infancy/Ren zhi Cu* (also scr.), *The Singing Girl's Spirit/Geyuan Xianghun, Five Sisters/Wu Zimei* (also scr.), *An Unhappy Woman's Love Song/Yuan Fu Qing Ge* (also scr.), *Autumn Tombs/Qiu Fen* **1951**; *The Satisfactory Wedding/Luanfeng Heming, A Bright Future/Jinxiu Qiancheng, Sisters Two/Zimei Hua, Life of Little Star/Xiao Mingxing Zhuan, Sister-in-Law in Danger/Xin Gusao Jie, Red Rose, the Songstress/Genü Hong Meigui, A Melancholy Melody, Parts One and Two/Gesheng Leiying* **1952**; *At Odds With Each Other/Tiecuo Menshen, The Temporary Wife/Kechuan Furen, The Sisters' Tragic Love/Qingjie Zimei Hua* (also scr.), *The Guiding Light/Kuhai Mingdeng, A Mother's Tears/Cimu Lei* (also scr.) **1953**; *Like the Cloud's Swift Passage/Liushui Xingyun, Autumn/Qiu* (also scr.), *This Wonderful*

Life/Jinxiu Rensheng (co-dir.), *Neighbours All/Jia Jia Hu Hu, The Spirit of Azalea/Dujuan Hua,* **1954**; *Love/Ai* (episode; in two parts co-dir. with others), *The Famous Beauty/Yidai Minghua, Parents' Hearts/Fumu Xin* (also scr.), *The More the Merrier aka We Owe It to Our Children/Ernü Zhai* **1955**; *Rouge Tigress/Yanzhi Hu, Lovelorn Monk's Visit to the Bamboo Lodge/Qingseng Toudao Xiaoxiang Guan, Dial 999 For Murder/999 Ming An, The Posthumous Child, Parts One and Two/Yi Fu Zi, The Newlyweds/Xinhun Fuqi* **1956**; *Bloodshed in the Valley of Love/Xueran Xiangsi Gu* (also scr.), *The Whispering Palms/Yelin Ye* (also scr.), *The Weeping Ghost /Gui Ye Ku* (also co-scr.) **1957**; *Those in Love/Youqing Ren* (also scr.), *Tears of the Flower/Xian Hua Can Lei* (also scr.), *Autumn Comes to Purple Rose Garden/Ziwei Yuan de Qiu Tian* **1958**; *Two Happy Couples/Huanxi Yuanjia, Her Last Gift/Qingtian Xuelei* (also scr.), *The Romantic Criminal/Qing Fan* **1959**; *Intimate Partners/Nanxiong Nandi, Blossom in Rainy May, Parts One and Two/Wu Yue Yu Zhong Hua* **1960**; *How to Get a Wife/Zhui Qi Ji* **1961**; *Between Hate and Love/Enyuan Qingtian* (co-scr.) **1963**; *The Beau/Huahua Gongzi* **1964**; *The Secret of Marriage/Jiehun de Mimi* **1965**.

MANDARIN FILMS: *Children's Hearts/Nüer Xin* **1954**; *The Big Circus/Da Maxi Tuan* **1964**; *The Story of Mini – Private Eye/Hutu Nü Zhentan, Pink Tears/Chiqing Lei* (also scr.) **1965**; *Till the End of Time/Heri Jun Zailai* (also scr.), *Rose Be My Love/Meigui Wo Ai Ni* **1966**; *Four Sisters/Dailu Nianhua* **1967**; *Three Swinging Girls/San Yan Ying Chun* **1968**; *Unfinished Melody/Bihai Qingtian Yeye Xin, Farewell My Love/Chun Can, River of Tears/Xiangsi Hepan* **1969**; *Double Bliss/Shuang Xi Lingmen* **1970**.

Allen Fong (name in pinyin: Fang Yuping; name in Cantonese: Fong Yuk-ping), b. 1947, Hong Kong. New wave director. After studies in US (1971–75), joins RTHK, directing outstanding realist works *Wild Child/Ye Haizi* and *The Song of Yuen Chau-chai/Yuanzhou Zai zhi Ge*, for the series *Below the Lion Rock/Shizi Shanxia* in 1977. Film debut with excellent melodrama *Father and Son/Fuzi Qing* in 1981. Has stuck since to realist, documentary-style format in his feature films. Also actor, appearing in Tsui Hark's *Shanghai Blues/Shanghai zhi Ye* (1984) and Wayne Wang's *Life is Cheap . . . but Toilet Paper is Expensive* (1990). Has directed for theatre and television.

FILMS: *Father and Son/Fuzi Qing* **1981**; *Ah*

Ying/Banbian Ren **1982**; *Just Like Weather/Meiguo Xin* (also appears in film) 1986; *Dancing Bull/Wu Niu* **1990**; *A Little Life Opera* **1997**.

Eddie Fong (name in pinyin: Fang Lingzheng; name in Cantonese: Fong Ling-ching), b. 1954, Hong Kong. Writer-director. He dabbled in experimental film-making before pursuing a professional career as writer for TV and films. Feature film debut as director in 1984 with *An Amorous Woman of the Tang Dynasty/Tang Chao Haofang Nü*, a remarkable piece of Hong Kong erotica. Has alternated as writer and director, but increasingly more in partnership with wife Clara Law (writing her screenplays and acting as producer on some of her films).

FILMS: *An Amorous Woman of the Tang Dynasty/Tang Chao Haofang Nü* (also co-scr.) **1984**; *Cherry Blossoms/Yu Dafu Zhuan* (also scr.) **1985**; *Kawashima Yoshiko* aka *The Last Princess of Manchuria/Chuandao Fangzi* **1990**; *Private Eye Blues/Feichang Zhentan* (also scr., ed.) **1994**.
AS WRITER: *Coolie Killer/Sha Chu Xiying Pan* (co-scr.) **1982**; *Nomad/Liehuo Qingchun* (co-scr.) **1983**; *Double Decker/Sanwenzhi* (co-scr.) **1984**; *Lai Shi, China's Last Eunuch/Zhongguo Zuihou de Yige Taijian*, *The Other Half and the Other Half/Wo Ai Taikong Ren* (also prod.), *Love Me and Dad/Youjian Yuanjia* (co-scr.) **1988**; *A Fishy Story/Bu Tuo Wa de Ren* (co-scr.) **1989**; *Farewell China/Ai Zai Bie Xiang de Jijie* **1990**; *Fruit Punch/Yes Yizu* **1991**; *Autumn Moon/Qiu Yue* **1992**; *Temptations of a Monk/You Seng* (co-scr.) **1993**; *Floating Life* (Australia) **1996**.

King Hu (name in pinyin: Hu Jinquan), b. 1931, Peking, d. 14 January 1997, Taipei. Seminal director of martial arts genre. Childhood and education (art school) in Peking. In Hong Kong in 1949; entered film industry in 1951 working for Long Ma and Great Wall in art department. Started acting in mid-50s. In 1958, joined Shaw Brothers as actor (billed as Jin Quan or 'King Chuan'), writer, and later, director, scoring success with swordfighting picture *Come Drink With Me/Da Zui Xia* (1966). Left Shaws for Taiwan to make *Dragon Inn/Longmen Kezhan*, which became top box-office draw in Taiwan, Hong Kong and S. E. Asia. International art-house success with *A Touch of Zen/Xia Nü*, winning a prize at 1975 Cannes Film Festival. Latter career

more erratic and less remarkable, taking in costumed ghost stories and modern-day comedy. Walked out of supposed comeback movie *Swordsman/Xiao'ao Jianghu* (1990).

FILMS (from 1965 onwards also scr.): *The Love Eterne/Liang Shanbo yu Zhu Yingtai* (co-dir. with Li Hanxiang) **1963**; *The Story of Sue San/Yu Tang Chun* (credited as 'executive director', direction supervised by Li Hanxiang) **1964**; *Sons of the Good Earth/Da Di Ernü* (also act.) **1965**; *Come Drink With Me/Da Zui Xia* **1966**; (IN TAIWAN) *Dragon Inn/Long Men Kezhan* (also co-prod. design) **1967**; *A Touch of Zen/Xia Nü* (also co-prod. design, ed.), *Anger/Nu* (episode in 'The Four Moods/Xi Nu Ai Le') **1970**; (IN HONG KONG) *The Fate of Lee Khan/Yingchun Ge zhi Fengbo* (also prod. design, exec. prod.) **1974**; *The Valiant Ones/Zhonglie Tu* (also prod. design, exec. prod.) **1975**; *Legend of the Mountain/Shanzhong Chuanqi* (scr. by Zhong Ling; also prod. design, ed.), *Raining in the Mountain/Kongshan Lingyu* (also prod. design, co-ed.) **1979**; (IN TAIWAN) *The Juvenizer/Zhongshen Dashi* (scr. Zhong Ling) **1981**; *All the King's Men/Tianxia Diyi* (also costumes), *The Wheel of Life/Da Lunhi* (directed first episode only) **1983**; (IN HONG KONG) *Swordsman/Xiao'ao Jianghu* (began film but left production, retains co-dir. credit with Tsui Hark, Raymond Lee, Ching Siu-tung) **1990**; (IN CHINA) *The Painted Skin/Huapi zhi Yinyang Fa Wang* **1993**.
AS ACTOR (selected films): *Red Bloom in the Snow/Xueli Hong*, *Golden Phoenix/Jin Feng*, *The Long Lane/Chang Xiang* **1956**; *A Mating Story/Yaotiao Shunü*, *Sisters Three/San Zimei*, *Little Angel of the Streets/Malu Xiao Tianshi*, *Frosty Night/Yue Luo Niao Ti Shuang Mantian* **1957**; *Laughter and Tears/Xiaosheng Leiying*, *Little Darling/Xiao Qingren*, *Young Shoe-shiners/Chaxie Tong*, *The Angel/Anqi'er*, *The Blessed Family/Quanjia Fu*, *The Magic Touch/Miaoshou Hui Chun* **1958**; *The Kingdom and the Beauty/Jiangshan Meiren* **1959**; *The Deformed/Jiren Yanfu*, *How to Marry a Millionaire/Kuang Lian*, *When the Peach Blossoms Bloom/Yishu Taohua Qianduo Hong* **1960**; *The Swallow/Yanzi Dao*, *Kiss For Sale/Maiwen Ji*, *The Girl Next Door/Geqiang Yanshi*, *The Fair Sex/Shenxian Laohu* **1961**; *The Love Parade/Huatuan Jincu*, *The Empress Wu/Wu Zetian* **1963**; *The Dancing Millionairess/Wanhua Yingchun* **1964**.

Ann Hui (name in pinyin: Xu Anhua; name in Cantonese Hui On-wah), b. 1947,

265

Liaoning Province. New Wave director. An assured stylist with a 'no frills' mentality; a graduate of London Film School. Worked as assistant to King Hu on return to Hong Kong. Career in TV between 1975-79, making among other films, *The Boy From Vietnam/Lai Ke* (1978), the first of her avowed 'Vietnamese trilogy' including her two feature films *The Story of Woo Viet/Hu Yue de Gushi* (1981) and *The Boat People/Touben Nuhai* (1982).

FILMS: *The Secret/Feng Jie* **1979**; *The Spooky Bunch/Zhuang Dao Zheng* **1980**; *The Story of Woo Viet/Hu Yue de Gushi* **1981**; *The Boat People/Touben Nuhai* **1982**; *Love in a Fallen City/Qingcheng zhi Lian* **1984**; *Romance of Book and Sword, Parts One and Two/Shujian Enchou Lu* (Part Two released under the title 'Princess Fragrance/Xiangxiang Gongzhu') **1987**; *Starry is the Night/Jinye Xingguang Canlan* **1988**; *Song of the Exile/Ketu Qiuhen* **1990**; *My American Grandson/Shanghai Jiaqi, The Zodiac Killers/Jidao Zhuizong* **1991**; *Summer Snow/Nüren Sishi* **1995**; *Ah Kam/A Jin* **1996**.

Michael Hui (name in pinyin: Xu Guanwen; name in Cantonese: Hui Kun-man), b. 1942, Guangdong Province. Cantonese comedian, popular on TV before making film acting debut in Li Hanxiang's *The Warlord/Da Junfa* (1972). Teaming up with brother Sam Hui, forms Hui Brothers Production Company in 1974 and signs co-production deal with Golden Harvest, making his famous series of self-directed comedies beginning with *Games Gamblers Play/Guima Shuangxing* (1975). Funny, even in rickety vehicles (often directed by others).

FILMS (all also act. and scr.): *Games Gamblers Play/Guima Shuangxing, The Last Message/Tianchai yu Baichi* **1975**; *The Private Eyes/Banjin Baliang* **1976**; *The Contract/Maishen Qi* **1978**; *Security Unlimited/Modeng Baobiao* **1981**; *The Trail/Zhui Gui Qi Xiong* (exec. prod. and scr. only) **1983**; *Teppanyaki/Tieban Shao* **1984**; *Happy Ding Dong/Huanle Dingdang* **1986**; *The Magic Touch/Shen Suan* **1991**. AS ACTOR: *The Warlord/Da Junfa* **1972**; *The Happiest Moment/Yi Le Ye* **1973**; *Scandal/Chouwen, Sinful Confessions/Sheng Si Quan Ma* **1974**; *Cannonball Run* (in US) **1981**; *Mr. Boo Meets Pom Pom/Zhiyong Sanbao* **1985**; *Inspector Chocolate/Shentan Zhu Guli* (also co-scr.) **1986**; *Chicken and Duck Talk/Ji Tong Ya Jiang* (also co-scr.) **1988**; *Mr.*

Coconut/Hejia Huan (also co-scr.) **1989**, *The Front Page/Xin Banjin Baliang* (also co-scr.) **1990**; *The Banquet/Haomen Yeyan* (cameo) **1991**; *Hero of the Beggars/Qigai Yingxiong* **1992**; *Always on My Mind/Qiangqian Fuqi* **1993**; *World of Treasure/Fugui Renjian* **1995**.

Sammo Hung (name in pinyin: Hong Jinbao; name in Cantonese: Hung Kam-bo), credited in early 70s as Zhu Yuanlong, b. 1950, Hong Kong. Kung fu actor-director; also martial arts director (with his own stunt team known as 'Hung Kar Ban'). One of the 'Seven Little Fortunes' in youth (cf. entry on Jacky Chan), who got into films through his expertise in martial arts. First appearance in the Mandarin film, *Education of Love/Ai de Jiaoyu* (1961). In the 1970s, choreographed martial arts action sequences for Bruce Lee, King Hu, John Woo. Directed first feature in 1977. Has occasionally acted in non-kung fu parts (most successfully in Alfred Cheung's *To Err is Humane/Biao Cuo Shen* and Mabel Cheung's *Eight Taels of Gold/Baliang Jin*). His weighty bulk has obviously not been an impediment to his doing strenuous kung fu stunts in the tradition of his colleague Jacky Chan. Has his own production company, Bo Ho Films; credited as executive producer on the *Mr. Vampire* series.

FILMS: *The Iron-Fisted Monk/Sande Heshang yu Zhuangmi Liu* (also act., MAD) **1977**; *Enter the Fat Dragon/Feilong Guojiang* (also act.), *Warriors Two/Zan Xiansheng yu Zhaoqian Hua* (also act. MAD) **1978**; *Knockabout/Zajia Xiaozi* (also act.) **1979**; *The Victim/Shen Bu You Ji* (also act.), *Encounter of the Spooky Kind/Gui Da Gui* (also act.) **1980**; *The Prodigal Son/Baijia Zai* (also act., co-scr.) **1981**; *Carry on Pickpocket/Tifang Xiaoshou* (also act.) **1982**; *Winners and Sinners/Qimou Miaoji Wu Fuxing* (also co-scr., act.) **1983**; *Wheels on Meals/Kuai Can Che* (also act.), *The Owl and Bumbo/Maotou Ying yu Xiao Feixiang* (also act.) **1984**; *My Lucky Stars/Fuxing Gaozhao* (also act.), *Twinkle Twinkle Little Star/Xiari Fuxing* (also act.), *Heart of the Dragon/Long de Xin* (also act.) **1985**; *The Millionaires' Express/Fugui Lieche* (also act.) **1986**; *Eastern Condors/Dongfang Tuying* (also act., co-MAD) **1987**; *Dragons Forever/Feilong Mengjiang* (also act.), *Spooky/Gui Meng Jiao* **1988**; *Pedicab Driver/Qunlong Xifeng* (also act.) **1989**; *Panty Hose Heroes/Zhifen Shuangxiong* (also prod., act.) **1990**; *Slicker Vs. Killer/Xianzhen Bianren* (also act.) **1991**; *Ghost Punting/Wu Fuxing*

Zhuang Gui (co-dir., also act.), *The Moon Warriors/Zhanshen Chuanshuo* 1992; *Blade of Fury/Yi Dao Qing Cheng* (also act.) 1993; *Don't Give a Damn/Mei Gei Mian* (also act.) 1995; *Mr. Nice Guy/Yige Hao Ren, Once Upon a Time in China and America/Huang Feihong zhi Xiyu Hongshi* 1997.

AS ACTOR: *Education of Love/Ai de Jiaoyu* 1961; *The Princess and the Seven Little Heroes/Gongzhu yu Qi Xiaoxia* 1962; *Father and Son/Ren zhi Cu* 1963; *A Touch of Zen/Xia Nü* 1970; *Lady Whirlwind/Tiezhang Xuanfeng Tui* (also MAD) 1972; *Enter the Dragon/Longzheng Hudou* 1973; *The Skyhawk/Huang Feihong Shaolin Quan* (also MAD) 1974; *The Valiant Ones/Zhonglie Tu* (also co-MAD), *Countdown in Kung Fu* aka *Hand of Death/Shaolin Men* (also MAD) 1975; *The Himalayan/Mizong Shengshou* (also co-MAD) 1976; *Winner Takes All/Mianmeng Xinjing* 1977; *Game of Death/Siwang Youxi* (also co-MAD), *Dirty Tiger, Crazy Frog/Laohu Tianji* (also prod., co-MAD) 1978; *The Incredible Kung Fu Master/Xingmu Zai Guhuo Zhao, Odd Couple/Duoming Dandao Duoming Qiang, The Magnificent Butcher/Lin Shirong* 1979; *The Dead and the Deadly/Ren Xia Ren* (also co-scr.) 1982; *Zu: Warriors From the Magic Mountain/Xin Shu Shan Jianxia, Project A/A Jihua* 1983; *Where's Officer Tuba?/Pili Da Laba, Lucky Stars Go Places/Zuijia Fuxing* 1986; *To Err is Humane/Biao Cuo Shen* 1987; *Lai Shi, China's Last Eunuch/Zhongguo Zuihou Yige Taijian* (also prod.), *Paper Marriage/Guofu Xinniang, Painted Faces/Qi Xiao Fu* 1988; *Eight Taels of Gold/Baliang Jin* 1989; *The Fortune Code/Fugui Bingtuan, Shanghai, Shanghai/Luanshi Ernü, Encounter of the Spooky Kind, Part Two/Gui Yao Gui, Skinny Tiger and Fatty Dragon/Shouhu Feilong* 1990; *The Gambling Ghost/Hongfu Qitian, Touch and Go/Yichu Jifa, Island of Fire/Huo Shao Dao* (Taiwan), *My Flying Wife/Menggui Ruqin Hei Shehui, The Banquet/Haomen Yeyan* (cameo), *Daddy, Father and Papa/Laodou Bupa Duo* 1991; *Lover's Tear/Shi Bu Wang Qing* 1992; *The Painted Skin/Hua Pi zhi Yinyang Fawang, The Kung Fu Cult Master/Yitian Tulong Ji zhi Mojiao Jiaozhu* (alsoMAD) 1993.

AS MARTIAL ARTS DIRECTOR: *The Fast Sword/Duoming Jinjian* 1971; *Hap-Ki-do/He Qi Dao* 1972; *When Taekwondo Strikes/Taiquan Zhen Jiu Zhou, The Fate of Lee Khan/Yingchun Ge zhi Fengbo* 1973; *The Manchu Boxer/Qi Sheng Quan Wang, The Tournament/Zhong Tai Quantan Shengsi Zhan* 1974; *The Dragon Tamers/Nüzi Taiquan*

Qunying Hui 1975; *Drunken Master/Zui Quan* (co-MAD) 1978; *Dongcheng Xijiu* 1993; *Ashes of Time/Dongxie Xidu* 1994.

Clifton Ko (name in pinyin: Gao Zhisen; name in Cantonese: Ko Chi-sum), b. 1958, Zhongshan, Guangdong Province. Director, writer. Television career (as writer and producer) followed his graduation from Hong Kong's Maryknoll College. He first worked in films in 1979, as a screenwriter. Joined Cinema City in 1982 and made his directing debut in 1984. Established his own production company in 1989. Ko's films are mainly lightweight affairs but he scored hits with *Chicken and Duck Talk/Ji Tong Ya Jiang* (1988), *Mr. Coconut/Hejia Huan* (1989) both starring Michael Hui; and the Chinese New Year movie *All's Well, Ends Well/Jia You Xishi* (1992).

FILMS: *The Happy Ghost/Kaixin Gui* (also co-scr.) 1984; *Merry Christmas/Shengdan Kuaile* (also co-scr.), *The Happy Ghost, Part Two/Kaixin Gui Fang Shujia* (also co-scr.) 1985; *Devoted to You/Chixin de Wo* (also scr.) 1986; *It's a Mad, Mad World/Fugui Biren* (also scr.), *Porky Meatballs/Guima Xiaoyuan* (also co-scr.) 1987; *It's a Mad, Mad World, Part Two/Fugui Zai Biren, Chicken and Duck Talk/Ji Tong Ya Jiang* (also co-scr.) 1988; *Mr. Coconut/Hejia Huan* (also co-scr.), *How To Be a Millionaire/Fada Miji* (co-dir. with Raymond Wong, also co-scr., co-prod.), *City Squeeze/Touqing Xiansheng* (also prod.) 1989; *The Happy Ghost, Part Four/Kaixin Gui Jiu Kaixin Gui* 1990; *The Gambling Ghost/Hongfu Qitian* (also prod.), *The Banquet/Haomen Yeyan* (co-dir., also co-scr.), *Daddy, Father and Papa/Laodou Bu Pa Duo* (also prod.) 1991; *All's Well, Ends Well/Jia You Xishi* (also prod.), *It's a Mad, Mad World Too/Fugui Huangjin Wu* (also prod.), *Summer Lovers/Xiari Qingren* (also prod.) 1992; *All's Well, End's Well Too/Huatian Xishi* (also co-scr.), *Laughter of Water Margin/Shuihu Xiaozhuan* 1993; *It's a Wonderful Life/Dafu zhi Jia, I Will Wait For You/Nian Nian You Jin Ri, I Have a Date With Spring/Wo He Chuntian You Ge Yuehui* (also prod.), *One of the Lucky Ones/Ban Wo Tongxing* (also ed.) 1994; *The Umbrella Story/Renjian You Qing, Paradise Hotel/Toucuo Geqiang Hua* 1995; *The Legend of the Mad Phoenix/Nanhai Shisan Lang* 1997.

Kwan Man-ching (name in pinyin: Guan Wenqing; also known as Moon Kwan), b. 1896, Guangdong Province, d. 1995.

267

Cantonese director. In America at an early age, Kwan hung around Hollywood after graduating from the University of California, eventually becoming the film colony's resident Chinese expert (advising Griffith on *Broken Blossoms*). In China in 1921, joining the Minxin Film Company, assisting on Li Minwei's *Lipstick/Yanzhi* (1925), and the company's documentary projects. Kwan became a director in 1926 in Guangzhou. In the early 30s, he worked for Shanghai's Lianhua studio and was associated with Chiu Shu-sun, his partner in the Grandview (Daguan) prodution company in Hong Kong. Much of their output in this period is considered lost. Continued directing in Hong Kong after the war. Author of an autobiograhy-cum-history entitled *A History of the Chinese Silver Screen/Zhongguo Yintan Waishi,* published (in Chinese) in Hong Kong, 1976.

CANTONESE FILMS: *Iron Bones and Heart of Orchid/Tiegu Lanxin* **1931**; *Midnight Shot/Yeban Qiangsheng* (silent) **1932**; *Pearl Shines in a Dark Room/Anshi Mingzhu* (also scr.) **1933**; *Broken Waves/Po Lang* (also scr.) **1934**; *Modern Miss/Modeng Xinniang* (also scr.), *Lifeline/Shengming Xian* (also scr.) **1935**; *Bandits of Shantung/Shandong Xiangma* (also scr.), *Gossip is Fearful/Renyan Kewei* (also scr.), *Resistance/Dikang* (also scr.), *Blood Money/Xue Sa Jinqian* **1936**; *Lady of West Lake/Xi Hu Nü* (also scr.), *Modern Warrior/Modeng Wu Dalang* (also scr.), *The Mad Director/Kuang Daoyan* (also scr.), *Tragedy at the Border/Bianfang Xuelei* (also scr.), *It's Life/Ruci Renjian* **1937**; *Public Enemy/Gong Di* (also scr.), *Gold Leaf Chrysanthemum/Jin Ye Ju* (also scr.), *Yan Ruisheng* (also scr.), *Chaimi Fuqi/The Fuel and Rice Couple* **1938**; *The Powder and Lipstick General/Zhifen Jiangjun, Tenth Madam Du Sinks the Hundred Treasure Chest/Du Shiniang Nu Chen Baibao Xiang* (also scr.), *The Sister's Grave/Gusao Fen* **1939**; *Tear of the Returned One/Fuyuan Lei* **1947**; *New Life/Xin Shengming Xian, The Groom and His Double/Zhenjia Xinlang* (also scr.), *The Lusty Thief Girl/Fengliu Nü Zei, Mr. Canton Exposes The Corrupted Temple/Guangdong Xiansheng Dapo Mouren Si* (also scr.), *Second Attempt/Zai Zhe Chang Ting Liu* (co-dir., also co-scr.) **1948**; *Third Madame Educating Her Son/San Niang Jiao Zi* **1949**; *The Rude Monk's Intrusion into Mount Wutai/Hua Heshang Da Nao Wutai Shan, Sorrows of a Neglected Wife/Lengluo Duanchang Hua* **1950**; *An Orphan's Sad Tale/Guchu Lei, Poor*

Mother/Nanwei Le Mama **1951**; *Between Her Own and the Concubine's Children/Di Shu zhi Jian Nan Wei Mu, Wealth Gone Like a Dream/Shi Zai Fanhua Yimeng Xiao, Daughter of a Humble House/Fengmen Xiao Feng* **1952**; *Flight of the Swallow/Li Chao Yan, The Crushed Flower/Canhua Lei* **1953**; *Tragedy of Divorce/Lihun Lei, Spring's Flight/Luohua Liushui, Orchid of the Valley/Kong Gu Lan* **1954**; *Romance in the West Chamber/Chunse Man Xi Xiang, Mystery of the Human Head/Rentou Qi An, Is Parents' Love Ever Rewarded?/Zhan Qian Di Shui* (also co-scr.) **1955**; *Filial Piety/Xiao Dao, General Kwan Seduced by Due Sim Under Moonlight/Guan Gong Yuexia Shi Diao Chan* (co-dir. with Chiu Shu-sun) **1956**; *General Kwan Escorts His Brother's Wife/Guan Gong Qianli Song Sao* (co-dir. with Chiu Shu-sun) **1957**; *An Immortal Refuses Love/Han Xiangzi Xueye Guo Qingguan* **1958**; *Poor Mother/Kelian de Mama* (also scr.) **1961**; *Girl in Danger/Weichao Xiaofeng* **1962**; *To Catch a Thief/Chali Zhuo Mao Ji* (also scr.) **1969**.

Stanley Kwan (name in pinyin: Guan Jinpeng; name in Cantonese: Kwan Kum-pang), b. 1957, Hong Kong. Second Wave director. Entered film industry by assisting Ann Hui, Tony Au, Patrick Tam, Leong Po-chih and others, after leaving HK-TVB in 1979. Became director in 1984, achieving international acclaim with *Rouge/Yanzhi Kou* (1988) and *Centre Stage/Ruan Lingyu* (1991).

FILMS: *Women/Nüren Xin* **1984**; *Love Unto Waste/Dixia Qing* **1986**; *Rouge/Yanzhi Kou* **1988**; *Full Moon in New York/Ren Zai Niu Yue* **1989**; *Centre Stage aka Actress/Ruan Lingyu* (also appears in film) **1991**; *Too Happy For Words/Liang Ge Nüren* (short) **1992**; *Red Rose White Rose/Hong Meigui Bai Meigui* **1994**.

Ringo Lam (name in pinyin: Lin Lingdong; name in Cantonese: Lam Leng-tung), b. 1955, Hong Kong. Director of the tough action school, whose stylish 1980s thrillers (*City on Fire/Longhu Fengyun, Prison on Fire/Jianyu Fengyun),* and subsequent movies, such as 1992's *Full Contact/Xia Dao Gao Fei* (starring Chow Yun-fat), although no less powerful, have been somewhat overshadowed by John Woo's films. Early career in HK-TVB. In Canada in the late 1970s, graduating from film studies at York University. On return to Hong Kong, helmed first feature in 1983. Quentin

Tarantino's *Reservoir Dogs* was re-worked from Lam's *City on Fire*.

FILMS: *Esprit d'Amour/Yinyang Cuo* **1983**; *The Other Side of Gentleman/Junzi Hao Qiu* **1984**; *Cupid One/Aishen Yihao* **1985**; *Aces Go Places, Part Four/Zuijia Paidang zhi Qianli Jiu Caipo* **1986**; *City on Fire/Longhu Fengyun, Prison on Fire/Jianyu Fengyun* **1987**; *School on Fire/Xuexiao Fengyun* **1988**; *Wild Search/Ban Wo Chuang Tianya* (also prod.) **1989**; *The Undeclared War/Shengzhan Fengyun, Rebel From China/Yongchuang Tianxia* (prod. only) **1990**; *Touch and Go/Yichu Ji Fa, Prison On Fire, Part Two/Jianyu Fengyun II Tao Fan* **1991**; *The Twin Dragons/Shuanglong Hui* (co-dir. with Tsui Hark), *Full Contact/Xia Dao Gao Fei* (also prod.) **1992**; *Burning Paradise/Huoshao Honglian Si* **1994**; *The Adventurers/Da Maoxian Jia* **1995**; (IN US) *Maximum Risk* **1997**.

Lau Kar-leong (name in pinyin: Liu Jialiang), b. 1935, Guangdong Province. One of the best post-Bruce Lee kung fu action directors. In Hong Kong in 1948, his background as kung fu artist (coached by his father) led to career as bit player and stuntman in Cantonese Wong Fei-hung serials of the 1950s and 1960s, then as martial arts director in 1960s, mainly on Zhang Che pictures. Switched to directing in 1975, making kung fu masterpiece *Dirty Ho/Lantou He* four years later. Brilliant action choreographer, and director of substance (in his best kung fu pictures). Also actor.

FILMS (as director, all films also MAD or co-dir.): *The Spiritual Boxer/Shen Da* **1975**; *Challenge of the Masters/Lu Acai yu Huang Feihong* **1976**; *Executioners From Shaolin/Hong Xiguan* **1977**; *36th Chamber of Shaolin/Shaolin Sanshiliu Fang, The Shaolin Mantis/Tanglang, Shaolin Challenges Ninja* (aka *Heroes of the East*)/*Zhonghua Zhangfu* **1978**; *The Spiritual Boxer, Part II/Maoshan Jiangshi Quan, Dirty Ho/Lantou He, Mad Monkey Kung Fu/Feng Hou* (also act.) **1979**; *Return to the 36th Chamber/Shaolin Dapeng Dashi, My Young Auntie/Zhang Bei* (also co-scr., act.), *Carry On Wise Guy/Pojie Dashi* (co-dir. under name of 'Kung Fu Leong') **1980**; *Martial Club/Wu Guan* **1981**; *Legendary Weapons of China/Shiba Ban Wuyi* (also scr., act.), *Cat vs. Rat/Yu Mao San Xi Jin Maoshu* **1982**; *The Lady is the Boss/Zhangmen Ren* (also co-scr., act.), *Shaolin and Wu Tang/Shaolin yu Wudang* (supervisory dir. under name of 'Kung Fu Leong', dir. by Lau Kar-fai) **1983**;

The Eight Diagram Pole Fighter/Wulang Bagua Gun (also co-scr., act.) **1984**; *Disciple of 36th Chamber/Bili Shijie* (also scr.) **1985**; *Martial Arts of Shaolin/Nanbei Shaolin* **1986**; *Tiger on Beat/Laohu Chugeng* **1988**, *Aces Go Places V/Zuijia Paidang Di Wu Ji* **1989**; *Tiger on Beat, Part Two/Laohu Chugeng II* **1990**; *Drunken Master, Part Two/Zui Quan II* (also act.), *Drunken Master, Part Three/Zui Quan III* (also act.) **1994**.

AS MARTIAL ARTS DIR., up to 1975 in partnership with Tong Kai (name in pinyin: Tang Jia): *South Dragon, North Phoenix/Nanlong Beifeng* **1963**; *Temple of the Red Lotus/Jianghu Qixia* **1965**; *The Jade Bow/Yunhai Yugong Yuan, The Magnificent Trio/Biancheng Sanxia* **1966**; *The Sword and the Lute/Qin Jian Enchou, The One-Armed Swordsman/Dubi Dao* **1967**; *The Golden Swallow/Jin Yanzi, The Tin Long Gang/Tianlang Zhai* **1968**; *Return of the One-Armed Swordsman/Dubi Daowang, The Invincible Fist/Tieshou Wuqing, Have Sword Will Travel/Baobiao* **1969**; *The Wandering Swordsman/You Xiaer, Vengeance/Baochou, The Heroic Ones/Shisan Taibao, The Singing Killer/Xiao Shaxing* **1970**; *King Eagle/Ying Wang, The Duel/Da Juedou, The Deadly Duo/Shuang Xia* **1971**; *The Boxer From Shantung/Ma Yongzhen, Trilogy of Swordsmanship/Qunying Hui, Man of Iron/Chou Lianhuan* **1972**; *Blood Brothers/Ci Ma* **1973**; *Heroes Two/Fang Shiyu yu Hong Xiguan, Men From the Monastery/Shaolin Zidi, Shaolin Martial Arts/Hong Quan yu Yong Chun, Five Shaolin Masters/Shaolin Wuzu* **1974**; *Disciples of Shaolin/Hong Quan Xiaozi, Marco Polo/Mage Bolo* **1975**; *Dirty Kung Fu/Guima Gongfu* **1978**; *Fists and Guts/Yi Dan, Er Li, San Gongfu* **1979**; *Clan of the White Lotus/Hong Wending Sanpo Bailian Jiao* **1980**; *The Barefooted Kid/Chijiao Xiaozi* **1993**.

Clara Law (name in pinyin: Luo Zhuoyao; name in Cantonese: Law Cheuk-yiu), b. Macao. Sensitive director of the Second Wave. A graduate of Britain's National Film School (1982-85). Has been associated with husband Eddie Fong (who has written all her screenplays and overseen the production of some of her films) since the start of her film career.

FILMS: *The Other Half and the Other Half/Wo Ai Taikong Ren* **1988**; *The Reincarnation of Golden Lotus/Pan Jinlian zhi Qianshi Jinsheng* **1989**; *Farewell China/Ai Zai Bie Xiang de Jijie* **1990**; *Fruit Punch/Yes Yizu* **1991**; *Autumn Moon/Qiu Yue* **1992**; *Temptations of a*

Monk/You Seng **1993**; *Erotique* (episode 'Wanton Soup') **1994**; *Floating Life* (Australia) **1996**.

Bruce Lee (name in pinyin: Li Xiaolong; name in Cantonese: Lee Siu-lung), b. 1940, San Francisco; d. 1973, Hong Kong. Kung fu superstar, perhaps the most highly skilled and graceful of all kung fu artists who made it to the screen. He started his career as a child actor, making his film debut at the age of three months (in *Golden Gate Girl/Jinmen Nü*, starring his father Lee Hoi-chuen, a Cantonese opera clown). After starring in Lee Sun-fung's *The Orphan/Renhai Guhong* (1960), he returned to the US in 1959 to resume his education. First presented his own kung fu technique of Jeet Kune Do in 1964 at the Karate World Championship in California, leading to TV career in Hollywood in *Green Hornet* and other series. In Hong Kong again in 1971, to make *The Big Boss/Tang Shan Da Xiong*. Directed *The Way of the Dragon/Menglong Guo Jiang* (1973) and began *Game of Death/Siwang Youxi*, shortly before his death (filmed footage later incorporated into movie concoction of same title but having no relationship with original project).

FILMS: (IN HONG KONG) *Wealth is Like a Dream/Fugui Fuyun* **1948**; *The Kid/Xilu Xiang* **1950**; *Infancy/Ren zhi Cu* **1951**; *The Guiding Light/Kuhai Mingdeng, A Mother's Tears/Cimu Lei, Blame it On Father/Fu zhi Guo, A Myriad Homes/Qianwan Renjia, In the Face of Demolition/Weilou Chun Xiao* **1953**; *Love, Part Two/Ai, Xia Ji, An Orphan's Tragedy/Guxing Xuelei, Orphan's Song/Guer Xing, The More The Merrier* aka *We Owe It To Our Children/Ernü Zhai* **1955**; *Wise Guys Who Fool Around/Zha Dian Na Fu, Too Late For Divorce/Zao Zhi Dangcu Wo Bu Jia* **1956**; *Thunderstorm/Lei Yu* **1957**; *The Orphan/Renhai Guhong* **1960**; (IN US) *Marlowe* **1969**; (IN HONG KONG) *The Big Boss/Tang Shan Daxiong* (US title: *Fists of Fury*) **1971**; *Fist of Fury/Jingwu Men* (US title: 'The Chinese Connection'), *The Way of the Dragon/Meng Long Guo Jiang* (US title: *Return of the Dragon*, also dir., scr., MAD) **1972**; *The Unicorn Fist/Qilin Zhang* (MAD only), *Enter the Dragon/Longzheng Hudou* **1973**; *Game of Death/Siwang Youxi* (incorporating original footage from Lee's project of the same title) **1978**; *Tower of Death* aka *Game of Death II/Siwang Ta*

(incorporates footage of Lee from previous films) **1981**.

Lee Sun-fung (name in pinyin: Li Chenfeng), b. 1909, Guangzhou, d. 1985, Hong Kong. Cantonese director. Entered drama school in 1927 in Guangzhou and was active in amateur drama groups. In Hong Kong in 1933. Entered the film industry in 1935 and directed first film in 1940. Over the next thirty years, Lee has worked in all major genres of Cantonese cinema but has proven most adept in the melodrama, making some of the best Cantonese films in the genre (such as *Humanity/Rendao* and *Cold Nights/Han Ye*). Also remembered for *The Orphan/Renhai Guhong* (1960), the first colour Cantonese film featuring a memorable performance from a teenage Bruce Lee. Has also directed Mandarin films and Chaozhou-dialect films.

CANTONESE FILMS: *An Encounter With the Fairy While Slaying the Dragon/Zhan Long Yu Xian Ji* (co-dir. with Lou Dun, also scr.) **1940**; *Three Heroes of the Ruan Family/Ruan Shi San Xiong* (co-dir. with Ng Wui, also co-scr.) **1941**; *Perserverance Rewarded/Shoude Yun Kai Jian Yue Ming* **1949**; *Blood-Stained Azaleas/Xueran Dujuan Hong, A Sad Tale of Rainbow Robes/Nishang Hen* (co-scr.); *A Love So Deep and Great/Enqing Shen Si Hai* (also scr.), *The Romantic Affair of Borrowing a Wife/Jie Qi Yanshi* (also scr.), *Everyone's Darling/Daochu Re Ren Lian* (also scr.) **1952**; *Soul of the Jade Pear/Yu Li Hun* (also scr.), *A Flower Reborn/Zaisheng Hua* (also scr.), *Sunrise/Ri Chu* (co-dir. with others, also scr.), *Her Pure Heart/Mingyue Bingxin* (also scr.), *Spring/Chun* (also scr.) **1953**; *The Good Earth/Da Di* (also scr.) **1954**; *Love, Parts One and Two/Ai* (dir. collectively with Chung-luen contract directors), *Cold Nights/Han Ye* (also scr.), *Humanity/Rendao, Broken Spring Dreams/Chun Can Meng Duan* (also scr.), *Lone Swan/Duanhong Lingyan Ji* (also scr.) **1955**; *Male or Female?/Daoluan Qiankun, Man of Prosperity/Fada zhi Ren, Beauty Raised From the Dead/Yanshi Huanhun Ji* (also scr.), *Oriole's Song/Chu Gu Huang Ying* (also scr.) **1956**; *Tale of Laughter and Tears/Tixiao Yinyuan* (also scr.) **1957**; *The Story of Her Life/Ta de Yisheng, The Wooden Hairpin/Jingcha Ji* (also scr.), *Sword of Blood and Valour, Parts One and Two/Bixue Jian* (also scr.) **1958**; *The Beautiful Ghost's Grievance/Ligui Yuanchou* (also scr.), *Feast of a Rich Family* aka *The Grand Party/Haomen*

270

Yeyan (co-dir. with Lee Tit, Ng Wui and Lo Chi-hung), *A Sketch of Humanity/Renlun* **1959**; *The Orphan/Renhai Guhong*, *The Book and the Sword/Shujian Enchou Lu* (in Three Parts, also scr.), *Rainbow/Hong* **1960**; *The House of Kam Topples, Parts One and Two/Jinfen Shijia* **1961**; *God of Wealth/Fugui Shenxian*, *So Siu Siu/Su Xiaoxiao*, *The Scholar and the Woman Ghost/Hushan Meng* **1962**; *Heartbroken Flower/Duanchang Hua*, *The Eternal Smile/Yongyuan de Weixiao* **1963**; *Men and Women/Nan Nan Nü Nü*, *The Heartless Lover/Lang Xin Ru Tie*, *Under Hong Kong's Roof/Xianggang Wuzhan Xia*, *Forever Together/Yongjie Tongxin* **1964**; *The Eternal Beauty of Hsi-Shih/Xi Shi*, *The Heroic Breed/Yingxiong Ernü*, *The Valley of Death/Ma Ling Dao*, *Eight Murderers/Bage Xiongshou* **1965**; *Tragedy of a Poet King/Li Houzhu* **1968**; *Dear Friends/Zhi Ai Qin Peng* **1976**; *The Devil Husband/Lashou Qingren* **1978**.

MANDARIN FILMS: *An Unforgettable Night/Yiye Nanwang*, *For Life or Death/Shengsi Pai* **1961**; *Liu Hai Meets Fairies/Liu Hai Yu Xian Ji* (also scr.) **1963**; *The Love Tide/Baba de Qingren* **1968**; *The Loner/Bansheng Niuma* **1972**; *Four Girls From Hong Kong/Qun Fang Pu* **1974**.

CHAOZHOU-DIALECT FILMS: *Liu Zhang Leaves the Mountain/Liu Zhang Xia Shan*, *Eternal Regret/Shengsi Hen* **1963**; *The Story of Chun Xiang/Chun Xiang Zhuan* **1964**.

Lee Tit (name in pinyin: Li Tie), b. 1913, Hong Kong, d. 27 September 1996, Hong Kong. Cantonese director. Educated in Guangzhou. An early interest in drama and cinema led to an acting role, aged eighteen, in Kwan Man-ching's silent film *Midnight Shot/Yeban Qiangsheng* (1932), made for the Lianhua Studio's Hong Kong branch. He enrolled in the studio's acting class in Shanghai and received a thorough training in film-making. His career as director began in the late 40s. Lee is today best known for the social-conscience melodrama *In the Face of Demolition/Weilou Chunxiao* (1953), and a famous series of opera films, all released in 1959: *The Purple Hairpin/Zichai Ji*, *Snow Storm in June/Liuyue Xue* and *Butterfly and Red Pear/Dieying Hongli Ji*.

CANTONESE FILMS: *House No. 66/Liushiliu Hao Wu* **1936**; *Resurrection/Fuhuo* (also scr.), *Song of Life/Rensheng Qu* (also scr), *The Elopement/Siben* **1937**; *Lone Swan/Duanhong Lingyan Ji*, *Master A Dou*, *A Native of Dailang/Dalang A Dou Guan* **1939**; *Flirts and Skirts/Xiaohun Liu*, *Tears for Society/Renhai Leihen* **1940**; *My Darling Daughter's Son/Qianjin zhi Zi* **1941**; *Hot Tempered Liang's Adventure in Hong Kong/Zhu Jingliang Da Nao Xianggang*, *Where is the Lady's Home?/Hechu Shi Nong Jia*, *War Criminal No. 1* (co-dir.) **1947**; *The Remorseful Rich/Zhumen Yuan*, *Villain/Yiguan Qinshou*, *My Daughter/A Nü* **1948**; *Kiss Me Again My Love/Yuanlang Chongwen Qie Zhu Chen* (also scr.), *The Story of Tung Siu Yuen/Dong Xiaowan*, *Kaleidoscope/Renhai Wanhua Tong* (episode 'Land is Precious/Cunjin Chitu'), *The Bloody Fight Between Big Knife Wang Wu and the Invincible Kid/Dadao Wang Wu Xuezhan Xiao Bawang*, *The Pearl Pagoda/Zhenzhu Da* **1950**; *Mutual Affections/Lianwo Liangqing*, *Big Sword Wang Wu's Revenge/Dadao Wang Wu Yu Xue Chanchou Ji* (co-dir., also co-scr.), *Sail On to Success/Yifan Fengshun* **1951**; *Lonely Moon on a Lonely Bed/Yi Wan Mei Yue Ban Han Qin* (co-dir.), *Return of the Soul/Zhuying Zhao Hun Fu*, *Gold and the Beauty/Huangjin Meiren* (also scr.), *Girl in Red/Yizhang Hong*, *A Sweet Girl's Fancies/Yunü Fanxin* **1952**; *Bird in the Sunset/Luoxia Guwu* (co-dir., also co-scr.), *Sunrise/Ri Chu* (co-dir. with several others), *In the Face of Demolition/Weilou Chunxiao* **1953**; *Pretty Girl From Kuala Lumpur* aka *Love in Penang/Bin Cheng Yan*, *The Dream Encounter Between Emperor Wu and Lady Wei/Han Wudi Menghui Wei Furen*, *Mrs. Cheng/Cheng Dasao* (also scr.) **1954**; *Love/Ai* (co-dir. with several others), *Her Unrequited Love/Hongfen Piaoling Wei Liao Qing*, *Everlasting Love/Tianchang Dijiu* **1955**; *The Sad Wife in a Grand House/Zhumen Yuan*, *Love and Hate/Bixue Enchou Wangu Qing*, *The King and the Beauty/Bawang Yaoji* **1956**; *The Love Thief/Heng Dao Duo Ai*, *Murderer in Town/Xiang Cheng Xiong Ying*, *The Tragic Story of Liang Shanbo and Zhu Yingtai/Liang Zhu Henshi* (also scr.) **1958**; *The Purple Hairpin/Zichai Ji*, *Snow Storm in June/Liuyue Xue*, *Feast of a Rich Family* aka *The Grand Party/Haomen Yeyan* (co-dir. with Lee Sun-fung, Ng Wui and Lo Chi-hung), *One Death, Three Criminals/Yiming San Xiongshou*, *Butterfly and Red Pear/Dieying Hongli Ji* **1959**; *We Want to Live/Wo Yao Huo Xia Qu*, *Blood Terror/Xue Wu Jing Hun* **1960**; *Father is Back/Huoku Youlan* **1961**; *Lotus in the Rain/Baoyu Honglian*, *The Princess Presents Her Petition/Nü Fuma Jin Dian Ming Yuan*, *Vampire Woman/Xixue Fu* **1962**; *The Dragon Lady/Long Nü San Niang*, *The Millionaire's Daughter/Qianjin zhi Nü*, *An Ill-Fated Woman/Qing A Bao Ming* **1963**; *The Bloody*

Paper Man/Xue Zhi Ren, Bitter Love/Ku Lian
1964; *The Lost Pearl/Canghai Yizhu* **1965**;
*Eternal Love/Qicai Hu Bugui, The Long Voyage
Home/Bihai Qingtian Yeye Xin, Between Justice
and Love/Fawang Qingsi, Duel in Moonlight
Bay/Roubo Mingyue Wan* **1966**; *Golden
Masked Heroes/Jinmian Xia, Love at First
Sight/Yi Jian Chiqing* **1967**; *The Little
Warrior/Xiao Wushi, Let's Build a
Family/Cheng Jian Lishi* (co-dir. with several
others), *The Gentleman Sword/Junzi Jian*
1969, *When Will it Rotate?/Chong Feng* (in
Mandarin) **1971**; *Laugh in the Sleeve/San
Xiao Yinyuan, Old Master Q/Lao Fuzi* (co-
dir.), *The Running Mob/Guhuo Lao Xun
Chun* **1975**; *The Modern Secretaries/Gun Nü
Wen Lao Qin* (in Mandarin) **1977**.

Leong Po-chih (name in pinyin: Liang
Puzhi), b. 1939, London. Director active
from the mid-1970s, a period just preceding
the Hong Kong New Wave. In Hong Kong
in 1967, employed by HK-TVB, setting up
its film unit and staying with the station
until 1969. Feature film debut in 1976. He
has consistently explored bicultural themes
in a rather mixed career highlighted by
Hong Kong 1941/Dengdai Liming (1984), an
allegorical work about 1997.

FILMS: *Jumping Ash/Tiao Hui* (co-dir. with
Josephine Siao) **1976**; *Foxbat/Hufu* **1977**;
Itchy Fingers/Shentou Miaotan Shou Duoduo
1979; *No Big Deal/You Ni Mei Ni* **1980**; *Super
Fool/Long Gam Wei* **1981**; *He Lives By
Night/Ye Jing Hun* **1982**; *Banana
Cop/Yinglun Pipa, Hong Kong 1941/Dengdai
Liming* (also act.) **1984**; *Welcome/Buhuo
Yingxiong* (also act.), *The Island/Shengsi Xian*
1985; (in UK) *Ping Pong* (also act.) **1986**;
*Fatal Love/Sha zhi Lian, Keep on Dancing/Jixu
Tiaowu* (co-dir. with Kam Kwok-leong)
1988; *Shanghai 1920* **1991**.

Li Hanxiang, b. 1926, Liaoning Province, d.
17 December 1996, Beijing. Representative
Mandarin film director of the 1950s and
1960s, and failed film mogul (he
established his own studio in Taiwan in
1964, calling it the Grand Motion Picture
Studio, or Guolian in Chinese, but by the
early 1970s had to call it quits). In Hong
Kong in 1948; started as an actor, then
screenwriter, set designer, and assistant
director. Claimed first real directing job
was on Yan Jun's *Golden Phoenix/Jin Feng*
(1956) on which he was credited as
assistant director and author of screenplay.
A specialist of historical costume epics and,

in the 1970s, softcore sex comedies with
period settings (known as *fengyue pian*),
produced by Shaw Brothers. Introduced
Michael Hui to the screen in *The
Warlord/Da Junfa* (1972).

FILMS: *Red Bloom in the Snow/Xueli Hong*
(also scr.), *Beyond the Blue Horizon/Shuixian*
(also scr.) **1956**; *A Mating Story/Yaotiao
Shunü* (also scr.), *Maiden in
Distress/Huanghua Guinü* (also scr.), *Little
Angel of the Streets/Malu Xiao Tianshi* (also
scr.), *A Mellow Spring/Chun Guang Wuxian
Hao, He Has Taken Him For Another/Yihua
Jiemu* **1957**; *A Kiss for Me/Gei Wo Yige Wen,
Diau Charn of the Three Kingdoms/Diao Chan,
The Angel/Anqi'er, Dan Fung Street/Danfeng
Jie* (also scr.), *The Blessed Family/Quan Jia Fu,
The Magic Touch/Miaoshou Huichun* **1958**;
*The Love-Letter Murder/Sharen de Qingshu,
The Kingdom and the Beauty/Jiangshan
Meiren, The Adventure of the 13th Sister/Ernü
Yingxiong Zhuan* **1959**; *Back Door* aka *Rear
Entrance/Hou Men, The Enchanting
Shadow/Qiannü Youhun* **1960**; *The Pistol* (co-
dir. with Gao Li) **1961**; *Yang Kwei Fei/Yang
Guifei, The Love Eterne/Liang Shanbo yu Zhu
Yingtai* (co-dir. with King Hu, also scr.), *The
Empress Wu/Wu Zetian* (also co-scr.), *Return
of the Phoenix/Feng Huan Chao* (co-dir. with
Gao Li), *The Adulteress/Yang Naiwu yu Xiao
Bai Cai* (co-dir. with He Menghua), *Seven
Fairies/Qi Xian Nü* (also scr.) **1963**; *The
Coin/Yi Mao Qian, The Story of Sue San/Yu
Tang Chun* (supervised direction with King
Hu as 'executive director'), *Beyond the Great
Wall of China/Wang Zhaojun;* (IN TAIWAN) *The
Imperial Scholar/Zhuangyuan Jidi* **1964**;*The
Beauty of Beauties/Xi Shi* (also prod.) **1965**;
*The Yangtze Incident/Yi Cun Shan He, Yi Cun
Xie, The Winter/Dong Nuan* **1969**; *A Tale of
Ghost and Fox/Guihu Waizhuan* (also scr.),
The Four Moods /Xi Nu Ai Le (episode:
'Happiness/Xi', also scr.) **1970**; *The Story of
Ti Ying/Ti Ying* (also scr.); (IN HONG KONG)
Legends of Cheating/ Pianshu Qitan (also
exec. prod., scr.) **1971**; *Cheating
Panorama/Pianshu Daguan* (also scr.), *The
Admarid Girl/Zhi Xian Yuanyang Bu Xian
Xian* (also co-scr.),*The Warlord/Da Junfa*
(also scr.), *Legends of Lust/Fengyue Qitan*
(also scr.) **1972**; *Tales of Larceny/Niu Gui She
Shen* (episode, also scr.), *Cheats to
Cheats/Pianshu Qi Zhong Qi* (also scr.), *Girls
From the North* aka *Facets of Love/Bei Di
Yanzhi* (also scr.), *Illicit Desire/Fengliu Yunshi*
(also scr.), *The Happiest Moment/Yi Le Ye*
(also scr.) **1973**; *The Golden Lotus/Jin Ping
Shuang Yan* (also scr.), *Scandal/Chouwen*

(also scr.), *Sinful Confessions/Sheng Si Quan Ma* (also scr., appearance) **1974**; *Forbidden Tales of Two Cities/Gang Ao Chuanqi* (also scr.), *The Empress Dowager/Qingguo Qingcheng* (also scr.), *That's Adultery/Zhuo Jian Qushi* (also scr.) **1975**; *The Last Tempest/Yingtai Qixue* (also scr.), *Wedding Nights/Dongfang Yanshi* (also scr.), *Crazy Sex/Nianhua Recao* (also scr.), *The Love Swindlers/Pian Cai Pian Se* (also scr.) **1976**; *Moods of Love/Fenghua Xueyue* (also scr.), *The Adventures of the Emperor Chien Lung/Qian Long Xia Jiangnan* (also scr.), *Dream of the Red Chamber/Jinyu Liangyuan Hong Loumeng* (also scr.), *The Mad Monk/Fo Tiao Qiang* (also scr.) **1977**; *Sensual Pleasures/Zi Yue: Shi Si Xing Ye, The Voyage of Emperor Chien Lung/Qian Long Xia Yangzhou* (also scr.) **1978**, *The Scandalous Warlord/Junfa Qushi* (also scr.), *The Ghost Story/Gui Jiao Chun* (also scr.), *Return of the Dead/Xiao Hun Yu* (also scr.) **1979**; *Emperor Chien Lung and the Beauty/Qian Long Huang yu San Guniang* (also scr.) **1980**; *Tiger Xu and the White Widow/Xu Laohu yu Bai Guafu* **1981**; *Passing Flickers/Sanshi Nian Xishuo Congtou* (also scr.), *Tiger Killer/Wu Song* (also scr.), *The Emperor and the Minister/Qian Long Huang Junchen Douzhi* **1982**; *Take Care, Your Majesty/Huangdi Baozhong,* (IN CHINA) *Burning of the Imperial Palace/Huoshao Yuanming Yuan* (also co-scr.), *Reign Behind the Curtain/Chuilian Tingzheng* (also co-scr.) **1983**; *The Last Emperor/Huo Long* **1986**; *Snuff Bottle/Ba Qi Zidi* (also scr.) **1988**; *The Empress Dowager/Xi Taihou* (also scr.) **1989**; *Golden Lotus Love and Desire/Jin Ping Fengyue* (also scr.), *Dunhuang Tales of the Night/Dunhuang Yetan* **1991**; *Lover's Lover/Qingren de Qingren* **1994**.

As producer, on his Guolian films (Li was often credited as 'supervising director'): *Dodder Flower/Tusi Hua* **1965**; *Many Enchanting Nights/Jidu Xiyang Hong, Black Bull and White Snake/Hei Niu yu Bai She, The Fourteenth Daughter of the Hsin Family/Xin Shisi Niang, The Proud Woman/Tian zhi Jiao Nü* **1966**; *Lady in the Tower/Ta Li de Nüren, Flower Drums of Fung Yang/Fengyang Hua Gu, Smile of the Distant Mountains/Yuanshan Han Xiao* **1967**; *The Dawn/Poxiao Shifen, The Stranger/Mosheng Ren, Love is Thicker Than Wine/Shenqing Bi Jiu Nong, Romance in the Northern Country/Beiji Fengqing Hua* **1968**.

Li Pingqian, b. 1901, Hangzhou, d. 1984, Hong Kong. Director, a veteran of Shanghai cinema and a stalwart of Hong Kong's Mandarin cinema in the 50s and 60s, working for the left-wing Great Wall film company. He got into films in 1920, enrolling in a film class run by the Mingxing studio. In 1924, he became a founder of the Shenzhou production company and acted in its first production, *Unbearable Memories/Bukan Huishou,* becoming a director the next year. He subsequently directed for Tianyi and Mingxing companies. An 'Orphan Island' director, Li was one of the directors who worked for the Japanese-controlled coalition of companies known as 'Zhonglian' and 'Huaying' during the Pacific War. In Hong Kong in 1948; prolific output, best films of which include the satire, *Awful Truth/Shuohuang Shijie* (1950) and the tragi-comedy *Laugh, Clown, Laugh/Xiao Xiao Xiao* (1960).

FILMS: (IN SHANGHAI) *Embarrassing Sister/Nanwei le Meimei, The Good Son/Hao Erzi* (co-dir.) **1926**; *Amazon Women/Xiyou Ji Nüer Guo* (co-dir.), *New Camellia/Xin Chahua; Hua Mulan Joins the Army/Hua Mulan Congjun, Princess Iron Fan/Tieshan Gongzhu* (co-dir. with Shao Zuiweng) **1927**; *The Lotus Flower Cave/Xiyou Ji Lianhua Dong, The Red Stone, Parts One and Two/Hong Baoshi* (also act.) **1928**; *The Emperor Goes South, Part Three/Qianlong You Jiangnan* (also scr.), *Burning of the Hundred Flower Fort, Parts One and Two/Huoshao Baihua Tai, Mirror of Desire/Qingyu Baojian, An Orphan After the Raid/Jiehou Guhong* (also scr.) **1929**; *University Queen, Parts One and Two/Daxue Huanghou* **1930**; *Tales of Sherlock Holmes/Fuermosi Zhentan An* (also act.), *Arsène Lupin/Yasen Luobin, Pleasures of the Dance Hall/Gechang Chunse, Between Husband and Wife/Fufu zhi Jian* **1931**; *Shanghai Socialite Han Xiuwen/Shanghai Xiaojie Han Xiuwen, The Married Woman/You Fu zhi Fu, Two Daughters of the Northeast/Dongbei Er Nüzi, Poem on the Banana Leaf/Bajiao Ye Shang Shi, Old and New Hatreds/Jiu Hen Xin Chou* **1932**; *Spring Sorrow of the Pipa/Pipa Chun Yuan, A Modern Woman/Xiandai Yi Nüxing, Children of the Times/Shidai de Ernü, Years of Plenty/Feng Nian* **1933**; *Three Sisters/San Zimei* (also co-scr.), *A Bible for Women/Nüer Jing* (episode) **1934**; *Human Being/Ren Lun* (also scr.), *Hot Blood and Faithful Heart/Rexue Zhonghun* **1935**; *Battle of Peach and Plum/Tao Li Zhengyan* (also scr.), *Rendezvous/Ye Hui* **1936**; *The Flower Blossoms and Wilts/Hua Kai Hua Luo* **1937**; *A Pair in Love/Feng Qiu Feng, Camille/Chahua Nü* (also scr.) **1938**; *Tragedy* of Life and Death/Shengsi Hen (also scr.), Beauty and the Tiger/Fei Zhen E Ci Hu (also scr.), The Young Mistress' Fan/Shao Nainai de Shanzi, Gold and Silver World/Jinyin Shijie **1939**; Du Shiniang (also scr.), Hongxian Steals the Box/Hongxian Dao He **1940**; Separated in Life and Death/Shengli Sibie (also scr.), Road of Life/Sheng Lu (also scr.), King of the Underground/Dicang Wang, The Heroes/Yinglie Zhuan (also scr.), The Merry Widow/Fengliu Guafu, Family/Jia (co-dir. with others) **1941**; The Happy Opponents/Huanxi Yuanjia (also scr.), The Amorous Lady/Guifu Fengliu **1942**; Madame Butterfly/Hudie Furen, Spring Battle of Peach and Plum/Tao Li Zheng Chun **1943**; Cloud-Capped Moon/Fuyun Yanyue, Four Sisters/Si Zimei **1944**; Spring on the Lake/Hu Shang Chun Hen (also scr.), Hang On to Your Relatives/Qun Dai Feng, Mother and Son/Mu yu Zi (also scr.) **1947**; Whither Spring?/Chun Gui He Chu, The Murderer/Xiong Shou **1948**; (IN HONG KONG) Our Husband/Chun Lei (also scr.) **1949**; A Strange Woman/Yidai Yaoji, Awful Truth/Shuohuang Shijie **1950**; A Night-time Wife/Jinhun Ji **1951**; Blossoms in the Heart/Baihua Qifang, A Bachelor is Born/Fang Maozi (co-dir. with Liu Qiong), Honeymoon/Miyue **1952**; Marriage Affair/Men, Daydream/Bairi Meng, Parents' Love/Cuncao Xin, The Peerless Beauty/Juedai Jiaren **1953**; Tales of the City/Duhui Jiaoxiang Qu **1954**; It So Happens to a Woman/Wo Shi Yige Nüren **1955**; Three Loves/San Lian **1956**; Forever Waiting/Wangfu Shanxia, Escape into a Trap/Nilü Fengyun **1957**; Miss Fragrance/Xiang Penpen Xiaojie, Green Swan Club/Lutian E Yezong Hui **1958**; Girl on the Front Page/Xinwen Renwu, Laugh, Clown, Laugh/Xiao Xiao Xiao, Rendezvous/Jiaren Youyue **1960**; The Seaman and the Dancing Girl/Hua Deng Cu Shang, A Dazzling Trap/Mihun Jing **1961**; The Princess Falls in Love/San Kan Yumei Liu Jinding **1962**; Between Vengeance and Love/Xuedi Qingchou **1963**; Three Charming Smiles/San Xiao **1964**; Romantic World/Yan Yu, Flame of Love/Fenghuo Yinyuan **1965**.

Lung Kong (name in pinyin: Long Gang), b. 1934, Anhui Province. Actor-director. He came from an acting family (his father was a female impersonator on the Cantonese opera stage, known as Siu San-san). A stockbroker before he entered Cantonese films in 1958 as an acting protégé of director Chow Sze-luk (name in pinyin: Zhou Shilu), the head of Shaw Brothers' Cantonese division. Directing debut in

1966, with The Broadcast Prince/Boyin Wangzi. Very much an issue-oriented director (he has tackled prostitution, juvenile delinquency, rehabilitation of ex-cons, the A-bomb). Turned to directing Mandarin films in early 70s. Retired in 1977 to concentrate on stockbroking, but has ocassionally returned to the screen as actor. His Story of a Discharged Prisoner/Yingxiong Bense (1967) was re-made by John Woo as A Better Tomorrow/Yingxiong Bense (1986).

CANTONESE FILMS: The Broadcast Prince/Boyin Wangzi (also scr.) **1966**; Story of a Discharged Prisoner/Yingxiong Bense (also scr., act.) **1967**; The Window/Chuang (also co-scr., act.) **1968**; Teddy Girls/Fei Nü Zhengzhuan (also co-scr., act.) **1969**; (MANDARIN FILMS) Yesterday, Today, Tomorrow/Zuori, Jinri, Mingri (also scr.) **1970**; My Beloved/Zuoye Menghun Zhong (also scr.) **1971**; Pei Shih/Pei Shi (also co-scr.) **1972**; The Call-Girls/Yingzhao Nülang (also co-scr., co-edit, act.) **1973**; Hiroshima 28/Guangdao Ershiba (also co-scr., co-edit) **1974**; Lina/Ta (sequel to 'The Call-Girls'), Laugh-in/Haha Xiao (also co-scr., act.) **1976**; Mitra/Bosi Xiyang Qing (also prod., co-scr., act.) **1977**; Love Massacre/Ai Sha (prod. only, also act.) **1981**. AS ACTOR: Crime of Passion in the Hotel/Jiudian Qingsha An, The Virtuous Girl From a Humble House/Fengmen Shu Nü, The Prodigal's Return/Langzi Hui Tou **1958**; Young Rock/Qingchun Yue, Case of the Female Corpse/Yanshi An, Beseiged/Chongchong Wei Kun, Bride From Another Town/Guofu Xinniang, Fragrance of Durians/Liulian Piao Xiang **1959**; Greenhorn in Love/Cu Lian, A Night of Thrills/Yixi Jinghun **1960**; Murder on the Black Dragon Street/Xuejiu Heilong Jie, Teenage Beat/Qingchun Re, Chase/Shentong Zhui Xiong **1961**; 999 The Mysterious Body/999 Guaishi An, Phantom of the Jade Chamber/Qionglou Moying **1962**; Between Love and Hatred/Enyuan Qingtian **1963**; Track of a Chase/Zhuizong **1964**; Two Swordswomen/Daojian Shuanglan, Eight Murderers/Bage Xiongshou **1965**; Legacy aka A Million Dollar Inheritance/Yichan Yibai Wan, Ghost Chasers/Yeban de Guiying **1966**; The Man From Interpol/Lanse Yezonghui, Beauty's Trap/Shentan Zhipo Meiren Ji **1967**; Winter Love/Dong Lian, Love With a Prodigal/Langzi Jiaren **1968**; Don't Kill Me, Brother/Wu Du Bu Zhangfu **1980**; Shanghai Blues/Shanghai zhi Ye **1984**; Gun of Dragon/Huxue Tulong zhi Hongtian Xianjing **1993**; The Black Mask/Hei Xia **1996**; Once Upon a Time in China and

America/Huang Feihong zhi Xiyu Hongshi **1997**.

Luo Wei, b. 1918, Jiangsu Province, d. 1996, Hong Kong. Corpulent actor-director. Began career as an actor in the Mainland, mainly on the stage. In Hong Kong in 1949, acting for various companies before turning to directing. Founded his own production company, Si Wei in 1957. Directing career in the 1960s marked by lush melodramas, spy thrillers and martial arts extravaganzas for the two major studios, MP and GI and Shaw Brothers. In the 1970s, directed Bruce Lee (*The Big Boss, Fist of Fury*) and discovered Jacky Chan.

FILMS: *Diary of a Husband* (co-dir. with Tang Huang, also act.), *Woman of Throbbing Passions/Dangfu Qingchi* (also act.) **1953**; *Blood-Stained Flowers* aka *The 72 Martyrs of Canton/Bixue Huang Hua* (co-dir. with several directors, also act.) **1954**; *River of Romance/Duoqing He* (also scr., act.) **1957**; *Jade Green Lake/Feicui Hu, Golden Phoenix/Jin Fenghuang* (also act.) **1958**; *Song From a Haunted House/Guiwu Gesheng* (also act.) **1959**; *Tragic Melody/Taohua Lei* (also act.), *The Tender Trap of Espionage/Zhifen Jiandie Wang* (also act.), *Black Butterfly/Hei Hudie* (also act.) **1960**; *Meng Lisi, Maid of the Jungle/Yuannü Meng Lisi* (also act.), *Song Without Words/Wuyu Wen Cantian* (also act.) **1961**; *The Golden Arrow/Jin Jian Meng* (also act.) **1963**; *The Magic Lamp/Baolian Deng* (co-dir.), *The Better Halves/Luanfeng Heming* (also act.), *An Affair to Remember/Qingtian Changhen* (also scr.) **1964**; *Crocodile River/Eyu He* (also act.), *Call of the Sea/Nuhai Qingchou* (also act.) **1965**; *The Golden Buddha/Jin Pusa* (also act.) **1966**; *Angel With the Iron Fists/Tie Guanyin* (also act.), *Madame Slender Plum/Yuhai Qingmo* (also act.) **1967**; *Forever and Ever/Jinshi Qing* (also act.), *Black Butterfly/Nüxia Hei Hudie* (also act.), *Angel Strikes Again/Tie Guanyin Yongpo Baozha Dang* (also act.), *Death Valley/Duanhun Gu* (also act.) **1968**; *Dragon Swamp/Du Long Tan* (also act.), *Raw Courage/Hu Dan* (also act.), *The Golden Sword/Longmen Jin Jian* (also scr., act.) **1969**; *Brothers Five/Wuhu Tulong* (also co-scr.) **1970**; *The Invincible Eight/Tianlong Bajiang* (also scr.), *The Shadow Whip/Yingzi Shenbian* (also scr., act.), *The Comet Strikes/Gui Liu Xing* (also scr., act.), *Vengeance of a Snow Girl/Bingtian Xianü, The Big Boss/Tangshan Daxiong* (also co-scr.) **1971**; *The*

Hurricane/Jin Xuanfeng* (also scr.), *Fist of Fury/Jingwu Men* (also scr., act.) **1972**; *A Man Called Tiger/Lengmian Hu* (also scr.), *Back Alley Princess/Malu Xiao Yingxiong* (also scr.), *Seaman No. 7/Haiyuan Qi Hao* (also scr.), *None But the Brave* aka *Kung Fu Girl/Tie Wa* (also scr., act.), *The Tattooed Dragon/Longhu Jingang* (also scr.) **1973**; *The Chinese Enforcers* aka *Chinatown Capers/Xiao Yingxiong Danao Tangren Jie* (also scr.), *Naughty! Naughty!* aka *Naughtier Than Thee/Zhuotou Zhuangyuan* (also co-scr.), *Yellow-Faced Tiger/Huangmian Laohu* (also co-scr.) **1974**; *The Bedevilled/Xin Mo* (also scr.), *The Girl With the Dexterous Touch/Jinfen Shenxian Shou, Shantung Man in Hong Kong/Xiao Shandong Dao Xianggang* (also scr.) **1975**; *New Fist of Fury/Xin Jingwu Men, The Killer Meteors/Fengyu Shuangliu Xing* **1976**; *To Kill With Intrigue/Jianhua Yanyu Jiangnan* **1977**; *The Magnificent Bodyguard/Feidu Juan Yunshan, Spiritual Kung Fu/Quan Jing* **1978**; *Dragon Fist/Long Quan* **1979**; (IN US) *Slaughter in San Francisco* (credited under name of William Lowe) **1981**.

AS ACTOR: *Sorrows of the Forbidden City/Qing Gong Mishi* **1948**; *Virtue in the Dust/Chun Cheng Hua Luo, Sins of Our Father/Da Liang Shan Enchou Ji* **1949**; *Quest for a Long-Lost Husband/Haiwai Xunfu* **1950**; *Witch, Devil, Gambler/Shen Gui Ren* (in 'Gambler' episode), *The Troubled Love of Wang Kui and Gui Ying/Wang Kui yu Gui Ying, Sweet Memories/Man Yuan Chun Se, Prisoner of Love/Ai de Fulu* **1952**; *Love Eternal/Wu Shan Meng, Heaven of Love, Sea of Sin/Niehai Qingtian, The Notorious Woman/Ming Nüren Biezhuan* **1953**; *Rose I Love You/Meigui Meigui Wo Ai Ni* **1954**; *Yang E, What Price Beauty?* aka *The Little Girl Named Cabbage/Xiao Bai Cai, Tokyo Interlude/Yingdu Yanji, New Song of the Fishermen/Xin Yuguang Qu* **1955**; *Miss Kikuko/Juzi Guniang, Songs of the Peach Blossom River/Taohua Jiang, The Error/Hong Chen, Red Bloom in the Snow/Xueli Hong, The Flame of Love* aka *Flesh and Flame/Lian zhi Huo, Surprise/Jinghun Ji, Always in My Heart/Mang Lian, Beyond the Blue Horizon/Shui Xian, Madame Butterfly/Hudie Furen, Fresh Peony/Xian Mudan, The Chase/Zhui* **1956**; *A Mating Story/Yaotiao Shunü, Booze, Boobs and Bucks/Jiuse Caiqi, Love and Crime/Ai yu Zui, Lady Sings the Blues/Tianya Genü* **1957**; *Diau Charn of the Three Kingdoms/Diao Chan, The Little Darling/Xiao Qingren, Blood-Stained Lantern/Xueying Deng, Torrents of Desire/Shan Hu, Wild Fantasies/Xiangru Feifei* **1958**;

Calendar Girl/Longxiang Fengwu, Full of
Joy/Mantang Hong, Love by the Beach/Haibin
Chunse, The Love-Letter Murder/Sharen de
Qingshu, Sophisticated Lady/Fengqing Youwu,
All in the Family/Jia You Xishi, The Adventure
of the 13th Sister/Ernü Yingxiong Zhuan 1959;
Nobody's Child/Kuer Liulang Ji, A Shadow
Over the Chateau/Honglou Mo Ying 1960;
Beauty Parade/Tiyu Huanghou, The Girl With
the Golden Arm/Zei Meiren 1961; Crusade
Against Daddy/Zao Sheng Guizi 1962; The
Empress Wu/Wu Zetian, Little Lotus/He Hua
1963; Romance of the Forbidden City/Shen
Gong Yuan, The Crisis/Shengsi Guantou 1964;
Squadron 77/Qiqi Gansi Dui 1965; The
Eunuch/Gui Taijian (also scr.) 1971; The
Forbidden Past/Xiaolou Canmeng 1976; Life is
Cheap . . . but Toilet Paper is Expensive 1990.

Karl Maka (also Carl Mak, name in pinyin:
Mai Jia; name in Cantonese: Mak Kar), b.
1944, Taishan, Guangdong Province. Actor-
comedian, director-producer. In Hong
Kong in 1958. Education in USA 1963-
1973. Returned to Hong Kong in 1973 to
work as assistant director on Robert
Clouse's *Golden Needles* and Guy Hamilton's
007 adventure *Man With the Golden Gun*
(1974). Directed first feature in 1976.
Founder of Cinema City (with actors Dean
Shek and Raymond Wong), hugely
successful production company in early
1980s. Active also in Taiwan, mainly as
producer e.g. *Papa Can You Hear Me
Sing?/Da Cuo Che* and *That Day on the
Beach/Haitan de Yi Tian* (both 1983).

FILMS: *The Good, the Bad, and the Loser/Yi Zhi
Guanggun Zou Tianya* (also scr.) 1976;
Winner Takes All/Mianmeng Xinjing (also
scr.) 1977; *Dirty Tiger, Crazy Frog/Laohu
Tianji* (also co-scr.) 1978; *His Name is
Nobody/Wuming Xiaozu* (also act.), *Crazy
Crooks/Fengkuang Da Laoqian* (also act.), *By
Hook or By Crook/Xianyu Fansheng* (also act.)
1980; *Chasing Girls/Zhui Nüzai* 1981; *It Takes
Two/Nan Xiong Nan Di* (also act.) 1982; *The
Thirty Million Rush/Hengcai Sanqian Wan*
(also act.) 1987.
AS PRODUCER (selected films): *Laughing
Times/Huaji Shidai* (also act.), *Beware of
Pickpockets/Huanle Shenxian Wo* (also act.),
*All the Wrong Clues (for the Right
Solution)/Guima Zhiduo Xing* (also act.)
1981; *Aces Go Places/Zuijia Paidang* (also
act.), *He Lives By Night/Ye Jing Hun* 1982;
*Aces Go Places, Part II/Zuijia Paidang Daxian
Shentong* (also act.), *All the Wrong Spies/Wo
Ai Ye Laixiang* 1983; *Aces Go Places, Part III:*

*Our Man in Bond Street/Zuijia Paidang
Nühuang Miling* (also act.), *Banana
Cop/Yinglun Pipa, The Happy Ghost/Kaixin
Gui, The Occupant/Lingqi Biren, Merry
Christmas/Shengdan Kuaile* (also act.),
Lifeline Express/Hongyun Dangtou 1984; *Kung
Hei Fat Choy/Gongxi Facai, The Happy Ghost,
Part Two/Kaixin Gui Fang Shujia* 1985; *Aces
Go Places, Part IV/Zuijia Paidang Qianli Jiu
Chaipo* (also act.) 1986; *City on Fire/Longhu
Fengyun, Prison on Fire/Jianyu Fengyun* 1987;
Tiger on Beat/Laohu Chu Geng 1988; *Aces Go
Places, Part V/Xin Zuijia Paidang* (also act.)
1989.

Johnny Mak (name in pinyin: Mai
Dangxiong; name in Cantonese: Mak Tong-
hung), b. 1949, Hong Kong. TV career in
1970s as director-producer, eventually
becoming controller of station (RTV).
Resigned in 1981 to form own film
production company, producing
controversial hit *Lonely 15/Liang Meizai*
(1982), based on the German film
Christiane F. In 1984 directed *Long Arm of
the Law/Sheng Gang Qibing*, his sole
directorial effort so far. But has acquired
reputation as 'creative producer' on
subsequent pictures, particularly the series
of gangster biographies known as 'Big
Timer' movies (*To Be Number One/Bie Hao*
and *Lord of the East China Sea/Shanghai
Huangdi*).

FILMS (as producer): *Lonely 15/Liang Meizai,
Happy 16/Qiaopi Nü Xuesheng, Crimson
Street/Sha Ru Aiqing Jie* 1982; *Possessed/Meng
Gui Chu Long* 1983; *Everlasting Love/Ting Bu
Liao de Ai, Long Arm of the Law/Sheng Gang
Qibing* (also dir.), *Possessed, Part II/Yan Gui
Fakuang* 1984; *Seven Angels/Huan Chang*
1985; *Midnight Girls/Wuye Liren* 1986; *Tragic
Hero/Yingxiong Haohan, Rich and
Famous/Jianghu Qing, Spiritual Love/Gui
Xinniang, Long Arm of the Law, Part II/Sheng
Gang Qibing Bing Fen Liang Lu* 1987; *The
Truth/Fa Nei Qing, The Greatest Lover/Gongzi
Duo Qing, Midnight Whispers/Jin Su Xinzhong
Qing* 1988; *Long Arm of the Law, Part
III/Sheng Gang Qibing Disanji, The Iceman
Cometh/Ji Dong Qixia* 1989; *Underground
Express/Sheng Gang Qibing Disiji, Dixia
Tongdao* (co-scr. only) 1990; *To Be Number
One/Bie Hao, Sex and Zen/Yu Pu Tuan zhi
Touqing Baojian* 1992, *Lord of the East China
Sea, Parts One and Two/Shanghai Huangdi,
The Sword of Many Love/Feihu Waizhuan*
(also co-scr.) 1993.

Ma-Xu Weibang, b. 1905, Zhejiang province; d. 1961, Hong Kong. China's most famous horror film director, he joined Shanghai's Mingxing Company as an actor in 1924. He appeared in such films as *The Seducer/Youhun* (1924, directed by Zhang Shichuan), *A Shanghai Woman/Shanghai Yi Furen* (1925, directed by Zheng Zhengqiu), *Master Feng/Feng Da Shaoye* (1925, directed by Hong Shen), *Orchid of the Vacant Valley/Kong Gu Lan* (1925, directed by Zhang Shichuan), *Repentance/Liangxin Fuhuo* (1926, directed by Bu Wancang), *Love and Gold/Aiqing yu Huangjin* (1926, directed by Hong Shen and Zhang Shichuan). He became a director in 1926 when he switched to the Langhua Film Company. He subsequently directed for the Tianyi, Jinlong, Lianhua and Xinhua companies, achieving instant fame with the horror classic *Song at Midnight/Yeban Gesheng* (1937), a reworking of Hollywood's *Phantom of the Opera*. He stayed in Shanghai during the 'orphan island' period and through the period of its full occupation when he directed *Qiu Haitang*, a film which immediately acquired notoriety due to the fact that it was made for the 'Huaying' corporation and the supposed 'weak' depiction of its central hero – a female impersonator on the Peking opera stage. He migrated to Hong Kong in 1949 where he worked for the Great Wall, Asia and other minor companies. He spent his last years directing opera films in the Amoy dialect. Died in a car accident.

FILMS: (IN SHANGHAI) *The Love Freak/Qingchang Guairen* (also scr.) **1926**; *Freak of the Night/Heiye Guairen* (co-dir. with Hong Ji) **1928**; *The Devil Incarnate/Hunshi Mowang* (also scr., act.) **1929**; *The Ape Cries in the Empty Valley/Kong Gu Yuan Sheng* **1930**; *Prison of Love/Ai Yu* (also act.), *Pear Flower in the Storm/Baoyu Lihua* (also scr.) **1934**; *The Goose Drops in the Cold River/Hanjiang Luo Yan* (also scr.) **1935**; *Song at Midnight/Yeban Gesheng* (also scr.) **1937**; *Corpse Walking in the Old Mansion/Guwu Xingshi Ji* (also scr.), *The Poetic Ghost on a Cold Moon/Leng Yue Shihun* (also scr.) **1938**; *The Leper Girl/Mafeng Nü* (also scr.) **1939**; *The Clan of Diao and Liu/Diao Liu Shi* (also scr.) **1940**; *Song at Midnight, Part Two/Yeban Gesheng Xuji* (also scr.), *Modern Youth/Xiandai Qingnian* **1941**; *Tears of the Mandarin Ducks/Yuanyang Lei* (also scr.) **1942**; *Qiu Haitang* (in two parts) **1943**; *Dragnet/Tianluo Diwang* (also co-scr.), *Broken Spring Dream/Chuncan Mengduan* (co-dir. with Sun Jing) **1947**; *The Beautiful Prince/Meiyan Qinwang* (also scr.); (IN HONG KONG) *A Maid's Bitter Story* aka *The Haunted House/Qionglou Hen* **1949**; *Blood-Stained Flowers* aka *The 72 Martyrs of Canton/Bixue Huanghua* (dir. with several others) **1953**; *New Song of the Fisherman/Xin Yuguang Qu* **1955**; *The Unconquered/Woxin Changdan, Foggy Night, Fright Night/Wuye Jinghun* (also scr.) **1956**; *Resurrected Rose/Fuhuo de Meigui, Booze, Boobs and Bucks/Jiuse Caiqi, The Dog Murderer/Gou Xiongshou* **1957**; *Young Vagabond/Liulang'er* **1958**; *The Elopment/Hongfu Siben, Snow Storm in June/Liu Yue Xue* (Amoy-dialect opera films) **1959**; *The Lovers and the Python/Dumang Qing Yuan* **1961**.

Ng See-yuen (name in pinyin: Wu Siyuan), b. 1944, Shanghai. Director, producer. Entered the film industry in 1966 through enrolment in an acting class organised by Shaw Brothers. Employed by Shaws in various junior jobs behind the scenes. Left Shaws in 1971 to direct first film *The Mad Killer/Fengkuang Shashou* (co-dir. with Luo Zhen). Established his own company, Seasonal Film Corporation, in 1973. Produced *Snake in the Eagle's Shadow/Shexing Diaoshou* and *Drunken Master/Zui Quan* (both 1978), which made Jacky Chan a star, and *The Butterfly Murders/Die Bian* (1979), which gave Tsui Hark his first big break. Currently serving as chairman of the Director's Guild of Hong Kong.

FILMS: *The Mad Killer/Fengkuang Shashou* (co-dir. with Luo Zhen) **1971**; *The Bloody Fists/Dangkou Tan* (also scr.), *The Good and the Bad/E Hu Kuang Long* (also scr.) **1972**; *Little Godfather From Hong Kong/Xianggang Xiao Jiaofu* (also scr.) **1974**; *A Haunted House/Shisan Hao Xiong Zhai, Anti-Corruption/Lianzheng Fengbo* (also scr.), *Little Super Man/Shenglong Huohu Xiao Yingxiong* (also scr.) **1975**; *The Secret Rivals/Nan Quan Bei Tui* (also co-scr.), *Million-Dollar Snatch/Qi Baiwan Yuan Da Jie An* (also scr.), *Bruce Lee – True Story/Li Xiaolong Chuanqi* (also scr.) **1976**; *The Secret Rivals, Part Two/Nan Quan Bei Tui Dou Jin Hu* (also scr.), *The Invincible Armour/Ying Zhao Tie Bushan* (also scr.) **1977**; *Tower of Death* aka *Game of Death, Part Two/Siwang Ta* **1981**; *The Unwritten Law/Fawai Qing* (also scr., prod.) **1985**.

AS PRODUCER: *Snake in the Eagle's Shadow/Shexing Diaoshou* (also co-scr.), *Drunken Master/Zui Quan* (also co-scr.) **1978**; *Dance of the Drunk Mantis/Nan Bei Zui Quan, The Butterfly Murders/Die Bian* (also scr.) **1979**; *Lackey and the Lady Tiger/She Mao He Hunxing Quan* **1980**; *The Sweet and Sour Cops/A Can Dang Chai* (also co-scr.) **1981**; *Ninja in the Dragon's Den/Long de Renzhe* (also co-scr.) **1982**; *Gun is Law/Tuixiu Tanzhang* **1983**; *Host for a Ghost/Haocai Zhuang Dao Ni* (also co-scr.) **1984**; *No Retreat, No Surrender* (US, also co-story) **1985**; *No Retreat, No Surrender, Part Two: Raging Thunder* (exec. prod. only, US) **1987**; *No Retreat No Surrender, Part Three: Blood Brothers* (exec. prod. only, US) **1989**; *All For the Winner/Du Sheng* **1990**.

Ng Wui (name in pinyin: Wu Hui), b. 1913, Guangzhou, d. 1996 Hong Kong. Cantonese director-actor. Employed by Grandview (Daguan) as an actor in 1940. Directed first film in 1941 and maintained prolific output until the 1970s, working in all genres. His best work was done in the 50s: *The Prodigal Son/Baijia Zai* (1952), *Family/Jia* (1953), *Father and Son/Fu yu Zi* (1954) are classics of Cantonese cinema.

FILMS: *Reunion at Full Moon/Jin Xiao Chong Jian Yue Tuanyuan, Three Heroes* (co-dir. with Lee Sun-fung, also co-scr.) **1941**; *Tears for An Impossible Love/Lei Sa Xiangsi Di, Romance From Heaven/Tian Ci Liangyuan* **1947**; *To Steal a Sweetheart/Miao Shou Tou Xiang, Hundreds of Children and Thousands of Grandchildren/Bai Zi Qian Sun, A Golden World/Huangjin Shijie* (also scr.), *Bat Thief/Bianfu Da Dao* (co-dir. with Cheung Ying, also co-scr.), *Man or Woman?/Dian Luan Dao Feng, Fight For Champion/Xuehai Zheng Xiong, Separated Too Soon/Hong Yan Wei Lao En Xian Duan* (co-dir. with Ch'un Kim, also co-scr.) **1948**; *Double Happiness at the Door/Shuangxi Lingmen, When A Woman Enters a Man's Home/Feng Ru Long Lou, The Orphan's Rescue/Guer Jiu Zu, End of the Day/Meng Duan Can Xiao, The Honest and the Dishonest/Yixin Nüzi Fuxin Lang, Purple-Misted Cup/Zixia Bei, Night Discovery of the Women's Trap/Yepo Cang Xiang Dong, A Pitiable Wife/Kelian Guili Yue* **1949**; *Flower Drops By the Red Chamber/Hua Luo Honglou, How Inspector Daisen Shattered the Strange Cloaks Gang/Daisen Qi An, Dark Paradise/Hei Tiantang, Bird on the Wing/Ling Xiao Gu Yan, The Haunted House/Gui Wu, Kaleidoscope/Renhai Wanhua Tong* (episode 'Black Market Marriage/Heishi Hunyin'), *The Blundering General/Wulong Jiangjun, The Waves of Sin, Parts I and II/Zui E Suolian, Love Tears of a Buddhist Recluse/Fan Gong Qing Lei, The War Baby/Jie Hou Guer, The Son Who Broke Mother's Heart/Erxin Sui Muxin, Lovers Caught in 10,000 Perils/Wanjie Qingyuan, The End of the Year Means Money/Nian Wan Qian* **1950**; *When a Lovely Girl Bestows Her Favours/Meiren En, Queen of the Devil's Palace/Mo Gong Yao Hou, Plum Blossom in the Snow/Xue Ying Han Mei, Marriage By Mistake/Wulong Hunyin, The Neglected Wife/Lengluo Chun Xiao, Drifting Swallow/Piaoling Yan, Orphan Girl in Love/Qingtian Guyan, Sunset Rendezvous/Renyue Huanghun Hou, Fathomless Love, Fathomless Hate/Wuxian Enqing Wuxian Hen, A Sad Tale of Rainbow Robes/Nichang Hen* (co-dir. with Lee Sun-fung, also co-scr.), *From Now On We Are Strangers/Cong Ci Xiaolang Molu Ren* (also scr.), *Lucky Strike/Fu Zhi Xinling, The Wrongly Accused Lover/Guai Cuo Youqing Lang, Why Not Return?/Xin Hu Bugui, How Liang Tianlai Was Thrice Beaten By Ling Guixing/Ling Guixing San Da Liang Tianlai, Dream of the Red Chamber/Honglou Xin Meng* **1951**; *Wedding Candles/Longfeng Huazhu, A Prayer for Happiness/Ruyi Jixiang, Love's Bliss/Huahao Yueyuan, Everything Goes Wrong For a Poor Couple/Pinjian Fuqi Baishi Shuai, A Song of Everlasting Sorrow/Changhen Ge, He Returns By the Lonely Moon/Lengyue Ban Lang Gui, Timely Fortune/Shilai Yundao, Poor Daddy/Nanwei Le Baba, The Swallow's Return/Huakai Yanzi Gui, Funny Fellows/Guling Jingguai, Sweet Love Lingers On/Ernü Qingchang* (co-dir. with Cheng Gang), *Ten Fat Brides For Skinny/Shi Ge Fei Nü Jia Shou Lang, Why Not Return? – The Musical/Gechang Hu Bugui* (also scr.), *How Two Naughty Girls Thrice Insulted Xiao Yuebai/Liang Ge Diaoman Nü San Xi Xiao Yuebai* (also scr.), *A New Story of A Niu/A Niu Xin Zhuan* (also scr.), *Two Naughty Girls/Yidui Yanzhi Ma, The Prodigal Son/Baijia Zai* (also scr.) **1952**; *Family/Jia; The Scholar Tang Bohu and the Maid Qiuxiang/Xin Tang Bohu Dian Qiuxiang, Fallen Petals in the Autumn Rain/Qiu Yu Can Hua, Two Heroic Rivals/Shuang Xiong Dou Zhi, The Newly-Weds/Xin Hun Ji, Never Too Late/You Xin Bu Pa Chi, All in the Family/Yijia Qin, Bright Nights/Huoshu Yinhua Xiangying Hong* (co-dir. with Chu Kea and Cheng Gang), *Sunrise/Richu* (co-dir. with several others), *Honour Thy Father and Mother/Yangzi Dang Zhi Fumu En* **1953**;

Father and Son/Fu yu Zi, We'll Meet
Again/Shanshui You Xiangfeng, Madam
Yun/Yun Niang, The Hills Divide Us/Ren Ge
Wan Zhong Shan, Lady Ping/Ping Ji (also co-
scr.), The Postponed Wedding/Gaiqi Jiehun,
The Big Thunderstorm/Da Leiyu (also scr.),
Love Killed at Midnight/Wuye Qingsha An,
Mother/Muqin, The Fall/Shizu Hen, Her Fickle
Heart/Baibian Furen Xin, The Noble
Family/Haohua Shijia, Sworn Sisters/Jinlan
Zimei 1954; Love, Parts One and Two/Ai,
Shangxia Ji (dir. with several others), The
Story of Chau Hoi-tong/Qiu Haitang, Action
Speaks Louder Than Words/Zhen Jin Bu Pa
Honglu Huo, The Renewal of an Ancient
Garden/Guyuan You Fengchun (also co-scr.),
In Different Lands We Still Long for Each
Other/Liang Di Xiangsi (also scr.), The
Devoted Lover/Qing Chi, Family Mottos/Jia
Jiao, Lady Chiu Kwun's Departure/Zhaojun
Chu Sai, The Hypocritical Heart/Liang
Chongxin, The Pagoda of Long Life/Chang
Sheng Da, The Matchmaker/Yuanyang Pu,
Rear Window/Hou Chuang (co-dir. with
Chan Pei and Chu Kea) 1955; The Peacock's
Sad Tale/Kongque Dongnan Fei (co-dir. with
Chu Kea), Wilderness/Yuanye, The Romantic
Story of the West Chamber/Xixiang Ji, An
Unusual Crime at Night/Heiye Qiyuan, Petals
in the Wind/Yipian Fei Hua, The Soul
Stealer/Gouhun Shizhe, The Precious Lotus
Lamp/Baolian Deng, The Seven Heavens/Qi
Chongtian, The Ghost of the Pot Comes to
Life/Wa Gui Huan Shen, The Strange
Adventures of a Strange Man/Qiren Qiyu,
Matching the Beauty and the Handsome/Hua
Hao Yue Yuan, Three Expeditions to Hell/San
Ru Yan Wang Dian, The Dunce Attends a
Birthday Party/Ailao Bai Shou 1956; The Lotus
Lamp, Part Two/Baolian Deng Xuji, The
Dunce Gets a Son/Ailao Tianding, A Fairy
Brings a Son/Tianji Songzi, Love in the Perilous
Sea/Wuqing Dahai You Qing Tian,
Thunderstorm/Leiyu, Tale of the Lychee/Lizhi
Ji, Taking the Birthday Gifts Caravan by
Strategy/Shuihu Zhuan: Zhiqu Shengchen
Wang (also scr.), The Story of See-ma Seong-
yu/Sima Xiangru, Pigsy's Marriage/Zhu Bajie
Zhaoqin, Little Women/Xiao Furen, Who is the
Killer?/Shui Shi Xiongshou, Caught in the
Act/Zhuojian Ji, Darling Girl/Tian Jie'er 1957;
A Beautiful Girl at War/Fenghuo Jiaren (also
scr.), The Lotus Lantern, Part Three/Baolian
Deng Sanji, Big Clumsy Melon/Da Donggua,
You Are the Murderer/Ni Shi Xiongshou,
Murder on a Wedding Night/Sharen Huazhu
Ye, The Tripod and the Pearl/Baoding
Mingzhu, Valley of the Lovebirds/Yuanyang Gu,
Little Songstress/Xiao Genü, Lau Ngai Sends

His Letters/Liu Yi Chuan Shu, Ah Chiu is
Getting Married/A Chao Jiehun, Rent a
Bride/Jie Xinniang 1958; Money/Qian, The
Impossible Son-in-Law/Huangtang Nüxu, Ten
Brothers/Shi Xiongdi, Feast of a Rich Family
aka The Grand Party /Haomen Yeyan (dir.
with Lee Sun-fung, Lee Tit and Lo Chi-
hung), The Road/Lu (also scr.), Dear
Love/Hao Yuan Jia, Daughter of a Grand
Household/Jinzhi Yuye, Beauty Slain by the
Sword/Daoxia Meiren Hun, The Cruel
Husband/Du Zhangfu 1959; They All Say I
Do/San Feng Qiu Huang, Humanity/Ren, The
Ten Brothers vs. the Sea Monster/Shi Xiongdi
Nuhai Chu Mo, The Outcast Woman, Parts
One and Two/Qi Fu Shangxia Ji, Forever
Lovers, Parts One and Two/En Qing Shangxia
Ji, The Wonderful Partner/Jiming Goudao,
Talented Children Getting Robbers/Shentong
Qinxiong Ji, The Last Five Minutes/Zuihou
Wufen Zhong, Adventure on a Deadly
Island/Huang Dao Jinghun, A Story About
Three Families/A Fu Guonian 1960; Long Live
the Money/Yinzhi Wansui, The Seven Kids/Qi
Xiaofu, The Story of a Family, Parts One and
Two/Tianlun Shangxia Ji 1961; Her Majesty's
Imperial Warrant/Jinpai Ji, The Chase/Bubu
Zhuizong, Autumn Melancholy/Qiufeng Qiuyu,
It's Hard to Get a Loving Man/Nande Youqing
Lang, The Wise Bride/Niuji Xinniang, 999 The
Mysterious Body/999 Guaishi An, The
Reunion/Pojing Chongyuan, Mysterious
Murder/Shenmi Xiongsha An, Longing for
Mother's Return/Yeye Wang Niang Gui 1962;
Take a Husband/Zhao Lang Ru She, The
Sea/Hai, When Spring Comes/Chun Dao
Renjian, The Unfortunate Couple/Wanjie
Yuanyang, The Lady Detective/Nü Zhentan,
The Strange Hero Flying Swallow/Guaixia
Yanzi Fei (also act.), Let's Be Happy/Jieda
Huanxi, An Ill-Fated Beauty/Boming Hongyan,
I Am the Murderer/999 Woshi Xiongshou,
Passionately in Love/Chiqing Ernü 1963;
Murder of a Woman/Xiangcheng Yanshi, Last
Flight to Freedom/Mimi Wenjian San Ling San,
Getting Married/Nanhun Nüjia, All Are
Happy/Mantang Jiqing 1964; The Chauffeur
Was a Lady/Nü Siji (also scr.), The
Pursuit/Wanli Zhuizong (also scr.), The Ring
of Spies/Xuezi Diyi Hao, An Eye for an
Eye/Xuezhai Xuezhai, Agent Black Spider/Tewu
Hei Zhizhu 1965; But How Cruel You
Are/Lang Xin He Tai Ren, Ghost
Chasers/Yeban de Guiying 1966; They Fought
Shoulder to Shoulder/Hukou Yuanyang, Miss,
Mr, Mrs/Xiaojie, Xiansheng, Shinai (co-dir.
with Cheung Ying), Divorce
Brinkmanship/Lihun zhi Xi 1967; The
Admirers of the Girl in the Mini-skirt/Baidao

279

Mini Qun, The Magic Bow/Shen Gong **1968**;
The Twin Swords/Duoming Cixiong Jian, Two
Sisters Who Steal/Shentou Zimei Hua, Money
From Heaven/Tianci Hengcai **1969**; To Crack
the Dragon Gate/Duzhang Zhen Longmen (co-
dir. with Fung Chi-kong) **1970**; Fun, Hong
Kong Style/Taiping Shanxia **1974**; My
Bewitched Wife/Shenhua Waimu Guhuo Qi
1975; Star Wonderfun/Xingzuo Qiqu Lu **1976**;
No Money No Talk/Luan Long Bo Meng **1977**;
Crazy Hustlers/Mengzai Shamei Miao Zhentan
(co-dir. with Do Ping) **1979**.
MANDARIN FILMS: The Shadow/Moying **1957**;
Affairs of Kitty/Xiao Mi Qushi **1958**; The
Golden Beauty/Jin Meiren **1959**; Beautiful
Vixen/Hutian Hudi **1976**.

Shu Kei (name in pinyin: Shu Qi), b. 1956,
Hong Kong. Writer-director. Also film
critic, distributor and promoter. Early
career as TV writer. 1979, wrote script of
Yim Ho's Happenings/Ye Che, also Yim's
assistant director on this and subsequent
film, Wedding Bells, Wedding Belles/Gongzi
Jiao (1980). Debut as director in 1981.
Founded Creative Workshop in 1986, to
handle distribution and publicity of films
such as A City of Sadness/Beiqing Chengshi,
Raise the Red Lantern/Dahong Denglong Gao
Gao Gua, and Farewell My Concubine/Bawang
Bieji.

FILMS: Sealed With a Kiss/Liang Xiao Wu Zhi
(also co-scr.) **1981**; Soul/Lao Niang Gou Sao
(also co-scr.) **1986**; Sunless Days/Wu Taiyang
de Rizi (documentary, also co-scr.) **1989**;
Stage Door (aka Hu-Du-Men)/Hu Du Men
1996; A Queer Story/Jilao Sishi (also scr.),
Love Amoeba Style/Aiqing Amiba **1997**.
AS WRITER: Happenings/Ye Che (co-scr.) 1979;
To Hell with the Devil/Modeng Tianshi (co-
scr.) 1982; Temptress Moon/Fengyue 1996.

Patrick Tam (name in pinyin: Tan Jiaming,
name in Cantonese Tam Kar-ming), b.
1948, Hong Kong. New wave director.
Published film criticism as student. Entered
HK-TVB in 1967, developing as producer
and director with penchant for
experimentation. Left TVB 1977, making
debut as director in 1980 with The
Sword/Ming Jian. Well-versed in formal
properties of film, often showing
fascination for French and Japanese new
wave styles. An underrated director.

FILMS: The Sword/Ming Jian (also co-scr.)
1980; Love Massacre/Ai Sha **1981**;
Nomad/Liehuo Qingchun (also co-scr.) **1982**;
Cherie/Xue'er (also co-scr.) **1984**; Final

Victory/Zuihou Shengli (also prod. design)
1987; Burning Snow/Xue Zai Shao (also co-
scr. and prod. design) **1988**; My Heart is
That Eternal/Shashou Hudie Meng (also
co prod. design) **1989**.
FURTHER CREDITS: art director on Mak Tai-
kit's To Spy With Love/Xiaoxin Jiandie (1990);
supervising editor on Wong Kar-wai's Days
of Being Wild/A Fei Zhengzhuan (1990) and
co-editor on same director's Ashes of
Time/Dongxie Xidu (1994).

Tang Huang, b. 1916, Shanghai; d. 1976,
Hong Kong. Director. Started in newsreel
documentaries in 1939, employed by the
KMT-run Central Film Studio (Zhong
Dian), and making his first feature for that
studio's No. 1 branch in Shanghai in 1949.
Directing career in Hong Kong in 1953.
Bulk of output made for MP and
GI/Cathay.

FILMS: (IN SHANGHAI) Fantasies of the Silver
Screen/Yinhai Huanmeng (compilation film),
Search for a Dream/Xunmeng Ji 1949; (IN
HONG KONG) Diary of a Husband/Zhangfu
Riji (co-dir. with Luo Wei), The Notorious
Woman/Ming Nüren Biezhuan (co-dir. with Yi
Wen), Crooks' Haven/Mogui Tiantang **1953**;
Tradition/Chuantong **1955**; The Story of a Fur
Coat/Jin Lü Yi **1956**; Immortal Tunes of Show-
Biz/Yinhai Xian Ge Chuchu Wen, Love and
Crime/Ai yu Zui, Life With Grandma/Man
Ting Fang **1957**; Love and Hate in the
Underworld/Jianghu Enchou (co-dir. with
Wan Fang) **1958**; Love by the Beach/Haibin
Chunse, Love and War/Hongfen Gange (also
scr.), Her Tender Heart/Yunü Siqing,
Cinderella and Her Little Angels/Yunchang
Yanhou **1959**; June Bride/Liu Yue Xinniang,
Sister Long Legs/Changtui Jiejie, Devotion/Mu
yu Nü, Miss Pony-tail/Bianzi Guniang,
Between Tears and Laughter/Yu Lou San Feng,
Sleeping Beauty/Shui Meiren **1960**; Beauty
Parade/Tiyu Huanghou, The Girl With the
Golden Arm/Zei Meiren **1961**; Crusade Against
Daddy/Zao Sheng Guizi, Come Rain, Come
Shine/Yehua Lian **1962**; Little Lotus/He Hua,
Four Brave Ones/Diehai Si Zhuangshi (co-dir.
with Wang Liuzhao) **1963**; The Magic
Lamp/Baolian Deng (co-dir. with several
others) **1964**; Fairy, Ghost, Vixen/Liaozhai
Zhiyi, Three Smart Girls/San Duo Meigui Hua
1965; Seventh Heaven/Qi Chongtian **1966**; The
Magic Fan/Shan Zhong Ren, The
Haunted/Liaozhai Zhiyi Xuji, Operation
Bangkok/Diehai Jiaolong (also scr.), Operation
Macao/Yingxiong Dan **1967**; The Persian
Cat/Bosi Mao, No Time for Love/Youlong

Xifeng, Song of Our Family/Chun Nuan Renjian (also scr.) **1968**; The Monkey in Hong Kong/Sun Wukong Da Nao Xiang Gang, My Father In-Law/Cheng Long Kuai Xu, The Spirits/Liaozhai Zhiyi Sanji **1969**; Monkey Comes Again/Sun Wukong Zai Nao Xianggang **1971**; (IN TAIWAN) No Rest on Sunday/Xingqi Tian Bu Fangjia, The Iron Fist/Tiequan Zhengduo **1972**; A Resort Called Hell/Shewang yu Yan Wang **1973**.

Tang Shuxuan, b. 1941, Yunnan Province. Director. USC graduate, whose first two films The Arch/Dong Furen (1969) and China Behind/Zaijian Zhongguo (1972) have given her something of an underground reputation: they are two of Hong Kong's most significant art movies of the 1970s (the latter not released until 1987, in part due to political censorship). Started film magazine Close-Up/Da Texie in 1975, closing it in 1979, the year she also gave up her film career and emigrated to US.

FILMS: The Arch/Dong Furen (also scr.) **1969**; China Behind/Zaijian Zhongguo (also scr.), completed in **1974**, not released until **1987**; Sup Sap Bup Dup/Shisan Buda (also scr.) **1975**; The Hong Kong Tycoon/Baofa Hu (also co-scr.) **1979**.

Tao Qin, b. 1915, Zhejiang Province; d. 1969, Hong Kong. Writer-director. Writing career in Shanghai during 'Orphan Island' period, associated with producer Zhang Shankun (he was sometimes credited under his real name Qin Fuji). In Hong Kong in 1949, debuting as director in 1952. Has directed for Great Wall, MP and GI, and Shaw Brothers. A neglected master of Hong Kong's Mandarin cinema, Tao's films are marked by stylish mise-en-scène and literate dialogue, his forte being the melodrama (but also comedies, musicals). Best remembered for two superior melodramas, Love Without End/Bu Liao Qing (1963) and The Blue and the Black/Lan yu Hei (1967), both starring Lin Dai.

FILMS (majority of films also scr.): Father Marries Again/Yijia Chun, Tomorrow/Mingtian **1952**; Aren't the Kids Lovely?/Ernü Jing, Night and Every Night/Pipa Xiang, A Song to Remember/Han Chan Qu, The Third Life/Can Sheng **1953**; Beyond the Grave/Ren Gui Lian, Temptation/Youhuo **1954**; A Deep-Love Well/Chixin Jing, Followed Birds/Tonglin Niao **1955**; Our Lovely Baby/Xiling Men, The Error/Hong Chen, A Lonely Heart aka The Love Bird/Ling Yan,

Surprise/Jinghun Ji, Secret of a Married Woman/Shao Nainai de Mimi, Our Good Daughter/Hao Nüer **1956**; Murder in the Night/Wutou An, Our Sister Hedy/Si Qianjin **1957**; Beware of Pickpockets/Tifang Xiaoshou **1958**; Calendar Girl/Longxiang Fengwu, The More the Merrier/Sanxing Banyue, Darling Daughter/Qianjin Xiaojie, Tragedy of Love/Tian Chang Di Jiu, The Scout Master/Tongjun Jiaolian, Wedding Bells for Hedy/Langui Fengyun, Desire/Yu Wang **1959**; Spring Tide/Chun Chao, Twilight Hours/Xiaofeng Canyue, How to Marry a Millionaire/Kuang Lian **1960**; All the Best/Jieda Huanxi, Les Belles/Qianjiao Baimei, Love Without End/Bu Liao Qing **1961**; The Love Parade/Huatuan Jincu, The Lady and the Thief/Nüren yu Xiao Tou **1963**; The Dancing Millionaire/Wanhua Yingchun **1964**; Hong Kong, Manila, Singapore/Xin Hua Duo Duo Kai **1965**; The Blue and the Black/Lan yu Hei **1966**; That Tender Age/Shaonian Shiwu Ershi Shi, My Dreamboat/Chuan **1967**; When the Clouds Roll By/Yun Ni **1968**; Twin Blades of Doom/Yinyang Dao **1969**. AS WRITER: (IN SHANGHAI) The Guiding Vessel/Renhai Cihang **1942**; Fiery Reds and Pleasing Purples/Wanzi Qianhong **1944**; Orioles Soar on Earth/Ying Fei Renjian (credited under real name Qin Fuji) **1946**; Bad Dream of the Red Chamber/Honglou Canmeng, Hot Blood/Re Xue, Demons of Humanity/Renhai Yaomo, In the Sea of Life/Hai Mangmang (HK) **1948**; Tying the Knot/Tongxin Jie; (IN HONG KONG) The Unmarried Mother/Wei Chujia de Mama, Blood-Stained Begonia/Xueran Haitang Hong **1949**; The Flower Street/Hua Jie, Awful Truth/Shuohuang Shijie (co-scr.) **1950**; A Night-Time Wife/Jinhun Ji **1951**; Blossoms in the Heart/Baihua Qifang, A Bachelor is Born/Fang Maozi, Unknown Father/Bu Zhidao de Fuqin **1952**; Rainbow Rhythms/Caihong Qu **1953**.

Johnny To (name in pinyin: Du Qifeng; name in Cantonese: To Kei-fung), b. 1955, Hong Kong. Director. Entered entertainment industry in 1972, employed by HK-TVB. Directed first film in 1980 but returned to TV work until 1986 when he switched full-time to directing films. Best known for his comedies, particularly The Eighth Happiness/Baxing Baoxi (1987) and the fantasy action movie The Heroic Trio/Dongfang Sanxia (1993).

FILMS: The Enigmatic/ Bishui Hanshan Duoming Jin **1980**; The Happy Ghost 3/Kaixin

Gui Zhuang Gui (co-dir.) **1986**; *The Seven Year Itch/Qi Nian zhi Yang* **1987**; *The Eighth Happiness/Baxing Baoxi* **1988**; *All About Ah Long/A Lang de Gushi* **1989**; *The Fun, The Luck, and the Tycoon/Jixing Gongzhao, The Story of My Son/Ai de Shijie* (also co-scr.) **1990**; *The Royal Scoundrel/Shatan Zai yu Zhou Shinai, Casino Raiders II/Zhijun Wushang II zhi Yong Ba Tianxia* **1991**; *Lucky Encounter/Ti Tao Bao, Justice My Foot/Shensi Guan* **1992**; *The Heroic Trio/Dongfang Sanxia, The Barefooted Kid/Chijiao Xiaozi, The Mad Monk/Ji Gong, Executioners/Xiandai Haoxia Zhuan* (co-dir. with Ching Siu-tung) **1993**; *Loving You/Wuwei Shentan* **1995**; *A Moment of Romance 3/Tian Ruo You Qing III Fenghuo Jiaren* **1996**; *Lifeline/Shiwan Huoji* **1997**.

Eric Tsang (name in pinyin: Zeng Zhiwei; name in Cantonese: Tsang Chi-wai), b. 1954, Hong Kong. Actor-director. A professional soccer player before he entered films as part of Zhang Che's stable of stuntmen (in the director's independent company, Chang Gong). After various jobs as martial artist, actor, writer, he was given his first chance to direct in 1979. Known as a good team player, his films often display the qualities of collective endeavour (*Aces Go Places/Zhuijia Paidang, The Tigers/Wu Hu Jiang zhi Juelie*).

FILMS: *The Challenger/Ti Guan* **1979**; *The Loot/Zei Zang* **1980**; *The Crazy Chase/Hefang Shensheng* **1981**; *Aces Go Places/Zuijia Paidang* **1982**; *Aces Go Places, Part Two/Zuijia Paidang Daxian Shentong* **1983**; *Double Trouble/Daxiao Buliang* (also act.) **1984**; *Strange Bedfellows/Liang Gongpo Ba Tiao Xin* (episode, also act.), *Shyly Joker/Xiaosheng Xianchou* (co-dir. with Wu Ma, also act.) **1986**; *Trouble Couple/Kaixin Wuyu* (also act.), *You're My Destiny/Yong Ai Zhuo Yiren* **1987**; *Little Cop/Xiaoxiao Jingcha* (also act.) **1989**; *Fatal Vacation/Anle Zhanchang* (also act.) **1990**; *The Tigers/Wu Hu Jiang zhi Juelie* **1991**; *Ghost Punting/Wu Fuxing Zhuang Gui*(co-dir., also act.), *Handsome Siblings/Juedai Shuangjiao* **1992**; *Come Fly the Dragon/Fadou Houzi,Vampire Family/Yi Wu Xiaoya Gui* (co-dir., also act.) **1993**; *Those Were the Days/Sige 32A He Yige Xiangjiao Shaonian* **1996**.
AS ACTOR: *The Iron-Fisted Monk/Sande Heshang yu Zhuang Miliu* **1977**; *Dirty Tiger, Crazy Frog/Laohu Tianji* (also co-scr.), *Enter the Fat Dragon/Feilong Guojiang* **1978**; *Crazy Couple/Wuzhao Sheng Youzhao* **1979**; *Legend of the Owl/Maotou Ying, Chasing Girls/Zhui*

Nüzai **1981**; *Once Upon a Rainbow/Caiyun Qu, Till Death Do We Scare/Xiao Sheng Pa Pa* **1982**; *The Perfect Wife/Zhuan Qiao Qiang Jiao* **1983**; *Heaven Can Help/Shang Tian Jiuming, Beloved Daddy/Shihun Laodou* **1984**; *Funny Triple/Kaixin San Xiang Pao, Friendly Ghost/Laoyou Guigui, Affectionately Yours/Huazai Duoqing, Funny Face/Chou Xiaoya, Those Merry Souls/Shilai Yunzhuan* **1985**; *The Millionaires' Express/Fugui Lieche, Lucky Stars Go Places/Zuijia Fuxing* **1986**; *It's a Mad, Mad World/Fugui Biren, The Seven Year Itch/Qi Nian zhi Yang, Scared Stiff/Xiao Sheng Meng Jing Hun, Final Victory/Zuihou Shengli, The Romancing Star/Jingzhuang Zhui Nüzai, The 30 Million Rush/Hengcai Sanqian Wan, Naughty Cadets on Patrol/Datou Bing* (also co-scr.), *Golden Swallow/JinYanzi* **1987**; *The Romancing Stars, Part Two/Jingzhuang Zhui Nüzai zhi Er, The Other Half and the Other Half/Wo Ai Taikong Ren, Keep on Dancing/Jixu Tiao Wu, Double Fattiness/Shuang Fei Ling Men, Criminal Hunter/Longhu Zhiduo Xing, Into the Night/Jinghun Jinwan Ye, Mister Mistress/Hunwai Qing, How to Pick/Qiu Ai Gansi Dui, Greatest Lover/Gongzi Duoqing, Eighteen Times/Hao Nü Shiba Jia* **1988**; *Lucky Guys/Fuxing Ling Men, Return of the Lucky Stars/Fuxing Chuang Jianghu, Dream of Desire/Huaxin Mengli Ren* **1989**; *The Sniping/Qi Bing, Sunshine Friends/Xiaoxing Zhuang Diqiu, The Other Half/Laopo Ni Hao Ye* **1990**; *The Last Blood/Jingtian Shier Xiaoshi, Alan and Eric/Shuangcheng Gushi, The Banquet/Haomen Yeyan* **1991**; *Days of Being Dumb/A Fei yu A Ji, Once Upon a Time, a Hero in China/Huang Feihong Xiaozhuan* **1992**; *Master Wong Vs. Master Wong/Huang Feihong Dui Huang Feihong, Yesteryou, Yesterme, Yesterday/Jide Xiangjiao Chengshu Shi, Chez 'n Ham/Zishi Huotui, Lady Super Cop/Nüer Dang Ziqiang, Moonlight Boy/Yueguang de Shaonian* (Taiwan) **1993**; *Always be the Winners/Shenlong Dusheng zhi Qikai Desheng, Oh Yes Sir/Shen Tan Power zhi Wen Mi Zhui Xiong, He's a Woman, She's a Man/Jinzhi Yuye, Over the Rainbow Under the Skies/Jide ... Xiangjiao Chengshu Shi II Cu Lian Qingren* **1994**; *The Age of Miracles/Mama Fanfan, How to Meet the Lucky Stars/Yun Cai Wu Fu Xing, Who's the Woman, Who's the Man?/Jinzhi Yuye 2, Comrades Almost a Love Story/Tian Mimi* **1996**.

Tsui Hark (name in pinyin: Xu Ke), b. 1951, Vietnam. Director, New Wave wunderkind. In Hong Kong in 1966 for his secondary school education, then to US to study in a Texas university. He interrupted his studies to co-direct a 45-minute documentary *From Spikes to Spindles;* also edited a Chinatown newspaper in NYC, developed a community theatre group and was active in a Chinatown cable TV programme. Returned to Hong Kong in 1977 and was immediately employed in TV. Made his first feature in 1979. Founded Film Workshop in 1984, producing his own films and those directed by others. Also actor, notably in Patrick Tam's *Final Victory/Zuihou Shengli* (1987) and John Woo's *Run Tiger Run/Liang Zhi Laohu* (1985).

FILMS: *The Butterfly Murders/Die Bian* **1979**; *We're Going to Eat You/Diyu Wumen, Dangerous Encounter – 1st Kind/Diyi Leixing Weixian* **1980**; *All the Wrong Clues (for the Right Solution)/Guima Zhiduo Xing* **1981**; *Zu: Warriors From the Magic Mountain/Xin Shu Shan Jianxia* **1983**; *Aces Go Places, Part Three: Our Man in Bond Street/Zuijia Paidang III: Nühuang Miling, Shanghai Blues/Shanghai zhi Ye* **1984**; *Working Class/Dagong Huangdi* (also act.) **1985**; *Peking Opera Blues/Dao Ma Dan* 1986; *A Better Tomorrow, Part Three/Yingxiong Bense III* **1989**; *Swordsmen/Xiao'ao Jianghu* (co-dir. with King Hu, Ching Siu-tung, Raymond Lee, also prod.) **1990**; *The Raid/Cai Shu zhi Hengsao Qianjun* (co-dir. with Ching Siu-tung, also co-scr.), *Once Upon a Time in China/Huang Feihong* (also prod., co-scr.), *The Banquet/Haomen Yeyan* (co-dir. with others, also co-scr.) **1991**; *The Twin Dragons/Shuang Long Hui* (co-dir. with Ringo Lam, also co-scr.), *Once Upon a Time in China, Part Two/Huang Feihong II zhi Nan'er Dang Ziqiang* (also co-prod., co-scr.), *The Master/Huang Feihong 92 zhi Long Xing Tianxia, King of Chess/Qi Wang* (co-dir. with Yim Ho, also prod.) **1992**; *Once Upon a Time in China, Part Three/Huang Feihong zhi San: Shiwang Zheng Ba* (also co-scr., prod.), *Green Snake/Qing She* (also co-scr., prod.) **1993**; *The Lovers/Liang Zhu* (also co-scr., prod.), *Once Upon a Time in China, Part Five/Huang Feihong zhi Wu Long Cheng Jian Ba* (also co-prod., co-scr.) **1994**; *The Chinese Feast/Jinyu Mantang* (also co-prod.), *Love in the Time of Twilight, Huayue Jiaqi, The Blade/Dao* (also co-scr.) **1995**; *Tristar/Da San Yuan* (also co-scr.) 1996; *Double Team* (in US) **1997**.
AS PRODUCER: *A Better Tomorrow/Yingxiong Bense* **1986**; *A Chinese Ghost Story/Qiannü Youhun, A Better Tomorrow, Part Two/Yingxiong Bense II* **1987**; *I Love*

Maria/Tiejia Wudi Maliya (also act.), *Gunmen/Tianluo Diwang* **1988**; *A Chinese Ghost Story, Part Two/Qiannü Youhun II Renjian Dao* **1990**; *Swordsman, Part II/Xiao'ao Jianghu II: Dongfang Bubai, Dragon Inn/Xin Longmen Kezhan* (also co-scr.), *The Wicked City/Yaoshao Dushi* (also co-scr.) **1992**; *The East is Red/Dongfang Bubai Fengyun Zai Qi* (also co-scr.), *Once Upon a Time in China, Part Four/Huang Feihong zhi Si: Wang Zhe zhi Feng* (also co-scr.), *The Magic Crane/Xin Xianhe Shenzhen* (also co-scr.) **1993**; *Shanghai Grand/Xin Shanghai Tan* 1996; *Once Upon a Time in China and America/Huang Feihong zhi Xiyu Hongshi* **1997**.

Tu Guangqi, b. 1914, Shaoxing; d. 1980, Los Angeles. Mandarin director-actor. A graduate of the National Drama School in Nanjing, he acted on the stage in Shanghai in 1937 and was brought into films by director Zhu Shilin as an actor. Directing debut in 1940. In Hong Kong in 1949, directing for Yonghua, Asia, Xinhua, Shaws, and Cathay. Best remembered films: *The Little Phoenix/Xiao Fengxian* (1953), *Half-Way Down/Ban Xialiu Shehui* (1957), and *The First Sword/Diyi Jian* (1967). As actor mostly in character roles (e.g. Fei Mu's 1940 *Confucius/Kong Fuzi*, King Hu's 1975 *The Valiant Ones/Zhonglie Tu*). Also directed numerous Cantonese features.

MANDARIN FEATURES: (IN SHANGHAI) *Meng Lijun, Parts One and Two* (co-dir. with Zhu Shilin) **1940**; *New Song of the Fishermen/Xin Yuguang Qu* **1941**; *Falling Plum Blossoms/Meihua Luo* (also scr.) **1942**; (IN PEKING) *Code Number One/Tianzi Diyi Hao* (also scr.) **1946**; *From Night Till Dawn/Heiye Dao Tianming* (also scr.), (IN SHANGHAI) *Murder Under the Black Moon/Yuehei Fenggao* (also scr.), *Wedding Candles/Longfeng Huazhu, Birds Sing Everywhere/Chuchu Wen Niao Ti* **1947**; *Like a Ghost/Shen Chu Gui Mo* (also scr.), *Tragedy of Two Sisters/Xuejian Zimei Hua* (also scr.), *Broken Love/Duanchang Xiangsi, Return of the Scented Spirit/Fanghun Guilai* (also scr.) **1948**; *The Woman Who Played With Fire/Wanhuo de Nüren, The Female Robber/Nü Zei* (also scr.), *Female Bandit Number Thirteen/Shisan Hao Nü Dao* (also scr.) **1949**; (IN HONG KONG) *Twenty-Four Hours of Marriage* aka *The Wedding Day/Jiehun Ershisi Xiaoshi, The Tiger and the Dog/Huluo Pingyang* **1950**; *Modern Wives/Modeng Taitai, To See the Clouds Roll/Chuhai Yunxia* **1951**; *The World Turned*

Upside Down/Tianfan Difu, *The Goddess and the Devil/Yue'er Wanwan Zhao Jiu Zhou* (also scr.), *The Closer the Better/Jinshui Loutai* (also scr.), *Fatal Attraction/Nie Yuan* (co-dir., also scr.), *The Troubled Love of Wang Kui and Gui Ying/Wang Kui yu Gui Ying*, *Sweet Memories/Manyuan Chunse* (co-dir. with others, also co-scr.) **1952**; *Heaven of Love, Sea of Sin/Niehai Qingtian* (also scr.), *A Songstress Called Hong Lingyan/Genü Hong Lingyan*, *New West Chamber/Xin Xixiang Ji*, *Meal Time/Guifang Le*, *The Little Phoenix* aka *General Choi and Lady Balsam/Xiao Fengxian*, *The Dawn of China's Revolution/Qiu Jin* **1953**; *Rose, I Love You/Meigui Meigui Wo Ai Ni*, *The Wind Withers/Feng Xiaoxiao* (also scr.), *Blood-Stained Flowers* aka *The 72 Martyrs of Canton/Bixue Huanghua* (co-dir. with several others, also act.) **1954**; *Love and Duty/Lian'ai yu Yiwu* (also scr.) **1955**; *Love's Elegy/Duanchang Fengyue*, (IN TAIWAN) *Code Number One* (remake)/*Xin Tianzi Diyi Hao* (also scr., act.), *The Black Widow/Hei Guafu* (also scr.) **1956**; *Half-Way Down/Ban Xialiu Shehui*, *The Great Wall of China/Wanli Changcheng*, *You Are My Soul/Ni Shi Wo de Linghun* **1957**; *Love With An Alien/Yiguo Qingyuan* (co-dir. with others), *Where Is My Bride?/Feng Qiu Feng* (also scr.) **1958**; *Red Turn the Flowers When Down Come the Showers/Yu Bu Jiu Hua Hua Bu Hong* **1959**; *Nineteen Swordsmen of Ching City /Qingcheng Shijiu Xia*, *A Shadow Over the Chateau/Honglou Moying* (also scr.), *Flash and Shadow of the Sword/Dao Guang Jian Ying* (also scr.), *Bloodbath in Emerald Valley/Cuiganggu Xue Ji* (also scr.) **1960**; *Heroic Lovers From the Tomb/Gumu Xialü*, *The Witch Girl/Yao Nü He Yue'er* **1961**; *How the Oil Vendor Won the Beauty Queen/Maiyou Lang Duzhan Huakui Nü* **1964**; *The First Sword/Diyi Jian* **1967**; *The Invisible Sabre/Yanling Dao* **1968**; *The Violet Mansion/Yijian Qingshen* (also scr.), *Lotus Camp/Lianhua Zhai* **1969**; *The King's Sword/Zhuangshi Xue* (also scr.), *Night is Not Made For Stealing/Qianmian Zei Meiren*, *Way Ching Killed the Dragon/Weizheng Zhan Long* (also scr.) **1970**; *Crush/Tangshou Taiquan Dao* **1972**.

Wang Tianlin (name in Cantonese: Wong Tin-lam), b. 1928, Shanghai. Prolific director of Cantonese and Mandarin films. In Hong Kong in 1945. Entered film industry in 1947, debuted as director in 1950 in Cantonese cinema. Began working in Mandarin films with producer Zhang Shankun in 1951. Proficient in martial arts

flicks, melodramas, musicals (working for MP and GI/Cathay). *The Wild, Wild Rose/Ye Meigui zhi Lian* (1960), based on *Carmen*), suggests that Wang's oeuvre may be a rich source for cult-movie discoveries. Active in TV from early 1970s on. Father of director Wong Jing.

CANTONESE FILMS: (selected) *The Flying Swordsman of O Mei, Parts One and Two/Emei Feijian Xia*, *Three Girl Musketeers/Nü San Jianxia*, *Magnificent Hero/Shen Xia Jin Luohan*, *Strange Hero/Jianghu Qixia* **1950**; *The Lightning Sword/Leidian Zhuifeng Jian*, *The Flying Daggers/Feidao Li Fengjiao*, *Darts of Fury/Wudi Lianhuan Biao*, *The Chivalrous Pair/Cixiong Shuangxia* **1951**; *Bloody Fight by the Golden Sand Beach/Xuejian Jinsha Wan*, *Black Swirling Wind/Qixia Hei Xuan Feng*, *Heroine in Red/Nüxia Yizhang Hong* **1952**; *Not All Umbrellas Have Similar Handles/Tongzhe Butong Bing* **1953**; *Heroine of a Hundred Faces/Baibian Meihua Xia* **1955**; *The Scatterbrain/Shichi Jiawan*, *How Wong Fei-hung Vanquished the Terrible Hound/Huang Feihong Shamian Fu Shen Quan* **1956**; *The Dragon's Daughter/Long Nü* **1957**; *The Seven Lucky Ones/Qi Xiling Men*, *Second Spring/Cuilou Chun Xiao* **1960**; *Mankiller Against the Tricky Man/Sharen Wang Dazhan Niuji Tan* **1961**; *Soaring High/Yifei Chongtian*, *Double Date/Fuhui Shuangxiu* **1962**; *Romantic Dreamer/Zizuo Duoqing* **1966**; *My Darling Love/Tixiao Fuqi* **1974**; *The Utmost Greatness/Da Dou Da* (also scr.) **1979**; *Pursuit/Mengnü Dazei Sha Zhentan* **1980**. MANDARIN FILMS: *The Legend of Madame White Snake/Baishe Zhuan* (co-dir.) **1952**; *Blood-Stained Flowers* aka *The 72 Martyrs of Canton/Bixue Huanghua* (co-dir. with several others) **1954**; *The Magic Monk and His Double/Zhenjia Jigong*, *Lady Balsam's Conquest/Xiao Fengxian, Xuji* (co-dir.) **1955**; *Songs of the Peach Blossom River* (co-dir. with Zhang Shankun), *Who Isn't Romantic?/Nage Bu Duo Qing*, *Angela of the Vineyard/Putao Xianzi*, *Season of Budding Roses/Qiangwei Chuchu Kai* **1956**; *The Nightingale of Alishan/Alishan zhi Ying*, *The Case of the Walking Corpses/Xiangxi Gan Shi Ji*, *Storm in the Peach Blossom Village/Fengyu Taohua Cun* **1957**; *Flying Together/Fenghuang yu Fei*, *Stand Up and Cheer/Yinhai Sheng Ge* (co-dir.) **1958**; *Flower Princess/Baihua Gongzhu*, *Riots in Outer Space/Liang Sha Danao Taikong* (also scr.), *All in the Family/Jia You Xishi*, *Lady on the Roof/Liang Shang Jiaren* **1959**; *A Challenge of Love/Ru Shi Jiaren*, *Secret Affairs/Si Lian*, *The Innocent Girl/Xiao Niao Yiren*, *The Iron*

284

Fist/Tiebi Jingang, The Lady Musketeer/Nüxia Wen Tingyu, The Wild, Wild Rose/Ye Meigui zhi Lian, The Amorous Pussy Cat/Duo Qing de Ye Mao **1960**; The Greatest Civil War on Earth/Nanbei He, Venture of the Lady Musketeer/Wen Tingyu Huohai Jianchou, You Were Meant For Me/Youxi Renjian **1961**; Lily of the Valley/Huo Zhong Lian, Her Pearly Tears/Zhenzhu Lei, The Greatest Wedding on Earth/Nanbei Yijia Qin **1962**; Because of Her/Jiao Wo Ruhe Bu Xiang Ta (co-dir. with Yi Wen), Father Takes a Bride/Xiao Ernü **1963**; The Magic Lamp/Baolian Deng (co-dir. with several others), The Story of Three Loves, Parts One and Two/Tixiao Yinyuan, The Greatest Love Affair on Earth/Nanbei Xixiang Feng, Romance of the Forbidden City/Shen Gong Yuan **1964**; A Beggar's Daughter/Jin Yu Nu **1965**; The Lucky Purse/Suo Lin Nang **1966**; Little Matchmaker/Qilin Songzi, Wife of a Romantic Scholar/Su Xiaomei **1967**; The Crimson Rose/Xuejiu Hong Meigui, Darling, Stay at Home/Taitai Wansui, Travels With a Sword/Juedou Ehu Ling, Red Plum Pavilion/Hongmei Ge, Desperate Seven/Qi Da Dao **1968**; The Royal Seal/Dao Er, Mad, Mad Sword/Shenjing Dao, How Love is Tested/Shi Qing Ji **1969**; The Unknown Swordsman/Yixiang Ke **1970**; The Chase/Zhui Ji (also scr.) **1971**.

Wang Yu (also billed as Jimmy Wang Yu), b. 1944, Wuxi, Jiangsu Province. Actor-director. A swimming athlete and karate expert who auditioned for the lead in Zhang Che's Tiger Boy/Huxia Jianchou and got the part. Successful career followed as martial arts star and later, director. Wang directed the first kung fu movie to hit the markets, The Chinese Boxer/Longhu Dou (1970), pre-empting the success of Bruce Lee the following year. In Taiwan in the 1970s; intermittently in Hong Kong (with Golden Harvest). Married actress Lin Cui (1969–75). Career hampered by murder charge in 1981 in Taiwan.

FILMS: The Chinese Boxer/Longhu Dou (also scr., act.) **1970**; (IN TAIWAN) The Brave and the Evil/Heibai Dao (also scr., act.) **1971**; The One-Armed Boxer/Dubi Quanwang (also prod., scr., act.); (IN HONG KONG) The Sword/Jian (dir. some action sequences only, also act.) **1972**; Beach of the War Gods/Zhanshen Tan (also scr., act.) **1973**; (IN TAIWAN) Four Real Friends/Sida Tianwang (also act.) **1974**; The Man From Hong Kong/Zhi Dao Huang Long (uncredited co-dir. with Brian Trenchard-Smith, also act.;

Australia/Hong Kong) **1975**; The One-Armed Boxer vs. The Flying Guillotine/Dubi Quanwang Dapo Xue Dizi (also scr., act.), The Savage Killers/Hu He Shuangxing (also act.) **1976**; The Two One-Armed Heroes/Dubi Shuangxiong (co-dir. with David Chiang, also act.), Duel of Fist and Gun/Quanqiang Juedou (also prod., act.) **1977**.
AS ACTOR: (IN HONG KONG) Temple of the Red Lotus/Jianghu Qixia, The Twin Swords/Yuanyang Jianxia **1965**; Tiger Boy/Huxia Jianchou, The Magnificent Trio/Biancheng Sanxia **1966**; Auntie Lan/Lan Yi, Trail of the Broken Blade/Duanchang Jian, The Sword and the Lute/Qinjian Enchou, Asia-Pol/Yazhou Mimi Jingcha, The One-Armed Swordsman/Dubi Dao, The Assassin/Da Cike **1967**; The Golden Swallow/Jin Yanzi, The Sword of Swords/Shen Dao **1968**; Return of the One-Armed Swordsman/Dubi Dao Wang **1969**; My Son/Chun Huo **1970**; The Desperate Chase/Zhuiming Qiang **1971**; (IN TAIWAN) The Invincible Sword/Yifu Dangguan, Furious Slaughter/Bawang Quan, Showdown/Tianwang Quan, Chow Ken/Qiu Jin, Ma Su Chen/Ma Suzhen Bao Xiong Chou, The Gallantry/Yishen Shidan, King of Boxers/Tangren Biaoke **1972**; (IN HONG KONG) A Man Called Tiger/Lengmian Hu, Knight Errant/Yingxiong Bense, Zatoichi and the One-Armed Swordsman/Dubi Dao Dazhan Mang Xia (Japan/Hong Kong), Seaman No. 7/Haiyuan Qi Hao, The Two Cavaliers/Shuanglong Chuhai, The Tattooed Dragon/Longhu Jingang **1973**; A Cookbook of Birth Control/Biyun Da Quan (Taiwan) **1975**; A Queen's Ransom/Etan Qunying Hui (HK), The Killer Meteors/Fengyu Shuangliu Xing (Taiwan) **1976**; (IN TAIWAN) One-Arm Chivalry Fights Against One-Arm Chivalry/Dubi Xia Da Zhan Dubi Xia, To Kill With Intrigue/Jianhua Yanyu Jiangnan **1977**; Brotherly Love/Qingtong Shouzu **1978**; One-Armed Swordsman Annihilates the Nine Disciples of Chu/Dubi Quanwang Yongzhan Chumen Jiuzi **1979**; The Battle of Guningtou/Guningtou Dazhan **1980**; Shanghai 13/Shanghai Tan Shisan Taibao **1984**; Island of Fire/Huoshao Dao **1991**; Shogun and Little Kitchen/Huotou Fuxing (HK) **1992**.

Wong Jing (name in pinyin: Wang Jing), b. 1956, Hong Kong. Director-writer. Entered film industry in the early 1970s aged seventeen, employed as script continuity man in the Fu Kwok Company. 1975, employed by HK-TVB as writer. 1980, debut as director in Shaw Brothers' Challenge of the

Gamesters/*Qianwang Dou Qianba*. A commercially-minded director, Wong's lightweight films have weighed heavily at the box-office. Son of director Wang Tianlin.

FILMS (also scr.): *Challenge of the Gamesters/Qianwang Dou Qianba* 1981, *Winner Takes All/Zeiwang zhi Wang* 1982; *Mercenaries From Hong Kong/Liemo Zhe, Hong Kong Playboy/Huaxin Dashao* 1983; *Prince Charming/Qingwa Wangzi, I Love Lolanto/Wo Ai Luo Landu* (also act.) 1984; *The Flying Mr. B/Guima Feiren, Girl With the Diamond Slipper/Modeng Xianlü Qiyuan* (also act.) 1985; *The Magic Crystal/Mo Feicui* (also act.) 1986; *Born to Gamble/Landu Yingxiong* (also act.), *The Romancing Star/Jingzhuang Zhui Nüzai* 1987; *The Romancing Star, Part II/Jingzhuang Zhui Nüzai Er, The Crazy Companies/Zuijia Sunyou, Mr. Possessed/Zhuangxie Xiansheng* (also act.), *How to Pick/Qiu Ai Gunsidui, The Crazy Companies, Part Two/Zuijia Sunyou Chuangqing Guan* 1988; *Doubles Causes Troubles/Shenyojng Shuangmei Mai, Casino Raiders/Zhizun Wushang* (co-dir., co-scr.), *Crocodile Hunters/Zhuandiao Da E, God of Gamblers/Du Shen* (also act.) 1989; *No Risk No Gain/Zhizunji Zhuangyuan Cai, Perfect Girls/Liangzu Yibai Fen, The Big Score/Jueqiao Zhiduo Xing* (also act.), *God of Gamblers, Part II: Back to Shanghai/Du Xia II Shanghai Tan Dusheng* 1990; *Tricky Brains/Zhenggu Zhuanjia, The Last Blood/Jiangtian Shier Xiaoshi, Dance With the Dragon/Yu Long Gong Wu* 1991; *Casino Tycoon/Ducheng Daheng zhi Xin Ge Chuanqi, Royal Tramp/Luding Ji, Casino Tycoon, Part II/Ducheng Daheng zhi Zhizun Wudi, Royal Tramp, Part II/Luding Ji II Shenlong Jiao* 1992; *Fight Back to School, Part III/Tao Xue Weilong zhi Long Guo Ji Nian, City Hunter/Chengshi Lieren, The Last Hero in China/Huang Feihong Tieji Dou Wusong, Boys are Easy/Zhui Nanzai, The Kung Fu Cult Master/Yitian Tulong Ji zhi Mojiao Jiaozhu* 1993; *New Legend of Shaolin/Hong Xiguan* (co-dir. with Yuen Kwai), *Hail the Judge/Jiupin Zhima Guan Baimian Bao Qingtian, Return to A Better Tomorrow/Xin Yingxiong Bense* (also prod.), *To Live and Die in Tsimshatsui/Xin Bianyuan Ren* (co-dir., also prod.), *God of Gamblers' Return/Du Shen 2, Whatever You Want/Zhuguang Baoqi* 1994; *The Saint of Gamblers/Du Sheng 2 Jietou Du Sheng* 1995; *Twinkle Twinkle Little Star/Yuncai Zhili Xing, God of Gamblers 3/Du Shen 3 zhi Shaonian Du Shen* (also scr.) 1996. AS WRITER: *Cunning Tendency/Guima*

Kuangchao (co-scr.), *Old Soldiers Never Die/Wenni Pawei* (co-scr.) 1978; *Itchy Fingers/Shentou Miaotan Shou Duoduo, The Lama Avenger/Da Chutou* (co-scr.), *The Ghost and I/Guigan Guoyin, Murder Most Foul/Huang Shishi* (co-scr.), *The Magnificent Butcher/Lin Shirong* (co-scr.) 1979; *Pursuit/Meng Nü Da Zei Sha Zhentan, Notorious Eight/Qianmen Bajiang* (also act.) 1980; *Dreadnaught/Yongzhe Wuquan, The Treasure Hunters/Longhu Shaoye* 1981; *Mahjong Heroes/Daque Yingxiong Zhuan, The Prodigal Son/Bai Jiazai* 1982; *Mad Mad 83/Fengkuang Basan* (co-scr.) 1983; *The Seventh Curse/Yuanzhen Xia yu Weisili* (co-scr.) 1986; *The Evil Cat/Xiong Mao* (also act.), *You're My Destiny/Yong Ai Zhuo Yiren* 1987; *Return of the Lucky Stars/Fuxing Chuang Jianghu* (co-scr.), *Vampire Buster/Zhuo Gui Dashi* (co-scr.), *Ghost Busting/Huagui Youxian Gongsi, The Romancing Stars, Part Three/Jingzhuang Zhui Nüzai Lang zhi Yizu* (also act.) 1989; *Ghostly Vixen/Tianshi Zhuojian, Kung Fu vs. Acrobatic/Modeng Rulai Shenzhang* 1990.

Kirk Wong (name in pinyin: Huang Zhiqiang; name in Cantonese: Wong Chi-keung), b. 1949, Hong Kong. Director. Studied fashion and stage design in England; while there gained TV and theatre experience. Returned to Hong Kong 1978, employed in TV on drama and action mini-series. 1980, feature film debut. Has since specialized in action flicks. Also actor, in character parts.

FILMS: *The Club/Wuting* (also prod. design) 1980; *Health Warning/Da Leitai* (video title: 'Flash Future Kung Fu') 1983; *Lifeline Express/Hongyun Dangtou* 1985; *True Colours/Yingxiong Zhengzhuan* 1986; *Gunmen/Tianluo Diwang* 1988; *Taking Manhattan/Mai Qi Mankedun* 1992; *Crime Story/Zhong'an Zu* 1993; *Organized Crime and Triad Bureau/Zhong'an Shilu Ling Ji, Rock 'N' Roll Cop/Sheng Gang Yihao Tongji Fan* (also prod.) 1994.

Wong Kar-wai (name in pinyin: Wang Jiawei), b. 1958, Shanghai. Second Wave director. Graduate of Hong Kong Polytechnic employed by HK-TVB in script department. Entered film industry in 1982 as writer (used more as an 'ideas man'). Debut as director in 1988 with *As Tears Go By/Wangjiao Kamen*. Receives acclaim as Hong Kong's latest and newest auteur with next film, *Days of Being Wild/A Fei*

Zhengzhuan (1990), originally planned in two parts (but second part was cancelled after commercial disaster of original).

FILMS: As Tears Go By/Wangjiao Kamen (also scr.) **1988**; Days of Being Wild/A Fei Zhengzhuan (also scr.) **1990**; Chungking Express/Chongqing Senlin (also scr.), Ashes of Time/Dongxie Xidu (also scr.) **1994**; Fallen Angels/Duoluo Tianshi **1995**; Happy Together/Chunguang Zhaxie **1997**.
AS WRITER: Once Upon a Rainbow/Caiyun Qu (co-scr.) **1982**; Just for Fun/Kongxin Da Shaoye (co-scr.) **1983**; Silent Romance/Yiren Zaijian (co-scr.) **1984**; Chase a Fortune/Jiren Tianxiang, The Intellectual Trio/Longfeng Zhiduo Xing (co-scr.), Unforgettable Fantasy/Xiao Huxian **1985**; Sweet Surrender/Woyao Jingui Xu (co-scr.), Rosa/Shenyong Shuangxiang Pao Xuji (co-scr.), Goodbye My Love/E Nan (co-scr.) **1986**; Final Victory/Zuihou Shengli (co-scr.), Flaming Brothers/Jianghu Longhu Dou, The Haunted Cop Shop/Menggui Chaiguan (co-scr.) **1987**; Saviour of the Soul/Jiu Yi Shendiao Xialü (uncredited) **1991**.

John Woo (name in pinyin: Wu Yusen; name in Cantonese: Ng Yu-sum) b. 1948, Guangzhou. Director. Career began in 1969 when he joined the Cathay Studio (now Golden Harvest) as a production assistant; switched over to Shaw Brothers in 1971, becoming assistant director to action maestro Zhang Che. Made his first feature as director in 1973, Farewell Buddy but not released until 1975 as The Young Dragons. 1986, made breakthrough movie, A Better Tomorrow/Yingxiong Bense. International success with The Killer/Diexue Shuangxiong (1989). Acts occasionally, mostly in his own films. Re-located to Hollywood in 1992.

FILMS (also scr. or co-scr.): Farewell Buddy/Guo Ke (released in 1975 as 'The Young Dragons/Tiehan Rouqing') **1972**; The Dragon Tamers/Nüzi Taiquan Qunying Hui **1975**; Princess Chang Ping/Dinü Hua, Countdown in Kung Fu aka Hand of Death/Shaolin Men (also act) **1976**; The Pilferers' Progress aka Money Crazy/Faqian Han **1977**; Follow the Star/Da Shaxing yu Xiao Meitou, Hello, Late Homecomers/Haluo, Yegui Ren (episode only) **1978**; Last Hurrah for Chivalry/Hao Xia **1979**; From Riches to Rags/Qian Zuo Guai **1980**; Laughing Times/Huaji Shidai (credited under name of 'Wu Shangfei') **1981**; To Hell With the Devil/Modeng Tianshi, Plain Jane to the Rescue/Bacai Lin Azhen **1982**; The Sunset

Warrior/Huanghun Zhanshi (released in 1986 as 'Heroes Shed No Tears/Yingxiong Wulei') **1983**; (IN TAIWAN) The Time You Need a Friend/Xiao Jiang **1984**; Run, Tiger, Run/Liangzhi Laohu **1985**; (IN HONG KONG) A Better Tomorrow/Yingxiong Bense (also act.), True Colours/Yingxiong Zhengzhuan (credited as 'creative director', d. Kirk Wong) **1986**; A Better Tomorrow II/Yingxiong Bense Xuji **1987**; The Killer/Diexue Shuangxiong (also ed.), Just Heroes/Yidan Qunying (co-dir. with Wu Ma) **1989**; Bullet in the Head/Diexue Jietou (also ed.) **1990**; Once a Thief/Zongheng Sihai **1991**; Hardboiled/Lashou Shentan (also act., ed.) **1992**; (IN US) Hard Target **1993**, Broken Arrow, Once a Thief (TVM) **1996**; Face/Off **1997**.

Wu Ma (sometimes credited under his real name, Feng Wuma; name in Cantonese: Ng Ma), b. 1942, Tianjin. Actor-director. Graduate of first acting class run by Shaw Brothers. Acting debut: Butterfly Chalice/Hudie Bei (released 1965). 1970, began as assistant director to Zhang Che; debuted as full director that year with Wrath of the Sword/Nujian Kuangdao. Active in Taiwan in latter part of 1970s, as part of Zhang Che's independent production company, Chang Gong. Found niche in horror-kung fu genre in 1980s Hong Kong cinema, both as director and actor (his masterpiece: The Dead and the Deadly/Ren Xia Ren, 1982).

FILMS: Wrath of the Sword/Nujian Kuangdao **1970**; Deaf and Mute Heroine/Long Ya Jian (also act.) **1971**; The Water Margin/Shuihu Zhuan (co-dir. with Zhang Che and Bao Xueli, also act.) **1972**; The Pirate/Da Haidao (co-dir. with Zhang Che and Bao Xueli), The Young Tiger/Xiao Laohu **1973**; Manchu Boxer/Qisheng Quanwang, Wits to Wits aka The Conman and the Kung Fu Kid/Langbei Weijian (also act.), The Dumb Ox/Da Tieniu (also act.; Video Title: 'Return of the Panther') **1974**; All Men Are Brothers/Dangkou Zhi (co-dir. with Zhang Che, also co-scr.) **1975**; New Shaolin Boxers/Cai Lifo Xiaozi (co-dir. with Zhang Che) **1976**; The Naval Commandos/Haijun Tuji Dui (co-dir. with Zhang Che) **1977**; The Handcuff/Shoukou **1979**; The Heroes/Yingxiong **1980**; Beware of Pickpockets/Huanle Shenxian Wo (also act.) **1981**; The Dead and the Deadly/Ren Xia Ren (also act.) **1982**; Mr. Boo Meets Pom Pom/Zhiyong Sanbao **1985**; Shyly Joker/Xiaosheng Xianchou (co-dir. with Eric

Tsang, also act.) **1986**; *My Cousin, the Ghost/Biaoge Dao* (also act.) **1987**; *Picture of a Nymph/Huazhong Xian* (also co-scr., act.) **1988**; *Burning Sensation/Huozhuo Gui* (also act.), *Just Heroes/Yidan Qunying* (co-dir. with John Woo) **1989**; *Stage Door Johnny/Wutai Zimei* (also act.), *Story of Kennedy Town/Xihuan de Gushi* (also act.) **1990**, *Fox Legend/Ling Hu* (also act.) **1991**; *Kickboxer/Huang Feihong zhi Gui Jiao Qi* (also act.) **1993**; *The Chinese Ghostbuster/Zhong Kui Jia Mei* (also act.), *Circus Kids/Maxi Xiaozi* (also act.), **1994**.

As ACTOR (selected films): *Lady General Hua Mulan/Hua Mulan* **1964**; *The Butterfly Chalice/Hudie Bei* **1965**; *Tiger Boy/Huxia Jianchou, The Sword and the Lute/Qinjian Enchou, Rape of the Sword/Dao Jian* **1967**; *The Golden Swallow/JinYanzi, Bells of Death/Duohun Ling, Divorce, Hong Kong Style/Se Bu Mi Ren Ren Zi Mi* **1968**; *The Flying Dagger/Feidao Shou, The Invincible Fist/Tieshou Wuqing* **1969**; *The Wandering Swordsman/You Xiaer* **1970**; *King Eagle/Ying Wang, Mad Killer/Fengkuang Shashou* **1971**; *Young People/Nianqing Ren* **1972**; *The Iron Fisted Monk/Sande Heshang yu Zhuangmi Liu* **1977**; *By Hook or By Crook/Xianyu Fansheng* **1980**; *Laughing Times/Huaji Shidai* **1981**; *Hong Kong 1941/Dengdai Liming* **1984**; *The Millionaires' Express/Fugui Lieche, New Mr. Vampire/Jiangshi Fansheng, Mr. Vampire, Part Two/Jiangshi Jiazu, Peking Opera Blues/Dao Ma Dan* **1986**; *A Chinese Ghost Story/Qiannü Youhun, To Err is Humane/Biaocuo Shen* **1987**; *Lai Shi, China's Last Eunuch/Zhongguo Zuihou Yige Taijian, Mr. Vampire, Saga Four/Jiangshi Shushu* **1988**, *Mr. Canton and Lady Rose/Qi Ji* **1989**; *Swordsman/Xiao'ao Jianghu, A Chinese Ghost Story, Part Two/Qiannü Youhun: Renjian Dao* **1990**; *The Gambling Ghost/Hongfu Qitian, My American Grandson/Shanghai Jiaqi, Once Upon a Time in China/Huang Feihong, The Magnificent Scoundrels/Qing Sheng* **1991**; *All Men Are Brothers/Shuihu Zhuan zhi Yingxiong Bense, The Painted Skin/Hua Pi zhi Yinyang Fawang* **1993**; *Dreadful Melody/Liuzhi Qinmo, Switch Over/Xin Qiao Langjun, Master of Zen/Damo Zushi* **1994**; *Kam Ping Mui of Deep Throat/Liaozhai Jin Ping Mei zhi Shen Hou* **1995**; *Iron Monkey 2/Jietou Shashou* **1996**.

Yan Jun, b. 1917, Peking; d. 1980, USA. Actor-director. Entered the film industry on the introduction of his uncle, Yan Hua, husband of actress Zhou Xuan. Active in the Shanghai film industry and in theatre in 'Orphan Island' period and during the Japanese occupation, acting in films for various companies including the 'Huaying' group. In Hong Kong in 1949, acting and directing for Great Wall, Yonghua, MP and GI, and Shaws. Founded his own production company, Golden Dragon (Jin Long) in 1957 (producing only four pictures). As director, best known for *Golden Phoenix/Jin Feng* (1956), starring Lin Dai, and Shaws' historical melodrama *The Grand Substitution/Wangu Liufang* (1965). As actor, remembered for his superb performances in *A Strange Woman/Yidai Yaoji, Awful Truth/Shuohuang Shijie, The Flower Street/Hua Jie* (all 1950) and *The Little Phoenix* aka *General Choi and Lady Balsam/Xiao Fengxian* (1953), where he starred opposite his wife, Li Lihua.

FILMS: *Love Eternal/Wu Shan Meng* (also act.), *Singing Under the Moon/Cui Cui* (also act.) **1953**; *Spring is in the Air/Chun Tian Bushi Dushu Tian* (also act.) **1954**; *Miss Kikuko/Juzi Guniang* (also scr., act.), *Golden Phoenix/Jin Feng* (also act.), *The Orphan Girl/Mei Gu* (also act.), *Rainstorm in Chinatown/Feng Yu Niucheshui* (also act.), *Autumn Affair/Qiu Ba, The Chase/Zhui* (also act.), *Nonya and Baba/Niangre yu Baba* (also act.) **1956**; *The Greatest Circus on Earth/Maxi Chunqiu* (also act.), *Frosty Night/Yue Luo Niao Ti Shuang Mantian* (also act.), *No Time for Love/Youlong Xifeng* (also prod., act.), *Valley of the Lost Soul/Wanghun Gu* (also act.), *A Marriage for Love/Longfeng Pei* (also act.) **1957**; *Laughter and Tears/Xiaosheng Leiying* (also prod., act.), *The Story of Yuanyuan Hong/Yuanyuan Hong* (also prod., act.) **1958**; *A Romantic Lady/Guifu Fengliu* (also prod., act.), *The Long Voyage Home/Fengyu Guizhou* (also act.), *The Pink Murder/Fen Hongse de Xiongshou* (also act.), *Appointment With Death/Siwang de Yuehui* **1959**; *A Shot in the Dark/Heiye Qiangsheng* (also act.) **1960**; *I Murderer/Woshi Sharen Fan* (also act.) **1961**; *Bride-Napping/Huatian Cuo, The Black Fox/Hei Huli* (also act.) **1962**; *Three Sinners/Yan Xijiao* (also act.); *Mung Li Chuen/Meng Lijun* (also act.) **1963**; *Qin Xianglian* (co-dir. with Chen Yixin, also act.), *Liang San Poh and Chu Ing Tai/Liang Shanbo yu Zhu Yingtai* (also act.) **1964**; *The Grand Substitution/Wangu Liufang* (also act.), *Squadron 77/Qiqi Gansi Dui* (also act.) **1965**; *That Man in Chang-an/Mengmian Daxia* (also act.), *Moonlight Serenade/Jing Jing* (also act.), *Lady Jade Locket/Lian Suo* **1967**; *Mist Over Dream Lake/Hanyan Cui* (also act.), *That Fiery Girl/Hong Lajiao* **1968**;

Golden Leaf/Jin Yezi, The Iron Buddha/Tie Luohan (also act.) **1970**; The Jade-Faced Assassin/Yumian Hu **1971.**

AS ACTOR: (IN SHANGHAI) New Hell/Xin Diyu, Li Amao and Miss Tang/Li Amao yu Tang Xiaojie **1939**; The Amorous Lady/Guifu Fengliu, Eternal Fame/Wan Gu Liufang **1942**; Alarm Conscious/Caomu Jiebing, Cloud-Capped Moon/Fuyun Yanyue, Fiery Reds and Pleasing Purples/Wanzi Qianhong, Sorrows Left at Spring River/Chunjiang Yihen **1944**; Heaven Helps a Good Man/Jiren Tianxiang, Spring on the Lake/Hu Shang Chun Hen, Mother and Son/Mu yu Zi, Murder Under the Black Moon/Yuehei Fenggao, Green Grass by the River/Qingqing Hebian Cao, Birds Sing Everywhere/Chuchu Wen Tiniao **1947**; All in the Same Boat/Tongshi Tianya Lunluo Ren, The Man Who Sold His Shadow/Chumai Yingzi de Ren, Light of the Pearl/Zhuguang Baoqi, No Words for Heaven/Wuyu Wen Cangtian **1948**; Storm in the Night/Yelai Fengyu Sheng, A Night for Killing/Sharen Ye, The Beautiful Corpse/Senlin Da Xue An, The Woman Who Played With Fire/Wanhuo de Nüren, A New Life/Zaisheng Nianhua, (IN HONG KONG) The Lexicon of Love/Fengliu Baojian, An Unfaithful Woman aka A Forgotten Woman/Dangfu Xin, Blood-Stained Begonia aka Blood Will Tell/Xue Ran Haitang Hong **1949**; A Strange Woman/Yidai Yaoji, The Flower Street/Hua Jie, Awful Truth/Shuohuang Shijie, Home Sweet Home/Nanlai Yan **1950**; Modern Red Chamber Dream/Xin Honglou Meng, Nonya/Niangre, Fatal Attraction/Nie Yuan, The Stormy Night/Fengkuang zhi Ye, Unknown Father/Bu Zhidao de Fuqini, A Moment of Bliss/Yike Chunxiao **1952**; Meal Time/Guifang Le, Night and Every Night/Pipa Xiang, Marriage Affair/Men, The Little Phoenix aka General Choi and Lady Balsam/Xiao Fengxian, The Story of Begonia/Qiu Haitang 1953; The Wind Withers/Feng Xiaoxiao **1954**; The Fisherman's Daughter/Yu Ge, Love is Like a Running Brook/Xinghua Xi zhi Lian, Merry Go Round/Huanle Niannian, Siren, Parts One and Two/Luanshi Yaoji **1956**; Hong Kong-Tokyo Honeymoon/Xianggang Dongjing Miyue Lüxing, Happy Union/Tianzuo zhi He **1957**; The Story of Lü Siniang/Lü Siniang **1958**; Darling Daughter/Qianjin Xiaojie **1959**; The Wild Girl/Ye Guniang **1960**; The Golden Silence/Youkou Nanyan, Yang Kwei-fei/Yuang Guifei **1962**; The Empress Wu/Wu Zetian **1963**; My Dreamboat/Chuan **1967**; Five Plus Five/Wudui Jia'ou **1971.**

Yi Wen (aka Evan Yang), b. 1920, Jiangsu

Province; d. 1978, Hong Kong. Director-writer. Graduated from St. John's University, Shanghai. Started working life as journalist in Chongqing during the anti-Japanese war, and in Shanghai after the war. Entered film industry as screenwriter in 1949 for KMT-controlled Zhong Dian (Central Film Studio), No. 1 studio in Shanghai, writing script of Search for a Dream/Xunmeng Ji under his real name, Yang Yanqi. 1950s, continues career in Hong Kong, first as writer, then director with sophisticated style (mainly for MP and GI). Best remembered for the musical Mambo Girl/Manbo Nülang (1957), starring Ge Lan (Grace Chang).

FILMS: The Notorious Woman/Ming Nüren Biezhuan (co-dir. with Tang Huang) **1953**; Blood-Stained Flowers aka The 72 Martyrs of Canton/Bixue Huanghua (co-dir. with several others, also co-scr.) **1954**; Yang E (co-dir. with Hong Shuyun, also scr.), What Price Beauty? aka The Little Girl Named Cabbage/Xiao Bai Cai (co-dir. with Zhang Shankun, also scr.), Lady Balsam's Conquest/Xiao Fengxian Xuji (co-dir. with Zhang Shankun and Wang Tianlin), Camille/Chahua Nü (co-dir. with Zhang Shankun, also scr.), Tokyo Interlude/Yingdu Yanji, Blood Will Tell/Haitang Hong (also scr.) **1955**; The Flame of Love aka Flesh and Flame/Lian zhi Huo (also scr.), Always in My Heart/Mang Lian, Madame Butterfly/Hudie Furen, Gloomy Sunday/Chunse Naoren (also scr.), Over the Rolling Hills/Guan Shan Xing (HK/Taiwan), Black Tulip of Inkabongh/Hei Niu (also co-scr.) **1956**; Holiday Express aka Express Train/Tebie Kuaiche (also scr.), Mambo Girl/Manbo Nülang (also scr.), Riot at the Studio/Liang Sha Danao Sheying Chang (also scr.), Happy Union/Tianzuo zhi He (also scr.) **1957**; Spring Song/Qingchun Ernü (also scr.), Air Hostess/Kongzhong Xiaojie (also scr.), Our Dream Car/Xiangche Meiren (also scr.), My Darling Sister/Zimei Hua (also scr.), 48 Hours in Escape/Taowang 48 Xiaoshi (also scr.) **1959**; Miss Secretary/Nü Mishu Yanshi (also scr.), Corpses at Large/Guwu Yiyun, Forever Yours/Qing Shen Si Hai (also scr.), The Loving Couple/Xinxin Xiangyin (also scr.), Bachelors Beware/Wenrou Xiang (also scr.) **1960**; Debt of Love/Tianlun Lei, Till the End of Time/Hongyan Qingdeng Wei Liao Qing, Sun, Moon and Star, Parts One and Two/Xingxing, Yueliang, Taiyang **1961**; It's Always Spring/Taoli Zheng Chun, The Male Bride/Pingshui Qiyuan (also scr.), Ladies First/Haoshi Chengshuang **1962**; Mad About

289

Music/*Ying Ge Yan Wu* (also scr.), *Because of Her/Jiao Wo Ruhe Bu Xiang Ta* (co-dir. with Wang Tianlin, also scr.) **1963**; *The Imperial Lady/Xi Taihou yu Zhen Fei, The Magic Lamp/Baolian Deng* (co-dir., also co-scr.), *The Crisis/Shengsi Guantou* (also scr.) **1964**; *The Longest Night/Zui Chang de Yi Ye* (also scr.) **1965**; *The Fugitive/Caomang Diexue Ji* (also scr.), *Forget Me Not/Konggu Lan* (also scr.) **1966**; *Isle of Gold/Huangjin Dao* **1967**; *The Boat Girl/Shuishang Renjia* (also scr.), *The Search for Monita/Mengnida Riji, Springtime Affairs/Yueye Qintiao* **1968**; *Iron Bones/Tiegu Bo, Gunfight at Lo Ma Lake/Luoma Hu* (also scr.) **1969**; *The Magnificent Gunfighter/Shenqiang Shou, Unconquered/Tu Long* (co-dir., also scr.) **1970**; *The Decisive Battle/Jingzhong Baoguo* (also scr., Taiwan) **1971**.

Yim Ho (name in pinyin: Yan Hao), b. 1952, Hong Kong. New wave director. Attended the London Film School (1973-75), and joined HK-TVB on return to Hong Kong, directing drama series and documentaries. Switched to films in 1978, making breakthrough movie *Homecoming/Sishui Liunian* in **1984**.

FILMS: *The Extras/Kalefei* (also co-scr.) 1978; *Happenings/Ye Che* (also co-scr.) **1980**; *Wedding Bells, Wedding Belles/Gongzi Jiao* (also scr.) 1981; (China/HK) *Homecoming/Sishui Liunian* **1984**; *Buddha's Lock/Tian Pusa* **1987**; (IN TAIWAN) *Red Dust* aka *Till the End of the World/Gungun Hongchen* (also co-scr., act.) **1990**; *King of Chess/Qi Wang* (began, completed by Tsui Hark; also co-scr., act.) **1992**; *The Day the Sun Turned Cold/Tianguo Nizi* (also co-scr., China/HK) **1994**; *The Sun Has Ears/Taiyang You Er* **1996**; *Kitchen/Chufang* **1997**.

Ronny Yu (name in pinyin: Yu Rentai; name in Cantonese: Yu Yan-tai), b. 1950, Hong Kong. Director. Educated in the US. After graduating from the University of Southern California, he worked with the ABC's news department. Returned to Hong Kong in 1975 where he produced Leong Po-chih's *Jumping Ash/Tiaohui* (1976) and Yim Ho's *The Extras/Kalefei* (1978). Directed his first film in 1979 but did his best work in 1993 with the stunning martial arts extravaganza *The Bride With White Hair/Baimao Monü Zhuan*.

FILMS: *The Servant /Qiang Nei Qiang Wai* (co-dir. with Philip Chan, also co-scr.) **1979**; *The Saviour/Jiushi Zhe* **1980**; *The Postman Strikes Back/Xuncheng Ma* (also co-scr.) **1982**; *The Trail/Zhuigui Qixiong* (also co-scr.) **1983**; *The Occupant/Liqi Biren* **1984**; *Legacy of Rage/Long Zai Jianghu* **1986**; *China White/Hongtian Longhu Hui* **1989**; *Shogun and Little Kitchen/Huotou Fuxing* **1992**; *The Bride With White Hair* aka *Jianghu: Between Love and Glory/Baifa Monü Zhuan* (also co-scr., prod.), *The Bride With White Hair, Part Two* (co-dir., co-scr., prod.) **1993**.

Yue Feng, b. 1901, Shanghai. Director. Entered Shanghai film industry in late 1920s as camera apprentice. Won praise for debut feature as director, *Angry Tide of China's Seas/Zhongguo Hai de Nuchao;* later a capable director working throughout 'Orphan Island' period and during full Japanese occupation of Shanghai. Shunned by colleagues for making 'Huaying' pictures, in particular *Sorrows Left at Spring River/Chun Jiang Yihen* (aka *Signal Fires Over Shanghai*), co-directed with Japanese director Hiroshi Inagaki in 1944. Continued directing career after the war in Shanghai and, from 1949, in Hong Kong. A stalwart of Mandarin cinema, directing for Great Wall, MP and GI, and Shaw Brothers.

FILMS: (IN SHANGHAI) *Daybreak/Chen Xi* (uncredited direction, also scr.), *Angry Tide of China's Seas/Zhongguo Hai de Nuchao* **1933**; *Escape/Taowang* **1935**; *Candle Night/Huazhu zhi Ye, Joy Comes to the Door/Xi Ling Men, Map of a Hundred Treasures/Baibao Tu* **1936**; *Spring in the Garden/Manyuan Chunse, Mystery Flower/Shenmi zhi Hua* **1937**; *A Generation of Heroes/Ernü Yingxiong Zhuan, The Lady is the Boss/Nü Shaoye, Sunrise/Ri Chu* **1938**; *Beast of Desire/Yu Mo, The Light of Women/Yunchang Xianzi* (also scr.) **1939**; *The Three Smiles/San Xiao, Three Sinners/Yan Xijiao* **1940**; *Family/Jia* (co-dir. with several others), *Murder in the Forest/Senlin Enchou Ji, Spring Dream/Chunfeng Huimeng Ji* (also scr.), *Blue Sea and Clear Sky/Bihai Qingtian* (also scr.), *The Little Room/Xiao Fangzi, Little Wife/Xiao Furen, Camille/Xin Chahua Nü* **1941**; *The Little Tiger/Xiao Laohu* (also scr.) **1942**; *Sorrows Left at Spring River* aka *Signal Fires Over Shanghai/Chun Jiang Yihen* (co-dir. with Hiroshi Inagaki) **1944**; *Roses Have Many Thorns/Meigui Duo Ci*, (IN HONG KONG) *Three Women/San Nüxing* **1947**; (IN SHANGHAI) *A Heartbroken Life, Parts One and Two/Duanchang Tianya, The Love Grumble/Luanfeng Yuan* **1948**; *A Night for Killing/Sharen Ye, Green Mountain, Jade Valley/Qing Shan Cui Gu, The Beautiful*

Corpse/Senlin Da Xue An, (IN HONG KONG)
An Unfaithful Woman aka *A Forgotten Woman/Dangfu Xin, Blood-Stained Begonia* aka *Blood Will Tell/Xueran Haitang Hong* **1949**; *The Flower Street/Hua Jie, Home, Sweet Home/Nanlai Yan* **1950**; *Modern Red Chamber Dream/Xin Honglou Meng* (also scr.), *Nonya/Niangre, The Stormy Night/Kuangfeng zhi Ye* **1952**; *Rainbow Rhythms/Caihong Qu* **1953**; *Pavilion in the Spring Dawn/Xiaolou Chun Xiao* (also scr.) **1954**; *Merry-Go-Round/Huanle Niannian, Green Hills and Jade Valleys/Qing Shan Cui Gu* (also scr.) **1956**; *Golden Lotus/Jinlian Hua* (also scr.), *The Battle of Love/Qingchang ru Zhanchang* **1957**; *A Tale of Two Wives/Rencai Liangde, Scarlet Doll/Hong Wa* **1958**; *The Wayward Husband/Taohua Yun, For Better, For Worse/Yu Guo Tian Qing* (also scr.), *The Other Woman/Zhangfu de Qingren, Spring Frolic/Xichun Tu* (also scr.) **1959**; *The Deformed/Jiren Yanfu, Street Boys/Jie Tong, When the Peach Blossoms Bloom/Yi Shu Taohua Qian Duo Hong* **1960**; *The Swallow/Yanzi Dao, The Husband's Secret/Zhangfu de Mimi* **1961**; *Madame White Snake/Baishe Zhuan* **1962**; *Revenge of a Swordsman/Yuanye Qixia Zhuan, Bitter Sweet/Weishui Xinku Weishui Mang* **1963**; *Lady General Hua Mulan/Hua Mulan, The Last Woman of Shang/Da Ji* **1964**; *The Lotus Lamp/Baolian Deng* (also scr.), *The West Chamber/Xi Xiang Ji* **1965**; *Auntie Lan/Lan Yi* (also scr.), *The Dragon Creek/Longhu Gou* (also scr.), *Rape of the Sword/Dao Jian* **1967**; *Flower Blossoms/Chun Nuan Hua Kai, The Magnificent Swordsman/Guai Xia* (co-dir. with Cheng Gang), *The Bells of Death/Duohun Ling* **1968**; *The Three Smiles/San Xiao* **1969**; *The Younger Generation/Ernü Shi Wo Men De, The Golden Knight/Jinyi Daxia, A Taste of Cold Steel/Wulin Fengyun* **1970**; *The Silent Love/Yaba yu Xinniang* **1971**; *The Avenger/Xiao Dulong, Trilogy of Swordsmanship/Qunying Hui* (episode) **1972**; *A Gathering of Heroes/Ganjin Shajue, The Two Cavaliers/Shuanglong Chuhai* **1973**; *Village for Tigers/E Hu Cun* (co-dir. with Wang Ping) **1974**.

Yuen Woo-ping (name in pinyin: Yuan Heping), sometimes billed as Yuen Wo-ping, b. 1945, Guangzhou. Director, whose first feature film, *Snake in the Eagle's Shadow/Shexing Diaoshou* (1978) propelled Jacky Chan to stardom. Like Chan, Sammo Hung, and many others, Yuen's childhood was steeped in the martial arts, taught him by his Peking-born father Yuan Xiaotian, an

actor who appeared in the Cantonese Wong Fei-hung series and who also starred in his son's *Snake in the Eagle's Shadow* and the follow-up hit, *Drunken Master/Zui Quan.* The junior Yuen also appeared as a bit player in the Wong Fei-hung films, and was employed as martial arts director in the early 1970s on a number of action flicks by director Ng See-yuen.

FILMS: *Snake in the Eagle's Shadow/Shexing Diaoshou* (also co-MAD), *Drunken Master/Zui Quan* (also co-MAD) **1978**; *Dance of the Drunk Mantis/Nanbei Zui Quan, The Magnificent Butcher/Lin Shirong* **1979**; *The Buddhist Fist/Fozhang Luohan Quan* (prod. only) **1980**; *Dreadnaught/Yongzhe Wuju* **1981**; *Legend of a Fighter/Huo Yuanjia, The Postman Strikes Back/Xuncheng Ma* (prod. only), *The Miracle Fighters/Qimen Dunjia* **1982**; *Shaolin Drunkard/Tianshi Zhuangxie* (also co-scr.) **1983**; *Drunken Tai Chi/Xiao Taiji* (also co-scr.) **1984**; *The Mismatched Couple/Qing Feng Dishou* (also ac.t) **1985**; *Close Encounter of a Vampire/Jiangshi Pa Pa* **1986**; *Tiger Cage/Tejing Tulong* **1988**; *In the Line of Duty, Part Four/Huangjia Shijie IV: Muji Zhengren* **1989**; *Tiger Cage, Part Two/Xi Hei Qian* **1990**; *Tiger Cage, Part Three/Lengmian Zuji Shou* **1991**; *Iron Monkey/Shaonian Huang Feihong zhi Tie Houzi* (also co-MAD), *Heroes Among Heroes/Su Qier* (co-dir.), *The Tai Chi Master/Taiji Zhang Sanfeng* (also co-MAD) **1993**; *The Fiery Romance/Huoyun Chuanqi, Wing Chun/Yong Chun* **1994**; *The Red Wolf/Hu Meng Wei Long* **1995**; *Tai Chi 2/Tiaji Quan* (co-dir.) **1996**.
AS MARTIAL ARTS DIRECTOR: *The Mad Killer/Fengkuang Shashou* **1971**; *The Bloody Fists/Dangkou Tan* (also act.), *The Lizard/Bi Hu, The Good and the Bad/E Hu Kuang Long* **1972**; *The Rage of Wind/Meng Hu Xia Shan, The Bastard/Xiao Zazhong* **1973**; *Tower of Death* aka *Game of Death II/Siwang Ta* **1981**; *Twin Dragons/Shuang Long Hui* (co-MAD), *Once Upon a Time in China, Part Two/Huang Feihong II zhi Nan'er Dang Ziqiang* **1992**; *The Last Hero in China/Huang Feihong Tieji Dou Wu Song* **1993**; *Fist of Legend/Jingwu Yingxiong* **1994**.

Zhang Che, b. 1932, Zhejiang Province. Director-writer. 1947, screenwriter in Shanghai's Guotai company. 1949, in Taiwan; co-directed *Storm Cloud Over Alishan/Alishan Fengyun,* first Mandarin film ever made in the island (Zhang also wrote lyrics for theme song). 1950, involved in anti-communist propaganda work for KMT

291

government in Taiwan. 1957, in Hong Kong to direct *Wild Fire/Ye Huo;* stays on in Hong Kong as screenwriter, journalist and novelist. 1960, joined MP and GI as resident writer. 1962, joins Shaw Brothers as head of script department. 1964, directed *Tiger Boy/Huxia Jianchou,* starting the craze for swordfighting martial arts flicks. 1974, established his own production company, Chang Gong (meaning 'long bow'), in Taiwan. The scripts of many of his martial arts films were written in collaboration with writer Ni Kuang.

FILMS: *Storm Cloud Over Alishan/Alishan Fengyun* (co-dir. with Zhang Ying, also scr., Taiwan) 1949; *Wild Fire/Yehuo* (also scr.) **1957**; *The Butterfly Chalice/Hudie Bei* (co-dir. with Yuan Qiufeng) **1965**; *Tiger Boy/Huxia Jianchou* (also scr.), *The Magnificent Trio/Biancheng Sanxia* (also scr.) **1966**; *Trail of the Broken Sword/Duanchang Jian* (also scr.), *The One-Armed Swordsman/Dubi Dao* (also co-scr.), *The Assassin/Da Cike* (also scr.) **1967**; *The Golden Swallow/Jin Yanzi* (also co-scr.) **1968**; *The Singing Thief/Dadao Gewang, Return of the One-Armed Swordsman/Dubi Dao Wang* (also scr.), *The Flying Dagger/Feidao Shou* (also co-scr.), *The Invincible Fist/Tieshou Wuqing, Dead End/Si Jiao, Have Sword Will Travel/Baobiao* **1969**; *The Wandering Swordsman/You Xiaer, Vengeance/Baochou* (also co-scr.), *The Heroic Ones/Shisan Taibao* (also co-scr.) **1970** *King Eagle/Ying Wang, The New One-Armed Swordsman/Xin Dubi Dao, The Duel/Da Juedou, The Anonymous Heroes/Wuming Yingxiong, Duel of Fists/Quan Ji, The Deadly Duo/Shuang Xia* **1971**; *The Boxer From Shantung/Ma Yongzhen* (co-dir. with Bao Xueli), *The Angry Guest/E Ke, The Water Margin/Shui Hu Zhuan* (co-dir. with Wu Ma and Bao Xueli), *Trilogy of Swordsmanship/Qunying Hui* (episode only), *Young People/Nianqing Ren, Delightful Forest/Kuaihuo Lin* (co-dir. with Bao Xueli), *Man of Iron/Chou Lianhuan* (co-dir. with Bao Xueli, also co-scr.), *Four Riders/Si Qishi* (also co-scr.) **1972**; *The Delinquent/Fennu Qingnian* (co-dir. with Gui Zhihong), *Blood Brothers/Ci Ma, The Generation Gap/Pan Ni* (also co-scr.), *The Pirate/Da Haidao* (co-dir. with Wu Ma, Bao Xueli) **1973**; *Heroes Two/Fang Shiyu yu Hong Xiguan, The Savage Five/Wu Hu Jiang, Men From the Monastery/Shaolin Zidi, Friends/Pengyou, Shaolin Martial Arts/Hong Quan yu Yong Chun* (also co-scr.), *Na Cha the Great/Nezha* (also co-scr.), *Five Shaolin Masters/Shaolin*

Wuzu **1974**; *All Men Are Brothers/Dangkou Zhi* (co-dir. with Wu Ma, also co-scr.), *Disciples of Shaolin/Hongquan Xiaozi, The Fantastic Magic Baby/Hong Haier, Marco Polo/Mage Bolo* **1975**; *The Boxer Rebellion/Ba Guo Lian Jun, New Shaolin Boxers/Cai Lifo Xiaozi* (co-dir. with Wu Ma), *The Shaolin Temple/Shaolin Si* (co-dir. with Wu Ma) **1976**; *The Naval Commandos/Haijun Tuji Dui* (co-dir. with Wu Ma), *The Brave Archer/She Diao Yingxiong Zhuan, The Chinatown Kid/Tangren Jie Xiaozi* (also co-scr.) **1977**; *The Brave Archer, Part Two/She Diao Yingxiong Zhuan Xuji,The Five Venoms/Wu Du* (also co-scr.) **1978**; *The Daredevils/Zhaji Wangming, The Magnificent Ruffians/Maiming Xiaozi* (also co-scr.), *The Kid With the Golden Arm/Jinbi Tong* **1979**; *Heaven and Hell/Di San Lei Da Dou, Two Champions of Shaolin/Shaolin yu Wudang* **1980**; *The Sword Stained With Royal Blood/Bixue Jian, Masked Avengers/Cha Shou* **1981**; *House of Traps/Chongxiao Lou, The Brave Archer and His Mate/Shediao Xialu, Five Element Ninjas/Wudun Renshu, The Brave Archer, Part III/Shediao Yingxiong Zhuan Disan Ji* **1982**; *The Weird Man/Shentong Shu yu Xiao Bawang, The Ghost/Zhuang Gui* **1983**; *Shanghai 13/Shanghai Tan Shisan Taibao* (also scr., prod.) **1984**; *Great Shanghai 1937/Da Shanghai 1937* (also scr.) **1986**; *Cross the River/Guo Jiang* (also scr.) **1988**; (IN CHINA) *Slaughter in Xi'an/Xi'an Shalu* (also scr.) **1990**; (IN TAIWAN) *The Magic Kid/Shen Tong* **1993**.

AS WRITER: (IN SHANGHAI) *The Woman With the False Face/Jiamian Nülang* **1947**; *Love in the Wild/Huangyuan Yanji* 1949; (IN HONG KONG) *The Tender Trap of Espionage/Zhifen Jiandie Wang, Black Butterfly/Hei Hudie* **1960**; *Song Without Words/Wu Yu Wen Cangtian, The Girl With the Golden Arm/Zei Meiren, You Were Meant For Me/Youxi Renjian* **1961**; *It's Always Spring/Taoli Zheng Chun, Come Rain, Come Shine/Yehua Lian, Her Pearly Tears/Zhenzhu Lei* **1962**; *The Female Prince/Shuangfeng Qiyuan, The Warlord and the Actress/Xue Jian Mudan Hong* **1964**; *The Mermaid/Yu Meiren, Crocodile River/Eyu He, Inside the Forbidden City/Song Gong Mishi, Call of the Sea/Huhai Qingchou* **1965**; *The Perfumed Arrow/Nu Xiucai* **1966**.

Zhang Zengze, b. 1931, Qingdao, Shandong Province. Director, resident in Taiwan. Early career developed in Taiwan after drama and film studies. A theatre director before he entered films, making documentaries for the government-run

292

Central Motion Picture Studio. His first feature films were Taiwanese-dialect productions. In Hong Kong in 1968 to direct Cathay's *From the Highway/Lu Ke yu Dao Ke* (mostly shot in Taiwan), a superior martial arts picture that foreshadowed the kung fu fad. Joined Shaw Brothers in 1971, then going independent in 1974.

FILMS: (IN TAIWAN) *Girl in the Chamber/Zaishi Nü* **1961**; *The Wish of the Orphan Girl/Gunü de Yuanwang, Love and Hate in the Prairies/Muye Enchou* **1962**; *The Surprised Husband/Jing Mou Da Zhangfu* **1963**; *Dodder Flower/Tusi Hua* **1965**; *Village Raid/Guxiang Jie* (also scr.), *The Bridge/Qiao* **1966**; *The Age of Tears and Joy/Beihuan Suiyue,* **1967**; *Coral/Shanhu* (also co-scr.) **1968**; (IN HONG KONG) *From the Highway/Lu Ke yu Dao Ke* (also scr.) **1970**; *Redbeard/Hong Huzi* (also scr.) **1971**; *The Casino/Jixiang Dufang, The Fugitive/Wangming Tu* **1972**; *River of Fury/Jianghu Xing* **1973**; *Sex for Sale/Mian Ju* **1974**; *Blue Dream/Lanse de Meng* (also scr.), *Queen Hustler/Da Laoqian, Bar Girl/Jiuba Nülang* (also co-scr.), *Gambling Syndicate/E Ba* **1975**; (IN TAIWAN) *Heroes in the Eastern Sky* aka *Combat the Air Raider/Jian Qiao Yinglie Zhuan* **1977**; *Pursued/Xiashi Zhuiming Ke, The Battle of Baoshan* (co-dir. with several others) **1978**; *The Perils of Chu Lao-san/Zhu Laosan Sanxiao Tan* (also prod.) **1979**; *The Battle at Guningtou/Guningtou Da Zhan* **1980**; *Soldiers From Heaven/Tianjiang Shenbing, Fragile Soldiers of the Tiger Unit/Laohu Budui Baobei Bing* **1981**.

Zhu Shilin, b. 1899, Guangdong Province; d. 1967, Hong Kong. Mandarin director. Early education in Shanghai. In films from the early 1920s, as publicist and translator in Beijing, employed by producer Luo Mingyou. When Luo founded the Lianhua Film Company in Shanghai in 1930, Zhu headed the production department. He made his debut as a director that year with a short film starring Ruan Lingyu, *Suicide Pact/Zisha Hetong*. Zhu wrote a number of screenplays in this early phase of his career. In 1934, he took charge of Lianhua's Number Three Studio and directed his first feature film, *Homecoming/Guilai*. Stayed in Shanghai during the anti-Japanese war as an 'orphan island' director. In Hong Kong in 1946, directing for Da Zhonghua (Great China), Yonghua and Longma film companies. Helped set up Fenghuang studio in 1954. Throughout the 1950s, Zhu's career in Hong Kong was wholly

spent in left-wing studios where he directed some of the finest films of that decade including *The Flower Girl/Hua Guniang* (1951), *Spoiling the Wedding Day/Wu Jia Qi* (1951), and *Festival Moon/Zhongqiu Yue* (1953). Acquired political notoriety in the Mainland as Cultural Revolution critics severely lashed his 1948 film *Sorrows of the Forbidden City/Qing Gong Mishi*. Zhu was credited as art director on two films produced in Shanghai: Sang Hu's *Two Women/Renhai Shuangzhu* (1945), and Cen Fan's *Dream of the Red Chamber/Hong Loumeng* (1962).

FILMS: (IN SHANGHAI) *Suicide Pact/Zisha Hetong* (silent short) **1930**; *Homecoming/Guilai* (also scr.), *Youth/Qingchun* (also scr.) **1934**; *Song of the Nation/Guo Feng* (co-dir. with Luo Mingyou), *Looking for a Wife/Zheng Hun* (short, also scr.) **1935**; *Lianhua Symphony/Lianhua Jiaoxiang Qu* (episode 'The Devil/Gui', also scr.), *Song of a Mother/Cimu Qu* (also scr.), *The Lost Pearl/Renhai Yizhu* (also scr.), *Old and New Times/Xinjiu Shidai* (also scr.), *Vistas of Art/Yihai Fengguang* (episode 'Film City/Dianying Cheng', also scr.) **1937**; *Wen Suchen, Parts One and Two* (also scr.) **1939**; *Xiangfei, Wen Suchen, Parts Three and Four* (also scr.), *Sai Jinhua* (also scr.), *Meng Lijun, Parts One and Two* (co-dir. with Tu Guangqi, also scr.) **1940**; *Xue Yanniang* (also scr.), *Incense of Reincarnation/Fanhun Xiang, Princess Ivy/Biluo Gongzhu* (also scr.), *Dangerous Mission/Longtan Huxue, Flesh/Rou, Wild Flowers Are Sweeter/Yehua Na You Jia Hua Xiang* (also scr.) **1941**; *The Wedding Night/Dongfang Huazhu Ye, Rendezvous in the Late Afternoon/Ren Yue Huanghun Hou, Grand View Garden on Sea/Haishang Daguan Yuan* (also scr.), *Love for Everyone/Bo Ai* (episode 'Marital Love/Fuqi zhi Ai'), *Romance of the Night/Liangxiao Hua Nong Yue, Eternal Fame/Wanshi Liufang* (dir. with several others) **1942**; *The Second Generation/Di Er Dai, Independence/Bu Qiu Ren* **1943**; *Alarm Conscious/Caomu Jiebing, Modern Couple/Xiandai Fuqi, National Treasure/Guo Bao* **1944**; (IN HONG KONG), *Two Persons in Trouble/Tongbing Bu Xiang Lian, You're Smart in One Way, I in Another/Ge You Qianqiu* (also scr.), *A Dream of Spring/Chun zhi Meng* (also scr.) **1946**; *Where is My Darling?/Yuren Hechu* (also scr.) **1947**; *The Third Generation/Di San Dai* (also scr.), *Sorrows of the Forbidden City/Qing Gong Mishi* **1948**; *Life and Death/Sheng yu Si* **1949**;

293

*The Flower Girl/Hua Guniang, Spoiling the
Wedding Day/Wu Jia Qi* (co-dir. with Bai
Chen) **1951**; *The Show Must Go On* aka *Sons
of the Earth/Jianghu Ernü, The Dividing Wall*
aka *Mr Chen vs. Mr. Chen/Yi Ban zhi Ge, Map
of 100 Treasures/Baibao Tu* **1952**; *Festival
Moon/Zhongqiu Yue, Keep Your Chin
Up/Shuihong Ling* (also scr.) **1953**; *Flight of a
Pair of Swallows/Yan Shuang Fei* (also scr.),
Joyce and Deli/Zimei Qu (also scr.), *House
Removal Greeting/Qiaoqian zhi Xi, Between Fire
and Water/Shuihuo zhi Jian* **1954**; *Love at First
Sight/Shandian Lian'ai, Welcome to the Whole
Family/Hedi Guangling, Beauty Parlour
Girls/Ding Xiang Guniang* **1955**; *The Foolish
Heart/Jimo de Xin* **1956**; *All About a
Baby/Taitai Quanqi* **1957**; *Husband
Hunters/Qiang Xinlang* (also scr.), *The Way
of Husband and Wife/Fuqi Jing* (also scr.)
1958; *A Well-To-Do Family/Jinwu Meng* (also
scr.) **1959**; *Eternal Love/Tongming Yuanyang*
(also scr.) **1960**; *Chen San and
Wuniang/Chen San yu Wuniang* (Chaozhou
opera film), *Thunderstorm/Lei Yu* (also scr.)
1961; *Three Men and a Girl/San Feng Qiu
Huang* (also scr.) **1962**; *Tung Hsiao
Wan/Dong Xiaowan* **1963**; *Hsu Hsueh
Mei/Fengxue Yizhi Mei, Garden of
Repose/Guyuan Chun Meng* (also scr.) **1964**.

Films in which Zhu was credited as
'executive director', essentially supervising
the work of younger directing protégés:
Year In Year Out aka *Springtime/Yinian zhi Ji,
To Marry or Not to Marry/Kongque Ping, They
All Want a Baby* aka *The Lady Fascinates/Xiao
Nainai zhi Mi* **1955**; *The Wedding Night/Xin
Hun Diyi Ye* (also scr.) **1956**; *A Widow's
Tears/Xin Gua* (also scr.), *The Lone
Woman/Xue Zhong Lian* **1957**; *Return of the
Prodigal Youth/Yeye Pan Lang Gui* **1958**; *The
Precious Little Moon/Xiao Yueliang, Mutual
Hearts/Tongxin Jie* **1959**; *Wild Rose/Ye Meigui*
1960.

Index

Gao Li 78
Gao Yuan 76
Garden of Repose/Guyuan Chunmeng (1964)
19
Garfield, John 76
Gaynor, Janet 208
Ge Lan (Grace Chang) 25, 31, 32, 33, 34,
35, 74
Ghost Woman of the Old Mansion/Guyuan Yaoji
(1949) 45, 221
Glickenhaus, James 130
Godard, Jean-Luc 156, 196
Goddess, The/Shen Nü (1934) 20, 191–2, 209
Godfather III (1990) 231
Golden Harvest 80, 114, 119, 125, 140, 165,
238
Golden Lotus, The/Jin Ping Mei 84n, 223
Golden Lotus/Jin Lianhua (1957) 23
Golden Phoenix/Jin Feng (1955) 79
Golden Swallow, The/Jin Yanzi (1968) 36,
99–100, 103
Grand Party, The/Haomen Yeyan (1959) 53
Grand Substitution, The/Wangu Liufang
(1965) 78
Great Wall (studio) 11, 15, 16, 18, 24, 25,
45, 97, 112
Green Card (1990) 188
Greene, Graham 150
Grow Up in Anger/Qingchun Nuchao (1986)
156
Gu Eryi 14, 15, 17, 18
Gu Feng 102
Gu Long 108
Guan Shan 75, 76, 77
Gui Yalei 81
Guiding Light, The/Kuhai Mingdeng (1953)
46, 47
Guolian (the Grand Motion Picture Co.)
80–2, 84n

Ha, Pat 156, 184
Half Way Down/Ban Xialiu Shehui (1955) 24
Hammer (production co.) 223
Han Fei 18, 19
Han Yingjie 92, 93
Han Ziyun 29
Hand-to-Hand Combat/Roubo (1937) 7
Happenings, The/Ye Che (1980) 147–8
Happiest Moment, The/Yi Le Ye (1973) 84
Happiness/Xi (episode in *The Four Moods*)
(1970) 81–2
Happy Ding Dong/Huanle Dingdang (1986)
144
Hard Target (1993) 182
Hardboiled/Lashou Shentan (1992) 178, 180,
181–2

Haunted House, The (**see** *A Maid's Bitter Story*)
Haunted Night, The/Huihun Ye (1962) 222
Hawks, Howard 169
Hayakawa, Sessue 110
He Fan 82, 137
He Feiguang 12
He Zhaozhang, 30
He's a Woman, She's a Man/Jinzhi Yuye (1994)
253
Health Warning/Da Lei Tai (1983) 158
Heart of the Dragon/Long de Xin (1985) 124
Heart to Hearts/Sanren Shijie (1988) 160
Heavenly Souls/Caifeng Zhan Youlong (1949)
50
Her Fatal Ways/Biaojie Ni Haoye (1990) 158
Heroes Two/Fang Shiyu yu Hong Xiguan
(1974) 103
Heung Wah-keung 235
Heung Wah-sing 235
Heung Wah-yim 235
Hiroshima 28/Guangdao Ershiba (1974) 138
Hitchcock, Alfred 147
HK–TVB 144, 146
Ho Tung, Sir Robert 4
Ho, Lily 32, 35, 36, 37
Home at Hong Kong/Jia Zai Xianggang (1983)
158
Home at Taipei/Jia Zai Taibei (1969) 60n
Homecoming/Sishui Liunian (1984) 154,
213–14
Hong Kong Nocturne/Xiangjiang Huayue Ye
(1967) 35, 36, 37
Hong Kong, Hong Kong/Nan yu Nü (1983)
158
Hongkong 1941/Dengdai Liming (1984) 155
Hou Xiaoxian 28n, 81, 87
Hou Yao 8
House of 72 Tenants, The/Qishi'er Jia Fangke
(1973) 57, 59, 144–5
House-Removal Greeting/Qiaoqian zhi Xi
(1954) 18
Hu Die (aka Butterfly Wu) 11, 12, 79
Hu, Jenny 76
Hu, King 4, 33, 79, 81, 87–100, 102, 163,
169, 199, 200, 201, 220, 222
Huang He 27, 76
Huaying (production co.) 5, 10, 16, 21
Hudson Hawk (1991) 180
Hui, Ann 84, 92, 112, 140, 146, 149–52, 153,
154, 155, 158, 161n, 184, 188, 192, 196,
207, 211–13, 214–15, 217n, 221, 225, 236
Hui, Michael 52, 54, 57, 58, 59, 80, 140–4,
145, 160
Hui, Ricky 54, 141–4
Hui, Samuel 54, 141–4, 200
Humanity/Ren (1960) 54, 55

300

301

303